Theory and Practice of Illegitimate Finance

Abdul Rafay
University of Management and Technology, Pakistan

A volume in the Advances in Finance, Accounting, and Economics (AFAE) Book Series

IGI Global
PUBLISHER of TIMELY KNOWLEDGE

Published in the United States of America by
IGI Global
Business Science Reference (an imprint of IGI Global)
701 E. Chocolate Avenue
Hershey PA, USA 17033
Tel: 717-533-8845
Fax: 717-533-8661
E-mail: cust@igi-global.com
Web site: http://www.igi-global.com

Library of Congress Cataloging-in-Publication Data

Names: Rafay, Abdul, 1973- editor.
Title: Theory and practice of illegitimate finance / edited by Abdul Rafay.

Description: Hershey, PA : Business Science Reference, [2023] | Includes bibliographical references and index.
Identifiers: LCCN 2023037192 (print) | LCCN 2023037193 (ebook) | ISBN 9798369311905 (hardcover) | ISBN 9798369311912 (ebook)
Subjects: LCSH: Finance--Corrupt practices.
Classification: LCC HG101 .T45 2023 (print) | LCC HG101 (ebook) | DDC 332--dc23/eng/20230907
LC record available at https://lccn.loc.gov/2023037192
LC ebook record available at https://lccn.loc.gov/2023037193

This book is published in the IGI Global book series Advances in Finance, Accounting, and Economics (AFAE) (ISSN: 2327-5677; eISSN: 2327-5685)

British Cataloguing in Publication Data
A Cataloguing in Publication record for this book is available from the British Library.

Advances in Finance, Accounting, and Economics (AFAE) Book Series

Ahmed Driouchi
Al Akhawayn University, Morocco

ISSN:2327-5677
EISSN:2327-5685

Mission

In our changing economic and business environment, it is important to consider the financial changes occurring internationally as well as within individual organizations and business environments. Understanding these changes as well as the factors that influence them is crucial in preparing for our financial future and ensuring economic sustainability and growth.

The **Advances in Finance, Accounting, and Economics** (**AFAE**) book series aims to publish comprehensive and informative titles in all areas of economics and economic theory, finance, and accounting to assist in advancing the available knowledge and providing for further research development in these dynamic fields.

Coverage

- Health Economics
- Fiscal Policy
- Labor Economics
- Interest Rates and Annuities
- Economics of Risks, Uncertainty, Ambiguity, and Insurance
- E-Accounting
- Public Finance
- Development Economics
- Auditing
- Macroeconomics

IGI Global is currently accepting manuscripts for publication within this series. To submit a proposal for a volume in this series, please contact our Acquisition Editors at Acquisitions@igi-global.com or visit: http://www.igi-global.com/publish/.

The Advances in Finance, Accounting, and Economics (AFAE) Book Series (ISSN 2327-5677) is published by IGI Global, 701 E. Chocolate Avenue, Hershey, PA 17033-1240, USA, www.igi-global.com. This series is composed of titles available for purchase individually; each title is edited to be contextually exclusive from any other title within the series. For pricing and ordering information please visit http://www.igi-global.com/book-series/advances-finance-accounting-economics/73685. Postmaster: Send all address changes to above address.

Titles in this Series

For a list of additional titles in this series, please visit: www.igi-global.com/book-series

The Importance of Entrepreneurship in Fostering Economic Progress
Mohammed El Amine Abdelli (University of Western Brittany, France) Naima Bentouir (Ain Temouchent University, Algeria) and Esra Sipahi Döngül (Aksaray University, Trkey)
Business Science Reference • © 2024 • 300pp • H/C (ISBN: 9781668471272) • US $240.00

Perspectives on the Transition Toward Green and Climate Neutral Economies in Asia
Patricia Ordóñez de Pablos (The University of Oviedo, Spain) Mohammad Nabil Almunawar (Universiti Brunei Darussalam, Brunei) and Muhammad Anshari (Universiti Brunei Darussalam, Bunei)
Business Science Reference • © 2023 • 465pp • H/C (ISBN: 9781668486139) • US $325.00

Revolutionizing Financial Services and Markets Through FinTech and Blockchain
Kiran Mehta (Chitkara Business School, Chitkara University, India) Renuka Sharma (Chitkara Business School, Chitkara University, India) and Poshan Yu (Soochow University, China & Australian Studies Centre, Shanghai University, China)
Business Science Reference • © 2023 • 340pp • H/C (ISBN: 9781668486245) • US $265.00

Circular Economy Implementation for Sustainability in the Built Environment
Nicoleta Cobîrzan (Technical University of Cluj-Napoca, Romania) Radu Muntean (Transilvania University of Braşov, Romania) and Raluca - Andreea Felseghi (Technical University of Cluj-Napoca, Romania)
Business Science Reference • © 2023 • 300pp • H/C (ISBN: 9781668482384) • US $250.00

Concepts and Cases of Illicit Finance
Abdul Rafay (University of Management and Technology, Pakistan)
Business Science Reference • © 2023 • 330pp • H/C (ISBN: 9781668485873) • US $250.00

Sustainable Growth and Global Social Development in Competitive Economies
Andrei Jean Vasile (Petroleum-Gas University of Ploiesti, Romania) Mile Vasić (European Marketing and Management Association, Banja Luka, Bosnia And Herzegovina) and Predrag Vukovic (Institute of Agricultural Economics, Belgrade, Serbia)
Business Science Reference • © 2023 • 320pp • H/C (ISBN: 9781668488102) • US $250.00

The Past, Present, and Future of Accountancy Education and Professions
Nina T. Dorata (St. John's University, USA) Richard C. Jones (Hofstra University, USA) Jennifer Mensche (St. Joseph's University, USA) and Mark M. Ulrich (CUNY Queensborough Community College, USA)
Business Science Reference • © 2023 • 240pp • H/C (ISBN: 9781668454831) • US $215.00

IGI Global
PUBLISHER of TIMELY KNOWLEDGE

701 East Chocolate Avenue, Hershey, PA 17033, USA
Tel: 717-533-8845 x100 • Fax: 717-533-8661
E-Mail: cust@igi-global.com • www.igi-global.com

Great things are done when men and mountains meet;
this is not done by jostling in the street –
William Blake in "Great things are done"
(c. 1807-1809)

This book by Professor Abdul Rafay, is dedicated to (the late) **Sheikh Ejaz Ahmad (1940-1998)** and **Dr. Gohar Ejaz.**

Sheikh Ejaz Ahmad (the late) was a visionary Pakistani businessman of his time. Sheikh Ejaz Ahmad laid the foundation of the Ejaz Group of companies in 1950 for the international trading of commodities. From 1962 to 1985, he was an iconic leader of the business community and gained the monumental title of 'King of Commodities' in Karachi. In fact, he was an institution in himself, and the history of commodity trading is incomplete without him. He became a member of the Senate of Pakistan in 1985.

May Allah rest his soul in peace.

Currently, **Dr. Gohar Ejaz**, a visionary businessman and philanthropist in Pakistan, is the torch bearer for this father's mission.

Being a philanthropist, his services in the field of health and education have uplifted the lives of millions of Pakistanis. He demonstrated exemplary humanitarian service during natural disasters in Pakistan. He is the founder/chairman of Sheikh Ejaz Ahmad Trust and Gohar Ejaz Foundation. Sheikh Ejaz Ahmad Trust provides premium quality medical equipment for the care and comfort of patients. The trust established state of art free of cost dialysis center at Jinnah Hospital, a public sector hospital in Lahore Pakistan. Gohar Ejaz Foundation provides merit-based scholarships to students from across the country.

Being the Patron-in-Chief of the All-Pakistan Textile Mills Association (ATMA), he is a staunch supporter of Export-led economic growth and worked tirelessly for improving the export-oriented textile sector of Pakistan. He was the force behind the 40% increase (FY18: $13 billion to FY22: $19.4 billion) in textile exports of Pakistan.

Dr. Gohar was awarded Hilal-i-Imtiaz (2023) & Sitara-i-Imtiaz (2014) by the Government of Pakistan for business leadership and philanthropic services. He is also a regular guest speaker at seminars organized around the globe by academic institutions, multilateral and bilateral economic institutions and NGOs.

Editorial Advisory Board

Table of Contents

Section 4
Corruption in Public Finance

Detailed Table of Contents

management and their effects on a company's reputation, economic performance, and financial stability. Additionally, the chapter includes relevant case studies from previous literature to illuminate the effects of earnings management on corporations and other organizations.

Section 2
Corruption, Fraud, and the Society

In this chapter, a renowned historical case study is explored, focusing on the resurgence of the plague in 18th-century Europe. The center stage is occupied by the port of Marseille in this narrative, as a contaminated cargo ship from the Levant inadvertently brought back the dreaded disease. Despite the implementation of effective protective measures across Europe since the Renaissance, all existing protocols mysteriously managed to be evaded by this particular vessel and its valuable cargo. The rapid spread of the plague is argued by researchers to be directly attributed to an instance of "crime of the powerful." It is emphasized by the authors that corruption, contrary to the prevailing notion that it is a victimless crime, can have devastating consequences in extreme cases like this, leading to tens of thousands of deaths.

This study investigates how the Anti-Money Laundering and Countering Financing of Terrorism (AML/CFT) regime influences the economic performance of developing countries, with a specific focus on Sri Lanka. By utilizing the AML/CFT effectiveness index and assessing ratings from the 11 immediate outcomes, as outlined in the latest mutual evaluation reports, the research evaluates the effectiveness of the AML/CFT regime. Additionally, the study analyzes the GDP growth rate of these developing countries as an indicator of their economic performance. The results of the study indicate a positive correlation between the strength of the AML/CFT regime and the economic performance of developing countries. As a result, the study emphasizes the critical importance of continuously implementing and enhancing a robust AML/CFT regime. It advocates for the prudent application of such measures to foster sound economic performance in developing nations.

This study analyzes empirical outcomes to understand the causal linkages between the rule of law, regulatory quality, and electricity theft in regulated industries. It provides a brief and explicit theoretical framework on the rule of law and its impact on electricity theft, using panel data for income groups. When the rule of law is not well established, poor governance in the regulatory process leads to larger social and economic costs associated with electricity theft. The analysis demonstrates that the rule of law has a uni-directional causality effect on transmission and distribution losses across all income groups. In the upper-middle and low-income panels, transmission and distribution losses granger cause regulatory quality, while this relationship cannot be validated in the high and lower-middle-income samples. These findings highlight the significance of the rule of law in reducing electricity theft by emphasizing regulatory quality as a transmission channel.

Section 3
Financial Scams

Electronic banking (e-banking) has played an important role in the development and economic growth of developing countries. E-Banking also acts as a catalyst for the development of the financial sector, capital markets, and digital economy. India's rapidly growing banking sector paved the way for development and fraud in the e-banking regime. The present chapter seeks to assess the techniques of detection of fraud from a global perspective and will also validate the boom of E-Banking with a thought of precaution and awareness. Secondary data has been collected through bank statements, journals, and the internet. The results will help banks and regulators to better understand online banking frauds and to strengthen the existing fraud prevention systems. It is recommended that the government should provide adequate infrastructural facilities in the telecommunications and energy sectors, coupled with encouraging the use of information and communication technologies among the masses for beneficial impact.

The concept of this chapter is to review the literature for a research gap on risk perception among online consumers and the intention for online purchases in Malaysia. Online platforms and digital payments make online shopping easier. During the year 2020 - 2021, online shopping had become increasingly active with the spike of the novel coronavirus pandemic. Online users who share their personal information online are most likely getting into the scammer's trap. Malaysia executed the national cyber security policy to defend the country's critical national information infrastructure. Financial awareness among online users plays a crucial role in fighting cybercrime. Digital guardianship should exist to prevent irresponsible parties from taking advantage. The routine activity theory has been proposed to explain the phenomenon whereby the offender makes the selection to commit a crime based on an online shopper as his target and the guardianship.

Preface

The editing of a book on illegitimate finance has never been more thrilling and demanding. Over the past few decades, this field of interest has experienced remarkable growth, garnering attention from the G20[1] to the World Economic[2] Forum and influencing both global and national economic agendas. In today's world, the alarming surge in illegitimate finance has elevated the importance of addressing this issue in developed and developing countries alike. Consequently, a new regulatory regime, characterized by strict compliance and robust processes, has emerged as a response to combat this challenge.

CORRUPTION AND FRAUD: A LIFELINE FOR ILLEGITIMATE FINANCE

Human nature presents a highly complex phenomenon, making it challenging to pinpoint the underlying motives that drive individuals to engage in accumulating illegitimate finance. The main sources of illegitimate finance comprise corruption and fraud. Corruption and fraud manifest differently for various people - for some, it arises as an opportunity crime, while for others, poverty and powerlessness serve as compelling motivation. Regardless of the approach used to gauge corruption and fraud - be it a rational choice, structural, or cultural - one thing remains evident: corruption and fraud are severely damaging to societies.

While high-level corruption is undeniably a significant reason for illegitimate finance, the primary factor often attributed to the challenges faced by developing countries is the fragmented nature of their state institutions. This problem arises particularly in regions where the legitimacy of the state and its institutions is under question. Corruption, by itself, does not directly cause poverty. Rather, its impact lies in its consequences on economic and governance factors, which act as intermediaries in generating poverty. Powerful elites exploit this fragmentation to their advantage, seeking rent-seeking opportunities at various levels of interaction with citizens. In some cases, this phenomenon has been labeled as *"State Capture"* in South Africa, *"Family Fiefdom"* in countries like Angola and Guinea Equatorial, or the *"Oligarch"* model in Russia and former Soviet states. Similarly, conflict of interest is a multifaceted social phenomenon that emerges in both the public and private sectors. In the context of the public sector, it represents a misuse of power and corrupt practice. This insidious issue poses a significant threat to the core principles on which modern democratic states rest, including legal equality, the separation of powers, and the rule of law.

While establishing a direct link between corruption and economic growth can be challenging, it is evident that corruption exerts significant negative impacts on crucial economic structures, including investment (particularly foreign direct investment), competition, entrepreneurship, government efficiency, and human capital formation. Moreover, the correlation between corruption and poverty is more evident, as impoverished individuals are more likely to fall victim to corrupt practices by government officials.

Fraud, on the other hand, constitutes a violation of the law, perpetuated by individuals or organizations seeking personal or corporate gain, and has proven to be a significant impediment to economic growth. Both individuals and companies engage in fraudulent practices for many reasons, with the most prevalent motives being the acquisition of money, property, or services, evasion of payments, and pursuit of personal or business gains. Intentional in nature, fraud aims to harm others and encompasses various illicit activities such as stealing, conspiracy, embezzlement, money laundering, bribery, and extortion.

Business organizations that possess valuable assets, be it cash, goods, information, or services, often become prime targets for fraudsters. Perpetrators of fraud can come from any age group or gender, and they may appear trustworthy, making it difficult for companies to identify potential threats. The assumption of trustworthiness in business is a common but potentially detrimental oversight, as business owners often place unwavering trust in their employees. Unfortunately, this naive confidence can lead to workplace fraud, enabling employees to misappropriate company assets.

Irrespective of an organization's size, industry, or geographical location, fraud remains a pervasive challenge faced by most entities in today's world. Small businesses are more vulnerable to fraud and tend to experience higher average losses compared to larger enterprises. The impact of a major fraud incident can be particularly severe for small companies, as they might struggle to absorb the resulting damage when compared to their larger counterparts. Viewing fraud from the perspective of small businesses, proprietors and managers reveals a host of significant challenges, including issues related to interpersonal relationships. Regrettably, some employees within small businesses betray the trust of their employers by exploiting their positions for personal financial gain.

The legal definition of fraud may vary from one country to another, but at its core, it involves deception, dishonesty, and ethical misconduct. Briefly, fraud encompasses any illegal act involving deceit, breach of trust, or concealment, irrespective of whether it involves the threat of violence or physical force. In other words, fraudulent actions encompass an array of deceptive behaviors, such as false statements, misrepresentations, and deceitful conduct.

The term *"White-collar crime"* refers to fraudulent activities perpetrated by individuals in positions of authority, who exploit their power and influence to manipulate legislative decisions in their favor. White-collar crimes encompass a range of deceptive acts, including theft, making false statements, evasion, and manipulation of information, among others. This type of fraud is a classic example of abuse of power within the workplace, often arising when there are unclear policies or procedures to control deceitful behaviors.

Understanding fraud requires a comprehensive approach that recognizes its dynamic nature and necessitates proactive know-how of its methodologies. Over time, various fraud models have been developed to understand and combat fraudulent activities. The *"Fraud Triangle"* was one of the initial models, highlighting three key factors—pressure, opportunity, and rationalization—that may drive individuals to commit fraud. However, as fraud schemes evolved, a more comprehensive model called the *"Fraud Hexagon"* emerged as a powerful tool for identifying and preventing fraud effectively. The *"Fraud Hexagon"* provides a broader perspective on risk management for fraud and includes six main factors that can contribute to fraudulent behavior.

- *Stimulus*: External events or internal pressures that may create a motive or incentive for fraud.
- *Capability*: The individual's ability to carry out fraudulent acts, such as possessing specific skills, knowledge, or authority.

- *Collusion*: The involvement of multiple parties working together to perpetrate fraud, making it more complex to detect.
- *Ego/Entitlement*: An individual's sense of superiority or belief that they are entitled to certain privileges, which might justify fraudulent actions in their minds.
- *Rationalization*: The process by which individuals justify their fraudulent behavior, often by convincing themselves that it is acceptable due to certain circumstances.
- *Opportunity*: The presence of vulnerabilities or weaknesses in control systems that allow fraud to occur without being detected.

By utilizing the *"Fraud Hexagon"* businesses and organizations can gain a comprehensive understanding of potential fraud risks and vulnerabilities. This model helps in developing robust measures and controls to safeguard against fraud and protect the integrity and reputation of the business. Emphasizing prevention rather than solely relying on detection, the "*Fraud Hexagon*" serves as a valuable tool in the ongoing fight against fraudulent activities in today's complex business landscape.

Detecting and Combating the Illegitimate Sources of Corruption and Fraud

Addressing the growing threat of illegitimate finance is crucial not only for financial stability but also for safeguarding the trust and confidence that underpin global economic systems. As awareness of the pervasive nature of illegitimate finance grows, attention has shifted toward detecting and combating the problems of corruption and fraud. Corruption and fraud are deemed to be exceptionally challenging activities to identify and even harder to justify. Fraud remains one of the most complex issues to combat. The most challenging aspect of combating corruption and fraud lies in their ever-evolving nature, with a multi-layered and entrenched presence within societies and businesses. Fraudsters constantly innovate new methods to execute their schemes and skillfully cover their tracks, evading detection. This complexity adds to the difficult and lengthy process of confronting fraudulent activity, demanding a profound comprehension of its underlying reasons and effective mitigation strategies.

Businesses must adopt a proactive approach to prevent and detect fraud, such as implementing comprehensive, robust, and stringent internal controls, regular audits, whistleblower hotlines, clear policies and procedures, thorough background checks on employees and regular employee training on fraud awareness. Moreover, fostering a culture of integrity and ethics can create a strong deterrent against fraudulent behavior within organizations. By acknowledging the presence of potential threats and staying informed through ongoing research, businesses can better safeguard their interests and protect themselves from the damaging consequences of workplace fraud. By remaining vigilant and proactive, organizations can protect themselves from the damaging impact of white-collar crimes and foster an environment of trust and accountability within their ranks. To address the reality that no organization is immune to occupational fraud, continued research on occupational fraud and workplace monitoring procedures is essential.

Employing modern technology and data analytics can enhance fraud detection capabilities. The continuous advancements in technology have also provided counterfeiters with opportunities to produce fake products with greater ease, posing additional challenges to businesses and consumers alike. Staying abreast of emerging technologies and adopting fraud prevention measures can aid in countering the ever-evolving tactics employed by fraudsters. Despite recent advancements in regulatory activities and data analytics, the detection and prevention of financial fraud still face challenges characterized by uncertainty and variability.

The complexity of fraud detection necessitates continuous collaboration between regulatory agencies, technology experts, and experienced fraud investigators. Regulatory agencies should make efforts to integrate technology into their anti-fraud strategies and standards. However, even with advanced tools, fraud investigators may encounter difficulties in obtaining sufficient evidence during examinations, leading to subjectivity in reporting fraud cases. Additionally, they may find it challenging to cope with the complexities of certain fraud schemes or to adapt to the ever-evolving analytical procedures and data mining technologies.

Businesses and regulatory bodies must work together to implement robust measures that can better safeguard their interests and protect the global economy from the harmful impact of fraudulent activities. Vigilance, education, and cooperation are crucial in the ongoing battle against fraud and its detrimental impact on economic prosperity.

CONCLUDING REMARKS

Illegitimate Finance remains a widely recognized global concern, yet its elusive nature often prevents timely detection, resulting in its acknowledgment only when it's too late. The far-reaching consequences of illegitimate finance underscore the urgency of combatting the pervasive issue of corruption and fraud. Promoting a culture of ethics and transparency within societies and organizations can act as a strong deterrent against corruption and fraud.

Understanding the tricky relationship between corruption and poverty is crucial for devising effective strategies to tackle both issues. Addressing corruption at all levels, along with comprehensive economic and governance reforms, is essential to break the cycle of poverty and create a more equitable and sustainable society. Implementing robust anti-corruption measures, strengthening institutions, and encouraging citizen engagement are vital steps in this ongoing battle against corruption and its detrimental effects on communities worldwide. Efforts to curb corruption and promote transparent governance are essential for fostering sustainable economic growth, reducing poverty, and creating a fair and just society for all.

The impact of fraud is widespread, affecting all sectors. The global financial crisis of 2008 and the subsequent corporate scandals, particularly within the financial industry, brought to the forefront the grave repercussions of fraud, underscoring its status as a significant worldwide problem. Accounting fraud can lead to substantial financial losses, with far-reaching consequences for both the economy and the state. In many instances, fraud can be attributed to weak or nonexistent controls within the organization, further exacerbating the problem.

In essence, understanding illegitimate finance and combating corruption and fraud requires a multifaceted approach that acknowledges the intricate nature of human behavior, while also addressing the systemic weaknesses in governance and societal and corporate structures that perpetuate corrupt and fraudulent practices. Only by addressing both the individual and systemic dimensions, one can hope to effectively curtail corruption and promote a more just and equitable society.

In conclusion, illegitimate finance arises because of a complex range of deceptive practices that can have severe legal, financial, and personal consequences.

CONTEXT AND ORGANIZATION OF THIS VOLUME

Regardless of whether you are a beginner or a seasoned researcher, this book will deepen the discourse about illegitimate finance. I am hopeful that this book is a fascinating and invaluable guide for understanding the theory, practice and cases of illegitimate finance in today's world.

This book consists of sixteen chapters by writers from fifteen countries. Thirty-one authors contributed from disparate parts of the world.

Americas: USA, Mexico
Europe: Switzerland, Italy, France, Sweden, Monaco, Türkiye
Oceania: Australia
Asia: India, Pakistan, Sri Lanka, Malaysia
Africa: Uganda, Nigeria

The first chapter "Targeted Enforcement against Illicit Trade in Tobacco Products: The Case of the United States" by James E. Prieger, examines that Illicit trade in tobacco products (ITTP) thrives on corruption and terrorism financing. Enforcing ITTP rules involves tradeoffs among objectives. The chapter discusses (1) efficient enforcement resource allocation, (2) targeting violent ITTP and terrorism funding differentially, (3) effective enforcement development, (4) insights from illicit drug markets, and (5) theoretical enforcement strategies. Targeted enforcement is the most efficient crime deterrent. Upcoming US policy changes may increase ITTP incentives, necessitating early enforcement for greater impact.

The second chapter "Entry Bans based on Foreign Criminal Proceedings: The Case of Switzerland" by Fabian Teichmann and Sonia Ruxandra Boticiu is about the role of the Swiss Federal Office of Police (Fedpol) has the authority to enforce entry bans on foreign nationals using the Foreign Nationals and Integration Act (FNIA). Due to migration and counterterrorism challenges faced by European countries, the Schengen Information System (SIS) plays a vital role. SIS facilitates information exchange among Schengen area authorities, including entry bans, wanted individuals, terrorism threats, extremism, and organized crime. Eastern European countries with corruption-plagued judiciaries like Moldova, Romania, Ukraine, Russia, and Bulgaria raise concerns about politically influenced manipulation of international criminal proceedings. As many entry bans depend on foreign criminal proceedings that could be politically motivated or manipulated, Fedpol's practices require careful examination.

The third chapter, "Consequences of Corruption on Economy, Politics and Society: The Case of India" by Asim Kumar Karmakar, Priyanthi Bagchi and Somnath Karmakar, explains that corruption, as the misuse of public office for private gain, has persisted in human societies throughout history. It takes various forms like fraud, embezzlement, theft, kickbacks, and bid rigging, causing detrimental consequences. The chapter aims to assess corruption levels and its impact on India's economy, politics, and society. It examines corruption worldwide and its effects on business and different sectors, proposing strategic policy implications for India and other countries grappling with this issue.

The fourth chapter, "Insider Trading and Front Running as the Basis of Money Laundering: The Case of Pakistan" by Tooba Akram, Muhammad Naveed, Suresh Ramakrishnan and Adnan Ali, analyses the fine line between insider trading and front running, highlighting their connection to global money laundering. Focusing on Pakistan's vulnerability, it examines three cases involving illicit activities by a politically exposed person, a corporate executive, and mid-level managers at a brokerage house. These cases provide detailed insights into these financial crimes and underscore the essential role of regulators and investigators. The chapter also emphasizes their significant impact on the financial economy, particularly concerning FATF measures.

The fifth chapter, "Earnings Management or Earnings Manipulation: A Narrative Review of Organizational Profitability" by Daniele Giordino, conducts a narrative review of earnings management, the strategic manipulation of financial reports to influence external stakeholders' perceptions. It examines accrual and real earnings management techniques, exploring motives and incentives. The review contributes to discussions on long-term profitability implications and emphasizes the need for systematic research on various forms of earnings management, including their effects on reputation, economic performance, and financial stability. Relevant case studies from previous literature are also included to illustrate the impact on corporations and organizations.

The sixth chapter, "Le Grand Saint-Antoine's Cargo: A Worst alleged case of Corruption in human history" by Jean Michel Rocchi and Ivan Topalovic looks at a historical case study of the plague's resurgence in 18th-century Europe, with a focus on the port of Marseille. A contaminated cargo ship from the Levant brought back the disease, evading existing protective measures. Researchers attribute the rapid spread to a "crime of the powerful," highlighting how corruption can have devastating consequences, causing tens of thousands of deaths.

The seventh chapter, "The Impact of AML/CFT Regime on the Economic Performance: The Case of Sri Lanka" by A P L J Dulanjali Thilakaratne, examines the impact of the Anti-Money Laundering and Countering Financing of Terrorism (AML/CFT) regime on developing countries, focusing on Sri Lanka. Using the AML/CFT Effectiveness Index and Mutual Evaluation Reports' ratings, it evaluates the regime's effectiveness. Additionally, GDP growth rate analysis is employed as an economic performance indicator. Findings show a positive correlation between a strong AML/CFT regime and economic performance in developing countries, emphasizing the need for continuous implementation and enhancement of such measures to foster sound economic growth.

The eighth chapter, "Electricity Theft, Regulatory Quality and the Rule of Law: A Cross-Country Analysis" by Gamze Kargın-Akkoç and Fuat Oğuz investigates examines the causal connections between the rule of law, regulatory quality, and electricity theft in regulated industries. The study demonstrates that a well-established rule of law reduces electricity theft and its associated social and economic costs. The analysis shows a unidirectional causality effect on transmission and distribution losses across income groups. Transmission and distribution losses granger cause regulatory quality in upper-middle and low-income panels, but not in high and lower-middle-income samples. These findings underscore the rule of law's importance in reducing electricity theft and highlight regulatory quality as a transmission channel.

The ninth chapter, "Electronic Banking Frauds: The Case of India" by Ruchi Gupta, Shilpi Gupta and Clement Chiahemba M. Ajekwe, explains that E-Banking plays a vital role in developing countries' economic growth and the digital economy's progress. India's booming banking sector brings both development and fraud in E-Banking. The chapter examines global fraud detection techniques, emphasizing caution and awareness. Utilizing secondary data, it aids banks and regulators in understanding and fortifying online banking fraud prevention. The government should invest in telecommunications and energy infrastructure and promote information and communication technologies for widespread benefits.

The tenth chapter, "Consumers' Risk Perception towards Cybercrimes and E-Commerce: The Case of Malaysia" by Hui Nee Au Yong, Yoke Chin Kuah, Chooi Yi Wei and Abdul Rafay, explores the research gap on risk perception and online purchasing intention among Malaysian consumers. The surge in online shopping during the pandemic raises concerns about scams targeting users sharing personal information.

Malaysia's cyber security policy defends critical information infrastructure. Financial awareness is crucial to combat cybercrime, and digital guardianship is needed to protect users. The routine activity theory explains offender selection based on targeting vulnerable online shoppers and the role of guardianship.

The eleventh chapter, "Investigations of Financial Frauds: Literature Analysis of Selected Financial Scams" by Martynas Damulis, focuses on securities fraud as a form of financial fraud, involving manipulation strategies for profit. Cases are analyzed to understand the impact on individuals' lives, and the use of cognitive biases and behavior heuristics in identifying potential fraud is explored. The literature review highlights the role of cognitive psychology in detecting red flags. However, limitations exist in understanding the impact on victims' lives, the social structure, the psychology of fraudsters, and their exhibited cognitive biases/heuristics. Further research is needed to comprehensively analyze this complex topic.

The twelfth chapter, "Accounting Fraud and Bankruptcy: The Case of Wirecard AG" by Barani Siddharthan S, Clement Chiahemba M. Ajekwe and Marie G Nakitende, discusses the Wirecard AG scandal, a German payment processing firm that gained substantial value on the stock exchange from 2010 to 2018. However, in 2019, investigative reports by the Financial Times raised concerns about Wirecard's accounting practices. A massive accounting fraud, involving missing €1.9 billion ($2.1 billion), was exposed in 2020, leading to bankruptcy. Several executives, including the CEO, faced charges of fraud and market manipulation. Regulators and auditors were criticized for their failure to detect and prevent fraud.

The thirteenth chapter, "Corruption and the Resource Curse: The Case of Timor-Leste" by Michael King and Abdul Rafay examines a corruption case in Timor-Leste, involving a tax lawyer who orchestrated a 'taxation miracle' for the country. He was charged with $3.51 million wire fraud by the US Department of Justice and received a six-year prison sentence. However, the case reveals complexities beyond fraud and official corruption, with misadventures in hiring, management, cybercrime, and weak internal controls playing a role. Collusion with multinational resource companies allowed the fraud to persist, causing a potential cost of $176 million to Timor-Leste taxpayers.

The fourteenth chapter, "Public Sector Frauds Control in the Caliphate of Umar bn Abdul-Aziz: Lessons for Contemporary Nigeria" by Adebayo Rafiu Ibrahim and Muftau Abdulrauph explores the exceptional achievements of Islamic caliph Umar bn Abdul-Aziz in combatting fraud, considered unparalleled after Prophet Muhammad (May peace be upon him). Examining Umar's strategies to reduce fraud in the public sector, valuable insights for contemporary Nigeria's political officeholders are revealed. Utilizing a phenomenological approach and Islamic ethical values, the study analyzes fraudulent activities in Nigeria. It concludes that public sector fraud is a global issue but draws hope from the Umayyad period, where effective leadership, exemplified by Umar bn Abdul-Aziz, eradicated corruption. Nigeria can follow a similar path by demonstrating a genuine commitment to fight fraud among public figures, inspired by the remarkable efforts during Umar bn Abdul-Aziz's caliphate.

The fifteenth chapter, "The Impact of Corruption on Tax Revenues: The Case of Türkiye" by Nagihan Özkanca Andıç, explains that in this interconnected world, rising corruption leads to harmful consequences such as tax evasion, irregular exemptions, and weakened tax administration, affecting both developed and underdeveloped nations. Corruption involving public employees is particularly destructive, causing a loss of tax revenue and other social problems. The research aims to investigate the relationship between tax types and corruption vulnerability, using a conceptual framework to explore causes and effects before conducting a regression analysis on tax revenues in Turkey.

The sixteenth chapter, "Difference between the real and estimated size of a company: A potential cause of Tax Evasion" by Gerardo Reyes Ruiz, analyses that Small and Medium-sized Enterprises

(SMEs) play a crucial role in modern economies, contributing significantly to wealth generation and job creation. The study explores the correlation between specific financial ratios to construct a synthetic measure for understanding the business size of selected Catalan SMEs. By utilizing Discriminant Analysis and Principal Components Analysis with financial ratios as input variables, the methodology precisely explains the "size" classification variable, addressing potential tax evasion. The study's valuation of the classification process reveals discrepancies between reported and actual company sizes, providing valuable insights into the business sizes of analyzed Catalan SMEs.

I express my gratitude to all the contributors and external reviewers who have provided valuable critiques to ensure the chapters meet the minimum acceptable standard. While the publisher and I, as the Editor, have made our best efforts in preparing this book, we do not make any representations or warranties regarding the accuracy or completeness of its contents. Specifically, we disclaim any implied warranties of merchantability or fitness for a particular purpose. The strategies, suggestions, or any information in this book may not be suitable for every specific situation, and individuals should consult with a professional as needed. Neither the publisher nor the Editor will be liable for any loss of profit or any other commercial damages, including but not limited to special, incidental, consequential, or other damages.

Abdul Rafay
University of Management and Technology, Pakistan
September 2023

ENDNOTES

[1] Group of Twenty (G20): It is an intergovernmental forum comprising of the European Union and nineteen industrialized and developed countries. It is a primary venue for international economic and financial cooperation.

[2] World Economic Forum (WEF): It *is an international non-governmental forum based in Switzerland, to discuss the state of the world by engaging business, political, academic, and other leaders of society.*

Section 1

Illegitimate Finance in the Economy

Chapter 1
Targeted Enforcement Against Illicit Trade in Tobacco Products:
The Case of the United States

James E. Prieger
https://orcid.org/0000-0002-5521-5557
Pepperdine University, USA

ABSTRACT

Illicit trade in tobacco products (ITTP) is often facilitated by corruption and in some cases helps terrorism financing. Enforcement against ITTP is vital but involves tradeoffs among competing objectives. This chapter examines (1) the efficient allocation of enforcement resources against ITTP (2) whether to differentially target ITTP that involves violence or funding for terrorism (3) the development of effective enforcement (4) lessons learned from illicit drug markets and (5) theoretical insights about enforcement targeting. It is concluded that targeted enforcement is the most efficient way to deter crime. Some upcoming policy changes in the US may increase the rewards to ITTP, and enforcement resources applied before illicit markets grow further will have a greater impact than enforcement resources applied later. Comparison among the results shows that focused deterrence aimed at ITTP-related violence is most promising and that the goal of reduced funding for terrorism may be more difficult, although combating the former may also help lessen the latter.

INTRODUCTION

Illicit trade in tobacco products (ITTP), much of which is carried out by organized criminal groups, is a substantial and growing economic activity around the world[1]. Estimates vary due to the nature of the market, but about one out of every 12 cigarettes smoked worldwide in 2020 was illicit, either contraband to avoid taxes or counterfeit. Figures from Euromonitor International (2021) show that the volume of illicit trade in terms of cigarettes sold grew by 7.7% from 2015 to 2019 (even as total consumption of

DOI: 10.4018/979-8-3693-1190-5.ch001

cigarettes fell by 7.6%), and illicit trade is expected to rise by 2025 to a worldwide market share of 8.8%. ITTP's national market share in the US is in the range of 4.2% to over 20%, depending on the source, methodology, and timeframe of the estimates (which are discussed below). ITTP creates much harm: to health, to governments' streams of tax revenue, and to social order by creating violence in illicit markets and by funding terrorist organizations (Reuter & Majmundar, 2015). As with other instances of smuggling and illicit trade, ITTP around the world is often facilitated by corruption, whether large-scale or petty or involving law enforcement or customs officials (Chionis & Chalkia, 2016; Kupatadze, 2021; Joossens & Raw, 2012).

To date, enforcement against ITTP in the US and in many other countries has had some isolated successes but overall has neither quashed the trade nor prevented its growth in most places. Increasing enforcement is costly, and enforcement can have unintended and unwanted consequences of its own, such as stimulating illicit revenue and violence (Prieger & Kulick, 2014, 2015). Thus, indiscriminate ramping-up of enforcement efforts is likely not the best strategy, and a careful look at alternatives is warranted. In this chapter, options to combat efficiently organized crime engaged in ITTP are examined.

The multiplicity of potential goals and evaluative dimensions — promoting public health, protecting tax revenue, suppressing violence, cutting off financing for terrorism, maintaining public order and the rule of law, fostering respect for government and removing possibilities for corruption (Rafay, 2023a) and improving relations between police and communities—creates difficulties for policy directed at criminals and organizations engaged in ITTP. Some tobacco-related policy goals work at cross-purposes to one another; promoting public health by taxing tobacco makes achieving the other goals more difficult. However, efficient enforcement strategies can improve the terms of the tradeoffs involved.

Three approaches—not necessarily mutually exclusive—to combat ITTP are broad-spectrum enforcement against ITTP in general, targeted enforcement against ITTP-related violence, and targeted enforcement against ITTP that funds terrorism. Lessons from experience with other organized illicit markets, most notably those for illicit drugs, insights from law and economics, and theories of enforcement swamping and strategic dynamic concentration are brought to bear on finding efficient options to combat ITTP and the related violence and funding for terrorist activity.

In the next section, ITTP in the US, its links to violence and terrorism, and current enforcement efforts are described. The subsequent section discusses the three alternative approaches: general suppression of ITTP, deterrence focused on violence, and deterrence focused on ITTP-enabled funding for terrorism. Aspects of *Pulling Levers*, a particular form of focused deterrence successful in reducing gun crime in drug markets, are discussed and applied to ITTP. The discussion of targeted enforcement encompasses both theoretical and practical aspects. The policy implications of the results are discussed in the recommendations section, including a discussion of how recent and likely future regulation may increase the scale of ITTP and its consequences. A summary of the pros and cons of the various approaches for policymakers leads to the conclusion that deterrence focused against violence is a promising strategy. Future research directions to address the increasing need for interagency cooperation to fight ITTP, particularly as some of it moves into cybermarkets, are discussed. A final section draws together the conclusions of the research.

BACKGROUND

This section takes the US as a case study and reviews the current state of ITTP and existing efforts to combat it. The US is chosen for examination because of the size of its market, its severe challenges regarding intranational cross-border ITTP, and the significant interest in the study of its ITTP (Kulick *et al.*, 2016; Pelfrey, 2015; von Lampe *et al.*, 2016). Furthermore, the capacity of the U.S to combat ITTP is middle-of-the-pack among developed countries (Ulep *et al.*, 2021), and thus recommendations developed here could likely be adopted feasibly by many other countries. Finally, the difficulty in the US in fighting ITTP due to the many regulatory and law enforcement agencies involved or with potential jurisdiction, at many levels of government, is a familiar problem around the world. Even in countries with more centralized (i.e., less federalist) governments and law enforcement, ITTP touches on so many different areas of concern—tax evasion, illicit trafficking, trademark violation and counterfeiting, money laundering, funding for terrorism, and violent crime—that the need for coordination among many agencies remains.

ITTP in the US

ITTP takes several forms (Kulick *et al.*, 2016), but at the root of each is the profit motivation to evade taxes. Excise taxes on cigarettes in the US consist of a federal tax of $1.01 per pack levied on manufacturers and state taxes most often levied on distributors. Every state has an excise tax on cigarettes but the rates vary widely, from $0.17 per pack in Missouri to $4.35 in New York; additionally, Washington, D.C. has a tax of $4.50 per pack (all as of year-end 2021). In a few areas, counties, or cities (and sometimes both, in the case of the city of Chicago and Cook County, Illinois) levy additional taxes on tobacco.

The most common ITTP in the US is the smuggling of genuine cigarettes from lower-tax to higher-tax jurisdictions, often at scale by criminal operators.[2] In New York, the state with the highest smuggling rate, about half of untaxed cigarettes come from outside the state are estimated to be from commercial (i.e., organized) criminal smuggling (LaFaive *et al.*, 2016). How much of ITTP is perpetrated by groups falling into narrower definitions of organized crime (i.e., large, sophisticated, hierarchical organizations using violence and corruption of government officials to facilitate criminal activity (Finckenauer, 2005) is unknown, but ITTP in the US has been linked to criminal organizations ranging from small gangs to the Genovese, DeCavalcante, and other crime families of La Cosa Nostra and international smuggling rings (Bender & Palmer; 2016, United States Attorney's Office, 2015; Associated Press, 2016). Criminal organizations sometimes use proceeds from ITTP as "venture capital" for other illicit activities (Shelley, 2018).

The large differences in excise taxes among the states or other jurisdictions provide a profit motive for ITTP (Baltagi & Levin, 1986; Bishop, 2018; Chiou & Muehlegger, 2008; DeCicca, Kenkel, & Liu, 2013; Galbraith & Kaiserman, 1997; Goel, 2008; Lovenheim, 2008; Prieger & Kulick, 2018; Saba *et al.*, 1995; Stehr, 2005; Thursby & Thursby, 2000). For example, the difference in taxes between Virginia and New York City amounts to almost $90 per carton of cigarettes, a differential that supports a sizeable Virginia-to-New York smuggling trade (ATF, 2018; Green, 2012). Purchasers masquerading as consumers or retailers buying in bulk from legitimate sources (Green, 2015a). Those purchases are then smuggled to higher-taxed states, either in personal vehicles or by common carrier, and sold or transferred to scofflaw shopkeepers and street sellers. Some of those smuggling operations constitute substantial criminal enterprises. One bust in Mississippi in 2009 led to the seizure of 200 million cigarettes valued at $20 million; another takedown of an organization smuggling from Maryland to New York involved $55 million in illegal cigarette sales (Mississippi Office of the State Auditor, 2009; New York State Office of the Attorney General, 2013). Despite the high profits, the easy availability of products in low-tax states means that the whole process is nowhere near as complex as smuggling controlled drugs from Mexico or growing or manufacturing them domestically. Trafficking in counterfeit products is much less common (excluding counterfeit tax stamps).[3] While as recently as 2003, 44% of commodities seized at the national borders were counterfeit cigarettes (General Accounting Office, 2004), by 2013 that figure had fallen to 1% (DHS, 2014) and in 2019 it was still only 3% (DHS, 2020). Organized crime in counterfeit tobacco can be a larger problem elsewhere in the world (Aziani, Dugato & Meneghini, 2020; McEwen & Straus, 2009).

One widely cited source, Euromonitor International (2021), estimates that untaxed or counterfeit products accounted for 4.2% of the trade volume of cigarettes in the US in 2020 (see Figure 1), or 9.6 billion cigarettes. Estimates from other sources and periods are higher. A report from the National Research Council estimates that between 8.5% and 21% of cigarette sales were subject to tax evasion and avoidance in 2010-2011 (Reuter & Majmundar, 2015). The estimates in Figure 1 show that illicit trade in the US as a share of all retail trade in cigarettes grew each year from 2008 through 2020, excepting a minor drop in 2015. Worldwide, the market share of ITTP declined slowly between 2006 and 2015, after which it begins to rise. In 2020, the year of the global pandemic, both the global level and share of ITTP fell, perhaps because illicit trade routes were disrupted by lockdowns and increased border and customs vigilance due to COVID-19.

Figure 1. Estimated illicit trade in cigarettes in the United States
Source: Euromonitor International (2021)

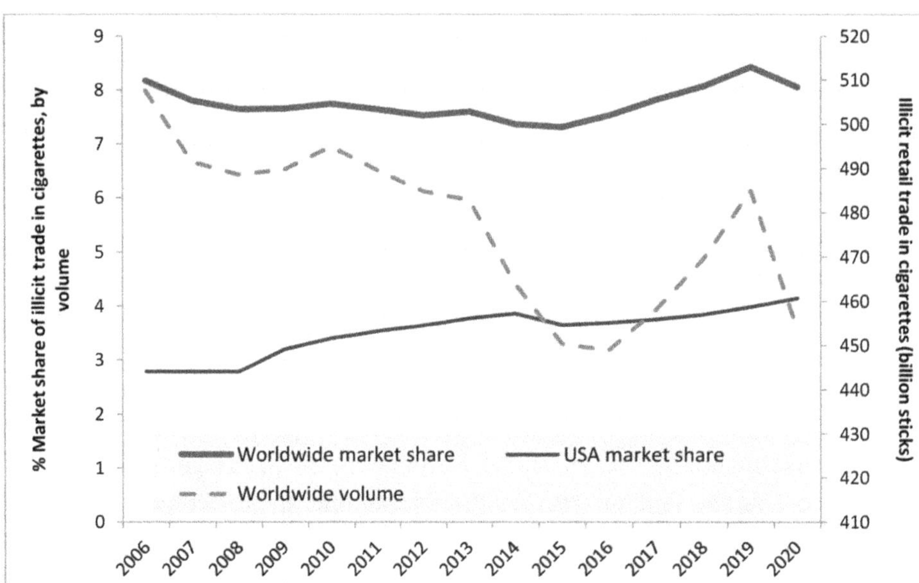

ITTP and Violence

With illicit trade comes the potential for organized crime and violence, but illicit markets vary widely along both dimensions. Illicit drug markets have proven to be particularly susceptible to violence (Andreas & Wallman, 2009; Goldstein, 1985; Rafay, 2021a). Some violence in and around illicit markets stems from calculation: participants may shoot competitors to gain or protect market share, customers to collect on business debt, suppliers to retaliate for having been cheated, employees to punish theft, or potential witnesses to prevent testimony (Caulkins *et al.*, 2010; Goldstein, 1989; Kleiman, 2011; Reuter, 2009). Many drug-related homicides in the US stem from robbery or interpersonal disputes instead of "business-related" reasons, however. Robberies of drug dealers, a common occurrence (Jackall, 1997), are often triggered by expectations that dealers have large amounts of cash or valuable product on their person and are further encouraged by the reluctance of the victims to call the police (Goldstein, 1985). Once dealers are armed to protect themselves from a robbery (and with their purchases of weapons financed from illicit-market revenue), they become potential sources of deadly violence. Furthermore, participants in the supply side of illicit drug markets are often pre-disposed to violence because they tend to be recruited from communities with above-average rates of violent crime (Moeller & Hesse, 2013).

Moreover, open-air illicit markets with many sellers and buyers create numerous opportunities for interpersonal disputes, often among young men for whom a reputation for dangerousness confers prestige and has practical value (Topalli *et al.*, 2002). Those perceived as less dangerous either become targets for others' aggression or take steps (such as arming themselves) to put themselves on a footing of equality (Jacobs *et al.*, 2000). The mentality of the "code of the street" can feed back into purely business-related violence; for example, unpaid debt is the sort of affront that cannot be safely tolerated in heavily-armed street culture.

Flagrant drug markets—where strangers meet in public spaces or dedicated drug-dealing locations such as crack houses—thus create circumstances much more conducive to deadly violence than discreet markets, where acquaintances connect in multi-purpose locations such as bars or where transactions are consummated by delivery to the buyer's residence (Boyum & Kleiman, 2003; Reuter, 2009). One reason current ITTP in the US has not been as violent as illicit drug markets to date is that the retailing is often indoors and discreet, due to the preferences of the buyers (von Lampe *et al.*, 2016). A corner store selling smuggled cigarettes is not markedly more exposed to robbery than any other corner store; the proprietor will not fear to call the police if he is robbed; nor is it likely that ITTP significantly increases the amount of cash on premises beyond that necessary for normal retail operations. While sales of "loosies" (single cigarettes, which are illegal to sell) by petty criminals occur in open-air locations, such sellers are often individuals engaged in small-volume operations, with small amounts of cash involved, rather than members of organized criminal networks (Smith *et al.*, 2007).

However, illicit tobacco markets are not violence-free. Criminal organizations are often diversified, and the Virginia Crime Commission reports that cigarette smuggling is often accompanied by credit card fraud, money laundering, burglary, and robbery (Dyson, 2015). The Bureau of Alcohol, Tobacco, Firearms, and Explosives (ATF, 2018) states that ITTP can have a "nexus to violent organized crime," and the Attorney General of New York also raised concern about violence associated with illicit tobacco (NY State, 2013). Much of the violence appears to occur up the supply chain, away from the retail level. In 2015 in Virginia, robbers accosted at gunpoint two traffickers loading cigarettes into a vehicle and escaping with $90,000 worth of cigarettes and $25,000 in cash (Green, 2015b). Overall, nevertheless, the levels of ITTP-related violence in the United States appear to be dramatically lower than the levels of violence in dealing with "hard" drugs. Reuter and Majmundar (2015) assert, based on experience in Europe, that illicit tobacco markets are not violent. Their report also notes that analogous research has not been performed in the United States, although various domestic incidents involving violence and ITTP have appeared in the media. For just one example, in November 2009, 14 people tied to a contraband cigarette ring were arrested in Virginia; members of the ring had asked undercover investigators to murder two of their competitors (Johnson, 2010). Statements from law-enforcement agencies tend to stress the violence associated with ITTP. For example, several law enforcement agencies state that trafficking has become increasingly violent in Virginia as competition increases between various trafficking organizations (Green, 2015a, 2015c). With the potential profits to be made and the history of other forms of organized crime such as firearm and human trafficking, experts expect organized crime networks to expand their market share (Green, 2015b; Pelfrey, 2015). Despite these plausible expectations, it is impossible to measure accurately the level of or trends in ITTP-related violence in the US, because crime is not tracked systematically by that category. Regardless, ITTP is not currently close to involving as much violence as the market for illicit drugs from Mexico.

Links to the Financing of Terrorist Organizations

In addition to concerns about violent crime, ITTP also raises questions about where its criminal proceeds are directed. Criminal organizations often traffic illicit tobacco and other goods as a form of trade-based money laundering (FATF, 2020, 2022; Rafay, 2021b), but in some instances, the movement of value through trading illicit tobacco is intended to fund terrorism. In some cases, in the US, criminal organizations have sent the proceeds from ITTP to terrorist organizations (Reuter & Majmundar, 2015; Sanderson, 2004; Shelley & Melzer, 2008). ITTP has been linked in various ways to al Qaeda, Hezbollah, Hamas, ISIL, FARC, and other terrorist groups (Exploring the Financial Nexus of Terrorism, 2018; Shelley, 2020; Tamekamta, 2021). The importance of the link between the illicit tobacco market and terrorism is contested. Reuter and Majmundar (2015) find that the connection to terrorism seems to be minor in the United States, based on cases examined from 2004 and 2005. The Financial Action Task Force, the lead inter-governmental body promulgating policy to fight terrorist financing, notes that the relatively small number of confirmed cases linking ITTP and terrorism may be due to local jurisdictions predominantly investigating and prosecuting only the predicate offense—the ITTP—but not the associated money laundering or financing of terror (FATF, 2012).

Some law-enforcement personnel and official government sources indicate that the problem of ITTP financing terrorism is larger than Reuter and Majmundar (2015) suggest. In 2007 and 2008, officials in New York and from the ATF estimated that cigarette smugglers earned, in the aggregate, between $200,000 and $300,000 per week (i.e., up to $15.6 million per year) in New York. These officials believed that a large fraction of the money was sent to the Middle East to finance Hezbollah, Hamas, and al Qaeda (Republican Staff, 2008). More recently, the ATF (2015) stated that the illegal trafficking of tobacco products by organized criminal groups was increasing and that some such groups had ties to terrorist organizations, although no statistics were presented. A US Department of State (2015) report adds that cigarette smuggling is "a lucrative crime for some terrorist groups and a potential revenue source to finance acts of terror" and "encourages a convergence between organized crime, terrorist groups, and other threat networks," though without providing much in the way of specific, detailed evidence. The high priority given to violent crime compared to mere tax evasion creates incentives for agencies seeking resources for ITTP enforcement to stress the violent aspects of the traffic; no comprehensive, quantitative study has yet been undertaken.

The publicly available evidence on ITTP and terrorism is based on case studies (Shelley & Melzer, 2008) and the few occurrences that appear in the media at the conclusion of successful law-enforcement operations. One international report documented some contemporary examples of how trafficking in illicit tobacco was used to fund terrorism in Syria and Iraq, for the benefit of the State of Iraq and the Levant (ISIL/Da'esh) and other Al-Qaeda affiliates (OECD, 2016). It is also worth noting that there is a high prevalence of immigrants from the Middle East involved in trafficking along the I-95 corridor. A Congressional report states that large-scale cigarette smuggling networks in New York are dominated by groups composed of closely connected individuals from the same extended family or country of origin—primarily Lebanon, Yemen, Jordan, and Palestine (Republican Staff, 2008). Typical of the close ethnic connections of many of these criminal enterprises was one operating in Maryland and New York, all of whose indicted members were Palestinian, that had distributed $55 million in untaxed cigarettes to Arab markets and grocery stores in New York (New York State Office of the Attorney General, 2013). Such anecdotes are common; about half of individuals engaging in ITTP along the Virginia to New York pipeline mentioned in print news media between 2015 and 2021 had Middle Eastern surnames or connections.[4] Of course, not all criminals with Middle Eastern backgrounds have connections to terror groups. Conversely, one of the non-Middle Eastern criminals included in these counts openly declared he wanted to send the proceeds of the trafficking to Hamas for purposes of perpetrating terrorist acts in New York City (Crudele, 2015).

Given the high potential profits from and current relatively low risk of ITTP, the prevalence of involvement in ITTP by criminals of Middle Eastern nationality or descent out of proportion to their population (even in New York City, with its large communities of Middle Easterners, where only 1.2% of residents are of Arab ancestry),[5] and the growing trend toward low-budget terrorism, there is a case for vigilant monitoring of possible links between ITTP and terrorism. Nevertheless, the current extent of the problem, and whether it is increasing or decreasing, remains unknown. The high ratio of potential financial return to likely penalties would seem to make ITTP an attractive target for those interested in financing terrorism, as for criminals with other uses for their money.

Existing Efforts to Combat ITTP

When it is nonviolent, the legal system often treats crime involving illicit tobacco as less serious than possession of drugs or weapons and accordingly assigns it a low priority for prosecution (Ross, 2015). Thus, current enforcement efforts against ITTP are generally limited, sporadic, and small compared to the scope of the traffic itself. The federal regulator covering tobacco products, the Food and Drug Administration (FDA), has only a small staff devoted to conducting criminal investigations (FDA, 2020).[6] For the most part, however, the FDA appears to view enforcement of its tobacco regulations as an administrative matter. For example, the only significant document from the agency regarding ITTP mentions sending warning letters to offending retailers (FDA, 2018). Organized criminal groups engaged in ITTP are unlikely to be deterred by such weak enforcement mechanisms.

Apart from the occasional high-profile sting operation (US State Dept., 2015), often only when ties to terrorism are involved, other federal enforcement of tobacco laws is also remarkably lax. Primary responsibility for criminal investigation and enforcement of tobacco laws (apart from the tax laws) is in the ATF, which apparently considers the area a "backwater" (Watkins & Apuzzo, 2018) and spends less than 2% of its budget on fighting tobacco diversion (Office of the Inspector General, 2009). Primary responsibility for federal excise tax compliance is in the Alcohol and Tobacco Tax and Trade Bureau (TTB), a Treasury Department agency created to monitor and enforce compliance with federal tobacco and alcohol tax laws but which lacks the power to make arrests. In 2015, TTB completed about 400 revenue investigations of alcohol and tobacco tax fraud, but these contributed to the identification of additional excise tax revenue of only $57 million (TTB, 2016). This amount, which includes alcohol taxes, is a pittance of the value of tax revenue due on all ITTP. There has been little change in the TTB's activity in recent years; in 2020, the recovery of additional revenue had risen only slightly to $60 million (TTB, 2021).

State and local enforcement is limited by the perception of ITTP as a low-priority crime. New York City and other areas with a high incidence of ITTP occasionally conduct sweeps of retail outlets likely to sell illicit tobacco, and law-enforcement agencies in sourcing states such as Virginia occasionally investigate suppliers of illicit products. Few states have entire investigative units dedicated to combatting ITTP. New York's Cigarette Strike Force, formed in 2013, is a rare exception; in 2017 it confiscated $6.6 million worth of contraband tobacco and levied $7 million in fines (New York State Office of the Governor, 2014, 2017). However, seizures and fines were abnormally high that year in New York and the Strike Force has been relatively quiet since; in any event, New York is one of the few states that devotes serious effort to enforcement. Even so, the direct financial disincentive to smuggle from this level of enforcement activity is trivial, accounting for roughly one percent of the total margin on illicit sales in New York.[7]

Municipal resources to enforce tobacco laws are even lower. The sheriff of New York City has the resources to inspect only 5% of tobacco retailers each year (Elstein, 2016). With such a low probability of detection, even the strengthened penalties since 2020 against retailing untaxed cigarettes, which include temporary suspension of the business registration,[8] would be expected to do little to deter violation. Legal disincentives to engage in smuggling would be much lower in most other locations.

Efforts to seize products entering the US from abroad likely lead to the interception of only a small fraction of the illegal products crossing the border. If so, smugglers would consider such trivial border seizures as merely a minor cost of doing business (Ross, 2015).

Such low probabilities of detection and sanction against ITTP of all forms lead to the problem of enforcement swamping, in which low expected penalties due to constrained enforcement resources lead to a self-reinforcing trend toward greater lawbreaking (Kleiman, 1993). Thus, targeting enforcement efforts in efficient ways to focus deterrence to achieve specific goals is important, as discussed in the following section.

ALTERNATIVE APPROACHES TO COMBAT ITTP

In this section, three alternative goals are discussed. The goals are not mutually exclusive but are different enough that the methods used to attain them may need to be quite different. The first goal is the suppression of ITTP generally. For any given expenditure, general suppression could be attempted through uniform but thin enforcement means or by targeted (a.k.a. focused) deterrence; these are examined in turn in the first two subsections. The other goals, discussed in the subsequent subsections, are narrower, and therefore probably more feasible to attain. The second goal is to alleviate or prevent violence in ITTP, and the third is to disrupt the use of ITTP to finance terrorist organizations.

Suppression of Market Volume

The first option is to aim for law enforcement efforts against the scale of the entire illicit market. Two approaches to achieve the goal of decreasing the market supply of illicit products are discussed. In this subsection, it is assumed that enforcement will be untargeted, i.e., uniform or random enforcement directed at ITTP across the entire range of potential lawbreakers. Most current enforcement against ITTP in the US appears to be of this type of general crackdown. The consequences of attempting to suppress market volume this way are increased costs of supplying the illicit market, increased revenue, increased violence, and ultimately difficult political questions regarding the will to sustain such outcomes.

In the microeconomic modeling approach adopted in the field of law and economics, enforcement against an illicit market can be treated as raising the effective cost of doing business. Costs rise through perceived risks of arrest, sanction, fine, incarceration, and product seizure. Modeling enforcement as a cost shifter allows supply and demand analysis to be used to explore likely outcomes (Prieger & Kulick, 2014, 2015). As an (unrealistic) example of how enforcement can be linked to suppliers' costs, note that if that one out of every four units intended to be placed on the illicit market were expected to be seized by authorities, then to actually supply an additional unit to customers would require the production and distribution costs for one and third units. Thus supply-side enforcement shifts upward the supply curve, which represents the marginal costs in the illicit industry. Enforcement unambiguously raises the illicit market price of the good and lowers the quantity sold. See Figure 2, in which the equilibrium in the illicit market moves from point A to point B, where the latter has higher prices and lower quantity sold. As long as demand is in the inelastic region, it follows that an increase in enforcement will increase revenue in the market (Prieger & Kulick, 2015).

Since Goldstein (1985) it has been common to assume that violence rises with revenue earned in illicit drug markets. For example, the larger amounts of cash transacted may attract more violent robberies of dealers. If this is indeed so, then the ultimate impact of increased enforcement against the illicit market is to increase violence.[9]

Figure 2. The impact of untargeted enforcement on equilibrium in a competitive market

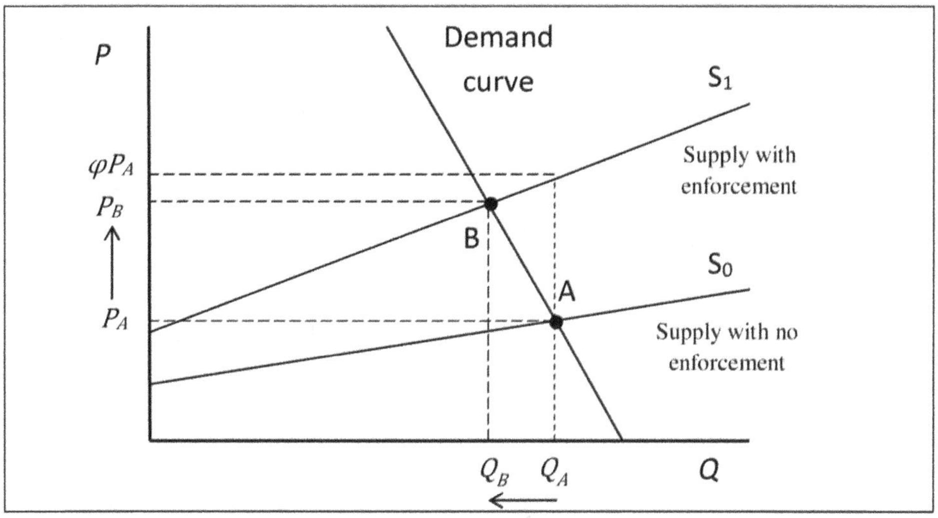

The empirical literature examining the enforcement of drug laws mainly supports the conclusion of this model regarding violence. Evidence suggests that enforcement initiatives against illicit drug markets in the 1980s increased the street price of drugs (Caulkins *et al.*, 1993; Zimmer, 1990). Comprehensive surveys show that the great majority of studies find a positive association between drug law enforcement and violence (Kulick *et al.*, 2016; Werb et al., 2011). Of course, enforcement can disrupt criminal markets and generate a turnover of organizations and their personnel, and each such disruption of equilibrium creates uncertainty and opportunities for profitable contestation, temporarily increasing the returns to violence against competitors and informants (Hobbs, 2003; Moeller & Hesse, 2013).

Prieger & Kulick (2014, 2015) and Kulick *et al.* (2016) show that the market characteristics of ITTP make it likely that enforcement will raise illicit revenue and therefore violence. For example, under the conditions likely to apply to proposed national bans on menthol cigarettes or even all cigarettes with a non-trivial amount of nicotine (as discussed in the Recommendation section below), enforcement is likely to be aimed primarily at suppliers and demand is more inelastic than supply. Under these conditions, the model implies that enforcement would increase revenue and violence. Thus attempts to suppress the market volume of illicit cigarettes may be likely to have the unintended consequence of fostering additional ITTP-related violence. If in fact, more intensive enforcement led to more violence, or even to more arrests, prosecutions, and sentences, two difficult questions would arise:

(1) Would the gains from reducing ITTP be sufficient to counterbalance the social losses, especially considering the already tense relationships between police and residents in low-income neighborhoods where the retail aspects of ITTP tend to flourish? and
(2) Even if the answer to (1) is yes, does the political will exist to implement such a strategy and keep it in place long enough to substantially shrink the market?

Given the recent retreat from aggressive policing in some cities following the Black Lives Matter protests and calls to "defund the police" in 2020, the answer to (2) is likely no in most places. However, if the answer to either question is no, there is good reason to doubt the practicability of a generalized crackdown.

Focused Deterrence and Dynamic Concentration

If unfocused deterrence aimed indiscriminately at all participants in an illicit market leads to problematic outcomes, what alternatives are available? For any given expenditure on enforcement, it turns out that targeting some potential lawbreakers more than others can increase overall compliance. The general notions of targeted enforcement, focused deterrence, and dynamic concentration of enforcement pressure are discussed here. The theoretical notions behind the improved efficacy of focused deterrence are explained first, followed by empirical evidence showing that the theory translates to improved outcomes in an application. This subsection concludes with a close examination of Pulling Levers, a particular implementation of focused deterrence that has been implemented successfully to curtain drug violence in several US cities.

Why Focus Deterrence?

In Becker's (1968) approach to modeling crime and punishment, a rational, self-interested potential lawbreaker commits a crime if and only if the expected gain from doing so is larger than the expected loss from punishment. The economic approach to crime sets punishment and allocates enforcement effort to equate the marginal social benefit of enforcement with its marginal cost. Given the assumed calculus of potential criminals, economic efficiency then requires that the largest feasible fine be set in order to make expenditure on enforcement as small as possible. This approach to optimality uses high fines or imprisonment (i.e., severe punishment) to overcome the low probabilities of detection of lawbreaking (Polinsky & Shavell, 2007).

In practice, the information required to calculate the optimal level of enforcement—the distribution of the gains from crime and the true value of the social harm from crime, int. al.—is unavailable. Furthermore, the basic model from law and economics leaves out many phenomena that would affect the social calculus: unintended consequences of enforcement such as increased violence in illicit markets, additional heterogeneity of individuals beyond the gain from crime, and so forth. Finally, it is unlikely to be politically feasible to spend the necessary amount for the optimal, high level of enforcement. These considerations lead to a more modest objective: given any particular amount of money to be spent on enforcement, how to best allocate it to reduce crime? This question leads to an exploration of the benefits of the particular form of targeted enforcement considered here: focused deterrence.

First, consider focused deterrence in the static case. Uniform application of enforcement efforts against crime is inefficient in many cases. Targeting efforts against a subset of potential criminals can increase compliance for the same expenditure on enforcement (Lando & Shavell, 2004). To demonstrate the logic, consider splitting the set of potential criminals in a market into two identical groups. For any given enforcement budget, focusing deterrence on one of the two groups causes compliance to (weakly) rise in the focal group and (weakly) fall in the other. However, the gain in compliance from the focal group can outweigh the loss in deterrence in the group with less enforcement.

This simple yet powerful result follows from the sharp threshold for compliance resulting from a rational potential criminal's calculus, as the following example demonstrates. Consider the set of retail outlets that sell cigarettes in an area and assume that each shop could gain $300 per week from selling illicit products. Assume that if law enforcement in the form of inspections and undercover purchases is evenly allocated among shops to detect illicit sales, then 10% of the shops can be inspected each week. For simplicity, assume that inspection leads to certain detection of illicit activity and that the fine for violation of the law is $2,000 (the fine in New York City for the first violation of selling counterfeit or improperly taxed cigarettes). The expected net gain of each shop, if risk-neutral, is, therefore, $300 – ($2,000 × 10%) = $100. Since expected gains are positive, all shops will violate the law. Thus any reallocation of enforcement effort that induces *any* compliance increases deterrence in the market. Such reallocation could be as simple as inspecting only one randomly selected shop each month, announced in advance; then all other shops are undeterred as before but the shop of focus will be compliant since the gain no longer outweighs the expected penalty, which has risen to the full $2,000.

Reallocation of enforcement need not be so extreme. If the authorities announced that half of the shops (e.g., those with odd street address numbers) were the focus of enforcement next week, then the detection and punishment rate would double to 20% for them. Those shops would face an expected penalty of $400, large enough to deter the crime. In this example, the compliance rate rises from zero to one-half through focused deterrence, with no increase in expenditure on enforcement. In this market, compliance can in fact be pushed as high as two-thirds by focusing deterrence on that proportion of the shops.[10] This example sets aside the question of how much ITTP would merely shift to the other shops. However, as long as illicit trade is less than fully shifted—the expected outcome, given imperfect information among consumers—the same principle applies: focusing deterrence can increase compliance. The benefits of focused deterrence accrue under much more general situations than the simple example above (Lando & Shavell, 2004).

It is important to note that the amount of punishment actually levied also falls. In the example with unfocused enforcement, 10% of the shops are punished each period. With focused deterrence, complete compliance is achieved and there is no punishment. Punishment is costly to perform and may cause harm to individuals and firms apart from the direct fine in ways not modeled above. For example, reputational effects may harm the future business of firms (Baucus & Baucus, 1997) or the earnings prospects of individuals (Raphael, 2014), and if punishment involves incarceration there are other potentially severe costs to the individual, his family, his community, and the state (CA LAO, 2022; Lynch & Sabol, 2004; Rose & Clear, 1998; Travis & Waul, 2003).[11] Given these costs, optimal enforcement strategies minimize the amount of actual punishment required to achieve any given level of compliance (Kleiman & Kilmer, 2009).

Next, consider focused deterrence via dynamic enforcement. Enforcement budgets can be allocated even more efficiently once repeated play is added to the thinking and modeling about enforcement. In the simplest form, a dynamic enforcement strategy can increase deterrence by endogenizing membership in the group upon which enforcement is focused. Harrington (1988) shows that when included in the focal group is state dependent—in particular, based on the past violation—then deterrence increases in both groups. In this approach, the non-target group faces a lesser but still positive probability of detection. Compliance increases in the non-target group because its members do not want to be placed into the focal group, where punishments are higher. Thus, by making the profit opportunities sufficiently attractive in the non-target group, all potential lawbreakers increase their compliance. By allowing the target of enforcement effort to change over time, the policymaker can potentially design more effective mechanisms for deterrence.

The dynamic concentration of enforcement offers even greater possibilities for the effective use of targeting (Kleiman, 1993, 2009; Kleiman & Kilmer, 2009). This approach employs an enforcement mechanism that places potential lawbreakers into a game in which strategic considerations multiply the impact of the enforcement expenditure. The basic insight from Kleiman and Kilmer (2009) is that more compliance does not necessarily require more punishment if the threat of punishment is appropriately placed. Consider first a one-shot, sequential-move game with n risk-neutral players (individuals or organized groups). Each player chooses to comply with or violate a law. Violation creates a gain for the player but will be detected by the agency. The players move sequentially, observing all previous moves by other players. Without loss of generality, the budget for enforcement restricts the enforcement agency to a sanction against a single player. After all, players have chosen whether to comply, and the agency observes violations and punishes one of the violating players if and only if at least one player has violated. The interesting case is when the gains from violation, the sanction cost to the player, and n are such that if a player knew he would be sanctioned he would not violate but if he expected all others to violate then he would, too. If so, and if the enforcement agency's policy is random, uniform enforcement, then in the unique subgame perfect Nash equilibrium of the sequential game there is no deterrence, all players violate, and one player will be punished.[12]

This replicates the outcome from the example of unfocused enforcement in the previous section: even with spending the entire enforcement budget, there is no deterrence. Why this occurs when $n = 2$ is clear. Player 2 will violate if player 1 violated and will comply if player 1 complied. But then player 1 faces the choice between complying and violating knowing that in the latter case both players will violate; by assumption, the latter case is preferred. With more than two players, the game tree has more branches but the result is the same through backward induction. At each decision, "comply if all have complied before me" and "violate if all have violated before me" are part of the player's optimal strategy. In the first move of the game, then, player 1 is faced with that same choice as in the two-player case—comply knowing all will comply or violate knowing all will violate in response—and chooses to violate, triggering the chain of subsequent violations.

The enforcement agency can do better by targeting the enforcement. If the agency establishes a priority order for the punishment of the players, then the threat of enforcement will be fully concentrated upon each player at the time it must choose whether to commit the crime. Kleiman and Kilmer (2009) term this *dynamic concentration.* To illustrate, imagine that there are two players and that the agency announces that if both players violate then player 1 will receive a single sanction in the enforcement budget. If only one player violates, that player is punished with certainty as before. The unique outcome of the game, whether the moves are simultaneous or sequential, is no violation and no enforcement. Since there is no longer "safety in numbers," player 1 will not violate. In response, player 2 will comply to avoid the full penalty that would accrue if he violated. Kleiman and Kilmer (2009) show that full compliance remains the unique equilibrium of the simultaneous or sequential game with n players with any complete ordering of priority for enforcement. Thus, under the assumptions of full information and rationality, *any* number of players can be deterred from violation with the threat of a single, dynamically concentrated sanction. Kleiman (2009) likens this counterintuitive outcome to the proverbial Texas Ranger who stops a large, angry mob in its tracks, even though he is down to his last bullet, with the threat to shoot the first person who steps forward.

Consider now the more realistic case in which each player decides many times whether to violate as time passes but has limited information (Kleiman, 1993; Kleiman & Kilmer, 2009). What happens when players do not observe whether others commit crimes or receive punishment, do not know what the enforcement strategy of the agency is, and do not know what the probability of punishment p is? Under these conditions, the situation reverts from a game to a decision problem where a player's beliefs about p are updated over time based on past experience. When the beliefs about p converge to the actual probability,[13] then Kleiman and Kilmer (2009) arrive at the following conclusions about the equilibria of the dynamic system with two players:

1) With a budget of one sanction, if players' prior beliefs about p are low enough then they will always reach a stable violate-violate equilibrium, whereas with sufficiently high priors they will always reach a comply-comply equilibrium;
2) Adding a second sanction, even temporarily, can tip the outcome to the comply-comply equilibrium, which will be stable even after the possibility of the second sanction is removed.

With more than two players and more than one sanction available, the same results obtain as in outcome 1 above. Furthermore, the same tipping from the high-violation equilibrium to the low-violation equilibrium as in outcome 2 above can be accomplished by the dynamic concentration of the punishment. Prioritizing the players for punishment will more rapidly increase the perceived probability of punishment held by players at the top of the list. Once they stop violating, the perceived probability of punishment of the next prioritized players begins to rise, and so on. Compared to random enforcement, with dynamic concentration, it takes fewer budgeted sanctions to tip the system to the low-violation outcome. Thus, the practical import of this work is to highlight 1) how increasing the capacity to punish offenders, even temporarily, can tip the system to a low-violation equilibrium while reducing the level of sanctions (and therefore their cost) actually imposed; and 2) that dynamic concentration will outperform equal-probability sanctioning.

Evidence on Targeted Enforcement

The theoretical case for targeted enforcement discussed above can be supplemented with evidence concerning how focused deterrence performs in real-world, real-crime settings. Criminologists have studied whether various forms of targeted enforcement work better in actual practice than the status quo of unfocused deterrence. The findings from this literature are first discussed in general and second, in the next subsection, with regard to Pulling Levers, a specific form of targeting enforcement against high-violence individuals in drug markets. Although the results are necessarily specific to the particular cases studied, the literature concludes that targeted enforcement is generally—but not uniformly—effective at reducing crime (Goldkamp and Vîlcică, 2008).

The meta-analysis conducted by Mazerolle, Soole, and Rombouts (2006) concludes that enforcement targeting geographic areas with high drug-related crime (what they term "geographically focused problem-oriented/partnership policing") is the most effective enforcement strategy. In particular, they found that such targeting reduces crime more than unfocused community-wide policing efforts. A meta-analysis of 78 studies on "hot spots policing"—enforcement targeted to small, high-crime areas within a city—also found a small but statistically significant causal effect of targeting, relative to similar crime hot spots that were not targeted (Braga *et al.*, 2019). Furthermore, targeting does not merely displace crime to other locations (Braga *et al.*, 1999, 2018; Braga *et al.*, 2019; Weisburd *et al.*, 2006). Targeted enforcement in high-crime areas has also been found to diffuse benefits by lowering crime in non-targeted areas (Braga *et al.*, 2019; Goldkamp and Vîlcică, 2008).

Focused Deterrence in Action: Pulling Levers

The premier implementation of focused deterrence against individuals involved in drug and gang-organized crime is *pulling-levers policing* (PL) (Kennedy, 1997). A PL intervention attempts to reduce crime through the strategic application of enforcement against specific individuals, not just areas, coupled with social service resources to encourage desirable behaviors (Braga & Weisburd, 2015). The essential features of PL in practice are the following (Kennedy & Braga, 2006; Braga & Weisburd, 2015). An interagency state and federal enforcement group is formed to combat a particular area of crime such as gun violence in a city. After research to identify key repeat offenders, their organizations, and their contexts, the group designs an enforcement intervention directed at these offenders. The group communicates to the targeted individuals to inform them that they are under scrutiny, which particular crimes will receive the heightened punishment, and when other targeted individuals have been so punished. The intervention employs all available possibilities for enforcement—pulling on all available "levers"—to sanction offenders who commit violence so that they face high costs of offending. Face-to-face meetings with police, social service workers, and community leaders such as clergy instruct the targeted individuals on what they can do to avoid enforcement action.

PL was first implemented in Boston with apparent success during the mid-1990s with Operation Ceasefire (Braga *et al.*, 2001). Operation Ceasefire differed from previous crackdowns on gang violence in two ways: the target of enforcement was violence rather than drug sales, and prevention of violence (through the carrots and sticks mentioned above) was prioritized over prosecution. Subsequently, PL has been applied to reduce homicides and gang violence in Boston, Chicago, Cincinnati, Detroit, Lowell, MA, Indianapolis, Los Angeles, New Orleans, Newark, Oakland, Stockton, CA, and the Quad Cities in Iowa.[14] In other areas it has been implemented specifically as a drug market intervention (High Point, NC, Nashville, Peoria, and Rockford, IL). PL is generally found to be successful at reducing violence and homicide (Braga & Weisburd, 2012; Corsaro & Engel, 2015). Braga, Weisburd, and Turchan (2018, 2019) perform a meta-analysis of 24 studies examining focused deterrence interventions. Of these, 19 studies reported statistically significantly reduced crime associated with the intervention. Furthermore, all 12 studies that specifically assessed the impacts of focused deterrence on violence by gangs and other criminal groups found statistically significant negative effects on crime. The meta-analysis yielded a moderate standardized, overall effect of PL on crime. It is worth noting that an earlier, similar analysis found (from the 11 earliest studies) that the effect size was "relatively large" (Braga & Weisburd, 2012), which may indicate that PL was implemented and studied first in the cities where it had the greatest effect.

Applying Focused Deterrence to ITTP

Targeted enforcement, the dynamic concentration of punishment, and PL have not yet been applied to ITTP. While there have been many enforcement actions in the US against ITTP, all seem to have stemmed from general enforcement against ITTP or from sting operations against particular, often small, groups engaged in organized crime, sometimes with an anti-terrorism angle. Such stings typically take the opposite approach from PL. Instead of informing the targeted group that it is under scrutiny, the secrecy of the investigation is maintained until the enforcement sweep and arrests begin.

What might the application of PL look like against ITTP? Drawing on the discussion of PL in Braga and Weisburd (2015), the effort would begin with the formation of an interagency—and likely multistate—task force involving police, federal and state prosecutors, probation agencies, and state and federal agencies with knowledge of ITTP (such as the TTB and the enforcement division of the Northern Virginia Cigarette Tax Board). The currently operating High-Intensity Drug Trafficking Area (HIDTA) program, headed by The White House's Office of National Drug Control Policy, is a potential model for such a cooperative arrangement. The HIDTA program was created to coordinate drug-control activities among federal, state, and local enforcement agencies, facilitate the sharing of data and manage relevant funding across the federal government (The White House, 2022). Operation Xcellerator of the US Drug Enforcement Agency (DEA) provides another example of a successful multistate, multiagency operation against illegal drugs. The operation, concluded in 2009, resulted in 775 arrests, seizures of 23 tons of narcotics worth almost $60 million, and 169 weapons (BBC, 2009). The operation comprised six federal law enforcement bodies and benefited from more than 200 federal, state, local and foreign law enforcement resources. Even though these efforts were not examples of PL, such cooperative arrangements demonstrate that interagency cooperation is possible.

The next steps would be to bring the enforcement capacity of these agencies to bear on the single or multiple priority targets (the choice of which to be discussed below) (Kleiman, 2009). Once enough offenders have been incarcerated or deterred from engaging in ITTP, equilibrium in the selected area should tip from the high-offending to the low-offending outcome. Then the temporary increase in enforcement effort toward that specific group or area can be diminished while maintaining the stability of the low-violation equilibrium. The enforcement resources so freed up can next be applied to tip a new target, and so on.

There are certain practicalities that must be observed for this scheme to work. Under what conditions are PL and dynamic concentration likely to succeed? Kleiman and Kilmer (2009) note that subjects must be susceptible to deterrence, which is to say that they must weigh the costs and benefits of illegal behavior (even if not in a perfectly rational manner) and that they perceive punishment as sufficiently costly to influence behavior if the probability of enforcement exceeds some threshold. Since ITTP, at least on the supply side, is pursued as a business activity instead of impulsive behavior or a crime of passion, this condition is likely to be satisfied. Dynamic concentration and PL are also best suited for situations in which detection is relatively easy and the set of potential offenders is known. When detection is difficult it is harder to issue credible threats of punishment, but even in that case, the logic of the example presented above makes it clear that focused deterrence is more efficient than an untargeted effort at detection and enforcement. More problematic is the case in which potential offenders cannot be easily identified. In such settings, certain practical aspects of PL, such as the face-to-face warnings about the new enforcement of "rules of the game" become infeasible. Alternatives to direct communication can include informal methods of spreading warnings such as through informants, parolee networks, and ethnic communities with disproportionate representation among ITTP actors to accomplish the same task. Regardless, the model with Bayesian learning by violators about the probability of punishment described above does not require an a priori known set of offenders.

The next important question is which criminal activities and set of offenders to target. The main choice of which crime to target is among ITTP in general (goal 1), violent crime committed in the course of (or ancillary to) ITTP (goal 2), and ITTP that funds terror (goal 3). Given the existing widespread, large-scale interstate smuggling operations in the US, and the difficulty in detecting the illicit activity, attempting indiscriminately to targ*et al*l ITTP—at least any further up the supply chain than the retail level—may be difficult. For this reason, goals 2 and 3 are more likely to be attained through focused deterrence, as the next two sections discuss.

Focused Deterrence Against ITTP-Related Violence

The second of the three potential goals for combating ITTP is to target enforcement resources at alleviating or preventing violence in ITTP.[15] Focusing deterrence on violence associated with ITTP may be more promising than trying to quell all ITTP in general because ITTP-related violence is not nearly as prevalent as ITTP, is easier to detect, and is likely to involve a smaller number of potential offenders. Furthermore, attempting to stamp out all ITTP raises the stakes for participants in ITTP by putting the entire industry's profits at risk. On the other hand, high levels of violence are not essential to ITTP, and it is possible that participants could be easily persuaded to abandon it. A focus on violence would, however, require a re-orientation of the current enforcement effort, which mainly focuses on the trade-in and flow of illicit cigarettes. This section first discusses how PL may be applied toward this end and then examines challenges to successful implementation. Despite the current apparently low level of violence in illicit tobacco markets, given the potential for violence to increase for the reasons discussed above it is well worth considering in advance targeted enforcement against ITTP-related violence.

Implementation

To apply the principle of PL, particular acts of violence must be able to be linked to ITTP and to specific individuals or criminal organizations (unless the target for enforcement is to be an area rather than a set of people). In principle, this should be no more difficult for illicit tobacco markets than it is for illicit drug markets, where PL has been successfully applied.

Next is the choice of which offenders to target. If violence reduction is the goal, then the choice is between targeting offenders in particularly violent areas and those who are members of particularly violent criminal organizations or networks. The best choice here depends on whether it is easier to link illicit products detected at the retail level with a source *area* or a source *organization*. Genuine cigarettes from major manufacturers, as long as they are still in their packs, are relatively easy to trace back to their state of intended sale and often also to the first (legitimate) step in the supply chain, the sale from the manufacturer to a wholesaler or retailer in a low-tax state. For example, in Virginia, cigarettes intended for resale in higher-tax states may be purchased legitimately in bulk from large retailers such as Walmart and Sam's Club or from wholesalers and other distributors by retail companies set up as fronts for ITTP (Green, 2015a; such retail "fronts" buying wholesale avoid retail sales taxes but not excise taxes). Tracing illicit products to the particular criminal organizations that supplied them is more difficult but still possible in some cases.

With these choices in mind, it is now possible to imagine how focused deterrence against ITTP-related violence might proceed. After the formation of the interagency enforcement task force, the authorities publicly identify the target area or organization and announce that ITTP-related violence will no longer be tolerated there. This is the *supply target*. As a practical matter, the most violent supply group or area should be targeted first. Policymakers will have to decide how to establish a scoring system that will prioritize potential targets (Chi *et al.*, 2014). The priority scores can depend not only on the extent of violence but on other considerations such as the identity of the victims (e.g., shooting a law enforcement officer may warrant a higher score than shooting a competitor). Community input from a range of stakeholders can be an important part of developing the scoring system (Paul *et al.*, 2011). This has the advantage of creating some disincentive for violence even in non-targeted areas since the dealers in those areas will reasonably want to avoid having their location chosen next.

Then the authorities should go after the retail outlets likely to carry illicit products from the supply target. These outlets become the *retail target*. For example, if the supply target is violent criminal organizations in the Richmond area (a hub of ITTP in Virginia [Green, 2016]), then small convenience stores (known as bodegas) in the Bronx may be a natural starting point given smokers' preference for purchasing untaxed cigarettes at those stores (von Lampe *et al.*, 2016) the past history of enforcement against ITTP in New York City. (Between half and three-fifths of locations inspected in New York City between 2011 and 2015, many of them bodegas, were in possession of illicit cigarettes (Green, 2015a; von Lampe, *et al.*, 2016), and 92 percent of the contraband was from Virginia.) The authorities make known to such stores in the area that they face a high probability of inspection for the illicit product and that if it is found and can be traced back to the supply target, the legal repercussions will be severe. The possibility that retailers are intimidated or coerced into maintaining supply-chain relationships with violent organizations may mean that sole reliance on retail targeting is ineffective without some direct pressure on the supply targets. To take advantage of dynamic concentration, the retail targets may also be subdivided for focus or prioritized for enforcement, as described above. Once equilibrium tips toward compliance, another retail target or (if violence from the supply target has been suppressed) another supply target can be chosen.

The advantage of leaning on the retail targets instead of solely on the supply targets directly is twofold. First, detection is likely much easier at the point of retail sale. For example, authorities in New York City regularly conduct such stings and sweeps to combat ITTP. Petty criminals selling single, untaxed cigarettes (i.e., loosies) on street corners and in parks are well-known to police in at least some areas of New York (Baker *et al.*, 2015). On the other hand, membership in, or even the existence of, some supply organizations may be less well-known to authorities (although this is less likely to be true with the most violent organizations). The second advantage of focusing on retail targets is that the supply target may involve activity outside the US, as with counterfeiting operations, importation of cheap whites, or the future possible involvement of violent Mexican drug trafficking organizations in ITTP if more types of tobacco products are banned in the US (Kulick *et al.*, 2016).

To paraphrase Kleiman's (2009) conclusion for the application of dynamic concentration to drug markets, adapted for ITTP-related violence: If the authorities focus enforcement and punishment on the most violent organizations, and do so in a highly visible manner, then a supplier of illicit tobacco would have to weigh the benefits of violence—the intimidation of witnesses, the creation of bargaining power against other market participants, and the direct profit from the violent robbery of rivals—against the disadvantage of moving himself up on the list of supply targets for enforcement. Moreover, those individuals and organizations (or, alternatively, geographic areas) most prone to violence would be taken out of the market by enforcement action at a higher rate than their less violent rivals, exerting evolutionary pressure toward less-violent ITTP.

Challenges to Successful Implementation

Some challenges would need to be met to implement focused deterrence against ITTP-related violence. The current pattern in New York City of under-the-counter ITTP retailing in corner stores might produce less violence than would ensue if the same volume of traffic were handled by street vendors. That in turn suggests a potential unwanted side-effect of cracking down on retail targets: if the increased enforcement were to drive ITTP back to street vendors, the result might be increased violence. That offers a reason to approach a crackdown on discreet retailing with caution; police should be vigilant about the re-emergence of flagrant retailing and prepared to shift their focus as necessary to prevent such a re-emergence. However, a third market format, in which customers order by text message and dealers deliver, now reportedly dominates illicit drug retailing in New York. This format might combine two attractive features from a law-enforcement perspective: less convenient access than corner-store availability (especially for new buyers in the marketplace) and less flagrancy and therefore less violence than open-air dealing (Reuter, 2009). For example, changes in illicit drug market transactions such as the use of mobile phones to connect dealers with customers and the lower prevalence of open-air street markets have reduced drug market violence (Rosenfeld, 2016; Zimring, 2011). A retail ITTP market that is off the street, out of the corner store, and more difficult for potential buyers to access might be the best available outcome. Enforcement practices could encourage such an outcome by putting less pressure on the home-delivery market than on the other two potential market forms. However, managing the repression of open-market ITTP without exacerbating police-community tensions will be challenging in the post-Eric Garner world, assuming that it is possible at all; the best hope would be early detection and quick mobilization of enforcement pressure to keep that market from growing to a size where large numbers of arrests would be required to get it under control.

There are further challenges for focused deterrence. Investigative bodies must have or be able to develop the capacity to connect identified violent actors to ITTP-linked organizations or ITTP-related activities. Traffickers in ITTP may also perpetrate violence that is unrelated to their conduct of ITTP, and such activities should not be conflated with ITTP-related violence. Making these connections between individuals, ITTP, and violence may require more thorough investigative methods, coordination, and technologies than are currently employed. The lack of coordination among agencies (and nations, where cross-border flows are involved) is a major contributor to ineffectiveness in combating illicit trade (Shelley, 2018). A successful program of investigation and enforcement would need the capacity to store, process, and analyze attribution data to create priority targets. A template, discussed by Chi *et al* (2014), is the Department of Justice's Organized Crime Drug Enforcement Task Forces which created a regionally organized system to gather comprehensive intelligence on targeted organizations.

Fiscal politics and constraints within and among agencies may present additional challenges. Focused deterrence and Pulling Levers would require higher-than-usual levels of flexibility and cooperation across agencies, which can strain limited staffing and budgets. The complicated task of reaching an agreement to prioritize ITTP among the participating agencies could face internal resistance. Decision makers in some agencies might perceive that the opportunity costs of such a commitment to fighting violence and ITTP are too high.

Finally, following a strategy that eliminates large, violent players in the ITTP market could create short-term dynamics that temporarily offset the anticipated reductions in violence. Leadership removals and fragmentation inside criminal organizations can lead to increased violence as the potential successors in the organizations seek to signal their comparative advantage in violence (Chi *et al.*, 2014; Dickenson, 2014). Enforcement that disrupts established hierarchies among criminal groups in the market can also spur renewed competition among groups, with attendant violence (Moeller & Hesse, 2013). These considerations enhance the benefits of targeting violent players in the market, however. If the intervention is successful at communicating (and proving) that "violence does not pay," then violence would no longer serve as a signal of fitness for leadership or an effective method of gaining market share.

Focused Deterrence Against Terrorism

The third possible enforcement goal is to reduce the flow of funds created by ITTP that finance terrorist groups or acts. Individual terrorists and small terrorist cells have much lower financial needs than parent organizations such as ISIL, since the costs of planning and executing a terrorist attack are lower than maintaining a fighting force, recruiting fighters, running propaganda operations, etc. (FATF, 2016). Some recent terrorist acts have been carried out with very limited funding (Shelley, 2015)—less than €10,000 in the case of the attack on Charlie Hebdo in Paris in November 2015 (one of which attackers was also engaged in ITTP). ISIL is making increasing use of small-cell terrorism, which is typically self-financed, implying that modest amounts of money from ITTP or other sources could go a long way toward the spread of terror. As discussed above, there are historic and current links between cigarette smuggling and terror organizations like the Irish Republican Army, Hezbollah, Hamas, al Qaeda, ISIL, and others (US Dept. of State, 2015). As with targeting violence, a scoring system could be developed to prioritize targets engaged in ITTP to fund terrorism. The goals and scores could interact; for example, an organization using more violent tactics on American streets while sending revenue abroad to support terror could receive a higher score than another potential target generating the same amount of funding for terrorists.

At first glance, the difficulties in applying Pulling Levers to this target are large. In particular, the targets may be difficult to identify, the targeted individuals may be less prone to be deterred than others involved in ITTP, and greater federal enforcement effort would be required. These issues are discussed in turn.

Given the nature of the severe punishment for financing terrorism, criminal organizations conducting ITTP for this purpose may be expected to hide their links to terrorism. However, when detection is difficult, communication of the threatened punishment becomes harder to accomplish and less credible. Furthermore, the community-involvement aspects of PL are problematic if individuals are difficult to identify and target. There are additional difficulties in this respect if the perpetrators are immigrants with weak ties to the larger communities in which they live and operate. For example, as mentioned above many smuggling networks in New York State are run by tightly knit, family-based groups of Middle Eastern descent (Republican Staff, 2008).

Targeted individuals must be susceptible to deterrence. Ideological or religious convictions may make some perpetrators of ITTP for purposes of funding terrorist activity immune to deterrence. However, it appears to be unlikely that all, or even most, targets would be at this ideological extreme. Furthermore, extremists transact with many service providers and other partners up and down the supply chain, and these partners may be more able to be deterred. If doing business with a terrorist-linked ITTP outfit is sufficiently risky, some other players may choose to deal with firms not linked to terrorism. An example of direct pressure on the supply target would be to freeze the assets of individuals or organizations that seek to fund terrorism via ITTP.

To date, applications of PL against gun and drug violence have made heavy (although not exclusive) use of local enforcement resources. The agencies most involved in combating terrorism and its funding, on the other hand, are customs and border authorities, law enforcement agencies, financial intelligence units, and taxation authorities at the federal or international level (FATF, 2022). For example, a recent high-profile case involving the smuggling of $8 million worth of cigarettes and providing material support to Hezbollah was investigated by Immigration and Customs Enforcement's (ICE) Homeland Security Investigations, the Federal Bureau of Investigation (FBI), ATF, US Citizenship and Immigration Services, the Internal Revenue Service, and the local police department and sheriff's office, with assistance from Canadian national security and police agencies (Immigration and Customs Enforcement, 2011). A recent counter-terrorism financing report called for better cooperation and coordination between agencies (FATF, 2012). Whether a task force with a heavy representation of federal enforcement agencies could achieve the necessary "local customization" that has been important to the success of PL in the past is an open question.

The international community of agencies involved with the counter-financing of terrorism is already familiar with the notion of targeted enforcement, at least in the general meaning of the term, which may help to bridge the institutional and historical differences among the many agencies involved. For example, FATF (2022) recommends and discusses the targeted freezing of funds and assets without delay of people engaged in the funding of terrorism. These financial sanctions are intended to be carried out by the relevant domestic authorities expeditiously and nimbly, regardless of whether criminal proceedings have begun. This flexibility gives enforcement agencies a "quick strike" option to put pressure on domestic ITTP operators channeling funds to terrorist groups even before criminal sanctions can be brought to bear.

The intervention could be designed to make use of the greater information held by illicit market participants about links to terrorism. As discussed in the previous section, pressure can be applied indirectly to the supply target by proximately pressuring the retail target. The goal would be to disincentivize retailers and dealers from doing business with the supply target so that the supply target no longer has a market for its illicit tobacco. Once that supply target is out of business or at least deterred from financing terrorism, the authorities can target the next largest funder of terrorism and repeat the process (Chi *et al.*, 2014). This requires linking the source of retail supply to the specific supply targets, which may be difficult as discussed above.

RECOMMENDATIONS

With the above examination of the strengths and weaknesses of untargeted and targeted enforcement in hand, recommendations for policy going forward can now be made. Specific suggestions for policymakers include 1) expecting and planning for increased ITTP and possibly violence as tobacco regulation increases the prices of or takes away altogether legal options for consuming nicotine and 2) applying enforcement resources earlier before illicit markets grow further to maximize the impact of the enforcement dollar. This section concludes with tables summarizing the advantages and disadvantages of untargeted enforcement, targeted enforcement in general, targeted enforcement against violence and funding terrorist organizations.

The exploration of targeted enforcement against ITTP is predicated upon there being substantial violence or funding of terrorism resulting from the illicit market. The publicly available data make it difficult to know the exact scale of either outcome. However, even if violence is low in ITTP at the present time, targeted anti-violence enforcement would be a promising approach if the scale of ITTP (or untargeted enforcement against it) increases the level of violence. Planning now to prevent future violence may be of heightened importance, given that there are several potential policy changes looming that might increase such harms from ITTP.

The US Food and Drug Administration (FDA) is currently considering whether to require manufacturers to reduce nicotine in cigarettes to non-addictive levels and, separately, has proposed to ban menthol cigarettes and all flavored cigars. As of August 2022, the FDA had not yet issued its final determination in either case. In 2016, the FDA extended its authority to include the regulation of e-cigarettes. New e-cigarette products now require authorization from the FDA before they can be marketed, which requires submission of health studies, product warning labels, and other requirements that will raise the costs of introducing new products and potentially lower their demand. Some states place additional regulations on tobacco and e-cigarettes, including bans on menthol cigarettes and using e-cigarettes anywhere combustible cigarettes are prohibited.

Voluminous evidence in the economic literature on regulation in general (not necessarily specific to health and product safety regulation) shows that regulation can increase costs, discourage innovation and introduction of new products, and raise barriers to entry for potential competitors (Joskow & Rose, 1989). With higher costs and less competition from the smaller manufacturers who are likely to drop out of the market, prices of illicit products may be expected to rise. In addition to regulatory pressure, the increasing tax burden on tobacco is expected to increase ITTP. Figure 3 shows that the average tax rate and the tax share of the total retail price increased dramatically from 2000 to 2009 and that the tax rates have continued to climb since then. Since increased taxes have been shown to decrease the incidence of smoking, public health experts continually call for higher tobacco excise taxes. However, there is much evidence that higher prices for legal tobacco products stimulate demand for the illicit substitute of ITTP (Freitas-Lemos *et al.*, 2021; Prieger & Kulick, 2018).

Figure 3. Growth in the tax burden on cigarettes in the US
Source: CDC (2021) and Campaign for Tobacco-Free Kids (2021)

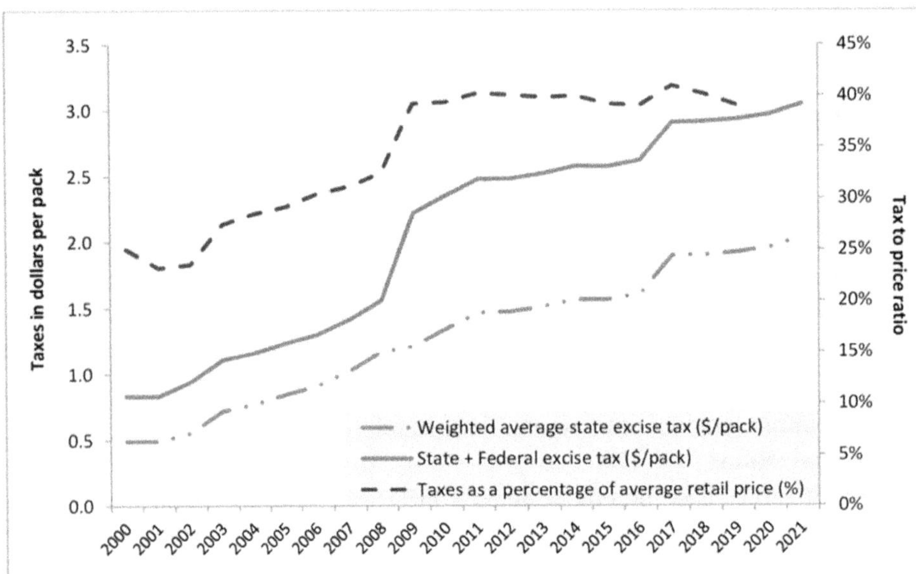

Should the FDA decide to ban menthols, demand for the illicit products would nearly certainly rise. Surveys of menthol smokers find that about one-quarter say that they would find menthol cigarettes regardless of a ban (O'Connor *et al.*, 2012; Zatoński *et al.*, 2018). Given the well-known tendency of survey respondents to underreport socially undesirable intentions (Fisher, 1993) such as engaging in criminal activity, the potential fraction of menthol smokers turning to ITTP after a menthol ban may be larger than this statistic suggests. Evidence on actual behavior also shows that many menthol smokers are reluctant to give up their preferred product. A study of a municipal partial ban on menthol found that 46% of cigarette packs smoked six months after the ban was menthol, even though the product was available only from specialist shops (about one in seven tobacco retailers) (Kurti *et al.*, 2020). Analysis of menthol bans in Canada indicates that although in at least one province authorities seized few menthol cigarettes after a ban (Stoklosa, 2019), trade-in menthol sourced from First Nations reservations appears to be widespread (Carpenter & Nguyen, 2020). In Europe, 13% of those who smoked menthol cigarettes before the EU-wide ban a few years ago indicated in a survey that they were buying menthol cigarettes from "other sources"—in the context of the survey question, nearly certainly a euphemism for illicit sources—after the ban (Janazzo, 2021). Banning all but trivial amounts of nicotine in cigarettes would similarly create new possibilities for ITTP.

If violations of the law are expected to increase in response to changes in tobacco regulation, it will make sense to precede the regulation with heightened (or more intelligently focused) enforcement (Kulick *et al.*, 2016). Suppose that ITTP increases in response to a ban on a tobacco product (a menthol ban, for instance), with no change in enforcement effort. The higher the overall violation rate, the smaller the risk of punishment for any individual violator. But then a spiral of enforcement swamping (Kleiman, 1993) would ensue, leading to the high-violation equilibrium described above. Since the enforcement-swamping analysis shows that preventing an increase in ITTP would be less costly than attempting to reduce the size of an established market, it follows that enforcement effort will be more efficiently allocated if applied before market growth rather than after.

To further guide policymakers' choices about how and against what to enforce, the present research results are summarized in Table 1 and Table 2. Table 1 contains a summary of the advantages and disadvantages of untargeted enforcement, targeted enforcement in general, and targeted enforcement against the funding of terrorist organizations. Table 2 summarizes targeted enforcement against ITTP-related violence, which differs by the specific supply-side and retail targets. The clearest—and easiest—choice is whether to target enforcement at all. It seems apparent that focusing effort to deter the targets (whatever those targets may be) is the most efficient method. Focused deterrence has the advantage of increasing the amount of compliance obtained from enforcement, may in the long run require less actual punishment, and can increase the legitimacy of the law enforcement effort in the eyes of the community. Evidence from the application of the Pulling Levers variant of focused deterrence is promising. While there may be higher setup costs associated with a Pulling Levers style intervention, compared with the status quo untargeted and limited enforcement directed against ITTP in the US, it seems clear that the status quo is not achieving its current goal of significantly reducing flows of illicit tobacco.

Once the policy decision is made to focus deterrence, next is the choice of targets. Given its past success against violent offenders in other drug markets, Pulling Levers appears to be well-suited to target ITTP-related violence. Combatting terrorism is an important current goal of public policy and national security, but there may be fewer levers for a focused deterrence program to pull. Part of the value of Pulling Levers, when it works, is that the threat of punishment can obviate the need to undertake actual costly enforcement. However, since uncovering terrorist links would presumably require expensive intelligence work just to identify the players, that advantage may be lost. However, no stark choice of target between violence and terrorism is required. Based on some of the media reports cited above, some participants in ITTP linked to terrorism may also be violent and targeting the latter will also target the former even if unwittingly. Furthermore, the decision is not binary but instead a question of how to optimally allocate resources between the two targets. Since it is likely that the marginal benefit of the last dollar spent on reducing violence is lower than the marginal benefit of the first dollar spent on targeting ITTP related to terrorism, efficient allocation of enforcement efforts will likely involve both targets.

Decisions remain to be made on whether to target specific organizations involved in violence (or terrorism) or any organizations operating in violent areas. While more specific targeting (the former option) would be more efficient, area targeting may require less investigatory expense. And in either case, applying pressure to the supply target through retailers and dealers can alleviate problems of asymmetric information about suppliers' activities and proclivities for violence.

Table 1. Comparison of aspects of various options for untargeted and targeted enforcement

General Target	Advantages	Disadvantages
ITTP (status quo; untargeted enforcement)	• No need to trace retail illicit products to a particular source	• Current approach is largely ineffective • Enforcement budget required for a significant reduction in supply may be prohibitively high • The more successful at reducing supply, the higher the illicit revenue and violence
Any focused deterrence	• Leverages impact of any given expenditure on enforcement • Evidence shows it has worked well applied to some other targets (gun crime, drug/gang violence) • Can increase the perceived legitimacy of police action • If works, it requires less actual punishment • Full rationality of the targets is not necessarily required	• May require higher fixed costs for the design of the intervention, setting up interagency enforcement groups, community outreach, etc. • Some forms (e.g., full information dynamic concentration) depend heavily on individuals' assumed rationality and ability to think strategically
ITTP funding for terrorist organizations	• Requires more detective/intelligence work to identify targets • May require buy-in from federal agencies with little experience or interest in combatting ITTP • Targets may be less deterrable if highly ideologically motivated	• Local success can create global benefits

Table 2. Comparison of aspects of various options for enforcement against ITTP-related violence

Supply Target	Retail Target	Advantages	Disadvantages
Any	Any or none	• Focuses on the greater problem (violence, not ITTP per se) • It is easier to discourage violence than to shut down an organization	• Requires detective/intelligence work to link violent acts to particular individuals and organizations
Violent organizations	Any or none	• Applies pressure most directly against the producers of violence.	• More difficult to link seized retail products to an organization than an area.
Violent areas	Any or none	• Easier to link seized retail products to an area than an organization.	• Only indirectly applies pressure against the producers of violence.
Any	A specific target is chosen	• Retail targets may be easier to identify than supply targets • Leverages the greater information possessed by ITTP retailers/dealers	• Perceived legitimacy of police action may be lower if the logic of the intervention is not adequately explained

FUTURE RESEARCH DIRECTIONS

Further work will be required to craft an operational intervention to combat ITTP-related violence or terrorist financing in the US Key to the success of Pulling Levers is the creation of an interagency working group with authority and responsibility for action. A powerful network of capacity for enforcement and administration of the intervention is required. The collaboration among the agencies in the group will require crossing boundaries that typically separate criminal justice agencies, human service agencies, and the community (Braga & Weisburd, 2015). This may not be easy; criminal justice agencies often have difficulty working together due to the costs of coordination and bureaucratic frictions (Braga, Kennedy & Tita, 2002), and intelligence dissemination has proven to be a barrier to multi-agency enforcement against organized crime (Schneider & Hurst, 2008). When collaboration with foreign agencies is required to fight the transnational aspects of ITTP such as illicit importation or terrorism, further barriers arise

(Small & Taylor, 2006). Even within the US, responsibility for the investigation and enforcement of cases related to ITTP is currently spread across several different federal agencies, including the ATF, US Customs and Border Protection, the TTB, and the FBI, making it difficult to know which agencies would be most appropriate for involvement with focused deterrence aimed at ITTP-related targets. The best ways to encourage interagency and intergovernmental cooperation to target enforcement against ITTP as desired remains a topic for future research. Interagency efforts, involving cybercrime units as well as traditional law enforcement agencies, may become even more important as some ITTP moves online to crypto markets (Munksgaard *et al.*, 2021; Shelley, 2018).

CONCLUSION

Resources for enforcing the law are limited and always involve tradeoffs among the multiple priorities to which they can be directed. Tobacco-related crime, whether involving illicit trafficking, violence, or funding for terrorism, is only one of a multitude of candidates for the law enforcement dollar. Thus any improvements in the compliance-related efficiency—the "bang for the buck"—of enforcement expenditure are of paramount interest. This chapter has discussed targeting enforcement efforts in ways that multiply the impact of enforcement efforts. In the static case, focusing efforts at deterring illicit behavior on subsets of potential lawbreakers can improve overall compliance with the law. More powerful applications of targeted enforcement are available in dynamic settings, where brief but intense monitoring and sanctioning of key individuals at key times can dramatically reduce lawbreaking. Indeed, in the long run, violations may disappear altogether as illicit market participants learn the probability and consequences of lawbreaking.

These theoretical results come to life in the Pulling Levers mechanism, which has demonstrated real-world success against drug and violent crime. Pulling Levers shows great promise for application toward ITTP, particularly against violence should it grow in frequency and scale in these markets. Apart from the particular application of targeted enforcement and focused deterrence discussed here, these notions and mechanisms could also be applied to fighting fraud and corruption (Rafay, 2023b) more generally.

RESEARCH SUPPORT

This research was supported by BOTEC Analysis, which was under contract with Cornerstone Research, which was under contract with Altria Client Services (ACS). ACS had no role in the writing of the paper and had no editorial control.

DECLARATION

The author declares that the manuscript follows ethical standards and there are no potential conflicts of interest with respect to the research, authorship and/or publication of this chapter.

DISCLAIMER

The contents and views of this chapter are expressed by the author in his personal capacity. It is not necessary for the Editor and the Publisher to agree with these viewpoints, and they are not responsible for any duty of care in this regard.

ACKNOWLEDGMENT

The author extends sincere gratitude to

- The Editor and the International Editorial Advisory Board (IEAB) of this book who initially desk reviewed, arranged a rigorous double/triple blind review process, and conducted a thorough, minute, and critical final review before accepting the chapter for publication.
- All anonymous reviewers who provided very constructive feedbacks for thorough revision, improvement, extension, and fine tuning of the chapter.
- All colleagues, assistants and well-wishers who assisted to complete this task.

REFERENCES

Andreas, P., & Wallman, J. (2009). Illicit markets and violence: What is the relationship? *Crime, Law, and Social Change*, *52*(3), 225–229. doi:10.100710611-009-9200-6

Associated Press. (2016, December 16). Genovese family mobsters busted for offshore gambling ring. *Fox News*. https://www.foxnews.com/us/genovese-family-mobsters-busted-for-offshore-gambling-ring

ATF. (2015, February). Fact sheet - Explosives Enforcement Officer (EEO). *Bureau of Alcohol, Tobacco, Firearms, and Explosives, United States Department of Justice*. https://www.atf.gov/file/10976/download

ATF. (2018, May). Fact sheet - tobacco enforcement. *Bureau of Alcohol, Tobacco, Firearms, and Explosives, United States Department of Justice*. https://www.atf.gov/resource-center/fact-sheet/fact-sheet-tobacco-enforcement

Aziani, A., Dugato, M., & Meneghini, C. (2020). A methodology for estimating the illicit consumption of cigarettes at the country level. *Global Crime*, *21*(2), 154–184. doi:10.1080/17440572.2020.1724786

Aziani, A., Kulick, J., Norman, N., & Prieger, J. E. (2017). Empty discarded pack data and the prevalence of illicit trade in cigarettes. SSRN *Electronic Journal*. https://ssrn.com/abstract=2906015 doi:10.2139/ssrn.2906015

Baker, A., Goodman, J. D., & Mueller, B. (2015, June 14). Beyond the chokehold: The path to Eric Garner's death. *New York Times*. https://www.nytimes.com

Baltagi, B. H., & Levin, D. (1986). Estimating dynamic demand for cigarettes using panel data: The effects of bootlegging, taxation and advertising reconsidered. *The Review of Economics and Statistics*, *68*(1), 148–155. doi:10.2307/1924938

Baucus, M. S., & Baucus, D. A. (1997). Paying the piper: An empirical examination of longer-term financial consequences of illegal corporate behavior. *Academy of Management Journal, 40*(1), 129–151. doi:10.2307/257023

BBC. (2009, February 26). US raids target Mexican drug gang. *BBC News*. http://news.bbc.co.uk

Becker, G. S. (1968). Crime and punishment: An economic approach. *Journal of Political Economy, 76*(2), 169–217. doi:10.1086/259394

Bender, W., & Palmer, C. (2016, August 4). Joey Merlino arrested in federal mob crackdown. *The Philadelphia Inquirer*. https://www.inquirer.com

Bishop, J. M. (2018). Does cigarette smuggling prop up smoking rates? *American Journal of Health Economics, 4*(1), 80–104. doi:10.1162/ajhe_a_00094

Boyum, D., & Kleiman, M. A. (2003). Breaking the drug-crime link. *The Public Interest, 152*, 19–38.

Braga, A. A., Kennedy, D. M., & Tita, G. E. (2002). New approaches to the strategic prevention of gang and group-involved violence. *Gangs in America, 3*, 271–286. doi:10.4135/9781452232201.n17

Braga, A. A., Kennedy, D. M., Waring, E. J., & Piehl, A. M. (2001). Problem-oriented policing, deterrence, and youth violence: An evaluation of Boston's operation ceasefire. *Journal of Research in Crime and Delinquency, 38*(3), 195–226. doi:10.1177/0022427801038003001

Braga, A. A., Turchan, B., Papachristos, A. V., & Hureau, D. M. (2019). Hot spots policing of small geographic areas effects on crime. *Campbell Systematic Reviews, 15*(3), e1046. doi:10.1002/cl2.1046 PMID:37133274

Braga, A. A., Weisburd, D., & Turchan, B. (2018). Focused deterrence strategies and crime control: An updated systematic review and meta-analysis of the empirical evidence. *Criminology & Public Policy, 17*(1), 205–250. doi:10.1111/1745-9133.12353

Braga, A. A., Weisburd, D., & Turchan, B. (2019). Focused deterrence strategies effects on crime: A systematic review. *Campbell Systematic Reviews, 15*(3), e1051. doi:10.1002/cl2.1051 PMID:37133287

Braga, A. A., & Weisburd, D. L. (2012). The effects of focused deterrence strategies on crime: A systematic review and meta-analysis of the empirical evidence. *Journal of Research in Crime and Delinquency, 49*(3), 323–358. doi:10.1177/0022427811419368

Braga, A. A., & Weisburd, D. L. (2015). Focused deterrence and the prevention of violent gun injuries: Practice, theoretical principles, and scientific evidence. *Annual Review of Public Health, 36*(1), 55–68. doi:10.1146/annurev-publhealth-031914-122444 PMID:25494051

Braga, A. A., Weisburd, D. L., Waring, E. J., Mazerolle, L. G., Spelman, W., & Gajewski, F. (1999). Problem-oriented policing in violent crime places: A randomized controlled experiment. *Criminology, 37*(3), 541–580. doi:10.1111/j.1745-9125.1999.tb00496.x

Brooks, C. (2019). Federal Law Enforcement Officers, 2016 – Statistical Tables. *US Department of Justice, Office of Justice Programs, Bureau of Justice Statistics* (NCJ 251922). https://tinyurl.com/2wr6zkhy

CA LAO. (2022, January). How much does it cost to incarcerate an inmate? *California Legislative Analyst's Office*. https://lao.ca.gov/policyareas/cj/6_cj_inmatecost

Campaign for Tobacco-Free Kids. (2021). *Cigarette tax increases by state per year 2000-2021*. Tobacco Free Kids. https://www.tobaccofreekids.org/assets/factsheets/0275.pdf

Carpenter, C. S., & Nguyen, H. V. (2021). Intended and unintended effects of banning menthol cigarettes. *The Journal of Law & Economics*, *64*(3), 629–650. doi:10.1086/713978

Caulkins, J. P., Kleiman, M. A. R., & Kulick, J. D. (2010). *Drug production and trafficking, counterdrug policies, and security and governance in Afghanistan*. New York University Center on International Cooperation.

Caulkins, J. P., Larson, R. C., & Rich, T. F. (1993). Geography's impact on the success of focused local drug enforcement operations. *Socio-Economic Planning Sciences*, *27*(2), 119–130. doi:10.1016/0038-0121(93)90012-8

CDC. (2021). *The Tax Burden on Tobacco, 1970-2019*. Centers for Disease Control and Prevention, United States Department of Health and Human Services. https://chronicdata.cdc.gov/Policy/The-Tax-Burden-on-Tobacco-1970-2019/7nwe-3aj9

Chi, J., Hayatdavoudi, L., Kruszona, S., Rowe, B., & Kleiman, M. A. R. (2014, April). *Reducing drug violence in Mexico: Options for implementing targeted enforcement*. UCLA Luskin School of Public Affairs. https://www.ojp.gov/pdffiles1/nij/grants/246358.pdf

Chionis, D., & Chalkia, A. (2016). Illicit tobacco trade in Greece: The rising share of illicit consumption during crisis. *Trends in Organized Crime*, *19*(3), 236–253. doi:10.100712117-016-9273-4

Chiou, L., & Muehlegger, E. (2008). Crossing the line: Direct estimation of cross-border cigarette sales and the effect on tax revenue. *The B.E. Journal of Economic Analysis & Policy*, *8*(1), 48. doi:10.2202/1935-1682.2027

Corsaro, N., & Engel, R. S. (2015). Most challenging of contexts. *Criminology & Public Policy*, *14*(3), 471–505. doi:10.1111/1745-9133.12142

Crudele, J. (2015, November 5). This teacher-turned-arms dealer is lucky he only got 15 years. *New York Post*. https://nypost.com/

DeCicca, P., Kenkel, D., & Liu, F. (2013). Excise tax avoidance: The case of state cigarette taxes. *Journal of Health Economics*, *32*(6), 1130–1141. doi:10.1016/j.jhealeco.2013.08.005 PMID:24140760

Department of State. (2015). *The global illicit trade in tobacco: A threat to national security*. DoS. https://2009-2017.state.gov/documents/organization/250513.pdf

DHS. (2014). Intellectual property rights seizures statistics: Fiscal year 2013. *Department of Homeland Security*. https://tinyurl.com/3vtrpp43

DHS. (2020). Intellectual property rights seizures statistics: Fiscal year 2019. *Department of Homeland Security*. https://tinyurl.com/2p8ktjrt

Dickenson, M. (2014). The impact of leadership removal on Mexican drug trafficking organizations. *Journal of Quantitative Criminology*, *30*(4), 651–676. doi:10.100710940-014-9218-5

Dyson, C. (2015, April 12). King George County has earned a dubious distinction for the role it plays in the highly profitable world of cigarette smuggling. *The Free Lance-Star*. https://fredericksburg.com

Elstein, A. (Nov. 13, 2016). High taxes and limited enforcement have New York City awash in illegal booze and cigarettes. *Crain's New York Business*. https://www.crainsnewyork.com/

FATF. (2012). FATF report: Illicit tobacco trade. *Financial Action Task Force*. https://tinyurl.com/2uytf5ay

FATF. (2016, February 19). Consolidated FATF strategy on combatting terrorist financing. *Financial Action Task Force*. https://tinyurl.com/y9fuwt8t

FATF. (2020, December). Trade-based money laundering: Trends and developments. *Financial Action Task Force*. https://www.fatf-gafi.org/media/fatf/content/Trade-Based-Money-Laundering-Trends-and-Developments.pdf

FATF. (2022). International standards on combating money laundering and the financing of terrorism & proliferation: The FATF recommendations: Updated March 2022. *Financial Action Task Force*. https://tinyurl.com/3fbncvur https://tinyurl.com/yptjyvca

FDA. (2018). Illicit trade in tobacco products after implementation of an FDA product standard. *United States Department of Health and Human Services*. https://tinyurl.com/3crar53d

FDA. (2020). Justification of estimates for appropriations committees: Fiscal year 2021. *Food and Drug Administration, United States Department of Health and Human Services*. https://www.fda.gov/media/135078/download

Finckenauer, J. O. (2005). Problems of definition: What is organized crime? *Trends in Organized Crime*, *8*(3), 63–83. doi:10.100712117-005-1038-4

Fisher, R. J. (1993). Social desirability bias and the validity of indirect questioning. *The Journal of Consumer Research*, *20*(2), 303–315. doi:10.1086/209351

Freitas-Lemos, R., Stein, J. S., Tegge, A. N., Kaplan, B. A., Heckman, B. W., Cummings, K. M., & Bickel, W. K. (2021). The illegal experimental tobacco marketplace I: Effects of vaping product bans. *Nicotine & Tobacco Research: Official Journal of the Society for Research on Nicotine and Tobacco*, *23*(10), 1744–1753. doi:10.1093/ntr/ntab088 PMID:33955478

Galbraith, J. W., & Kaiserman, M. (1997). Taxation, smuggling and demand for cigarettes in Canada: Evidence from time-series data. *Journal of Health Economics*, *16*(3), 287–301. doi:10.1016/S0167-6296(96)00525-5 PMID:10169302

General Accounting Office. (2004, May). *Cigarette smuggling: Federal law enforcement efforts and seizures increasing*. GAO-04-641. https://www.gao.gov/new.items/d04641.pdf

Goel, R. K. (2008). Cigarette smuggling: Price vs. nonprice incentives. *Applied Economics Letters*, *15*(8), 587–592. doi:10.1080/13504850600721981

Goldkamp, J. S., & Vîlcică, E. (2008). Targeted enforcement and adverse system side effects: The generation of fugitives in Philadelphia. *Criminology*, *46*(2), 371–409. doi:10.1111/j.1745-9125.2008.00113.x

Goldstein, P. J. (1985). The drugs/violence nexus: A tripartite conceptual framework. *Journal of Drug Issues*, *15*(4), 493–506. doi:10.1177/002204268501500406

Goldstein, P. J. (1989). Drugs and violent crime. In N. A. Weiner & M. E. Wolfgang (Eds.), *Pathways to Criminal Violence* (pp. 16–48). Sage Publications.

Green, F. (2012, September 5). Va., US aim to crack down on cigarette smuggling. *Richmond Times-Dispatch*. http://www.richmond.com

Green, F. (2015a, March 14). Garner case brings cigarette trafficking to light. *Richmond Times-Dispatch*. http://www.richmond.com

Green, F. (2015b, March 28). Cigarette trafficking spawning other crimes and possibly violence. *Richmond Times-Dispatch*. http://www.richmond.com

Green, F. (2015c, December 20). Major player in cigarette trafficking to be sentenced Tuesday. *Richmond Times-Dispatch*, 1A.

Green, F. (2016, July 25). 2 plead not guilty in cigarette case. *Richmond Times-Dispatch*, 6B.

Harrington, W. (1988). Enforcement leverage when penalties are restricted. *Journal of Public Economics*, *37*(1), 29–53. doi:10.1016/0047-2727(88)90003-5

Hobbs, D. (2003). Organized Crime and Violence. In W. Heitmeyer & J. Hagan (Eds.), *International Handbook of Violence Research* (pp. 679–699). Springer. doi:10.1007/978-0-306-48039-3_33

Immigration and Customs Enforcement. (2013, January 27). Mohamad Youssef Hammoud sentenced to 30 years in terrorism financing case. *United States Department of Homeland Security*. https://tinyurl.com/9x9sk552

Jackall, R. (1997). *Wild cowboys: Urban marauders and the forces of order*. Harvard University Press.

Jacobs, B. A., Topalli, V., & Wright, R. (2000). Managing retaliation: Drug robbery and informal sanction threats. *Criminology*, *38*(1), 171–198. doi:10.1111/j.1745-9125.2000.tb00887.x

Janazzo, D. (2021, January 28). EU menthol cigarette ban survey. *Foundation for a Smoke Free World*. https://www.smokefreeworld.org/eu-menthol-cigarette-ban-survey-2

Joossens, L., & Raw, M. (2012). From cigarette smuggling to illicit tobacco trade. *Tobacco Control*, *21*(2), 230–234. doi:10.1136/tobaccocontrol-2011-050205 PMID:22345257

Joskow, P. L., & Rose, N. L. (1989). The effects of economic regulation. Handbook of Industrial Organization, 2, 1449-1506.

Kennedy, D. M. (1997). Pulling levers: Chronic offenders, high-crime settings, and a theory of prevention. *Valparaiso University Law Review. Valparaiso University. School of Law*, *31*(2), 449–484.

Kennedy, D. M., & Braga, A. (2006). Advocate: Old wine in new bottles: Policing and the lessons of pulling levers. In D. Weisburd (Ed.), *Police Innovation* (1st ed., pp. 155–170). Cambridge University Press. doi:10.1017/CBO9780511489334.008

Kleiman, M. A. R. (1993). Enforcement swamping: A positive-feedback mechanism in rates of illicit activity. *Mathematical and Computer Modelling*, *17*(2), 65–75. doi:10.1016/0895-7177(93)90240-Y

Kleiman, M. A. R. (2009). *When brute force fails: How to have less crime and less punishment*. Princeton University Press. doi:10.1515/9781400831265

Kleiman, M. A. R. (2011). Surgical strikes in the drug wars: Smarter policies for both sides of the border. *Foreign Affairs*, *90*(5), 89–101.

Kleiman, M. A. R., & Kilmer, B. (2009). The dynamics of deterrence. *Proceedings of the National Academy of Sciences of the United States of America*, *106*(34), 14230–14235. doi:10.1073/pnas.0905513106 PMID:19706505

Kulick, J., Prieger, J., & Kleiman, M. A. R. (2016). Unintended consequences of cigarette prohibition, regulation, and taxation. *International Journal of Law, Crime and Justice*, *46*, 69–85. doi:10.1016/j.ijlcj.2016.03.002

Kulick, J., & Prieger, J. E. (2019). Empty discarded pack data and the prevalence of illicit trade in cigarettes in California. SSRN *Electronic Journal*. https://ssrn.com/ abstract=3320922. doi:10.2139/ssrn.3320922

Kupatadze, A. (2021). Corruption and illicit tobacco trade. *Journal of Illicit Economies and Development*, *3*(2), 217–223. doi:10.31389/jied.94

Kurti, M. K., Schroth, K. R., Ackerman, C., Kennedy, M., Jeong, M., & Delnevo, C. D. (2020). Availability of menthol cigarettes in Oakland, California after a partial flavor ban. *Preventive Medicine Reports*, *20*, 101200. doi:10.1016/j.pmedr.2020.101200 PMID:32995144

LaFaive, M., Nesbit, T., & Drenkard, S. (2016). Cigarette taxes and smuggling: A 2016 update. *Mackinac Center for Public Policy*. https://www.mackinac.org/S2016-09

Lando, H., & Shavell, S. (2004). The advantage of focusing law enforcement effort. *International Review of Law and Economics*, *24*(2), 209–218. doi:10.1016/j.irle.2004.08.005

Lovenheim, M. F. (2008). How far to the border? The extent and impact of cross-border casual cigarette smuggling. *National Tax Journal*, *61*(1), 7–33. doi:10.17310/ntj.2008.1.01

Lynch, J. P., & Sabol, W. J. (2004). Assessing the effects of mass incarceration on informal social control in communities. *Criminology & Public Policy*, *3*(2), 267–294. doi:10.1111/j.1745-9133.2004.tb00042.x

Mazerolle, L., Soole, D. W., & Rombouts, S. (2006). Street-level drug law enforcement: A meta-analytical review. *Journal of Experimental Criminology*, *2*(4), 409–435. doi:10.100711292-006-9017-6

McEwen, A., & Straus, L. (2009). Counterfeit tobacco in London: Local crime requires an international solution. *Trends in Organized Crime*, *12*(3-4), 251–259. doi:10.100712117-009-9068-y

Mississippi Office of the State Auditor. (2009, April 15). *State Auditor and Tax Commissioner Uncover Warehouse Containing Estimated $20 Million Of Contraband Tobacco* [Press release]. MS OSA. https://tinyurl.com/sz4cyvuv

Moeller, K., & Hesse, M. (2013). Drug market disruption and systemic violence: Cannabis markets in Copenhagen. *European Journal of Criminology*, *10*(2), 206–221. doi:10.1177/1477370812467568

Munksgaard, R., Décary-Hétu, D., Malm, A., & Nouvian, A. (2021). Distributing tobacco in the dark: Assessing the regional structure and shipping patterns of illicit tobacco in crypto markets. *Global Crime*, *22*(1), 1–21. doi:10.1080/17440572.2020.1799787

National Network for Safe Communities. (n.d.). *Group violence intervention.* MSC. https://nnscommunities.org/strategies/group-violence-intervention

New York State Office of the Attorney General. (2013, May 16). *A.G. Schneiderman & NYPD Commissioner Kelly Announce Take Down of Massive Eastern Seaboard Unstamped Cigarette Trafficking Enterprise*. NY SoAG. https://tinyurl.com/u8j2cbhs

New York State Office of the Governor. (2014, July 14). *Governor Cuomo Announces New Cigarette Strike Force Seizes Nearly $1.7 Million in Contraband and Cash Within First 6 Months*. NY SoAG. https://tinyurl.com/mkzeynjn

New York State Office of the Governor. (2017, August 3). *Governor Cuomo Announces $6.6 Million in Illegal Tobacco Removed from New York State Streets in 2017.* NY SoAG. https://tinyurl.com/3mke4cbp

O'Connor, R. J., Bansal-Travers, M., Carter, L. P., & Cummings, K. M. (2012). What would menthol smokers do if menthol in cigarettes were banned? Behavioral intentions and simulated demand. *Addiction (Abingdon, England)*, *107*(7), 1330–1338. doi:10.1111/j.1360-0443.2012.03822.x PMID:22471735

OECD. (2016, April 18). Illicit trade: Converging criminal networks. *Organisation for Economic Cooperation and Development.* https://www.oecd.org/corruption-integrity/reports/charting-illicit-trade-9789264251847-en.html

Office of the Inspector General. (2009, September). The Bureau of Alcohol, Tobacco, Firearms and Explosives' efforts to prevent the diversion of tobacco. *United States Department of Justice, Office of the Inspector General, Evaluation and Inspections Division.* OIG. http://oig.justice.gov/reports/ATF/e0905.pdf

Paul, C., Schaefer, A. G., & Clarke, C. P. (2011). *The challenge of violent drug-trafficking organizations: An assessment of Mexican security based on existing RAND research on urban unrest, insurgency, and defense-sector reform.* RAND National Defense Research Institute.

Payton, M. E., Young, L. J., & Young, J. H. (1989). Bounds for the difference between median and mean of beta and negative binomial distributions. *Metrika*, *36*(1), 347–354. doi:10.1007/BF02614111

Pelfrey, W. V. Jr. (2015). Cigarette trafficking, smurfing, and volume buying policy, investigation, and methodology recommendations from a case study. *Criminal Justice Policy Review*, *26*(7), 713–726. doi:10.1177/0887403414540518

Polinsky, M. A., & Shavell, S. (2007). The theory of public enforcement of law. In M. A. Polinksy & S. Shavell (Eds.), *Handbook of Law and Economics* (Vol. 1, pp. 403–454). Elsevier.

Prieger, J. E., & Kulick, J. (2014). Unintended consequences of enforcement in illicit markets. *Economics Letters*, *125*(2), 295–297. doi:10.1016/j.econlet.2014.09.025

Prieger, J. E., & Kulick, J. (2015). Violence in illicit markets: Unintended consequences and the search for paradoxical effects of enforcement. *The B.E. Journal of Economic Analysis & Policy*, *15*(3), 1263–1295. doi:10.1515/bejeap-2014-0184

Prieger, J. E., & Kulick, J. (2018). Cigarette taxes and illicit trade in Europe. *Economic Inquiry*, *56*(3), 1706–1723. doi:10.1111/ecin.12564

Rafay, A. (Ed.). (2021a). *HandBook of Research on Theory and Practice of Financial Crimes*. IGI Global. doi:10.4018/978-1-7998-5567-5

Rafay, A. (Ed.). (2021b). *Money Laundering and Terrorism Financing in Global Financial Systems*. IGI Global. doi:10.4018/978-1-7998-8758-4

Rafay, A. (Ed.). (2023a). *Concepts, Cases, and Regulations in Financial Fraud and Corruption*. IGI Global. doi:10.4018/978-1-6684-5007-9

Rafay, A. (Ed.). (2023b). *Concepts and Cases of Illicit Finance*. IGI Global. doi:10.4018/978-1-6684-8587-3

Raphael, S. (2014). The effects of conviction and incarceration on future employment outcomes. In D. P. Farrington & J. Murray (Eds.), Advances in Criminological Theory: Vol. 18. *Labeling Theory: Empirical Tests* (pp. 237–262). Transaction Publishers.

Reuter, P. (2009). Systemic violence in drug markets. *Crime, Law, and Social Change*, *52*(3), 275–284. doi:10.100710611-009-9197-x

Reuter, P., & Majmundar, M. (Eds.). (2015). Understanding the US illicit tobacco market: Characteristics, policy context, and lessons from international experiences. National Academies of Science and Engineering, National Research Council, Committee on the Illicit Tobacco Market: Collection and Analysis of the International Experience and Division of Behavioral and Social Sciences and Education, Committee on Law and Justice; Institute of Medicine, Board on Population Health and Public Health Practice. National Academies Press.

Rose, D. R., & Clear, T. R. (1998). Incarceration, social capital, and crime: Implications for social disorganization theory. *Criminology*, *36*(3), 441–480. doi:10.1111/j.1745-9125.1998.tb01255.x

Rosenfeld, R. (2016). *Documenting and explaining the 2015 homicide rise: Research directions*. National Institute of Justice, Office of Justice Programs, US Department of Justice.

Ross, H. (2015). Measures to control illicit tobacco trade. *University of Illinois at Chicago, Institute for Health Research and Policy, Tobacconomics*. UIC. https://tinyurl.com/nm3n6hu4

Saba, R. R., Beard, T. R., Ekelund, R. B. Jr, & Ressler, R. W. (1995). The demand for cigarette smuggling. *Economic Inquiry*, *33*(2), 189–202. doi:10.1111/j.1465-7295.1995.tb01856.x

Sanderson, T. M. (2004). Transnational terror and organized crime: Blurring the lines. *SAIS Review (Paul H. Nitze School of Advanced International Studies)*, *24*(1), 49–61. doi:10.1353ais.2004.0020

Schneider, S., & Hurst, C. (2008). Obstacles to an integrated, joint forces approach to organized crime enforcement: A Canadian case study. *Policing*, *31*(3), 359–379. doi:10.1108/13639510810895759

Shelley, L. (2015, November 28). How to beat Islamic State? Crack down on cigarette smuggling. *The Guardian*. https://www.theguardian.com/commentisfree/2015/nov/27/isis-cigarette-smuggling-isis-middle-east

Shelley, L. I. (2018). *Dark commerce: How a new illicit economy is threatening our future*. Princeton University Press. doi:10.2307/j.ctv346n56

Shelley, L. I. (2020). Illicit trade and terrorism. *Perspectives on Terrorism*, *14*(4), 7–20.

Shelley, L. I., & Melzer, S. A. (2008). The nexus of organized crime and terrorism: Two case studies in cigarette smuggling. *International Journal of Comparative and Applied Criminal Justice*, *32*(1), 43–63. doi:10.1080/01924036.2008.9678777

Small, K., & Taylor, B. (2006). State and local law enforcement response to transnational crime. *Trends in Organized Crime*, *10*(2), 5–17. doi:10.100712117-006-1033-4

Smith, K. C., Stillman, F., Bone, L., Yancey, N., Price, E., Belin, P., & Kromm, E. E. (2007). Buying and selling "loosies" in Baltimore: The informal exchange of cigarettes in the community context. *Journal of Urban Health*, *84*(4), 494–507. doi:10.100711524-007-9189-z PMID:17431795

Staff, R. (2008). *Tobacco and terror: How cigarette smuggling is funding our enemies abroad*. United States House of Representatives, Committee on Homeland Security. https://tinyurl.com/2p8d9pfz

Stehr, M. (2005). Cigarette tax avoidance and evasion. *Journal of Health Economics*, *24*(2), 277–297. doi:10.1016/j.jhealeco.2004.08.005 PMID:15721046

Stoklosa, M. (2019). No surge in illicit cigarettes after implementation of menthol ban in Nova Scotia. *Tobacco Control*, *28*(6), 702–704. doi:10.1136/tobaccocontrol-2018-054552 PMID:30309981

Tamekamta, A. (2021). Terrorism and privatization of state spaces in the Sahel: Case of the Polisario Front. *Revista Universitară de Sociologie*, *17*(1), 186–196.

The White House. (2022, July 13). *The White House Announces Newly Designated High Intensity Drug Trafficking Areas* [Press release]. The White House. https://tinyurl.com/y74yzhbe

Thursby, J. G., & Thursby, M. C. (2000). Interstate cigarette bootlegging: Extent, revenue losses, and effects of federal intervention. *National Tax Journal*, *53*(1), 59–77. doi:10.17310/ntj.2000.1.04

Topalli, V., Wright, R., & Fornango, R. (2002). Drug dealers, robbery and retaliation: Vulnerability, deterrence and the contagion of violence. *British Journal of Criminology*, *42*(2), 337–351. doi:10.1093/bjc/42.2.337

Travis, J., & Waul, M. (2003). Prisoners once removed: The impact of incarceration and reentry on children, families, and communities. *The Urban Institute*. https://webarchive.urban.org/publications/210900.html

TTB. (2016). FY 2017 president's budget. *Alcohol and Tobacco Tax and Trade Bureau, United States Department of the Treasury*. https://www.ttb.gov/images/pdfs/fy2017-enacted.pdf

TTB. (2021). Congressional Budget Justification and Annual Performance Plan and Report. *Alcohol and Tobacco Tax and Trade Bureau, United States Department of the Treasury*. TTB. https://www.ttb.gov/images/pdfs/fy2022-cj.pdf

Ulep, V. G., Lavares, M. P., & Francisco, A. (2021). Measuring the capacity to combat illicit tobacco trade in 160 countries. *Globalization and Health*, *17*(1), 1–8. doi:10.118612992-021-00783-4 PMID:34789289

United States Attorney's Office. (2015, March 12). *Ten members and associates of decavalcante organized crime family arrested* [press release]. USAO. https://tinyurl.com/mkars347

von Lampe, K., Kurti, M., Johnson, J., & Rengifo, A. F. (2016). "I wouldn't take my chances on the street": Navigating illegal cigarette purchases in the South Bronx. *Journal of Research in Crime and Delinquency*, *53*(5), 654–680. doi:10.1177/0022427816637888

Watkins, A., & Apuzzo, M. (2018, January 19). Trump envisions an A.T.F. without the A or T. *New York Times*. http://www.nytimes.com

Weisburd, D., Wyckoff, L. A., Ready, J., Eck, J. E., Hinkle, J. C., & Gajewski, F. (2006). Does crime just move around the corner? A controlled study of spatial displacement and diffusion of crime control benefits. *Criminology*, *44*(3), 549–592. doi:10.1111/j.1745-9125.2006.00057.x

Zatoński, M., Herbeć, A., Zatoński, W., Przewoźniak, K., Janik-Koncewicz, K., Mons, U., Fong, G. T., Demjén, T., Tountas, Y., Trofor, A. C., Fernández, E., McNeil, A., Willemsen, M., Hummel, K., Quah, A. C. K., & Kyriakos, C. N. (2018). Characterising smokers of menthol and flavoured cigarettes, their attitudes towards tobacco regulation, and the anticipated impact of the Tobacco Products Directive on their smoking and quitting behaviours: The EUREST-PLUS ITC Europe Surveys. *Tobacco Induced Diseases*, *16*(Suppl. 2), A4. doi:10.18332/tid/96294 PMID:31516460

Zimmer, L. (1990). Proactive policing against street-level drug trafficking. *American Journal of Police*, *9*(1), 43–74.

Zimring, F. E. (2011). *The city that became safe: New York's lessons for urban crime and its control*. Oxford University Press. doi:10.1093/acprof:oso/9780199844425.001.0001

ADDITIONAL READING

Exploring the Financial Nexus of Terrorism, Drug Trafficking, and Organized Crime: US House of Representatives Financial Services Committee, Subcommittee on Terrorism and Illicit Finance, 115th Cong. (2018) (Testimony of Louise Shelley). https://tinyurl.com/98tkwr3h

KEY TERMS AND DEFINITIONS

Alcohol and Tobacco Tax and Trade Bureau (TTB): An interdisciplinary agency within the US Treasury Department created to monitor and enforce compliance with federal tobacco and alcohol tax laws.

Bureau of Alcohol, Tobacco, Firearms and Explosives (ATF): The federal agency in the US with primary responsibility for criminal investigation and enforcement of tobacco laws (apart from tax laws). The agency is known as the ATF (not ATFE) due to its original name.

Dynamic Concentration: A strategic approach to enforcement that multiplies the impact of the enforcement expenditure. The threat of enforcement is dynamically and fully concentrated upon each potential criminal at the time he must choose whether to commit the crime. Dynamic concentration is a particular example of targeted enforcement.

Excise Taxation: The legislated taxation of specific commodities. Excise taxes are typically levied on manufacturers or distributors of the goods. The profit motive provided by the avoidance of excise taxation on tobacco products is the main motivating factor for criminal organizations engaging in ITTP.

Focused Deterrence: An approach to targeted enforcement in which monitoring and sanctioning crime are focused on a subset of potential lawbreakers in such a manner that overall compliance is higher than if enforcement effort were applied uniformly. In the criminology literature (but not in this chapter) the term often refers specifically to Pulling Levers.

Illicit Trade in Tobacco Products (ITTP): The trafficking of contraband or counterfeit tobacco. The main form of ITTP in the US is smuggling of genuine cigarettes from lower-tax to higher-tax jurisdictions, but other forms include trafficking counterfeit products, diversion of untaxed products destined for export back into the US, and trafficking cigarettes produced abroad for the purpose of illicit sales elsewhere.

Pulling Levers (PL): A crime-prevention intervention applying enforcement strategically against individuals, along with social services to encourage desirable behaviors. The intervention focuses on a particular type of crime in a certain area and targets key repeat offenders, using all available enforcement possibilities—pulling on all available "levers".

ENDNOTES

1 Early versions of this research were aided greatly by collaboration with co-authors Jonathan Kulick and Mark A.R. Kleiman. While Mark is no longer with us, many of his ideas and no doubt some of his words live on in this article.

2 Many cross-border purchases involve casual bootlegging by consumers, which may be legal depending on the state and the amounts involved.

3 Counterfeit tax stamps have been found on up to three in five illicit packs consumed in New York City 2011-2014 (Aziani *et al.*, 2017) and California in 2012 (Kulick & Prieger, 2019).

4 An exhaustive search was performed of Lexis-Nexis Academic of US newspaper articles from January 2015 through June 2021 mentioning "illicit cigarettes" or "illegal cigarettes" and "New York" or "Virginia". Out of the 82 distinct individuals mentioned by name or whose nationality was otherwise identified who were charged with or convicted of ITTP-related crimes, 42 (51%) had surnames of Arabic origin or were otherwise identified in the articles as nationals of Middle Eastern countries (including Palestine).

5 The estimate is computed using data from the 2018 5-year American Community Survey.

6 Criminal investigation at the FDA originates in the Office of Criminal Investigations (OCI), which the FDA itself describes as a small staff. There are relatively few special agents in OCI: 231 in 2016, compared to over 4,000 other employees in the Office of Regulatory Affairs, the division within the FDA that houses the OCI. Per its own description on its website, the OCI appears mainly to investigate matters involving pharmaceuticals and medical treatments and devices, not tobacco. (For ORA headcount, see FDA [2020]; for the count of special agents, see Table 2 of Brooks [2019].)

7 Taking LaFaive, Nesbit, and Drenkard's (2016) estimate that 26.5% of cigarette sales in New York State are from commercial smuggling operations, about 75 million smuggled packs were sold in 2017 in the state. The per-pack margin is about $8 (based on an estimate of $8.8 per pack on Virginia to New York City price differential (ATF, 2018), lowered because not all illicit sales are in NYC). Fines of $7 million would be about 1.2% of the resulting $600 million in organized smuggling revenue from that margin.

8 See New York State Public Health Law Art. 13-F § 1399-EE

9 When enforcement raises risk and the perceived price of the illicit products for consumers on the demand side as well, the effect on market revenue is ambiguous (Prieger & Kulick, 2015). In general, therefore, the impact of general enforcement on revenue and violence is indeterminate. In practical terms, this ambiguity is of little significance to tobacco markets, since anti-consumer enforcement is almost unknown.

10 This can be seen as follows. The probability of punishment is $p = 0.1/a$, where a is the fraction of the market under focus. The expected penalty $p\times\$2000$ can be lowered no more than to equal the gain of \$300 to still ensure compliance. Solving $\$300 = p\times\$2000 = (0.1/a)\times\$2000$ yields $a = 2/3$.

11 As an example of costs to the state, in California it costs an average of $106,000 per year to incarcerate an inmate in a state prison (CA LAO, 2022)

12 Kleiman and Kilmer (2009) discuss another Nash equilibrium in the two-player game, with the outcome comply-comply, but this equilibrium is not subgame perfect since it relies on an incredible threat from the second player to comply if the first player violated.

13 Beliefs about p converge to the true value, for example, if the player is Bayesian with prior distribution Beta(α,β) on p. To see this, denote the number of rounds in which the player chose to violate as m and the number of times the player has experienced punishments as k. Whether the player updates beliefs with the Bayesian posterior mean, median, or mode does not matter. The Bayesian posterior mean is $(\alpha+k)/(\alpha+\beta+m)$, the posterior mode is $(\alpha+k\text{-}1)/(\alpha+\beta+m\text{-}2)$, and (at least for some values of α and β) the posterior median is sandwiched between the two (Payton, Young & Young, 1989). Thus all converge to k/m as m grows large, a ratio that would converge to the true value of p by the law of large numbers.

14 In Iowa, the program is known by its new "brand name" of Group Violence Intervention (National Network for Safe Communities, n.d.).

15 Mark A.R. Kleiman contributed heavily to this section.

Chapter 2
Entry Bans Based on Foreign Criminal Proceedings:
The Case of Switzerland

Fabian Teichmann
Teichmann International (Schweiz) AG, Switzerland

Sonia Ruxandra Boticiu
Teichmann International (Schweiz) AG, Switzerland

ABSTRACT

The Swiss Federal Office of Police (Fedpol) has the authority to impose entry bans on foreign nationals under the Foreign Nationals and Integration Act (FNIA). Given the challenges faced by European countries, particularly in migration and counterterrorism efforts, the Schengen Information System (SIS) has become an essential tool. This system enables authorities and police within the Schengen area to exchange crucial information, including details about individuals subjected to entry bans, wanted persons, terrorism threats, violent extremism, and organized crime activities. It is widely acknowledged that certain Eastern European countries, such as Moldova, Romania, Ukraine, Russia, and Bulgaria, have a judiciary plagued by corruption. Consequently, there is a potential risk of politically influenced manipulation of international criminal proceedings. Given that many entry bans rely on foreign criminal proceedings, which could be politically motivated or subject to manipulation, it is essential to scrutinize the Fedpol's current practices critically.

INTRODUCTION

The judiciary in Western countries is frequently confronted with the results of investigations in foreign criminal proceedings (Mendelski, 2010). The results of criminal proceedings in Eastern Europe must be evaluated in rogatory commissions and domestic criminal proceedings. However, international criminal proceedings also play an increasingly important role in domestic administrative proceedings (Wilkitzki, 1995). This raises how international criminal proceedings should be monitored and evaluated (Mc Gonigle, 2011).

DOI: 10.4018/979-8-3693-1190-5.ch002

This article explains why national authorities should not blindly rely on the findings of foreign prosecuting authorities and why the actual results of foreign prosecuting authorities must be critically analysed. Further clarification is also needed on the powers and obligations of Schengen States when using the SIS database, especially given recent national developments affecting EU principles of democracy and the rule of law.

Entry bans are an essential foreign policy tool for the EU to intervene when necessary to ensure the security of Member States. They can also be an essential tool in the fight against corruption and aim to deter and sanction corruption at national borders (Moiseienko, 2018). However, this article also wishes to emphasise that such immigration measures can be a flexible tool for states to use when necessary and can also present a potential risk of abuse. In corrupted Eastern European countries, it is often possible to initiate criminal proceedings against disgraced political or business opponents to weaken them further (Teichmann, 2017).

Switzerland cannot rely on such criminal proceedings in Eastern Europe, as they would be incompatible with the principles of the rule of law and a thorough examination of each case is required (Elbasani, 2018). Therefore, both lawyers and employees of the judiciary must be aware of the aspects of criminal procedural law.

This study has identified gaps and challenges both Swiss and Western European authorities encountered when dealing with foreign criminal proceedings, particularly regarding entry bans. The study contributes to the existing literature by explaining the benefits of entry bans, highlighting possible abuses that states can make through immigration measures as well as offering suggestions to avoid these potential abuses. Indeed, there have been several criticisms of these immigration measures in the literature, however, the literature has not adequately described how entry bans could be used against political opponents or disgraced businesspeople. There is thus a significant research gap. This research gap has practical relevance because there is also a risk that international criminal proceedings are politically motivated in many Eastern European countries where we face high-level corruption (Popova, & Post, 2018). Many entry bans are regularly issued based on criminal proceedings in these countries.

UNIQUE CHARACTERISTICS OF INTERNATIONAL CRIMINAL PROCEEDINGS

In some Eastern European countries, such as Russia, Moldova, Romania, Bulgaria, and Ukraine, the judiciary is highly corrupt (Skoryk, 2019; Transparency International, 2020). In these countries, it is possible to bribe prosecutors and judges or exert political pressure on the judiciary (World Justice Project, 2020). This is unheard of in Switzerland, known for its excellent standards regarding the law.

Practices such as opening criminal proceedings on uncertain grounds against political and business opponents have become commonplace in these countries (Teichmann, 2021). Often, the state opens criminal proceedings against disgraced businesspeople or oligarchs to further weaken them (Anderson, 2007). Often businesspeople also report to such tactics to weaken their competitors. Prosecutors are often bribed for this purpose (Karklins, 2002). Frequently, the person in question is charged with money laundering offences (Teichmann & Sergi, 2018). They resort to such approaches to keep the person concerned busy with these criminal proceedings without being able to intervene in other areas (Oxford Analytica, 2021).

This eases the seizure of assets belonging to the person concerned, both in Switzerland and abroad. The persons involved are often convicted in their absence (Kühne, 2020).

At least at first glance, it can be exceedingly difficult for Western countries to differentiate between politically motivated or bribery-based criminal proceedings and legitimate criminal proceedings (Zabyelina, 2020). Therefore, it is impossible to refer to facts in the countries mentioned without further ado (Cosgrove, 2005). The results of investigations by prosecution authorities in Eastern Europe must be critically questioned (Kühne, 2020). Therefore, Fedpol should not rely on the results of foreign investigations without examining in detail the facts presented by foreign authorities. Adopting national measures based on these would not align with the rule of law (Andreas & Nadelmann, 2008).

ENTRY BANS AND ASSET FREEZES AS A POTENTIAL SOLUTION AGAINST CORRUPTION

Globally, the world is currently facing significant challenges in migration and terrorism (Kinnvall & Lindén, 2010). For this reason, entry bans are issued when a country's security is threatened by terrorism, organised crime, or violent extremism. Such restrictive measures are essential in the EU's Common Foreign and Security Policy (CFSP). The EU can intervene when necessary to protect the peace and security of Member States (European Commission, 2021).

For example, if a third-country national no longer has a residence permit and has already been charged for irregular stay, then such a case qualifies for an entry ban (Rutz, 2014). Persons posing a risk to public policy, national security or public safety are also grounds for imposing an entry ban. The legislation also provides for the possibility of withdrawing an entry ban. The persons concerned must present arguments demonstrating that there has been a material change in their situation since the entry ban was imposed (Li, Sommarribas & Baltes-Löhr, 2014). Lifting the entry ban means stopping it (Ministry of Justice and Security, 2021).

In many situations, entry bans are used to fight against corruption (Moiseienko, 2019). Since many corrupt individuals can exploit borders to launder their ill-gotten gains in foreign jurisdictions and hide from prosecution. Thus, denial of entry is a new attempt to deter and sanction the corrupt across national borders (Transparency International, 2014). However, it is important to note that in many Eastern European countries, where the judiciary is highly corrupt, there is a risk that the state will initiate criminal proceedings against disgraced businesspeople or oligarchs to weaken them further. For this reason, investigations by prosecution authorities in Eastern Europe should be critically questioned (Teichmann, 2017).

The European Court of Auditors, on the other hand, criticised in a report issued in 2021 the ineffectiveness of the European Union's anti-corruption initiatives. Specifically, the report concluded that EU member states must work with the European Commission to prevent oligarchs from Eastern European countries and other people suspected of grand corruption from using their assets and travelling to the EU. The report also pointed to the US as an example of the use of the entry ban as a tool to fight corruption. In 2021, Antony Blinken, US Secretary of State, banned a Ukrainian oligarch from entering the United States for alleged corruption and financial fraud. The ban was also extended to his children and wife (Kaleniuk, 2021).

On 7 December 2020, the European Union adopted the European Magnitsky Act, which allows the EU to impose travel bans and freeze the assets of individuals involved in serious human rights violations wherever they are. The EU thus joined Canada, the UK and the US, which have similar Magnitsky legislation. However, the US version of the Magnitsky Act also targets corrupt actors in addition to human rights violators. The laws are named after Russian whistle-blower Sergei Magnitsky, who died in

Russia in 2009 while in custody. Initially, the US Magnitsky Act sanctioned those guilty of his death, but subsequent legislation built a global sanctions campaign that allowed the US to target corrupt actors and human rights abusers globally (Chemali, 2020).

In the case of Switzerland, the 2016 Federal Act on the Freezing and Return of Illicit Assets (Foreign Illicit Assets Act), allows for the freezing of assets of politically exposed persons when there is reason to believe that these assets have been acquired through corruption and may be imposed for the purpose of mutual legal assistance or domestic confiscation if cooperation from the country where the corruption took place fails or is not initiated. Four cumulative steps are required for this to be initiated. First, the foreign government must have lost or be about to lose. Second, the home country must have a notorious level of corruption. Third, the assets must be likely to have been criminally acquired. Finally, the freezing action must be necessary to protect Switzerland's interests (Cizmaziova, 2021).

In addition, in the case of politically exposed persons (PEPs), the Swiss asset freezing provisions are linked to a special administrative legal regime, which makes very swift action possible. To protect the interests of the country, the Federal Council can issue ordinances and decisions to freeze the assets of foreign individuals. This allows Switzerland to act even in the absence of freezing requests from other jurisdictions, or the opening of criminal investigations and even in the absence of suspicious transactions reported to the Financial Intelligence Unit (Cizmaziova, 2021).

SCHENGEN ENTRY BANS

The SIS database is a computerised alert system containing information on missing or stolen objects, persons wanted for extradition or subject to an entry ban in a particular country. SIS is jointly used by all Schengen countries (Fedpol, 2020b). EU countries must determine whether the case is sufficiently important and relevant to be entered into SIS II before issuing an alert (EUR-Lex, 2019).

An entry ban can only be imposed based on a return decision. The return decision is the one that formally establishes that a person is illegally present in one of the Schengen countries (Drakopoulou, Konstantinou & Koros, 2020). In case of an entry ban, the person concerned cannot travel to the EU, EEA and Switzerland (Majcher, 2020). An entry ban applies only to third-country nationals (Ministry of Justice, 2021). The form of expulsion for residence is imposed on EEA nationals, Swiss nationals and privileged third-country nationals if they stay illegally or if public policy is endangered and the conditions for residence are no longer met. Another means of termination of stay which only concerns EEA nationals, Swiss nationals and privileged third-country nationals is the exclusion order which can be imposed in cases where the behaviour of these persons seriously endangers public order (Rutz, 2014).

A third-country national may be reported to the SIS either on the grounds of expulsion, refusal of entry or removal as a measure of immigration law resulting in an entry ban or on the grounds of public policy or security, as set out in Article 24 of the SIS II Regulation. An SIS alert may be based either on a conviction of a Member State for an offence punishable by at least one year's imprisonment or when there are reasonable grounds to believe that a person has committed serious crimes or there are indications of intent to commit such crimes on the territory of a Member State (Brouwer, 2018). Once an alert is entered into the SIS database in one Member State, it is notified in all other Member States (European Commission, n.d.).

These grounds have been heavily criticised because they offer the possibility that a minor offence in one Member State could lead to a very long-term ban throughout the Schengen territory and, at the same time, give the Member States a broad margin of discretion as to what should be considered a serious crime and who should be considered at risk of committing a serious crime (Brouwer, 2018).

We can use as an example the case of a Ukrainian human rights activist and resident in Poland for 10 years, who was detained at Brussels airport in August 2018 based on an entry ban to Poland and deported the next day to Kyiv (Brouwer, 2018). Her entry ban was entered into SIS II and for this reason, all Schengen member states must refuse her entry to Schengen territory (Bellanova & Glouftsios, 2022). If her residence status were to be withdrawn, a return decision would first have to be issued, not automatically reported in SIS II. An SIS alert can also be issued because of a conviction for a crime committed on the territory of a Member State or when there are clear indications that a person intends to commit a crime on the territory of a Member State. She has been identified as a danger to Poland because she is the president of the Open Dialogue Foundation, which has been often described as a "Polish anti-government group". In her case, the entry ban affected her right to family life, as she has family in Poland and is married to a Polish citizen and her right to freedom of expression. This example highlights the need for remedies against decisions reported in large-scale databases like SIS (Brouwer, 2021). Although SIS II is based on the principle of mutual trust, a state may have an obligation to check its legality if its application would violate the fundamental rights of the person concerned. For this reason, the legality of the Belgian decision to expel the person mentioned above in Kyiv and the legitimacy of the entry ban in Poland could be questioned. Therefore, the authorities must first ensure that such an expulsion does not violate the right to family life, freedom of expression or the right of residence as a family member of an EU citizen (Majcher, 2019a).

SWISS ENTRY BANS

Fedpol has also been tasked with developing its technical infrastructure for operating the SIS database, to which all Schengen Member States have access (Fedpol, 2020b). Fedpol issues entry bans because of information on foreign criminal proceedings. The entry ban is designed to complement the return decision by prohibiting the persons concerned from entering and remaining on the territory of the State (Majcher, 2019b).

Fedpol's mission is to investigate, analyse and coordinate severe complex crime cases in Switzerland. Although the cantons are primarily responsible for public security, the Fedpol plays an essential role in case of foreign countries (Fedpol, 2020c). Fedpol fights serious crimes under federal jurisdiction. It also directs police response to emergencies such as terrorist attacks, hostage-takings, kidnappings, money laundering, human trafficking, and counterfeit money, among others. Fedpol also plays an essential role in managing national and international police cooperation with Interpol, Europol and the UN (Fedpol, 2020c).

Fedpol meets many criminal proceedings from all over the world. It is important to note that many of these criminal proceedings have legitimate objectives and origins. International law enforcement agencies have a legitimate interest in supporting Swiss authorities. But at the same time, it is significant for an institution such as the Fedpol, and those international facts are critically examined.

For foreign offences, Fedpol uses the results of investigations carried out by foreign law enforcement agencies. This raises how carefully the Fedpol examines foreign facts and critically evaluates them from the criminal procedure.

Fedpol has relied partly upon the obligation to review and evaluate the results of international investigations rests with the prosecutor's office. For example, the Money Laundering Reporting Office Switzerland (MROS), a member of the Egmont Group, is an international association of financial intelligence units (FIUs) that enables the exchange of information to combat money laundering and terrorist financing (Fedpol, 2020a). However, MROS operates based on unverified suspicions since the obligation to verify these suspicions lies with the public prosecutor's office and must occur before proceedings are initiated and, in particular, before coercive measures are taken and must be reviewable by the courts (Fedpol, 2020a).

The impact of entry bans on the economy or society is relatively narrow since only a few people are affected by these measures. Instead, there have been numerous instances where entry bans have impacted private property rights. There have been cases where Eastern European businesspeople have seized their assets in Switzerland and banned them from entering the country. In Eastern European countries, where the legal system is already notoriously corrupt, politically motivated proceedings can sometimes be brought against disgraced businesspeople to weaken them further (Mendelski, 2015). In this case, foreign countries may want Switzerland to issue an entry ban to target political opponents. As a result, it can be argued that many businesspeople might refrain from investing in Switzerland and this could affect the country's economic growth.

The Procedure of the Fedpol

Before issuing an order, Fedpol usually tries to contact the persons concerned to receive a fair trial. This explains why an entry ban is taken into account. In particular, the persons involved are regularly requested to disclose their present location and their whereabouts within a certain period (Perrin, Rémy & Roubaty, 2011). These persons are given 30 days to submit observations. They are also asked to submit extracts from criminal records not older than three months. They are also requested to present extracts from criminal records from countries where they have lived for a specific time, not older than three months old. In addition, the persons concerned are often asked to submit a list of all criminal proceedings pending against them (Fedpol, 2020).

International procedures are often not evaluated from the point of view of criminal procedures, although Fedpol usually takes these procedures into account in its decision-making. There have been cases where decisions have been made based on foreign press reports without the case files being accessed. In addition, the case files are regularly not fully translated (Teichmann, 2021).

Critical Assessment of the Fedpol's Approach

It is important to mention that the persons in question may not even be in Switzerland and may not have requested legal proceedings in Switzerland. It is also possible that they may not even be charged in criminal proceedings in Switzerland. They are also asked to send Fedpol a list of the criminal proceedings pending against them worldwide. In this situation, the question arises about how such a list can be relevant to the Swiss authorities. Finally, the presumption of innocence applies in ongoing criminal proceedings (Teichmann, 2021).

In practice, the requirement to provide a global list of all ongoing criminal proceedings against individuals can lead to significant challenges. In corrupted Eastern European countries, in particular, it is possible to initiate criminal proceedings by bribing public prosecutors against political or business opponents in order to weaken those involved (Dionisie & Checchi, 2008). Switzerland could not rely on such criminal proceedings from Eastern Europe because they would be incompatible with the rule of law principles. Therefore, thorough scrutiny of each criminal case is necessary.

However, it does not seem acceptable under any circumstances that foreign criminal proceedings are not sifted through. It would have to be checked whether the results of the investigations taken into account in the decision-making process in Switzerland satisfy generally recognised principles of criminal procedural law. If they are not, the results in question should not be considered (Teichmann, 2021).

Procedural Aspects

1) Local and Subject-Matter Jurisdiction

It should be noted that appeals against such entry bans are in principle excluded. Exceptions exist only to the extent that international law grants the right to a judicial evaluation as provided for in Article 32 para. 1. Such an exception applies in principle to EU nationals (Teichmann, 2021).

2) Restoration of the Suspensive Effect

Fedpol regularly withdraws the suspensive effect of the appeal. Therefore, it is needed to make a procedural request in the appeal to restore the suspensive impact within the meaning of Art. 55 para. 3 VwVG. The same requirements apply to the withdrawal of the suspensive effect. Specifically, sufficient interest must be shown to make the suspensive effect's restoration appear justified and proportionate (Kiener, 2018).

Administrative Grounds of Appeal

1) Infringement of the Right to Be Heard

As addressees of the Fedpol order, the persons in question are parties to it and are therefore entitled to be heard. A violation of the constitutional right to be heard leads to the annulment of the order in question. A remedy may be granted in the proceedings before the appeal authority in extraordinary cases. Nonetheless, this is subject to the condition that the appellate authority has the same knowledge. Remittal to the lower court would only lead to an unneeded delay in the proceedings (Teichmann, 2021).

Fedpol also frequently refers to foreign sources that can be difficult to verify in detail and sometimes even foreign press reports are considered. It is inconsistent with the rule of law principles to base the order on foreign newspaper reports. In many Eastern European countries, journalists have to choose between obeying orders from high-ranking politicians or financial masters and losing their jobs (Boros & Cusick, 2017). Many journalists also decide to maintain their loyalty to corrupt politicians and, for this reason, agree to publish negative news against their competitors to destroy their reputation (Örnebring, 2012). For this reason, it is necessary to critically question whether the information has been manipulated.

Fedpol frequently uses international files in connection with the issuance of entry bans. These are usually not translated into a national language or English, thus making it more challenging to verify and understand Fedpol's claims. This is especially true concerning any time limits for appeal, which must be observed by the parties concerned. Nonetheless, according to Art. 9 para. 1 of the Language Act, the Fedpol is obliged to use the official language of the Confederation (Teichmann, 2021).

2) Unfair Federal Information Requirements in the Fedpol Order

The Fedpol tends to impose supplementary obligations on the persons involved to respect the right to be heard. Generally, this lacks a legal basis and is not proportionate. The request to disclose the last place of residence and all pending criminal proceedings and the request to hand over the criminal record is inadmissible. Among other things, this concerns personal data that is particularly worthy of protection. These data belong to the private sphere of the persons concerned (Teichmann, 2021).

3) Breach of the Principle of Inquiry

Fedpol also violates the procedure's maximum investigation applicable in administrative proceedings. In particular, it does not clarify the facts of the case but constructs a possible set of points based on foreign data.

In some cases, it is unclear what the Fedpol wishes to prove with the foreign data. Nonetheless, it is inadmissible that the person to whom the order is addressed should have to rebuild the facts of the case. Apart from the risk of a flawed reconstruction, such a procedure also makes it more challenging to comply with the time limit for appeals and the obligation to justify (Teichmann, 2021).

4) Absence of Evidence of Consultation of the Intelligence Service

Furthermore, it can be criticised that the intelligence service was not sufficiently well founded. Fedpol must hear the FIS in advance. It must be possible for the persons concerned and the appeal authorities to verify that this hearing occurred (Teichmann, 2021).

5) Incorrect and Incomplete Establishment of the Facts

In this context, too, it can be argued that the Fedpol relies on foreign public sources. In countries with a high level of corruption, it is still possible to bribe journalists. Articles in foreign newspapers, especially in Eastern Europe, should not be considered without further formalities. In Eastern European countries, media ownership is excessively concentrated in corrupt politicians and oligarchs, putting editorial independence at risk (Zgaga, 2018).

It can be argued that reports in national newspapers might clarify, but they cannot be considered accurate without further evidence (Ngcamu, & Mantzaris, 2021). Unverifiable reports in foreign newspapers may find even less use in domestic proceedings. It remains unclear who the websites are operated by in many cases, and it is not even verified who is behind the sources mentioned. For this reason, the credibility of the information should be questioned (Oberlechner, & Hocking, 2004). In particular, it can often be argued that the Fedpol did not try to find out to what extent an alternative account of the facts would be possible or more likely to correspond to the truth. So, it can be argued that in some countries where there is high-level corruption, neither the judiciary nor the media can be trusted. For this reason, it is imperative that where constitutional and democratic requirements in the Swiss sense are not met, foreign information must be critically examined and evaluated (Teichmann, 2021).

Administrative Aspects

The Fedpol does not always succeed in clearly demonstrating to what extent the entry ban is justified by an accurate and sufficiently serious threat to Switzerland's internal security. It is often not even explained how the alleged threat should be present. Frequently, facts are referred to that lie clearly in the past. Also, an entry ban, in the case of white-collar criminals who may carry out their actions on the internet or by telephone, is not adequate for the protection of Switzerland.

Fedpol often does not specify the extent to which there are accurate and current suspicions that the persons concerned might commit crimes in Switzerland. Although it is regularly mentioned that the entry ban order is intended to help prevent the persons concerned from committing crimes on Swiss territory. Thus, without concrete grounds for suspicion, it cannot be assumed that the persons concerned would commit offences on Swiss territory. The purely theoretical possibility that offences were committed on Swiss territory is insufficient. An entry ban would only be justified if there were concrete grounds for suspicion, concrete crimes planned or in preparation. There is a real and serious danger for Switzerland in such a situation. On the other hand, amusing is Fedpol's remarks that entry bans should also help prevent those concerned from escaping foreign criminal authorities. These statements are made regularly and can hardly be reconciled with the rule of law principles (Teichmann, 2021).

LESSONS FROM CRIMINAL PROCEEDINGS

In addition to the administrative law aspects described above, various aspects of criminal procedure must be considered. In particular, an insufficient suspicion can be objected to. It can be argued that there is no sufficient suspicion to justify the measure taken. Ultimately, for an entry ban to be issued, the information obtained must substantiate sufficient suspicion that a criminal offence may have been committed abroad or could be committed within the country in the near future (Moiseienko, 2021).

It follows that an assessment of the information must be carried out (Teichmann, 2021). In particular, mere rumours or suppositions do not satisfy the requirements for suspicion (Moiseienko, 2021). Furthermore, the inadmissibility of proceedings in absentia and violations of the presumption of innocence may be invoked (Teichmann, 2021).

The Role of Suspicion

The question arises as to how far the criminal procedural assessment of suspicion could be relevant for entry bans in Switzerland. The Fedpol bases its decision on entry bans on criminal proceedings abroad should be borne in mind. Therefore, it is of fundamental importance that, before issuing an entry ban, it should be ascertained whether the criminal proceedings abroad on which the ban is based are based on factual suspicion. If this requirement is not met, it would not be consistent with the rule of law principles to issue an entry ban on the basis of foreign criminal proceedings. If the foreign criminal proceedings were not based on sufficient suspicion substantiated by facts, the entry ban imposed by the Fedpol would not be based on such suspicion either. Since criminal prosecution authorities abroad are sometimes corrupt, a review of the foreign criminal proceedings on which the ban is based is unavoidable (Cameron, 2003).

It could be argued that it is not justifiable for reasons of procedural economy and practicability to review foreign proceedings. At the same time, however, foreign proceedings that are not based on factual suspicion should not be arbitrarily referred to. Otherwise, Switzerland would degrade itself into a helper of corrupt regimes.

Therefore, it must be ensured that the foreign proceedings are based on plausible, verifiable facts that constitute sufficient suspicion. If the facts are not verifiable, it would not be permissible to issue coercive measures on the basis of suspicion. This makes it all the less permissible to permanently interfere with the rights of the persons concerned (Teichmann, 2021).

Absence Procedure

Another problem connected with foreign criminal proceedings is so-called judgments in absentia (Riedo, Fiolka & Niggli, 2011). The accused is entitled to a right of presence in Switzerland. The ECtHR also emphasises the need for the accused to be present. Finally, the accused can only exercise the rights granted in Art. 6 para. 2 ECHR - inter alia to defend himself - if he is present in person (Pierini, 2014). In systems based on the rule of law, this view is generally shared. The extradition of foreign nationals to their home state is refused if they are to be transferred to the penal system there on the basis of a judgment in absentia (Kühne, 2010).

Proceedings in absentia can then only be considered in accordance with the principles of the rule of law in exceptional cases (Pieth, 2016). This applies in particular in the case of very minor criminality. However, these exceptional cases do not consider the present case, as they would not be sufficiently serious, even in total, to justify an entry ban.

Presumption of Innocence

Everyone is presumed innocent unless proven otherwise by judicial evidence (Kindhäuser, 2015). The burden of proof lies with the state (Stuckenberg, 1998). It follows that citizens do not have to exonerate themselves. Nor do they have to contribute to their dismissal. Instead, the burden is solely on the state to prove that they engaged in tortious conduct (Kühne, 2010).

It is conceivable that an entry ban could also be issued on the basis of suspicion (and thus without a final judgment). This would be to keep away dangers emanating, for example, from terrorists. However, the hurdle for this must be high. Otherwise, one could arbitrarily interfere seriously with the rights of the persons concerned on the basis of vague suspicions. Therefore, the presumption of innocence must not be forgotten (Teichmann, 2021).

CONCLUSION

The Swiss Federal Office of Police (Fedpol) is used as an example in this study to highlight the challenges they face in handling foreign criminal proceedings and what principles of criminal procedure need to be considered in administrative law. However, it should be noted that this article is not limited to Switzerland or even Fedpol, rather the implications are relevant to all Western countries.

Fedpol can be used as a good example, as it deals permanently with a large number of important international criminal proceedings, particularly those concerning Eastern European countries. Consequently, criminal and administrative proceedings are frequently initiated in Switzerland based on investigations by foreign authorities. By regularly proceeding in this way, the glaring shortcomings of foreign proceedings are completely ignored, which is possible, among other things, on the basis of the argument that entry bans within the meaning of Article 67(4) of the AIG are primarily administrative measures.

In addition to the usual administrative remedies against such entry bans, it has also been pointed out which aspects of the criminal procedure deserve special attention when the Swiss authorities issue orders on the basis of international criminal proceedings. Suspicion and judgments in absentia as well as the presumption of innocence play a special role. It is also difficult to challenge SIS alerts promptly, as third-country nationals reported in SIS II only learn about the existence of such a report when they are refused a visa, entry or extension of their residence permit. However, it should be noted that persons for whom an alert has been issued in the SIS II can initiate legal proceedings in any Schengen Member State and, if the national authority of the Member State decides that the entry ban is illegal, the reporting State must delete the entry ban from the SIS II. This provision can form an important basis for appeals against entry bans (Brouwer, 2018).

Both Swiss and foreign authorities are advised to examine the events underlying criminal proceedings on the basis of their standards of criminal procedure. Provided that it is concluded that there is also a suspicion under Swiss criminal procedural law (or applicable criminal procedural law) supported by facts and verified, the other requirements for an entry ban can be examined. Otherwise, the exercise can already be terminated after examination of the suspicion. It is therefore clear that the Federal Police Office has in the past ignored the principles of criminal procedural law and thus issued unlawful entry bans.

An excellent state governed by the rule of law, such as Switzerland, should only rely on foreign criminal procedures if these procedures do not suffer from serious procedural shortcomings that could not be reconciled with Western legal standards. Therefore, a full and fair exposition of the facts is impossible without a well-founded criminal procedural analysis of foreign proceedings.

DECLARATION

The authors declare that the manuscript follows ethical standards and there are no potential conflicts of interest with respect to the research, authorship and/or publication of this chapter.

DISCLAIMER

The contents and views of this chapter are expressed by the authors in personal capacities. It is not necessary for the Editor and the Publisher to agree with these viewpoints, and they are not responsible for any duty of care in this regard.

ACKNOWLEDGMENT

The authors extend sincere gratitude to

- The Editor and the International Editorial Advisory Board (IEAB) of this book, who initially desk reviewed, arranged a rigorous double/triple-blind review process, and conducted a thorough, minute, and critical final review before accepting the chapter for publication.
- All anonymous reviewers who provided very constructive feedback for thorough revision, improvement, extension, and fine-tuning of the chapter.
- All colleagues, assistants and well-wishers who assisted to complete this task.

REFERENCES

Anderson, J. H., & Gray, C. W. (2007). Transforming judicial systems in Europe and Central Asia. In F. Bourguignon & B. Pleskovic (Eds.) *Annual World Bank Conference on Development Economics – Regional: Beyond Transition*, (pp. 329–356). World Bank.

Andreas, P., & Nadelmann, E. (2008). *Policing the globe: Criminalization and crime control in international relations*. Oxford University Press.

Bellanova, R., & Glouftsios, G. (2022). Controlling the Schengen Information System (SIS II): The infrastructural politics of fragility and maintenance. *Geopolitics*, *27*(1), 160–184. doi:10.1080/14650045.2020.1830765

Boros, C., & Cusick, J. (2017, November 22). Bought and paid for – how Romania's media is pressured by corporate and political masters. *Open Democracy*. https://www.opendemocracy.net/en/bought-and-paid-for-how-romania-s-media-is-pressured-by-corporate-and-polit/

Brouwer, E. (2018, August 2018). Schengen entry bans for political reasons? The Case of Lyudmyla Kozlovska. *Verfassungsblog: On Matters Constitutional*. https://verfassungsblog.de/schengen-entry-bans-for-political-reasons-the-case-of-lyudmyla-kozlovska/

Brouwer, E. (2021). Schengen and the administration of exclusion: Legal remedies caught in between entry bans, risk assessment and artificial intelligence. *European Journal of Migration and Law*, *23*(4), 485–507. doi:10.1163/15718166-12340115

Cameron, I. (2003). UN targeted sanctions, legal safeguards and the European Convention on Human Rights. *Nordic Journal of International Law*, *72*(2), 159–214. doi:10.1163/157181003322560556

Chemali, H. H. (2020, December 10). The European Magnitsky Law—A milestone with a lot of potential. *Atlantic Council*. https://www.atlanticcouncil.org/blogs/new-atlanticist/the-european-magnitsky-law-a-milestone-with-a-lot-of-potential/#:~:text=The%20European%20Magnitsky%20Act%20has%20some%20limitations%2C%20but,States%20and%20Europe%20to%20coordinate%20their%20efforts%20together

Cizmaziova, L. (2021). *Sanctions as a tool for asset recovery: A global perspective (CIFAR Research Paper)*. CIFAR. https://cifar.eu/wp-content/uploads/2021/05/CiFAR_Sanctions-as-a-Tool-for-Asset-Recovery_Global-Perspective.pdf

Cosgrove, E. (2005). Examining targeted sanctions: Are travel bans effective? In C. Staibano & P. Wallensteen (Eds.), *International Sanctions: Between Wars and Words* (pp. 225–246). Routledge.

Dionisie, D., & Checchi, F. (2008). *Corruption and anti-corruption agencies in Eastern Europe and the CIS: A practitioners' experience*. United Nations Development Programme.

Drakopoulou, A., Konstantinou, A., & Koros, D. (2020). Border management at the external Schengen borders: border controls, return operations, and obstacles to effective remedies in Greece. In S. Carrera & M. Stefan (Eds.), *Fundamental Rights Challenges in Border Controls and Expulsion of Irregular Immigrants in the European Union: Complaint Mechanisms and Access to Justice* (pp. 175–196). Routledge. doi:10.4324/9780429203275-11

Elbasani, A. (2018). International promotion of rule of law: Facing connections between patronage, crime and judiciary corruption. In *Rule of law in the Eestern Balkans: Exploring the new EU enlargement strategy and necessary steps ahead.* Aspen Institute. https://www.aspeninstitute.de/wp-content/uploads/Reader-Rule-of-Law.pdf#page=28

EUR-Lex. (2019). *Second generation Schengen Information System (SIS II).* EUR-Lex. https://eur-lex.europa.eu/legal-content/RO/TXT/?uri=LEGISSUM%3Al14544

European Commission. (2021). *Restrictive measures (sanctions).* EC. https://ec.europa.eu/info/business-economy-euro/banking-and-finance/international-relations/restrictive-measures-sanctions_en

European Commission. (n.d.). *Migration and Home Affairs*. EC. https://ec.europa.eu/home-affairs/policies/schengen-borders-and-visa/schengen-information-system/alerts-and-data-sis_en

European Council. (2022). *EU sanctions against Russia explained.* EC. https://www.consilium.europa.eu/en/policies/sanctions/restrictive-measures-against-russia-over-ukraine/sanctions-against-russia-explained/

Fedpol. (2020a). *Money Laundering Reporting Office Switzerland MROS.* Fedpol. https://www.fedpol.admin.ch/fedpol/en/home/kriminalitaet/geldwaescherei.html

Fedpol. (2020b). *The Schengen Information System SIS*. FedPol. https://www. fedpol.admin.ch/fedpol/en/home/polizei-zusammenarbeit/international/schengen /sis.html

Fedpol. (2020c). *At the centre of policing in Switzerland – fedpol in focus.* Fedpol. https://www.fedpol.admin.ch/fedpol/en/home/fedpol/fedpol.html

Kaleniuk, D. (2021). *The EU must stop serving as a playground for corrupt Ukrainian oligarchs and officials.* Atlantic Council. https://www.atlanticcouncil.org/blogs /ukrainealert/the-eu-must-stop-serving-as-a-playground-for-corrupt-ukrainian-oligarchs-and-officials/

Karklins, R. (2002). Typology of post-communist corruption. *Problems of Post-Communism*, *49*(4), 22–32. doi:10.1080/10758216.2002.11655993

Kiener, R. (2018). Art. 55. In C. Auer, M. Müller, & B. Schindler (Eds.), *VwVG Kommentar*. Dike.

Kindhäuser, U. (2015). Strafprozessrecht, 4th ed. Baden-Baden, 219, Nomos.

Kinnvall, C., & Lindén, J. (2010). Dialogical selves between security and insecurity: Migration, multiculturalism, and the challenge of the global. *Theory & Psychology*, *20*(5), 595–619. doi:10.1177/0959354309360077

Kühne, H. H. (2010). *Strafprozessrecht: eine systematische Darstellung des deutschen und europäischen Strafverfahrensrechts*. CF Müller GmbH.

Kühne, H. H. (2020). Die internationale Bekämpfung von Wirtschaftskriminalität und die Konstitution des Verdachts. *Goltdammer's Archiv für Strafrecht*, 356–363.

Li, L., Sommarribas, A., & Baltes-Löhr, C. (2014). Good practices in the return and reintegration of irregular migrants: Member states' entry bans policy & use of readmission agreements between member states and third countries - Luxembourg. Walferdange: University of Luxembourg.

Majcher, I. (2019a). Conclusion: Schengen-Wide Entry Ban: A Triple Peine? In The European Union Returns Directive and its Compatibility with International Human Rights Law (pp. 333–342). Brill Nijhoff.

Majcher, I. (2019b). The European Union returns directive and its compatibility with international human rights law: Analysis of return decision, entry ban, detention, and removal. In *The European Union Returns Directive and its Compatibility with International Human Rights Law*. Brill Nijhoff.

Majcher, I. (2020). The Schengen-wide entry ban: How are non-citizens' personal data protected? *Journal of Ethnic and Migration Studies*, *48*(8), 1944–1960. doi:10.1080/1369183X.2020.1796279

Mc Gonigle, B. N. (2011). *Procedural justice? Victim participation in international criminal proceedings* [Doctoral Dissertation, The Netherlands Institute of Human Rights, Utrecht University].

Mendelski, M. (2010). Where does the European Union make a difference? *Rule of law development in South-Eastern Europe (APSA 2010 Annual Meeting Paper.* SSRN. https://papers.ssrn.com/sol3/papers.cfm?abstract_id=1644729

Mendelski, M. (2015). The EU's pathological power: The failure of external rule of law promotion in South Eastern Europe. *Southeastern Europe. L'Europe du Sud-Est*, *39*(3), 318–346. doi:10.1163/18763332-03903003

Ministry of Justice and Security. (2021). *Entry ban.* IND. https://ind.nl/en/Pages/Entry-ban.aspx

Moiseienko, A. (2018). Legal Protections from the accusations of corruption. In Corruption and Targeted Sanctions: Law and Policy of Anti-Corruption Entry Bans (pp. 177–211). Brill Nijhoff. doi:10.1163/9789004390478_006

Moiseienko, A. (2019). *Corruption and targeted sanctions: Law and policy of anti-corruption entry bans*. BRILL. doi:10.1163/9789004390478

Moiseienko, A. (2021). Due process and unilateral targeted sanctions. In C. Beaucillon (Ed.), *Research Handbook on Unilateral and Extraterritorial Sanctions*. Edward Elgar Publishing. doi:10.4337/9781839107856.00033

Ngcamu, B. S., & Mantzaris, E. (2021). Biased and falsified reporting: The Government's perspectives. In *Addressing Xenophobia in South Africa: Drivers, Responses and Lessons from the Durban Untold Stories*. Emerald Publishing Limited. doi:10.1108/978-1-80262-479-320211006

Oberlechner, T., & Hocking, S. (2004). Information sources, news, and rumors in financial markets: Insights into the foreign exchange market. *Journal of Economic Psychology*, *25*(3), 407–424. doi:10.1016/S0167-4870(02)00189-7

Örnebring, H. (2012). Clientelism, elites, and the media in Central and Eastern Europe. *The International Journal of Press/Politics*, *17*(4), 497–515. doi:10.1177/1940161212454329

Oxford Analytica. (2021). Russia's EU entry bans may close these sanctions round. *Emerald Expert Briefings*, (oxan-es).

Perrin, B., Rémy, M., & Roubaty, R. (2011). Electronic evidence in Swiss criminal procedure. *Digital Evidence & Electronic Signature Law Review*, *8*, 70.

Pierini, J. P. (2014). Violation of ECHR procedural guarantees and redress using the example of the Italian trial in absentia. *Zeitschrift für die gesamte Strafrechtswissenschaft*, 951.

Pieth, M. (2016). *Schweizerisches Strafprozessrecht* (3rd Revised Ed.). Helbing Lichtenhahn.

Popova, M., & Post, V. (2018). Prosecuting high-level corruption in Eastern Europe. *Communist and Post-Communist Studies*, *51*(3), 231–244. doi:10.1016/j.postcomstud.2018.06.004

Riedo, C., Fiolka, G., & Niggli, M. A. (2011). Strafprozessrecht sowie Rechtshilfe in Strafsachen. 1st ed. Basel, 425. Retrieved from Helbing Lichtenhahn Verlag.

Rutz, J. (2014, November). Austria's Return Policy: Application of entry bans policy and use of readmission agreements. *European Migration Network (EMN)*. https://www.emn.at/wp-content/uploads/2017/01/EMNReturnStudy2014_AT-NCP_eng.pdf

Skoryk, M. (2019). Theoretical aspects of the transformation of the institute of corruption in Eastern Europe. *Baltic Journal of Economic Studies*, *5*(1), 201–206. doi:10.30525/2256-0742/2019-5-1-201-206

Stuckenberg, C. F. (1998). Untersuchungen zur Unschuldsvermutung, 1st ed. Berlin: de Gruyter. DEG. doi:10.1515/9783110906349

Swissinfo. (2022, April 13). *Swiss tighten Russia sanctions and increase support for refugee*. Swiss Info. https://www.swissinfo.ch/eng/swiss-tighten-russia-sanctions-and-increase-support-for-refugees/47515750

Teichmann, F. (2017). Bribery and corruption–Challenges and potential solutions in multinational corporations. *SEER: Journal for Labour and Social Affairs in Eastern Europe*, *20*(2), 247–268. doi:10.5771/1435-2869-2017-2-247

Teichmann, F. (2021). Einreiseverbote aufgrund ausländischer Strafverfahren – Straf- und verwaltungsverfahrensrechtliche Herausforderungen für das schweizerische Bundesamt für Polizei (Fedpol). *Kriminalistik*, *1*, 48–53.

Teichmann, F. (2021). Korruption in osteuropäischen Staatsanwaltschaften und ihre Implikationen für Rechtshilfe - und Wirtschaftsstrafverfahren. *Kriminalistik*.

Teichmann, F. M., & Sergi, B. S. (2018). *Compliance in Multinational Corporations: Business Risks in Bribery, Money Laundering, Terrorism Financing and Sanctions*. Emerald Group Publishing. doi:10.1108/9781787568679

The Federal Council. (2022, February 28*). Switzerland adopts EU sanctions against Russia*. The Federal Council. https://www.admin.ch/gov/en/start/documentation/media-releases.msg-id-87386.html

Transparency International. (2014). *Leaving the corrupt at the door: From denial of entry to passport sales*. Federal Council. https://transparency.eu/wp-content/uploads/2018/02/Golden-Visas-TI-S-Leaving-the-Corrupt-at-the-Door.pdf

Transparency International. (2020). *World Map*. Transparency International. https://www.transparency.org/en/cpi/2019/results.

Wilkitzki, P. (1995). On judicial mutual assistance in criminal matters between the states of Western and Eastern Europe. *European Journal on Criminal Policy and Research*, *3*(4), 91–98. doi:10.1007/BF02243036

World Justice Project. (2020). *Rule of Law Index*. World Justice Project. https://worldjusticeproject.org/sites/default/files/documents/WJP-ROLI-2020-Online_0.pdf. (Accessed 09.05.2020).

Zabyelina, Y. (2020). The Long arm of anti-corruption: Extraterritoriality and anti-corruption targeted sanctions. *Global Policy*, *11*(4), 535–540. doi:10.1111/1758-5899.12850

Zgaga, B. (2018). Slovene media owned by oligarchs, corrupt politicians. *Reporters without borders*. https://rsf.org/en/slovene-media-owned-oligarchs-corrupt-politicians

Chapter 3
Consequences of Corruption on Economy, Politics, and Society: The Case of India

Asim Kumar Karmakar
Netaji Subhas Open University, India

Priyanthi Bagchi
Netaji Subhas Open University, India

Somnath Karmakar
https://orcid.org/0000-0002-1427-7938
University of Gour Banga, India

ABSTRACT

Corruption, defined as 'the abuse and misuse of public office for private gain,' has been a part of human societies since ancient times. Fraud, embezzlement, theft, black money, kickbacks, and bid rigging in the form of providing poorly delivered goods and services with the bad intention of making money by hook or by crook, are all features of corruption. Corruption under the garb of many tricks has existed for ages. History is evidence of the fact that it had extended its hands at different times at different places, with varying degrees of damaging consequences. Against the above backdrop, the objective of this chapter is to find out the levels of corruption and its impact on the economy, politics, and society with special reference to India. The main objective of this study is to examine the status of corruption in the world and its impact on business and various sectors of the economy and society as well. The study endeavors to suggest strategic policy implications for India and other countries engrossed in corruption.

DOI: 10.4018/979-8-3693-1190-5.ch003

INTRODUCTION

Corruption (*Bhrashtecher* in Hindi), defined simply as 'the abuse and misuse of public office for private gain) has been a part of human societies since time immemorial. Fraud, embezzlement, theft, black money, bribes (in order to obtain business, for example), kickbacks and bid rigging, in the form of providing poorly delivered goods and services with the bad intention of making the building collapse and roads to wash away, when sub-standard labor or materials are used, are all features of corruption.

Corruption under the garb of many tricks existed for ages. History is evidence of the fact that it had extended its hands at different times at different places, with varying degrees of damaging consequences. Dating back to the Fourth Century B.C. in India, Kautilya writes in *Arthashastra* about the high prevalence of corruption in the then government. In fact, the *Arthashastra* enlisted at least 40 ways in which public officials make these practices. Even the fruits of the toil of millions, when taken away by a few to build colossal fortunes in their favors, is also a form of corruption. In ancient Egypt, the practice of corruption in the guise of bribery and nepotism was in vogue. But, in recent times, it is reported to have taken a high jump and the issue of corruption has come to the fore with a great deal of attention. In the absence of good governance and a good system of accountability, the occurrence of serious neglect of duties plays a pivotal role with damaging consequences for which nothing moves in the intended direction, but many temptations for officials lie in wait for them in camera to earn extra money. Corruption now has that topic that is resonating even more loudly that the modern history has ever seen. It is found that companies were active in countries where the risk of corruption is high face a greater task in exerting due diligence and carrying out auditing procedures. Countries with dictatorships, whether the dictators are families or overweening parties, are the most corrupt. As Lord Action (1834-1902), the great 19th century British historian and moralist, in a letter to Bishop Creighton in 1887, succinctly commented, "*Power tends to corrupt and absolute power corrupts absolutely. Great men are almost always bad men.*" His comment is true even today. Individuals or families that stay in power for a long time build up coteries that rely on the patronage of their leaders. Even if the country has had a system requiring transparency and accountability that can be evaporated with the oncoming of individuals who have an inherent tendency to protect their sources of wealth (Kochan & Goodyear, 2011). But there is no denying the fact that there has not been a serious effort to fight against corruption, money laundering, and the black market and its associated forms of corruption around the world as well as the fight for the recognition of the importance of governance (Rafay, 2021a, 2023a).

OBJECTIVE OF THE STUDY

The present study is the study on the levels of corruption and its impact on the economy, politics, and society with special reference to India. The main objective of this study is to examine the status of corruption in the world and its impact on business and various sectors of the economy and society as well. The study endeavors to suggest strategic strategies for policy implications for India and other countries engrossed in corruption. The study is conducted with the help of secondary data from various national and international reports, government websites, books, and various journals.

WHAT IS CORRUPTION?

Although disagreements exist, corruption can be simply defined as the misuse of public power for personal gains. To make it elaborate, one can say that corruption refers to decisions that politicians and public bureaucrats make, and those decisions are conferred on them based on authority delegated to them by the populace. When these decisions are directed to have personal gains rather than by the public's interest, this is considered corruption. Corruption exists in a broad framework although there are many variations like administrative corruption, political corruption, etc. Administrative or petty corruption refers to acts of bribery, kickbacks, and grease money when public officials make money from bribes and a part of the profit favoring a particular contractor in an existing decision.

Political corruption was an issue from early times in many developed and developing countries (Nakitende *et al.*, 2021). The two words 'fraud' and 'corruption' appeared on their maps frequently. The close ties between big businesses and politicians occurred at the center of discussion concerning the abuse of public power, office, or resources for personal gain, including protection and /or strengthening of one's position in the system. Some of the common forms of political corruption are buying of votes and rigging of elections, non-transparent and illegal political campaigns, and party financing (Yogesh & Choudhary, 2014). Examples abound when political leaders either allocate national budgets from which either they themselves or their close associates' benefit. In developing countries, there exists a vicious nexus among voters, politicians, and businessmen by compulsion. Here voters (the poor and the unprivileged) know that politicians will provide patronage, give jobs, and help them acquire public services. The self-centered shrewd politicians are in dire need of the businessman to provide the funds that allow them to supply patronage to the poor and fight elections. The corrupt businessman is in dire need of this politician to have monopoly rights, public resources, and contracts cheaply. Politicians need the vote of the poor. Thus, the cycle is complete, and every constituency is tied to such a system (Rajan, 2019). From the local to the central, election campaigns are being fought on the strength of money power, and politics (Karmakar & Jana, 2022). Also, there are ample examples of political dictators who have managed to enrich themselves while impoverishing their countries abound: Haiti under Francois Duvalier (1907-1971) also called 'Papa Doc', Nigeria under Kwame Nkrumah (1909-72) and Uganda under Idi Amin (c. 1925-2003), Ben Ali (of Tunisia), Mubarak of Egypt, Ghaddafy (of Libya), and others-- are just some examples in this context. What follows is that political corruption dominates the ballot-box, the Legislature and the then prevailing Government thus leading to the misallocation of the country's economic resources and the political system, not to say about political dictators.

MEASUREMENT OF CORRUPTION

It is very difficult to measure corruption, but it exists in all countries. In countries where corruption is not endemic, corrupt acts are carried out under secrecy. In countries where corruption is not endemic, or widespread, corrupt incomes take so many forms that measurement becomes meaningless.

Due to a burgeoning global protest movement and growing across-the-global public intolerance against corrupt practices, transnational anti-corruption agencies emerge for its measurement and are playing an increasingly vital role in setting the agenda and shaping the direction of campaigns against corruption and bribery. There are major international drivers for the anti-corruption agenda—Transparency International (TI), Global Witness (GW), and Human Rights Watch (HRW).

TI is the leading activist group in this field. This TI, a Berlin-based non-governmental organization (NGO), founded in 1993 by a former regional director of the World Bank, Peter, has chapters in over 90 countries (Eigen, 2005). TI is best known for its annual publication of the Corruption Perception Index (CPI), a measure of corruption. TI draws attention to the problems created by corruption. IT campaigns to promote transparency in elections, public administration, procurement, and business, and lobbies governments to bring about change. The organization also develops and distributes practical guidance to help businesses operate ethically.

In addition, TI also publishes a Bribe Payers Index and since September 2010, the only worldwide public opinion on corruption is called a Global Corruption Barometer. From the drafting stage in the preparation of the UN Convention against Corruption and the African Union Convention on Preventing and Combating Corruption, it goes even further by involving in international agreements on corruption.

Its biggest achievement so far, however, has been to raise awareness in governments, businesses, and the general population—in its own words, to "challenge the inevitability of corruption."

Also founded in 1993, GW, a London and Washington-based NGO, is motivated to end the impunity of individuals, companies and governments that exploit natural resources for their own benefit at the expense of their people and the environment. The group campaigns for financial transparency to expose corrupt relationships. For example, it exposes that in 2008, exports of oil and minerals from Africa were worth $393 billion. If used properly in a prudent way, this wealth could lift millions of people out of poverty. However, the main benefits of resource extraction were shared by political, military, and business elites in producer countries, and oil, timber, and other companies overseas.

The phenomenon whereby countries rich in natural resources end up poorer and more unequal than countries without them because of corruption that happens. Countries relying on oil and mining revenues are often poor, badly run, corrupt, and prone to violent instability. This is in large part because the political elite place their own vested interests above their responsibilities to their population, undermining democracy, and basic human rights. The GW describes the above phenomenon as a 'resource curse' – also known as the paradox of plenty.

The World Bank Group highlighted its efforts to advance the fight against fraud and corruption in the development projects it finances, with the release of its *Sanctions System Annual Report for fiscal year 2022*.

WHY DOES CORRUPTION GROW AND PERSIST?

All countries have laws against corruption. Yet corruption persists. Democratic institutions cannot act properly against the growth of corruption, as there exist lacunas in the administrative, legislative and judiciary systems. Through these loose systems, corruption finds its way to act in the hands of those who have the power to exercise it. Corruption persists when in democratic countries, most of the elected members of the Parliament and State Legislative Assemblies are dishonest and few are honest. In the absence of a free press, corruption persists; it persists when public officials tempt to take advantage of their authority. To wipe out corruption, well-developed legal, political, and social institutions within the society and the country are required. Offending public officials and corrupt politicians are to be identified and punished by an independent and honest judicial system. Good institutions with good governance play an important role in controlling corruption. Research clearly confirms that the absence of corruption within countries correlates with the level of development of these institutions. Nay, the strengths of institutions and control mechanisms much be greater than the powers of public officials.

CORRUPTION REIGNS SUPREME IN PUBLIC SERVICES: IT CALLS FOR INSTITUTIONAL CHANGES

Corruption reigns supreme in public services. The causes of the prevalence of corruption in public services are many. First, corruption, being a secretive affair, emerges and flourishes through informational asymmetry. To arrest bribery and embezzlement, an institutional change that fosters transparency and accessibility of information will be effective. Secondly, it is found that the general belief among the population, still now, is that corruption is 'standard behavior' and must be tolerated. This notion acts in favor of the prevalence of corruption. Thirdly, in the absence of a realistic threat of prosecution and sanction, the unholy wave of corruption cannot be abated.

It is in this context what is essentially required for an effective anti-corruption strategy is to focus on institutional reforms as well as to generate effective measures to reduce the 'demand' and the 'supply side' of corruption so that a new, simpler, and effective procedure can be launched. Institutional reform along with legal reform is necessary to reduce the number of agencies if a country is engaged with so many agencies involved in the anti-corruption drive. A prudent institutional change can foster and accessibility of information, which in turn can be an effective tool for curbing the intensity of bribery and embezzlement. A culture of corruption persists when the unholy nexus like informational lacuna, social leniency and prosecution difficulty (due to the cumbersome nature of the administrative system) works (Drèze, 2015).

Moreover, the alienation of government concerns from the lives of ordinary masses has weakened customary forms of accountability and, on occasion, has led to a highly corrupt and self–seeking, awkward partisan state. In these cases, political parties and leaders, government officials and other vested interests connive to divert enormous public resources for narrow and selfish private benefit and use. The policies, laws and procedures play no role or when applied, make selection. The politics of vote banks is used to reinforce existing divisions within society and to create a new one by pampering one community and ignoring others. In this way emerges a diverse society—often fragmented and conflict-ridden. The public services have become too loyal to the ruling party. Corruption and self-seeking behavior that persist heavily on political leaders and public officials damage the 'trust' that citizens have in their governments. The citizens feel ignored or even betrayed either by their representatives or the government's policy ineffectiveness criterion. Very often, they become suspicious of the very programs that are created to meet their needs. The result is a wholesale collapse of citizens' faith in institutions:

The leaders have big salaries and people are without food (a citizen in Zimbabwe).

The result is a sense of powerlessness:

We are in a position to complain to anyone as there is nobody to listen to us—not even the police (a citizen in Gambia).

Poor people like us have no role to play...No one ever listens to us (a free-trade worker in Sri Lanka).

Political leaders and public officials abstain from criticisms from citizens, blame and 'bad news'—they always welcome praise, flattery and 'good news.' The problem is that governments everywhere have nearly always been driven by forces of oligarchy surrounding, rather than democracy; and government, political leaders and officials are very keen to enjoy power, no matter whether their deeds are doing good or bad to the society as a whole. As we have seen governments tend to become corrupted when pursuing a narrowly private agenda, rather than acting for the public benefit. This leads to corruption with a small capital 'c'. With such corruption, the call for institutional reform with good governance falls even on deafer ears (Knight, Chigudu, & Tandon, 2006).

CONSEQUENCES OF CORRUPTION

The Economic Effects of Corruption

Corruption is a huge drag on the economy – and on the lives of the people. Corruption, it being an important component of 'governance' -- is extremely a hindrance to economic growth and development (Jain, 2001). Misallocation of resources, distortion of labor markets, discouragement of investments and altering income distribution is the common outcome arising out of the practice of corruption. The myth that corruption helps the market by "greasing the wheels of commerce" has been proven false. In a remarkable study of bribery, Wade (1985) shows that once bribes are introduced, bureaucracies redirect their attention from providing services to the public to maximize bureaucrat's illicit incomes. In the Indian case, once in the decade of 1950s, there was a system that left government officers effectively in sole command—or oligarchic dominance—over giving licenses (say, import or mining licenses), without checks and invigilation, became a free playfield of corrupt practices (Das, 2012).

There is a negative correlation between the performance of stock markets and corruption as corruption increases volatility in the economy and hinders investors from long-term investment. Across the global international financial markets, corruption increases borrowing costs significantly higher, lowers stock valuations and augments bad Corporate Governance. Corruption if not checked can erode the very pillars of the growth prospects of the economy.

Corruption also distorts the selection of public-sector projects. Corruption also discriminates against FDI because dealing with corrupt officials requires familiarity. It also affects labor markets by distorting returns for various activities.

Corruption facilities direct tax evasion and can also lead to further unaccounted (bribe) income. Unaccounted bribe income has been alleged to be a major source of unaccounted funds held outside the country, leading to further revenue loss (Das-Gupta, 2015). The intensity of corruption is such that only a wholesale transformation of the society covering the politicians, bureaucracy, judiciary, private sector, media, and NGOs can be expected to cure this malady.

Corruption negatively affects and deteriorates the systemic delivery of public services, for example, health care and education. Such deterioration affects the poor more than the rich first because they must pay a bribe to agents engaged in those sectors to receive the services and second because they depend wholly on services. In this way, common men's respect for 'the rule of law' and honesty is bound to dampen.

Banerjee's (1997) important insight into this connection is that corruption is indirectly responsible for higher delivery costs since corrupt bureaucrats have the incentive to generate excessive red tape which adds to costs. This theory is supported in the Indian context by a recent field experiment.

The negative impact of corruption on business costs clearly reduces international competitiveness. Bardhan's (1997) review of the negative impact of corruption on efficient resource allocation; investment, particularly foreign investment, and economic growth suggest that these costs are appreciable. As

Bardhan (1997) points out, efficiency and growth costs are not limited to direct costs. Indirect cost channels include the reduced information transmitting efficiency of markets since corruption is necessarily secretive. Another indirect channel identified is the two-way link between corruption and unaccounted wealth, including wealth held outside the country in secretive foreign jurisdictions. Conspicuous consumption from 'black' wealth and curtailed investment opportunities further reduce growth. In a recent book, the same author mentioned the case of demonetization in November 2016 in the BJP regime that has turned out to be one of the '*grandest hoaxes ever in Indian political history*'-- failed miserably to vaporize the corrupt cash hoarded by the rich. The author also mentioned the gigantic Vyapam scam in the BJP regime in Madhya Pradesh, India in which 40 mysterious deaths of the witnesses and the accused had been reported. Then there is the cricket–related scams. Alongside, many stories about continuing corruption in government procurement and land grabs continue in India, (Bardhan, 2022). Yet the rhetoric of slaying the demon of corruption continues in full force.

The most harmful consequence of corruption may be summarized in the following manner: it inhibits investment in the economy. Research clearly shows that countries with high corruption exhibit lower levels of investment and economic growth (World Bank, 2001). It also undermines investor confidence across all sectors of business, as mentioned. Corruption in poor overall governance makes it difficult for entrepreneurs to invest because in that case, the cost of starting a business venture rises. Once the investment is made, corruption creates uncertainties for entrepreneurs, because the public officials' option to extract bribes from the venture increases the entrepreneur's risk and lowers their returns. However, the pernicious effects of corruption are not merely confined to the economic domain; they pervade all layers of society.

The Social Effects

One of the major effects of widespread corruption is its highly devastating and destabilizing impact on a country's social order. A culture of bribery can effectively hold society captive, slow, or stop social progress, and empower despots. Where corruption is rampant in the countries in question, bribery sharply divides between the ruling elite and the have-nots, with potentially long-run consequences.

Corruption prevents good change in society, constrains development, and damages the economic and social fabric of the countries where it occurs-- be it in developing countries, developing developed or developed countries. It destroys the rule of law and democratic institutions. It is no coincidence that those countries with systemic corruption have no respect for the rule of law, do not respect the independence of the judges and the enforcement authorities, and do not look into democratic accountability. It is also no coincidence that this results in the impoverishment of the citizens of those countries.

In addition, TI observes that high levels of inequality in the distribution of income predict high levels of corruption. The Corruption Perception Index (CPI), supported by various other studies, shows that per capita income is inversely related to corruption, and those countries with greater economic inequalities are perceived as substantially more corrupt.

Exacerbating inequality and deprivation can contribute to social instability, even in some cases the condition of even civil war as happened in Russia during Bolshevik Revolution in 1917. In today's Russia, we also witness a corrupt shadow economy; rampant corruption and bribery function like a parallel tax system for the personal enrichment of elites—at the cost of the rest of the society.

TI's observation goes even further. It has identified three of the UNs Millennium Development Goals -- "Reduced child mortality, improved maternal health, and the fight against HIV/AIDS, malaria and other diseases"—that have particularly suffered because of corruption (TI, 2006)

In this context, Labelle's (2010) comments are worth noting: Allowing corruption to continue is unacceptable: too many poor, kicked and vulnerable people continue to suffer its consequences, across the world. We need to see more enforcement of existing rules and laws. There should be nowhere to hide the corrupt or their money.

The Political Effects

Needless to say, corruption and bribery have darkened the political atmosphere across the world. In the political arena, corruption occurs in the shadows. Sometimes, through secret negotiation, self-centered shoddy politicians and business elites obtain money corruptly either by distorting markets or selling state assets. The TI study of Vietnam finds that bribery and corruption are associated with "the loss of state assets, reduction in business opportunities and competitiveness due to increased production costs, reduce foreign investors' confidence, under-utilization and loss of competent civil servants and officials, increased social inequality and environmental degradation (Gainsborough, 2006).

Bribes are such notorious things that they can even weaken democratic governments, bereft of hampering economic and social development; impede the consolidation of democratic structures and their functions for smooth processes. Bribes can have a dampening effect on justice in the country in which they occur. There is solid evidence that businesspeople in developed countries have offered bribes to foreign public officials to prevent investigation so that they can wipe away their financial misconduct.

Today most of the international business is captured and conducted by multinational companies. Their global reach, economic power, and intelligence capabilities now exceed those of many small and many developing countries. Taking this opportunity, they enter where usual weal governance prevails. In these cases, bribery can misappropriate the infrastructure of developing countries for commercial gains. Besides, when a particular government is identified with the closest proximity to corruption, it can erode social capital and foster support for various forms of extremism and organized crime (Rafay, 2021b, 2023b). Nay, bribery in real life leads to a wider loss of trust in the very fabric of government and the administration law. This erosion of trust between the government and the people can ultimately add fuel to fire uprising the forces of anarchy and revolution; corruption surrounding the high and over-powerful rules has been cited as a central reason for the uprisings currently taking place in Africa and the Middle East.

These are the few examples that serve as illustrations of the damage that corruption and bribery have on the economic, social, and political order in the countries in which they occur.

CORRUPTION AND BRIBES: THE INDIAN STORY

Despite various measures taken by the present and earlier governments to reduce the intensity of corruption in the administrative and political system, India's rank in the CPI and Global Corruption Barometer is relatively low. In the latest Index for 2021, India's score is 40 on a scale of 0 to 100 where 0 is "totally corrupt" and "100" is "very clean". India is the 85 least corrupt nation out of 180 countries, according to the 2021 Corruption Perceptions Index reported by Transparency International.

The Indian political virtue in the 1950s was marked by the near- absence of corruption; but the birth of the License-Permit-Quota Raj in India following the import-substitution industrialization strategy during the 1950s and its growth overtime, especially in the 1970s during the socialist-era policies of Prime Minister Indira Gandhi had created a parallel economy through which government officials, politicians and bureaucrats started devising restrictive laws that ultimately increased their private wealth and corruption skyrocketed (Sen & Sen, 2019).

The early stage of the liberalization episode in the mid-1980s initiated by the Prime Minister (PM), Rajiv Gandhi was accompanied by the Bofors scandal, which for the first time in Independent India, placed the now-mentioned PM and his office in the talk of the scandal. In India, corruption is the go of everyday life. A person who bribes the ticket collector to get a better birth on a train might be considered corrupt, or when a traffic police constable collects money for a truck or scooter–driver for 'teas and water'. In the latter case, a portion of money transfers is passed up through government hierarchies—from the first person to police inspectors to superintendents – and on up to politicians, who use these funds in part to finance elections and pay off supporters. (Jeffrey & Hariss, 2014).

It is no surprise that corruption is widely discussed in India. The abuse of public office for private gain is endemic in the country. The post-1991 neo-liberal reforms that were more systemic than the Rajiv era, have propelled a rise in corruption more boldly, more vividly- bigger in magnitude. It manifests itself when huge scams come to light – the notorious '2G scam' for example.

Money power and politics or to speak specifically the nexus between black money and political parties is one of the principal causes of corruption in India, though to break this vicious circle, several Committees were set up in the 1990s and the 2000s (*for example* Goswami Committee on Electoral Reforms 1990, Election Commission of India Report on Proposed Electoral Reforms 2004, and Second Administrative Reform Committee (ARC) 2008). In this context, the Delhi High Court's judgment is worth mentioning:

"Money power should not be allowed to distort the conduct of free and fair election … Political parties must maintain properly audited accounts of income received through various sources. Unless this is done, the political parties cannot claim an exemption on income tax."

In September 2018, to discourage elected leaders from criminal activities, the Supreme Court issued some injunctions to the political parties about the distribution of tickets for election and thereby warning that each candidate must fill out forms disclosing whether he/she is not involved in criminal cases, or any cases pending against him/her (Jalan, 2019). Despite these attempts, none of these have been successful in doing so. The magnitude of the illicit money power remains high in the hands of political parties endangering the democratic credibility itself. It is of no surprise that India has ranked the lowest on account of political finance regulation (according to the Global Integrity Report), scoring zero, out of 100 in case of disclosure of the fund of political parties. India also scored a zero on the effectiveness of party financing (Varma, 2019).

In India in 2011, officers in the top and middle management of various public sector banks and financial institutions received illegal gratification from the private financial services company which was acting as a mediator and facilitator for corporate loans and other facilities from financial institutions (Singh, 2010). Reuter reports that a large proportion of the companies in this "bribes for loans" scandal are major players in India's booming infrastructure and construction industry (Mukherjee & Tripathy, 2010). It came to global media when Anna Hazare, an Indian anti-corruption campaigner, Anna Hazare was arrested in mid-August 2011. International Accountancy firm KPMG states that in its experience with clients, construction is extremely vulnerable to corruption in general and bribery payments in particular (McDermott, 2010).

Recognizing the gravity of the situation that corruption will pose a serious threat to the security, freedom and well-being of ordinary citizens and their long-cherished values, and of new avenues created for corruption of the older variety, and because the reforms have still not been covered and extended to the new areas, the government had no other option but to curb corruption in the light of deepening and the broadening of the reforms to new areas. The reform of the antiquated Land Acquisition Act of 1894, the issuance of land titles that would improve access to credit, transparency in government procurement and competitive auctions of mineral rights and telecom spectrum are among such measures (Bhagwati & Panagariya, 2012). Along with strengthening the Right to Information (RTI) Act, ratification of the United Nations Convention Against Corruption (UNCAC), placing information on assets of government officers in the public domain, setting up additional special CBI courts, introduction of e-governance and a direct benefit scheme, enactment of the Prevention of Corruption (Amendment) Act, 2018 is an important step in this direction. A special investigation team (SIT) has also been formed to detect black money.

Even under the NDA Modi government, the fight against black money came to the fore in getting the black money stashed in foreign accounts. But the sudden bold launching of the 'hastily-thought-out' demonetization program in November 2016 did not yield the desired result and went in the wrong direction, though the objective was to wash away the corrupt money hoarded by the rich. Bardhan (2021) says: "What was done in the name of demonetization was a cruel joke on the Indian poor, particularly those in the informal sector."

There is no doubt that an effective anti-corruption strategy enveloping institutional reform as well as the supply and demand sides will help accelerate poverty eradication and improve the public delivery system (Jalan, 2019)

A TIME TO ACT ON CORRUPTION

The fight against corruption is the need of the hour, as corruption is endowed with such a story that has heroes, villains, and victims -- heroes in the guise of the individuals (whether journalists, members of NGOs, private citizens, or others including big politicians) in the country or society, villains in the form of individuals or companies that do business with the corrupt politicians and officials not caring what the ill- results will be for the poor, and the victims are the many people in the countries who suffer utmost as a result of corruption. There is solid evidence that countries rich in the quality of their resources and the talents of their citizens are held back by a culture of corruption that favors the few and causes great damage to the many. For example, many students who on October 23, 2022, were in *Dharna* and *geraoed* Education Department in the State of West Bengal of India were being pulled out and beaten severely by the working governments' policemen from their legitimate jobs due to corrupt politicians activities, that takes a huge amount of money and ornaments as bribes from unqualified students in the examinations in lieu of their confirmed jobs. In the era of greed, foul becomes fair.

Recognizing that corruption is a serious obstacle to fighting poverty and inequality, many international and non-governmental organizations since the latter half of the 1990s and beyond have been leading the fight to reduce corruption in the world. The fight focuses on three areas: civil societies in which the public plays a key role, a top-down commitment from the political leadership to fight corruption, and a proactive private sector that accepts its social responsibility to operate in a corruption-free manner. The current fashion in fighting corruption is transparency, the idea that the working of governments should be available for scrutiny by outsiders like independent public auditors, the media and the public (Banerjee & Duflo, 2019; Ramzan *et al.*, 2020). There is solid evidence that in many situations' transparency helps.

CONCLUSION AND POLICY POINTERS

Increased corruption reduces most of the fundamentals of an economy, including governance factors. It has a great role in eroding the institutional capacity of government and augmenting poverty and income inequalities, among others. Because corrupt practices have such far-reaching negative consequences, eliminating them from every sphere of the public and private sectors can bring about widespread beneficial effects. When corruption and bribery are ruled out, it is obvious that benefits accrue to all from the domestic as well as from the global economy.

Moreover, to have "just, honest, transparent, accountable, and participatory government and probity in public life and poverty–free situation, countries should come forward to sign the Protocol on the Fight against Corruption by strengthening their parliamentary capacity to fight corruption and promote good governance and at the same time to establish an international cooperation framework to improve mutual law enforcement and facilitate asset confiscation.

Following are some of the suggestions in this regard:

- The lines of authority should be well-defined and streamlined.
- The new generation becoming more active in politics and with a sunlit vision should come forward to help remake the political system more vibrant than before.
- A no-corruption grass route movement is required. The chain must come from the people first. The laws and regulations against corruption must be rigid and need to be in place and in practice. There must be a more visible and clearer message from the government to abolish systematic corruption in the government structure.
- There must be some fear of the law.
- There should be some monitoring to see whether the proper functioning of good governance is going on or not.
- Emphasis should be on the moral character of the individuals.
- Emphasis should be on strengthening the functional aspects of institutions.
- There must be incentive payments for civil servants.
- Anti-corruption campaigns will do well for society; and
- To curb the spread of corruption and other allies, the most effective course of action available to the government is clearly the deepening and the broadening of the reforms to new areas.

DECLARATION

The authors declare that the manuscript follows ethical standards and there are no potential conflicts of interest with respect to the research, authorship and/or publication of this chapter.

DISCLAIMER

The contents and views of this chapter are expressed by the authors in personal capacities. It is not necessary for the Editor and the Publisher to agree with these viewpoints, and they are not responsible for any duty of care in this regard.

ACKNOWLEDGMENT

The authors extend sincere gratitude to

- The Editor and the International Editorial Advisory Board (IEAB) of this book, who initially desk reviewed, arranged a rigorous double/triple-blind review process, and conducted a thorough, minute, and critical final review before accepting the chapter for publication.
- All anonymous reviewers who provided very constructive feedback for thorough revision, improvement, extension, and fine-tuning of the chapter.
- All colleagues, assistants and well-wishers who assisted to complete this task.

REFERENCES

Banerjee, A. V. (1997). A theory of misgovernance. *The Quarterly Journal of Economics*, *112*(4), 1289–1332. doi:10.1162/003355300555484

Banerjee, A. V., & Duflo, E. (2019). *Good economics for hard times*. PublicAffairs.

Bardhan, P. (1997). Corruption and development: A review of issues. *Journal of Economic Literature*, *35*(3), 1320–1346.

Bardhan, P. (2021). *Indian Polity and economy: A mirror to difficult times*. Frontpage.

Bhagwati, J., & Panagariya, A. (2012). *India's tryst with destiny: Debunking myths that undermine progress and addressing new challenges*. HarperCollins Publishers.

Das, G. (2013). *India grows at night*. Penguin.

Das-Gupta, A. (2015). Corruption. In K. Basu & A. Maertens (Eds.), *The New Oxford Companion to Economics in India* (Vol. I). Oxford University Press.

Drèze, J. (2018). On corruption. In B. C. Nirmal, B.C& Bandyopadyay, S. (Eds.) Combating Corruption, Black Money and Money Laundering: Issues and Challenges Ahead. New Delhi: Satyam Law International.

Eigen, P. (2005). *Corruption Perception Index*. Transparency International.

Gainsborough, M. (2006). *Country study report: Vietnam 2006*. Transparency International.

Jain, A. K. (2001). Corruption: A review. *Journal of Economic Surveys*, *15*(1), 71–121. doi:10.1111/1467-6419.00133

Jalan, B. (2019). *Resurgent India: Politics, economics and governance*. HarperCollins Publishers India.

Jeffrey, C., & Harriss, J. (2014). Corruption. In *Keywords for modern India*. Oxford University Press.

Karmakar, A. K., & Jana, S. K. (2018). Corruption in India - An introspective view. In S. Bandyopadyay & B. C. Nirmal (Eds.), *Combating Corruption, Black Money and Money Laundering: Issues and Challenges*. Satyam Law International.

Karmakar, A. K., & Jana, S. K. (2022). Governance reform from global perspectives: Some dimensions. In R. C. Das (Ed.), *Social Sector Spending, Governance and Economic Development - Theoretical and Empirical Perspectives from Across the World* (Vol. I). Routledge.

Knight, B., Chigudu, H., & Tandon, R. (2006). *Reviving democracy: Citizens at the heart of Governance*. Earthscan Publications.

Kochan, N., & Goodyear, R. (2011). *Corruption: The new corporate challenge*. Palgrave Macmillan. doi:10.1057/9780230343344

Labelle, H. (2010, October 26). Response to global crises must prioritize zero tolerance for corruption. *Transparency International*. https://www.transparency.org/en/press/20101026-global-crisis-zero-tolerance-for-corruption

Lane, D. (2002). *Russian Banking: Evolution, problems, and prospects*. Edward Elgar. doi:10.4337/9781781950586

McDermott, R. (2010). *UK Bribery Act 2010—a blessing in disguise? Construction industry briefing*. KPMG.

Mukherjee, K., & Tripathy, D. (2010, November 26). India probes 21 companies in bribes-for-loans scandal. *Reuters*. https://www.reuters.com/article/us-india-corruption-idUSTRE6AO19P20101126

Nakitende, M. G., Rafay, A., & Waseem, M. (2021). Frauds in Business Organizations: A Comprehensive Overview. In A. Rafay (Ed.), *Handbook of Research on Theory and Practice of Financial Crimes* (pp. 21–38). IGI Global. doi:10.4018/978-1-7998-5567-5.ch002

Rafay, A. (Ed.). (2021a). *Money Laundering and Terrorism Financing in Global Financial Systems*. IGI Global. doi:10.4018/978-1-7998-8758-4

Rafay, A. (Ed.). (2021b). *HandBook of Research on Theory and Practice of Financial Crimes*. IGI Global. doi:10.4018/978-1-7998-5567-5

Rafay, A. (Ed.). (2023a). *Concepts, Cases, and Regulations in Financial Fraud and Corruption*. IGI Global. doi:10.4018/978-1-6684-5007-9

Rafay, A. (Ed.). (2023b). *Concepts and Cases of Illicit Finance*. IGI Global. doi:10.4018/978-1-6684-8587-3

Rajan, R. (2019). *The third pillar: How markets and the state leave the community*. HarperCollins Publishers India.

Ramzan, M., Ahmad, I., & Rafay, A. (2020). Is auditor independence influenced by Non-audit services? A stakeholder's viewpoint. *Pakistan Journal of Commerce and Social Sciences*, *14*(1), 388–408.

Sen, S., & Sen, A. (2019). *India Emerging: From Policy Paralysis to Hyper Economics*. Bloomsbury Publishing.

Singh, R. (2010, December 27). RBI joins bribes-for-loans scam probe. *Economic Times*. https://economictimes.indiatimes.com/news/politics-and-nation/rbi-joins-bribes-for-loans-scam-probe/articleshow/7169716.cms?from=mdr

TI. (2006). *Global Corruption Report 2006: Corruption and Health*. Transparency International.

Varma, P. K. (2019). *Chanakya's View: Understanding India in Transition*. Tranquebar Press.

Wade, R. (1985). The market for public office: Why the Indian state is not better at development. *World Development*, *13*(4), 467–497. doi:10.1016/0305-750X(85)90052-X

World Bank. (2001). *Governance and Corruption*. World Bank Group.

Yogesh, A., & Choudhary, S. K. (2014). *Combating corruption: The Indian case*. Orient BlackSwan.

Chapter 4
Insider Trading and Front Running as the Basis of Money Laundering:
The Case of Pakistan

Tooba Akram
https://orcid.org/0000-0002-7039-1591
Universiti Teknologi Malaysia, Malaysia

Muhammad Naveed
https://orcid.org/0000-0002-1764-6110
Bahria University, Pakistan

Suresh Ramakrishnan
Universiti Teknologi Malaysia, Malaysia

Adnan Ali
https://orcid.org/0000-0003-4051-3153
Shaheed Benazir Bhutto University, Pakistan

ABSTRACT

This chapter explores the fine line between insider trading and front running, providing a categorical analysis of these financial crimes. It highlights how insider trading serves as a predicate offense for money laundering on a global scale and focuses on Pakistan as a vulnerable market for such malpractices. The chapter examines three cases investigated by the apex regulator: one involving a politically exposed person engaged in illicit activities, another exposing a corporate executive's involvement in insider trading and front running, and a third case revealing front running by mid-level managers at a brokerage house. These cases offer detailed insights into the execution of these crimes and underscore the crucial role of regulators and investigators. Additionally, the chapter emphasizes the significant impact of these activities on the financial economy, particularly in connection with FATF measures.

DOI: 10.4018/979-8-3693-1190-5.ch004

INTRODUCTION

The purpose of this chapter is to provide a foundational knowledge of insider trading, as well as front running, and the components that comprise these practices. This chapter elucidates the relevance of insider trading, which is a crime that can serve as a predicate for money laundering. In addition, the chapter examines three distinct situations from a developing nation to demonstrate how criminals profit from their activities. The most important takeaway from the chapter is to understand the significance of insider trading, which is defined as an offence for money laundering, and have an in-depth grasp of the components of insider trading as well as the subsequent steps to crime proceeds.

THE CONCEPTS

Insider Trading

Insider trading describes a situation in which a person engages in stock trading in violation of a fiduciary duty or other relationship of trust and confidence, while in possession of material non-public information about a company's shares (Hansen, 2021). This expression refers to the dissemination of such information, the trading of stocks by the individual who has been "tipped off," and the trading of stocks by those who have misused such information. In addition, illegal insider trading earnings can be laundered through the stock market. As a result, money laundering is both a predicate offense and a mechanism for laundering illegal funds.

Hence, Insider Trading is an offensive trade carried out based on any insider information. An insider trade must encompass the three elements including (i) insider, (ii) inside information, and (ii) insider trade.

Front Running

Also known as "*Tailgating*", is the illegal practice of entering an equity trade, to profit from advance, non-public knowledge of a large block pending transaction that will affect the price of the underlying security. Front running is the illicit activity of purchasing securities based on non-public information about an anticipated significant transaction that would affect its price.

Front running, also known as tailgating, is the illegal practice of entering an equity trade, to profit from non-public knowledge of a large block pending transaction that will affect the price of the underlying security.

Thin Line between Insider Trading and Front Running

"Insider trading" and "Front running" are often used interchangeably as synonyms but, there is a distinction. When a trader places an order to trade based on information he or she has about another trader's order, the trade goes through, and the trader makes money from it, we say that the trader is "front running" the orders of other traders. This benefit could be making a profit or preventing a loss in the future. Insider trading happens when a person trade based on price-sensitive information that is not known to the public. This could be a company's good earnings, healthy financial results, dividend announcements, a new project, or a large investment. To be exact, all front running can be considered insider trading, but not all insider trading can be considered front running.

Mandatory Elements of Insider Trading

To prove any case of insider trading, one must have proved these four elements.

***Inside Information*:** Any information which is not yet publicly disclosed and, is price-sensitive information is "inside Information". To endorse the act of insider trading, one must prove what was the inside information.

***Insider*:** A person who possesses inside information is an "insider". Typically, this becomes evident upon summoning the minutes of meetings and attendance sheets of the meeting wherein it is suspected that price-sensitive information is discussed.

***Insider trading*:** Buying or selling of the stock based on inside information and insider trading.

The Passing of inside information: How the information is passed. There should be a shred of shreds of evidence that attests that the insider possesses the inside information or if he passed that information to someone, then how it is passed (any circumstantial evidence that leads to substantial evidence).

Insider Trading Across the Globe: A Predicate Offence of ML/CFT

ML and FT originated in Paris in the 1980s and gradually the whole world came under this umbrella of organized crime. During the past 25 years, ML and FT elements are being studied, however, gained a lot of attention after the 9/11 terrorist attack. First time in 2001, the EU agreed to investigate whether the terrorists were engaged in insider trading before the attacks (Euractiv, 2010). A considerable number of preliminary reports concluded that criminals use financial markets to launder money and finance terrorist activities (Hanif *et al.*, 2023).

It is observed that most of these reports explained the phenomenon through qualitative analysis and concluded various typologies. These typologies rendered the following aspects of ML and FT research.

(i) Sources/Medium of organized crime
(ii) Measure ML and FT values using the Walker gravity model.
(iii) Due Diligence to curb ML and FT and evolution of the theory of crying wolf.
(iv) Detection and Prediction using conventional technology and artificial intelligence.
(v) Rules, Regulations and Enforcement Laws.

Surprisingly, all the aforementioned dimensions take the account of insider trading and front running. FATF Recommendations regarding the stock market designated insider trading, market manipulation, and market fraud as money laundering offences (FATF, 2012; Rafay, 2021a, 2023a). Therefore, to expand the scope of stock market surveillance, the global jurisdiction needs to expand the scope to cross-market surveillance. Nonetheless, Insider trading is not easy to prosecute by the authorities (Barnes, 2010). Many cases established that money launderers and insider traders use almost identical methods: they conceal their illegal operations via the use of strawmen and (offshore) business structures, and they often operate in several countries at the same time. As a result, both are not easy to curb. Both activities are often used as a medium for each other. Thence, the connection appears significant. Insider trade can be executed in any stage of money laundering whether it is layering, placement, or integration.

Theoretically, "*The classic theory of insider trading*" determines that the infringement in insider trading is based on the relationship of the Parties in the transaction or those who have a fiduciary obligation. When the classic theory of insider trading is employed to solve the problem of insider trading, a person who has no fiduciary obligation but trades stocks using non-public information material is not considered to be an insider trading perpetrator. As a result of this theory, the objective of insider trading regulation to be a form of protection for investors will not be maximized because of the classic theory that fiduciary obligation based provides an opportunity to a party who has no fiduciary obligation to conduct insider trading. For example, if a tippee obtains information material from the insider and the tippee does not have the fiduciary obligation, then the tippee cannot be held liable. Hence, keeping in view the sensitivity of these financial crimes (Rafay, 2021b), jurisdictions have even designated insider trading as ML/TF Offense.

Considering, the measures to curb crime in developed countries, followed by emerging and developing ones, it is observed that Financial Conduct Authority (FCA) in the USA has already fired the caution at capital markets over money laundering acquaintances and disclosures. FCA also focused on identifying stock market offences at the expense of spotting money laundering, and many firms had failed to appreciate that market abuse could also be indicative of money laundering (Amjad *et al.*, 2021). On the other hand, in the past, the Obama administration planned strategies to equip all US agencies with access to a huge database (Flitter, Dawson & Hosenball, 2013). This database contains financial data of US citizens and the individuals keeping banking channels in the US. This proposed plan was to identify and hunt down terrorist networks and crime syndicates. This became possible only by fetching all the data of financial transactions, military intelligence, and records of the criminal. It is pertinent to mention here that aforesaid data is not accessible to public researchers, therefore, academic literature deeply lacks such studies.

Moreover, The Eurasian group combating money laundering and financing of terrorism (EAG) is a FATF-style regional body that comprises 9 countries: Belarus, China, Kazakhstan, Kyrgyzstan, India, and Russia, Tajikistan, Turkmenistan, and Uzbekistan. EAG is an associate member of the FATF. Out of these 9 countries, three countries did not designate Insider Trading as ML/TF offenses. Figure 1 is the snapshot from the Eurasian group report by FATF in 2013.

Brown & Gillespie (2015) explained that there are two main reasons why organized crime has infiltrated the capital markets: the first is to make money, which is primarily accomplished through fraud, share manipulation, insider trading, deceptive and coercive telemarketing; the second is to launder money, which is primarily accomplished through drug trafficking and other profit-oriented crimes.

CASE STUDIES

Pakistan: A Developing Country With an Emerging Market

Unfortunately, any piece of literature in existing studies pertaining to money laundering and Terrorism financing is not complete without the name "Pakistan". Whether the literature is related to highlighting the proceeds, measuring in terms of value, detection, or enforcement regarding organized crimes, the name "Pakistan" is always there, and the vulnerability of Pakistan's Financial market is high in terms of financial crimes.

Figure 1. EAG jurisdictions designated insider trading

3.1 Designation of offences in the securities markets as ML/TF offences

As already mentioned, the FATF standards[3] require that securities market related offences, such as, insider trading, market manipulation and securities related fraud should be designated as ML/TF offences. Therefore, jurisdictions were requested to inform if these offences had been designated as ML/TF offences. The responses are received below.

Jurisdiction	Whether Insider Trading is designated as ML offence (Yes/No)?	Whether Market Manipulation is designated as ML offence (Yes/No)?
Belarus	Yes	Yes
China	Yes	Yes
India	Yes	Yes
Kazakhstan	No	No
Kyrgyz Republic	Yes	Yes
Russia	Yes	Yes
Tajikistan	Yes	Yes
Turkmenistan	Yes	Yes
Uzbekistan	Yes	Yes
Armenia	Yes	Yes
Turkey	Yes	Yes
Ukraine	No	Yes
Mongolia	No	No

Even though Pakistan has implemented administrative and legislative steps to combat terrorist funding, the Financial Action Task Force put Pakistan on its 'grey list' in 2018, citing 'structural inadequacies' in tackling terrorism financing and money laundering. Pakistan was ordered by the FATF to adhere to the action plan and strengthen legal frameworks to conform to international norms to maintain the global financial system's integrity. Between 2015 and 2018, the Federal Investigation Agency (FIA) filed 1,111 charges against suspected terrorist financiers, confiscated PKR 2 billion, detained 1,466 suspects, and obtained 254 convictions in various courts (Daily Times, 2018). According to the US State Department, $10 billion in money is laundered out of Pakistan each year. Pakistan keeps its high significance, summarizing the situation of money laundering and terrorism in Pakistan during the last ten years. This can be seen in Figure 2.

Also, the below graph (Figure 3) depicts how Pakistan has remained vulnerable to organized crimes of money laundering and terrorism financing. From 2004 till 2016, not only the terrorism activities were at large but the financial system was also weak.

Refer to the operational framework of ML and FT in Pakistan, Section 3 of Pakistan's Anti-Money Laundering Act (AMLA), 2010 defines "Money Laundering" and "Terrorism" which is followed by the National Accountability Bureau (NAB), the Federal Investigation Agency (FIA), the Anti-Narcotics Force (ANF), the Securities and Exchange Commission of Pakistan (SECP) and other relevant authorities to investigate offenders involved in the crime. Pakistan enacted the Anti-Money Laundering (AML) Ordinance in 2007, establishing regulations for AML and combating money laundering and terrorist financing. The Financial Monitoring Unit (FMU) was formed by legislation. It is accountable for Suspicious Transaction Reports and Cash Transaction Reports, as well as the associated due diligence processes. The FM Unit, in collaboration with the FIA and the Provincial Police Counter Terrorism Department, has disrupted several illegal money trades. Whereas the Financial Investigations Agency (FIA) investigates money laundering, terrorism, human smuggling and trafficking, and cybercrime (Mukhtar, 2018). The State Bank of Pakistan (SBP) and the Securities and Exchange Commission of Pakistan (SECP) are the primary money regulators. Despite the absence of AML legislation, the SBP and SECP have established AML teams to close systemic loopholes. The stock market of Pakistan concluded that the market is of high volatility for handsome gains but also the stock market is vulnerable to ML and TF.

Figure 2. Money laundering in Pakistan (2012-2021)

Year	ML/TF Risk Score	ML Cases registered	Global terrorism Index
2021	6.40	423	7.48
2020	6.30	450	7.54
2019	6.45	542	7.63
2018	6.49	150	7.45
2017	6.64	478	8.35
2016	6.62	443	8.55
2015	6.52	422	8.89
2014	6.53	401	9.23
2013	6.75	390	8.75
2012	6.75	545	8.63

Figure 3. Terrorism financing in Pakistan (2001-2019)

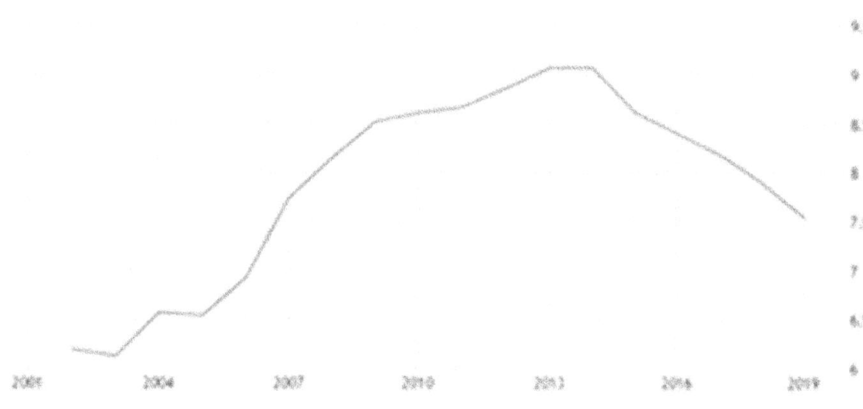

Case One: White Collar Crime by Politically Exposed Person (PEP)

One of the famous cases was by a Politically Exposed Person (PEP), Mr. Jahangir Khan Tareen (JKT) for his act of insider trading, which perhaps, be followed by money laundering acts. Besides, the general secretary of the party, JKT is a wealthy businessman, owns thousands of acres of farmland, a private plane, and runs some of the largest sugar mills in the country (Iqbal, 2017).

JKT is a Director of "*JDW Sugar Mills Ltd*" and was aware of the fact that the said company will be buying the majority of the shares, taking over United Sugar Mills Ltd. (Scrip code - USML). JKT admitted that he did insider trading and bought shares of USML from November 2004 to November 2005 through his "gardener" and "cook," whose names were "Haji Khan" and "Allah Yar," so that he could get an unfair advantage from this inside information. Table 1 exhibits the structure of insider trading cases for politically exposed persons.

Table 1. Structure of insider trading case

Inside information	Insider Trader	Insider Trading
"JDW will be taking over USML"	Main – JKT In acquaintance with – Haji Khan and Allah Yar	Heavy buying id USML shares before disclosure of public information.
Shreds of evidence:		
Trading Pattern before and after the announcement Connection of highest beneficiaries with JKT Minutes of the meeting & attendance Sheet evident that Mr. JKT was privy to the insider information. Money Trail – Transaction sent to the accounts of Haji Khan and Allah Yar from JKT		

Allah Yar has worked for Tareen since 1975, and he is currently in charge of the Lodhran farm. Haji Khan has worked for Tareen since 1980, and he is in charge of taking care of Tareen's homes in Lahore and Islamabad. The trading pattern was as follows:

Table 2. PEP Case: insider trading pattern

Insider Trading Pattern								Gain from Trade		
Allah Yar				Haji Khan				Total		
Buy Volume	Buy Value (mil)	Sell Volume	Sell Value (mil)	Buy Volume	Buy Value	Sell Volume	Sell Value	Buy	Sell	Gain
Jan – Oct 2005				May 2005						
141,780	12.97	141,780	46.12	200,000	29.01	200,000	66.6	41.98	112.7	70.80

Ulterior Between January 12, 2005, and October 27, 2005, Allah Yar bought 141,780 shares of ASB firm for Rs12.97 million. The shares were sold for Rs 46.115 million, which was Rs 33.145 million more than they were bought for. Between May 3, 2005, and November 19, 2005, Haji Khan bought 200,000 shares of ASB company worth Rs 29 million. Haji Khan got Rs 66.666 million for the shares he sold, which was a net gain of Rs 37.666 million. The two employees bought shares for a total of Rs 41.9 million and then sold them for Rs 112.7 million, making a profit of more than Rs 70 million. Tareen gave them both the money they needed to buy shares of stock.

Legal Action

In fact, he has violated Sections 15-A, 15-B, and 15-E of the Securities and Exchange Ordinance of 1969 (now known as the "Securities Act of 2015") Through this insider trading, the respondent gained Rs.70.811 million by selling USML shares after JDW Sugar Mills Ltd.'s public offer to acquire the company. In this context, the SECP initiated proceedings against the respondent under Section 217 of the Companies Ordinance, 1984 (Ordinance, 1984) and Section 15-A, etc. of the Ordinance, 1969 and some other laws; he was served with a show cause notice/letter dated 3.12.2007 regarding the aforementioned violation of the relevant laws, which was also a criminal offense under Section 15-B. The Securities and Exchange Commission of Pakistan (SECP) later in 2007 accused Tareen of insider trading violations. Tareen accepted his wrongdoing and paid SECP a sum of $70.811 million derived through insider trading (The Express Tribune, 2016).

Well, as a result of SECP investigations, Tareen admitted his illegal doings and wrote to the commission that he is ready to pay a fine: for which the commission replied as follows:

"The Commission considered your Letter in its meeting held on January 3, 2007. After due deliberation and taking into account all circumstances, including your offer to repay the gain made by you, the Commission has accepted your offer to make payment of the said gain of Rs.70.811 million, in terms of Section 15B(3) of the Securities & Exchange Ordinance 1969, in the admission of your obligation under the law, in addition to maximum applicable fines totalling Rs.1.256 million under the following relevant provisions of law as detailed below:

Table 3.

Sr.	Section	Amount
1.	Securities & Exchange Ordinance 1969 15-B(3)	70,811,000
2.	Companies Ordinance 1984 214	5,000
3.	Companies Ordinance 1984 216	5,000
	Listed Companies (Substantial Acquisition of Voting Shares & Takeovers) Ordinance, 2002	1,000,000

Additionally, and as agreed by you through your counsel, you shall also pay the Commission's legal costs totalling Rupees one million, thereby aggregating to Rs.73.067 million".

JKT's claimed failure to disclose assets, the presence of offshore firms and the party's receipt of foreign funds are moving forward. It was uncovered that Tareen's children possess a British Virgin Islands firm for conducting business and holding properties. Moreover, he has omitted to mention the vast sums of money he receives from his children on his tax forms. Perhaps, converting black into white? - laundering money through the stock market?

Case Two: "Insider Trading Is a too Sophisticated Crime to be Caught"

The Securities and Exchange Commission of Pakistan (SECP) filed a criminal complaint of insider trading and fraud against a former employee of one of the country's largest banks in court (SECP, 2017).

The case was filed because of an analysis of Karachi Automated Trading System (KATS) data for the period of 01.09.2015 to 31.01.2016 concerning unusual transactions in illiquid shares of Gharibwal Cement Limited (Scrip Code: GCWL); during the investigation, insider trading through front running transactions with UBL was established. The aforementioned analysis led to the suspicion that one of the accused, Khalid Iqbal (former Head of Capital Markets at UBL), who was authorized to trade on behalf of UBL, abused his position to carry out manipulated deals with the connivance of *Khurram Shahzad Sindhu, Muhammad Tousif Peracha, and Abdur Rafiq Khan.* Consequently, an investigation was conducted for the aforementioned time frame.

In addition, the UBL conducted an internal inquiry in this regard, which revealed that Khalid Iqbal admitted his involvement in rogue trading while misusing his position to conduct manipulated transactions in a few listed scrips. Khurram Shahzad Sindhu was identified as the chief conspirator in the dealings involving Gharibwal Cement Limited stock certificates. During the course of the inquiry, it was determined that both of the accused were involved in insider trading through front-running trade conducted through the account of *Hafza Maryam Khurram* (wife of Khurram Shahzad), who maintained her trading account with Escort Capital Limited.

Figure 4.

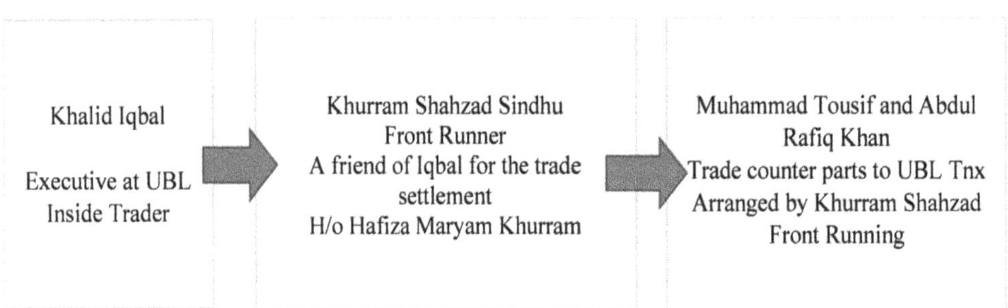

During the examination, the close connection between order placement and simultaneous purchasing and selling on Haza Maryam Khurram's account was also determined. On 31.12.2015, UBL through accused Khalid Iqbal purchased a total of 6.5 million shares of Gharibwal Cement Limited, whereas on 06.01.2016, accused Muhammad Tousif and Abdul Rafiq Khan acted as counter parties and purchased 6.009 million shares.

By engaging in insider trading/front running, the accused made illegal profits and caused financial loss to the UBL, constituting violations of insider trading, market manipulation, and use of fraudulent or deceptive devices to trade in listed shares in violation of Sections 128 and 135 of the Securities Act. The summary is as follows.

Table 4. Insider trading: UBL case

Time Period	Scrip Code	No. of shares	Shares worth	Buyer (s)	Seller (s)
31.12.2015 06.01.2016	GWCL	6.5 million 6.009 million		UBL	Muhammad Tousif and Abdul Rafiq Khan

Table 5. Insider trading case structure: UBL case

Insider information	Insider Trader	Insider Trading	Front Runner
UBL has decided to purchase shares of GWCL	Khalid Iqbal – privy to the information as he was an attendee of the meeting	As above	Khurram Shahzad Arranged two counterparts and traded from his wife's trading account

In addition, later the record reflects money laundering, as UBL filed a criminal case against *Khalid Iqbal and Khurram Shahzad Sindhu* at Dubai Court, with the charge against Khalid Iqbal being that he took a bribe of AED 541,000 in exchange for purchasing undesirable inactive stocks in the market from six companies in Pakistan with a total value of AED 69,787,689 in violation of his job, whereas the charge against Khurram Shahzad.

Case Three: Investigation—Front Running at Brokerage House

SECP filed a very interesting and classic case of front running involving equity traders and KATS Operators. In July 2017, frequent harmonized trades worth Rs. 1.2 million from the trading account of Mr. X from A-Securities (Pvt.) Ltd was observed with the high-net-worth individuals/clients (HNWI) of B-Securities (Pvt.) Ltd as a counterparty which automatically rose a red flag at the SECP headquarters. The investigation officer (IO) found it suspicious and decided to examine the trading activities of all the trades executed from A-Securities for the period of the last 2 years (FY 15-16 & FY 16-17).

As an extension to his inquiry, the officer, while exercising his investigation powers under Section 131 of the Securities Act 2015, sought a certain set of information from both brokerage houses. The information included the account opening forms of traders, Central Depository Centre (CDC) A/c opening forms, and the list of all the associated employees working with the brokerage house. In addition, the brokerage houses were directed to provide telephonic recordings according to the officers, as per rule. A careful look into all this information revealed that there are employees namely Ali, Zahid, and Akram of the same brokerage house, therefore connected to each other in respect of their common employer. Furthermore, contrary to the usual observation, all three of them possessed common contact details provided in their sub-account opening forms. In addition, the IO raised his eyebrows in suspicion when he figured out that all three of them used a common KATS terminal* for the majority of the trades.

Table 6. Trading pattern: UBL case

Date	Share	Trade Time	Traded Qty	Trade Price	Amount	B/S	Counter Party	Counter Party Brokerage House
2017-01-06	KTML	09:55:08	4,000	38.00	152,000	B	FFC FUND	MAZDA Securities (Pvt.) Ltd.
2017-01-06	KTML	09:55:11	40,000	38.00	1,520,000	B	HAMMAD	Alan Securities (Pvt.) Ltd.
2017-01-06	KTML	09:55:17	6,000	38.00	228,000	B	HASSAN	DJM Securities (Pvt.) Ltd.
2017-01-06	KTML	09:55:21	10,000	38.00	380,000	B	FFC FUND	DJM Securities (Pvt.) Ltd.
2017-01-06	**KTML**	**09:59:29**	**5,000**	**38.30**	**191,500**	**S**	**HUMA**	**B-Securities (Pvt.) Limited**
2017-01-06	**KTML**	**09:59:29**	**5,000**	**38.49**	**192,450**	**S**	**HUMAIRA**	**B-Securities (Pvt.) Limited**
2017-01-06	**KTML**	**10:01:13**	**47,500**	**38.90**	**1,847,750**	**S**	**NASEEM**	**B-Securities (Pvt.) Limited**
2017-01-06	**KTML**	**10:02:40**	**2,500**	**38.75**	**96,875**	**S**	**RANGOONWALA**	**B-Securities (Pvt.) Limited**

Activity	Start Time	End Time	Qty.	Trade Price	Value
Buy	9:55:08:00:15	9:55:21:00:63	60000	38	2280000
Sell	9:59:29:00:73	10:02:40:00:15	60,000	38.61	2,328,575
Total Activity Duration	07 Minutes 32 seconds		**Profit**		48,575

Date	Share	Trade Time	Traded Qty	Trade Price	Amount	B/S	Counter Party	Counter Party Brokerage House
2016-12-08	SSGC	09:55:21	40,000	38.00	1,520,000	B	MOHAMMAD	Alpha Securities (Pvt.) Ltd.
2016-12-08	SSGC	09:55:29	25,000	38.01	950,250	B	BARKAT	MRA Securities Limited.
2016-12-08	SSGC	**10:01:13**	**65,000**	**38.74**	**2,518,100**	S	**NASEEM**	**B-Securities (Pvt.) Limited**

Shreds of Evidence

Furthermore, an in-depth analysis of the trading data of the last 2 years revealed approximately 450 events of such activities, *prima facie* appeared to be traded based on inside information, approximately earned a substantial profit of Rs.14. 2 million. Two of these suspicious activities are illustrated in Table 1 and Table 2.

As shown in Exhibit, on January 6, 2017, Akram purchased 60,000 shares of the textile company "KTML" for Rs. 38.00 between 09:55:08 and 09:55:21 (13 seconds). Four minutes later, he sold all the shares to B-SECURITIES clients at an average rate of Rs. 38.61, generating a profit of Rs. 48,575.00 in 7 minutes and 32 seconds. Similarly, exhibit 2 demonstrates that on December 8, 2016, Zahid purchased 65,000 shares of SSGC at Rs. 38.00 between 09:55:21 and 09:55:29 (8 seconds), and after 6 minutes, he sold all the shares to B-SECURITIES clients at Rs. 38.74, earning Rs. 47,850 within 5 minutes.

An obvious shortcut to establishing the linkages between the employees of the two brokerages houses was to see evidence of any financial transaction between them. For this purpose, the IO sought information on all suspects from the banks including bank account opening forms, bank statements, and copies of cheques, drafts, and any instrument through which payment is made through their accounts. All the information together evidently substantiated the passing of inside information among the accused to execute the fraudulent activity of front running by the group as a whole in DICE. The evidence of the process can be seen in Exhibits 3 and 4.

Exhibit 3 shows that at 02:40 PM HNWI client "SHAFI (Pvt.) Limited" placed a buy order for APCL shares at 02: 40 pm through telephones placed at B-SECURITIES and despite restrictions1 on the use of cell phones, Sidney exchanged cellular calls with Ali at 14:53 prima facie to set up the trades for front running. Accordingly, Ali bought the shares from the market at a comparatively low price and sold these to B-SECURITIES HNWI client in connivance with Akram executed the trades based on clients' order information tipped off by Sidney.

Table 7. Trading pattern and call: UBL case evidence

Telephonic call recording of HNWI client "SHAFI Pvt. Ltd" to place buy order for APCL shares at 02: 40 pm									
Call placed by Sidney to Ali at 14:53:09 (Call Time Period: 60 seconds)									
Share	**Date**	**Trader Name**	**Time**	**Qty.**	**Share Price**	**Value**	**B/S**	**Counter Party**	**Counter Party Brok House**
ACPL	2016-05-13	ALI	14:59:16	200	234.99	46,998	B	SOHAIL	DICE
ACPL	2016-05-13	ALI	14:59:16	3,000	235.00	705,000	B	NAFA	Elixir (Pvt.) Ltd
ACPL	2016-05-13	ALI	14:59:16	200	235.00	47,000	B	AZHAR SHAH	B-SECURITIES
ACPL	2016-05-13	ALI	14:59:16	2,500	235.00	587,500	B	MUHAMMAD MUNIR	Munir Khanani
ACPL	2016-05-13	ALI	14:59:16	2,500	235.50	588,750	B	NAFA	Elixir (Pvt.) Ltd
ACPL	2016-05-13	ALI	14:59:27	1,600	235.50	376,800	B	NAFA	Elixir (Pvt.) Ltd
ACPL	2016-05-13	ALI	15:01:45	3,000	235.00	705,000	B	NAFA	Elixir (Pvt.) Ltd
ACPL	**2016-05-13**	**ALI**	**15:02:04**	**3,000**	**235.99**	**707,970**	**S**	**SHAFI (PVT.) LIMITED**	**B-SECURITIES**
ACPL	**2016-05-13**	**ALI**	**15:02:04**	**10,000**	**237.50**	**2,375,000**	**S**	**SHAFI (PVT.) LIMITED**	**B-SECURITIES**
Call also placed by Ali to Sidney at 15:28:53 and Zahid to Sydney at 15:57: 43 (Call Time Period: 163 and 180 seconds)									

Table 8. Trading pattern and call: UBL case evidence

At 12: 35 :17 , Client "Asif" called equity trader-B-SECURITIES to place buy order for 130,000 shares of NCPL									
Call placed by Sidney to Akram at 12:57:53 (Call Time Period: 180 seconds)									
Call placed by Sidney to Zahid at 13:05:42 (Call Time Period: 60 seconds)									
Call placed by Akram to Sidney at 13:21:28 (Call Time Period: 180 seconds)									
Share	**Date**	**Trader Name**	**Time**	**Qty.**	**Share Price**	**Value**	**B/S**	**Counter Party**	**Counter Brokerage H**
NCPL	2015-11-05	ZAHID	13:22:22	125,000	50.00	6,250,000	B	NASEEM	B-SECURITI
NCPL	2015-11-05	ZAHID	13:22:24	2,500	50.00	125,000	B	NASEEM	B-SECURITI
NCPL	**2015-11-05**	**ZAHID**	**13:54:22**	**2,500**	**50.45**	**126,125**	**S**	**ASIF SAEED**	**B-SECURIT**
NCPL	**2015-11-05**	**ZAHID**	**13:54:22**	**125,000**	**50.48**	**6,310,000**	**S**	**ASIF SAEED**	**B-SECURIT**
NCPL	2015-11-05	ARIF	13:36:54	500	50.08	25,040	B	RIAZ AHMED	BIPL
NCPL	2015-11-05	ARIF	13:36:54	1,000	50.15	50,150	B	UMER KHAYYAM	M.M. Securiti
NCPL	**2015-11-05**	**ARIF**	**13:54:22**	**1,500**	**50.40**	**75,600**	**S**	**ASIF SAEED**	**B-SECURIT**
NCPL	**2015-11-05**	**ARIF**	**13:54:22:**	**1,000**	**50.45**	**50,450**	**S**	**ASIF SAEED**	**B-SECURIT**
Call placed by Sidney to Akram at 14:15:36 (Call Duration: 60 seconds)									
Call placed by Sidney to Akram at 15:19:32 (Call Duration: 60 seconds)									

Exhibit 4 shows that Sidney exchanged frequent calls with Akram and Zahid prima facie to set up the trades for front running between 12:57:53 to 13:21:28. Before that, it was noted that B-SECURITIES Client "Asif" called equity trader Sydney to place a buy order for 130,000 shares of NCPL At 12: 35:17. Zahid bought the shares of NCPL from market worth RS 6,375,000 and sold to B-SECURITIES Clients for Rs. 6,426,125, earned a substantial profit of Rs. 51,125. Hence, Zahid and Ali in connivance with Akram (as Akram was KATS Operator at DICE as well) executed the trades based on inside information on B-SECURITIES's client (Asif) sell orders prima facie tipped off by Sidney.

Conclusion by IO

The IO concluded that at B-SECURITIES, Sidney, the equity trader, and Aslam, the KATS Operator was privy to inside information on the placement of orders by respective clients of B-SECURITIES and accordingly, shared the inside information with the front runners Akram, Zahid, and Ali who were successful in front running the clients of B-SECURITIES and earned a hefty profit of Rs.14. 2 million during the process. This act was in clear violation of the provisions of Section 128 of the Act punishable under Section 159 of the Act. The equity trader of B-SECURITIES front ran transactions of B-SECURITIES clients by either tipping the front runners to purchase shares from the market and then securing the position with B-SECURITIES clients or by tipping the front runners to purchase shares from B-SECURITIES clients and then sell the shares in the market. Sidney, serving as the equity trader for investments at B-SECURITIES, was hence responsible for the placement of orders of equity investment/disinvestment. It means that Sidney was an insider and he had inside information regarding B-SECURITIES clients' decisions to invest/disinvest.

Furthermore, the relationship between Aslam and Akram as brothers and their similar residence accentuates the fact that both had inside information. In addition, the majority of the trades being front run were through the Terminal ID of Aslam who had also been noticed through telephonic recordings of taking orders from clients in the absence of Sidney.

In addition, the call record patterns matched the times of trades performed by the front runners, since both Sidney and Akram had been in communication with one another throughout trading hours and near trades being front run. Sidney, who was privy to inside knowledge, tipped the abovementioned information to his close friends at DICE. As a result, the frontrunners leveraged the provided information to generate enormous profits over an extended period. Sidney admitted that, as an Equity Trader, he is privy to inside information on potential buy/sell orders from B-SECURITIES clients; therefore, as an insider, he violated the law on inside information by tipping price-sensitive information to the front runners through the use of cell phones (not permitted at B-SECURITIES).

Legal Action

Sidney had access to his clients' order information at B-Securities (Pvt) Ltd, as described by Section 130(g) and Section 129 (d) of the Act, as evidenced by the call logs. The relationship between the cases and ML/FT has not yet been established, mostly for political reasons; nonetheless, circumstantial evidence exists.

IMPACT ON THE FINANCIAL ECONOMY IN LIGHT OF FATF

Present values, risk management, and diversification are regarded as two fundamental elements of the financial economy. The financial economy includes price fixing, money mobilisation, risk sharing, easy access, liquidity, capital development, transaction cost reduction, and information provision. It is challenging to quantify the negative effects of money laundering on economic development, but it is clear that such activity hurts the financial industry by diverting resources, increases crime and corruption (Rafay, 2023b), and distorts international trade indices. As a result, the securities market's financial crimes flee, with insider trading and front running being the most serious.

Small investors and company sectors are viewed as being negatively affected by insider trading. Illegal insider trading assures that there is no reasonable play and no reasonable demand and supply of stocks, all of which are averse to the operation of a healthy capital market. Insider trading lowers investor confidence in the capital-raising system, and unrestricted insider trading could deter individuals from investing capital, which could be bad for the economy. Consequently, trading based on inside information has a detrimental influence on market liquidity, resulting in higher transaction costs and lower returns for investors. Because so many people have a stake in the financial markets — over half of U.S. households' own stocks in some form – this behavior is bad for the majority of Americans.

As far as Pakistan is concerned, the country is already facing a financial crunch. A surge in such crimes will only highlight the inability of Pakistan to curb the crimes resulting in a grey list of FATF. This will further impact the country's financial indicators and its deal with IMF and World Bank.

CONCLUSION

The influence, degree, and consequences of insider trading vary by jurisdiction, although any amount is detrimental to a nation's standing. Every investor makes investments with simplicity and efficiency in mind. Any investor determining whether to invest (sell, purchase, or retain stock) relies on the company's price-sensitive stock market data. Recently, market interest in safeguards has increased. Insider trading has become illegal; thus, no replacement is necessary. If insider trading restrictions prevent managers from obtaining specific information from the stock market, they can create a virtual market to achieve this objective. Virtual markets can isolate the precise causes of share price fluctuations, which is not achievable in the real stock market. Design and motivational concerns hinder virtual marketplaces from serving as a complete substitute. Thus, can aid the apex regulator in combating insider trading, and the authors anticipate their success in the future.

This chapter provides a basic understanding of insider trading and front running proceeds and further explains it in the context of money laundering. For an in-depth understanding of proceeds, the chapter highlights three different cases. Moreover, real time case studies are limited to a developing country wherein the market is more prone to money laundering. The chapter does not target to provide any literature review but to explain the concept considering applied research with practical and on-ground cases. Lastly, the chapter forged and disguised some names to avoid any conflicts in the future, hence ethical consideration is considered.

DECLARATION

The authors declare that the manuscript follows ethical standards and there are no potential conflicts of interest with respect to the research, authorship and/or publication of this chapter.

DISCLAIMER

The contents and views of this chapter are expressed by the authors in personal capacities. It is not necessary for the Editor and the Publisher to agree with these viewpoints, and they are not responsible for any duty of care in this regard.

ACKNOWLEDGMENT

The authors extend sincere gratitude to

- The Editor and the International Editorial Advisory Board (IEAB) of this book, who initially desk reviewed, arranged a rigorous double/triple-blind review process, and conducted a thorough, minute, and critical final review before accepting the chapter for publication.
- All anonymous reviewers who provided very constructive feedback for thorough revision, improvement, extension, and fine-tuning of the chapter.
- All colleagues, assistants and well-wishers who assisted to complete this task.

REFERENCES

Akram, T., Ramakrishnan, S. A. I., & Naveed, M. (2022). (Forthcoming). Prevalence of money laundering and terrorism financing through stock market: A comprehensive conceptual review paper. *Journal of Money Laundering Control*. doi:10.1108/JMLC-06-2022-0094

Amjad, R., Rafay, A., Arshed, N., Munir, M., & Amjad, M. (2021). Non-Linear impact of globalization on financial crimes: A case of developing economies. *Journal of Money Laundering Control*, *25*(2), 358–375. doi:10.1108/JMLC-03-2021-0023

Barnes, P. (2010). Stock market efficiency, insider dealing and market abuse: The UK experience. *International Journal of Business Governance and Ethics*, *5*(1-2), 38–50. doi:10.1504/IJBGE.2010.029554

Brown, R., & Gillespie, S. (2015). Overseas financial investigation of organised crime. *Journal of Money Laundering Control*, *18*(3), 371–381. doi:10.1108/JMLC-03-2014-0010

Euractiv. (2010, January 29). *EU investigates possible insider trading by terrorists*. Euractiv.com. https://www.euractiv.com/section/financial-regulation/news/eu-investigates-possible-insider-trading-by-terrorists/

FATF. (2012, July 17). *Revisions to the Financial Action Task Force (FATF) Standard - Information note to the executive board* (IMF Policy Papers). International Monetary Fund. https://www.imf.org/en/Publications/Policy-Papers/Issues/2016/12/31/Revisions-to-the-Financial-Action-Task-Force-FATF-Standard-Information-Note-to-the-PP4683

Flitter, E., Dawson, S., & Hosenball, M. (2013, March 13). Exclusive: U.S. plans to let spy agencies scour Americans' finances. *Reuters*. https://www.reuters.com/article/usa-banks-spying-idINDEE92C0EH20130313

Hanif, N., Javaid, A., Arshed, N., & Rafay, A. (2023). (Forthcoming). Foreign exploration of immature markets and incidence of money laundering. *Journal of Money Laundering Control*. doi:10.1108/JMLC-10-2022-0153

Hansen, L. (2021). Regulatory ambiguity: The underbelly of insider trading. In A. Rafay (Ed.), *Handbook of Research on Theory and Practice of Financial Crimes* (pp. 132–148). IGI Global., doi:10.4018/978-1-7998-5567-5.ch008

Iqbal, N. (2017, October 19). Tareen's employees involved in insider trading, counsel tells SC. *Dawn*. https://www.dawn.com/news/1364754

Rafay, A. (Ed.). (2021a). *Money Laundering and Terrorism Financing in Global Financial Systems*. IGI Global. doi:10.4018/978-1-7998-8758-4

Rafay, A. (Ed.). (2021b). *HandBook of Research on Theory and Practice of Financial Crimes*. IGI Global. doi:10.4018/978-1-7998-5567-5

Rafay, A. (Ed.). (2023a). *Concepts, Cases, and Regulations in Financial Fraud and Corruption*. IGI Global. doi:10.4018/978-1-6684-5007-9

Rafay, A. (Ed.). (2023b). *Concepts and Cases of Illicit Finance*. IGI Global., doi:10.4018/978-1-6684-8587-3

SECP. (2017, April 27). *SECP files criminal case of insider trading against a bank employee*. Retrieved from https://www.secp.gov.pk/media-center/press-releases/secp-files-criminal-case-of-insider-trading-against-a-bank-employee/

The Express Tribune. (2016, November 23). PTI leader had returned Rs73.1 million: SECP. *The Eastern Tribune*. https://tribune.com.pk/story/1240182/pti-leader-returned-rs73-1-million-secp

ENDNOTE

1 Under brokers regulation code of conduct, persons dealing with client's order are not allowed to keep their phones during trading hours.

Chapter 5
Earnings Management or Earnings Manipulation?
A Narrative Review of Organizational Profitability

Daniele Giordino
https://orcid.org/0000-0001-5507-6270
University of Turin, Italy

ABSTRACT

Earnings management is the strategic use of accounting principles to manipulate financial reports and influence external stakeholders' perceptions of a company's financial position. This chapter conducts a narrative review of the literature examining the long-term impact of earnings management on future profitability. It focuses on two main dimensions: accrual earnings management (AEM) and real earnings management (REM) techniques, exploring the motives and incentives driving companies towards this practice. The chapter seeks to contribute to discussions on earnings management and its implications for long-term profitability while emphasizing the need for systematic research on various forms of earnings management and their effects on a company's reputation, economic performance, and financial stability. Additionally, the chapter includes relevant case studies from previous literature to illuminate the effects of earnings management on corporations and other organizations.

INTRODUCTION

Corporations often engage in earning management (Teixeira & Rodrigues, 2022; Vagner et al., 2021). Earnings management has been defined as the processes utilized by firms to achieve/manipulate and report desirable levels of earnings by taking advantage of the accounting principles in place in the country in which the firm operates (Al-Shattarat, Hussainey & Al-Shattarat, 2022; Christensen et al., 2022; Dyreng, Hillegeist & Penalva, 2022; Sofian et al., 2022; Teixeira & Rodrigues, 2022; Vagner et al., 2021). By manipulating their financial reports, companies can publicly disclose information that

DOI: 10.4018/979-8-3693-1190-5.ch005

presents an overly positive outlook of their economic performance (Healy & Wahlen, 1999). In doing so, organizations can influence shareholders', and potential investors' opinions, as well as influence future contract conditions (Al-Shattarat, Hussainey & Al-Shattarat, 2022).

The current body of literature has categorized earning management under two main dimensions: accruals earnings management (AEM) (Sofian et al., 2022; Teixeira & Rodrigues, 2022) and real earning management (REM) (Roychowdhury, 2006). Corporations utilizing the AEM approach use accounting accruals to report their desired earning levels (Sofian et al., 2022; Teixeira & Rodrigues, 2022). Whereas organizations engaging in REM practices manipulate their earnings by programming and manipulating their business transactions. For example, organizations engaging in REM can: affect sales through price changes, manipulate their production expenses to boost their earnings or actively manage their inventory stock to reduce the costs of goods sold (Roychowdhury, 2006; Sadiq & Shafie, 2017).

Several empirical studies have gathered empirical evidence which highlights the utilization of various forms and dimensions of earnings management techniques by corporations and other organizations all over the world (Cussatt et al., 2018; Putra et al., 2018). Hence, this topic is of relevance because of its global implications for the trustworthiness of organizations' reported financial and economic information (Abou-El-Sood & El-Sayed, 2022; Al-Shattarat, Hussainey & Al-Shattarat, 2022; Christensen et al., 2022; Dyreng, Hillegeist & Penalva, 2022; Sofian et al., 2022; Teixeira & Rodrigues, 2022).

Due to this topic's relevancy, multiple studies have investigated various organizations' dimensions and multiple forms and techniques of earning management. For example, some researchers have investigated the effects that financial information manipulation through earning management has on companies' short-term reputation (Ariza, Ferrero & Sànchez, 2015), while others have gathered empirical findings to better understand how earnings management affects companies' market capitalization (Azizi, 2018) and more. Nonetheless, as far as the authors are concerned, little efforts have been directed toward a more discursive and narrative approach to earnings management and its implications for companies' future profitability. Therefore, the following research question has been formulated: "How does earnings management affect companies' future profitability?".

To better comprehend the current understanding of earnings management, the author conducts a review of previously published articles to create a narrative chapter. This body of work seeks to review previously published articles to create a narrative chapter that focuses on the long-term effects that various dimensions of earnings management have on organizations' stability and performance. Moreover, companies' case study examples are fragmented and lack a narrative presentation. This is particularly relevant for the long-term effects that earning management techniques have on companies' profitability and longevity (Christensen et al., 2022; Sofian et al., 2022; Teixeira & Rodrigues, 2022). Furthermore, the author seeks to provide some case study examples of companies' utilization of various forms of earnings management. In doing so, the present body of work seeks to further contribute to the existing literature on earnings management and its long-term effect on companies' economic and financial performance, by investigating different motives that push management to adopt the foregoing techniques and to present a comprehensive view of this phenomenon by referring to studies from multiple geographical areas and industrial sectors.

This chapter has the following theoretical and practical implications. First, this body of work underlines the lack of consensus amongst researchers concerning the impact that earnings management techniques might have on a company's future profitability. Therefore, this chapter calls for future empirical studies to further investigate whether various techniques of earnings management affect companies' future profitability. Furthermore, this chapter should prove particularly useful to companies that are taking into consideration earnings management to achieve performance targets imposed by stakeholders. This chapter should help companies better understand to what extent various forms of earnings management impact their future. In doing so, managers can use this narrative review to make better-informed decisions concerning earnings management and its potentially negative effects on companies.

The book chapter is structured as follows. Section two contains a narrative discussion of which earnings management techniques are most utilized by firms. Section three outlines the key motives which have been discovered to have a positive and significant relationship in motivating firms and management to adopt earnings management techniques to meet stakeholders' expectations. Section four highlights the current discourse relating to earnings management and firms' future profitability. Section 5 compares the use of earnings management with fraud, and it highlights possible common elements between the two techniques of manipulation. Section 6 outlines relevant case studies which have been selected so to further support the previously reported empirical findings indicated within the current literature. Finally, section seven provides this chapter with the concluding remarks, as well as some avenues for future research.

EARNINGS MANAGEMENT MOST COMMONLY ADOPTED TECHNIQUES

Earnings management can be achieved through a multitude of techniques that boost companies' financial statements (El Diri, 2017; Vagner et al., 2021). Researchers believe that it is necessary to highlight the most adopted earnings management techniques to shed light on this phenomenon (Toumeh & Yahya, 2019).

Firstly, there are improper revenue recognition techniques which consist of early recognition or the recognition of potentially unrealizable revenue in full (Stallworth & Digregorio, 2004). The above-mentioned technique is one of the most adopted forms of earnings management (Toumeh & Yahya, 2019). For example, with reference to the IFRS, which is one of the most adopted accounting standards, IFRS 15, IAS 18 and IAS 11 indicated that companies must recognize revenues when the firm has satisfied its performance obligation (Toumeh & Yahya, 2019). Therefore, organizations can recognize revenues before completing any performance obligation (Schilit & Perler, 2010). In doing so, firms can boost their earnings by recording future sales (Schilit & Perler, 2010). Past studies have also presented empirical evidence which suggests that the above-mentioned technique is often utilized when committing fraud too (Hurtt et al., 2000). Therefore, improper revenue recognition reduces the quality and reliability of financial reporting since it presents manipulated results to investors (Wasiuzzaman et al., 2015).

Secondly, another approach to earnings management is associated with the big bath technique which consists of "a wholesale write-down of assets and accrual of liabilities in an effort to make the balance sheet conservative so that there will be fewer expenses to serve as a drag on future earnings" (Mulford & Comiskey, 2002). The above-mentioned technique is often utilized to worsen current financial reporting to show growth and better results in future reporting periods (Toumeh & Yahya, 2019). Nonetheless, the big bath technique does not necessarily indicate corporate failure (Toumeh & Yahya, 2019). In fact, the degree of conservatism associated with companies' big bath is a good indicator of whether they are trying to manage their earnings or not (Toumeh & Yahya, 2019). However, there is a multitude of studies that present empirical evidence that oftentimes managers use the above-mentioned technique to manipulate future performance and present stakeholders with future growth (Omar et al., 2014; Zhou & Habib, 2013).

Thirdly, earnings management is often achieved using income smoothing which consists of leveling amplitudes of periodic net income fluctuations to create consistent earnings growth (Kighir et al., 2014). This is often done by allocating capitalization costs utilizing a straight-line method over time as costs incurred by the organization (Toumeh & Yahya, 2019). Income smoothing is used to signal somewhat of a degree of persistence of companies' earnings since fluctuations level in earnings sometimes indicates a probability of a firm going bankrupt (Safdar & Yan, 2016).

Fourthly, managers can manipulate earnings by aggressively accrual expenses to push positive results into the next reporting period (Chhabra, 2016). The above-mentioned approach to earnings management is like income smoothing but it is defined as cookie jar reserves since its aim is to reallocate today's positive earnings in future, uncertain reporting periods (Toumeh & Yahya, 2019). Thus, managers can build up reserves by recognizing later their revenues in financially strong years and then using the previous year's unrecognized revenues in years in which their earnings are lower to present a manipulated financial statement and reassure stakeholders about the company's profitability (Caylor & Chambers, 2015).

Finally, the last most used technique for earnings management is depreciation, amortization and depletion (Franceschetti, 2018). Intangible assets, property plant and equipment, as well as natural resources such as oil and gas, require management decision and judgment to select an appropriate depreciation, amortization or depletion method which consequently allows management to change the above-mentioned asset's useful life to influence the companies' reported earnings within their income statement (Franceschetti, 2018; Omar et al., 2014). In fact, experts believe that such techniques provide managers with ample space for discretionary judgment that can be utilized and exploited to manage companies' earnings (Toumeh & Yahya, 2019).

EARNINGS MANAGEMENT INCENTIVES

Capital Market Incentives

Investors and financial analysts must rely on companies' reports to assess firms' financial and economic position, as well as to assess companies' future capabilities to generate value for them. Therefore, organizations' managers are incentivized by capital markets and investors' expectations to disclose certain results (Bartov, Givoly & Hayn, 2002; Dyreng, Hillegeist & Penalva, 2022). Therefore, to affect the perceived value of a publicly listed company, managers might seek to engage in earnings management to manipulate the perception of said company and mislead investors about the firm's shares value (Bartov, Givoly & Hayn, 2002; Dyreng, Hillegeist & Penalva, 2022).

Shareholders that own a majority stake in a specific company have the power, as well as the interest, to safeguard their capital and position within a company. Therefore, previous studies have gathered empirical evidence which suggests that shareholders with the majority of votes often force management to engage in earnings management in an attempt to grow or maintain their investment portfolio value within a specific organization (Duo et al., 2016). This is because investors' sentiment and market conditions are reported to have an impact on organizations' decisions to engage with earnings management techniques (Dyreng, Hillegeist & Penalva, 2022). For example, empirical evidence reported that investors' sentiment is positively correlated with the adoption of earnings management techniques within the Brazilian capital market (Miranda et al., 2018). Moreover, empirical findings indicate that earnings management techniques are commonly adopted by firms and organizations during periods of uncertainty since firms seek to report a positive outlook in an attempt to manipulate share valuation and prices (Sofian et al., 2022; Stein & Wang, 2015).

Finally, there are multiple bodies of work that indicate that during uncertain times companies often engage in earnings management by creating revenue reserves that can then be recognized later so to offset potentially negative financial and economic performance (Christensen et al., 2022; Sofian et al., 2022; Teixeira & Rodrigues, 2022). In doing so, companies smoothen their revenues and financial performance fluctuation; hence presenting a less volatile business economic performance (Christensen et al., 2022; Sofian et al., 2022; Teixeira & Rodrigues, 2022).

Regulatory Incentives

Organizations might decide to engage in earnings management manipulation because of the regulators' incentives and motives. Antitrust and other governmental entities can limit companies' future mergers and acquisitions, as well as limit companies' profit margins by introducing new windfall taxes during times of crisis (Abou-El-Sood & El-Sayed, 2022; Teixeira & Rodrigues, 2022). For example, the US government intervened to limit oil and gas prices after the Katrina and Rita hurricane. This is because companies operating within the oil and gas industry were engaging in price gouging (Byard et al., 2007). Consequently, the US government has investigated the issue and has proposed windfall profit taxes (Byard et al., 2007). Nonetheless, oil and gas companies engaged in earnings management techniques to report lowered financial performance and avoid political costs and taxes (Byard et al., 2007). The previously reported example underlines that corporations and other organizations might want to engage in earnings management to lower their financial and economic performance during times of increased profitability in an attempt to lower their tax rate (Teixeira & Rodrigues, 2022). For instance, banks often engage in earnings management manipulation to reduce their taxable income, influence their deferred tax assets and manipulate their future profitability outlook by manipulating their valuation allowances (Schrand & Wong, 2003; Rafay & Ajmal, 2014). The previously presented evidence is further supported by a multitude of studies that gather empirical findings and obtain similar results (Balachndran, Hanno & Hanghang, 2013; Zeng, 2014). Therefore, it is evident that regulatory norms do incentivize firms to engage with earnings management techniques (Teixeira & Rodrigues, 2022).

Contracting Incentives

Companies might seek to engage in earnings management techniques when subscribing to contracts whose conditions are influenced by the firms' performance and results (Hou et al., 2015). Companies that subscribe to such contracts adopt earnings management techniques to meet the pre-specified contract conditions to obtain more favorable contracts and reduce their costs and expenses associated with the foregoing style of contracts (Hou et al., 2015). There is empirical evidence that suggests that by looking at the contract conditions, it is possible to better comprehend which styles and techniques of earnings management the company will engage with (Hou et al., 2015).

Secondly, organizations might seek to engage in earnings management when looking to obtain loan contracts. Similarly, to previous style contracts, companies engage in earnings management to achieve and get access to loans at favorable conditions and pay lower rates (Kim et al., 2017). Moreover, by engaging in earnings management, companies might be able to avoid covenant restrictions on loan contracts (Kim et al., 2017).

Finally, there is empirical evidence which suggests that firms' management might seek to engage in earnings management based on management remuneration and compensation type. This is because managers might seek to positively influence companies' share value through earnings management techniques if they receive equity-based compensation (Wang et al., 2017; Xian et al., 2015). Managers might seek to engage in earnings management manipulation when their reported performance is taken into consideration when assigning bonuses. For example, managers can get bonuses if they successfully reduce the level of tax expenses (Beebeejaun et al., 2023). To do so, managers often engage in various dimensions of earnings management manipulation (Armstrong, Blouin & Larcker, 2012).

EARNINGS MANAGEMENT AND ITS RELATIONSHIP WITH FUTURE PROFITABILITY

Future profitability is defined within this book chapter as the ability of an organization to successfully employ its resources and capabilities to generate profit during its financial years. To generate said profit, organizations must engage in operations aimed at the economic and financial growth of the firm. To evaluate a company's future profitability, empirical studies have also adopted the evaluation of various tools and indicators to assess the effects that REM and AEM have on companies' ability to generate long-term profit (Al-Shattarat, Hussainey & Al-Shattarat, 2022; Beyer, Nabar & Rapley, 2018; Vagner et al., 2021). Various earnings management techniques are adopted by firms seeking to report positive short-term performance. This means organizations prioritize their need to meet a specific target or objective by the end of a fiscal year (Xu, 2016). Nonetheless, earnings management might have a negative effect on companies' long-term performance (Al-Shattarat, Hussainey & Al-Shattarat, 2022; Ehsan et al., 2022; Kallunki et al., 2003). Therefore, within this section of the book chapter, the author seeks to provide a narrative review of previous empirical findings concerning REM and AEM effects and implications for future profitability.

Real Earnings Management: Implications for Future Profitability

There are empirical findings that suggest that organizations engaging in REM to meet analysts' and investors' expectations often incur negative effects on their future profitability (Ehsan et al., 2022; Osma et al., 2022). In fact, there are studies that indicate that firms that have engaged in REM suffered losses from an operating and stock price performance perspective (Bhojraj et al., 2009). Moreover, it is highlighted within empirical research that managers do know the potentially negative effects that REM might have on companies' future fiscal years. Nonetheless, managers decide to engage in REM practices to favor short-term performance (Bhojraj et al., 2009).

Research has investigated the opinion of chief financial officers (CFOs) through the utilization of a survey aimed at exploring their views of REM and its impact on companies' future performance (Dichev et al., 2013). In the above-mentioned study, the authors were able to gather empirical findings which suggest that CFOs' view the manipulation of earnings through REM as extremely dangerous for the organizations' long-term profitability and performance (Dichev et al., 2013). This is because managers that engage in REM often cut costs normally associated with the following business activities: research and development, maintenance and marketing expenses (Dichev et al., 2013). The foregoing business activities are extremely relevant to the business and do add value to its core activities (Dichev et al.,

2013). Analysts looking into a company's reports do not have enough information to understand whether the reduction in expenses associated with the foregoing activities is because the business is struggling; hence, management seeks to reduce the business expenses, or whether the management is chasing rather opportunistic reasons (through REM) (Dichev et al., 2013). Therefore, analysts and stakeholders might interpret the reduction in expenses in a way that would negatively affect the firms' perception and future position (Dichev et al., 2013). Additionally, there are empirical bodies of work that highlight the risks associated with the reduction of investments toward business research and development activities to engage with REM practices. Firstly, by reducing their investments in research and development, organizations might incur long-term disadvantages and reduction of their perspectives and competencies because the business has decreased its ability to adapt to changes and innovate within its industry sector (Roychowdhury, 2006). Secondly, by reducing research and development expenses to partake in REM, firms reduce their capability to achieve new patents. Patents can be utilized by analysis to predict a firm's future profitability and operating performance while also reducing a firm's ability to obtain technological competencies (Bereskin, Hsu & Rotenberg, 2017). Finally, the reduction of expenditures in research and development activities tends to reduce companies' share repurchase; thus, weakening and impacting their future profitability.

Zhao et al., (2012) have gathered empirical evidence which suggests that REM does have a negative effect on companies' ability to generate cash flows. This further underlines the negative effects that have been reported within the body of literature.

Despite the previously reported empirical evidence, there is a part of the literature which argues that the relationship between REM and a company's future profitability is not clear (Beyer, Nabar & Rapley, 2018). Within their study, Beyer, Nabar & Rapley (2018) analyze the following performance elements of companies: tax rates, market share and financial health. They obtain empirical findings which highlight that REM effects vary depending on the information environment in which organizations operate. Companies that operate in less robust information environments (lower focus on firms' performance by stakeholders, high stock return volatility) are less likely to engage in REM to meet short-term objectives and goals. Nonetheless, if managers seek to engage with REM practices anyway, they are less likely to have negative consequences on their firm's future profitability (Beyer, Nabar & Rapley, 2018).

Gunny and Zhang (2014) have published an article that suggests that corporations that engage in REM manipulation to meet their expected targets and goals do have improved economic and financial performance in subsequent fiscal years in comparison to firms that do not engage in REM and fail to meet their target goals. Furthermore, additional bodies of literature support the literature stream which indicates that REM does not negatively impact companies' future profitability and performance since the short-term achievement of an organization's goals might act as a positive signal to investors and stakeholders (Lanier et al., 2019).

Finally, there is empirical evidence which suggests that REM manipulation is likely to cause litigation between investors and the organization engaging with it. This is because analysts and investors often seek to discover businesses' use of AEM rather than REM practices. Hence, they are less likely to pursue litigation and legal actions (Ibrahim et al., 2011).

Accruals Earnings Management: Implications for Future Profitability

Most of the literature concerning AEM indicates that AEM manipulations have a negative effect on companies' capability to be profitable in subsequent fiscal years (Ehsan et al., 2022).

A study presents evidence that suggests that companies that have adopted AEM techniques for long periods of time struggle to report increasing levels of income in subsequent fiscal years (Mosebach & Simko, 2010). As a matter of fact, companies often report decreasing levels of income after they have engaged for long periods with AEM techniques (Mosebach & Simko, 2010).

Empirical findings suggested that investors are less likely to engage in litigation with firms that engage in REM instead of firms partaking in AEM (Ibrahim et al., 2011). This is because investors focus more on the potentially negative effects that AEM techniques might have on future companies' profitability and performance (Ibrahim et al., 2011). Thus, investors perceive AEM to have a stronger negative impact on firms' long-term profitability. Therefore, they are more likely to engage in legal actions when they feel like organizations are taking advantage of AEM to disclose overly positive information concerning their economic and financial stability (Ibrahim et al., 2011).

Kallunki and Martikainen (2003) further corroborate the foregoing findings concerning AEM's negative effect on companies' future profitability. They present findings that indicate that within Finnish firms, AEM does have a negative effect on firms' future profitability (Kallunki & Martikainen, 2003). In fact, they suggest within their published paper that lagged earnings in relation to past earnings can be utilized as predictive tools for the firm's future profitability (Kallunki & Martikainen, 2003).

There are also multiple studies that indicate that the eventual reversal effect of AEM might negatively impact companies' future fiscal year performance and profitability (Chen, 2009; Ehsan et al., 2022). Moreover, similar studies have been conducted within the Indian context and they were able to identify that AEM does negatively impact Indian manufacturing firms' ability to generate economic and financial value in future fiscal years (Gill et al., 2013; Rafay et al., 2018). Furthermore, they report that AEM has an adverse effect on the company's rate of return on assets in the following fiscal year (Gill et al., 2013). Additionally, they have discovered that when a company is decreasing its earnings reported quality to meet its benchmarks and goals, the market responds by lowering the company's share value thus reducing its market capitalization (Gill et al., 2013).

When it comes to the auditing of AEM, prior literature presents evidence that suggests that big accounting and auditing firms do try to restrict organizations' utilization of AEM because they seek to protect and maintain their reputation in auditing appropriately their clients' reports and financial statements (Becker et al., 1998; Francis et al.,1999; Ramzan et al., 2020). Consequently, it is possible to assume that the adoption of AEM techniques not only affects the future profitability of companies engaging with AEM but also affects the competitive advantage of the organizations conducting the auditing process for those companies engaging in AEM.

AEM is therefore considered to be an extremely risky and drastic earnings management technique. In fact, most companies that seek to engage with it are organizations on the edge of bankruptcy. In fact, there are empirical studies that support the foregoing statement. For example, within Spanish firms, researchers were able to identify a significant relationship between AEM and managers of bankrupt firms (Campa & Cmacho-Miñan, 2014). Moreover, they indicate that they were able to identify a pattern that suggests that managers' utilization of AEM often starts 3 years before the company fails and goes bankrupt (Campa & Cmacho-Miñan, 2014). Consequently, it is safe to assume that AEM does not positively affect companies' capabilities to generate profit in the next fiscal years. Instead, it simply provides a decrease in earnings quality reports to better their short-term position.

Nonetheless, there are empirical bodies of work that argue that there is not a positive relationship between the adoption of earnings management techniques and an organization's future profitability (Ahmadpour & Shahsavari, 2016). In fact, some may argue that past earnings cannot be utilized to predict the future earnings performance of companies. Additionally, some argue that strong protection of investors does reduce companies' usage of AEM and REM; thus, governments and entities should focus on those elements to maintain high quality and accuracy in firms' reporting practices (Enomoto et al., 2015).

Finally, empirical findings indicate that despite the use of AEM, analysts and stakeholders can correctly price and hence, adjust accordingly to companies' usage of earnings management techniques (Athanasakou, Strong & Walker, 2011).

EARNINGS MANAGEMENT AND FRAUD

Earnings management is generally restricted to practices within the generally accepted accounting principles (GAAP) limits and bounds, whereas fraud is not (Dechow et al., 1995). Nonetheless, a relationship between earnings management in various dimensions and fraud exists since both elements are perceived to be unethical and unlawful utilization of discretionary accruals management (Ramírez-Orellana et al., 2017). However, earnings management differs from fraud. Fraud is outside the scope of GAAP whereas earnings management involves management's personal judgment (Perols & Lougee, 2011; Xu et al., 2007). Consequently, the adopted definition of fraud within this chapter is the following: financial statement fraud occurs when managers use accounting principles that are not allowed by GAAP to either mislead stakeholders about the economic performance of a company or influence contractual outcomes by manipulating reported accounting numbers (Healy, 1985). According to previous publications, investors and external stakeholders (which are the main users of statements of financial reports) are more worried by fraud (Rafay, 2021, 2023a, 2023b) than earnings management since the act of fraud can create larger monetary losses to shareholders in comparison to losses caused by earnings management (Rosner, 2003). In fact, various models concerning fraud detection exist such as financial statement analysis, and digital analysis based on Benford's Law (Ramírez-Orellana et al., 2017).

When firms inflate their obtained and reported economic and financial performance by adopting earnings management techniques, they generate incomes that must be offset over the coming financial years (Healy, 1985) otherwise they must engage in fraud to offset the reversals to cancel the necessity to rebalance their financial statements (Beneish, 1997; 1999). However, when confronted with lowered earnings management workability, managers might adopt fraudulent activities since they are pressured to accomplish previously obtained results by managing earnings (Perols & Lougee, 2011). In fact, previous empirical research underlines that firms and managers which have engaged in earnings management techniques in the past three years are more likely to engage in fraudulent behaviors (Beneish, 1997). There are multiple studies that highlight how earnings management is something that can be a warning sign for stakeholders since it is most likely to cause fraudulent behaviors (Dechow et al., 1996; Dechow et al., 2011; Jones et al., 2010; Perols & Lougee, 2011). This is because firms that have already engaged in earnings management activities are prone to commit fraud since they have limited earnings flexibility due to previous fiscal years' aggressive adoption of earnings management techniques which results in the company's need to resolve the foregoing issue (Perols & Lougee, 2011).

Most of the existing literature provides evidence that supports that financial reports fraud is produced through accruals earnings management before organizations engage in fraudulent practices (Ali, Razzaque & Ahmed, 2018). Nonetheless, there is an empirical finding which suggests that REM can also be utilized prior to fraud occurrence (Ali, Razzaque & Ahmed, 2018). In fact, some publications suggest that using real earnings management facilitates manipulations and is more believable in comparison to

AEM (Graham et al., 2005; Hashemi and Rabiee, 2011; Hashim et al., 2012). REM activities are often preferred over AEM in countries that safeguard stakeholders and investors (Ali, Razzaque & Ahmed, 2018; Bansal et al., 2022).

EARNINGS MANAGEMENT CASE EXAMPLES

The following case studies are utilized to underline how and to what extent various forms of earnings management can impact companies' future profitability. The following case studies further underline how both academic and professional understanding of the effects that earnings management has on companies' future profitability is fragmented and various empirical data provide contrasting findings. Finally, the presented case studies underline that investors engage in litigations concerning the utilization of AEM rather than litigations surrounding REM. This is in line with the current literature since there is empirical evidence which suggests that AEM is considered by stakeholders to be dangerous and that might lead to fraud. Therefore, the use of REM is more likely to remain unnoticed in comparison to the use of AEM.

Microsoft

Following an investigation by the US attorney general, they discovered that Microsoft adopted an extremely conservative approach when it came down to its earnings management (Degeorge et al., 1999). The Securities and Exchange Commission (SEC) accused the company of misstating its financial results between 1994 and 1998 (Belverd, Powers & Şenyiğit, 2018 Belverd, Powers & Şenyiğit, 2018; Dechow & Skinner, 2000). The company was accused of overstating its income in quarters and under-reporting its income during other quarterly financial reports. SEC thought that Microsoft set aside large quantities of reserves to reduce revenues during profitable periods thus utilizing said reserves during less profitable periods; reserves were estimated to be between 200 million dollars and 900 million dollars during the above-mentioned period (Belverd, Powers & Şenyiğit, 2018; Dechow & Skinner, 2000). The technique adopted by Microsoft has been previously defined within this chapter as the "cookie jar" and it is often used to give investors and other stakeholders an inaccurate view of the firm's economic and financial position. Despite the above-mentioned accusation, the SEC and Microsoft have agreed to refrain from the earnings management accusation and no fine was imposed on the company (Mohanram, 2003). This is a clear example of earnings management usage which did not cause the company to suffer any meaningful consequences which negatively impacted its future profitability or performance. The company was not punished by ruling bodies. Moreover, the company did not suffer from reduced profitability over the coming fiscal years despite its utilization of the cookie jar method.

The Time Warner

Time Warner is reported to have established reserves consisting of 2 billion during its 2009 and 2008 financial years. This decision has been made by management and it is grounded on the vendor selloff of product and historical returns, economic conditions and changes in customers (Time Warner Inc., 2010). The foregoing example is considered by the literature as another example of earnings management that has been utilized during the 2008 financial crisis to potentially mislead the company's financial performance (Belverd, Powers & Şenyiğit, 2018). Despite their use of earnings management, the company did not suffer any meaningful consequences which can be directly associated with the management's decision to adopt earnings management to disclose improved financial performance. Therefore, this example further supports the literature strand which believes that various forms of earnings management do not have a significant and positive relationship with companies' future profitability.

Dell

The US SEC accused Dell of misleading investors by managing their earnings by presenting money received from Intel to boost its quarterly earnings statement to meet Wall Street's expectations (Luong, 2015; Penman, 2009). Intel paid Dell through rebates as part of an accord that forced Dell to avoid the utilization of chips produced and branded by Advanced Micro Devices (AMD) within its computers (Luong, 2015). Those rebates, under the US government, are subject to US federal antitrust scrutiny and inspection. Thus, when Dell eventually selected and approached AMD as their second supplier of chips, Intel decided to cut its concession to AMD. Consequently, Dell's financial and economic performance suffered (Belverd, Powers & Şenyiğit, 2018; Penman 2009). The SEC reported that investors were not aware of the conditions of the agreement between Dell and Intel. Moreover, the SEC reported that Dell was able to achieve Wall Street's expectations in its fiscal year from 2002 up to 2006 only because of the payments issued by Intel under the above-mentioned agreement (Belverd, Powers & Şenyiğit, 2018; Luong, 2015). If Dell did not make such an agreement, the company would not have been able to meet investors' expectations concerning their earnings per share (Belverd, Powers & Şenyiğit, 2018). Dell reported the exclusivity payments as operating income slowly increasing its reported earnings from 2003 up to 2007 (Belverd, Powers & Şenyiğit, 2018; Penman, 2009; Luong, 2015). Thus, Dell has adopted earnings management techniques to recognize the above-mentioned payments as operating income. Moreover, the earnings management utilization has led the company towards the accusation of fraud (Wyatt, 2010). In fact, Dell's founder and former executive have settled with the SEC to pay more than 100 million dollars in sanctions (Wyatt, 2010). This is a clear example of how earnings management can fall within the fraud definition of manipulation of companies' performance. Therefore, Dell suffered consequences that negatively impact the company's future performance. This case study can be utilised to further support the strand of literature which believes that the adoption of earnings management techniques by companies can negatively impact their future performance.

AT&T Inc. and Verizon Communications

During the market crisis of 2008 and 2009, companies such as AT&T Inc. and Verizon Communications Inc. incurred large losses of over 10 million dollars. In accordance with US standards, the above-mentioned companies decided to amortize the losses over future years (Rapoport, 2011). However, in later fiscal years, AT&T Inc. and Verizon Communications changed their accounting for pension funds to mark-to-market accounting following international standards which would allow them to restate prior financial statements (An, Lee & Zhang, 2014; Belverd, Powers & Şenyiğit, 2018; Hsieh et al., 2020). Consequently, the above-mentioned change in their accounting approach allows AT&T Inc. and Verizon Communications to improve their financial statements concerning 2008 and 2009, as well as improve future earnings since the change will never reflect the large losses incurred during 2008 and 2009 (Lew, 2009; Belverd, Powers & Şenyiğit, 2018). The companies believe that this change would make their financial statement more transparent for investors and stakeholders by changing the value of pension assets and obligations (Belverd, Powers & Şenyiğit, 2018). However, scholars believe that such change is a prime example of earnings management since, by changing their accounting approach, they were able to drastically improve their companies' performance, as well as, offset the negative effects that the market crisis of 2008 and 2009 had on their earnings results (Belverd, Powers & Şenyiğit, 2018; Bergstresser, Desai & Rauh, 2006; Morais & Pinto, 2019). This is another example that identifies a technique of earnings management that does not decrease the company's future profitability. As far as the author is concerned, no empirical studies were able to identify a significant and positive relationship between the foregoing company's usage of earnings management and the organization's future profitability.

CONCLUSION

Overall, this narrative analysis helps us conclude that the current body of literature does not provide a definitive conclusion as to whether REM has a relevant effect on companies' future profitability (Beyer, Nabar & Rapley, 2018). As previously highlighted, empirical evidence suggests that companies might incur consequences when engaging in earnings management manipulation depending on the environment in which they operate (Morais & Pinto, 2019). For example, there are findings suggesting that companies that operate in environments that are not strongly driven by information normally do not suffer any consequences after engagement with various dimensions of earnings management (Beyer, Nabar & Rapley, 2018; Enomoto et al., 2015). This is because less information-driven environments do not rely too heavily on corporations or organizations meeting and reporting expected benchmarks and future results (Beyer, Nabar & Rapley, 2018). Therefore, organizations operating in the foregoing style of environments do not usually suffer consequences on their future and long-term capabilities to generate economic and financial profits (Beyer, Nabar & Rapley, 2018).

The above-stated might not be applicable to organizations operating within strong information environments. Therefore, firms engaging with REM might suffer from negative effects after engaging in manipulation (Zhao et al.,2012). This is because robust information environments operate under the assumption that firms disclose accurate and rigorous information. By manipulating their disclosed performance, stakeholders and investors might no longer feel compelled to rely on public information; hence, they might deem the company unreliable (Zhao et al.,2012). There is empirical evidence which suggests that the utilization of REM techniques does have a negative impact on a company's stock price and cash flows (Bhojraj et al., 2009). The foregoing further underlines the negative impact that REM might have on organizations operating in robust information environments. Additionally, there is empirical evidence that highlights the negative effects that companies might suffer when engaging in earnings management manipulation by reducing a company's expenses toward research and development processes (Dichev et al., 2013; Roychowdhury, 2006; Zhao et al.,2012). This is because the reduction of investments in research and development might cause analysts and investors to misinterpret a firm's vision, position and future development strategy (Dichev et al., 2013; Roychowdhury, 2006; Zhao et al.,2012). Furthermore, cost reduction on research and development expenses to meet profitability benchmarks might also cause firms to miss allocate their resources; thus, creating long-term prospects and disadvantages (Dichev et al., 2013; Roychowdhury, 2006; Zhao et al.,2012).

Finally, within the current literature and the presented case studies, it was possible to observe that investors engage more often in litigations concerning the utilization of AEM rather than litigations surrounding REM manipulation. This is because investors often seek to identify companies' manipulations through AEM. Therefore, organizations can safely assume that REM is more likely to go unnoticed.

When it comes to AEM, most of the literature highlights the negative impact that such manipulation techniques might have on companies' future profitability. For example, there are published bodies of work that indicate that AEM techniques do have a negative effect on organizations' market value and share price (Gill et al., 2013). This is because investors and external stakeholders can identify the manipulation from the managers' side to achieve goals or meet investors' expectations by reducing the quality of the reported information (Gill et al., 2013). Furthermore, there is empirical evidence that suggests that AEM has a negative effect on corporates' rate of return on assets of a company's future financial years (Chen, 2009).

Nonetheless, AEM's negative impact is not limited to companies' future profitability. There are studies that indicate that organizations that engage with AEM do suffer from reputational losses, as well as a decrease in their competitive advantage when getting audited by a company to approve their statement of financial position (Becker et al., 1998; Francis et al.,1999).

However, it is important to note that the negative effects of AEM are also tied to the environment in which firms operate. Similarly, to REM, AEM effects on companies' future profitability depend on the robustness of the information environment (Enomoto et al., 2015).

Nonetheless, there is a stream of literature that argues that AEM does not necessarily negatively affect companies' future profitability and market valuation (Ahmadpour & Shahsavari, 2016; Athanasakou, Strong & Walker, 2011). This is because investors and analysts often fail to price corporations and organizations despite their use of AEM. Therefore, they argue that it is not possible to identify a relevant and positive relationship between AEM and companies' future profitability (Ahmadpour & Shahsavari, 2016; Athanasakou, Strong & Walker, 2011).

Additionally, this chapter further delineates through the adoption of multiple case studies and examples, that periods of financial distress do promote companies' utilization of earnings management manipulation since firms might seek to meet stakeholders' expectations despite the financial and economic struggles. Consequently, this chapter should further motivate investors and analysts to monitor companies' financial statements (Li et al., 2020). In doing so, they should be able to recognize different reporting models and standards (Li et al., 2020). Differences in companies' reports might further reduce investors' and analysts' ability to assess reports' transparency and accuracy (Li et al., 2020).

Finally, this narrative review highlights the need for future studies to further explore and clarify the relationship between companies' long-term economic and financial performance and organizations' use of various techniques and dimensions of earnings management. Additionally, future research could further explore how earnings management impacts an organization's relationship with its supplier, creditors, as well as market capitalization.

DECLARATION

The author declares that the manuscript follows ethical standards and there are no potential conflicts of interest with respect to the research, authorship and/or publication of this chapter.

DISCLAIMER

The contents and views of this chapter are expressed by the author in personal capacity. It is not necessary for the Editor and the Publisher to agree with these viewpoints, and they are not responsible for any duty of care in this regard.

ACKNOWLEDGMENT

The author extends sincere gratitude to

- The Editor and the International Editorial Advisory Board (IEAB) of this book, who initially desk reviewed, arranged a rigorous double/triple-blind review process, and conducted a thorough, minute, and critical final review before accepting the chapter for publication.
- All anonymous reviewers who provided very constructive feedback for thorough revision, improvement, extension, and fine-tuning of the chapter.
- All colleagues, assistants and well-wishers who assisted to complete this task.

REFERENCES

Abou-El-Sood, H., & El-Sayed, D. (2022). Abnormal disclosure tone, earnings management and earnings quality. *Journal of Applied Accounting Research*, *23*(2), 402–433. doi:10.1108/JAAR-07-2020-0139

Ahmadpour, A., & Shahsavari, M. (2016). Earnings management and the effect of earnings quality in relation to bankruptcy level. *Iranian Journal of Management Studies*, *9*(1), 77–99.

Al-Shattarat, B., Hussainey, K., & Al-Shattarat, W. (2022). The impact of abnormal real earnings management to meet earnings benchmarks on future operating performance. *International Review of Financial Analysis*, *81*, 101264. doi:10.1016/j.irfa.2018.10.001

Ali, M. J., Razzaque, R. M., & Ahmed, K. (2018). Real earnings management and financial statement fraud: Evidence from Malaysia. *International Journal of Accounting & Information Management*, *26*(4), 508–526. doi:10.1108/IJAIM-03-2017-0039

An, H., Lee, Y. W., & Zhang, T. (2014). Do corporations manage earnings to meet/exceed analyst forecasts? Evidence from pension plan assumption changes. *Review of Accounting Studies*, *19*(2), 698–735. doi:10.100711142-013-9261-8

Ariza, L. R., Ferrero, J. M., & Sànchez, M. B. (2015). Consequences of earnings management for corporate reputation. Evidence from family firms. *Accounting Research Journal*, *29*(4), 457–474. doi:10.1108/ARJ-02-2015-0017

Armstrong, C. S., Blouin, J. L., & Larcker, D. F. (2012). The incentives for tax planning. *Journal of Accounting and Economics*, *5*(1), 391–411. doi:10.1016/j.jacceco.2011.04.001

Athanasakou, V., Strong, N. C., & Walker, M. (2011). The market reward for achieving analyst earnings expectations: Does managing expectations or earnings matter? *Journal of Business Finance & Accounting*, *38*(2), 58–94. doi:10.1111/j.1468-5957.2010.02219.x

Azizi, F. (2018). Effect of information asymmetry and mutual funds ownership on earnings management in companies listed in Tehran Stock Exchange. *International Journal of Management. Accounting and Economics*, *5*(7), 516–534.

Balachndran, B., Hanno, D., & Hanghang, T. (2013). Tax-induced earnings management within a dividend imputation system. *Australian Tax Forum, 28*(3), 555–582.

Bansal, M., Kumar, A., Bhattacharyya, A., & Bashir, H. A. (2022). Predictors of revenue shifting and expense shifting: Evidence from an emerging economy. *Journal of Contemporary Accounting & Economics*, *19*(1), 100339. doi:10.1016/j.jcae.2022.100339

Bartov, E., Givoly, D., & Hayn, C. (2002). The rewards to meeting or beating earnings expectations. *Journal of Accounting and Economics*, *33*(2), 173–204. doi:10.1016/S0165-4101(02)00045-9

Becker, C. L., Defond, M. L., Jiambalvo, J., & Subramanyam, K. R. (1998). The effect of audit on earnings management. *Contemporary Accounting Research*, *15*(1), 1–25. doi:10.1111/j.1911-3846.1998.tb00547.x

Beebeejaun, A., Gunputh, R., & Rafay, A. (2023). Base Erosion and Profit Shifting (BEPS) in International Taxation System: The Case of Mauritius in the light of OECD/G20 initiatives. In A. Rafay (Ed.), *Concepts, Cases, and Regulations in Financial Fraud and Corruption* (pp. 259–277). IGI Global. doi:10.4018/978-1-6684-5007-9.ch011

Belverd, E., Powers, M., & Şenyiğit, Y. B. (2018). Earnings management: A review of selected cases. *Muhasebe Enstitüsü Dergisi*, *16*(59), 23–36.

Beneish, M. D. (1997). Detecting GAAP violation: Implications for assessing earnings management among firms with extreme financial performance. *Journal of Accounting and Public Policy*, *16*(3), 271–309. doi:10.1016/S0278-4254(97)00023-9

Beneish, M. D. (1999). Incentives and penalties related to earnings overstatements that violate GAAP. *The Accounting Review*, *74*(4), 425–457. doi:10.2308/accr.1999.74.4.425

Bereskin, F. L., Hsu, P., & Rotenberg, W. (2018). The real effects of real earnings management: Evidence from innovation. *Contemporary Accounting Research*, *35*(1), 525–557. doi:10.1111/1911-3846.12376

Bergstresser, D., Desai, M., & Rauh, J. (2006). Earnings manipulation, pension assumptions, and managerial investment decisions. *The Quarterly Journal of Economics*, *121*(1), 157–195.

Beyer, B. D., Nabar, S. M., & Rapley, E. T. (2018). Real earnings management by benchmark-beating firms: Implications for future profitability. *Accounting Horizons*, *32*(4), 59–84. doi:10.2308/acch-52167

Bhojraj, S., Hribar, P., Picconi, M., & McInnis, J. (2009). Making sense of cents: An examination of firms that marginally miss or beat analyst forecasts. *The Journal of Finance*, *64*(5), 2361–2388. doi:10.1111/j.1540-6261.2009.01503.x

Byard, D., Hossain, M., & Mitra, S. (2007). US oil companies' earnings management in response to hurricanes Katrina and Rita. *Journal of Accounting and Public Policy*, *26*(6), 733–748. doi:10.1016/j.jaccpubpol.2007.10.006

Campa, D., & Cmacho-Miñan, M. D. M. (2014). Earnings management among bankrupt non-listed firms: Evidence from Spain. *Revista Española de Financiación y Contabilidad*, *43*(1), 3–21. doi:10.1080/02102412.2014.890820

Caylor, M. L., & Chambers, D. J. (2015). Reaching into the cookie jar? Why conservative accounting is sometimes a problem. *Journal of Corporate Accounting & Finance*, *26*(5), 73–77. doi:10.1002/jcaf.22066

Chen, J. Z. (2009). *The choice between real and accounting earnings management* [Doctoral Dissertation). University of Houston]. https://pdfs.semanticscholar.org/491e/97e6eaca3e6d2cf8986cb8e03b5a5568cf2f.pdf

Chhabra, S. (2016). Earning management: A study. *Splint International Journal of Professionals*, *3*(11), 40–44.

Christensen, T. E., Huffman, A., Lewis-Western, M. F., & Scott, R. (2022). Accruals earnings management proxies: Prudent business decisions or earnings manipulation? *Journal of Business Finance & Accounting*, *49*(3-4), 536–587. doi:10.1111/jbfa.12585

Cussatt, M., Huang, L., & Pollard, T. J. (2018). Accounting quality under U.S. GAAP versus IFRS: The case of Germany. *Journal of International Accounting Research*, *17*(3), 21–41. doi:10.2308/jiar-51997

Dechow, P. M., Ge, W., Larson, C. R., & Sloan, R. G. (2011). Predicting material accounting misstatements. *Contemporary Accounting Research*, *28*(1), 17–82. doi:10.1111/j.1911-3846.2010.01041.x

Dechow, P. M., & Skinner, D. J. (2000). Earnings management: Reconciling the views of accounting academics, practitioners, and regulators. *Accounting Horizons*, *14*(2), 235–250. doi:10.2308/acch.2000.14.2.235

Dechow, P. M., Sloan, R. G., & Sweeney, A. P. (1995). Detecting earnings management. *The Accounting Review*, 193–225.

Dechow, P. M., Sloan, R. G., & Sweeney, A. P. (1996). Causes and consequences of earnings manipulation: An analysis of firms subject to enforcement actions by the SEC. *Contemporary Accounting Research*, *13*(1), 1–36. doi:10.1111/j.1911-3846.1996.tb00489.x

Degeorge, F., Patel, J., & Zeckhauser, R. (1999). Earnings management to exceed thresholds. *The Journal of Business*, *72*(1), 1–33. doi:10.1086/209601

Dichev, I. D., Graham, J. R., Harvey, C. R., & Rajgopal, S. (2013). Earnings quality: Evidence from the field. *Journal of Accounting and Economics*, *56*(3), 1–33. doi:10.1016/j.jacceco.2013.05.004

Duo, Y., Hope, O., Thomas, W. B., & Zou, Y. (2016). Individual large shareholders, earnings management and capital market consequences. *Journal of Business Finance & Accounting*, *43*(7), 872–902.

Dyreng, S. D., Hillegeist, S. A., & Penalva, F. (2022). Earnings management to avoid debt covenant violations and future performance. *European Accounting Review*, *31*(2), 311–343. doi:10.1080/09638180.2020.1826337

Ehsan, S., Tariq, A., Nazir, M. S., Shabbir, M. S., Shabbir, R., Lopez, L. B., & Ullah, W. (2022). Nexus between corporate social responsibility and earnings management: Sustainable or opportunistic. *MDE. Managerial and Decision Economics*, *43*(2), 478–495. doi:10.1002/mde.3396

El Diri, M. (2017). *Introduction to Earnings Management*. Springer.

Enomoto, M., Kimura, F., & Yamaguchi, T. (2015). Accrual-based and real earnings management: An international comparison for investor protection. *Journal of Contemporary Accounting & Economics*, *11*(3), 183–198. doi:10.1016/j.jcae.2015.07.001

Franceschetti, B. M. (2018). *Financial Crises and Earnings Management Behavior*. Springer International Publishing. doi:10.1007/978-3-319-54121-1

Francis, J. R., Maydew, E. L., & Sparks, H. C. (1999). The role of big 6 auditors in the credible reporting of accruals. *Auditing*, *18*(2), 17–35. doi:10.2308/aud.1999.18.2.17

Gill, A., Biger, N., Mand, H. S., & Mathur, N. (2013). Earnings management, firm performance, and the value of Indian manufacturing firms. *International Research Journal of Finance and Economics*, *116*(1), 120–132.

Graham, J. R., Harvey, C. R., & Rajgopal, S. (2005). The economic implications of corporate financial reporting. *Journal of Accounting and Economics*, *40*(1), 3–73. doi:10.1016/j.jacceco.2005.01.002

Gunny, K., & Zhang, T. C. (2014). Do managers use meeting analyst forecasts to signal private information? Evidence from patent citations. *Journal of Business Finance & Accounting*, *41*(8), 950–973. doi:10.1111/jbfa.12082

Hashemi, S. A., & Rabiee, H. (2011). The relation between real earnings management and accounting earnings management: Evidence from Iran. *Business and Management Review*, *1*(8), 25–33.

Hashim, J., Haniff, M. N., & Rahman, I. K. A. (2012). Tax waiver year effect on earnings management practices in Malaysia. *Journal of Financial Reporting and Accounting*, *10*(2), 171–189. doi:10.1108/19852511211273714

Healy, P. M. (1985). The effect of bonus schemes on accounting decisions. *Journal of Accounting and Economics*, *7*(1-3), 85–107. doi:10.1016/0165-4101(85)90029-1

Healy, P. M., & Wahlen, J. M. (1999). A review of the earnings management literature and its implications for standard setting. *Accounting Horizons*, *13*(4), 365–383. doi:10.2308/acch.1999.13.4.365

Hou, Q., Jin, Q., Yang, R., Yuan, H., & Zhang, G. (2015). Performance commitments of controlling shareholders and earnings management. *Contemporary Accounting Research*, *32*(3), 1099–1127. doi:10.1111/1911-3846.12111

Hsieh, S. J., Su, Y., & Chang, C. C. A. (2020). The role of discretionary pension accruals in earnings management. *Journal of Applied Accounting Research*, *22*(1), 1–21. doi:10.1108/JAAR-06-2019-0095

Hurtt, D. N., Kreuze, J. G., & Langsam, S. A. (2000). Auditing to combat revenue recognition fraud. *Journal of Corporate Accounting & Finance*, *11*(4), 51–59. doi:10.1002/1097-0053(200005/06)11:4<51::AID-JCAF8>3.0.CO;2-V

Ibrahim, S., Xu, L., & Rogers, G. (2011). Real and accrual-based earnings management and its legal consequences: Evidence from seasoned equity offerings. *Accounting Research Journal*, *24*(1), 50–78. doi:10.1108/10309611111148779

Jones, K. L., Krishnan, G. V., & Melendrez, K. (2010). Do models of discretionary accruals detect actual cases of fraudulent and restated earnings? An empirical evaluation. *Contemporary Accounting Research*, *25*(2), 499–531. doi:10.1506/car.25.2.8

Kallunki, J. P., & Martikainen, M. (2003). Earnings management as a predictor of future profitability of Finnish firms. *European Accounting Review*, *12*(2), 311–325. doi:10.1080/0963818032000089409

Kighir, A., Omar, N., & Mohamed, N. (2013). Opportunities, motivations and approaches of earnings management: A structured theoretical review of the corporate virus. *International Journal of Auditing Technology*, *1*(3-4), 312–329. doi:10.1504/IJAUDIT.2013.057730

Kim, J. B., Song, B. Y., & Wang, Z. (2017). Special purpose entities and bank loan contracting. *Journal of Banking & Finance*, *74*, 133–152. doi:10.1016/j.jbankfin.2016.10.006

Lanier, D. Jr, Wempe, W. F., & Swink, M. (2019). Supply chain power and real earnings management: Stock market perceptions, financial performances effects, and implications for suppliers. *The Journal of Supply Chain Management*, *55*(1), 48–70. doi:10.1111/jscm.12186

Lew, J. F. (2009). Pension actuarial incentive for earnings management. *Asia Pacific Management Review*, *14*(3), 313–334.

Li, Y., Li, X., Xiang, E., & Djajadikerta, H. G. (2020). Financial distress, internal control, and earnings management: Evidence from China. *Journal of Contemporary Accounting & Economics*, *16*(3), 100210. doi:10.1016/j.jcae.2020.100210

Luong, L. (2015). *Earnings management through accrual-based analysis: Case study: Stockmann Oy Abp 2005-2014* [Doctoral Dissertation, Nyland's Swedish University of Applied Sciences].

Miranda, K. F., Machado, M. A. V., & Machedo, L. A. F. (2018). Investor sentiment and earnings management: Does analysts monitoring matter? *Revista de administração Mackenzie, 19*(4), 1–29.

Mohanram, P. S. (2003). How to manage earnings management. *Accounting World*, *10*(1), 1–12.

Morais, A. I., & Pinto, I. (2019). Pension plans assumptions: The case of discount rate. *Accounting Research Journal*, *32*(1), 36–49. doi:10.1108/ARJ-02-2018-0041

Mosebach, M., & Simko, P. (2010). Discretionary accruals and the emergence of profitability. *Journal of Accounting, Auditing & Finance*, *25*(3), 351–374. doi:10.1177/0148558X1002500304

Mulford, C. W., & Comiskey, E. (2002). *The Financial Numbers Game: Detecting Creative Accounting Practices*. John Wiley & Sons.

Omar, N., Rahman, R. A., Danbatta, B. L., & Sulaiman, S. (2014). Management disclosure and earnings management practices in reducing the implication risk. *Procedia: Social and Behavioral Sciences*, *145*, 88–96. doi:10.1016/j.sbspro.2014.06.014

Osma, B. G., Gomez-Conde, J., & Lopez-Valeiras, E. (2022). Management control systems and real earnings management: Effects on firm performance. *Management Accounting Research*, *55*, 100781. doi:10.1016/j.mar.2021.100781

Penman, S. H. (2009). Accounting for intangible assets: There is also an income statement. *Abacus*, *45*(3), 358–371. doi:10.1111/j.1467-6281.2009.00293.x

Perols, J. L., & Lougee, B. A. (2011). The relation between earnings management and financial statement fraud. *Advances in Accounting*, *27*(1), 39–53. doi:10.1016/j.adiac.2010.10.004

Putra, A. M., Pagalung, G., & Habbe, A. H. (2018). Culture and corruption-driven agency costs and earnings management. Evidence from southeast Asian countries. *Intangible Capital*, *14*(4), 499–517. doi:10.3926/ic.1289

Rafay, A. (Ed.). (2021). *HandBook of Research on Theory and Practice of Financial Crimes*. IGI Global., doi:10.4018/978-1-7998-5567-5

Rafay, A. (Ed.). (2023a). *Concepts and Cases of Illicit Finance*. IGI Global. doi:10.4018/978-1-6684-8587-3

Rafay, A. (Ed.). (2023b). *Concepts, Cases, and Regulations in Financial Fraud and Corruption*. IGI Global., doi:10.4018/978-1-6684-5007-9

Rafay, A., & Ajmal, M. M. (2014). Earnings management through deferred taxes recognized under IAS 12: Evidence from Pakistan. *Lahore Journal of Business*, *3*(1), 1–19. doi:10.35536/ljb.2014.v3.i1.a1

Rafay, A., Chen, Y., Naeem, M. A. B., & Ijaz, M. (2018). Analyzing the impact of credit ratings on firm performance and stock returns: An Evidence from Taiwan. *Indian Economic Review*, *22*(3), 767–786.

Ramírez-Orellana, A., Martínez-Romero, M. J., & Mariño-Garrido, T. (2017). Measuring fraud and earnings management by a case of study: Evidence from an international family business. *European Journal of Family Business*, *7*(1-2), 41–53. doi:10.1016/j.ejfb.2017.10.001

Ramzan, M., Ahmad, I., & Rafay, A. (2020). Is auditor independence influenced by non-audit services? A stakeholder's viewpoint. *Pakistan Journal of Commerce and Social Sciences*, *14*(1), 388–408.

Rapoport, M. (2011, March 9). Rewriting pension history. *Wall Street Journal*.

Rosner, R. L. (2003). Earnings manipulation in failing firms. *Contemporary Accounting Research*, *20*(2), 361–408. doi:10.1506/8EVN-9KRB-3AE4-EE81

Roychowdhury, S. (2006). Earnings management through real activities manipulation. *Journal of Accounting and Economics*, *42*(3), 335–370. doi:10.1016/j.jacceco.2006.01.002

Sadiq, M., & Shafie, R. B. (2017). The quality of financial reporting and its measurements. *International Journal of Economic Perspectives*, *11*(1), 392–401.

Safdar, R., & Yan, C. (2016). Managing accruals for income smoothing: Empirical evidence from Pakistan. *Journal of Accounting in Emerging Economies*, *6*(4), 372–387. doi:10.1108/JAEE-07-2014-0038

Schilit, H. M., & Perler, J. (2010). *Financial Shenanigans* (3rd ed.). McGraw-Hill.

Schrand, C., & Wong, M. H. F. (2003). Earnings management using the valuation allowance for deferred tax assets under SFAS No. 109. *Contemporary Accounting Research, 20*(3), 579–611. doi:10.1506/480D-098U-607R-5D9W

Sofian, F. N. R. M., Mohd-Sabrun, I., & Muhamad, R. (2022). Past, present, and future of corporate social responsibility and earnings management research. *Australasian Accounting. Business and Finance Journal, 16*(2), 116–144.

Stallworth, H. L., & Digregorio, D. (2004). Improper revenue recognition: To help clients avoid SEC violations, internal auditors need to understand the revenue management practices that can lead to material misstatements. *Internal Auditor, 61*(3), 53–57.

Stein, L. C. D., & Wang, C. C. Y. (2015). *Economic uncertainty and earnings management* (Working Paper 16-103). Harvard Business School Accounting & Management Unit.

Teixeira, J. F., & Rodrigues, L. L. (2022). Earnings management: A bibliometric analysis. *International Journal of Accounting & Information Management, 30*(5), 664–683. doi:10.1108/IJAIM-12-2021-0259

Time Warner Inc. (2010). *Time Warner Annual Report, 2009.* Annual Report Owl. https://www.annualreportowl.com/Time%20Warner%20Cable/2009/Annual%20Report

Toumeh, A. A., & Yahya, S. (2019). A review of earnings management techniques: An IFRS perspective. *Global Business and Management Research, 11*(3), 1–13.

Vagner, L., Valaskova, K., Durana, P., & Lazaroiu, G. (2021). Earnings management: A bibliometric analysis. *Economia e Sociologia, 14*(1), 249–262.

Wang, Y., Butterfield, S., & Campbell, M. (2017). Effects of earnings management, compensation, insider equity holding on tax structure. *International Management Review, 13*(2), 5–15.

Wasiuzzaman, S., Sahafzadeh, I., & Nejad, N. R. (2015). Prospect theory, industry characteristics and earnings management: A study of Malaysian industries. *Review of Accounting and Finance, 14*(3), 324–347. doi:10.1108/RAF-07-2014-0075

Wyatt, E. (2010, July 22). Dell to pay $100 million settlement. *The New York Times.* https://www.nytimes.com/2010/07/23/business/23dell.html#:~:text=Dell%2C%20agreed%20Thursday%20to%20pay,pad%20its%20quarterly%20earnings%20statements.

Xian, C., Sun, F., & Zhang, Y. (2015). Book-tax differences: Are they affected by equity-based compensation? *Accounting Research Journal, 28*(3), 300–318. doi:10.1108/ARJ-12-2013-0088

Xu, R. Z., Taylor, G. K., & Dugan, M. T. (2007). Review of real earnings management literature. *Journal of Accounting Literature, 26*, 195–228.

Xu, W. (2016). Accruals Management to avoid losses. *Journal of Business Finance & Accounting, 43*(9), 1095–1120. doi:10.1111/jbfa.12215

Zeng, T. (2014). Earnings management around tax rate reduction: Evidence from China's 2007 corporate tax reform. *Asian Review of Accounting*, *22*(3), 304–317. doi:10.1108/ARA-01-2014-0012

Zhao, Y., Chen, K. H., Zhang, Y., & Davis, M. (2012). Takeover protection and managerial myopia: Evidence from real earnings management. *Journal of Accounting and Public Policy*, *31*(1), 109–135. doi:10.1016/j.jaccpubpol.2011.08.004

Zhou, D., & Habib, A. (2013). Accounting standards and earnings management: Evidence from China'. *Accounting Perspectives*, *12*(3), 213–236. doi:10.1111/1911-3838.12016

Section 2
Corruption, Fraud, and the Society

Chapter 6
Le Grand Saint-Antoine's Cargo: A Worst Alleged Case of Corruption in Human History

Jean Michel Rocchi
Sciences Po Aix, France

Ivan Topalovic
https://orcid.org/0000-0002-0221-3929
Independent Researcher, Monaco

ABSTRACT

In this chapter, a renowned historical case study is explored, focusing on the resurgence of the plague in 18th-century Europe. The center stage is occupied by the port of Marseille in this narrative, as a contaminated cargo ship from the Levant inadvertently brought back the dreaded disease. Despite the implementation of effective protective measures across Europe since the Renaissance, all existing protocols mysteriously managed to be evaded by this particular vessel and its valuable cargo. The rapid spread of the plague is argued by researchers to be directly attributed to an instance of "crime of the powerful." It is emphasized by the authors that corruption, contrary to the prevailing notion that it is a victimless crime, can have devastating consequences in extreme cases like this, leading to tens of thousands of deaths.

INTRODUCTION

"Historically, the crimes of the powerful have managed to avoid or escape criminalization and stigmatization (p. 21)". Barak (2015)

If the literature review recognizes with great consensus the illicit nature of corruption and the link between the bribe giver and the bribe taker, there is on the other hand a debate on its impact on third

DOI: 10.4018/979-8-3693-1190-5.ch006

parties and a fortiori on its supposed cost at the societal level. Based on a case of supposedly extremely serious corruption from the history of France, which had a great impact in Europe, the authors will demonstrate that the economic and societal cost of a mundane case of corruption can be considerable. The authors share the classic definition of Misangyi *et al.* (2008) *"From an economic perspective, corruption generally is defined as the misuse of a position of authority for private or personal benefit (p.751)"*.

As researchers in social science, it is not up to us to rewrite history, we are respectful of what has been judged: the first alderman of the city of Marseille (equivalent to the mayor), who was suspected for a while, was soon cleared of any wrongdoing, and the captain of the ship, who was quickly incarcerated, was finally released after three years in prison on remand for lack of evidence. By relying on the work of historians, we will try to demonstrate that there are many suspicions of corruption and that the impunity observed can be explained in terms of the "Crimes of the powerful" theory. We do not, of course, make a final decision on the debate, which would risk leading us into the realm of judicial error at best or revisionism at worst, but rather we intend to fuel it. Nevertheless, our conclusions are rather in the direction of a strong suspicion of organizational corruption initiated by the 4 owners of the ship's cargo, including the owner of the ship and the first alderman. The first section of this chapter will be classically devoted to the literature review, section two to the voyage of the ship ''*le grand Saint-Antoine*'', section three to the death toll in Marseille and its consequences, and the fourth and final section to the scope of the case, and the prospects for future research

LITERATURE REVIEW

We will successively address these three notions which will then enlighten us and enrich our case study.

CORRUPTION: A PHENOMENON AS OLD AS HUMAN SOCIETY AND INCREASINGLY WELL KNOWN

The phenomenon of corruption is not recent; in 1984, John Noonan, federal judge for the State of California, stated: *"Everybody does it: Romans and Visigoths, English and Africans, Catholics and Jews, Pagans and Protestants, Capitalists and Communists, Imperialists and Patriots"*. But first things first, a definition of corruption needs to be addressed. From the two Latin words "*cum*" and "*rumpere*", literally translated as breaking together, the first idea that appears is that corruption involves two people who act together in order to break something, be it the law or moral behavior. The following dictionary definitions show in different orders the following meanings; to break or destroy a whole; to spoil by decomposition; to deprave; to alter in a bad way; to gain something from someone through bribery. For many years, the phenomenon has been perceived in developing countries as a necessary evil, an unavoidable step to ease the growth of a country, facing a lack of bureaucracy and arguable governance (Rafay, 2021a, 2023a). This was the "*grease the wheels*" notion, as opposed to the "*sand*" that might block the system (Wei, 1999). The idea of corruption efficiency emerged (Aidt, 2003). Viswanathan (2008) in India even opposed the *"warm nature of corruption" to the "coldness of bureaucratic rationality"*.

However, since the middle of the XXth century, corruption is studied through the prism of morality, being described in 1996 in a speech by James Wolfensohn, President of the World Bank, as a "*modern society's cancer*". Pervert effects of corruption are extracted through academic research, such as; loss of revenue for governments, preventing public investment and leading to poor quality infrastructure (Fjeldstad & Tungodden, 2003); overhead costs for companies engaging in these behaviors, and lack of opportunities for the virtuous ones (Caiden *et al*., 2001); a distortion in the perception of the efficiency of the law (Hamir, 1999); impossibility for the population to have access to infrastructure or medical care that should be financed by the State (Everett, Neu & Rahaman, 2006). Effects are therefore observed, and researchers tried to define corruption in order to prevent it. Torsello and Venard (2016) classified the phenomenon into three categories: firstly, corruption as an organizational behavior deviation; bribes, interest conflicts, and treason; secondly, the narrow academic definition targeting the public sector; corruption is the misuse of public empowerment for private interests; thirdly, a broader definition, required when the public sector is not involved; the misuse of an entrusted power for a private or organizational gain (Anand *et al.* 2004). Corruption is not a private-to-public phenomenon, but can also be seen in private-to-private relationships.

Klitgaard (1991) described the determinants of corruption through a mathematical formula;

$$C = M + D - A$$

i.e.

$$\text{Corruption} = \text{Monopoly} + \text{Discretion} - \text{Accountability}$$

Goudie & Stasavage (1997) related this equation with bureaucracy; its complexity, diluted responsibility, lack of transparency and elevated discretionary power might open the door to a corrupt behavior. The researchers will enlighten these determinants in this case study.

A consensus emerges on the ''what''. Firstly, corruption involves two parties, the corruptor and the corrupt, in a mutual agreement for a common interest (Park, 2003). The relationship will pursue as long as the value of the illegal act is superior to the value of honesty (Lavallée *et al.* 2008). The rent-seeking, the perceived bribe and the sanction probability will be the determinants for the corrupt. The financial and moral cost, mixed with the expected gain are the determinants for the corruptor. Secondly, corruption is a crime with no direct victims, only involving two parties with illegal and secret mutual benefits. The victims should be looked at outside of this relationship (Von Arnim, 2003), with consequences such as an unbalance, a competition distortion, a breach in a development possibility (Rafay, 2021b, 2023b). Engaging in a corrupt act is often correlated with a diminished perceived sensation of committing a crime, as when compared to murder or theft; there is often no identified or identifiable victim (Lascoumes & Nagels, 2014)

The authors through this case study beg to differ from this idea, aiming to highlight a direct link between a phenomenon of corruption and the death of individuals, which is rare to find and prove.

The question of the ''why'' and the ''how'':

According to Merton's strain theory (1938), there is tension between the goal (success, power, wealth) and the means to achieve it. In a competitive environment, social pressure imposes goals but does not ethically frame the way. Disengagement is perceived as a failure. Therefore, social structures can exert pressure on individuals that can lead them to crime when individuals do not feel they can achieve societal goals without resorting to such methods. Two complementary theories can also be mentioned. Firstly, the culturalist theories postulate that a culture within an organization can contribute to the endorsement of a transgressive act (Sutherland, 1973), and the culture of organizational loyalty will lower the moral standards of the members for the good of the organization, or lower the perception of colleague misbehavior. Corruption can emerge even when the organization didn't require it (Box, 1983). Through this culturalist lens, Vaughan (2007) states that illegal actions are not considered as such, because they are considered common acts, while Shover (2007) believes the elites perceive themselves as culturally superior, therefore the laws do not apply to them and are negotiable. In Shover's analysis, the actor knows he is out of the law, but considers himself as above the law. Secondly, the rational choice theory is based on an analysis by a rational individual with regard to the cost/benefit prism (Becker, 1968a, 1968b). In Becker's view, the possibility of the death penalty is in principle a strong deterrent, but it is combined with the likelihood of being caught and the likelihood of such a sentence being passed, especially if one believes, rightly or wrongly, that one has protections in high places.

WHITE-COLLAR CRIME VERSUS OCCUPATIONAL CRIME: SUTHERLAND LEGACY VERSUS YALE TRADITION

In 1939, Edwin Sutherland pronounced a revolutionary criminology speech at the American Sociological Association. According to a definition that has become classic, (Sutherland, 1940), a "*white collar crime*" constitutes a *"crime in relation to business"*. A more precise definition is provided by him later: *"a crime committed by a person of high social status and respectability in the course of his occupation"* (Sutherland 1949: 9). Without the great interest of business, behaviors of total recklessness, or even obvious corruption could only come from irrational, not to say crazy, individuals. Sutherland's (1945) famous question 'Is "White Collar Crime" Crime?', finds in this case an undeniably important element to contribute to the debate. Sutherland's (1945: 139) concluding remark is clear: *"The relation between the law and the mores tends to be circular. The mores are crystallized in the law and each act of enforcement of the laws tends to re-enforce the mores. The laws regarding white collar crime, which conceal the criminality of the behavior, have been less effective than other laws in re-enforcement of the mores."*

Benson & Simpson (2014) emphasizes that *"it would be a mistake to think that white-collar crime is a new invention of the criminal mind. Unfortunately, criminals have engaged in white-collar type crimes literally for thousands of years .... For example, in the fourth century BC, the Greek philosopher Aristotle wrote about the embezzlement of funds by road commissioners and other officials (p. 3)"* In other words, it is clear that this is a new name for behaviors that date back to antiquity and continue through the ages to the present day.

Engaging in a corrupt act is often correlated with a diminished perceived sensation of committing a crime, as when compared to murder or theft, there is often no identified or identifiable victim (Lascoumes & Nagels, 2014) The authors are interested in the "Sociology of delinquent elites" (*"sociologie des élites délinquantes"* in French), i.e. those assimilated to white-collar crime.

Rothe & Kauzlarich (2016, First Edition) seminal book entitled *"Crimes of the Powerful"* responds to the *Routledge International Handbook of the Crime of the powerful* (Barak, 2015).

Firstly, the Sutherland legacy emphasizes mainly power and status, and hence the organizational aspect of white-collar crime (See left side of Figure 1) conversely unlike the Yale tradition which focuses on crimes committed mainly by individuals for one's self-interest or self-gain which is called occupational crime (See right side of Figure 1). Secondly, occupational crimes are most of the time associated with middle-class crimes, committed by people less wealthy than the bourgeoisie, even if there are some counter-examples. On the other hand organizational crimes are crimes committed by individuals in the name and interest of the organization. The concept of *"Crimes of the powerful"* is, therefore, more naturally associated with the notion of "organizational crime" than with that of "occupational crime", because the latest consists of small scams and low-level thefts committed in the office by individuals working alone.

This distinction is the consequence of a difference of focus which generated two schools of thought as shown in Figure 2 below.

Benson & Simpson (2014) propose to analyze white-collar crime from an "*opportunity perspective*", which in fact leads to analytically separate answers to "*why*" and "*how*". We will see in our case study that the "*why*" is finally easy to understand, while the "*how*" consists of making the impossible

Figure 1. The two types of white-collar crime
Source: Rothe & Kauzlarich (2022), p.7.

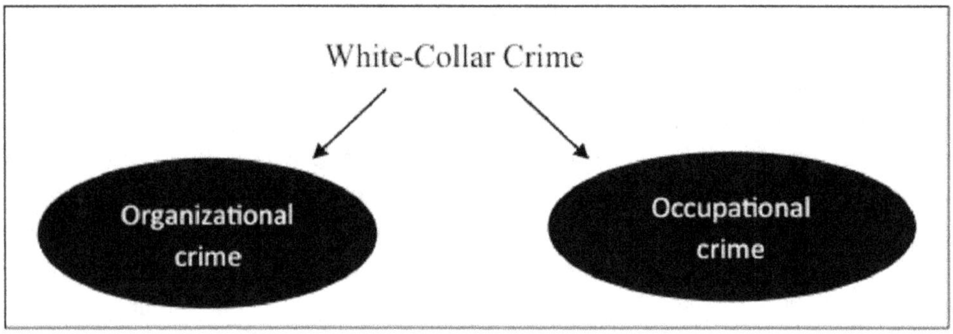

Figure 2. The Sutherland/Yale History
Source: Rothe & Kauzlarich (2022), p.5.

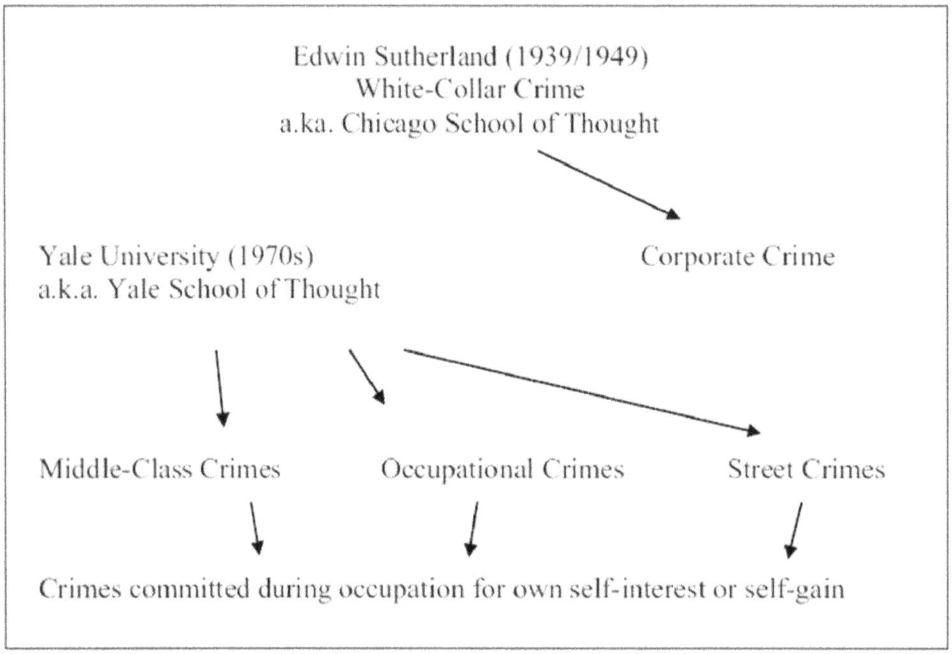

possible. Lange (2008:710) explains that "*Organizational corruption*" can be defined as follows: "*the pursuit of individual interests by one or more organizational actors through the intentional misdirection of organizational resources or perversion of organizational routines, is commonly understood to be highly undesirable for any parties holding a stake in the organization's performance. Even when the actors ostensibly direct the corrupt behavior on behalf of rather than against the organization, the behavior may ultimately impede the organization's ability to accomplish its legitimate purpose and may threaten its very survival*". Following Pinto *et al* (2008), we will examine the nature of the relationships between the various cargo owners: "*Corrupt organizations or organizations of corrupt individuals?*". This should lead us to study the two dimensions of a corruption case, first, the "*primary beneficiary*", and second, the nature of the "*collusion among organizational members*". Baker and Faulkner (1993) define organizational crime as a "*type of white-collar crime that is enacted by collectivities or aggregates of discrete individuals in the context of complex relationships and expectations among boards of directors, executives, and managers, and among parent corporations, corporate divisions, and subsidiaries. (p. 842)*". This recent definition of an organizational crime applies, in our opinion, quite well to an old *ad hoc* organization created to finance a maritime expedition, the acceptance of a high level of risk of loss of goods (storm, pirates, crew mutiny, risk of fire, seizure of goods by the port authorities, long quarantine...) creating a culture of wanting to save the cargo at any cost, at any place and at any time, whatever the occurring risk.

Crimes of the Powerful: Is There an Inversion of Values Consisting in Focusing on the Less Serious but More Common Crimes?

Are the powerful, because they are powerful, above the law? Moreover, don't we tend to consider that their crimes, however serious, are not really crimes? These are the questions that agitate this field of research. For Michalowski (2013) it is the state "*that determines what behaviors are legal, which are illegal, and among those that are illegal, which will be nominated as serious crimes, which will be lesser offenses or minor infractions, and which will be treated as non-criminal administrative matters.*" This fact introduces a bias that conventional forms of crime—crimes committed by the powerless (easier for a quantitative analysis) tend to distract and lessen the perception of an unconventional but severe form of criminality. For him, the consequence of the forms of state definition produces an inverted criminology focus, which in practice consists of the highest social harms benefiting from the lowest attention. Friedrichs (2009) emphasizes the paradox of "*an inverse relationship between the level of harms caused by some human (individual or organizational) activity and the level of criminological concern. (p.1)*". Lastly, Ruggiero (2021) is helpful when he emphasizes that: "*the crimes of the powerful are the result of the different features displayed in the exercise of power itself: coercion, legitimacy, violence, secrecy, consensus, and hegemony.*"

Let us now turn to the case study.

LE GRAND SAINT-ANTOINE'S VOYAGE IN A NUTSHELL: MAIN FACTS AND FIGURES

In 1720, Marseilles was the main French port in the Mediterranean, notably because of the monopoly on trade with the Levant granted to the city in 1669 by Minister Colbert. This 700-ton merchant ship has a flat-bottomed hull, with a carrying capacity of around 7000 quintals or 266 tons of cargo. Rigged as a three-masted square-rigged vessel, it is approximately 37 meters long with a beam of 7.50 meters and a beam of 3.80 meters. On July 22, 1719, the Grand Saint-Antoine, a large Dutch-made ship, left for the Levant (now the Middle East) to buy precious silk and cotton fabrics that were to be sold at a very high price at the Beaucaire fair, which was synonymous with great profits for the ship's cargo owners. In the Levant, the plague[1] was still raging, while in Europe it was a very painful but already ancient story with the Black Death's great epidemic in 1348, which had hit Marseille as early as 1347, causing 16,000 deaths.

The Answer to the "Why" or Who Benefits From the Crime?

The ship's cargo, which had a considerable resale value, belonged to the city's notables, including the first alderman (equivalent to a mayor) Jean Baptiste Estelle, who owned a quarter of it. The captain of the ship was informed that he had to be back in the spring and in any case before the beginning of the Beaucaire fair held from July 22 - 28, 1720. He himself is motivated to meet the deadline because he owns another quarter of the cargo. His brother-in-law Jean Chaud who bought the ship will be entitled to another quarter of the profits. The Saint-Jean-Baptiste, renamed Grand Saint-Antoine, was bought for 12000 livres tournois[2]. In the holds of the ship, nearly 900 bales of cotton, wool, silk and brightly colored cloth sought after at the fairs of Provence were to be stored. This cargo was insured for 100,000 livres tournois (more than eight times the value of the ship alone, the equivalent of more than 31 kilos of pure gold in 1720 or nearly 900,000 euros today). The last quarter belongs to Antoine Bourguet, who works as a shipowner.

The ship left Syria in February 1720, and in addition to the goods, a Turkish passenger who paid for the crossing was taken on board. It then stopped at Larnaca in Cyprus before setting sail for Marseilles. The Turkish passenger died on April 5, 1720. At the end of the month of April, two crew members died again. At the beginning of May two other crew members and the surgeon passed away. In the mid of May two sailors and a ship's boy died in turn. And lastly, a sailor died on May 26, 1720 after the arrival in Marseille.

Therefore, the total number during the return trip and including the final stopover in Livorno sums up to 9 deaths.

A Presumption of Corruption That Was not Recognized by the Authorities

While the plague was progressively eradicated in Europe from the Renaissance onwards, it continued to ravage the Levant and Barbary (the current Middle East) with which trade, particularly maritime trade, remained important. These successes in the face of the disease can be explained by the establishment of a strict and efficient sanitary system in the European ports of the Mediterranean, particularly in Marseille.

The Patents System and its Practical Consequences

From then on, the already existing "health patents" were made compulsory and had to be handed over by the French consul of the "*Échelle*" where the vessel embarked its cargo or stopped over. They were of three kinds: "*Patente nette*" means good health in the port; "*Patente soupçonnée*" or "*touchée*" in the case of rumors of an epidemic or its proximity; "*Patente brune*" or "*grosse*" is the worst-case scenario; it occurs when the port is affected by the plague.

Figure 3. The round trip of the ship Grand Saint-Antoine from Marseille to the Levant
Source: Buti (2020)

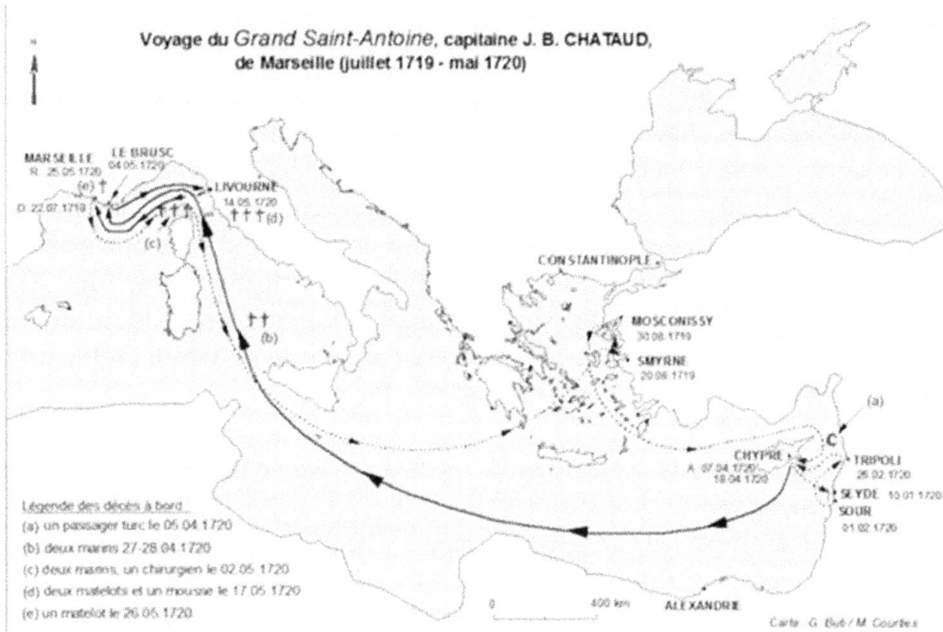

Strangely enough for our contemporary perception, the members of the health office (*bureau de santé* in French) do not usually belong to the medical staff but on the contrary "will be taken among the people of the lodge, merchants, traders" according to the edict of 1717 as emphasizes Buti (2020). The lodge (*la loge* in French) is the meeting place of the merchants. Therefore, giving the role of stewards of health (*intendants de santé* in French) to merchants and empowering them to deliver the patents for goods, which belong to them or to people they relate personally or professionally, wouldn't that constitute a risk to be at the same time judge and party?

In 1720, there were sixteen merchants among the twenty stewards of health. Is there not by design a risk of business first? There were, for example, former merchants who knew the Levant, some former captains, the men who had experience in the international trade of goods. Stewards of health were elected annually on October 29 to take office on January 2 the following year, which in the absence of support threatened their re-election and encouraged them to remain popular.

As Buti (2020) points out, the stewards had a great deal of statutory autonomy in their decision-making by virtue of the texts that governed them. Indeed, they were able to decide on *"all that they*

Table 1. Number of days of quarantine imposed in Marseille, at the end of the 18th century

	Gross Patents	Suspected Patents	Net Patents
Passengers	32 to 35 days	25 days	14 to 18 days
Ships	35 to 50 days	25 to 30 days	20 to 28 days
Goods	40 to 60 days	35 to 40 days	30 to 38 days

Source: Biraben (1975)

judged appropriate for the preservation of the plague and contagious disease ... the treasurer will pay the expenses that will be made on this occasion, in any amount that may rise". It can be seen that there is a contradiction between considerable decision-making powers and theoretically unlimited financial means and a very precarious personal status.

In the building of the Consignor (*Consigne*), the captain, his second in command, or the on-board ship's writer has an obligation of an oath which is made the hat in hand (*Chapeau bas*) in a high and intelligible voice of any sanitary incident that one would have noticed on board. As well as the ships met during the crossing which there would have been "*communications*" with. The stewards and their staff would listen behind a screen the statements and documents on board were previously tempered in a wine vinegar purifier. They are then dried over a purifying smoke before being filed. At the time of filing, it is therefore the responsibility of the ship's manager to transmit the health certificate issued by the competent authorities of the port of Marseilles (as the port of origin), which itself must be stamped at each port of call, with three possible qualifications:

- Net patent (*patente nette*) which corresponds to the case where the departure and the calls are made in healthy countries;
- Affected (*touchée*) or suspected (*soupçonnée*) patent when the departure or stopover is in a country in a suspected contagion zone
- Brown patent (*patente brune*) in case of contact with a contaminated territory.

Figure 4. Map of Marseille and the city's health protection organization (Arrow: North)
Source: Buti (2020).

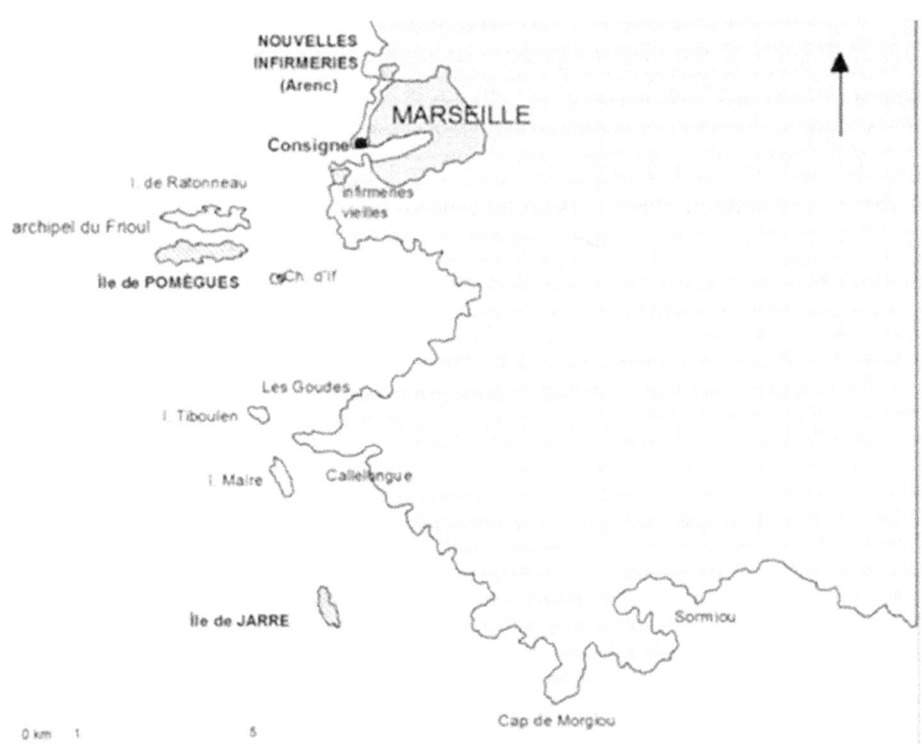

The sanitary decision that is taken at the arrival of the ship depends on the nature of the patent shown to the health stewards. In case of falsification of the patent, the death penalty is incurred.

The slowness of the crossings to the Levant and/or Barbary (30 to 40 days) acted as a first level of "sanitary barrier", but it was not sufficient. In addition, the ship was subjected to quarantine on the islet of Pomègues in the Frioul archipelago, while the passengers were isolated in a Lazaretto (*Lazaret*) called the New Infirmaries (*Les Nouvelles Infirmeries*). The first Lazaretto was built in 1423 in Venice, progressively imitated by many European ports. In August 1663, the foundation stone of the Lazaretto was laid in the city of Marseille. The purpose of the building was to "contain and quell the plague". Called the "New Infirmaries", the building was completed in 1668 and was located in the north of the city in the Arenc district.

According to Biraben (1975), from 1710 to 1792, in Marseilles, 22,651 ships were received from the Levant or Barbary. Of this total, 140 ships arrived contaminated (0.6%), while in 1720, the plague affected 8 ships out of 212 (3.8%). The statistics above mentioned testify to the great efficiency of the Royal procedures. When faced with the improbable, three explanations were possible: a curse, negligence and/or the possibility of corruption, which was quickly dismissed despite legitimate suspicions in the face of the accumulation of strange phenomena and behaviors.

How Was it Possible for the Ship to Reach Marseilles and Probably Bypass the Very Strict Quarantine Rules?

For Michelet (2016), author of a classic monumental history of France, the case of the great Saint-Antoine is *''revealing frauds, or, at least, the great deficiencies of the quarantine in force''*. Nevertheless, it is important to place the case in the context of time, as Devaux (2013) points out; *"At that time, the plague had virtually disappeared from France for several decades and only a few cases were reported from time to time in port cities. Health checks tended to loosen and smuggling tended to increase."*

Irregularities and/or Incompetence

The first inconsistency is noted at the departure from Syria where the plague was rife; the ship obtained a "net patent", i.e. an authorization to go to sea due to the absence of risk (a "brown patent" in case of risk imposes a quarantine to a ship). Then once again upon departing from Cyprus, when deaths have occurred on board, a new "net patent" is issued to the captain. On the return trip, *Le Grand Saint-Antoine* first stopped in the harbor of Le Brusc, north of the island of Les Embiez, 5 miles northwest of Cap Sicié. Le Brusc is definitely not a normal stopover for a ship returning from the Levant. It was not planned when the ship left. It is even more surprising that the captain headed east, to Livorno, before returning to Marseille. This round trip, which represents an additional distance of more than 400 nautical miles, has no apparent commercial justification. This secret stopover at Le Brusc (near Marseille) occurs when the ship's owners are informed of the deaths on board; the captain then seems to be ordered to head for Livorno to obtain death certificates that do not mention the plague. This is consistent with a "white collar crime" and not an "occupational crime", as it cannot be attributed to the captain alone, but rather to a collective decision of the business partners. Hence this defines it as an "organizational crime" and, considering the eminent personalities involved, a "crime of the powerful". A document preserved in the French National Archives, a letter signed by Benoît de Maillet, official correspondent of the *Ministry of the Navy*, describes this meeting. Moreover, according to Vitaux (2021), before joining Livorno, the ship would have made a clandestine stopover in La Ciotat to unload contraband goods. The chief physician of the port of Livorno, a man named Marcello Ittieri, had to examine the last three deaths that had recently occurred on board (after the first 6 deaths that had already occurred) and qualified the 3 new deaths as victims of pestilential fevers. This qualification was different from the plague for the contemporaries and corresponded to fevers related to tropical diseases or malaria. Based on this diagnosis, he was able to hand over travel documents from Livorno which attested to a clear patent, so the return to Marseilles was under the best of auspices. Was the doctor incompetent or corrupt? Besides, Livorno was not a stopover initially planned, so why did he choose this particular port, which is quite far from Marseilles?

Papon (1760) proposes another version: the authorities of Livorno would have informed the port of destination of the health risks observed on board. Devaux (2013) explains in a complementary way: *"The ship should have been immediately rerouted to the island of Jarre, -an island ranging between the inlet of Callelongue (at the South of the mountain of Marseilleveyre) and the island of Riou, to be burned with its goods. However, its Captain, Jean-Christophe Chataud, requested to drop anchor at Pomègues in the archipelago of Frioul ..., where the ''Grand Saint Antoine'' was quarantined as ordinary. There, the crew unloaded the ship cargo (then transported to the new lazaretto at ''La Joliette''), before returning to the island of Jarre. The reason behind this unusual conduct was that the owner of the ship, the deputy mayor of the city of Marseille, influenced the decision of the health office because he wanted to sell its cargo as soon as possible at the fairs in the South of France (so-called Provence), especially the one in Beaucaire (p. 174)"*

Captain Chataud, interviewed by the officers of the sanitary services, declared that the six deaths during the crossing were linked to "bad food" and for the last three, he had the explanations of Doctor Marcello Ittieri. In spite of Livorno's stratagem and the captain's reassuring statements, events again did not go as planned; two days after the ship's arrival in Marseille and while the ship was undergoing a normal quarantine at the island of Pomègues a new sailor died. The Marseille doctor Gueirard, who examined the body of the crew member, concluded in an extremely surprising way that he had died of old age, even though it was a young man. Ten deaths had now occurred and none of the deaths had been attributed to the plague, the word has never even been uttered.

What is even stranger is that on May 27, the health board deliberated twice to take two completely opposite decisions. The first decision was that the ship should head for the island of La Jarre where the contaminated ships were waiting; a logical decision considering the deaths that occurred on board, the last of which was on the same day. But by a second decision, it was decided that the ship could dock at the Grande-Prise, which was a cove for ships coming out of quarantine. Why such an inexplicable reversal? Were the stewards of health financially corrupted? Have they been pressured by threats of not being reelected or on the contrary were they granted support for their reelection in October?

On June 4, part of the cargo was authorized to disembark, particularly the most valuable goods (silk and cotton), which were transferred to the New Infirmaries in Arenc. Then on June 14th, it was the turn of the passengers to be allowed to disembark. Once again, the social status of the ship's owners seemed to have played a role in avoiding the normal execution of the quarantine.

Notwithstanding the disembarkation of "junk" was a custom to allow the crew members to bring back various objects. In spite of the quarantine, they were disembarked clandestinely and were kept for personal use or resold.

Even though we will see that this is not the official thesis, such an accumulation of facts allowing the goods to circulate and then disembark constitute too great an accumulation of facts to be the result of chance alone. Chance on the other hand lies in the fact that the ship was caught in a heavy storm in February 2021 from Syria and almost sank.

For the authorities, there was officially only one culprit, the ship itself, which was rumored to be cursed, and was then burned and sunk. The captain, in pre-trial detention, was released. The way he was treated could not be considered severe, since in 1733, in another less serious case, Pierre le Borel, captain of the ship *Sainte-Marthe*, was sentenced to death by the court of Aix-en-Provence and hanged.

THE DEATH TOLL AND ITS CONSEQUENCES

The plague epidemic that began in June 1720 did not decline until the end of 1722. The toll was very heavy as shown in Table 2.

Delays and Measures

The first measures have been delayed due to denial by local authorities. The plague spread outside the lazaret and struck the old city in June. The first victim, according to the doctor Jean-Baptiste Bertrand,

Table 2. Consequences of the epidemic

Population	Death toll	Mortality rate
Provence: 400,000	90,000 to 120,000	22.5% to 30%
Marseille: 80,000 to 90,000	30,000 to 40,000	33.33% to 50%

Source: Authors estimates based on Leskiewicz & Mourre (1964), Biraben (1975), Carrière *et al.* (2013), Mouton (2020).

was Marguerite Dauptane, who died on June 20, followed eight days later by Michel Cresp and his family. The alderman's office, which governs the city, took many weeks to recognize the existence of an epidemic and the word "plague" was never publicly pronounced by the authorities until September 1720. The first alderman of the city, Jean-Baptiste Estelle, who owned part of the cargo of the Grand Saint-Antoine, was sued but rapidly released due to lack of evidence. The port of Marseilles was closed for several years. On July the 31, the Parliament of Provence closed Marseilles and its suburbs with a cordon of troops, any crossing being punishable by death. On his side, the Regent sent doctors on August 12, 1720 and the financier Law sent funds to help the city and its inhabitants. As reported by Michelet (2016) *"The famous Chirac, doctor of the Regent, consulted, answered ''that it was especially necessary to be joyful"* This belief shared also by the Doctors of Montpellier had a part of verity; if in theory all the layers of the society were exposed, excess mortality was noted in the less well-nourished popular layers and within people with the most health fragility, supposed to be less cheerful.

The Regent's Decisions

The port of Marseille was closed for several years. The regent Philippe d'Orléans set up an army-controlled containment of Provence, which would divide France for many months. On July 28, 1720 in Versailles, the Regent decided that the goods and the Grand Saint-Antoine should be burned. On September 10, a Royal officer, Jean-Jacques de Gérin, arrived with clerks to draw up a list of all the merchandise before burning it, and also to interview the crew members. Captain Chataud had already left for the Chateau d'If to be incarcerated. He was finally released in September 1723; at the end of the trial, his guilt was not retained. On the island of La Jarre on September 25, the cargo was burned and the next day torches were thrown at the ship which caught fire and sank. While much of the cargo was burned, which probably protected the owners rather than the captain, goods were nonetheless offloaded; either goods intended to be sold or items bought and resold by the crewmen themselves in an established practice of turning a blind eye.

The Castle of If is a French fortress with a sinister reputation because of the very difficult living conditions and its isolation. The prison was built on the orders of King François the First, between 1527 and 1529 on the islet of If, part of the archipelago of Frioul, close to the islands of Ratonneau and Pomègues in the center of the roadstead of Marseilles. It became world-famous with the novel by Alexandre Dumas:

Figure 5. Drawing of the prison of the Chateau d'If fortress in 1641.
Source: Pen drawing by F. Blondel, Bibliothèque Nationale, Cabinet des Estampes.

The Count of Monte-Cristo (*Le Comte de Monte-Cristo*) published in 1844, in which an innocent victim of a plot is imprisoned there before managing to escape and take revenge. Captain Chataud escaped the death penalty but if he held any secrets, he was silenced by his detention; from his cell in the Chateau d'If he was not able to reveal anything to anyone, and secrets remained well kept.

A plague police force was organized to control the city and recruited new members to compensate for the desertions following the outbreak of the epidemic. The knight Charles-Claude Andrault de Langeron, who was already the squadron leader of the galleys in Marseille and marshal of camp, was appointed on September the 3, 1720 at the initiative of the Regent to *''command in the aforementioned city of Marseilles as much to the inhabitants as to the people of war who are and will be garrisoned there*'' (King's Commission). A government with a military component was thus substituted to the traditional "*échevinage*", however going as far as deposing the four aldermen (Estelle, Audimar, Moustiès, Dieudé). These were already fighting the plague and continued to work in concert with Langeron, but the final decision was his. The military commanders in Provence were endowed with full theoretical powers, turning the cities de facto into states of exception. In his time, Estelle was variously judged. At first and under pressure from the angry population, the government believed him guilty because he was one of the owners of the cargo. Son of a consul, he was himself a diplomat and the first alderman of the second city of France. He was a first rank notable who had a lot of connections, moreover, had he been declared guilty, the powerful and the court would have been inevitably scratched by a huge scandal. Hence, the Court was not long in reversing its initial severity. Maréchal de Villars wrote on November 6, 1721: *"His Royal Highness himself told me that Sieur Estelle, to whom one had initially wanted to attribute the beginning of the misfortunes, had justified himself of this false accusation and that he had served very well as well as his fellow fighters"*. (Carrière, Courdurié, Rebuffat, 1968). On January 19, 1722, Lebret proposed Estelle for the granting of letters of nobility and gratification of 6 000 livres. He was then ennobled in July and died shortly after in January 1723. A street in the 1st district of Marseille bears his name; this is not surprising since he is officially innocent. Furthermore, in front of the plague he showed courage both in the fight against the epidemic and in the provisioning of the city to avoid a famine. For his detractors, he simply sought to redeem himself. The heroes of the epidemic were the archbishop of Marseille, Monseigneur de Belsunce, and moreover, the Chevalier Roze, who led the operations to remove the bodies of the plague victims and greatly contributed to the eradication of the disease.

Looking for an Explanation: The Curse, a Convenient Cause

In the presence of a curse, it is therefore nobody's fault, with two close versions: fate or divine punishment. From then on there is no crime and it is not necessary to look for a culprit. One also avoids facing the very important popular discontent in the city and beyond in all of Provence, which was touched by the disease. Superstition pushes the population into the churches, which has the advantage of not seeing a violent and angry crowd taking the streets, and the fear of contamination during gatherings also avoids excesses. But on the other hand, gatherings in churches, if they relieve the fears of believers, can also be vectors for the spread of the disease. The words of a medieval prayer commonly used in Provence are edifying: *"A Bello, Fame e Peste libera nos, Domine"* (deliver us, Lord, from war, hunger and pestilence) emphasizes Mouton (2020).

Looking for an Explanation: Suspicion of "Crimes of the Powerful"

The power in Marseille was very concentrated: on the one hand, there were the king's representatives with the Marquis de Pilles, governor of the city, and his superior, the Marquis de Brancas, governor of Provence, who depended directly on the Regent; on the other hand, there were the four aldermen (of which the first Jean-Baptiste Estelle), who represented the elite, such as the nobility, and above all, the bourgeoisie. They were enriched by the port trade, in spite of the fact that poverty was endemic in many districts of the city.

Table 3. The various presumed causes of the plague epidemic reflect a lack of consensus.

Causes	Remarks
The curse	This explanation, which spread with great success among the contemporaries of the affair, is of course no longer retained by any historian. Hence, this is being explained by the fact that we live in a largely dechristianized society and above all by the fact that we have a perfect knowledge of plague epidemics since the discovery of Alexandre Yersin at the end of the XIXth century of *"yersinia pestis"*, the bacillus responsible from the plague.
Contaminated sails	The purchase of contaminated sails constitutes a simple imprudence nevertheless explained by the will to make a good deal, simple greed without corruption. This decision was made at the discretion of the captain and did not bind his associates. (Mouton, 2020).
The Turkish passenger was the cause of the plague on board.	It is a common practice for cargo vessels to accept paying passengers to improve the profitability of the crossing. The fact that the Turkish passenger may have died of the plague by infecting the crew is the result of simple carelessness dictated again by greed but does not constitute corruption. This decision was made at the discretion of the captain and did not bind his associates. (Mouton, 2020).
The high value of the cargo is the ''why'' and determines the ''how'' (the continuous corruption process'').	Suspicion 1: Upon departing from Syria where the plague was rife, the ship obtained a "net patent". Did the captain corrupt port authorities? Suspicion 2: Upon departing from Cyprus, when deaths have occurred on board, a new "net patent" is issued to the captain. Suspicion 3: A secret stopover at Le Brusc (near Marseille) occurs, where the ship's owners are informed of the deaths on board. The captain is then ordered to head for Livorno to obtain death certificates that do not mention the plague. Suspicion 3 (alternative version): Livorno services informed Marseille authorities. Why is the ship sent to Pomèque island instead of Jarre island (the quarantine place)? Suspicion 4: Captain Chataud, interviewed by the officers of the sanitary services, declared that the deaths during the crossing were linked to "bad food". Suspicion 5: A sailor died two days after his arrival on the island of Pomegues located off the coast where the ship was in quarantine. The Marseilles doctor Gueirard, who examined the body, concluded that he had died of old age, even though the sailor was a young man. Suspicion 6: When the cargo on the Île de la Jarre was burned by the royal officers, was it complete? **The researchers in this chapter devoted to the case of the great Saint-Antoine is the existence of a continuous process of corruption within the framework of an organizational crime with the characteristics of a crime of the powerful.**
The crew goods were possibly contaminated	The practice of crew members bringing back goods and personal effects is widespread and tolerated, whether items are kept or resold is not monitored, and how items are removed from the ship remains a mystery. As a result, if items were fraudulently landed during quarantine, the fact is unverifiable because unlike the cargo they are not registered, and therefore not traceable. If there has been a corruption of port officials, we are in the presence of an "occupational crime" perpetrated by representatives of the lower strata of society to increase their income, if they are at the origin of the epidemic the small profits will have had disastrous consequences.
The accumulation of small negligence	*"It comes to the evidence that although the threat was known and health surveillance existed with quite effective preventive measures such as quarantine, the accumulation of small negligence led to one of the worst epidemics in the city (about 30% of casualties among the inhabitants)."* (Devaux, 2013).

continues on following page

Table 3. Continued

Causes	Remarks
Fraud or great deficiencies	The case of the great Saint-Antoine is *''revealing frauds, or, at least, the great deficiencies of the quarantine in force''*. (Michelet, 2016)
Le Grand Saint-Antoine is not the culprit?	As explained by Arnaud (2016) and Bos *et al.* (2016) a team from the *Max-Planck Institute* (Germany) has succeeded in reconstructing the genome of the bacillus *Yersinia pestis*, which ravaged Marseille between 1720 and 1722. *"The bacillus of this medieval black plague persisted locally for several centuries before suddenly resurfacing"* says paleopathologist Olivier Dutour, one of the authors of the study. For Spyrou *et al.* (2016) *"Historical Y. pestis Genomes reveal the European Black Death as the source of ancient and modern plague pandemics"*. As the plague bacillus traveled, it is conceivable that a European strain of the plague returned with *Le Grand Saint-Antoine*. Secondly, if the thesis of Bos *et al.* (2016) is confirmed, it does not invalidate the existence of a case of corruption (if any).
Captain's misrepresentation was covered up by health stewards.	Captain Chataud made false statements to the stewards of health because he knew that there was a plague on the ship, the stewards of health covered them up which allowed the court, based on the acts recorded by the stewards, to finally release him from prison (Leskiewicz & Mourre, 1964).
Corruption as an established fact	Beyond the many dissimilarities in behavior and negligence, Vitaux's (2021) most convincing argument is the one highlighting the fact that on May 27, 1720, in Marseilles, the stewards of health took two opposite decisions. The second positive decision was unintelligible in view of a suspicious death on board the ship the same day.

SCOPE OF THE CASE AND PROSPECTS FOR FUTURE RESEARCH

The subject of the Marseilles plague remains a source of study and the tercentenary of this event has given rise to numerous events, conferences and studies in 2020. Buti (2020) has published a book on the subject incorporating the latest historical work.

In support of this case, which is certainly extreme in scope, the researchers have demonstrated that corruption can prove to be a weapon of mass destruction in terms of its consequences, even if the main protagonists never intended it to be that way. On the other hand, they could not ignore the risks of their actions; the numerous irregularities noted show an economic choice in front of the sanitary concerns imposing the quarantine of the ship and its cargo.

Historians have identified cases of corruption dating back to antiquity, and the authors believe that researchers in organizational science can easily refer to ancient organizational forms to identify interesting case studies to advance scientific knowledge.

The collapse of the Morandi viaduct in Genoa, Italy, in 2018 appears to have occurred against a backdrop of repeated lies and corruption. Its toll was high, with 43 deaths. Even more emblematic is the case of the collapse of the Rana Plaza building causing 1 135 deaths in Dhaka, Bangladesh, in 2013, where factories of subcontractors in the textile industry were concentrated. Disasters linked to the construction industry due to the non-respect of quality and/or maintenance standards are particularly deadly in the world and often result in the opening of investigations for corruption. In the absence of a confession from the accused, the accusation is often difficult to prove. These two new cases also tend to weaken the idea that corruption is a crime without victims, at least not in all cases.

Another way of ensuring that a corruption crime goes unpunished is to invoke a curse. This is what the archbishop of Marseille did, but these days we're more likely to speak of bad luck, fate or an unpredictable event. When, as in the case of the earthquakes in Turkey in 2022 and 2023, it seemed clear that the buildings that complied with anti-seismic regulations were left standing, but the others were not, a reaction from the authorities became indispensable. The first arrests began on Friday, February 10, 2023 (some forty contractors and owners) and continued for several days.

Some 134 investigations were launched, and the Ministry of Justice asked the 148 public prosecutors in the ten provinces affected by the earthquake to open investigation offices to identify those responsible for the construction of the buildings that collapsed. But what about possible actors close to the ruling elites or benefiting from various forms of protection? Wouldn't it be a good thing if, in all countries, suspicions of large-scale corruption could bring the emergence of an independent and impartial international investigation and/or allow non-governmental organizations (NGOs) to start civil actions? Given the current state of international relations, it is to be feared that in many countries this is just wishful thinking.

CONCLUDING REMARKS

The reference to history shows us to what extent a presumed case of corruption can have considerable consequences; moreover, the case of *Le Grand Saint Antoine* had great repercussions well beyond the Kingdom of France, particularly in the United Kingdom, because the issue was the reintroduction of the plague in Europe. The authors also argue that the consensus that corruption is a victimless crime is a simplistic view that does not cover all cases, as there may be direct links between deaths and corruption. The researchers emphasize that the "crimes of the powerful" may come from powerful individuals who may benefit from voluntary protection, or by force of circumstance in order to avoid the implication of more important people by boomerang effect may affect the power itself, risking being accused of laxity, negligence or complicity. The consequences of serious cases of corruption can be insurrectionary or even revolutionary, like the Maïdan revolution in Ukraine in 2014. The French society under the Regency was very unequal, both in terms of wealth distribution, health care access, the burden of taxes or the treatment before the courts of justice; this will lead a few decades later to the French Revolution and the abolition of privileges during the night of August 4th, 1789.

Paul Krugman said:

"Both history and modern experience tell us that highly unequal societies also tend to be highly corrupt."[3]

The researchers do not claim to have solved the mystery, and besides, the charm of the mysteries isn't precisely to remain mysterious?

DECLARATION

The authors declare that the manuscript follows ethical standards and there are no potential conflicts of interest with respect to the research, authorship and/or publication of this chapter.

DISCLAIMER

The contents and views of this chapter are expressed by the authors in personal capacities. It is not necessary for the Editor and the Publisher to agree with these viewpoints, and they are not responsible for any duty of care in this regard.

ACKNOWLEDGMENT

The authors extend sincere gratitude to

- The Editor and the International Editorial Advisory Board (IEAB) of this book, who initially desk reviewed, arranged a rigorous double/triple-blind review process, and conducted a thorough, minute, and critical final review before accepting the chapter for publication.
- All anonymous reviewers who provided very constructive feedback for thorough revision, improvement, extension, and fine-tuning of the chapter.
- All colleagues, assistants and well-wishers who assisted to complete this task.

REFERENCES

Aidt, T. (2003). Economic analysis of corruption: A survey. *Economic Journal (London)*, *113*(491), 632–652. doi:10.1046/j.0013-0133.2003.00171.x

Anand, V., Ashforth, B. E., & Joshi, M. (2004). Business as usual: The acceptance and perpetuation of corruption in organizations. *The Academy of Management Perspectives*, *18*(2), 39–53. doi:10.5465/ame.2004.13837437

Arnaud, B. P. (2016, January 31). La Grande Peste de Marseille de 1720 n'est pas venue d'Asie. Le bacile tueur était sur place. *Science & Avenir*. https://www.sciencesetavenir.fr/archeo-paleo/archeologie/la-grande-peste-de-marseille-de-1720-n-est-pas-venue-d-asie-le-bacille-tueur-etait-sur-place_104165

Audoin-Rouzeau, F. (2003). *Les chemin de la peste. Le rat, la puce et l'homme*. Presses Universitaires de Rennes. doi:10.4000/books.pur.8382

Baker, W. E., & Faulkner, R. R. (1993). The social organization of conspiracy: Illegal networks in the heavy electrical equipment industry. *American Sociological Review*, *58*(6), 837–860. doi:10.2307/2095954

Barak, G. (Ed.). (2015). *The Routledge international handbook of the crimes of the powerful*. Routledge. doi:10.4324/9781315815350

Becker, G. S. (1968a). *The Economic approach to human behavior*. University of Chicago Press.

Becker, G. S. (1968b). Crime and punishment: An economic approach. *Journal of Political Economy*, *76*(2), 169–217. doi:10.1086/259394

Benson, M. L., & Simpson, S. S. (2014). *Understanding White-Collar crime. An opportunity perspective*. Routledge. doi:10.4324/9780203762363

Biraben, J. N. (1968). Certain demographic characteristics of the plague epidemic in France, 1720-1722. *Daedalus, 97*(2), 536–545. PMID:11609518

Biraben, J. N. (1975). Les hommes et la peste en France et dans les pays européens et méditerranéens des origines à 1850. *Population, 30*(6), 1143–1144. doi:10.2307/1531209

Bos, K. I., Herbig, A., Sahl, J., Waglechner, N., Fourment, M., Forrest, S. A., Klunk, J., Schuenemann, V. J., Poinar, D., Kuch, M., Golding, G. B., Dutour, O., Keim, P., Wagner, D. M., Holmes, E. C., Krause, J., & Poinar, H. N. (2016). Eighteenth century Yersinia pestis genomes reveal the long-term persistence of an historical plague focus. *eLife, 5*, e12994. doi:10.7554/eLife.12994 PMID:26795402

Box, S. (1983). *Crime, power and ideological mystification.* Tavistock.

Buti, G. (2020). *Colère de dieu, mémoire des hommes. La peste en Provence 1720-2020.* Les éditions du Cerf.

Caiden, G. E., Dwivedi, O. P., & Jabbra, J. (2001). Where Corruption Lives. Bloomfield: Kumarian Press.

Carrière, C., Courdurié, M., & Rebuffat, F. (1968). *Marseille ville morte: la peste de 1720.* Jeanne Laffite.

Devaux, C. A. (2013). Small oversights that led of the Great Plague of Marseille (1720-1723): Lessons from the past. *Infection, Genetics and Evolution, 14*, 169–185. doi:10.1016/j.meegid.2012.11.016 PMID:23246639

Everett, J., Neu, D., & Rahaman, A. S. (2006). The global fight against corruption: A Foucaultian, virtues-ethics framing. *Journal of Business Ethics, 65*(1), 1–12. doi:10.100710551-005-8715-8

Fjeldstad, O. H., & Tungodden, B. (2003). Fiscal corruption: A vice or a virtue? *World Development, 31*(8), 1459–1467. doi:10.1016/S0305-750X(03)00089-5

Friedrichs, D. (2009). *Trusted Criminals: White Collar Crime in Contemporary Society.* Wadsworth.

Goudie, A., & Stasavage, D. (1997). *Corruption: The Issues* (OECD Development Centre Working Paper No. 122). Paris: OECD Publishing.

Hamir, M. A. (1999). Keynote Address. In K. Frimpong & G. Jacques (Eds.), *Corruption, democracy and good governance in Africa: Essays on accountability and ethical behavior.* Lightbooks.

Klitgaard, R. (1991). *Controlling corruption.* University of California Press.

Lange, D. (2008). A multidimensional conceptualization of organizational corruption control. *Academy of Management Review, 33*(3), 685–709. doi:10.5465/amr.2008.32465742

Lascoumes, P., & Nagels, C. (2014). *Sociologie des élites délinquantes; De la criminalité en col blanc à la corruption politique.* Armand Colin.

Lavallée, E., Razafindrakoto, M., & Roubaud, F. (2008). *Les mécanismes à l'origine de la corruption: une analyse sur micro-données africaines* (Working Paper No. DT/2008-08). Paris: DIAL.

Leskiewicz, J., & Mourre, C. (1964). La peste de 1720 à Marseille et les Intendents du Bureau de Santé", Ch. Mourre," Provence Historique, t. XIV, fasc. 52, 1963: [recenzja]/JL. Kwartalnik Historii Kultury Materialnej, 12(4)

Merton, R. K. (1938). Social structure and anomie. *American Sociological Review*, *3*(5), 319–328. doi:10.2307/2084686

Michalowski, R. (2013). What is crime? Why is criminology? Presented at the *annual meeting of the* American Society of Criminology.

Michelet, J. (2016). *Histoire de France* (Vol. XVII). Lacroix et Cie. (Original work published 1877)

Misangyi, V. F., Weaver, G. R., & Elms, H. (2008). Ending corruption: The interplay among institutional logics, resources, and institutional entrepreneurs. *Academy of Management Review*, *33*(3), 750–770. doi:10.5465/amr.2008.32465769

Mouton, P. (2001). *La malédiction du Grand-Saint-Antoine: 25 mai 1720: la peste entre à Marseille.* Autres Temps.

Papon, P. (1760). Stories of the great day of history. Plague of Marseille in 1720. In H. Gautier (Ed.), *Vaugirard Press.*

Park, H. (2003). Determinants of corruption: À cross-national Aanalysis. *Multinational Business Review*, *11*(2), 29–48. doi:10.1108/1525383X200300010

Pinto, J., Leana, C. R., & Pil, F. K. (2008). Corrupt organizations or organzations of corrupt individuals? Two types of organization-level corruption. *Academy of Management Review*, *33*(3), 685–709. doi:10.5465/amr.2008.32465726

Rafay, A. (Ed.). (2021a). *Money Laundering and Terrorism Financing in Global Financial Systems*. IGI Global. doi:10.4018/978-1-7998-8758-4

Rafay, A. (Ed.). (2021b). *HandBook of Research on Theory and Practice of Financial Crimes*. IGI Global. doi:10.4018/978-1-7998-5567-5

Rafay, A. (Ed.). (2023a). *Concepts, Cases, and Regulations in Financial Fraud and Corruption*. IGI Global. doi:10.4018/978-1-6684-5007-9

Rafay, A. (Ed.). (2023b). *Concepts and Cases of Illicit Finance*. IGI Global. doi:10.4018/978-1-6684-8587-3

Rothe, D., & Kauzlarich, D. (2022). *Crimes of the powerful: White-collar crime and beyond*. Routledge. doi:10.4324/9781003124603

Ruggiero, V. (2021). The Crimes of the powerful: Between force and consensus. *Social Sciences (Basel, Switzerland)*, *10*(2), 51. doi:10.3390ocsci10020051

Shover, N. (2007). Generative worlds of white-collar crime. In H. Pontell & G. Geis (Eds.), *International Handbook of White-Collar and Corporate Crime*. Springer. doi:10.1007/978-0-387-34111-8_4

Spyrou, M. A., Tukhbatova, R. I., Feldman, M., Drath, J., Kacki, S., Beltran de Heredia, J., Arnold, S., Sitdikov, A. G., Castex, D., Wahl, J., Gazimzyanov, I. R., Nurgaliev, D. K., Herbig, A., Bos, K. I., & Krause, J. (2016). Historical Y. pestis Genomes Reveal the European Black Death as the Source of Ancient and Modern Plague Pandemics. *Cell Host & Microbe*, *19*(6), 874–881. doi:10.1016/j.chom.2016.05.012 PMID:27281573

Sutherland, E. H. (1940). White-collar criminality. *American Sociological Review*, *5*(1), 1–12. doi:10.2307/2083937

Sutherland, E. H. (1945). Is "white collar crime" crime? *American Sociological Review*, *10*(2), 132–139. doi:10.2307/2085628

Sutherland, E. H. (1949). *White collar crime*. Dryden.

Sutherland, E. H. (1973). Development of the theory. In K. Schuessler (Ed.), *Edwin H. Sutherland on analyzing crime Chicago*. University of Chicago Press.

Torsello, D., & Venard, B. (2016). The anthropology of corruption. *Journal of Management Inquiry*, *25*(1), 34–54. doi:10.1177/1056492615579081

Vaughan, D. (2007). Beyond macro- and micro-levels of analysis, organizations, and the cultural fix. In H. Pontell & G. Geis (Eds.), *International Handbook of White-Collar and Corporate Crime*. Springer. doi:10.1007/978-0-387-34111-8_1

Viswanathan, V. N. (2008). *Corruption and Human Rights*. Allied Publishers.

Vitaux, J. (2021). *Les grandes pandémies de l'histoire: De la peste au Covid*. Archipoche.

Von Arnim, H. H. (2003). Korruption in politik und verwaltung. In H. H. Von Arnim (Ed.), *Korruption. Netzwerke in Politik, Ämtern und Wirtschaft*. Knaur.

Wei, S. J. (1999). *Corruption in economic development: Beneficial grease, minor annoyance, or major obstacle?* (World Bank Policy Research Working Paper). National Bureau of Economic Research.

ENDNOTES

1 *In 1720, almost nothing was known about the plague, which was considered to be largely uncontrollable. It was perceived as a scourge of God that appeared to punish the sins of men. Some practices were rather healthy: ventilation of interiors, fumigation, disinfection with vinegar, and isolation of diseases. Superstition puts forward two remedies: the administration of viper's blood or toad pellets (Mouton, 2020) worthy of the potions of the Middle Ages witches. Worse still, the doctors' remedies are not only ineffective but probably harmful: bloodletting and purgation dominate. Very painful is the more sensible practice of incising the buboes and cauterizing them without mercy. Doctors approached the diseased wearing gloves and masks in the shape of a bird's beak (imagined a century earlier by Delorme, the physician of King Louis XIII) and topped with a hat. One practice is healthy; the dead are burned or thrown into mass graves on which lime is thrown. Other practices seem to us incensed today such as lighting huge braziers in the city to purify the air, or the massacre of dogs and cats that are rumored to be responsible of the propagation of the disease; they will end up burned in mass. Science has now revealed that the culprit was in fact the rat flea (Audoin-Rouzeau, 2003) "In the eighteenth century, men were as ignorant as in the sixth century of the causes of the plague and did not suspect the role of rats and even less fleas in its spread (p. 15)". Yersinia pestis is a gram-negative bacterium of the genus Yersinia that causes plague. This bacterium was discovered in 1894 in French Indochina with the work of Alexandre Yersin, a*

French-Swiss bacteriologist from the Pasteur Institute, during the third plague epidemic originating in Hong Kong. Today, a simple antibiotic-based treatment can greatly reduce the mortality rate, with the notable exception of Madagascar, where particularly resistant strains have developed. The disease, which has disappeared from Western Europe, now only exists in a few regions of the world.

2 *One of numerous currencies used in medieval France*

3 http://cpi.stanford.edu/_media/pdf/journalism/2.27.06%20Graduates%20Versus.html

APPENDIX

Table 4. Brief chronology of events and historical landmarks

Date	Event and if any consequences
531 – 558.	First Pandemic: ''Plague of Justinian.'' (China, Egypt, North Africa, Palestine, Syria, Europe). > 10,000,000 deaths.
1346-1353.	Second Pandemic. ''Great Black Death'' epidemic of 1348 in Europe. The consensus of historians estimates that one third of the population died as a result. Europe and Asia: > 50,000,000 deaths of which 16,000 in Marseille.
1649-1650.	Plague in Marseilles a few thousand deaths.
1665-1666.	''Great Plague of London''. > 100,000 deaths.
1668.	End of the construction of the Lazaretto or ''Nouvelles Infirmeries''.
1669.	Edict of emancipation of the port of Marseilles and monopoly of trade with the Levant and Barbary whose goods were subject to an *ad valorem* tax of 20% on non-provençal ships.
1701-1713.	Plague epidemic in Europe (Balkans, Hungary, Russia, Sweden). > 1,000,000 deaths.
1715	Beginning of the Regency of Philippe d'Orléans, Duke of Chartres, at the death of King Louis XIV.
1718	On October the 28th, J.B Estelle was elected first alderman of Marseille.
1719, July 22	Departure of the ship from Marseille to the Levant.
1720, May 26	Arrival of the ship in the Gulf of Marseilles.
1720, June 4	The most valuable part of the cargo is authorized to disembark (Silk and cotton)
1720, June 14	The passengers are allowed to disembark.
1720, June 20	Marguerite Dauptane is the first death noted in Marseille.
1720, July	Authorities in Marseille acknowledge the existence of an epidemic in the city
1720, July 22-28	Beaucaire Fair.
1720, September	For the first time the authorities in charge of the city pronounce in public the word ''plague''.
1720, September 25	The cargo of the great Saint-Antoine and then the ship are burned. It sinks off the coast.
1722	Crowning of King Louis XV.
1723	Death of Philippe d'Orléans.
1723	Captain Chataud is released from his cell in Château d'If
1723	Death in Marseilles of Jean-Baptiste Estelle.
1728	Death in Marseilles of Jean-Baptiste Chataud.
1733	Pierre le Borel, captain of the ship *Sainte-Marthe*, was sentenced to death for breaking the law by the court of Aix-en-Provence and hanged.
1894-1920.	Third pandemic: plague of Mongolia (China, India). > 10,000,000 deaths.
1978	The wreck of the ship *Le Grand Saint-Antoine* is discovered and formally identified by divers from Marseilles in a cove of the islet Jarron between 10 and 18 meters deep.
1982	The ship's anchor is discovered.
2016, January	A contrarian version, release of the Max-Planck study results: the plague bacillius was already there.
2016, April	The anchor is on display at the Museum of History of Marseille.
2020	Commemorative events of the tercentenary of the great plague of Marseille in 1720.
2022	All visitors to the Château d'If can still read on a commemorative plaque on the wall of the entrance to his cell: ''J.-B. Chataud commander of the *Grand Saint-Antoine* who brought the plague in 1720''.

Chapter 7
The Impact of AML/CFT Regime on the Economic Performance: The Case of Sri Lanka

A. P. L. J. Dulanjali Thilakaratne
https://orcid.org/0000-0002-5700-6521
Central Bank of Sri Lanka, Sri Lanka

ABSTRACT

This study investigates how the Anti-Money Laundering and Countering Financing of Terrorism (AML/CFT) regime influences the economic performance of developing countries, with a specific focus on Sri Lanka. By utilizing the AML/CFT effectiveness index and assessing ratings from the 11 immediate outcomes, as outlined in the latest mutual evaluation reports, the research evaluates the effectiveness of the AML/CFT regime. Additionally, the study analyzes the GDP growth rate of these developing countries as an indicator of their economic performance. The results of the study indicate a positive correlation between the strength of the AML/CFT regime and the economic performance of developing countries. As a result, the study emphasizes the critical importance of continuously implementing and enhancing a robust AML/CFT regime. It advocates for the prudent application of such measures to foster sound economic performance in developing nations.

INTRODUCTION

Money laundering and Terrorism Financing (ML/TF) are two-much discussed and debated topics in the present world. The undetectable processes involved and the resulting severe consequences to countries have led to many studies and interpretations about ML/TF.

DOI: 10.4018/979-8-3693-1190-5.ch007

Money Laundering

Money laundering has been interpreted by numerous global institutions in several ways. The UN made an indirect attempt to define money laundering as the transformation of assets earned from offences to legal status by concealing its illicit origin (UNODC, 1988). The Financial Action Task Force (FATF, 2022a) defines money laundering as the conversion of criminal proceeds to conceal their illegal origin. The FATF further states that money laundering could occur in any part of the world mainly in countries with weak anti-money laundering regimes. The European Commission identifies money laundering as a complex process designed to cleanse the unethical activities undertaken to generate funds from illegal sources (EC, 2022). At the same time, Interpol defines money laundering as a method of disguising the origins of illegally earned proceeds to make them appear to have originated from legitimate sources (Interpol, 2022). By taking into consideration the many definitions of money laundering, it can be simply defined as a cumbersome operation of introducing *(placement)*, blending *(layering)* and using *(integration)* funds earned from criminal activities with the primary objective of concealing the ultimate owner and source of such funds.

Money laundering as a process (Figure 1) has two main objectives. The first objective is to bring in illegally generated money to the legal financial system. The second objective is to conceal the true source and the generator of such funds.

Figure 1. Money laundering process
Source: Author

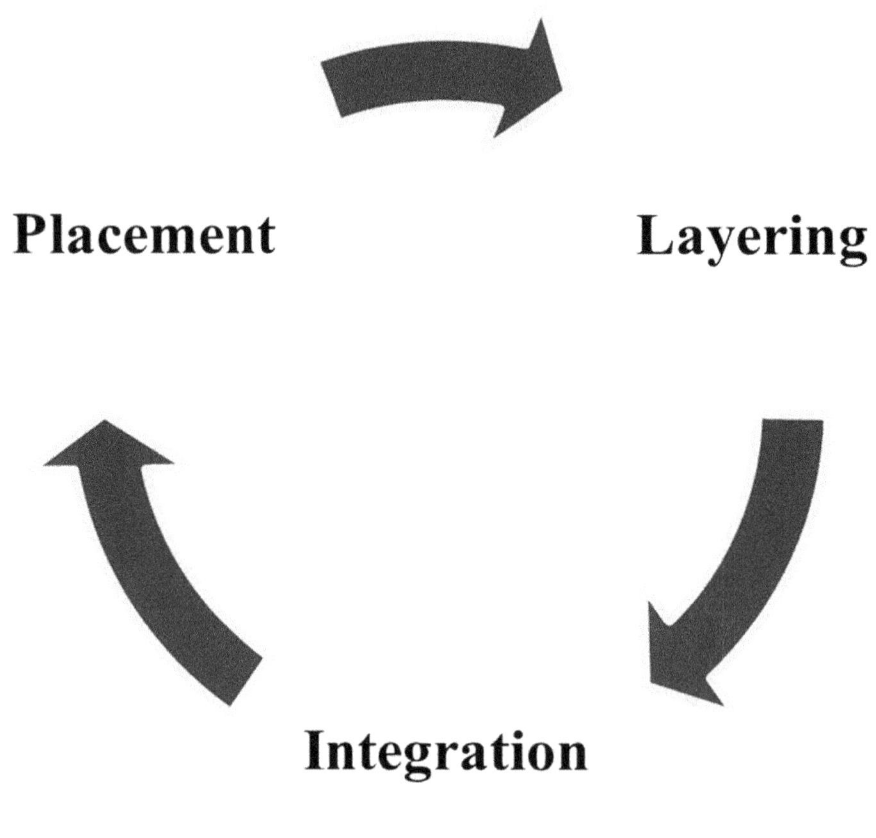

Even though money laundering is a highly evasive activity, several attempts have been made to quantify the amount of money laundered in the overall economy. The UNODC (2011) estimated the amount of money laundered globally in a year as 2% - 5% of global GDP which is $800 billion - $2 trillion in current US dollars. This estimation has been consistently used to date with slight variations to show the total amount of money laundered annually in the world.

To mitigate the risk of money laundering, countries use various tactics such as developing and enforcing anti-money laundering laws and imposing fines in the case of any violations of such laws (Rafay, 2021a, 2023a). Statistics published about anti-money laundering fines show that fines totaling $2,732,099,008 (approx.) involving 80 institutions were imposed during 2021 (Kyckr, 2021). The total amount of fines imposed was relatively reduced and the number of institutions subject to fines drastically increased from 2020 to 2021. The list of institutions charged with anti-money laundering fines in 2021 comprises several renowned brand names operating in different countries as given in Table 1.

Table 1. Charged institutions

Institution	Country	Fine Value in $ MN (approx.)
AmBank	Malaysia	700
Capital One Bank	USA	390
National Westminster Bank PLC	UK	356
Mashreq Bank	USA	100
HSBC	UK	85

Major factors that have supported the strength and the continuity of the money laundering process include its ability to evolve according to the global trends arising from time to time. One of the latest platforms for executing money laundering is through cryptocurrency. Dyntu and Dykyi (2018) state that the anonymity of the parties involved, easy access and the lack of a proper regulatory framework have encouraged the use of cryptocurrency for money laundering activities. Albrecht *et al.* (2019) identify the absence of intermediaries in cryptocurrency transactions as a major contributor to the rise in its popularity as a tool of money laundering. They further insist on strict Customer Due Diligence practices to discourage the improper use of cryptocurrency for money laundering. Blending cryptocurrency with money laundering ensures that only the technophiles understand such processes making it more difficult to trace and penalize money laundering.

Terrorism Financing

As per the UNODC (2022), terrorism financing encompasses various ways and means of securing funds for terrorist activities. The IMF identifies terrorism financing as an act of requesting, assembling, or supplying funds to assist terrorist acts or entities (IMF, 2000). The Asia/Pacific Group on Money Laundering defines terrorism financing as the funding of persons, acts and institutions associated with terrorism (APG, 2022). The numerous explanations about terrorism financing (Figure 2) can be narrowed down to a simple definition as any activity which directly or indirectly supports terrorism by collecting, transferring, or using funds.

Figure 2. Terrorism financing process
Source: Author

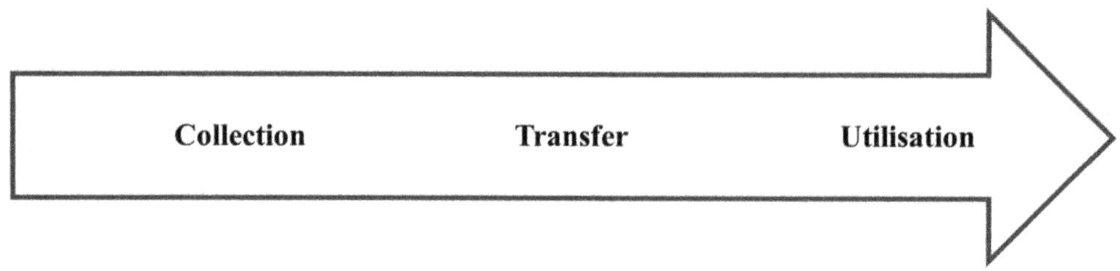

Terrorism financing has also evolved with time and modern methods are employed to gather funds for terrorism as well as to spread the concept of terrorism. Social media, cryptocurrency platforms, health and wellness websites and online gaming websites have been used to finance terrorism and to brainwash the users of such media, especially the young generation to spread the ideology of terrorism (IntelBrief, 2021). Further, terrorism trainings are also offered by terrorist organizations. Investigations into the Easter Sunday attack which took place in Sri Lanka on April 21, 2019, reveal that the suicide bombers had undergone training conducted by designated terrorist organizations abroad. The availability of such rigorous training programs using the latest arms and weapons indicates that a significantly large scale of funds is injected for the advancement of terrorism. Cyberterrorism is another concept that is spreading in the modern world where technology is exploited to attack information systems and databases of governments and government institutions (Wikipedia, 2023). Cyber terrorist activities are backed by political motives and try to instill terror among governments and people. However, as per the Global Terrorism Index (2022), the threat of terrorism financing has declined continuously and has recorded the lowest rate in 2021 after a considerable period.

ML/TF

The primary focus of money laundering is on the source of funds whereas the same of terrorism financing is on the use of funds. In the case of money laundering, the sources of funds are illicit, but the utilization of such funds may bring short-term benefits to the economy. During the integration stage of money laundering, such funds can be invested in construction projects such as hotels, and apartments and used to purchase automobiles and precious metals such as gems, and jewelry. However, what we must keep in mind is money laundering creates only a temporary boom in economic activities and will be followed by repercussions in the long run. The need for money laundering verily stems from the infinite greed for wealth and power and the absence of conscience of human beings. Once the money launderers taste the benefits of money laundering, there will be no end to it and that is the main reason why money laundering is a continuous process. This cycle must be broken because as per Stancu and Rece (2009), laundered money can be reinvested in illicit activities as well.

In the case of terrorism financing, the source of funds may either be legal or illegal. However, the ultimate use of such funds is always to commit the offence of terrorism. Terrorism financing is often felt by commoners more than money laundering due to the direct severe consequences resulting from it. Further, Kagan (2021) explains that there can be links between ML/TF because money generated from illegal sources (prior to laundering) and laundered money may be injected into terrorist activities and organizations. The possible link between ML/TF is shown in Figure 3.

Figure 3. ML/TFL link
Source: Author

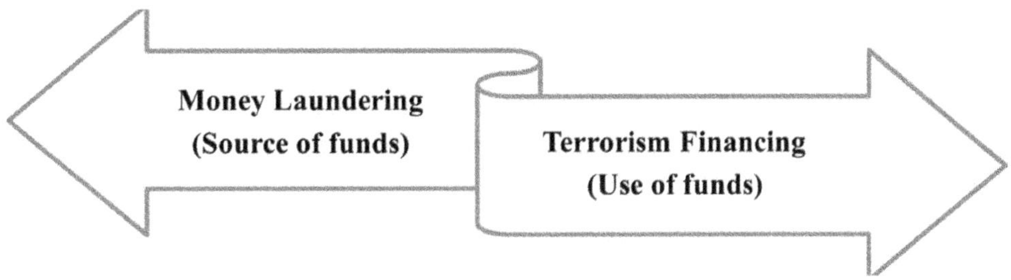

AML/CFT

A strong AML/CFT regime is mandatory for a country to ensure the smooth functioning of its economic activities as well as to maintain a good outlook on the world. Accordingly, there are several global institutions formed to make this world a better place to live. The FATF and the Basel Institute of Governance are two such institutions established for the purposes of formulating policies on AML/CFT as well as to give an indication of the level of exposure of countries to ML/TF risk.

The FATF is an intergovernmental body acting as a global policy setter for AML/CFT (FATF, 2022b). The FATF develops and issues recommendations with the objective of mitigating the ML/TF threat in the world. These recommendations must be followed by its member countries and any non-compliance will result in such countries entering their watch lists. Being included in watch lists will lead to grave consequences such as downgraded country ratings, discouraged foreign direct investments, reduced trade and finance offers and tourism, depreciated foreign exchange rates and depleted country reputation (Sharma, 2022).

The Basel Institute of Governance is another institution established to secure good governance in the world (BIG, 2022). This institution computes the Basel Anti-Money Laundering (AML) Index which assesses the degree of exposure of countries to ML/TF risk on a regional basis. The Basel AML Index 2021 pays particular attention to the weaknesses identified in several critical areas such as proper legislation covering cryptocurrencies, ultimate beneficial ownership records and designated non-financial businesses and professions which could lead to increased risks of ML/TF in countries (BIG, 2021). The findings of this report show that the European and North American regions have a relatively low exposure to the ML/TF risk while the Asian and African regions have a medium to high exposure to the ML/TF risk.

Transparency International is another global body operating with the mission of eliminating corruption and spreading transparency and integrity in the world. The Corruption Perceptions Index (CPI) is an outcome of this institution which is an indicator of the estimated level of public sector corruption of countries. CPI 2021 shows that since the previous year, the average level of corruption has remained the same across the world (TI, 2021).

ML/TF AND ECONOMIC PERFORMANCE OF DEVELOPING COUNTRIES

The UN and the World Bank classify countries on different bases to provide a better understanding of their economic and social performance. The UN classifies countries as developed and developing countries based on the Human Development Index (HDI) rating earned by each country. The World Bank classifies countries as low-income, lower middle-income, upper middle-income and high-income countries based on their Gross National Income level. The lower and upper middle-income countries under the World Bank classification and the developing countries under the UN classification can be treated in parallel. Currently, there are 100+ countries that have been classified as developing countries. Research studies show that the negative effects of ML/TF may be more damaging for developing countries than developed countries. This could be due to several reasons such as fragile AML/CFT regimes, illiterate population, delicate financial systems and a high tendency for corruption in developing countries (Sanction Scanner, 2020; Rafay, 2021b, 2023b). Reuter (2012) identifies inadequacies in the legal framework, low technological advancement and the existence of a large unregulated informal sector as factors encouraging high levels of money laundering in developing countries. Further, Javaid and Arshed (2021) identify two main factors namely high taxation on private sector profit and diversion of public funds that increase the demand for money laundering in developing countries.

To overcome these deficiencies, critical areas which support a country's overall development need to be strengthened. Accordingly, Vaithilingam and Nair (2007) identify the strength of the legal framework, technology, human capital, innovativeness and corporate governance as factors that slow down the level of penetration of money laundering. Strong AML/CFT regimes will bring loads of benefits to countries and will greatly stimulate their development in every aspect. Enhanced economic and financial stability, discouraged crimes, improved good governance and investor confidence attained by countries through a resilient AML/CFT regime will uplift them from developing status to developed status in the long run (Sanction Scanner, 2020).

AML/CFT REGIME IN THE CONTEXT OF SRI LANKA

Sri Lanka is currently ranked as a developing country by the UN and a lower middle-income country by the World Bank. Sri Lanka is also a founding member of the APG (1997) and was nominated as the APG co-chair for a two-year period 2016 - 2018 (FIU-SL, 2016). The AML/CFT regime of Sri Lanka is pillared by three acts (Figure 4) namely the Convention on the Suppression of Terrorist Financing Act, No. 25 of 2005 (CSTFA), Prevention of Money Laundering Act, No. 05 of 2006 (PMLA) and the Financial Transactions Reporting Act, No. 06 of 2006 (FTRA).

The Financial Intelligence Unit of Sri Lanka (FIU-SL) was established under the FTRA in 2006 as the central agency for combating ML/TF and predicate offences. It currently operates as an independent department attached to the Central Bank of Sri Lanka (CBSL). The FIU-SL refers analyzed Suspicious Transaction Reports (STRs) received from its Reporting Institutions on ML/TF to the relevant Law Enforcement Agencies (LEAs), issues guidelines and circulars and conducts awareness campaigns to mitigate the risk of ML/TF. Further, there have been 23 money laundering prosecutions and 3 money laundering convictions in Sri Lanka during the period 2015 – 2020 (FIU-SL, 2020).

Figure 4. AML/CFT regime of Sri Lanka
Source: Author

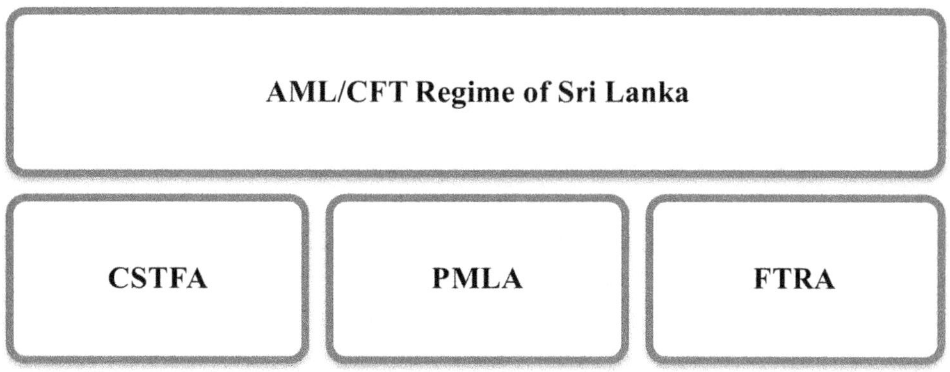

The National Risk Assessment (NRA) is a self-assessment undertaken by countries to assess its overall ML/TF risk and to formulate or upgrade the national AML/CFT regime. Sri Lanka conducted its last NRA in 2014 to formulate its national AML/CFT policy for the period 2015-2020. The overall ML/TF risk of the country was rated as Medium at the 2014 NRA and several key areas which needed significant improvements were also identified (FIU-SL, 2014). Sri Lanka commenced its second NRA in 2022 with the objective of upgrading its future AML/CFT regime.

The FIU-SL has gone through a rocky path with various challenges to its AML/CFT status. In 2017, Sri Lanka was subject to a review of the International Co-operation Review Group (ICRG) of the FATF and was listed as a jurisdiction with strategic AML/CFT deficiencies, commonly known as the grey list. Subsequently, the European Union (EU) also listed Sri Lanka in its list of High Risk Third Countries with AML/CFT deficiencies, referred to as the Blacklist, in February 2018. Upon bridging the deficiencies identified and fulfillment of the action plans given by the FATF and EU, Sri Lanka was delisted by the FATF from its Grey List in October 2019 (CBSL, 2019) and the EU delisted Sri Lanka from its Blacklist in May 2020 (CBSL, 2020).

The above details prove that ML/TF is a risk that affects the entire world. The past, present and future have been, are and will be vulnerable to this risk in varying degrees and the challenge faced by all countries is to mitigate such risk. A country's AML/CFT regime must be driven continuously with timely upgrades since this is a risk that cannot be underestimated due to its great evolving power. Accordingly, countries should join hands with both national as well as global authorities to take necessary steps to address the ML/TF risk through an effective AML/CFT regime to pave the way for a sustainable world.

METHODOLOGY

The selection of the sample, determination of the dependent and independent variables, extraction of the required statistics, the expectation of the outcome and descriptive statistics of this cross-sectional study are explained below.

Selection of the Sample

This cross-sectional study assessed the impact of the strength of the AML/CFT Regime on the economic performance of developing countries was performed across 50 developing countries. These 50 developing countries were selected after a three-step filtering process as given below.

1. The first step was to select the total list of developing countries. Since developing countries as per the UN are equivalent to the countries in the middle-income category as per the World Bank, the World Bank World Development Indicators (WDI, 2022) database was used to extract these details. Accordingly, a list of 110 countries was available which included 55 countries from the lower middle-income category and 55 countries from the upper middle-income category.
2. As the second step, the availability of the latest published Mutual Evaluation Reports (MERs) for the above list of developing countries was examined and it was noted that MERs for 60 developing countries were available.
3. The final step was to check the availability of the GDP annual growth rates of the relevant MER year concerning the above list of countries. This data was available in the World Bank WDI database only for the period 2015 – 2020. Accordingly, the sample size was finalized as 50 developing countries.

Determination of Variables

The dependent and independent variables of this research are given below.

Dependent variable: The dependent variable of this study is the Gross Domestic Product (GDP) annual growth rate of developing countries. GDP annual growth rate is a commonly used measure of the economic performance of countries. The GDP is the total value of goods and services produced within the domestic boundaries of a country during a given time period. The GDP annual growth rate is the depiction of the relative increase in the GDP when moving from one year to another year, as a percentage.

$$GDP\ Annual\ Growth\ Rate_{Y1} = GDP_{Y1} - GDP_{Y0} / GDP_{Y0}\ X\ 100$$

$_{Y1}$ = Current year

$_{Y0}$ = Previous year

Independent variables: The independent variables of this study are of two types as follows.

1) The AML/CFT Effectiveness Index (Jayasekara, 2021)

The AML/CFT Effectiveness Index is an indication of the strength of the AML/CFT regime of countries which is computed as a weighted average of the ratings earned for the level of effectiveness of the 11 Immediate Outcomes achieved by a country at a Mutual Evaluation.

2) The 11 Immediate Outcomes are used by the FATF to assess the effectiveness of the AML/CFT system of a country (FATF, 2021).

Since the AML/CFT Effectiveness Index is equivalent to the weighted summation of the 11 Immediate Outcomes, the independent variables were further broken down to encompass 11 more variables. Ratings given for each Immediate Outcome are low, moderate, substantial or high based on the degree of effectiveness attained by a country. The 11 immediate outcomes are listed in Table 2.

Extraction of Statistics

GDP Annual Growth Rate: For this analysis, the GDP annual growth rate relevant to the MER year of a particular country was used. All data were extracted from the World Bank WDI database (Table 3).

AML/CFT Effectiveness Index and Immediate Outcomes: The ratings attained for the effectiveness of the 11 Immediate Outcomes by each country were extracted from the latest published MER. To compute the AML.CFT Effectiveness Index, the 11 independent variables were assigned a weight based on the rating earned by them for their effectiveness in line with Jayasekara (2021) as given in Table 4. The AML/CFT Effectiveness Index values have been computed for the selected list of countries as given in Table 5.

Expectations of the Outcome

A positive relationship is expected between the AML/CFT Effectiveness Index as well as each of the 11 immediate outcomes with the GDP annual growth rates since the greater the strength of the AML/CFT regime, the greater shall be the economic performance of developing countries. The impact of the strength of the AML/CFT Regime on the economic performance of developing countries is assessed using the following model.

$$\log(EP) = \beta_1 \log(EI)$$

Where:

EP = Economic Performance (measured in terms of the GDP annual growth rate)
EI = AML/CFT Effectiveness Index

And

$$\log(EP) = \log(IOn)$$

Where:

EP = Economic Performance (measured in terms of the GDP annual growth rate)
IOn = Immediate Outcomes (n=1 to 11)

DESCRIPTIVE STATISTICS

Eviews statistical tool was used to derive the descriptive statistics as given in Table 6. These values have been calculated based on the original values of the variables considered for this empirical study. However, the negative GDP growth rates have been replaced by the median value of the EP variable (Table 3).

EMPIRICAL ANALYSIS

The empirical results of this study showed that a positive non-significant relationship exists between the GDP annual growth rate and the AML/CFT Effectiveness Index as well as with eight Immediate Outcomes. However, three Immediate Outcomes resulted in a negative non-significant relationship with the GDP annual growth rate (Table 7).

OVERALL EFFECTS ON DEVELOPING COUNTRIES

The results of this study prove that the strength of the AML/CFT regime of a country is indeed a positive influence on the economic performance of developing countries. However, the non-significance of this relationship suggests that the AML/CFT regime imposes a positive but indirect effect on a country's economy. The implementation of a strong AML/CFT regime will not merely bring about a good performance of the economy. Instead, necessary steps should be taken to direct the benefits received from the proper application of AML/CFT practices toward developing the economy.

On one hand, strong AML/CFT practices will ensure that money is generated from ethical sources. On the other hand, it also ensures that funds are used for ethical activities. However, the mere ethical generation of funds is not sufficient for the growth of an economy. Instead, such money must be both efficiently and effectively used to enhance production and service provision in the country. At the same time, clean money should not be wasted by allocating it to non-feasible and unproductive activities.

However, the GDP annual growth rate indicates the existence of a negative non-significant relationship with three Immediate Outcomes (IO6, IO8 and IO9 in Table 2). IO6 emphasizes the importance of capitalizing financial intelligence and all other relevant information by relevant LEAs when conducting ML/TF investigations. Even though ML/TF investigations done by LEAs receive the fullest support in terms of knowledge and expertise, if the positive outcomes of such investigations are wasted, it will both delay and deny growth in economic performance. As per IO8, proceeds and instrumentalities of crime need to be properly confiscated. This is of utmost importance to break the cycle of ML/TF since proceeds of crime may continuously pump ML/TF activities. However, the confiscated assets must be efficiently used without wasting or misusing them. IO9 which is about investigating terrorist financing offences and activities and prosecuting persons who finance terrorism while subjecting to effective, proportionate and dissuasive sanctions will ensure TF activities are discouraged. Sanction lists also indicate that TF-related activities are constantly under surveillance. However, prosecutions and sanction list alone will not support the economy.

EFFECTS ON SRI LANKA

The GDP annual growth rate of Sri Lanka during the mutual evaluation year was 5.00% (Table 3) and the AML/CFT Effectiveness Index value earned was 31.82 (Table 5). When scrutinizing the individual ratings earned for each Immediate Outcome (Table 8), a low rating has been earned for a majority. It shows that Sri Lanka needs significant improvement in many areas. However, from 2015 to 2022, Sri Lanka has taken many steps to strengthen its AML/CFT regime which is evident from the Follow-Up Reports issued. Sri Lanka has also undertaken the NRA at present with great confidence understanding the need for continuous execution and upgrade of the AML/CFT regime.

CONCLUSION

Scrutiny of literature, news, laws and indices shows that the prevention of ML/TF positively affects an economy. Money laundering may bring alluring benefits in the short-run but will pave the way to the downfall of good governance and ethics of a country in the long-run. This in return will adversely affect the country's economic performance. Even if funds are generated through legal means, if its use supports offences such as terrorism financing, again the country will suffer. The results of this study proved that the strength of the AML/CFT regime, measured in terms of the AML/CFT Effectiveness Index, has a positive effect on the economic performance, measured in terms of the GDP annual growth rate, of developing countries. The steps taken to develop the AML/CFT regime will indirectly boost the growth of the economy. Therefore, the benefits reaped from well-established AML/CFT practices must be effectively directed toward the betterment of the people and society.

LIMITATIONS AND RESEARCH GAPS

The limitations faced and research gaps identified when conducting this study are given below.

1. The latest MERs of several developing countries had been published in 2021 and 2022. However, such countries were not considered in this study due to the unavailability of the GDP annual growth rates for those years.
2. This research used data given only in the latest MERs and no Follow-Up Reports were considered.
3. Only one variable i.e., GDP annual growth rate was used to assess the economic performance of developing countries. The author encourages future researchers to use multiple variables to arrive at a more informed and comprehensive outcome.

DECLARATION

The author declares that the manuscript follows ethical standards and there are no potential conflicts of interest with respect to the research, authorship and/or publication of this chapter.

DISCLAIMER

The contents and views of this chapter are expressed by the author in personal capacity. It is not necessary for the Editor and the Publisher to agree with these viewpoints, and they are not responsible for any duty of care in this regard.

ACKNOWLEDGMENT

The author extends sincere gratitude to

- The Editor and the International Editorial Advisory Board (IEAB) of this book who initially desk reviewed, arranged a rigorous double/triple blind review process, and conducted a thorough, minute, and critical final review before accepting the chapter for publication.
- All anonymous reviewers who provided very constructive feedbacks for thorough revision, improvement, extension, and fine tuning of the chapter.
- All colleagues, assistants and well-wishers who assisted to complete this task.

REFERENCES

Albrecht, C., Duffin, K. M., Hawkins, S., & Morales Rocha, V. M. (2019). The use of cryptocurrencies in the money laundering process. *Journal of Money Laundering Control*, *22*(2), 210–216. doi:10.1108/JMLC-12-2017-0074

APG. (1997). *Members & Observers - Sri Lanka*. Asia Pacific Group. http://www.apgml.org/members-and-observers/members/details.aspx ?m=ff29a4ed-30d0-416b-a234-39aa780a2c9f

APG. (2022). *What is mone laudering*. Asia Pacific Group. http://www.apgml.org/about-us/page.aspx?p=5620f71b-1858-4ca1-85d7-f9eae97210a7

BIG. (2021). *Basel AML Index 2021*. Basel Institute of Governance. https://baselgovernance.org/publications/basel-aml-index-2021

BIG. (2022). *About us*. Basel Institute of Governance. https://baselgovernance.org/about-us

CBSL. (2019, October 21). *The Financial Action Task Force delisted Sri Lanka from the grey list*. Central Bank of Sri Lanka. https://www.cbsl.gov.lk/en/node/6701#:~:text=The%20Financial%20Action%20Task%20Force%20(FATF)%2C%20the%20global%20policy,as%20%E2%80%9Cthe%20Grey%20List%E2%80%9D

CBSL. (2020, May 12). *Delisting of Sri Lanka by the Eropean Commission from its list of high risk 3rd countries*. Central Bank of Sri Lanka. https://www.cbsl.gov.lk/en/news/delisting-of-sri-lanka-by-european-commission-from-its-list-of-high-risk-3rd-countries

Dyntu, V., & Dykyi, O. (2018). Cryptocurrency in the system of money laundering. *Baltic Journal of Economic Studies*, *4*(5), 75–81. doi:10.30525/2256-0742/2018-4-5-75-81

EC. (2022). *Money Laundering*. European Commission. European Commiccion. https://ec.europa.eu/home-affairs/policies/internal-security/organised-crime-and-human-trafficking/money-laundering_en#:~:text=EU%20legal%20measures%20against%20money,it%20through%20law%20enforcement%20response

FATF. (2021, October). *FATF Methodology for assessing compliance with the FATF Recommendations and the effectiveness of AML/CFT systems*. Financial Action Task Force. https://www.fatf-gafi.org/publications/mutualevaluations/ documents/fatf-methodology.html

FATF. (2022a). *Frequently asked questions*. Financial Action Task Force. https://www.fatf-gafi.org/en/pages/frequently-asked-questions.html

FATF. (2022b). *About*. Financial Action Task Force. Retrieved fom https://www.fatf-gafi.org/about/

FIU-SL. (2014). *National Risk Assessment Report*. Financial Intelligence Unit of Sri Lanka Central Bank of Sri Lanka. https://fiu.gov.sl/reports/national-risk-assessment-report-nra-report/

FIU-SL. (2016). *APG Co-Chair (for 2016-2018) acceptance speech by Director of the Financial Intelligence Unit of Sri Lanka*. Financial Intelligence Unit of Sri Lanka Central Bank of Sri Lanka. FIU-SL: http://www.fiusrilanka.gov.lk/docs/Other/APG_Co-Chair_Acceptance_Speech.pdf

FIU-SL. (2020). *FIU-SL Annual Report*. Financial Intelligence Unit of Sri Lanka Central Bank of Sri Lanka. https://fiu.gov.sl/reports/annual-reports/

IMF. (2000). *Anti-money laundering/combating the financing of terrorism (AML/CFT)*. International Monetary Fund. https://www.imf.org/external/np/leg/amlcft/eng/aml1.htm#:~:text=Terrorist% 20financing%20involves%20the%20solicitation,both%20legal%20and%20illicit%20sources.

IntelBrief. (2021, March 12). *Emerging terrorist financing threats and trends*. The Sofan Center. IntelBrief: https://thesoufancenter.org/intelbrief-2021-march-12/

Interpol. (2022). *Fighting money laundering goes hand in hand with investigating the crimes it is linked to*. Interpol. https://www.interpol.int/en/Crimes/Financial-crime/Money-laundering#:~:text=Money%20laundering%20is%20concealing%20or, drug%20trafficking%2C%20robbery%20or%20extortion.

Javaid, A., & Arshed, N. (2022). Demand for money laundering in developing countries and its deterrence: A quantitative analysis. *Journal of Money Laundering Control, 25*(3), 625–636. doi:10.1108/JMLC-06-2021-0063

Jayasekara, S. D. (2021). How effective are the current global standards in combating money laundering and terrorist financing? *Journal of Money Laundering Control, 24*(2), 257–267. doi:10.1108/JMLC-05-2020-0047

Kagan, J. (2021, July 25). *Combating the Financing of Terrorism (CFT) Definition* Investopedia. *Investiopedia*. https://www.investopedia.com/terms/c/combating-financing-terrorism-cft.asp

Kyckr. (2022, February 3). *AML Fines 2021*. Kyckr. https://www.kyckr.com/aml-fines-2021/

Rafay, A. (Ed.). (2021a). *Money Laundering and Terrorism Financing in Global Financial Systems*. IGI Global., doi:10.4018/978-1-7998-8758-4

Rafay, A. (Ed.). (2021b). *HandBook of Research on Theory and Practice of Financial Crimes*. IGI Global., doi:10.4018/978-1-7998-5567-5

Rafay, A. (Ed.). (2023a). *Concepts, Cases, and Regulations in Financial Fraud and Corruption*. IGI Global., doi:10.4018/978-1-6684-5007-9

Rafay, A. (Ed.). (2023b). *Concepts and Cases of Illicit Finance*. IGI Global., doi:10.4018/978-1-6684-8587-3

Reuter, P. (2012). *Draining development?: Controlling flows of illicit funds from developing countries* (Report 66815). The World Bank. https://documents1.worldbank.org/curated/en/305601468178737192/text/668150PUB0EPI0067848B09780821388693.txt

Sanction Scanner. (2020). *Effects of money laundering on development*. Sanction Scanner. https://sanctionscanner.com/blog/effects-of-money-laundering-on-development-291

Sharma, R. (2022). *Grey List*. EDUCBA. https://www.educba.com/grey-list/

Stancu, I., & Rece, D. (2009). The Relationship between economic growth and money laundering—a Linear Regression Model. *Theoretical & Applied Economics*, *16*(9), 1–8.

TI. (2021). *Corruption perceptions index*. Transparency International: https://www.transparency.org/en/cpi/2021

UNODC. (1988). *United Nations Convention against Illicit Traffic in Narcotics Drugs and Psychotropic Substances*. United Nations Office on Drugs and Crimes. https://www.unodc.org/unodc/en/treaties/illicit-trafficking.html

UNODC. (2011). *Money Laudering*. United Nations Office on Drugs and Crimes. https://www.unodc.org/unodc/en/money-laundering/overview.html

UNODC. (2022). *Combatting Terrorist Financing*. United Nations Office on Drugs and Crimes. https://www.unodc.org/unodc/en/terrorism/expertise /combating-terrorist-financing.html

Vaithilingam, S., & Nair, M. (2007). Factors affecting money laundering: Lesson for developing countries. *Journal of Money Laundering Control*, *10*(3), 352–366. doi:10.1108/13685200710763506

WDI. (2022). *Data Bank: World Development Indicators*. The World Bank. https://databank.worldbank.org/source/world-development-indicators

Wikipedia. (2023). *Cyberterrorism*. https://en.wikipedia.org/wiki/Cyberterrorism

APPENDIX

Table 2.

IO No.	IO
IO1	Money laundering and terrorist financing risks are understood and, where appropriate, actions coordinated domestically to combat money laundering and the financing of terrorism and proliferation.
IO2	International cooperation delivers appropriate information, financial intelligence, and evidence, and facilitates action against criminals and their assets.
IO3	Supervisors appropriately supervise, monitor and regulate financial institutions, DNFBPs and VASPs for compliance with AML/CFT requirements commensurate with their risks.
IO4	Financial institutions, DNFBPs and VASPs adequately apply AML/CFT preventive measures commensurate with their risks, and report suspicious transactions.
IO5	Legal persons and arrangements are prevented from misuse for money laundering or terrorist financing, and information on their beneficial ownership is available to competent authorities without impediments.
IO6	Financial intelligence and all other relevant information are appropriately used by competent authorities for money laundering and terrorist financing investigations.
IO7	Money laundering offences and activities are investigated, and offenders are prosecuted and subject to effective, proportionate and dissuasive sanctions.
IO8	The proceeds and instrumentalities of crime are confiscated.
IO9	Terrorist financing offences and activities are investigated and persons who finance terrorism are prosecuted and subject to effective, proportionate and dissuasive sanctions.
IO10	Terrorists, terrorist organisations and terrorist financiers are prevented from raising, moving and using funds, and from abusing the NPO sector.
IO11	Persons and entities involved in the proliferation of weapons of mass destruction are prevented from raising, moving and using funds, consistent with the relevant UNSCRs.

Source: FATF Methodology (2013)

Table 3.

No.	Country	MER Year	GDP Annual Growth Rate	No.	Country	MER Year	GDP Annual Growth Rate
1	Albania	2018	4.00	26	Mauritius	2018	3.80
2	Armenia	2015	3.20	27	Mexico	2018	2.20
3	Bangladesh	2019	8.20	28	Moldova	2019	3.70
4	Belarus	2019	1.40	29	Mongolia	2017	5.60
5	Bhutan	2016	8.10	30	Morocco	2019	2.60
6	Botswana	2017	4.00	31	Myanmar	2018	6.40
7	Cabo Verde	2019	5.70	32	Nicaragua	2017	4.60
8	Cambodia	2017	7.00	33	Pakistan	2019	1.10
9	China	2019	5.90	34	Panama	2018	3.70
10	Colombia	2015	3.00	35	Peru	2019	2.20
11	Costa Rica	2015	3.70	36	Philippines	2019	6.10
12	Cuba	2015	4.40	37	Russian Federation	2019	2.00
13	Dominican Republic	2018	7.00	38	Samoa	2015	4.30
14	Fiji	2016	2.40	39	Senegal	2018	6.20
15	Georgia	2020	3.75 *(Initial -6.80)*	40	Serbia	2016	3.30
16	Ghana	2018	6.20	41	Solomon Islands	2019	1.20
17	Guatemala	2016	2.70	42	Sri Lanka	2015	5.00
18	Haiti	2019	3.75 *(Initial -1.70)*	43	Tajikistan	2018	7.60
19	Honduras	2016	3.90	44	Thailand	2017	4.20
20	Indonesia	2018	5.20	45	Tunisia	2016	1.10
21	Jamaica	2017	1.00	46	Turkey	2019	0.90
22	Jordan	2019	2.00	47	Ukraine	2017	2.40
23	Kyrgyz Republic	2018	3.80	48	Vanuatu	2015	0.40
24	Malaysia	2015	5.10	49	Zambia	2019	1.40
25	Mauritania	2018	4.50	50	Zimbabwe	2016	0.80

Source: World Bank World Development Indicators (WDI, 2022)

Table 4.

Level of Effectiveness	Assigned Weight
High	4
Substantial	3
Moderate	2
Low	1

Source: Jayasekara (2021)

Table 5.

No.	Country	EI	No.	Country	EI
1	Albania	50.00	26	Mauritius	34.09
2	Armenia	59.09	27	Mexico	52.27
3	Bangladesh	47.73	28	Moldova	54.55
4	Belarus	59.09	29	Mongolia	29.55
5	Bhutan	29.55	30	Morocco	45.45
6	Botswana	29.55	31	Myanmar	27.27
7	Cabo Verde	25.00	32	Nicaragua	45.45
8	Cambodia	36.36	33	Pakistan	27.27
9	China	47.73	34	Panama	47.73
10	Colombia	52.27	35	Peru	54.55
11	Costa Rica	45.45	36	Philippines	38.64
12	Cuba	61.36	37	Russian Federation	68.18
13	Dominican Republic	52.27	38	Samoa	43.18
14	Fiji	38.64	39	Senegal	27.27
15	Georgia	52.27	40	Serbia	43.18
16	Ghana	38.64	41	Solomon Islands	31.82
17	Guatemala	59.09	42	Sri Lanka	31.82
18	Haiti	25.00	43	Tajikistan	52.27
19	Honduras	54.55	44	Thailand	52.27
20	Indonesia	59.09	45	Tunisia	36.36
21	Jamaica	38.64	46	Turkey	50.00
22	Jordan	45.45	47	Ukraine	52.27
23	Kyrgyz Republic	45.45	48	Vanuatu	25.00
24	Malaysia	59.09	49	Zambia	45.45
25	Mauritania	25.00	50	Zimbabwe	29.55

Source: Computations by the Author

Table 6.

Variable	Mean	Median	Maximum	Minimum	Std. Dev.
EP	3.534000	3.750000	8.200000	-6.800000	2.645258
EI	43.63636	45.45455	68.18182	25.00000	11.69733
IO_1	1.980000	2.000000	3.000000	1.000000	0.742033
IO_2	1.640000	2.000000	3.000000	1.000000	0.692820
IO_3	1.660000	2.000000	3.000000	1.000000	0.557326
IO_4	1.620000	2.000000	3.000000	1.000000	0.567486
IO_5	1.420000	1.000000	3.000000	1.000000	0.609114
IO_6	1.980000	2.000000	4.000000	1.000000	0.714000
IO_7	1.480000	1.000000	3.000000	1.000000	0.543609
IO_8	1.800000	2.000000	4.000000	1.000000	0.808122
IO_9	1.980000	2.000000	4.000000	1.000000	0.868731
IO_{10}	1.640000	2.000000	3.000000	1.000000	0.692820
IO_{11}	1.400000	1.000000	3.000000	1.000000	0.699854

Source: EViews based on original values

Table 7.

Variable (log form)	Coefficient	Std. Error	t-Statistic	Prob.
EI	0.146101	0.341676	0.427602	0.6709
IO_1	0.002463	0.236651	0.010408	0.9917
IO_2	0.111449	0.259824	0.428940	0.6699
IO_3	0.009755	0.272195	0.035837	0.9716
IO_4	0.044911	0.267215	0.168070	0.8672
IO_5	0.115698	0.258353	0.447827	0.6563
IO_6	-0.030155	0.252992	-0.119194	0.9056
IO_7	0.027832	0.271549	0.102493	0.9188
IO_8	-0.062190	0.218021	-0.285248	0.7767
IO_9	-0.241686	0.205250	1.177524	0.2448
IO_{10}	0.123854	0.235802	0.525246	0.6018
IO_{11}	0.013667	0.241411	0.056615	0.9551

Source: EViews

Table 8.

IO No.	Rating
IO1	2
IO2	1
IO3	1
IO4	1
IO5	1
IO6	1
IO7	1
IO8	1
IO9	3
IO10	1
IO11	1

Chapter 8
Electricity Theft, Regulatory Quality, and the Rule of Law:
A Cross-Country Analysis

Gamze Kargın-Akkoç
Ankara Yıldırım Beyazıt University, Turkey

Fuat Oğuz
Ankara Yıldırım Beyazıt University, Turkey

ABSTRACT

This study analyzes empirical outcomes to understand the causal linkages between the rule of law, regulatory quality, and electricity theft in regulated industries. It provides a brief and explicit theoretical framework on the rule of law and its impact on electricity theft, using panel data for income groups. When the rule of law is not well established, poor governance in the regulatory process leads to larger social and economic costs associated with electricity theft. The analysis demonstrates that the rule of law has a uni-directional causality effect on transmission and distribution losses across all income groups. In the upper-middle and low-income panels, transmission and distribution losses granger cause regulatory quality, while this relationship cannot be validated in the high and lower-middle-income samples. These findings highlight the significance of the rule of law in reducing electricity theft by emphasizing regulatory quality as a transmission channel.

INTRODUCTION

The connection between economic growth and electricity consumption is widely tested in empirical studies. The institutional framework of a country and energy efficiency underlie the growth-electricity nexus. Electricity losses are widely considered one of the important factors that harm energy efficiency, distort competition, and increase social and economic costs of end-users or distribution companies (Ozturk, 2010; Payne, 2010; Omri, 2014; Tiba & Omri, 2017).

DOI: 10.4018/979-8-3693-1190-5.ch008

Electricity losses refer to the difference between generated and delivered electricity. It takes two basic forms as technical and non-technical losses. Technical losses generally occur in the transmission grid due to the characteristics of the network, such as geography, transportation, length of lines, and the quality of the grid. Technical losses cannot be eliminated fully in the current technological environment. These losses fluctuate around 6 to 8 percent for transmission and distribution networks (Jimenez *et al.*, 2014)[1]. Any losses beyond this level are considered non-technical losses or pilferage[2].

Non-technical losses can also be named financial losses for electricity companies. Because, these types of losses include non-payment bills, energy theft, energy fraud, billing errors, and other kinds which induce revenue losses. According to studies estimates, the cost of electricity theft and fraud is as much as USD101.2 billion across 138 countries (Northeast-Group, 2021). A major component of non-technical losses is electricity theft. The economic cost of electricity theft reaches high levels in both developing and developed countries[3]. Even if illegal usage is limited in developed countries, the size of total consumption makes it an important social problem when compared to the costs of other illegal activities. For example, Ofgem (2014) estimates that the cost of electricity theft in the UK is around £ 250 million annually. In Canada, illegal drug producers use substantial amounts of illegal electricity, and electricity theft reaches high levels[4]. In the USA, the cost of electricity theft and fraud is USD6 billion in 2020.[5]

In developing countries, illegal usage of electricity rates is much higher. Countries such as India, Pakistan, Bangladesh, and Latin American countries do particularly have very high electricity theft levels. For example, the cost of electricity theft is estimated at USD16.2 billion in India[6]. Brazil and Russia also suffer from illegal usage. Half of Latin America and the Caribbean countries' losses are approximately 20%, and it costs almost USD 15 billion (Jimenez *et al.*, 2014). The annual worldwide economic cost of non-technical electricity losses is estimated to be around USD 100 billion (Glauner *et al.*, 2018).

Illegal electricity usage is not considered a major criminal issue in the developing world (Min & Golden, 2014; Joseph, 2010). As an example, electricity theft in Türkiye is accepted as a social issue rather than a strictly criminal one (Yurtseven, 2015). Governments in these countries tend to use the term 'illegal use of electricity' rather than calling it 'theft.' In many developing countries, illegal use is usually tolerated by governments, and society usually overlooks the issue as a social problem (Smith, 2004; Depuru *et al.*, 2011).

Electricity theft has both economic and social ramifications. On the one hand, unbilled consumption reduces revenues (Arango *et al.*, 2017), worsens energy efficiency (Cubbin & Stern, 2006; Jamil, 2013; Yurtseven, 2015), and slows down investments (Jamil & Ahmed, 2010; Lewis, 2015). On the other hand, governments may use it as a subsidy mechanism for political opportunism during electoral cycles[7]. Illegal use increases carbon emissions and causes environmental degradation[8], or promotes other illegal activities[9]. Generally, the use of regulatory policy for social policy goals weakens the belief in the rule of law in society. Since social issues should be dealt with by social policies, indirect methods to subsidize some groups in society create the problem of identification of the correct groups, and waste resources (Cooter & Ulen, 2016). Besides, being an economic, governance, or monitoring problem there is another aspect of high electricity losses. These losses threaten the financial sustainability of the electricity or energy industry considerably.

In this study, we take our cue from the fact that institutional endowments of economies have a significant impact on energy efficiency and electricity theft. Institutions are structures that link political, social, and economic interactions, and these components are formed by formal and informal rules. While formal rules include law, property rights, etc., informal rules are about norms, sanctions, taboos, customs, and so on (North, 1991). Numerous studies show the importance of institutional quality on economic performance (Knack & Keefer, 1995; Rodrik, 2000; Dollar & Kraay, 2003; Glaeser *et al.*, 2004). In this context, it is investigated whether it can be traced the effect of institutions, more specifically the rule of law, in electricity regulation and illegal electricity usage. This study seeks to explain the causal linkages of institutional and regulatory endowment with electricity theft, which mostly occur because of poor governance, lack of institutions and the rule of law, and regulatory capture that harms the efficiency of the regulatory process in the electricity industry.

The starting point of this chapter is to clarify how to understand the implications of the rule of law in regulated industries. If an institutional capability has an effective role in the development of a country, can a similar impact also emerge in a regulated industry? The dearth of empirical studies that connect the rule of law to the regulatory policy was the impetus for this chapter. The aim of the study is to follow the institutional linkages between the rule of law and electricity theft.

It is assumed that improvements in the rule of law and regulatory quality lead to lower electricity theft. Accordingly, the purpose of this study is to determine whether the illegal use of electricity affects the individual's compliance with the rules, institutional capacities, and regulatory quality. It is claimed that electricity theft is closely related to the deterioration of regulatory quality and the rule of law. The chapter begins with a brief discussion of the meaning of the rule of law and its connection with regulation and electricity theft. Then panel Granger causality is applied to present the empirical evidence on the relation between the rule of law, regulatory quality, and electricity theft in the third section. The fourth section presents the empirical findings. It is offered a discussion in the fifth section and concludes the chapter.

BACKGROUND: THE RULE OF LAW, REGULATION AND ELECTRICITY THEFT

The connection between the rule of law and economic growth shows the importance of the rule of law for the effectiveness of complex structures such as social, economic, and regulatory effects (Dam, 2007). In this context, the effectiveness of regulations and institutions are directly related. The rule of law ensures the existence of effective regulations (Berg & Desai, 2013). In a major study, Rigobon and Rodrik (2005) examine the relationship between economic institutions, democracy, openness, and income. They link political institutions and economic institutions to the rule of law. In this sense, the connection between separate institutions plays a more significant role than individual parts of a rule of law system (Acemoglu & Johnson, 2005), especially in developing countries. In this way, the rule of law has begun to be seen as a "cluster' of institutions. Previous empirical studies support the assumption that the rule of law, as an equilibrium or cluster of institutions, has a significant effect on the economy in developed countries. In other words, economic performance is found to be mainly driven by the rule of law (Law *et al.*, 2013).

The Rule of Law and Regulation

While the concept of the rule of law goes back to Aristotle, its modern evolution started with Albert Dicey and culminated with Friedrich A. Hayek's work (Bingham, 2011). In its simplest definition, the existence of the rule of law requires everybody in society, including those who wield government powers, to be bound by the same set of rules. These rules should be made publicly accessible to everybody, and predictable.

Some authors add a dynamic dimension to the concept. The sustainability of the rule of law, in the long run, is accepted as an element of the rule of law system (Hadfield & Weingast, 2014). During the implementation of regulatory reforms, the sustainability of the rule of law plays a central role. The existence of the rule of law reduces government opportunism and regulatory capture in regulated industries. The independence of regulatory authorities can be seen as an indicator of the rule of law in regulated industries. Cubbin and Stern (2006) characterize the rule of law as a formal requirement to establish good governance of regulatory systems. In countries where the rule of law has been established, it is assumed that the judiciary is relatively independent, and everyone is treated equally before the law. This assumption is held for regulatory authorities and other institutions of regulated industries (Hanretty & Koop, 2013).

The rule of law from an economic perspective refers to governance and focuses on the regulatory process. As infrastructure industries include a wide range of users with conflicting interests, the pricing and provision mechanisms are vulnerable to political and economic interventions. Some studies link the rule of law as a high-quality institution and regulatory independence, governance, or reforms for different infrastructure industries (Stern & Holder, 1999), especially in electricity (Cubbin & Stern, 2006; Erdogdu, 2014) and telecommunication (Levy & Spiller, 1994; Gual & Trillas, 2006).

The right institutional framework in the regulatory process brings about stabilization and legitimization to infrastructure industries (Rodrik *et al.*, 2004). Levy and Spiller (1994) state that different institutional endowments create a divergence in regulatory processes. They categorize the countries according to the quality of their institutional endowments. Where the institutional endowment is high, the regulatory system would be well-organized and restrict arbitrary behaviors. Regulations take the rule of law for granted. Such countries would manage the tension to provide some flexibility which could damage credible commitment within the process. The opposite situation may arise in low-income countries that do not have any institutions maintaining credible commitment.

The Rule of Law and Electricity Theft

Non-technical losses in the electricity system occur in one of the following ways. To begin with, customers may try to deceive the distribution company deliberately. Tampering with the meter is a widely used method to reduce electricity bills. A second method is to steal electricity from the power line. The third way of theft is not paying bills. Customers may accumulate their debts to utilities. Both households and businesses may defer their payments and create costs for the distribution companies. These methods support each other. Non-paying users may start to tamper with meters or steal directly from the grid. These behaviors are closely related to the level of the rule of law and the effectiveness of regulation.

The rule of law may influence illegal use through two separate channels: the state's impartiality and the transaction cost of non-economic pricing. When the state loses its impartiality on electricity theft, the whole society pays the price (Smith, 2004; Lewis, 2015). When electricity theft goes unpunished, this encourages more illegal activity, creating a slippery slope toward more avoidance of the rules in general. Since there is no market price for electricity theft, society pays a higher price for illegal use, as it involves deadweight losses and inefficient pricing because of high monitoring and enforcement costs. As non-technical losses are increasingly connected with some form of illegal use, international organizations such as the World Bank have begun to monitor them more closely.

Electricity theft is a crucial issue, both for developed and developing countries. While it has been regarded as criminal activity in developed countries, developing countries are tackling it mostly as a social issue. The problem is usually related to the lack of institutions, regulatory failures, political opportunism, and socioeconomic factors. The empirical studies generally focus on the determinants of electricity theft. For example, Gaur and Gupta (2016) and Yurtseven (2015) examine the determinants of electricity theft in India and Türkiye, respectively. They both find socioeconomic factors such as education, income, and rural population affect the loss ratios for these countries. Also, some studies (Jamil, 2013; Lewis, 2015) examine the cost of theft on electricity efficiency, tariff, and outages. Many recent studies stress that the presence of inefficient regulatory reforms leads to higher theft and losses in developing countries (Taşdöven *et al.*, 2012; Winther, 2012; Kessides, 2012). Nepal and Jamasb (2015) examine Nepal and Belarus. Their research indicates that the delay of independent regulatory agencies causes regulatory failure in the sense of electricity theft.

Most of the studies on illegal electricity usage find that poor governance results in higher levels of theft besides socioeconomic factors (Smith, 2004; Min & Golden, 2014; Steadman, 2011). Min and Golden (2014) and Baskaran *et al.* (2015) examine the relationship between electoral cycles and electricity theft in India. They state that fighting electricity theft has political costs for governments. This creates a public choice problem. The government may spread the cost to society, as the cost per person in society stays low. Still, the benefits for illegal users remain high enough to encourage them to continue theft (Bazilian *et al.*, 2014). They see illegal use as a victimless crime. In this sense, the rule of law and the role of institutions become significant. Never (2015) indicates that electricity theft is not a technical problem; it is closely associated with social norms, trust, and awareness. Similarly, Ullah *et al.* (2017) dwell on the institutional determinants of energy governance. Consequently, formal and informal laws, regulations, social norms, and institutions are closely related to electricity theft.

DATA AND METHODOLOGY

It is examined the relationship between the rule of law and electricity theft by using three indicators. The annual data of the study covers the period 1996 to 2014 for 64 countries from different parts and income levels of the world. To measure the rule of law and regulatory quality, we use the WGI. It is utilized the percentile rank that shows each country's position compared to others ranging between 0-100. While 0 indicates the lowest rank, 100 indicates the highest rank among countries (Kaufmann *et al.*, 2011). To quantify electricity theft, the transmission and distribution losses (% of output) are employed from the World Bank database, which includes our focal point pilferage, in our words "theft."

It is examined the causality relationship between the transmission and distribution losses (TDLOSS), the regulatory quality (RQ), and the rule of law (RL) in four different groups of countries following the World Bank classification. Accordingly, the panel data framework is utilized for each group of income levels named high-income countries, upper-middle-income countries, lower-middle-income countries, and low-income countries. A list of the country groups can be found in Appendix A. Figure 1 shows that TDLOSS tends to decrease in middle-income countries, but low-income countries have experienced surging losses. While RQ and RL are higher in the high-income group, and TDLOSS decreases as income rises. RQ and RL have noticeable decreases in low- and high-income groups.

According to Figure 1, it is seen that the electricity T&D losses differ across income groups significantly. For example, while the average of 1996-2014 in high-income countries is about 8%, this rate is 23.5% in low-income countries. Although the upper-middle and lower-middle-income groups show similar rates (11% and 16%, respectively), when it is evaluated all groups together, it is evident that the losses decrease as the income increases. Considering that technical losses that arise in any case may fluctuate between 1% and 12% depending on the efficiency of the networks, it can be said that non-technical losses (or electricity theft) are higher in lower-income groups.

Figure 1. The trend of variables for income groups
Notes: Red lines that represent the TDLOSS correspond to the second axes.

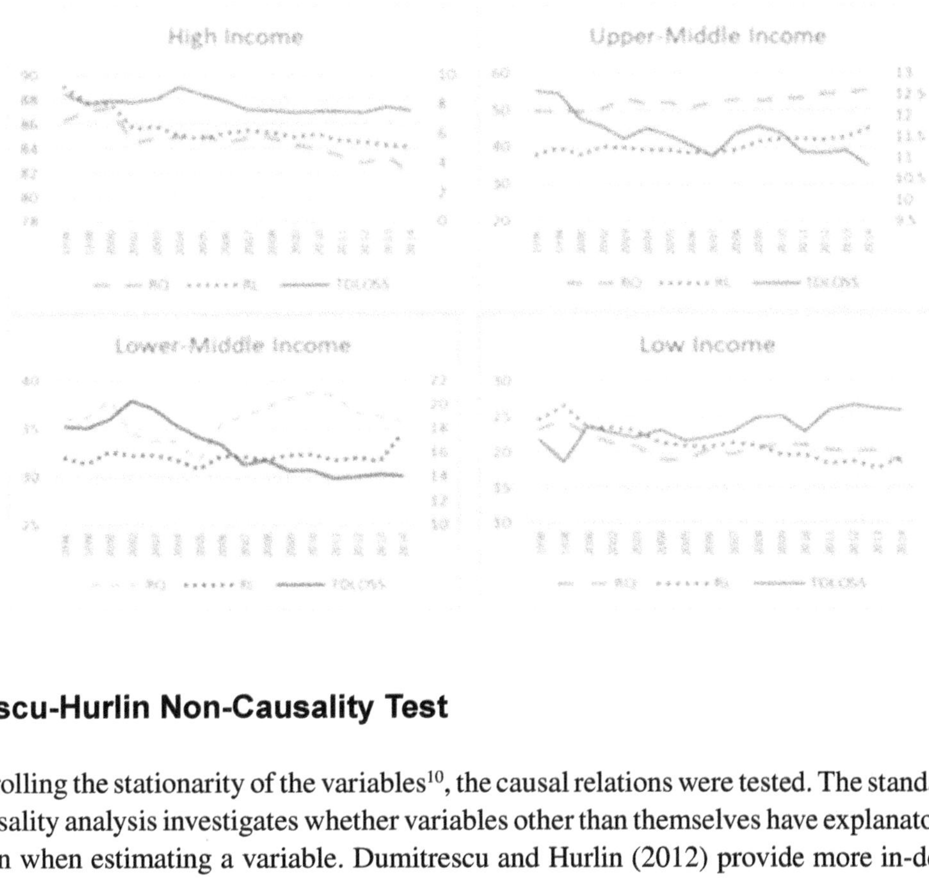

Dumitrescu-Hurlin Non-Causality Test

After controlling the stationarity of the variables[10], the causal relations were tested. The standard Granger (1969) causality analysis investigates whether variables other than themselves have explanatory or useful information when estimating a variable. Dumitrescu and Hurlin (2012) provide more in-depth insight into the Granger Causality approach for panel data analysis and testing non-causality relationships through cross-sections. The recent advances of this test are twofold: using the heterogeneity of causality relationships and having significant power testing for samples that consist of very small T and N. This method is particularly useful in both T>N and N>T samples. Then, we introduce the heterogeneous model specification of the Dumitrescu-Hurlin non-causality test:

$$y_{i,t} = \alpha_i + \sum_{k=1}^{K} \gamma_i^{(k)} y_{i,t-k} + \sum_{k=1}^{K} \beta_i^{(k)} x_{i,t-k} + \varepsilon_{i,t} \tag{1}$$

Where αi and βi are assumed to be fixed across time, and eit is the error term. Yit and xit represent stationary variables for N individuals in T periods. Also, this model tests the non-existence of a causal relationship for at least one of the cross-sections. So, the null hypothesis has no causal relationship for any of the cross-section units, and the rejection of the null hypothesis indicates the causality relationship for at least one cross-section. The null and alternative hypotheses are presented as follows:

$$H0 = \beta i = 0 \text{ for } \forall i = 1, \ldots, N \quad (2)$$

$$H_1 = \begin{cases} \beta_i = 0 & \text{for } \forall i = 1, \ldots, N_1 \\ \beta_i \neq 0 & \text{for } \forall i = N_1 + 1, \ldots, N \end{cases}$$

EMPIRICAL RESULTS

The results of the Dumitrescu Hurlin (hereafter DH) non-causality test for the first lag of variables are presented in Table 1. Empirical findings for each income group are explained below:

High-Income Panel

There is no bi-directional causality relationship between none of the three variables in the high-income group. The causality results indicate that a uni-directional causality exists from RQ and RL to TDLOSS. In other words, a deterioration in the rule of law and regulatory quality cause electricity losses in the high-income group. The significant causal effect that runs from RL to RQ is one of the most remarkable findings and is only valid for the high-income sample.

Upper-Middle-Income Panel

Upper-middle-income panel results present a bi-directional between RQ, RL, and TDLOSS. One exception to this result is that no causality is running from RL to RQ. The results of this group share some similarities with both high and lower-middle-income groups. While the uni-directional causality effects from RL and RQ to TDLOSS of the upper-middle-income group are similar to the high-income group, similar bi-directional causality between RQ and RL can be observed in the lower-middle-income group.

Table 1. Dumitrescu-Hurlin panel causality test results

Direction	High-income		Upper-Middle-income		Lower-Middle-income		Low-income	
	W-stat	p-value	W-stat	p-value	W-stat	p-value	W-stat	p-value
RQ→TDLOSS	2.979	0.000**	2.167	0.044**	4.043	0.000**	3.044	0.000**
TDLOSS→RQ	0.978	0.646	3.663	0.000**	1.494	0.541	2.321	0.042**
RL→RQ	2.159	0.046**	1.316	0.808	1.619	0.385	1.908	0.199
RQ→RL	1.838	0.185	3.483	0.000**	2.522	0.006**	3.638	0.000**
RL→TDLOSS	2.751	0.001**	2.053	0.076*	3.010	0.000**	2.948	0.001**
TDLOSS→RL	1.990	0.105	2.602	0.003**	3.394	0.000**	2.581	0.012**

Note: **, and * denote the 5% and 10% significance levels respectively.

Lower-Middle-Income Panel

Lower-middle-income panel results represent only bi-directional causal effects running from RL to TDLOSS. However, there is a uni-directional causality between RQ and TDLOSS. These results are contrary to upper-middle and low-income group outcomes, which show the bi-directional causality relationship between RQ and TDLOSS. Also, this result reflects the high-income sample observations that even RQ pass through TDLOSS. This relationship does not have any feedback effect.

Low-Income Panel

For low-income countries, bi-directional causality effects are identical to upper-middle countries. More specifically, the causal effect runs from RL to RQ is not significant in common with other income groups except high-income.

DISCUSSION

Previous studies stress the importance of institutions for economic performance. A limited number of empirical studies (Butkiewicz & Yanıkkaya, 2006; Law & Bany-Ariffin, 2008; Aixalá & Fabro, 2008; Law *et al.*, 2013) identify the rule of law as part of the institutional framework. Also, a few studies examine the impact of regulatory governance on electricity reform (Cubbin & Stern, 2006; Smith, 2004; Erdogdu, 2014).

Our findings shed light on the role of the rule of law in reducing electricity theft by focusing on regulatory quality as a transmission channel. The causality results strengthen the hypothesis that the rule of law and regulatory quality leads to higher economic efficiency (Levy & Spiller, 1994; Stern & Holder, 1999). As in many empirical studies, it is crucial to understand how institutions matter for the economy and society in terms of different levels of development by ascertaining the direction of causal linkages. The causality pattern of high-income countries between the rule of law and regulatory quality is different from that of other panel groups, as shown in Figure 2. While the rule of law leads to regulatory quality in high-income countries, there is no causality running from the rule of law to regulatory quality for other income groups. The consequence of having a significantly different pattern in high-income countries confirms the claim that ignoring the rule of law impedes effective regulations. Good and well-established governance (e.g., the rule of law) is necessary for the successful implementation of regulations (Cubbin & Stern, 2006; Maiorano & Stern, 2007).

The significant difference in the causality between RL and RQ in high and low-income countries leads us to examine the classification of Levy and Spiller (1994) more closely. According to them, countries with high institutional endowments can adapt their regulatory systems to changing conditions and prevent arbitrary actions. In such countries, well-designed institutional structures directly affect the quality of regulations. On the contrary, in low-income countries, institutions that provide credibility may be inefficient or even absent. In this context, existing uni-directional causality from the rule of law to the regulatory quality in high-income countries supports the new institutional thesis (Levy & Spiller, 1994). Similarly, in other income group countries, this relationship from regulatory quality to the rule of law shows that the regulatory structure in these countries is still influenced by the ongoing institutional capacity building.

Figure 2. Summary of causality relationships

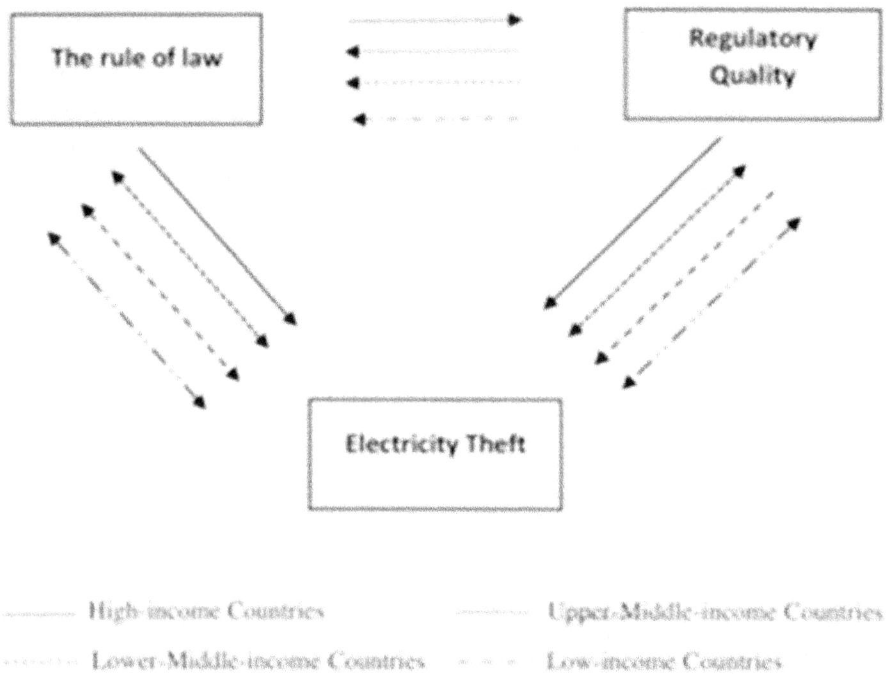

The enhancing impact of the rule of law on utilities for high-income countries appears to be one step ahead of the results of the previous studies on the effects of institutions on economic performance, as it shows the role of the rule of law on regulations. These findings support the theoretical literature on the importance of institutions for developing countries. Previous studies (Law & Bany-Ariffin, 2008; Law *et al.*, 2013; Aixalá & Fabro, 2008) emphasize that the effect of institutional variables is significant only when the rule of law is included in high-income country analysis. They state that the essential institution for developed countries is the rule of law. Regulatory evolution is still in progress in developing countries. The establishment of credible commitments in the regulatory framework is a major determinant of the causality relationship for this country group, from regulatory quality to the rule of law. The ability to reflect the cost of electricity theft to all end-users turns an economic problem into a political problem and encourages rent-seeking in these countries. The non-mark*et al*location of the cost of illegal use increases tariffs for the whole society and legitimizes electricity theft indirectly. This political process weakens regulatory quality and the rule of law as shown by our findings.

The Granger causality results of TDLOSS are an important indicator of electricity theft and the relative efficiency of the electricity market. TDLOSS results also indicate a social problem, confirming prior expectations. There are causal relationships between RL and RQ to TDLOSS for all income groups. As the quality of regulation improves, efficiency in the industry is expected to increase. Likewise, when the quality of regulation worsens, electricity theft tends to increase. Similarly, the rule of law is the most important factor of institutional capacity and demonstrates the tendency to comply with the rules. Development of the institutional capacity of the country results in an increased tendency to follow the rules of the game and increase the efficiency of the markets. As a result, a causality relationship from the rule of law to transmission and distribution losses shows that the relationship between the rule of law and economic development also applies to regulated industries, as the study shows in the case of electricity theft.

Another major finding supports the significant role of the rule of law and its dominant power. While a uni-directional causality in the high-income group from transmission and distribution losses to the rule of law is found, bi-directional causality for other income groups is valid. This shows that in countries where the rule of law is established, economic outcomes are positively affected by this environment. Consequently, miscellaneous causal linkages have been found between the rule of law and economic growth (Butkiewicz & Yanıkkaya, 2006), foreign direct investments (Bénassy-Quéré *et al.*, 2007) or environmental and energy efficiency (Mavragani *et al.*, 2016) for developing countries. On the one hand, institutions or the rule of law encourage economic activities; on the other hand, greater economic activity demands more rule of law and institutional accumulation in countries.

The causal relationships between regulatory quality and electricity losses also differ across income groups. While there is no significant causality from electricity theft to regulatory quality in high- and lower-middle-income country groups, it is significant in upper-middle and low-income countries. In developed countries, the share of technical losses is quite high, and illegal usage or non-technical losses are quite low in T&D losses. By contrast, in lower-middle-income countries, both technical and non-technical losses are quite high. The average rate of T&D losses is 7.56% for high-income countries and 14.09% for lower-middle-income countries in 2018. The same causality relationship can occur because of the quite low T&D loss rates in developed countries. These countries may not give priority to T&D losses due to well-designed rules and regulations.

Furthermore, the causality running from the rule of law to regulatory quality also indicates that the rule of law is a dominant factor in the effectiveness of existing systems through creating huge positive externalities in high-income countries. This finding of the lower-middle-income group may have been caused by the fact that the illegal use of electricity in countries is not considered a crime or illegal activity[11], and even it could be ignored in some specific periods (Min & Golden, 2014). Besides, some countries in our lower-middle-income sample stand out with this result. The countries with high losses such as India, Pakistan, Nigeria, and other countries where electricity theft is strictly a socio-economic problem are included in this group. In developing countries, energy or electricity is seen as a political good (Huda & McDonald, 2016; Oğuz *et al.*, 2014), and often the illegal usage of electricity is not seen as a problem to be solved by the regulatory authority, as the social cost of tackling theft is too high. The lack of causality relation from T&D losses to the quality of regulation supports this view.

CONCLUSION

This study sets out to examine causal relationships between electricity theft, the rule of law, and regulatory quality as an indication of institutional endowment using the panel Granger non-causality test. Most of the time, the failure to control electricity theft arises out of high social costs due to the political nature of electricity regulation. It is assumed that regulatory policy for social policy goals reduces the belief in the rule of law in society. Social issues should be dealt with by social policies. Using indirect methods to subsidize some groups in society creates the problem of identification of the correct groups and dissipates resources. That also weakens the rule of law and regulatory quality in developing countries. The rule of law would reduce electricity theft and lead to efficiency as in developed countries.

Electricity theft is mainly driven by the establishment of effective regulatory systems and driven by the huge externalities that arise from the rule of law.

The empirical findings suggest that the uni-directional causality effect running from the rule of law to transmission and distribution losses is valid for all groups. The uni-directional causality is also statistically significant for the transmission from regulatory quality to T&D losses for each group. However, Granger causality effects have unanticipated results for the same causality patterns in high-income and lower-middle-income groups. Transmission and distribution losses Granger causes regulatory quality in upper-middle- and low-income panels, whereas the high and lower-middle-income samples cannot validate this relation. It is also crucial to examine the direction of causal effects between the rule of law and regulatory quality for each sample to evince which institutional component drives the other.

Regulated industries can be considered as a microcosm of the aggregated economy that is highly influenced by existing institutions, the rule of law, and regulatory systems. Middle-income and low-income countries have relatively higher T&D losses and less efficient regulatory institutions, which in turn affects the rule of law. Characteristics of utilities are highly sensitive to regulatory commitment, rent-seeking, administrative capabilities, as well as norms, behaviors, and political cycles. While tackling illegal electricity usage, policymakers should not rule out the way theft is linked to political and social governance alongside pure economic and financial conditions. There must be a political will to support economic and technical policy changes to reduce electricity theft to acceptable levels regarding economic efficiency. Greater efforts should be performed to institutionalize the rule of law and regulatory commitment in electricity markets.

DECLARATION

- This Chapter is extracted from the unpublished doctoral dissertation titled "Three essays on the connection between the rule of law and regulatory governance in electricity market" by Gamze Kargın Akkoç. The thesis was submitted to the Ankara Yıldırım Beyazıt University, Türkiye in 2019 to fulfill doctoral degree requirements.
- The authors declare that the manuscript follows ethical standards and there are no potential conflicts of interest with respect to the research, authorship and/or publication of this chapter.

DISCLAIMER

The contents and views of this chapter are expressed by the authors in personal capacities. It is not necessary for the Editor and the Publisher to agree with these viewpoints, and they are not responsible for any duty of care in this regard.

ACKNOWLEDGMENT

The authors extend sincere gratitude to

- The Editor and the International Editorial Advisory Board (IEAB) of this book, who initially desk reviewed, arranged a rigorous double/triple-blind review process, and conducted a thorough, minute, and critical final review before accepting the chapter for publication.
- All anonymous reviewers who provided very constructive feedback for thorough revision, improvement, extension, and fine-tuning of the chapter.
- All colleagues, assistants and well-wishers who assisted to complete this task.

REFERENCES

Acemoglu, D., & Johnson, S. (2005). Unbundling institutions. *Journal of Political Economy*, *113*(5), 949–995. doi:10.1086/432166

Aixalá, J., & Fabro, G. (2008). Does the impact of institutional quality on economic growth depend on initial income level? *Economic Affairs*, *28*(3), 45–49. doi:10.1111/j.1468-0270.2008.00844.x

Andrews, C. J. (2008). Greenhouse gas emissions along the rural-urban gradient. *Journal of Environmental Planning and Management*, *51*(6), 847–870. doi:10.1080/09640560802423780

Arango, L. G., Deccache, E., Bonatto, B. D., Arango, H., & Pamplona, E. O. (2017). Study of electricity theft impact on the economy of a regulated electricity company. *Journal of Control. Automation and Electrical Systems*, *28*(4), 567–575.

Baskaran, T., Min, B., & Uppal, Y. (2015). Election cycles and electricity provision: Evidence from a quasi-experiment with Indian special elections. *Journal of Public Economics*, *126*, 64–73. doi:10.1016/j.jpubeco.2015.03.011

Bazilian, M., Nakhooda, S., & Van de Graaf, T. (2014). Energy governance and poverty. *Energy Research & Social Science*, *1*, 217–225. doi:10.1016/j.erss.2014.03.006

Bénassy-Quéré, A., Coupet, M., & Mayer, T. (2007). Institutional determinants of foreign direct investment. *World Economy*, *30*(5), 764–782. doi:10.1111/j.1467-9701.2007.01022.x

Berg, L. A., & Desai, D. (2013). *Background paper: overview on the rule of law and sustainable development for the global dialogue on rule of law and the post-2015 development agenda*. UNDP.

Bingham, T. (2011). *The rule of law*. Penguin.

Butkiewicz, J. L., & Yanikkaya, H. (2006). Institutional quality and economic growth: Maintenance of the rule of law or democratic institutions, or both? *Economic Modelling*, *23*(4), 648–661. doi:10.1016/j.econmod.2006.03.004

Cooter, R., & Ulen, T. (2016). *Law and economics*. Addison-Wesley.

Cubbin, J., & Stern, J. (2006). The impact of regulatory governance and privatization on electricity industry generation capacity in developing economies. *The World Bank Economic Review*, *20*(1), 115–141. doi:10.1093/wber/lhj004

Dam, K. W. (2007). *The law-growth nexus: The rule of law and economic development*. Brookings Institution Press.

Depuru, S. S. S. R., Wang, L., & Devabhaktuni, V. (2011). Electricity theft: Overview, issues, prevention and a smart meter-based approach to control theft. *Energy Policy, 39*(2), 1007–1015. doi:10.1016/j.enpol.2010.11.037

Dollar, D., & Kraay, A. (2003). Institutions, trade, and growth. *Journal of Monetary Economics, 50*(1), 133–162. doi:10.1016/S0304-3932(02)00206-4

Dumitrescu, E. I., & Hurlin, C. (2012). Testing for Granger non-causality in heterogeneous panels. *Economic Modelling, 29*(4), 1450–1460. doi:10.1016/j.econmod.2012.02.014

Erdogdu, E. (2014). The political economy of electricity market liberalization: A cross-country approach. *The Energy Journal (Cambridge, Mass.), 35*(3), 91–128. doi:10.5547/01956574.35.3.5

Gaur, V., & Gupta, E. (2016). The determinants of electricity theft: An empirical analysis of Indian states. *Energy Policy, 93*, 127–136. doi:10.1016/j.enpol.2016.02.048

Glaeser, E. L., La Porta, R., Lopez-de-Silanes, F., & Shleifer, A. (2004). Do institutions cause growth? *Journal of Economic Growth, 9*(3), 271–303. doi:10.1023/B:JOEG.0000038933.16398.ed

Glauner, P., Valtchev, P., State, R., & Duarte, D. (2018). *Non-technical losses in the 21st century: Causes, economic effects, detection and perspectives*. Research Gate. https://www.researchgate.net/publication/325297875_Non-Technical_Losses_in_the_21st_Century_Causes_Economic_Effects_Detection_and_Perspectives

Granger, C. W. (1969). Investigating causal relations by econometric models and cross-spectral methods. *Econometrica, 37*(3), 424–438. doi:10.2307/1912791

Gual, J., & Trillas, F. (2006). Telecommunications policies: Measurement and determinants. *Review of Network Economics, 5*(2), 249–272. doi:10.2202/1446-9022.1097

Hadfield, G. K., & Weingast, B. R. (2014). Microfoundations of the rule of law. *Annual Review of Political Science, 17*(1), 21–42. doi:10.1146/annurev-polisci-100711-135226

Hanretty, C., & Koop, C. (2013). Shall the law set them free? The formal and actual independence of regulatory agencies. *Regulation & Governance, 7*(2), 195–214. doi:10.1111/j.1748-5991.2012.01156.x

Huda, M. S., & McDonald, M. (2016). Regional cooperation on energy in South Asia: Unraveling the political challenges in implementing transnational pipelines and electricity grids. *Energy Policy, 98*, 73–83. doi:10.1016/j.enpol.2016.07.046

Jamil, F. (2013). On the electricity shortage, price and electricity theft nexus. *Energy Policy, 54*, 267–272. doi:10.1016/j.enpol.2012.11.034

Jamil, F., & Ahmad, E. (2010). The relationship between electricity consumption, electricity prices and GDP in Pakistan. *Energy Policy, 38*(10), 6016–6025. doi:10.1016/j.enpol.2010.05.057

Jimenez, R., Serebrisky, T., & Mercado, J. (2014). *Power lost: sizing electricity losses in transmission and distribution systems in Latin America and the Caribbean*. IADB. https://publications.iadb.org/en/publication/16883/power-lost-sizing-electricity-losses-transmission-and-distribution-systems-latin

Joseph, K. L. (2010). The politics of power: Electricity reform in India. *Energy Policy*, *38*(1), 503–511. doi:10.1016/j.enpol.2009.09.041

Kaufmann, D., Kraay, A., & Mastruzzi, M. (2011). The worldwide governance indicators: Methodology and analytical issues. *Hague Journal on the Rule of Law*, *3*(2), 220–246. doi:10.1017/S1876404511200046

Kessides, I. N. (2012). The impacts of electricity sector reforms in developing countries. *The Electricity Journal*, *25*(6), 79–88. doi:10.1016/j.tej.2012.07.002

Knack, S., & Keefer, P. (1995). Institutions and economic performance: Cross-country tests using alternative institutional measures. *Economics and Politics*, *7*(3), 207–227. doi:10.1111/j.1468-0343.1995.tb00111.x

Law, S. H., & Bany-Ariffin, A. N. (2008). Institutional infrastructure and economic performance: Dynamic panel data evidence. *Transition Studies Review*, *15*(3), 542–557. doi:10.100711300-008-0026-1

Law, S. H., Lim, T. C., & Ismail, N. W. (2013). Institutions and economic development: A Granger causality analysis of panel data evidence. *Economic Systems*, *37*(4), 610–624. doi:10.1016/j.ecosys.2013.05.005

Levy, B., & Spiller, P. T. (1994). The institutional foundations of regulatory commitment: A comparative analysis of telecommunications regulation. *Journal of Law Economics and Organization*, *10*(2), 201–246.

Lewis, F. B. (2015). Costly 'Throw-Ups': Electricity theft and power disruptions. *The Electricity Journal*, *28*(7), 118–135. doi:10.1016/j.tej.2015.07.009

Maiorano, F., & Stern, J. (2007). Institutions and telecommunications infrastructure in low and middle-income countries: The case of mobile telephony. *Utilities Policy*, *15*(3), 165–181. doi:10.1016/j.jup.2007.04.001

Marangoz, C. (2013). *Illegal electricity use in Türkiye: Causes and policy implications* [Doctoral dissertation, Vanderbilt University].

Mavragani, A., Nikolaou, I., & Tsagarakis, K. (2016). Open economy, institutional quality, and environmental performance: A macroeconomic approach. *Sustainability (Basel)*, *8*(7), 601. doi:10.3390u8070601

Min, B., & Golden, M. (2014). Electoral cycles in electricity losses in India. *Energy Policy*, *65*, 619–625. doi:10.1016/j.enpol.2013.09.060

Nepal, R., & Jamasb, T. (2015). Caught between theory and practice: Government, market, and regulatory failure in electricity sector reforms. *Economic Analysis and Policy*, *46*, 16–24. doi:10.1016/j.eap.2015.03.001

Never, B. (2015). Social norms, trust and control of power theft in Uganda: Does bulk metering work for MSEs? *Energy Policy*, *82*, 197–206. doi:10.1016/j.enpol.2015.03.020

North, D. C. (1991). Institutions. *The Journal of Economic Perspectives*, *5*(1), 97–112. doi:10.1257/jep.5.1.97

Northeast-Group. (2021). *Electricity theft and non-technical losses.* Northeast Group. https://Northeast-Group.com/2021/10/20/electricity-theft-non-technical-losses/

Ofgem. (2014). *Tackling Electricity Theft - The way forward.* Ofgem. https://www.Ofgem.gov.uk/sites/default/files/docs/2014/03/electricitytheft-iafinal_0.pdf

Oğuz, F., Akkemik, K. A., & Göksal, K. (2014). Can law impose competition? A critical discussion and evidence from the Turkish electricity generation market. *Renewable & Sustainable Energy Reviews*, *30*, 381–387. doi:10.1016/j.rser.2013.10.024

Omri, A. (2014). An international literature survey on energy-economic growth nexus: Evidence from country-specific studies. *Renewable & Sustainable Energy Reviews*, *38*, 951–959. doi:10.1016/j.rser.2014.07.084

Ozturk, I. (2010). A literature survey on energy–growth nexus. *Energy Policy*, *38*(1), 340–349. doi:10.1016/j.enpol.2009.09.024

Payne, J. E. (2010). A survey of the electricity consumption-growth literature. *Applied Energy*, *87*(3), 723–731. doi:10.1016/j.apenergy.2009.06.034

Rigobon, R., & Rodrik, D. (2005). Rule of law, democracy, openness, and income: Estimating the interrelationships. *Economics of Transition*, *13*(3), 533–564. doi:10.1111/j.1468-0351.2005.00226.x

Rodrik, D. (2000). Institutions for high-quality growth: What they are and how to acquire them. *Studies in Comparative International Development*, *35*(3), 3–31. doi:10.1007/BF02699764

Rodrik, D., Subramanian, A., & Trebbi, F. (2004). Institutions rule: The primacy of institutions over geography and integration in economic development. *Journal of Economic Growth*, *9*(2), 131–165. doi:10.1023/B:JOEG.0000031425.72248.85

Smith, T. B. (2004). Electricity theft: A comparative analysis. *Energy Policy*, *32*(18), 2067–2076. doi:10.1016/S0301-4215(03)00182-4

Steadman, K. U. (2011). *Essays on electricity theft.* State University of New York at Binghamton.

Stern, J., & Holder, S. (1999). Regulatory governance: criteria for assessing the performance of regulatory systems: an application to infrastructure industries in the developing countries of Asia. *Utilities Policy*, *8*(1), 33–50. doi:10.1016/S0957-1787(99)00008-9

Taşdöven, H., Emhan, A., & Dönmez, M. (2012). Liderlik tarzı ve mizaç-karakter ilişkisi: Polis teşkilatında bir uygulama. *Yönetim ve Ekonomi Dergisi*, *19*(2), 165–177.

Tiba, S., & Omri, A. (2017). Literature survey on the relationships between energy, environment and economic growth. *Renewable & Sustainable Energy Reviews*, *69*, 1129–1146. doi:10.1016/j.rser.2016.09.113

Ullah, K., Arentsen, M. J., & Lovett, J. C. (2017). Institutional determinants of power sector reform in Pakistan. *Energy Policy*, *102*, 332–339. doi:10.1016/j.enpol.2016.12.019

Wijayatunga, P. D., Fernando, W. J. L. S., & Shrestha, R. M. (2004). Impact of distributed and independent power generation on greenhouse gas emissions: Sri Lanka. *Energy Conversion and Management*, *45*(20), 3193–3206. doi:10.1016/j.enconman.2004.01.009

Winther, T. (2012). Electricity theft as a relational issue: A comparative look at Zanzibar, Tanzania, and the Sunderban Islands, India. *Energy for Sustainable Development*, *16*(1), 111–119. doi:10.1016/j.esd.2011.11.002

Yurtseven, Ç. (2015). The causes of electricity theft: An econometric analysis of the case of Türkiye. *Utilities Policy*, *37*, 70–78. doi:10.1016/j.jup.2015.06.008

ENDNOTES

1 Glauner *et al.* (2018) focus on the non-technical losses, specifically. They indicate the non-technical losses fluctuates between 1-2% in Western Europe and in less efficient systems, it fluctuates between 9-12%.

2 In the following sections, we have used transmission and distribution losses as a proxy of electricity theft in our estimations from the World Bank Database that covers illegal usages using the term as "pilferage."

3 There are differences in classifying countries based on their income or development levels. We leave aside these differences for practical reasons.

4 http://dtechsepm.com/power-theft/

5 https://www.networkedenergy.com/en/news-events/energy-theft-and-fraud-reduction?utm_medium=sei&utm_source=external&utm_campaign=article%20f&t

6 https://asian-power.com/ipp/in-focus/indian-power-sector-loses-162b-theft-every-year

7 Min and Golden (2014) revealed the electricity theft ratios increased 3% in political periods.

8 Wijayatunga et al. (2004) and Andrews (2008) emphasize the additive effect of transmission and distribution losses on carbon or greenhouse gas emissions.

9 Marangoz (2013) found the terrorist activities are also high in areas with high losses. Also, electricity theft is strictly accepted as drug-related crime, especially in Latin America. Please see https://digitalrepository.unm.edu/cgi/viewcontent.cgi?referer=https://www.google.com/&httpsredir=1&article=1032&context=la_energy_dialog.

10 The study begins with controlling the cross-sectional dependency across the countries in our study of the causality within the panel data framework. In the second step, the stationarity of variables is determined with unit root tests to provide protection from spurious results. The results of cross-dependency and unit root test are upon the request from the authors.

11 Jamil and Ahmad (2013) develop a model investigating the criminal motivations of electricity theft, although the recent studies overlooked the criminal characteristics of electricity theft.

APPENDIX A. LIST OF COUNTRY GROUPS

Table 2. List of country groups

High-income	Upper Middle-income	Lower Middle-income	Low-income
Australia	Algeria	Bangladesh	Congo, Dem. Rep.
Belgium	Belarus	Bolivia	Eritrea
Canada	Brazil	Cameroon	Ethiopia
France	Bulgaria	Egypt, Arab Rep.	Haiti
Greece	Dominican Rep.	Georgia	Mozambique
Ireland	Jamaica	India	Nepal
Italy	Malaysia	Indonesia	Senegal
Netherlands	Mexico	Kenya	Syrian Arab Rep.
Norway	Namibia	Nigeria	Tajikistan
Portugal	Paraguay	Pakistan	Tanzania
Spain	South Africa	Sri Lanka	Togo
Sweden	Thailand	Sudan	Yemen, Rep.
Switzerland	Türkiye	Ukraine	Zimbabwe
United Kingdom	Russian Fed.	Ghana	
United States	China	Kyrgyz Rep.	
Uruguay	Azerbaijan	Morocco	
Argentina	Colombia	Tunisia	

Section 3
Financial Scams

Chapter 9
Electronic Banking Frauds: The Case of India

Ruchi Gupta
ICFAI University, India

Shilpi Gupta
https://orcid.org/0000-0003-4382-3616
Amity University, India

Clement Chiahemba M. Ajekwe
https://orcid.org/0000-0001-9617-6438
Benue State University, Nigeria

ABSTRACT

Electronic banking (e-banking) has played an important role in the development and economic growth of developing countries. E-Banking also acts as a catalyst for the development of the financial sector, capital markets, and digital economy. India's rapidly growing banking sector paved the way for development and fraud in the e-banking regime. The present chapter seeks to assess the techniques of detection of fraud from a global perspective and will also validate the boom of E-Banking with a thought of precaution and awareness. Secondary data has been collected through bank statements, journals, and the internet. The results will help banks and regulators to better understand online banking frauds and to strengthen the existing fraud prevention systems. It is recommended that the government should provide adequate infrastructural facilities in the telecommunications and energy sectors, coupled with encouraging the use of information and communication technologies among the masses for beneficial impact.

INTRODUCTION

Due to rapid advances of information technology in the knowledge era of 21st century, electronic banking (E-Banking) has been adopted extensively as a channel of distribution for financial services (Salehi and Alipour, 2010). The literal meaning of "electronic" refers to the provision of banking products through

DOI: 10.4018/979-8-3693-1190-5.ch009

electronic networks. In India, the importance of E-Banking can be traced to the decision of the government of India to enact the IT Act 2000 with effect from October 17, 2000, which legalized electronic transactions to develop a cashless economy on trustworthy lines and provide financial stability to investors. The Basel Committee Report on Banking Supervision (1998) described E-Banking as the provision of retail and small-value banking products and services through electronic channels. Such products and services include deposit taking, lending account management, provision of financial advice, electronic bill payment, and the provision of other electronic payment products and services. Globally it has been established that E-Banking has increased the financial transactions both in volume and quantity. The growth stimulant hormone in E-Banking also led to an increase in fraudulent activities. The speedy expansion of E-Banking services carries risks as well as unmatchable benefits. Therefore, it is the responsibility of banks to identify, manage and deal with banking institutions prudently and sensibly in terms of the signs and challenges of E-Banking services with continual awareness programs for the normal man.

The traditional banking system had huge challenges in terms of manual operation, time consumption, data insecurity, data leakage and loss, less skilled manpower, etc. E-Banking is inevitable for growth as it counters the challenges being faced by traditional banking worldwide and facilitating online transactions with the click of a mouse. Speed and accuracy are the new mantras of the E-Banking system. In the era of E-Banking, new modes of transactions like RTGS [Real-time gross settlement], NEFT [National electronic fund Transfer], ECS [Electronic cleaning services], and EFT [Electronic Fund Transfer] has captured the limelight facilitating national and international transactions.

At the time of the pandemic, E-Banking played a very important role for the public and the government. If this innovation would not present, none of the work related to the bank can be done.

BACKGROUND OF E-BANKING FRAUD

The banking sector around the world plays an essential role in promoting sustainable growth and economic activity. As intermediaries between users and providers of funds, banks are successfully placed in a continuum that controls the pulse economy (Rampini & Viswanathan, 2019). Around the world, the failure of the banking sector to effectively perform its intermediation functions and the failure to control the financial problems it has faced so far have raised serious concerns. (Gertler & Nobuhiro, 2010). Rampini and Viswanathan (2010) state that the main feature of business in the banking sector is the performance of the functions of authorized observers and advisers of borrowers on behalf of legal depositors.

Banks face challenges in preventing and detecting fraud, and these challenges are often compounded by existing organizational structures, policies, regulatory frameworks, and new technological approaches. However, banks must protect themselves in this special relationship with borrowers and depositors' confidence and trust (Ali, Lei & Wei, 2018). The failure of banks to perform their role satisfactorily resulted from the risks they are exposed to that are not adequately controlled (Papazoglou, 2003). One of these risks that are gradually becoming a burden is the banking risk associated with fraud. In addition, fraud, an intentional deception act that causes society to suffer monetary or physical loss, is now a global threat to the entire banking industry (Ramamoorti, Morrison & Koletar 2013).

Accordingly, it is annoying that while the banking sector is persistently trying to fight the demands of the monetary authorities to recapitalize to the required minimum standards, fraudsters are always at work destroying and threatening the financial base of the banks (Mahdi, Rezaul & Rahman, 2010). According to Mannan and Oorschot (2008), the consistent fraud incidents in the banking sector are causing embarrassment and confusion at present in the country, which is evident from the apparent inability of the law enforcement agencies to effectively catch criminals. The development of banking services, from traditional banking to E-Banking, is complex not only in terms of banking risk management but also with international and national violations (Saranya & Gunasri, 2013; Chaturvedi & Meena, 2016; Abu-Shanab & Matalqa, 2015).

E-Banking fraud is fraud or theft committed using Internet technology to illegally withdraw money from a bank account and/or transfer money to an account at another bank (Rafay, 2019). Internet Banking Fraud is a form of identity theft and is usually made possible through various techniques.

Few of the Indian cases are described below.

Case One: The Case of Nirav Modi and Mehul Choksi—PNB Scam 2018

Nirav Modi, a once-famous diamond trader, is now a wanted man accused by Interpol and the Indian government of criminal conspiracy, criminal breach of trust, cheating, dishonesty, money laundering, and breach of contract. The fraudulent method by which Punjab National Bank (PNB) was tricked shook the nation in 2018, and the scam is now believed to be worth more than USD 2 billion. This PNB Scam involves the issuing of forged Letters of Undertaking [LoU] by bankers at the PNB's Brady House Branch in Fort, Mumbai. These Memorandums of Understanding (MoU) were signed in favor of Indian Bank branches in other countries for the import of pearls and other valuable stones for one year, even though the RBI had recommended a total period of 90 days only from the date of shipping. However, these criteria were ignored by Indian Bank's branches abroad, and is not even revealed what documents/ records were made available to them by the diamond merchant/his enterprises when they obtained credit guarantees from them.

These flaws in the banking system were brilliantly exploited by Nirav Modi, his uncle Mehul Choksi, and their crew, who got a total of 1212 LoUs in 74 months from his first fake guarantee received from PNB on March 10, 2011.

PNB employees who had collaborated with Nirav Modi used the international banking financial communication system SWIFT from the PNB banking network to send messages to overseas branches of other Indian banks, including Allahabad Bank, Union Bank of India, and Axis Bank, on fund requirements, for which the banking personnel used their allotted SWIFT Password, but the transactions were never recorded in the Bank's core system. Therefore, PNB's senior management was completely unaware of what was going on.

Furthermore, Nirav Modi got LoUs primarily in favor of fictitious corporations based in the British Virgin Islands (BVI), and funds collected through illegal LoUs were transferred into their accounts.

Somehow, the fraudulent method of fund withdrawal was brought to the attention of PNB's top management, and they filed a formal FIR with CBI on 29th January 2018, admitting a bank fraud worth INR 2.8 billion, with Nirav Modi, Ami Modi, Nishal Modi, and Mehul Choksi, all partners of M/s Diamond R US, M/s Solar Exports, and M/s Stellar Diamond, as the prime accused.

The incident is being investigated by the CBI, the ED, and INTERPOL, and the worth of the fraud has now risen to nearly INR 14000 crores because of the following inquiry. Mr. Nirav Modi is still fleeing arrest, and a lengthy court struggle is underway to extradite him to India.

Case Two: The Case of Vijay Mallya

Vijay Mallya, formerly a ROCKSTAR business tycoon, is now a fugitive businessman accused of a bank debt default case involving his now-defunct Kingfisher Airlines. This is a simpler example in which a consortium of banks, led by the Public Sector powerhouse, State Bank of India (SBI), continued to make loans without due diligence, causing the loan amount to balloon to over INR 9000 crores and Vijay Mallya's UB group [United Breweries Holding Limited] to default. The situation was exacerbated by the bankruptcy of Kingfisher Airlines, and the Consortium of Banks eventually brought a criminal prosecution against Vijay Mallya.

The lack of insight by banking regulators was evident in the fact that news about Vijay Mallya's business failures continued to surface in the media from early 2000, yet the banks, a total of 17, continued to lend to him to fulfill his demand for costly company development. He used the funds to purchase Deccan Airlines and integrate it with Kingfisher Airlines, however, the project proved to be a flop. At one point, the firm ran out of funds and was unable to pay its employees' salaries.

His company, Kingfisher, also kept back service tax collected from passengers, Provident Fund (PF) recovered from workers, and income tax recoveries made at source since it had no money to deposit with the IT Department or PF authorities. At one point, SBI declared Kingfisher Group bankrupt, but other banks continued to extend loans to him, and many Financial Observers attribute this to the fact that he was also a two-time Member of Parliament in the upper House and had very close connections with the power centers in the government, both in his state of Karnataka and at the center in New Delhi.

This matter is also being examined by the CBI and the ED; however, Vijay Mallya has fled to the United Kingdom. In June of this year, the ED published a statement indicating that the banks had recovered INR 1357 crores through the sale of shares attached by the ED under the Prevention of Money Laundering Act [PMLA]. He, like Nirav Modi, is facing extradition proceedings in the United Kingdom.

Besides the above two cases, there are other types of E-Banking fraud that are common in India:

1) Stolen or lost credit/debit cards and their abuse by fraudsters.
2) Cloning debit/credit cards.
3) Phishing or fraudulently influencing customers to give their information and thereafter duping money from their accounts.
4) Stolen PINs and banking passwords
5) Hacked accounts and mobile apps
6) Stolen CVV and OTP numbers
7) Fraudsters set up fake online shopping platforms.
8) Luring people to share their confidential information like AADHAR details, ATM PIN, an Account password, etc. in the name of some attractive gifts or lottery and duping money thereafter.

Challenges of E-Banking

Although many benefits are expected from the implementation of E-Banking, it does not mean that E-Banking does not face associated challenges. A study conducted by Chiemeke, Evwiekpaefe, and Chete (2006), identified the major factors hindering the adoption of internet banking in Nigeria such as lack of security, and inadequate operational facilities including telecommunication facilities and power supply. Challenges to E-Banking implementation as identified by Andoh-Baidoo and Osatuyi (2009) include inadequate electricity supply, inadequate telecommunications, customer literacy, cost of internet browsing, insufficient understanding of the benefits of internet banking, and security/trust issues in internet banking.

Fraud detection has been investigated by (Bashir *et al.* 2020) in E-Banking. The study reported three main types of fraud detection which are credit card fraud detection, telecommunication fraud detection, and computer intrusion detection.

Strategies to Address E-Banking Challenges

Efforts should be made by different E-Banking stakeholders to encourage and promote the use of E-Banking and commerce by the population of the country. The strategies include but are not limited to:

a) The government must ensure that the people it governs are literate in the use and application of computers in this information age.
b) The government should also take steps to privatize the telecommunication sector to improve efficiency and productivity in the sector, to increase efficiency and productivity in the sector thus increasing capacity is achieved.
c) Banks should design their website in such a way that consumers of their services are fully aware of the services provided electronically and develop ways to ask questions and fulfill requirements online.
d) Banks should regularly disseminate information about the security of E-Banking to remove consumers' fear about E-Banking services and thereby gain customers' trust. The bank should also encourage the do-it-yourself attitude of customers by providing necessary and sufficient information on how to use E-Banking services, making it user-friendly.

LITERATURE REVIEW

The focus of this chapter is to provide an overview of the literature related to the topic. The chapter focuses mainly on the study of fraud detection and prevention in E-Banking in India. The chapter provides an overview of the Indian banking system, the background of the Indian banking system, and the design of E-Banking, and highlights the impact of E-Banking fraud, E-Banking attacks and techniques, and factors contributing to the increase in E-Banking fraud. The discussion also includes fraud detection and prevention mechanisms in E-Banking, conclusion, and recommendation.

Globalization, the transformation of social trends, competition, and especially the development of information and communication technologies led to intensive reform of the banking system (Loonam & O'Loughlin, 2008; Rafay & Gilani, 2016). On the contrary, fraudulent electronic activities are increasing and becoming more sophisticated, seriously threatening the trust and security of E-Banking services (Mahdi, Rezaul & Rahman, 2010). E-Banking fraud has become a sophisticated and serious phenomenon for financial fraud and the fight against banking crime worldwide (John *et al.*, 2016).

Kuzic, Fisher & Scollary (2002) found numerous problems with E-Banking. They can be divided into three categories: technological, managerial, and business challenges. Technology issues related to security issues, cost of websites and technology, software, and infrastructure. Management challenges are related to people and organizational issues and gaining the support of top management. The business challenge concerns customer service, sustaining customer habits, and legal challenges.

Hani *et al.* (2020) researched the impact of fraud on the Indian banking sector. The objectives of the study were to review and analyze the trend of fraud plaguing the banking sector in India. It also examined the impact of fraud in the continuous rise of NPAs in the Indian banking sector. With the help of secondary data, the study concluded to elucidate the impact of rising bank frauds on the profitability of the banking sector in India.

Shah (2019) performed research on the rise in banking fraud in India. The goal was to figure out what was causing various forms of banking fraud and how to stop them so that diverse stakeholders might be protected. The researcher stated that there are several causes of fraud, the most common of which are a bad regulatory framework, employee carelessness, a lack of effective oversight by top management, wrong use of technology, a lack of consumer and staff knowledge, and poor coordination.

Sharma and Sharma (2017) conducted an empirical study on banking fraud in India with a particular emphasis on the role of employee awareness in banking fraud. This work is based on primary data. The research aims to examine the degree of implementation of internal control systems and distinguish between procedural fraud and other causes of bank fraud and learn about bank workers' attitudes regarding that.

Mostafa *et al.* (2020) reviewed about detection of fraud in E-Banking. The study presents a comprehensive review of the issues associated with the security of E-Banking and addresses the importance of ensuring the security of such systems. Furthermore, common types of fraud encountered on E-Banking platforms are also reviewed, along with prevention and detection of cyber-attack.

Mangala, & Soni (2023) evaluated the fraud in the banking sector and discussed the investigation conducted over the last 20 years. The study emphasized the comprehensive view of the causes and effects of bank fraud, as well as measures to prevent this scourge. Secondary data was employed in this work, with databases collected between 2000 and 2021. According to the survey, banking fraud has become a major problem for virtually all nations throughout the world, inflicting significant financial and non-financial harm to banks, consumers, other stakeholders, and the economy. Fraudulent incidences are caused by a variety of variables, including stress and opportunity. The survey also indicated that banks must have comprehensive fraud risk management in place to prevent, identify, and mitigate deployments.

Various studies examined the issue of detecting financial fraud risk and its implications for financial stability (Shams *et al.*, 2021; Rafay, 2021a, 2023a; Nakitende *et al.*, 2021). The primary purpose of this study was to focus on the link between financial fraud risk and financial stability, as well as to shed light on the gaps in financial fraud research. As an indicator for future study, it was discovered in this work that there was a possible effect on financial stability.

Rahman *et al.* (2014) investigated the effectiveness of fraud prevention and detection techniques in Malaysian Islamic banks. According to the findings of 146 questionnaires given to managers and officers of Islamic banks in Malaysia, the most effective components of fraud prevention methods were protection software/applications. Meanwhile, when examined separately, the most successful measures include bank reconciliation, password security, and internal control review and improvement. This research would ideally help both academics and practitioners analyze Malaysia's current level of protection against bank fraud.

Eneji *et al.* (2019) concentrated on E-Banking fraud, detection of E-Banking frauds, control of E-Banking frauds, and issues related to E-Banking fraud detection and control. According to the researchers, integrating biometric security and a system that reveals individuals' anonymity with E-Banking systems would aid in mitigating and combating E-Banking fraud.

Jeyanthi *et al.* (2020) explained the importance of fraud analytics in Indian financial sector. The research focused on false and fraud cases in the banking sector. This article focuses on bank personnel who manage day-to-day banking activities with the purpose of assisting them in identifying and predicting similar events in case of fraud. It is concluded that effective customer education and communications initiatives assist consumers in recognizing how to prevent fraud and in understanding their obligations about digital safety.

Ramana *et al.* (2017) explained a comprehensive assessment of banking fraud. Authors found and described strategies for detecting and preventing fraud in minor financial products. Furthermore, it is noted that the Indian banking industry was under strain due to an increase in fraud incidents in recent years. Retail banking was more volume driven, which exacerbated the number of fraud incidences in that sector, raising the need to promote a broader audit of procedures and measures to detect the fraud.

Ahmad *et al.* (2021) performed a study on an E-Banking scam using a comprehensive literature review. This study emphasized the technology that financial institutions are now adopting to safeguard the E-Banking system, as well as the strategies for a secure E-Banking system. Secondary information has been used. The detailed study provided a snapshot of the existing situation and highlighted advanced security solutions that can successfully counteract the negative impact on E-Banking performance.

Usman (2019) conducted research entitled critical success factors for preventing E-Banking fraud. The goal of this study is to better understand the aspects that may be important in enhancing fraud protection systems in E-Banking. The study identifies important success elements for fraud prevention in E-Banking. The findings suggest that, in addition to technology, additional elements such as internal controls, consumer education, and staff education, among others, must be addressed. These issues should be addressed to improve fraud prevention systems of banks.

Abu-Shanab and Matalqa (2015) discussed security and fraud issues of E-Banking, as well as the features and challenges of E-Banking fraud. E-Banking provides several advantages that increase customer happiness through improved service quality while also allowing banks to obtain a competitive advantage over other rivals. However, greater attention is needed to E-Banking security and fraud prevention because the lack of control over security makes E-Banking untrustworthy for many people even today. This study also discusses several forms of assaults, fraud detection systems, and preventive measures employed by electronic banks. To rate alternative security models and procedures, an expert opinion method was applied. According to the findings, the most effective model is "*Transaction Monitoring*," while the poorest models are "*Virtual Keyboards*", "*Browser Protection*," and "*Device Identification*."

Alsayed *et al.* (2017) discussed E-Banking Security such as internet hacking, phishing assaults, fraud analysis, and prevention. The goal of this study is to look at how phishing hackers try to steal users' data and commit financial fraud. In turn, it illustrates how bank customers may employ security solutions to protect their online transactions. The study concluded that there are numerous sorts of phishing assaults as well as several ways that a bank may utilize to prevent phishing attacks. These tactics are referred to as phishing assault countermeasures, and include E-mail and web page personalization, protection software, the usage of two-factor authentication, and raising consumer knowledge. Some of the strategies recommended in this section to lessen the danger of phishing assaults will protect consumers from being deceived by online phishing attackers.

Kibets *et al.* (2019) discussed anti-fraud technology in E-Banking. The goals of an efficient fight against fraud in the banking industry were revealed, taking into consideration the terms of the European Parliament and Council Directive on combatting fraud and counterfeiting of non-cash methods of payment, which replaced Council Framework Decision 2001/413/JHA, 2017. The EMA Association, as Ukraine's national representative in EAST - European Association for Secure Transactions, was given special attention to the resolution of issues of preventing fraud in the sector of financial services. The difficult components of the restoration of monies lost by a bank client due to third-party fraud were discovered.

Chaimaa *et al.* (2021) reviewed the overview of E-Banking. The major objective was to enable enterprises to increase the quality-of-service delivery while lowering transaction costs and providing consumers with service at any time and from any location. However, it made them more vulnerable to fraudulent operations such as spamming, phishing, and credit card fraud. The major obstacle to E-Banking is assuring financial security.

THE OBJECTIVE OF THE STUDY

The basic objective of the study is to detect E-Banking fraud and to suggest remedial measures to prevent E-Banking fraud in India.

DETECTION OF E-BANKING FRAUD

Phishing Hacks

Fraudsters design a phishing website that looks to be a real website, such as a bank's website, an E-commerce website, or a search engine. Scammers provide links to these websites via SMS, social media, email, and Instant Messenger, among other channels.

Many clients click on the link without first inspecting the Uniform Resource Locator (URL) and input security credentials such as a Personal Identification Number (PIN), One Time Password (OTP), Password, and so on, which fraudsters gather and use.

Vishing

Impersonators impersonating bankers, corporate executives, insurance agents, government officials, and others call or approach customers over the phone or through social media. To gain confidence, imposters reveal a few consumer data, such as the customer's name or date of birth. Imposters may pressure or trick customers into disclosing confidential information such as passwords, OTPs, PINs, and Card Verification Values (CVVs) by citing an urgency/emergency such as the need to block the unauthorized transaction, payment required to avoid a penalty, or an appealing discount, among other things. These credentials are then used to scam customers.

Frauds Using Online Sales Platforms

Fraudsters act as buyers on online sales platforms and indicate an interest in the seller's merchandise (s). To garner trust, some scammers act as defense personnel stationed in isolated areas. Instead of paying the vendor, they utilize the "request money" option in the Unified Payments Interface (UPI) app and demand that the seller authorize the request by inputting the UPI PIN.

Frauds Committed Because of the Use of Unverified/unknown Mobile Apps

According to RBI, fraudsters circulate through SMS, email, social media, Instant Messenger, etc., certain app links, are masked to appear like the existing apps of authorized entities. Fraudsters trick the customer to click on such links which result in downloading of unknown/unverified apps on the customer's mobile, laptop, desktop, etc. Once the malicious application is downloaded, the fraudster gains access.

ATM Card Skimming

Skimming devices are installed in ATMs by fraudsters who take data from the customer's card. According to the RBI release, "*Fraudsters may also install a dummy keypad or a small / pinhole camera, well-hidden from plain sight to capture ATM PIN. Sometimes, fraudsters pretending to be other customers standing nearby gain access to the PIN when the customer enters it into an ATM. This data is then used to create a duplicate card and withdraw money from the customer's account.*"

Frauds Using Screen Sharing App / Remote Access

RBI warns customers stating the procedure that fraudsters trick the customer to download a screen-sharing app. Using such an app, the fraudsters can watch/control the customer's mobile / laptop and gain access to the financial credentials of the customer. Fraudsters use this information to carry out the unauthorized transfer of funds or make payments using the customer's Internet banking/payment apps.

SIM Cloning

In cases such as SIM swapping or SIM cloning, "*Fraudsters may obtain a duplicate Subscriber Identity Module (SIM) card (including electronic-SIM) for the registered mobile number linked to the customer's bank account by gaining access to the customer's Subscriber Identity Module (SIM) card,*" according to the RBI. Fraudsters utilize the OTP obtained on such a duplicate SIM to conduct unauthorized transactions. Fraudsters often obtain personal / identity data from customers by acting as telephone / mobile network workers and requesting the customer details in the name of incentives such as free SIM card upgrades from 3G to 4G or extra perks on the SIM Card.

Frauds Committed by Compromising Credentials on Search Engine Results

Customers utilize search engines to locate contact information for their bank, insurance provider, Aadhaar updation center, and other organizations. Scammers routinely alter these contact data on search engines to look as though they belong to the corresponding business. Customers may find unknown/unverified contact numbers of fraudsters advertised on search engines as bank/company contact numbers. According to the RBI's pamphlet, "*When client's phone these contact numbers, the imposters ask for their card credentials/details for verification. Customers submit their security information because they believe the scammer is a legitimate representative of the RE.*"

QR Code Scanning Scam

"*Fraudsters frequently approach consumers under various pretexts and deceive them into scanning Quick Response (QR) codes using the applications on the clients' phones*," RBI added. Customers may unintentionally authorize fraudsters to take money from their accounts by scanning such QR codes.

Social Media Impersonation

Lots of people spending time on social media and updating their details has made it easy for fraudsters to get details to dupe people. As per the RBI booklet, "*Fraudsters create fake accounts using details of the users of social media platforms such as Facebook, Instagram, Twitter, etc. Fraudsters then send a request to the users' friends asking for money for urgent medical purposes, payments, etc. Fraudsters, using fake details, also contact users and gain users' trust over some time. When the users share their personal or private information, the fraudsters use such information to blackmail or extort money from the users.*"

PREVENTION FROM E-BANKING FRAUD.

SMS Challenge Code

This is used to ensure that the user is logging into their real mobile phone by receiving an activation code on the registered mobile numbers associated with their bank account. Such temporary passwords are generated by the bank and sent as an SMS to the user's mobile phone number. The code is then used by the user to access their account.

Verification of Image

This method is based on a shared secret (picture or verification phrase) between the user and the bank. After logging into the banking system with a username, a device ID is sent to the user with that username and delivered via an encrypted cookie stored on the user's device. The system then determines if the device ID matches the username stored in the system before directing the user to a login page where the passcode/passphrase will be verified before accessing the system.

Dynamic Security Skins (DSS)

Here, the user must select an image (containing hints of sensitive information) to be superimposed on the web forms. This image is equipped with a virtual hash and bound to a secure SSL session. This makes it impossible for attackers to spoof pop-ups like password prompts.

Blocking Software

An example of blocking software is a surf watch that can filter or block any apps that are suspicious or could cause a security breach.

V-Chip

V-chip is a software developed and used to control children's access to websites. V-chip restricts children from viewing information that is considered dangerous to them. It can be installed on computers or televisions.

Browsers With Ratings

Browsers such as kidDeck, chiBrow, and sea Monkey are browsers that are customized for use by a specific category of people, such as children, to help them avoid becoming victims of cybercriminals.

Audit Controls

Audit controls are software installed and run on most networks to track records and file transactions of Internet users. Logs can be used to track security breaches and their sources.

Encryption

Encryption is used in data communication to convert data in transit or stored to an indecipherable form such that the data will be meaningless to the fraudster in the cause of interception. The policy here is that it is only the owner of the message that can decrypt the data and make it meaningful. A Microsoft and Netscape Email program has a synCrypt and SIMIME encrypting program used in its data communication.

People Controls

Hence fraud is committed by people, people control is rather a policy that regulates the right to use the net and other network applications. It is expected that organizations that use the net should prevent misuse, or abuse by screening who to employ or give right of usage, have job specifications for employees, limiting coverage, and proper disposal of documents that may communicate the organization's secrets to the public.

Firewalls

A firewall is used on a computer to block suspicious programs from running on a system, thereby denying suspicious programs control or access to the system.

Access Authorization

Access authorization is a program that disguises an access point by asking for credentials or permission to access an application or network. The user will be required to enter the requirements in the form of a PIN (Personal Identification Number), username, password, or biometrics before gaining access.

Use of Anti-Virus Software to Debug Viruses and Malware

The use of cryptography (anti-virus software) to transform data or information before transmission so that an unauthorized interceptor cannot decipher it. Only the sender and the authorized recipient can decrypt the message.

Use of Biometric Authentication

Biometrics is a measure of a physical characteristic or behavior pattern of people. A scan of physiological features is analyzed using a mathematical algorithm. The analyzed physiological feature is stored in the database in the form of data (minutes), which are used to verify and authenticate the person in the next transaction. Biometric security is one of the most reliable security measures.

Legislations and Policies

Enactment and enforcement of laws and policies that prohibit e-fraud with penalties for perpetrators is a very important measure to control E-fraud. Humans are complex and trivial in their behavior. When allowed to control themselves, they find it difficult to do the right thing. Therefore, documented controls are needed to control their behavior from excesses. Such a document should clearly define the penalty for any violation. As a matter of necessity and priority, offenders should be held accountable for their misconduct as stated in the constitution. If this is enforced, humans are expected to shape their behavior to suit well in such a society, if this is equally implemented in electronic fraud, it should be a good control measure then. Following the September 2001 Pentagon attack in the United States, the Federal Information Security Management Act (FISMA) was passed in 2002, giving the Office of Management and Budget (OMB) responsibility for coordinating information security standards and guidelines developed by federal agencies.

Banking Frauds in India

Many bank fraud cases across India from the financial year 2009 to 2021.

FINDINGS AND SUGGESTIONS

The findings revealed that online banking fraud, mobile banking fraud, and ATM fraud are the current E-banking fraud risks relevant to Indian banks. This study will help banks and regulators better understand E-Banking fraud, to strengthen the existing fraud prevention systems and new remedial measures related to the prevention of E-Banking fraud. It has been found that integrating biometric security and a system that reveals individuals' anonymity with E-Banking systems would aid in mitigating and combating E-Banking fraud. It has also been found that much software is available through which prevention of E-Banking fraud can be done. It has been noted that inefficient banking operations and internal controls, improper bank management, lack of education and training of bank personnel, lack of sophisticated technological prevention and detection tools, insufficient customer awareness, ineffective legislation, and law enforcement, and insufficient infrastructural and financial resources, economic pressure and availability sophisticated technology in the hands of fraudsters are seen as the main problems being faced by E-Banking system of India.

Figure 1.
Source: https://www.statista.com/statistics/1012729/india-number-of-bank-fraud-cases/

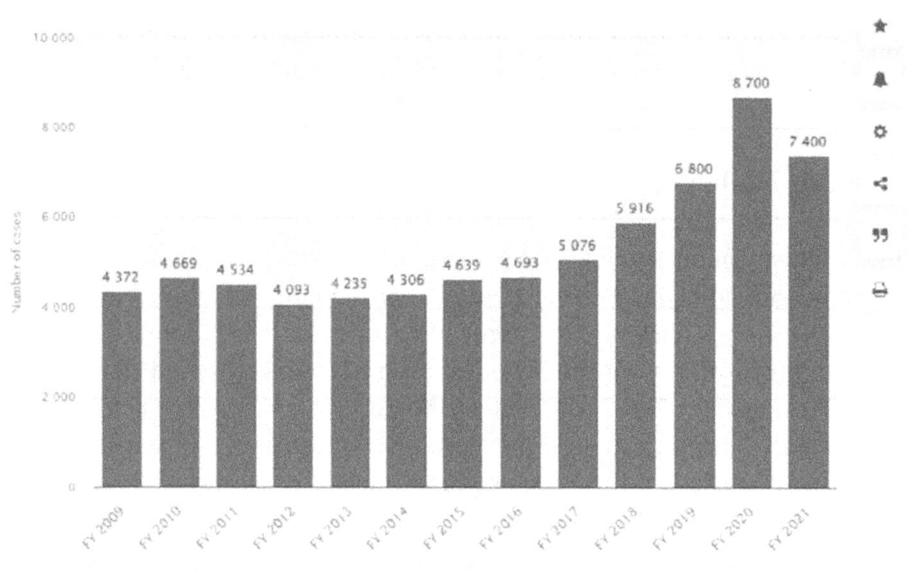

Figure 2. Fraud cases: Bank group-wise

(Amount in ₹ crore)

Bank Group/Institution	2018-19		2019-20		2020-21	
	Number of Frauds	Amount Involved	Number of Frauds	Amount Involved	Number of Frauds	Amount Involved
1	2	3	4	5	6	7
Public Sector Banks	3,704 *(54.5)*	64,207 *(89.8)*	4,410 *(50.7)*	1,48,224 *(79.9)*	2,903 *(39.4)*	81,901 *(59.2)*
Private Sector Banks	2,149 *(31.6)*	5,809 *(8.1)*	3,065 *(35.2)*	34,211 *(18.4)*	3,710 *(50.4)*	46,335 *(33.5)*
Foreign Banks	762 *(11.2)*	955 *(1.3)*	1026 *(11.8)*	972 *(0.5)*	521 *(7.1)*	3,315 *(2.4)*
Financial Institutions	28 *(0.4)*	553 *(0.8)*	15 *(0.2)*	2,048 *(1.1)*	25 *(0.3)*	6,839 *(4.9)*
Small Finance Banks	115 *(1.7)*	8 *(0.0)*	147 *(1.7)*	11 *(0.0)*	114 *(1.6)*	30 *(0.0)*
Payments Banks	39 *(0.6)*	2 *(0.0)*	38 *(0.4)*	2 *(0.0)*	88 *(1.2)*	2 *(0.0)*
Local Area Banks	1 *(0.0)*	0.02 *(0.0)*	2 *(0.0)*	0.43 *(0.0)*	2 *(0.0)*	0 *(0.0)*
Total	**6,798** ***(100.0)***	**71,534** ***(100.0)***	**8,703** ***(100.0)***	**1,85,468** ***(100.0)***	**7,363** ***(100.0)***	**138,422** ***(100.0)***

Note: 1. Figures in parentheses represent shares in total (in per cent).
2. Figures reported by banks & FIs are subject to change based on revisions filed by them.
3. Amounts involved reported do not reflect the amount of loss incurred. Depending on recoveries, the loss incurred gets reduced. Further, the entire amount involved is not necessarily diverted.
4. The dates of occurrence of these frauds are spread over several previous years.
5. The above data is in respect of frauds of ₹1 lakh and above reported during the period.

Source: RBI Supervisory Returns.

For the growth of E-Banking, the government is advised to provide adequate infrastructural facilities, especially in telecommunication and power, and take steps to encourage ICT usage amongst its public. The government should also strengthen the regulatory framework to ensure the security of the transaction. Banks on their part are recommended to improve their e-commerce and E-Banking facilities and ensure good connectivity for a hitch-free transaction via electronic means and carry out constant and extensive training of their employees and customers to make them abreast of the latest developments in e-commerce and e-banking.

Each bank should pay attention to E-Banking fraud because the study showed that the rapid implementation of E-Banking security has become important as banks have introduced E-Banking for all their customers. Execution of sophisticated prevention and detection mechanisms is needed, especially for the most popular types of E-Banking fraud in India: ATM fraud, Internet banking fraud, mobile banking fraud, and credit and debit card fraud. E-Banking fraudsters are unlikely to be caught by modern security systems in individual banks. Therefore, Indian banking systems need to create an external environment in terms of external IT structures, as these structures may be vulnerable to attacks from outside, which may result in significant losses. Indian banking institutions, jointly or individually, can test the best practices in E-Banking fraud prevention and detection in other banks or institutions around the world.

Customer awareness is another challenge. Banking institutions are reluctant to engage in customer awareness about E-Banking fraud because of the potential reputational damage. Brand identity is vital to retain and maintain customer loyalty to banks; therefore, the Indian banking system should take this important role by providing customer education and information materials to all Depository Banks (DMBs) on the causes and effects of E-Banking fraud, including how to report, prevent and detect it. This can prominently draw attention to the early warning system of customers without putting any bank's product brand and reputation at risk. In addition, the creation of a centralized fraud database would be very important and would increase the fraud investigation capabilities of the Depository Fraud Investigation Teams.

The Indian banking sector should provide antivirus software to all its customers through electronic bank accounts, they must be granted access to download and install it on their systems. This will protect individual E-Banking customers from fraudsters using viruses to capture their account information. Another recommendation is based on the prevention and detection of E-Banking fraud committed by fraudsters from abroad. The Indian banking system should tie up with foreign banking associations. Such relationships can enhance their capacity to prevent and detect E-Banking fraud both domestically and internationally and contribute to the development of international E-Banking fraud prevention and detection techniques for use in the Indian banking industry.

In a similar vein, almost all business and non-profit organizations are patronizing the banking industry and engaging in E-Banking such as Electronic points of Sale (EPoS) and Automated Teller Machines (ATMs). Therefore, Indian banks should establish relationships, interactions, or partnerships with government and non-government organizations, including other financial institutions in the country, to share information and technology to prevent and detect E-Banking fraud, and to improve knowledge and transfer of technology. It will also provide an opportunity to educate all organizations that the prevention and detection of E-Banking fraud is not only a struggle of one organization but also involves the cooperation of all organizations in the region.

CONCLUSION

The exponential rise of the Internet has greatly helped today's business environment (particularly the E-Banking industry). E-Banking transformed the banking industry by providing several customer-related benefits and new commercial platforms for banks. It did, however, come at a cost, mostly in terms of financial risks, problems, and security concerns. To safeguard against various types of fraud, financial firms must address security at all levels (Rafay, 2021b, 2023b). Several strategies for fraud prevention and detection have been proposed by several academics. This includes full biometric integration in E-Banking, user identity at each transaction, the usage of personal identity, and so on. Due to the significant weight of biometrics and its application in real-time transactions, as well as human rights abuses, not all the results have been integrated into E-Banking to combat fraud.

Hence, it can be concluded that e-commerce and E-Banking positively impact the economy by facilitating better exchange transactions, promoting active participation in the international market, enhancing effectiveness and efficiency, and lastly, it has led to significant improvement in the growth of the economy.

DECLARATION

The author declares that the manuscript follows ethical standards and there are no potential conflicts of interest with respect to the research, authorship and/or publication of this chapter.

DISCLAIMER

The contents and views of this chapter are expressed by the authors in personal capacities. It is not necessary for the Editor and the Publisher to agree with these viewpoints, and they are not responsible for any duty of care in this regard.

ACKNOWLEDGMENT

The authors extend sincere gratitude to

- The Editor and the International Editorial Advisory Board (IEAB) of this book who initially desk reviewed, arranged a rigorous double/triple blind review process, and conducted a thorough, minute, and critical final review before accepting the chapter for publication.
- All anonymous reviewers who provided very constructive feedbacks for thorough revision, improvement, extension, and fine tuning of the chapter.
- All colleagues, assistants and well-wishers who assisted the authors to complete this task.

REFERENCES

Abu-Shanab, E., & Matalqa, S. (2015). Security and fraud issues of E-Banking. *International Journal of Computer Networks and Applications*, *2*(4), 179–188.

Ahmad, I., Iqbal, S., Jamil, S., & Kamran, M. (2021). A Systematic literature review of E-Banking frauds: Current scenario and security techniques. *Linguistica Antverpiensia, 2*(2), 3509–3517.

Ali, M., Lei, S., & Wei, X. Y. (2018). The mediating role of the employee relations climate in the relationship between strategic HRM and organizational performance in Chinese banks. *Journal of Innovation & Knowledge, 3*(3), 115–122. doi:10.1016/j.jik.2016.12.003

Alsayed, A., & Bilgrami, A. (2017). E-Banking security: Internet hacking, phishing attacks, analysis, and prevention of fraudulent activities. *International Journal of Emerging Technology and Advanced Engineering, 7*(1), 109–115.

Andoh-Baidoo, F. K., & Osatuyi, B. (2009). Examining online banking initiatives in Nigeria: A value network approach. *The Electronic Journal on Information Systems in Developing Countries, 38*(1), 1–14. doi:10.1002/j.1681-4835.2009.tb00264.x

Basel Committee Report on Banking Supervision. (1998). *Risk Management for Electronic Banking and Electronic Money Activities*. Basel: Bank of International Settlements.

Bashir, M. A., Ali, M. H., Wai, L. M., Hossain, M. I., & Rahaman, M. S. (2020). Mediating effect of customer perceived value on the relationship between service quality and customer satisfaction of E-Banking in Bangladesh. *International Journal of Advanced Science and Technology, 29*(2), 3590–3606.

Chaimaa, B., Najib, E., & Rachid, H. (2021). E-banking overview: Concepts, challenges and solutions. *Wireless Personal Communications, 117*(2), 1059–1078. doi:10.100711277-020-07911-0

Chaturvedi, A., & Meena, A. (2016). Analyzing the impacts of phishing and vishing attacks in internet banking. *International Journal of Advanced Research in Computer Science and Software Engineering, 6*(3), 16–21.

Chiemeke, S. C., Evwiekpaefe, A. E., & Chete, F. O. (2006). The adoption of Internet banking in Nigeria: An empirical investigation. *Journal of Internet Banking and Commerce, 11*(3), 1–10.

Eneji, S. E., Angib, M. U., Ibe, W. E., & Ekwegh, K. C. (2019). A study of electronic banking fraud, fraud detection and control. *International Journal of Innovative Science and Research Technology, 4*(3), 708–711.

Gertler, M., & Kiyotaki, N. (2010). Financial intermediation and credit policy in business cycle analysis. In *Handbook of Monetary Economics* (Vol. 3, pp. 547–599). Elsevier.

Hani, P. (2020). Impact of frauds on the Indian Banking sector. *International Journal of Creative research Thoughts, 8*(4), 1602–1607.

Ingle, A., & Pardeshi, R. (2012). Internet banking in India: Challenges and opportunities. *IBMRD's. Journal of Management Research, 1*(1), 13–18.

Jeyanthi, P. M., Mansurali, A., Harish, V., & Krishnaveni, V. D. (2019). Significance of fraud analytics in Indian banking sectors. *Journal of Critical Reviews, 7*(4), 209–213.

John, S. N., Anele, C., Kennedy, O. O., Olajide, F., & Kennedy, C. G. (2016, December). Realtime fraud detection in the banking sector using data mining techniques/algorithm. In 2016 international conference on computational science and computational intelligence (CSCI) (pp. 1186–1191). IEEE.

Kibets, D., Lepei, O., Prokopenko, O., Chorna, A., & Shelukhin, M. (2019). Anti-Fraud technologies in E-Banking. *Journal of Legal, Ethical and Regulatory Issues*, *22*(SI2), 1–6.

Kuzic, J., Fisher, J., & Scollary, A. (2002). Electronic commerce benefits, challenges and success factors in the Australian banking and finance industry. *ECIS 2002 Proceedings, 60*, 1607–1616.

Loonam, M., & O'Loughlin, D. (2008). An observation analysis of e-service quality in online banking. *Journal of Financial Services Marketing*, *13*(2), 164–178. doi:10.1057/fsm.2008.13

Mahdi, M. D. H., Rezaul, K. M., & Rahman, M. A. (2010, February). Credit fraud detection in the banking sector in UK: a focus on e-business. In *2010 Fourth International Conference on Digital Society* (pp. 232–237). IEEE. 10.1109/ICDS.2010.45

Mangala, D., & Soni, L. (2023). A systematic literature review on frauds in banking sector. *Journal of Financial Crime*, *30*(1), 285–301. doi:10.1108/JFC-12-2021-0263

Mannan, M., & Van Oorschot, P. C. (2008, July). Security and usability: the gap in real-world online banking. In *Proceedings of the 2007 Workshop on New Security Paradigms* (pp. 1–14). ACM. 10.1145/1600176.1600178

Mostafa, R. B. (2020). Mobile banking service quality: A new avenue for customer value co-creation. *International Journal of Bank Marketing*, *38*(5), 1107–1132. doi:10.1108/IJBM-11-2019-0421

Nakitende, M. G., Rafay, A., & Waseem, M. (2021). Frauds in Business Organizations: A Comprehensive Overview. In A. Rafay (Ed.), *Handbook of Research on Theory and Practice of Financial Crimes* (pp. 21–38). IGI Global., doi:10.4018/978-1-7998-5567-5.ch002

Papazoglou, M. P. (2003, December). Service-oriented computing: Concepts, characteristics and directions. In *Proceedings of the Fourth International Conference on Web Information Systems Engineering, 2003. WISE 2003.* (pp. 3–12). IEEE. 10.1109/WISE.2003.1254461

Rafay, A. (Ed.). (2019). *FinTech as Disruptive Technology for Financial Institutions*. IGI Global. doi:10.4018/978-1-5225-7805-5

Rafay, A. (Ed.). (2021a). *Money Laundering and Terrorism Financing in Global Financial Systems*. IGI Global. doi:10.4018/978-1-7998-8758-4

Rafay, A. (Ed.). (2021b). *HandBook of Research on Theory and Practice of Financial Crimes*. IGI Global. doi:10.4018/978-1-7998-5567-5

Rafay, A. (Ed.). (2023a). *Concepts, Cases, and Regulations in Financial Fraud and Corruption*. IGI Global. doi:10.4018/978-1-6684-5007-9

Rafay, A. (Ed.). (2023b). *Concepts and Cases of Illicit Finance*. IGI Global. doi:10.4018/978-1-6684-8587-3

Rafay, A., & Gilani, U. J. (2016). Banking Competition and Stability: Evidence from Inter-continental Markets. *DLSU Business and Economics Review*, *25*(2), 24–40.

Rahman, R. A., & Anwar, I. S. K. (2014). Effectiveness of fraud prevention and detection techniques in Malaysian Islamic banks. *Procedia: Social and Behavioral Sciences*, *145*, 97–102. doi:10.1016/j.sbspro.2014.06.015

Ramamoorti, S., Morrison, D., & Koletar, J. W. (2009). *Bringing Freud to Fraud: Understanding the state-of-mind of the C-level suite/white collar offender through "ABC" analysis*. Institute for Fraud Prevention (IFP) at West Virginia University. https://ecommons.udayton.edu/acc_fac_pub/71/

Ramana, S. V., & Krishna, S. G. (2017). A study on impact of fraud in Indian banking sector (With special reference on retail banking products). *International Journal of Academic Research and Development*, *2*(6), 544–547.

Rampini, A. A., & Viswanathan, S. (2010). Collateral, risk management, and the distribution of debt capacity. *The Journal of Finance*, *65*(6), 2293–2322. doi:10.1111/j.1540-6261.2010.01616.x

Rampini, A. A., & Viswanathan, S. (2019). Financial intermediary capital. *The Review of Economic Studies*, *86*(1), 413–455. doi:10.1093/restud/rdy020

Salehi, M., & Alipour, M. (2010). E-banking in emerging economy: Empirical evidence of Iran. *International Journal of Economics and Finance*, *2*(1), 201–209. doi:10.5539/ijef.v2n1p201

Saranya, K., & Gunasri, K. S. (2013). Challenges in E-banking. *International Journal of Scientific Research and Management (IJSRM)*, *22*, 27.

Shah, M. (2019). A Case study on increasing of banking fraud in India. *Parichay: Maharaja Surajmal Institute Journal of Applied Research*, *2*(1), 20–23.

Shams, R., Sobhan, A., Vrontis, D., Belyaeva, Z., & Vukovic, D. (2021). Detection of financial fraud risk: Implications for financial stability. *Journal of Operational Risk*, *15*(4), 1–13.

Sharma, N., & Sharma, D. (2017). An empirical study on banking frauds in India-with a special reference to role of employee awareness in banking frauds. *International Journal of Business and Management*, *3*(1), 2055–2066.

Usman, A. K., & Shah, M. H. (1970). Critical success factors for preventing e-banking fraud. *Journal of Internet Banking and Commerce*, *18*(2), 1–14.

Chapter 10
Consumer Risk Perception Towards Cybercrimes and E-Commerce:
The Case of Malaysia

Hui Nee Au Yong
https://orcid.org/0000-0002-3337-213X
Universiti Tunku Abdul Rahman, Malaysia

Yoke Chin Kuah
Universiti Tunku Abdul Rahman, Malaysia

Chooi Yi Wei
Universiti Tunku Abdul Rahman, Malaysia

Abdul Rafay
https://orcid.org/0000-0002-0285-5980
University of Management and Technology, Pakistan

ABSTRACT

The concept of this chapter is to review the literature for a research gap on risk perception among online consumers and the intention for online purchases in Malaysia. Online platforms and digital payments make online shopping easier. During the year 2020 - 2021, online shopping had become increasingly active with the spike of the novel coronavirus pandemic. Online users who share their personal information online are most likely getting into the scammer's trap. Malaysia executed the national cyber security policy to defend the country's critical national information infrastructure. Financial awareness among online users plays a crucial role in fighting cybercrime. Digital guardianship should exist to prevent irresponsible parties from taking advantage. The routine activity theory has been proposed to explain the phenomenon whereby the offender makes the selection to commit a crime based on an online shopper as his target and the guardianship.

DOI: 10.4018/979-8-3693-1190-5.ch010

INTRODUCTION

In line with Industrial Revolution (IR) 4.0, advanced technologies have shifted by propelling Malaysians to enter a digital world. Moreover, the digital economy as the global network of economic activities is empowered by information and communication technologies. Online platforms and digital payment make life easier for consumers to do their online shopping. The economy is transforming into a cashless economy where day-to-day transactions are being completed by digital wallets such as TnG e-wallet, Grabpay and Boost.

According to Jones (2021), cybercrime cost the world GBP 1 trillion in 2020. In the United Kingdom (UK), there were more than six thousand COVID-19 related fraud and cyber-crime cases reported involving GBP 34.5 million in one year from March 2020 (Simmons & Quinton, 2021). Consequently, cybercrime issues in electronic payment systems deter consumers from purchasing online (Muhtasim *et al.*, 2022).

This chapter focuses on the overview of shopping trends in the new era, consumer risk perception, cybercrime, cybersecurity and area of improvement in terms of digital guidance and the intention to purchase online. The implication of this chapter will benefit the practitioners of online shopping to enhance their awareness and to make them more alert during online shopping.

The fear of cybercrime is a serious social problem as it will deter the development of a digital economy that signifies the era of the fourth industrial revolution. This is the problem for the next stage of economic development.

The main theme of the literature review is based on the Routine Activity Theory and its construct, digital guardianship (e.g., cybersecurity) and risky online lifestyles. It is important to contain cybercrime victimization risk so that the digital economy can further be developed with stronger online consumer intention to purchase. The chapter is significant as a wider understanding of the issue is much needed.

SHOPPING TREND IN NEW ERA: CONSUMER ONLINE LIFESTYLE

Consumer lifestyle will affect their own action in making the decision to purchase. A similar view by Herawaty and Tresna (2019) mentioned that purchase decision stems from the characteristics of a consumer's lifestyle. If a person has a habit of spending online, he or she will consume the products that they like, without much consideration of online reviews or word-of-mouth promotion. The growth of e-commerce in Malaysia has shifted dramatically at an unprecedented pace especially during the COVID-19 pandemic, leading to consumers changing from physical shopping to online shopping, especially during the Movement Control Order (MCO) period. Accordingly, the rapid shift to online shopping has also changed consumers' online lifestyles (Anastasiadou *et al.*, 2020). Consumers prefer online shopping for its efficiency and convenience as well as the pricing, relative to the pricing at the physical outlets. The increasing trend for online shopping has significantly affected consumers' purchases.

On the other hand, Stofkova, Laikep, and Stofkova (2022) further explained that consumers can purchase anything at any time with just a few clicks without having to leave their homes. Online shopping is integrated into the daily life of consumers, from purchases of apparel and groceries to hotel/flight bookings and others (Iqbal, 2019). In addition, online shopping allows consumers to draw comparisons among many online shopping websites so that they can decide upon the best-suited and reasonably priced purchases. Nonetheless, online shoppers who work five days a week from 9 am to 5 pm may face difficulties in collecting parcels physically when the delivery is made.

Hence, there is a need for online retailers to provide more delivery alternatives to cater to the needs of online shoppers and to complete transactions. Suggestions of the strategy include providing specific locations that are convenient for consumers to pick up goods after working hours such as 24-hour convenient stores. This will increase the efficiency of online shopping in this new era. Online shopping businesses also need to take any corrective actions arising from consumers' reviews and feedback (Wen, Salar, Ishak & Ating, 2020).

Perceived Risk

Even though e-commerce and online shopping activities are increasing especially during the Covid-19 pandemic period, there are also mounting challenges and problems identifying consumers' risk perception compared to traditional retail.

Despite the advantages of online shopping in terms of saving costs and time, online shopping also has its drawbacks. Taking the surface view from the dimension of product quality, there is the risk that online shoppers may be disappointed when the product they receive has a quality that is not up to their expectations. Additionally, there was also the possibility of delay and not receiving the items in the quantity purchased. When the online shopper checks on the review before they purchase the items, there is also a possibility that the reviews are fake or inaccurate.

In fact, there are several perceived risks that have an impact on online purchases, especially fraud risk. Fraud risk through e-commerce includes any illegal activities that enable the online sellers to gain profit which in turn, will harm the consumers financially, cause fear and become a security threat to e-commerce consumers (Kim, Ferrin, & Rao, 2008). Online fraudulent behavior is like conventional fraud. The dissimilarity is in the way of action, which is the operating computer systems (Thomas *et al.*, 2004) The speedy development of the usage of the Internet services has caused some adverse impacts in the type of crimes and violations, i.e., the cybercrime (Dashora, 2011). Internet hacker or scammer seems to act faster than cybersecurity protector companies. This situation will affect the trust among online shoppers which plays an important role in affecting the sustainability of businesses for the long term.

Apau, Koranteng and Gyamfi (2019) also found that trust in the Internet is an important consideration in less developed countries. The flaws associated with computer networks and the Internet have resulted in cybercrime. Internet users are aware of these fraudulent activities by cybercrime, leading them to exercise higher cautiousness when making online transactions. Thus, in the current digital era, reliable investigative skills are needed to uncover fraudulent practices (Sumartono *et al.*, 2020). However, if consumers spend time accessing more information about the web pages before making online transactions, they can predict the risks they face. For example, online shoppers could browse the company's website and Facebook, 'Google-search' on the company products to ensure the reliability of the company and the products from the said company. The more positive the information about web e-commerce, the smaller the fraud risk faced by consumers (Winarso, 2020). This is consistent with the study by Johan, Syed and Adnan (2022) which states that businesses need to provide enough security measure information to customers, that is on how their data and online transactions are being protected. Through this, businesses will gain higher trust among online shoppers to increase their purchasing intention. Perceived risk has a stronger negative influence on customer purchase behavior (Li *et al.*, 2019).

According to Meskaran, Ismail and Shanmugam (2013), security problems are understood to be the main worry of online consumers. The study reported that 70 percent of online consumers are willing to spend extra on online shopping if the security issues can be solved. The authors also reported that managing the online transaction risks with the purpose of increasing online purchases is the most important restriction for online purchase intention. Consumers will feel secure with online purchases. Nevertheless, Wei, Peng and Wu (2021) found that risk-preferred household head was among the variables that positively impact fraud detection.

Besides security, education level also influences the level of risk perception among online shoppers. Consumers with higher education levels are perceived to have the best risk perception mindset, so they will be more careful when they do online shopping. According to a field study by Hasan, Rahman, Abdillah and Omar (2015) on younger Internet users, the students with higher levels of education have higher risk perception. According to the study, higher learning institutions are recommended to play a role in educating young people with knowledge of cybercrime to increase their level of awareness and risk perception. On the other hand, gender may also play a role. The results from Yusof (2015) show that although people are autonomous in their financial decisions, female is to have less risk tolerance than males.

Overview of Cybercrime

Consistent with the development of the latest digital technology or the Fourth Industrial Revolution (IR4.0), the online shopping process becomes more efficient and is a contributing factor behind a country's economic growth. Kigerl (2012) found that richer countries with higher online users per capita have more cybercrime cases. However, Internet users who are also spammers were found more in countries with higher unemployment rates. This might be because this group tends to be searching for easy alternatives to obtain income. On the other hand, Kigerl (2021) added that online users per capita predicted all 3 types of cybercrime namely spam, fraud, and malware, while GDP was linked positively with spam, and negatively with fraud.

The case of First Commercial Bank is one of the earliest global organised crimes committed by the Cobalt group in Taiwan. The offenders concentrated on a German automatic teller machine model for utilising their programmed malware that activated a large amount of cash flow from automatic teller machines. Cybercriminals misused the susceptibility of the cybersecurity defense system (Hsieh & Wang, 2018). The hackers and tricksters took advantage of the situation by sabotaging the online platforms and causing trauma to the consumers. It is worrying that online consumers may underestimate the vulnerability of "transmission channels" namely chat rooms, discussion forums, emails, instant messaging, messenger, social media, and other online platforms that could be utilized for the penetration of the network (Antonescu & Birăub, 2015).

In cyberspace, despite geographical borders, culprits can victimise any online user if they activate the concealed malware in their computer or mobile phone (Taylor *et al.*, 2006; Eck & Clarke, 2003). It is crucial to have strong antivirus software, and Cybersecurity protection elements in online devices such as personal computers, mobile phones, and laptops for hackers to not be able to attack easily. Online users that used to share their personal photos and personal information online most likely have a higher possibility of getting into the scammer's trap.

In Malaysia, Basyir (2021) also highlights that people have lost RM2.23 billion because of cybercrime frauds since the year 2017. Fraud refers to deception deliberately committed for unlawful gain.

Online shopping scams engage scammers pretending to be lawful online merchants. Trends in online shopping increased drastically during the MCO implemented worldwide in relation to the spike of the novel coronavirus pandemic. There was a loss of RM58 million to online shopping scams in the first 10 months of 2021 with 8,162 reported online shopping fraud cases during the said duration in Malaysia. This indicates that many of the online consumers in Malaysia are in the high-risk group. Government and relevant stakeholders should investigate this issue seriously towards strategizing the possible alternatives to overcome or reduce the issue of cybercrime.

On the other hand, trust fraud in the online purchase can occur easily as the buyers in an online marketplace rely significantly on the reviews written by past customers (Wu *et al.*, 2015). Zhang *et al.* (2013) also agree that trust fraud has become the biggest obstacle since the expansion of the e-commerce market in China. A study finds that 92 percent of online consumers will review the comments of previous customers before making purchasing decisions (Li *et al.*, 2013). Yet, the reviews provided on the website cannot be confirmed as reliable, unless verified through the word of mouth from the website's own contact list. Hence, placing an order and purchasing without obtaining much information or obtaining the actual review prior to the online purchase will easily lead the consumer to an online shopping scam.

Cybercrime Victimization

Despite Malaysia moving into digital technology that benefits the nation, the cybersecurity issue and online scam cases are still crucial aspects to be given focus by all stakeholders (Muniandy *et al.*, 2017). Insecure Internet links and public access computers are developed as risk factors for both cyber-dependent and cyber-enabled crime victimization; specifically, personal information disclosure via online advertisement sites and social networking services has intensified the possibility of one being a phishing target (Akdemir & Lawless, 2020).

The study by Song *et al.* (2016) found that patrons who access the Internet only at home were positively related to people involved in cyber-theft victimization. Personal low self-control with attractive information on the Internet, lack of digital guardianship among online users, also online exposure often led the user to cyber scam victimization (Wilson *et al.*, 2022).

The study of Saridakis *et al.* (2016) shows that there is a negative relationship between the usage of multipurpose dominant social networking services (SNS) and online victimization. Nevertheless, actions on the SNS for the exchange of knowledge, e.g., LinkedIn and Blogger, have a positive relationship with online victimization. In addition, deviant online activities, e.g., free streaming or peer-to-peer sharing appear to intensify the risk of crime victimization (Akdemir & Lawless, 2020).

Different frauds committed online and victimization methods are related to media types (Lee, 2021). Amongst the wide-ranging Internet activities, ''targeted browsing'' leads to intensified risks (Leukfeldt, 2014). Most of the time, misleading information from the Internet will propel the users to browse further to the next webpage and at some point, they might be required to download certain software or files. Users will usually follow the instruction given as it is stated that an upcoming attractive return might be there for the users. This situation is common, especially on the online shopping website where it requires the user to key in the number of their bank account, credit card or debit card together with the security number from the payment card on the website. Money in the payment card will then be transferred out without any notification to the user until the user receives their bank transaction statement. As a result, a lot of misleading information will lead to occurrences of online shopping scams.

During the year 2020 - 2021, online shopping was on the rise significantly. This situation has been confirmed by Oki and Ngotshane (2021) who found that the number of cybercrime cases has increased drastically among online shoppers during the pandemic era. However, there were some irresponsible online sellers who intentionally grab the advantage by conducting their business unethically. Hence, this phenomenon turns the online shopping experience into a traumatic situation for certain online scam victims. As reported by Nuradzimmah (2022) in the New Straits Times, there were more than 51,600 online scam cases incurring a total loss of RM1.61 billion reported from the year 2020 - 2021. Online shopping scams were reported as the highest cases surrounding the 18,857 complaints during the said duration.

The risk of consumer victimization among the elderly is increasingly prominent as their level of awareness of fraud is low (Mears *et al.*, 2016). The reason is that the consumer's ability to make sound financial decisions is reduced as they become older. Moreover, the elderly people have savings and strong financial assets in comparison to the younger groups (Nguyen *et al.*, 2013). On the contrary, the youth is reasonably aware of financial cybercrime (Muhamad *et al.*, 2021). Based on the findings of Junger *et al.* (2017), the youth were more at risk of online purchase fraud, but the elderly ran more risk of being victims of online banking fraud.

According to Junger *et al.* (2017), there were few differences according to gender, and gender continues as a strong forecaster of adolescent victimization (Alam, 2018). A study by Whitty (2020) highlighted that online shopping scam victims are more likely to be women with lower education qualifications as well as senior males with a higher internal locus of control. Tharshini, Hassan and Mas'ud (2021) also indicate that females aged between 18 and 28 years old more easily fall prey as victims to online phishing/malware distribution and online sexual harassment.

In addition, consumers who are married, such as adults of the age of 25 to 45 years, with at least a diploma education level yet lacking in digital skills and low cyber fraud awareness are more probable to be victims of cyber romance scams (Saad, Abdullah, & Murah, 2018). Guedes, Martins and Cardoso (2022), report findings on victimization that those who have better higher computer skills are less fearful of online identity theft (OIT). In this respect, financial literacy and public awareness play a crucial role to combat the threat of cybercrime (Isa, Ibrahim & Mohamed, 2021).

WAY FORWARD: INCREASING THE SECURITY

Cybersecurity

One of the main attributes leading to the wave of cybercrime is the lack of cybersecurity defense awareness of online users (Zulkipli *et al.*, 2021). Tharshini, Mas'ud and Hassan (2022) also establish that online users must suffer from an elevated level of online phishing/malware distribution in addition to a moderate level of both online fraud and online sexual harassment. Furthermore, an analysis from Lallie *et al.* (2021) shows that COVID-19 related cybercrime cases have increased to 3 to 4 distinctive cybercrime cases on certain days.

According to Leukfeldt (2014), among eight Internet activities, ''targeted browsing'' leads to enlarged risk, where banks could play the function of a competent guardian. The finding of Muhamad *et al.* (2021) shows that youth are reasonably aware of financial cybercrime. According to Garba, Siraj and Othman (2022), students have knowledge of cybersecurity in Internet banking, while others such as cyber bullying, self-protection and Internet addiction display moderate awareness. Furthermore, youths who are more often involved in online risky social networking actions are at greater risk of being oppressed by cyberbullying in contrast to conventional bullying (Choi, Cho & Lee, 2019).

A higher number of cybercrime cases have been reported. Sviatun *et al.* (2021) found that the reasons for the increasing cybercrime cases are due to (i) electronization and computerization of most industries, public sector; (ii) low level of operational cooperation; (iii) inconsistency of legal policy with the realities of cybercrime; (iv) development of cyber-attack mechanism; (v) modernization of cybercrime; (vi) obstacles to international cooperation.

In contrast, De Kimpe *et al.* (2021) observed that people who feel well-informed about electronic safety were less susceptible to cybercrime and were less serious about taking additional protection to conduct security actions. In other words, a high trust level in Internet safety is related to individual sentiment: those less exposed to cybercrime, or who have never experienced cybercrime previously or perceived that cybercrime is not a severe risk. In relation to this, the study of Zahari, Bilu, and Said (2019) deduces that those with higher levels of confidence, familiarity and trust appear to have higher e-commerce trustworthiness levels. A person who has yet to experience the cybercrime trap can hardly imagine the impact or the seriousness of cybercrime.

Hence, Tamyez (2022) suggested that awareness and budget are crucial for the implementation of the cybersecurity element in the company operating system. Companies should focus on protecting critical applications in the pervasive environment to handle cyberspace attacks for the benefit of the company's revenue (Singh, Frank, & Zainon, 2021). An analysis by Buil-Gil, Lord and Barrett (2021) on the UK Cybersecurity Breaches Survey shows that the most secure method to reduce cyber-attacks is to provide in-house cybersecurity personnel and develop the personnel's cyber self-protection through cybersecurity education, instead of merely deploying software shield and management concerning robust passwords. A study by Back and Guerette (2021) assessed the effect of an anti-phishing training course provided to personnel which can enhance both the awareness and understanding of ways to well protect their "virtual places" against cybercrime.

Cyber threats are real, and the government should lay out c measures against them. There is a huge threat that the increasing wave of cybercrime impersonates not only various social, and commercial but also digital government applications. Consequently, Malaysia executed the National Cyber Security Policy (NCSP) to defend the country's Critical National Information Infrastructure against cyber threats, in which the NCSP initiatives require the commitment and participation of numerous stakeholders to safeguard the continuous momentum (Abdullah, Mohamad & Yunos (2018). All the relevant stakeholders such as sellers, buyers, the Government, non-profit organizations (NGOs), and even the Central Bank need to cooperate to combat the issues of cyber scams which impact the country's social and economic aspects. Furthermore, AlDaajeh *et al.* (2022) suggest that cybersecurity training programs made from the Goal-Question-Outcomes (GQO) + Strategies paradigm based on the 3 major cybersecurity strategic goals, i.e., defense against sophisticated cyber threats, the progress of digital and information technology securities, and the improvement of cybersecurity awareness.

Consequently, various stakeholders are required to consider measures that enhance cybersecurity and financial literacy. According to Isa, Ibrahim and Mohamed (2021), financial literacy and awareness among online users play a crucial role to fight threats of cybercrime. Nevertheless, due to the COVID-19 pandemic and the MCO period, the working from home concept demands the usage of digital systems and Internet services. It has exposed employees and employers to cybersecurity risks (Faisal & Ismail, 2022). Obviously, online shopping transaction increases significantly during MCO compared to the year 2019. Moreover, physical businesses also transform their business into an online or virtual platform during the MCO period. Thus, Internet traffic has heavily increased due to all sorts of sectors performing their work virtually, i.e., education, administration, and selling goods and services online. This phenomenon contributes to the increase of cybercrime where some irresponsible parties would seek to gain fast cash by performing cyber scam activities. Hence, Tientcheu (2021) analyzed the issue in 4 themes, i.e., cybercrime prevention policies, cybersecurity response plan, cybersecurity awareness culture, and end-users/employees training. With these categories, relevant stakeholders might be able to draft a comprehensive action plan and develop a task force to overcome the issues.

In Europe, Cook *et al.* (2022) showed that the anxiety of economic cybercrime differs across European Union members, other than the fact that the country's infrastructure and income inequality are projecting individual anxiety, individual routine activities and social demographic variables are linked with anxiety, and country infrastructure moderates the impacts of individual guardianship.

Digital Guardianship

The advanced technology has enabled the monitoring of Internet users' activities and ongoing exploration of human interaction and cybersecurity improvement (Ceccato, 2019). For instance, the history of websites browsed and pop-up messages for confirmation if one needs to download or browse a specific website can be monitored.

Recommendation of digital guardianship enhancement should be considered. Particularly, banks as financial intermediaries could play the role of capable guardians. Digital guardianship is important to prevent irresponsible parties from taking advantage of online scams. A study done by Reyns, Henson and Fisher (2016) reveal that students staying with their parents will have more effective guardianship compared to the students staying in the hostel with their peers. This may be explained by the fact that there are no adults to observe or advise them, and they are free to browse their preferred websites with their peers.

Online users should be aware of the online scam risk, especially during online shopping. According to Yoon (2002), awareness is defined as the individual's knowledge about a situation or fact and the level of risk. These include their awareness while purchasing things online in B2C contexts (Chin *et al.*, 2009). Therefore, Akdemir and Yenal (2020) suggest that personal guardianship actions, such as using complex and different passwords, are predictors of victimization.

The excellent design and branding of the online store will have an impact on the online consumer's judgment of whether they want to buy. As a result, the consumers may purchase the items due to the excellent surroundings of the online store instead of fulfilling their actual needs (Clow *et al.*, 1998). The user will be more confident in making a purchase if the desired website has greater exposure in the open market since the public's and individuals' trust on the website will increase. The level of confidence in purchasing from the vendor will also rise because of having a larger and more renowned website (Jarvenpaa *et al.*, 2000). At this stage, the consumers may make irrational buying decisions without considering the need to buy the said product.

Kuo (2021) recommends that the lifestyle-routine activity style in justifying crime patterns' applicability in burglary and cybercrime must be considered well. Findings from Kirwan, Fullwood, and Rooney (2018) reveal some victimization risk factors such as having higher scores in impulsivity, applying simple notification service devices, and having been on a simple notification service for a long.

On the other hand, Heinrich (2015) mentions that females were more likely to share their photos online be it on Facebook, Instagram, Tik Tok, WhatsApp and other relevant social media with the mindset of flaunting themselves and their lives to the public without considering its impact very much. This easily attracts potential hackers or perpetrators to access their personal profiles. Once the scammers obtain a great number of online users' personal details, they tend to commit their scamming activities on the targeted users. Wilson, Sheridan and Garratt-Reed (2022) also agree that females easily fall into a cyber-scam trap, especially those who lack digital guardianship. Additionally, a married person will have a constant level of guardianship compared to a person staying alone. Hence, it is crucial to have digital guardianship to reduce the likelihood of falling into cyber scams.

Intention to Purchase Online

Purchasing interest is the psychological aspect that influences a person's behavior. The stronger the consumer's behavioral intention, the more probable he/she is to accomplish the behavior. For instance, if an individual is led to be involved in a cyber-scam or suffers from these cases: poor product quality, delay in delivering products, product received not as shown on the website, and other negative issues. Hence, the individual will treat the first transaction as their final transaction. He or she will not repeat the online purchase. On the other hand, if the individual has performed his or her first online purchase smoothly, he or she will perform their online purchase again. This situation is very much related to an individual's psychological mindset.

In addition, the purchase decision is preceded by the intention in the buyer's mindset to make an online purchase transaction that was previously trusted. High purchasing interest will encourage consumers to make their purchase transactions online. Customer decision-making behavior is affected by the pre-purchase, during the purchase, and the post-purchase stages. The consumer will make their purchasing decision which starts with the consumer's awareness and moves on to the need to purchase. Consumers realize the difference between a need and a want. It causes them to look for more information related to their wanted or desired items. After the information is obtained, an evaluation of whether the purchase is essential or desired is carried out. They will drag the desired items to the virtual cart, and the items will be in the cart until the payment is made. Once the consumer has finalized the items to be purchased in the virtual cart, they will then proceed to make payment. During the purchase or at the payment web-page, the consumer will also browse again on the product list to ensure that the selected products have been confirmed in the list. Once the payment is made, a reference number will be generated, and the consumer will keep a record and wait for the products to reach him or her. During the post-purchase, consumers might browse other websites with similar products that have been purchased to compare the pricing. This psychological action in fact is not advisable since the consumer has made up his or her mind to purchase the product and has paid for the product on the previous website.

Similarly, the purchasing behavior of consumers is linked to how they make their purchase Choices on the products or services. In conclusion, online purchase intention is a consumer's willingness and intention to purchase through the Internet (Meskaran *et al.*, 2013). In Malaysia, generation Z (born in the range of 1997 to 2012) is more comfortable with mobile activities, causing them to contribute to higher online purchases compared with other generations. Thus, generation Z is known as the new market sector that brings a shift to the Internet platform in a hugely connected world (Johan *et al.*, 2022). This generation Z will continue the advancement of digital technology in all aspects of life for world sustainability.

Routine Activity Theory (RAT)

Confronting the increasing crime rate, researchers aim to describe the rate of crime and its projections of the cases. The Routine Activity Theory (RAT) was initially formed by Marcus Felson and Lawrence Cohen during the crime rate exposure in the United States in the 20th century. This theory stresses that crime happens when 3 elements come together, i.e., an inspired offender, an appropriate target, and the absence of a proficient guardian (Cohen & Felson, 1979). RAT was earlier intended to account for changes in urban crime rates and has been used for predictions of predatory criminal or victimization cases.

Figure 1. Routine activity theory (RAT)
Source: Nickerson (2022)

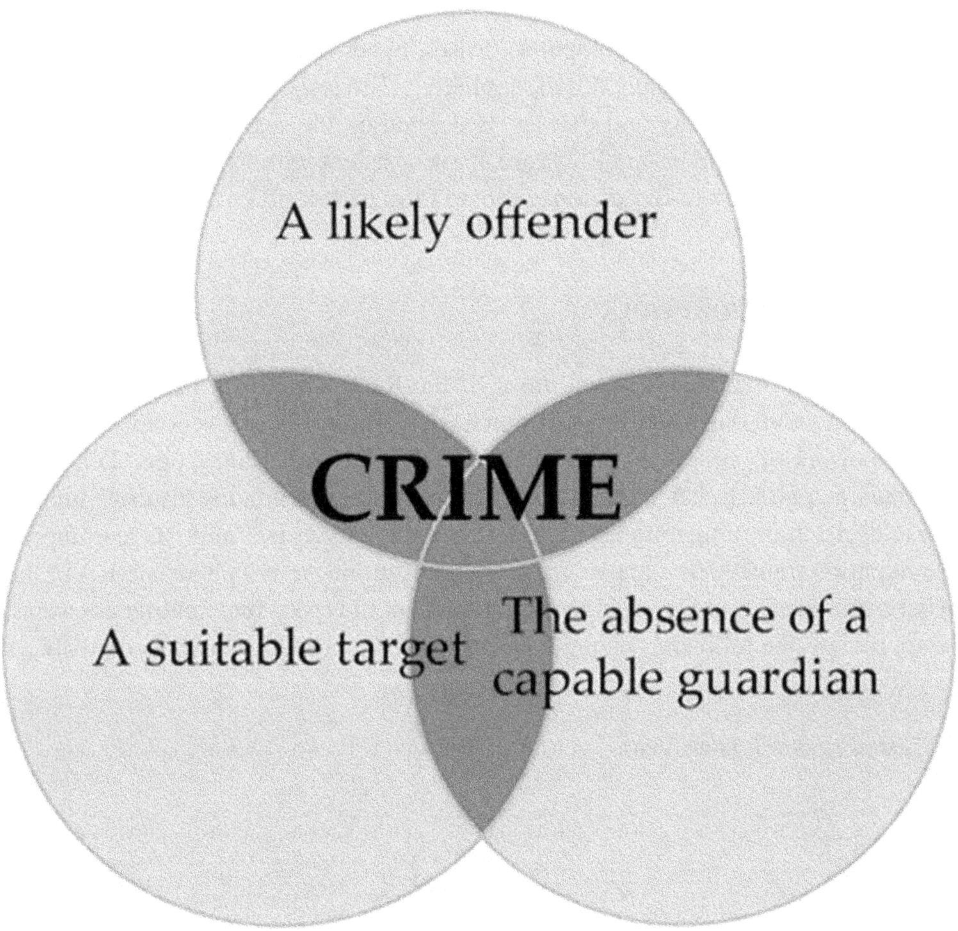

RAT expresses that offenders make selections whether to execute a crime based on a seemly target and the existence of efficient guardianship which might possibly affect the offender. Cohen and Felson (1979) invented RAT, supposing that the purpose of offenders continuously exists. This puts RAT separately from other criminological models, which pursue investigating the drive of the offenders, the suitable targets and the capable guardians. The target vulnerability varies on how satisfactory it can be seized and suppressed and its worth compared to its concealability. According to Cohen *et al.* (1981), individual lifestyles and routine activities leave people in risky situations that generate criminal opportunities, and individuals become the right targets through their lifestyles.

There are factors causing the increase in crime recently. People stay at home less frequently, in tandem with the fact that there has been a growing number of women beginning to work away from their homes. Hence, there are fewer people present in the housing zones. There are more homes for singles, and people begin to be outdoor more for various reasons, such as going on a vacation. With fewer people at home, the guardianship in the neighborhood also deteriorates, making it simpler for criminals to commit crimes. At the same time, there is an increasing number of suitable targets. Those who buy electrical appliances such as televisions could simply be pilfered and re-marketed. In short, it becomes simpler to commit crime as there are fewer people guarding (fewer guardians) and this means that there are extra suitable targets.

According to Hsieh and Wang (2018), some researchers utilize RAT on crimes that have occurred in a virtual environment, for instance, computer viruses, cyber stalking, fraud, identity theft, malware infection, and phishing. Hsieh and Wang (2018) applied RAT to test cybercrime where it was discovered that the usefulness of cybersecurity and risk levels depend on the scale of guardianship. In addition, findings from Johnson and Nikolovska (2022) are also consistent with Routine Activity Theory (RAT) demonstrating that people's day-to-day actions seem to form peaks and lows in stages of crime that have been committed electronically.

Proposed Research Framework

Based on the discussion in earlier sections, most of the RAT framework has not been successful in tackling a cybercrime issue that affects online purchase intention. In this section, the author proposes a conceptual framework of online purchase intention for cybercrime mitigation. This framework is a novel and promising approach that works against cybercrime, which helps the consumers to make an online purchase decision in mitigating any cybercrime incidents. It is a multistage comprehensive online purchase intention framework that extends from the Routine Activity Theory (RAT). It is aimed at resolving cybercrime issues and increasing awareness about the risky surrounding environment. Based on the literature review, the following Figure 2 showing the proposed research framework, is proposed.

Figure 2. Proposed research framework

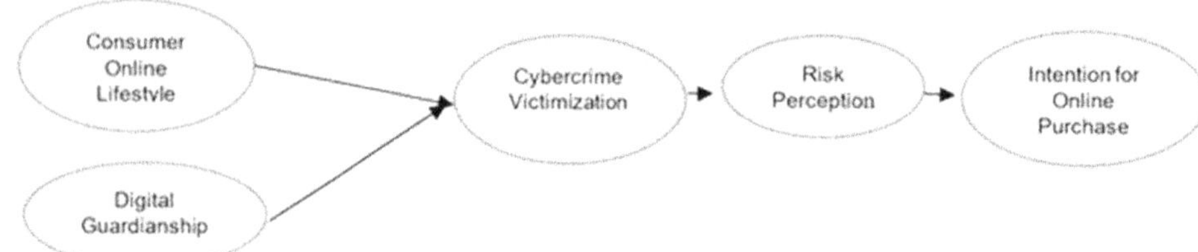

Cybercrime Victimization

According to Villarreal and Silva (2006), neighborhood social and physical disorders increase violent victimization but not the perceived risk of being victimized. Consequently, in the current research, the Routine Activity Theory (RAT) will be applied to test its applicability to cybercrime victimization. After collecting the intention source data for online purchasers, these cybercrime victimization's online consumer lifestyle and digital guardianship paths are used to predict cybercrime victimization.

Perceived Risk

Perceived risk of victimization and safety efficacy is found associated with worrying about safety, safety responses, and intervention intentions (Logan & Walker, 2021). In the current research, risk perception is predicted at this stage. The risk perception model is used to quantify the source data. This quantified data will be compared with the cybercrime victimization paths in the survey process to detect any suspicious activity. This model is used to contain increasingly serious risks.

Intention for Online Purchase

The intention to purchase among online consumers is linked to how they make their online purchase options. The findings of Fadare (2015) show that perceived risk contributes to explaining the intention to use. For internet banking users with high-risk acceptance, the intention to use is low (Marafon *et al.*, 2018). Badiora (2022) indicates that perceived crime risk significantly predicts travel intentions, while Hakim, Zanetta and da Cunha (2021) suggest that increased purchasers' risk perception affects their intentions. Specifically, there is a negative relation between perceived risk and online purchase intention (Jordan, Leskovar & Maric, 2018). In the current research, the intention stage will prevent the risk of data leakage. Finally, an extension of the Routine Activity Theory (RAT) framework will be assessed in relation to its usability.

CONCLUSION

This conceptual idea assists in bridging the research gap on the risk perception among Malaysian online consumers and the intention for online purchases towards the digital economic development of Malaysia. Healthy growth of the digital economy will contribute to the Malaysian economy with the aim to increase output, increase employment, and increase the GDP during the post-pandemic era. The growth of the digital economy would enhance and penetrate another market with scientific innovation. It would increase the competition among firms, and this would put pressure on their products and services to be world-class. Competition among businesses enables the business to put more effort to improve their product's quality to cater to the consumer's demand. The online shopping platform needs to be updated daily and needs to strengthen cybersecurity protection to reduce cyber scams or cyber fraud which will affect businesses, society, and country. The growth of the digital economy would ultimately alter the firm's work through state-of-the-art systems, targeted at updating and globalizing corporate procedures.

This chapter carries some limitations. The author uses only a few scientific articles from database sources. Furthermore, the author is not able to confirm that all relevant studies in the review are included.

DECLARATION

The authors declare that the manuscript follows ethical standards and there are no potential conflicts of interest with respect to the research, authorship and/or publication of this chapter.

DISCLAIMER

The contents and views of this chapter are expressed by the authors in personal capacities. It is not necessary for the Editor and the Publisher to agree with these viewpoints, and they are not responsible for any duty of care in this regard.

ACKNOWLEDGMENT

The authors extend sincere gratitude to

- The Editor and the International Editorial Advisory Board (IEAB) of this book who initially desk reviewed, arranged a rigorous double/triple blind review process, and conducted a thorough, minute, and critical final review before accepting the chapter for publication.
- All anonymous reviewers who provided very constructive feedbacks for thorough revision, improvement, extension, and fine tuning of the chapter.
- All colleagues, assistants and well-wishers who assisted to complete this task.

REFERENCES

Abdullah, F., Mohamad, N. S., & Yunos, Z. (2018). Safeguarding Malaysia's cyberspace against cyber threats: Contributions by cyber security Malaysia. *OIC-Cert Journal of Cyber Security*, *1*(1), 22–31.

Akdemir, N., & Lawless, C. J. (2020). Exploring the human factor in cyber-enabled and cyber dependent crime victimization: A lifestyle routine activities approach. *Internet Research*, *30*(6), 1665–1687. doi:10.1108/INTR-10-2019-0400

Akdemir, N., & Yenal, S. (2020). Card-Not-Present fraud victimization: A routine activities approach to understand the risk factors. *Güvenlik Bilimleri Dergisi*, *9*(1), 243–268. doi:10.28956/gbd.736179

Alam, M. K. (2018). *Situational Victimization Among Adolescents Exploring the Role of Morality, Self-control and Lifestyle Risk*. Degree Project in Criminology master's Program, Criminology. Malmo Universitet.

AlDaajeh, S., Saleous, H., Alrabaee, S., Barka, E., Breitinger, F., & Choo, K. K. R. (2022). The role of national cybersecurity strategies on the improvement of cybersecurity education. *Computers & Security, 119*, 102754. doi:10.1016/j.cose.2022.102754

Anastasiadou, E., & Chrissos Anestics, M. (2020). The coronavirus' effects on consumer behavior and supermarket activities: Insights from Greece and Sweden. *The International Journal of Sociology and Social Policy, 40*(9/10), 893–907. doi:10.1108/IJSSP-07-2020-0275

Antonescu, M., & Birăub, R. (2015). Financial and non-financial implications of cybercrime in emerging countries. *Procedia Economics and Finance, 32*, 618–621. doi:10.1016/S2212-5671(15)01440-9

Apau, R., Koranteng, F. N., & Gyamfi, S. A. (2019). Cyber-crime and its effects on E-commerce technologies. *Journal of Information, 5*(1), 39–59. doi:10.18488/journal.104.2019.51.39.59

Back, S., & Guerette, R. T. (2021). Cyber place management and crime prevention: The effectiveness of cybersecurity awareness training against phishing attacks. *Journal of Contemporary Criminal Justice, 37*(3), 427–451. doi:10.1177/10439862211001628

Badiora, A. I. (2022). Predictors of future travel intentions to Lagos Megacity: Exploring the crime-risk perceptions. [AJHTM]. *African Journal of Hospitality and Tourism Management, 3*(2), 1–22. doi:10.47963/ajhtm.v3i2.831

Basyir, M. (2021). Malaysians suffered RM2.23 billion losses from cyber-crime frauds. *New Straits Times*. https://www.nst.com.my/news/crime-courts/2021/07/708911/malaysians-suffered-rm223-billion-losses-cyber-crime-frauds

Buil-Gil, D., Lord, N., & Barrett, E. (2021). The dynamics of business, cybersecurity and cyber-victimization: Foregrounding the internal guardian in prevention. *Victims & Offenders, 16*(3), 286–315. doi: 10.1080/15564886.2020.1814468

Ceccato, V. (2019). Crime and control in the digital era. *Criminal Justice Review, 44*(1), 5–10. doi:10.1177/0734016818818688

Chin, A. J., Wafa, S. A. W. S. K., & Ooi, A. Y. (2009). The effect of internet trust and social influence towards willingness to purchase online in Labuan, Malaysia. *International Business Research, 2*(2), 72–81. doi:10.5539/ibr.v2n2p72

Choi, K. S., Cho, S., & Lee, J. R. (2019). Cyberbullying and traditional bullying victimization among Korean youth: Application of cyber-routine activities theory with latent class analysis. *Computers in Human Behavior, 100*, 1–10. doi:10.1016/j.chb.2019.06.007

Clow, K. E., Baack, D., & Fogliasso, C. (1998). Reducing perceived risk through advertising service quality cues. *Journal of Professional Services Marketing, 16*(2), 151–162. doi:10.1300/J090v16n02_08

Cohen, L. E., & Felson, M. (1979). Social change and crime rate trends: A routine activity approach. *American Sociological Review, 44*(4), 588–608. doi:10.2307/2094589

Cohen, L. E., Kluegel, J. R., & Land, K. C. (1981). Social inequality and predatory criminal victimization: An exposition and test of a formal theory. *American Sociological Review, 46*(5), 505–524. doi:10.2307/2094935

Cook, S., Giommoni, L., Trajtenberg Pareja, N., Levi, M., & Williams, M. L. (2023). Fear of economic cybercrime across Europe: A multilevel application of Routine Activity Theory. *British Journal of Criminology*, *63*(2), 384–406. doi:10.1093/bjc/azac021

Dashora, K. (2011). Cybercrime in the society: Problems and preventions. *Journal of Alternative Perspectives in the Social Sciences*, *3*(1), 240–259.

De Kimpe, L., Walrave, M., Verdegem, P., & Ponnet, K. (2022). What we think we know about cybersecurity: An investigation of the relationship between perceived knowledge, internet trust, and protection motivation in a cybercrime context. *Behaviour & Information Technology*, *41*(8), 1796–1808. doi:10.1080/0144929X.2021.1905066

Eck, J. E., & Clarke, R. V. (2003). Classifying common police problems: A routine activity approach. *Crime Prevention Studies*, *16*, 7–39.

Fadare, O. A. (2015). A survey on perceived risk and intention of adopting internet banking. *Journal of Internet Banking and Commerce*, *21*(1), 144.

Faisal, S. H. S., & Ismail, F. (2022). Cybersecurity threats and best practices of working from home. *Journal of Techno-Social*, *13*(2), 1–5.

Garba, A. A., Siraj, M. M., & Othman, S. H. (2022). An assessment of cybersecurity awareness level among Northeastern University students in Nigeria. *Iranian Journal of Electrical and Computer Engineering*, *12*(1), 572–584. doi:10.11591/ijece.v12i1.pp572-584

Guedes, I., Martins, M., & Cardoso, C. S. (2022). Exploring the determinants of victimization and fear of online identity theft: An empirical study. *Security Journal*, 1–26. doi:10.105741284-022-00350-5

Hakim, M. P., Zanetta, D., & da Cunha, D. T. (2021). Should I stay, or should I go? Consumers' perceived risk and visit to restaurants during the COVID-19 pandemic in Brazil. *Food Research International*, *141*, 110152. doi:10.1016/j.foodres.2021.110152 PMID:33642018

Hasan, M. S., Rahman, R. A., Abdillah, S. F. H. B. T., & Omar, N. (2015). Perception and awareness of young internet users towards cybercrime: Evidence from Malaysia. *Journal of Social Sciences*, *11*(4), 395–404. doi:10.3844/jssp.2015.395.404

Heinrich, P. A. (2015). *Generation iStalk: An examination of the prior relationship between victims of stalking and offenders* [Master's Thesis Marshall Digital Scholar]. Marshall University.

Herawaty, T., & Tresna, P. W. (2019). The influence of lifestyle on the process of purchase decision (A study on android users community). *Review of Integrative Business and Economics Research*, *8*(S I2), 344–351.

Hsieh, M.-L., & Wang, S. Y. K. (2018). Routine activities in a virtual space: A Taiwanese case of an ATM hacking spree. *International Journal of Cyber Criminology*, *12*(1), 333–352.

Iqbal, W. (2019). Impact of perceived risk on customer's online purchase intention towards branded apparels. *Journal of Marketing Strategies*, *1*(1), 38–62. doi:10.52633/jms.v1i1.3

Isa, M. Y. M., Ibrahim, W. N. W., & Mohamed, Z. (2021). The relationship between financial literacy and public awareness on combating the threat of cybercrime in Malaysia. *The Journal of Industrial Distribution and Business*, *12*(12), 1–10.

Jarvenpaa, S. L., Tractinsky, N., & Vitale, M. (2000). Consumer trust in an internet store. *Information Technology and Management*, *1*(1/2), 45–71. doi:10.1023/A:1019104520776

Johan, M. R. M., Syed, M. A. M., & Adnan, H. M. (2022). Digital media and online buying considerations among generation Z in Malaysia. *Jurnal Intelek*, *17*(1), 164–180. doi:10.24191/ji.v17i1.15920

Johnson, S. D., & Nikolovska, M. (2022). The effect of COVID-19 restrictions on routine activities and online crime. *Journal of Quantitative Criminology*, 1–20. doi:10.100710940-022-09564-7 PMID:36532607

Jones, N. (2021, May 14). The shape of fraud and cybercrime: 10 things we learned from 2020. *Computerweekly.com*. Retrieved from https://www.computerweekly.com/opinion/The-shape-of-fraud-and-cyber-crime-10-things-we-learned-from-2020

Jordan, G., Leskovar, R., & Marič, M. (2018). Impact of fear of identity theft and perceived risk on online purchase intention. *Organizacija*, *51*(2), 146–155. doi:10.2478/orga-2018-0007

Junger, M., Montoya, L., Hartel, P., & Heydari, M. (2017). Towards the normalization of cybercrime victimization: A routine activities analysis of cybercrime in Europe. *2017 International Conference on Cyber Situational Awareness, Data Analytics and Assessment*. IEEE. 10.1109/CyberSA.2017.8073391

Kigerl, A. (2012). Routine activity theory and the determinants of high cybercrime countries. *Social Science Computer Review*, *30*(4), 470–486. doi:10.1177/0894439311422689

Kigerl, A. (2021). Routine activity theory and malware, fraud, and spam at the national level. *Crime, Law, and Social Change*, *76*(2), 109–130. doi:10.100710611-021-09957-y

Kim, D. J., Ferrin, D. L., & Rao, H. R. (2008). A trust-based consumer decision-making model in electronic commerce: The role of trust, perceived risk, and their antecedents. *Decision Support Systems*, *44*(2), 544–564. doi:10.1016/j.dss.2007.07.001

Kirwan, G. H., Fullwood, C., & Rooney, B. (2018). Risk factors for social networking site scam victimization among Malaysian students. *Cyberpsychology, Behavior, and Social Networking*, *21*(2), 123–128. doi:10.1089/cyber.2016.0714 PMID:29048944

Kuo, T.-L. (2021). *Criminal Victimization in Taiwan: An Opportunity Perspective*. [Doctor of Philosophy Thesis, University College London].

Lallie, H. S., Shepherd, L. A., Nurse, J. R. C., Erola, A., Epiphaniou, G., Maple, C., & Bellekens, X. (2021). Cyber security in the age of COVID-19: A timeline and analysis of cyber-crime and cyber-attacks during the pandemic. *Computers & Security*, *105*, 102248. doi:10.1016/j.cose.2021.102248 PMID:36540648

Lee, C. S. (2021). Online fraud victimization in China: A case study of Baidu Tieba. *Victims & Offenders*, *16*(3), 343–362. doi:10.1080/15564886.2020.1838372

Leukfeldt, E. R. (2014). Phishing for suitable targets in The Netherlands: Routine activity theory and phishing victimization. *Cyberpsychology, Behavior, and Social Networking, 17*(8), 551–555. doi:10.1089/cyber.2014.0008 PMID:25080013

Li, M., Huang, L., Tan, C. H., & Wei, K. K. (2013). Helpfulness of online product reviews as seen by consumers: Source and content features. *International Journal of Electronic Commerce, 17*(4), 101–136. doi:10.2753/JEC1086-4415170404

Li, Z., Sha, Y., Song, X., Yang, K., Zhao, K., Jiang, Z., & Zhang, Q. (2019). Impact of risk perception on customer purchase behavior: A meta-analysis. *Journal of Business and Industrial Marketing, 35*(1), 76–96. doi:10.1108/JBIM-12-2018-0381

Logan, T. K., & Walker, R. (2021). The gender safety gap: Examining the impact of victimization history, perceived risk, and personal control. *Journal of Interpersonal Violence, 36*(1-2), 603–631. doi:10.1177/0886260517729405 PMID:29294904

Marafon, D. L., Basso, K., Espartel, L. B., de Barcellos, M. D., & Rech, E. (2018). Perceived risk and intention to use internet banking: The effects of self-confidence and risk acceptance. *International Journal of Bank Marketing, 36*(2), 277–289. doi:10.1108/IJBM-11-2016-0166

Mears, D. P., Reisig, M. D., Scaggs, S., & Holtfreter, K. (2016). Efforts to reduce consumer fraud victimization among the elderly. *Crime and Delinquency, 62*(9), 1235–1259. doi:10.1177/0011128714555759

Meskaran, F., Ismail, Z., & Shanmugam, B. (2013). Online purchase intention: Effects of trust and security perception. *Australian Journal of Basic and Applied Sciences, 7*(6), 307–315.

Muhamad, F. H., Muhammad, M. Z., Muhamad, S. F., & Samad, N. S. A. (2021). Awareness on Financial Cybercrimes among youth: Experience, exposure and effect. *Proceedings of the First International Conference on Society 5.0*. IEEE.

Muhtasim, D. A., Tan, S. Y., Hassan, M. A., Pavel, M. I., & Susmit, S. (2022). Customer Satisfaction with digital wallet services: An analysis of security factors. *International Journal of Advanced Computer Science and Applications, 13*(1), 195–206. doi:10.14569/IJACSA.2022.0130124

Muniandy, L., Muniandy, B., & Samsudin, Z. (2017). CyberSecurity behavior among higher education students in Malaysia. *Journal of Information Assurance and Cybersecurity, 800299*, 1–13. doi:10.5171/2017.800299

Nguyen, C. M., Barrash, J., Koenigs, A. L., Bechara, A., Tranel, D., & Denburg, N. L. (2013). Decision-making deficits in normal elderly persons associated with executive personality disturbances. *International Psychogeriatrics, 25*(11), 1811–1819. doi:10.1017/S1041610213001270 PMID:23906413

Nickerson, C. (2022). Routine activities theory. *Simply Psychology*. https://www.simplypsychology.org/routine-activities-theory.html

Nuradzimmah, D. (2022, March 14). Online scammers rake in RM1.6 billion, over 51,000 reports lodged in 2 years. *New Straits Times*. https://www.nst.com.my/news/nation/2022/03/779915/online-scammers-rake-rm16-billion-over-51000-reports-lodged-2-years

Oki, O. & in Buffalo City. *International Conference on Electrical, Computer, Communications and Mechatronics Engineering (ICECCME)*. (pp. 1–6). doi:10.1109/ICECCME52200.2021.9590998

Reyns, B. W., Henson, B., & Fisher, B. S. (2016). Guardians of the cyber galaxy: An empirical and theoretical analysis of the guardianship concept from routine activity theory as it applies to online forms of victimization. *Journal of Contemporary Criminal Justice*, *32*(2), 148–168. doi:10.1177/1043986215621378

Saad, M. E., Abdullah, S. N. H. S., & Murah, M. Z. (2018). Cyber romance scam victimization analysis using routine activity theory versus apriori algorithm. *International Journal of Advanced Computer Science and Applications*, *9*(12), 479–485. doi:10.14569/IJACSA.2018.091267

Saridakis, G., Benson, V., Ezingeard, J. N., & Tennakoon, H. (2016). Individual information security, user behavior and cybervictimization: An empirical study of social networking users. *Technological Forecasting and Social Change*, *102*, 320–330. doi:10.1016/j.techfore.2015.08.012

Simmons, D., & Quinton, M. (2021, March 24). Covid fraud: £34.5m stolen in pandemic scams. *BBC*. https://www.bbc.co.uk/news/technology-56499886

Singh, M. M., Frank, R., & Zainon, W. M. N. W. (2021). Cyber-criminology defense in pervasive environment: A study of cybercrimes in Malaysia. *Bulletin of Electrical Engineering and Informatics*, *10*(3), 1658–1668. doi:10.11591/eei.v10i3.3028

Song, H. J., Lynch, M. J., & Cochran, J. K. (2016). A Macro-Social exploratory analysis of the rate of interstate cyber-victimization. *American Journal of Criminal Justice*, *41*(3), 583–601. doi:10.100712103-015-9308-4

Stofkova, K. R., Laitkep, D., & Stofkova, Z. (2022). Shopping behavior in the context of the digital economy. *Journal of Risk and Financial Management*, *15*(2), 39. doi:10.3390/jrfm15020039

Sumartono, S., Urumsah, D., & Hamdani, R. (2020). Skills of the forensic accountants in revealing fraud in public sector: The Case of Indonesia. *Journal of Accounting and Investment*, *21*(1), 180–194.

Sviatun, O., Goncharuk, O., Roman, C., Kuzmenko, O., & Kozych, I. V. (2021). Combating cybercrime: Economic and legal aspects. *WSEAS Transactions on Business and Economics*, *18*, 751–762. doi:10.37394/23207.2021.18.72

Tamyez, P. F. (2022). The challenges and solutions of cybersecurity among Malaysian companies. In *Research Anthology on Business Aspects of Cybersecurity* (pp. 676–693). IGI Global. doi:10.4018/978-1-6684-3698-1.ch031

Taylor, R. W., Caeti, T. J., Loper, D. K., Fritsch, E. J., & Liederbach, J. (2006). *Digital crime and digital terrorism*. Pearson Prentice Hall.

Tharshini, N. K., Hassan, Z., & Mas'ud, F. (2021). Cybercrime threat landscape amid the movement control order in Malaysia. *International Journal of Business and Society*, *22*(3), 1589–1601. doi:10.33736/ijbs.4323.2021

Tharshini, N. K., Mas'ud, F., & Hassan, Z. (2022). Level of cybercrime threat during the outbreak of COVID-19 pandemic: A study in Malaysia. *International Journal of Academic Research in Business & Social Sciences*, *12*(5), 40–51.

Thomas, B., Clergue, J., Schaad, A., & Dacier, M. (2004). A comparison of conventional and online fraud. *Conference on Securing Critical Infrastructures* (pp. 25–27). IEEE.

Tientcheu, P. P. (2021). *Security Awareness Strategies Used in the Prevention of Cybercrime by Cybercriminals.* [MS Thesis. Walden University].

Villarreal, A., & Silva, B. F. A. (2006). Social cohesion, criminal victimization and perceived risk of crime in Brazilian neighborhoods. *Social Forces*, *84*(3), 1725–1753. doi:10.1353of.2006.0073

Wei, L., Peng, M., & Wu, W. X. (2021). Financial literacy and fraud detection - Evidence from China. *International Review of Economics & Finance*, *76*(C), 478–494. doi:10.1016/j.iref.2021.06.017

Wen, T. S., Satar, N. M., Ishak, N. A., & Ating, R. (2020). Consumer intention towards online shopping in Malaysia. *The International Journal of Accounting*, *5*(27), 93–117.

Whitty, M. T. (2020). Is there a scam for everyone? Psychologically profiling cyber scam victims. *European Journal on Criminal Policy and Research*, *26*(3), 399–409. doi:10.100710610-020-09458-z

Wilson, C., Sheridan, L., & Garratt-Reed, D. (2022). Examining cyberstalking perpetration and victimization: A scoping review. *Trauma, Violence & Abuse*, *15248380221082937*. Advance online publication. doi:10.1177/15248380221082937 PMID:35387506

Winarso, W. (2020). The impact of perceived of cyber fraud, ease of use and risk perception on the behavior of using e-commerce systems in Indonesia. *Journal of Critical Reviews*, *7*(4), 2394–5125.

Wu, K., Noorian, Z., Vassileva, J., & Adaji, I. (2015). How buyers perceive the credibility of advisors in online marketplace: Review balance, review count and misattribution. *Journal of Trust Management*, *2*(1), 1–18. doi:10.118640493-015-0013-5

Yoon, S. J. (2002). The antecedents and consequences of trust in online-purchase decisions. *Journal of Interactive Marketing*, *16*(2), 47–63. doi:10.1002/dir.10008

Yusof, S. A. (2015). Household bargaining, financial decision-making and risk tolerance. *International Journal of Business and Society*, *16*(2), 221–236.

Zahari, A. I., Bilu, R., & Said, J. (2019). The role of familiarity, trust and awareness towards online fraud. *Journal of Research and Opinion*, *6*(9), 2470–2480.

Zhang, Y., Bian, J., & Zhu, W. (2013). Trust fraud: A crucial challenge for China's e-commerce market. *Electronic Commerce Research and Applications*, *12*(5), 299–308. doi:10.1016/j.elerap.2012.11.005

Zulkipli, N. H. N., Rashid, N. A. M., Zolkeplay, A. F., & Buja, A. G. (2021). Synthesizing cybersecurity issues and challenges for the elderly. *Turkish Journal of Computer and Mathematics Education*, *12*(5), 1775–1781.

Chapter 11
Investigations of Financial Fraud:
Literature Analysis of Selected Financial Scams

Martynas Damulis
Jönköping University, Sweden

ABSTRACT

Financial fraud is a broad description including all frauds or scams that consist of credit card scams, insurance frauds, money laundering, securities frauds, or income statement misinformation to name a few. Out of all these misconducts, this chapter discussed only securities fraud that consists of any manipulation strategy to make a profit, whether income statement or market manipulation. Various cases are analyzed to describe the impact of frauds, how people's lives changed, and how cognitive biases/behavior heuristics can identify potential fraud. In the literature review section, it is analyzed how researchers and analyst who implements cognitive psychology can detect red flags of the phenomenon. The main limitations were the lack of research about the impact on victims' lives, the impact of fraud on social structure, the psychology of the frauds, and the cognitive bias/heuristics that a fraudster shows. The study laid the foundation for further research studies because more research is required to fully analyze this complex topic.

1. INTRODUCTION

Financial fraud (scam) can be defined as the manipulation of financial information as well as intentional deceit with the motivation to illegally make a profit (Reurink, 2018). It usually involves representing misleading information. Financial fraud is a broad description including all frauds or scams that are consisted of finance related topics like credit card scams, insurance frauds, money laundering, securities frauds, or income statement misinformation (Rafay 2021a, 2023a). Out of all these misconducts, the researcher of this chapter is going to discuss mainly securities frauds, which consists of any kind of

DOI: 10.4018/979-8-3693-1190-5.ch011

manipulation strategy to make a profit, either it is income statement manipulation or market manipulation. The public experienced what market manipulation can do when it developed into one of the biggest financial bubbles in history – the 2008 financial crisis. It was the biggest financial crisis since the great depression. Merle (2018) says that more than $2 trillion was wiped from the global economy. This much money was lost due to the irresponsible management of one of the biggest banks in the world and of course because the government was not regulating these banks strictly enough. One institution cannot have this much power, to lead the world to recession. This is when the term '*Too big to fail*' was popularized (Thoma, 2010). The worst thing about financial bubbles is that analysts notice it when the phenomenon is already been formed and do not know when it is going to explode. There is an argument called the greater fools' theory, which explains who drives financial bubbles and the researcher of this chapter will discuss the before-mentioned theory further in this chapter. On top of that, financial frauds are often associated with excessive greed, but greed is not the only factor that fuels scams or manipulative bubbles, which will also be explained in this chapter.

1.1 History of Financial Frauds: Brief Example of Nick Leeson

If we would look back at the history of financial crimes, we could see that some scammers had a reason to execute their fraud, even though they did not profit from it. For example, Nick Leeson – the rogue trader, who brought down the Barings bank, one of the oldest merchant banks in the world according to Pressman (1998). This issue started when Leeson's co-worker made a mistake, he instantly hides the mistake in a secret error account named '88888' and wanted to win back the losses by doing highly speculative trades with the bank's money. One billion dollars was lost, not in a day not in a week, but over a long period of time (Baxter & Ramasastry, 1996). The reason why Nick Leeson was not caught right away is because of his personality and the managers' lack of responsibility. First thing when Leeson went to the new office in Singapore, where he committed this fraud, he cleaned the place and brought back the money to Barings bank, which they did not know they had. He earned the trust of the senior managers, when he "showed" profits, when in fact he was making losses. Nisbett & Wilson (1977) describes a Halo effect and how one positive trait can alter someone's opinion about a person, in our case managers of Barings bank's opinion about Nick Leeson. After this fraud, Nick Leeson was charged with fraud and was sentenced to six and a half years in prison, despite the fact that he did not make any money from this fraud. Besides Nick Leeson, there were other fraudsters in History who committed even bigger scams, without a reasonable rationale and the focus will be on those that were the biggest in terms of stolen (lost) value and were impactful to society. So, Nick Leeson was a brief example of how heuristics can explain the occurrence of a financial scam.

Financial frauds are getting harder to detect and their scale is increasing over time, because of the cleverness of scammers, the availability of information fraudsters have, and the increasing usage of the internet (Singh, 2013). Their ability to adapt to old fraud detecting systems is getting impressive, but (Columbus, 2019) states that with the help of Artificial Intelligence (AI) there should be easier to detect more fraudsters that already started to commit a crime. AI in online fraud prevention delivers payment response and interprets data in 250 milliseconds. There's one thing that AI will never have, and that is the human factor and intuition to spot a misdemeanor, based on his decisions, behavior, or personality, which can help to prevent fraud from happening in the first place. The author of this work can agree that fraud detection strategies with AI can help reduce e-commerce scams, reduce insurance frauds and they can help detect financial scams that had previously occurred (Bolton & Hand, 2002). Although, experienced auditors and analysts apply cognitive psychology to accounting (Mostyn, 2012). Thus, not only detecting red flags and forensic warning signals but also learning the rationale of the fraudster and adapting his example to catch other scammers. So, to summarize, financial misconduct is a topic that is important to analyze, so that we could learn from previous fraudsters and their methods and also enlighten the public about the dangers of financial fraud and potential signals that they can notice.

As the chapter progresses, the researcher will discuss two different cases of financial fraud and also mention how they started, describe people and companies who committed such frauds, their motivation behind it and try to find similarities of cognitive biases/behavior heuristics in both examples. Chosen case studies were a couple of the biggest and the most impactful financial scams and corporate scandals in the financial world. The author of this work will use these examples to describe the impact they left after the frauds had been exposed and how people's lives had been changed. On top of that, in the literature review section, the author will analyze how researchers and analyst who implements cognitive psychology can detect red flags of the phenomenon, using other researchers' examples and their strategies. Further explanation can be seen in the Methodology chapter.

2. METHODOLOGY

For the chapter the author used an exploratory approach, to have a better understanding of the existing problem and acquire new insights into it to form a foundation for further research and for a better understanding of the basics of financial fraud (Jebb, Parrigon & Woo, 2017). Since the chosen topic is a broad and complex one, the author narrowed it down using only two case studies, which should help better understand the problem that the author is mainly describing. On top of that, this approach allows the author to evaluate the opinions of other authors and to analyse their research. This work is compared chosen case studies, also discussing how cognitive biases/behavior heuristics can identify potential fraud. The author laid a foundation for further research studies because more research is required to fully analyze this complex topic. This chapter did not conduct any statistical calculations, only secondary data, and scientific articles. Search engines that helped the author to find credible sources were google scholar, ResearchGate, emerald, JSTOR and other known journals and articles.

2.1 Rationale

The main reason for this chapter was to investigate causes and effect of the problem and to discuss the aftermath and consequences that these scandals faced. It also describes how these scandals affected investors, the public and families of fraudsters (Rafay, 2021b, 2023b). Another reason was to show that it is important to talk about this issue, because of the relevance it has in our everyday lives and that it is possible to educate people to avoid such scams. And thirdly, to describe that understanding psychology of the fraud can help to identify future scams. In 2006 alone, there were 25,000 websites that were running a Ponzi scheme and they were shut down by the U.S. Securities and Exchange Commission based on the data from the study of Gunestas, Mehmet & Wijesekera (2017). With internet usage increasing over the years, it creates an even bigger problem, because it is easier for fraudsters to get away and harder for authorities to regulate every single website, according to Armstrong (2021) there are over 1 trillion web pages on the internet. Ekins (2017) found that 64% of American citizens think that Wall Street bankers get paid a lot of money, for "*essentially tricking people*" on top of that, 65% of people do not believe in the term "*too big to fail*", they rejected the idea that banks are very important to the U.S. economy and do not agree with the idea that they should receive taxpayers money when facing bankruptcy. The public does not trust people that work in the finance sector, especially on Wall Street and the crimes that the author discussed earlier make the situation worse, also when media tries to portray bankers and brokers as corrupt and bad individuals, thus making stereotypes develop around them.

2.2 Limitations

The main limitation of this chapter was the lack of research about impact on victims' lives and the impact on the social structure that has been affected after the frauds. Then, the university did not have access to some of the journals or articles, so this chapter used information that was available to collect through the university's library. Also, the lack of research about the psychology of the frauds and cognitive bias/heuristics that a fraudster shows that should be important because then we could notice the pattern between the fraudsters. Due to the limited availability of research papers, the work of a selected number of authors is anlayzed thoroughly. Key authors that this chapter used were C. Hurt, W. Quisenberry, C.W. Thomas, A. Anandarajan and G. Kleinman, W.R. Bufkins and B.G. Dharan.

All the information and data that have been collected are publicly available. This study did not conduct any interviews or questionnaires and only used secondary data. With the information that was available, the author formed research objectives that are shown below.

3. RESEARCH OBJECTIVES

1. To review case studies and describe how chosen financial frauds were formed.
2. To show the impact of the frauds and the psychological side that victims faced due to the financial scams.
3. To analyze how cognitive psychology is a big part of financial misconduct formation and how can it be helpful in detecting signals and red flags of fraud.

This study will answer objectives 1 and 2 using chosen case studies, and objective 3 will be answered in the literature review, using other researchers' work and available data.

4. CASE STUDIES

4.1 Introduction: History of the Ponzi Scheme

The Ponzi scheme was pioneered by Charles Ponzi and used in his Securities Exchange Company (Frankel, 2012). This is one of the oldest tricks in financial history, where the operator pays off his earlier investors with the money obtained from later investors and usually assets in which the operator "invests" are not existent (Frankel, 2012; Asadov, 2021). The first recorded Ponzi scheme was around late 1800 by a woman named Sarah Howe (Robb, 2012). Often the scheme works, because it offers investors high returns (usually 50%-70%) with little or no risks. Jacobs & Schain (2011) found that a big part of the scheme is the personality of the fraud operator because he has to have an ongoing personality and people need to trust and listen to that person. But in the ever-developing world, people find innovative ways to implement this fraudulent strategy in their businesses.

4.2 Bernard Madoff: Biggest Ponzi Scheme in History

The good-old fashioned Ponzi scheme was the strategy Bernard Madoff was doing for 17 years (Quisenberry, 2017). Bernie Madoff also called the wizard of lies, had an investment fund called 'Bernard L. Madoff Investment Securities' (Heydenburg, 2015). He started with cultivating friendships with wealthy, influential people in New York and Florida, paying them high returns and using their recommendations to lure new investors. Also, Bernard Madoff made his investment fund exclusive (Hurt, 2009). This way he could attract serious, wealthy investors, who loved the idea of prestige. Madoff served as NASDAQ chairman for three one-year terms, which only build the trust In him (Stolowy, 2014). Madoff declined wealthy clients because he targeted those investors who were the least demanding and the least financially savvy (Hurt, 2009). Also gaining him a reputation as the maverick outsider, as his strategy was to lure trades off the NYSE. Potentially gaining him the respect of investors who did not trust traditional Wall Street types and the SEC, which had similar intentions. A couple of factors that contributed to this phenomenon are the 'magic' of accounting. With the accounting practices being so vast and complex Bernie Madoff was able to show fake profits every year in his financial statement, thus showing his investors that their investment is safe and increasing in value, making investors feel secure and not want to leave his fund. The second issue was the lack of experience from the regulators and the lack of supervision from senior employees (Smith, 2010). Then, the people that regulated Bernie Madoff were young and inexperienced and the Securities and Exchange Commission (SEC) was biased toward Bernie (Quisenberry, 2017). They thought that it is the person they can trust because he shared similar views with and also one of the officers in SEC was his relative.

The amount, that was stolen from clients of Madoff's firm, was around 65 billion US dollars (Hurt, 2009) and by December 2008 the advisory business part of Bernard L. Madoff Investment Securities managed 5,000 client accounts. But victims of these crimes say that the amount was calculated incorrectly by the Securities Investor Protection Corporation (SIPC). In their opinion if a client invests 100,000 US dollars with Bernard Madoff in 1985 and the investor believes that in 2008 it should grow to 400,000 US dollars, then the client should argue the loss of 400,000 US dollars. But SIPC argues that the loss is 100,000 US dollars. On top of that, the initial loss is estimated regardless of inflation or the idea of the time value of money. If Madoff would have actually been investing 100,000 US dollars, the amount may have turned profitable, but it also may have lost its value during economic fluctuations or unwise investment decisions. Hurt (2009) said that the goal behind SIPC is to reimburse for a sum the client has invested and not for economic fluctuations or to compensate for the promised return. In addition, there is a more basic reason for the Securities Investor Protection Corporation not to compensate for "phantom losses". They do not have enough funds to reimburse each of B. Madoff's investors for those losses (Hurt, 2009).

Stolowy (2014) stated that in 2008, when investors saw all indexes falling and when the financial crisis was around the corner, Madoff's clients, however, saw positive returns in their financial statements in September 2008. But when the financial crisis developed, they demanded to claim their funds and soon found out that they had no funds left at all and all numbers, that showed positive returns were made up. On December 11, Bernie Madoff was arrested. Bernard Madoff pleaded guilty to 11 criminal counts and was sentenced to 150 years in prison with a restitution of 170 billion US dollars (Smith, 2010).

Hurt (2009) says that this type of financial fraud can also be called affinity fraud. Because affinity fraud is when a person commits fraud in the family circle or around people within their own community. Madoff's first clients were from a circle of mostly Jewish friends and partners of his father-in-law (Hurt, 2009). All of his family and his closest friends were tricked by Madoff himself, even in court no one testified or wrote letters on Madoff's behalf, unlike any other financial fraud cases. Madoff's clients consisted not only of individuals, but it was also of charities like The Wunderkind Foundation, run by Steven Spielberg, and the Foundation of Humanity, which is Elie's Wiesel foundation. Also, Madoff had clients like Yeshiva University and Hadassah (Women's Zionist Organization of America) (Mandell, 2015). As Madoff had a largely Jewish clientele, Mandell (2015) states that comparisons to Adolf Hitler ware frequent. Although Hitler did not deceive his own friends and family. Hurt (2009) says that the Jewish community felt the ripple effect of the fraud, fearing that the public will look at the Jewish with hatred and will negatively stereotype them for participation in the financial markets, also enhancing anti-Semitism.

The effects of this Ponzi scheme on the community and the pain it left inside people are immeasurable. Firstly, Madoff distorted his own family, because the bankruptcy court, media and public targeted his family, due to misinformation about the fact that his family was also part of the fraudulent scheme Lewis, 2010). The family of Bernie Madoff did not know about the Ponzi scheme happening, even though both sons of Bernard Madoff worked in his company. Brody and Perri (2016) noted that the tragic side is, that despite Madoff's son Mark Madoff not being a part of the fraud, he was constantly receiving threats to kill him from people that lost money and he believed that he will forever be associated with the fraud, so he hanged himself in his own home next to a room, where his 2 children were sleeping.

Furthermore, it cannot be compared if the family or other victims suffered more, but people said that they feel that having their financial security disappear, as a result of a betrayal by a trusted advisor, is a fate worse than death (Hurt, 2009). Also, some victims described the effects of the scam as catastrophic and they believed that "they are eligible for government assistance, just as victims of natural disaster and terrorist acts are" (Hurt, 2009). Other authors even found that some victims had symptoms of PTSD syndrome, which often occurs after exposure to extreme or traumatic events. (Glodstein, Glodstein & Fornaro, 2010) states that people develop PTSD after the events of the war, violent death or natural disasters. Varcarolis *et al.*, (2006) also noted that post-traumatic stress disorder symptoms include hopelessness, intrusive thoughts, anger, depression, rage, panic attacks, anxiety, fear and nightmares. Even though victims of Madoff crime were not exposed to death or serious physical injury, they expressed severe psychological, emotional, and physical symptoms in language identical to those who suffered abuse, rape, trauma, and PTSD (Glodstein *et al.*, 2010).

Before the beginning of court, the judge asked victims to comment on Madoff's sentencing. Many of them admitted believing that no sentence would be proportionate to the magnitude of Madoff's crime because they assumed that the nature of the Ponzi scheme is that it can lead to thousands of potential individual crimes. Many of the victims were middle-aged people, so for them losing savings meant that their kids would not be able to attend college and their parents losing retirement savings, meant that those middle-aged victims will have to support three generations. The judge of the court noted that the symbolism of a large sentence was necessary to send a message, that this kind of manipulation of the system is not only a financial crime that takes place on paper, but it is instead one that influences victims' well-being and can shift their life decisions (Quigley & Williams, 2013). Judge note that victims' statements were important to illustrate the horror of this crime and the impact it has left on people.

4.3 Enron: Distrust in Wall Street

Besides Bernard Madoff's scheme of luring out lifetime savings from innocent people, there were other frauds that affected Wall Street in a different way and one of those frauds was the Enron scandal.

After the merger of two major natural gas companies Houston Natural Gas Corporation and Inter-North Inc. Enron was formed and the CEO was Kenneth Lay (Deakin & Konzelmann, 2004). He later hired Jeff Skilling, which was an architect of an accounting technique called Mark to Market, which Enron used and was the main component of the fraud, even though it was approved by SEC in 1992 (Ofori, 2016). This technique allowed Enron to adjust the value of an asset on the balance sheet from its historical cost up to the fair market value and capture the difference as a gain or revenue. For example, when they were building a factory, it allowed Enron to look at the value of the power plant today and then look at its future revenue and adjust the value based on the cashflow that it is expecting to generate. Allowing Enron to capture the projected revenue of that plant as revenue today. Even though revenue did not match the performance of the business, it was still an attractive investment idea for both retail investors and institutional investors, because what they saw was fascinating revenue growth and debt/equity ratio. It was very beneficial for the company's stock performance. The share price went from 8 dollars per share to the highest peak of 90.75 dollars per share (Abatecola, 2019).

The collapse of the company was beginning to start when they went into a deal with the company "Blockbuster" in 2000 to provide a service called video on demand (VOD) service. Blockbuster wanted to start streaming movies and shows, just like Netflix is doing right now, and Enron's part was to provide broad banding and internet services to them. What Enron did was they took the profits from the contract that they expect to make in the future and booked it as revenue today immediately after the deal. Thus, inflating the revenue and the stock price to new heights. But the worst part was that the deal was cancelled after a short while because the technology was not advanced enough to execute this kind of idea (Thomas, 2002). Another big mistake for Enron was that they were losing billions on natural gas projects. They invested 3 billion dollars in the power plant in India (Bratton, 2001). But they did not take into account that India cannot afford to buy electricity, so they abandoned the project but left the expected future profits in the balance sheet and handed themselves unearned bonuses Thomas (2002). What happened afterward was that the performance of the business was not matching up with the revenue that the balance sheet was showing and a reporter in Fortune magazine asked Jeffrey Skilling in an interview a simple question "How exactly does Enron makes its money?" he did not answer that question and left it to be answered by Enron's CFO, who also failed to answer the question. Thus, making mainstream reporters searched for more information and regulators started to uncover frauds that Enron was committing, the company's share price fell from 90 dollars per share to 0.12 dollars per share and Enron declared the largest bankruptcy filling in United States history (Prabakaran, 2010).

After all the scams of Enron were uncovered, the executives of the company and all who contributed to the scam went to court. Kenneth Lay was sentenced to 45 years in prison, but he died before going to jail due to a heart attack (Thomas, 2002). J. Clifford Baxter, who was one of the executives of Enron shot himself after the lawsuit had been filed by the shareholders. He noted in his suicide note that the pain he felt was overwhelming and that he could not live this way anymore (Koehler, 2007). Lastly, the main man Jeffrey Skilling was convicted of 18 counts of fraud and conspiracy and one count of inside trading for the role of forming a fraudulent accounting scheme that masked weak finances and Enron's debt (Benston, 2006). In 2006 he was sentenced to 24 years in prison and had to forfeit 45 million dollars, but later the term was reduced to 14 years, because of a mistake made by a judge (Johnsen, 2018).

Even though the impact on people was not as tragic as Madoff's crime, it still left 28,000 people unemployed, their medical insurance stripped away leaving them to have a meagre retirement (Edelman, 2011). The collapse of Enron made one of the biggest accounting firms in the world named Arthur Andersen LLP go out of business because they were the main auditors of Enron and contributed to the crime thus destroying their own reputation. It was one of the scandals that made the public even more pessimistic about Wall Street and the people who work there.

Analysts had the ability to stop the corruption, but they were tricked by the complexity of the company and the charisma of Skilling. He made analysts believe his words and those who had questions were fired (Ginzl, 2004). The personality traits of Executives such as the need to control situations and/or people, lack of ethical decision making and as well as extensive greed led to the collapse of the company (Reinstein & McMillan, 2004). The power dynamic in the workplace also contributed to some employees fueling the fraud, because Skilling's strategy in the company was that only the fittest survive, so he rated his employees between 1 and 5. 1 being the best and 5 being the worst and every year he fired people who were in the 20% worst performing employees and best performing employees had the chance to spend weekend vacations with the executives (Sims & Brinkmann, 2003). This kind of environment puts pressure on employees, who then have the motivation to commit financial fraud so they would not be fired. As Dr. Donald Cressey stated in his fraud triangle that in most occurrences of frauds these three factors were present: Opportunity, Pressure (also referred to as incentive or motivation) and rationalization (also known as justification or attitude) (Schuchter & Levi, 2016). In Enron's case, Skilling had the opportunity, because the SEC approved his accounting technique and Fastow constructed hundreds of "special purpose entities" designed to distribute Enron's debt to outside companies and get it off the ledgers without handing back control of the assets that was behind the debt (Michaels, 2003). Pressure - another side of the triangle can be explained as the before mentioned survive of the fittest dynamic in the workplace, motivating employees to do anything to keep their jobs. Lastly, the rationalization factor, which can be explained as the facto when the fraudsters do not perceive themselves as criminals, rather they think they are people in an unfortunate situation, who tried to do the best thing possible, thus creating a justification for their crime (Schuchter & Levi, 2016). This kind of method helps criminals to protect themselves from a guilty conscience.

Both examples were chosen, because they were impactful enough to demonstrate to what lengths can a deception take, starting with disappointing families and customers, ending with suicide and destroying lives. The idea is that neither Madoff's nor Enron's stolen amount of money can help them forget about their guilty consciences, which should haunt them for the rest of their lives. On top of that, no amount of remuneration can help restore the lives that these frauds destroyed.

5. LITERATURE REVIEW

5.1 Introduction

White-collar crimes refer to misconducts that were financially motivated and nonviolent. It is usually committed by government professionals and businesses. Rosoff *et al.*, (2002) said in their work, that white-collar crime is more dangerous to society than regular crime. It sounds cruel to compare unlawful behavior, especially when they compare murder with greed. But single murder does not affect society as a corporate fraud or manipulative bubble. Furthermore, financial misconducts are especially destructive to society since they are committed by people in control who are anticipated to set a moral example and behave responsibly. An ordinary viewpoint was expressed in a couple of observational studies that the public does not view white-collar crime as a serious crime. In addition, researchers have left essentially unexamined the harm to social ethics and structures caused by financial frauds (Nakitende, 2021). Areas that lack investigation include estrangement from society, resulting in feelings of normlessness and fragility, and public confidence in major institutions. People can lose their jobs, life savings, and investments. These problems then can lead to family problems, ruining friendships and careers. Pavlo (2018) investigates, that both the victim and the person who committed fraud are constantly feeling the pressure, can abuse alcohol and drugs, feeling of failure and being confused of what is happening around them can be overwhelming and lead to suicide. He talks that law enforcement, lawyers and attorneys need to be informed that there is a dark side to some white-collar criminals and although they are not counselors, they still should be aware of the propensity for violence or suicide. To describe the consequences and impacts of financial fraud this study used examples of Bernard Madoff and the biggest Ponzi scheme in history (Quisenberry, 2017), and Enron, the corporation that is an example of why people distrust Wall Street.

5.2 Irrationality Explained

"The nature of fraud is that it works outside our field of vision" (Davies, 2018). We do not see the fraud happening until investigators catch who is committing the crime. It is normal to miss it, because of human cognitive biases and irrational thinking. Malkiel (1999) said in his book that most of the scams and manipulative bubbles are driven by the 'Greater Fools Theory', which says that during a bubble, investors buy overvalued assets and hope to sell their investment to someone who is willing to pay a higher price. There is a similar theory that backs up this explanation formed by John Maynard Keynes called the "Castle in the air" theory. This approach shows that an investment (house, car, stocks, bonds, other assets) is only worth what someone else is willing to pay for it, also it takes more of a psychological perception of the stock market than a fundamental one, concentrating on how a mass of investors is going to behave in the future (Keynes, 1971). Such a psychological approach can explain how some financial frauds develop and hopefully detect a pattern between financial scams. The existence of cognitive biases can explain irrational investors, business owners or corporate employees' behavior. Such biases are overconfidence, loss aversion, halo effect, etc. Usually, we can spot cognitive biases in an irrational person. This kind of individual's judgement can influence his emotions and therefore he will not use logic or common sense to make decisions (Anandarajan & Kleinman, 2011). Believe that cognitive biases can partially explain the occurrence of financial frauds. What they meant was not that most irrational people commit fraud, but rather that seniors of a company or public can "oversee" the crime that is happening in front of their eyes. Either because of their positive opinion about the fraudster or because of the greediness of the public, wanting to get rich quicker and believing anyone, who offers such a solution (Anandarajan & Kleinman, 2011).

5.3 Similarities of Two Case Studies, Analyzing Potential Warning Signals Using Cognitive Psychology

To notice similar cognitive biases/heuristics this study compared cases of Madoff's Ponzi crime and Enron's crime. Firstly, both of those cases created a halo effect around them. This effect occurs when individuals use one trait of a business or a person to make an overall decision about them (Hong & Liskovich, 2015). In Bernard Madoff's case, the positive character attributes of the person who was suggesting an investment had a bigger influence than the investment itself. As Bernie Madoff was trusted by his fellow Jewish community, charities, and wealthy family members and being an executive of NASDAQ created a halo effect around him, when people did not have a reason to doubt Madoff's decisions, because they thought that their money was safe (Henriques, 2018). In Enron's case, the company was called the Darling of Wall Street for a reason. They offered a great return for investors, Enron was 7th largest corporation in the United States and the charisma of Jeffrey Skilling and Kenneth Lay made investors and even their own employees believe that they were geniuses in the natural energy business (Ekbia, 2004). These factors made people believe that Enron was capable of generating amazing returns forever. Due to the halo effect surrounding the company made analysts, auditors, and reporters not question the managers' behavior or motives and overlook the financial statements (Sood & Bushan, 2020).

Furthermore, other biases we can notice in both cases are the Ostrich effect and inattentional blindness. The Ostrich effect is a cognitive bias when people avoid information that they think is unpleasant. The name comes from the legend that ostriches hide their head in the sand to avoid hazards (Karlsson, Loewenstein & Seppi, 2009). When In attentional Blindness is a psychological phenomenon that occurs when an individual or public fail to see red flags or warning signals of the event or investment because the attention is focused on other things for example making a profit. (Kleinman & Anandarajan, 2011) In other words, not being able to see things that are actually there. In Madoff's case, Markopolos, a former securities industry executive, proved that Bernard Madoff's wealth management business was a massive Ponzi scheme. He discovered using math that Bernie Madoff could not produce 1% to 2% returns every month in positive territory 96% of the time, thus creating a 45-degree curve of profit with no volatility (Markopolos, 2011). He also stated that Madoff charged very little for his hedge fund activities, wondering why a good businessman working for pennies would. Markopolos (2011) tried to alert the United States Securities and Exchange Commission in 2000, 2001 and 2005 of the fraud, showing supporting documents, but SEC ignored it. They weren't the only institution that failed to do the math and were unsuccessful to see the fraud in front of their eyes, but also the smartest people on Wall Street - analysts and investors, overlooked the fraud because they did not want to notice bad information that could lead to discovering a fraud. Kleinman & Anandarajan (2011) States that investors saw what they wanted to see a consistently solid returns on an investment opportunity managed by someone with a strong reputation. The warning signals were around them, but they could not accept that one of the most respectable firms on Wall Street could be a scam. Red flags that (Kleinman and Anandarajan, 2011) found were:

- Bernard Madoff declined to explain his strategy, even to sophisticated analysts who requested information.
- He closely guarded his financial statements and was secretive about his business.
- B. Madoff mainly focused on one ethnic group, Jewish people.
- He rejected meeting directly with investors when they had questions.
- Markopolos's statement that according to his math, it was impossible to make the profits Madoff claimed was making.
- Bernard Madoff in the period 1995-2008 (i.e., 156 months) reported only seven loss-making months. Kleinman and Anandarajan (2011) compared it with a baseball player getting a 0.966 average batting score without cheating when the average baseball player's batting average score is between 0.25 and 0.27 (Beneventano, Berger & Weinberg, 2012).

- He never disclosed how much he was paying brokers for transactions. One explanation could be that there were no trades that have been made.
- He declined to provide his clients with online access to their accounts, so they could not monitor their investments' performance.
- Fraudster was audited by a small firm that had only one accountant. It would be impossible for one accountant to review all of Madoff's vast transactions. He also was a close friend of Madoff who had invested in a fraudster's fund himself.

These are the red flags and questions, that no one was able to ask, when investing in Madoff's firm, due to inattentional blindness, that (Kleinman & Anandarajan, 2011) could discover analyzing Madoff's crime.

The Ostrich effect and inattentional blindness in Enron's case could be explained as, that Enron used revenue and not profits as their primary financial objective, a measure of success and performance driver, resulting in investors believing that it was a smart financial decision (Bufkins & Dharan, 2004). Enron also revealed to their shareholders that the company had hedged downside risk in their own illiquid investments using "special purpose entities". However, shareholders were oblivious to the fact that the special purpose entities were the company's own stock and financial guarantees to finance the hedges (Healy & Palepu, 2003). Another red flag would be the attention of growing independent analysts, who did not see the profitability of Enron. Executives berated an analyst and used an obscene word to refer to him, when he asked for a balance sheet during a conference call says (Bufkins & Dharan, 2004). The net income in (Bufkins & Dharan, 2004) analysis did not grow at a similar rate as revenues, which grew 164.6% per year for the same five-year period, as a result, there was a stable decline in net profit margin from 4.4% in 1996 to 1% in 2001. Similarly, the company's gross profit margin (gross profits as a percentage of revenues) declined from 21.2% at the beginning of the 5-year period to 6.2% in 2000, in the same year when earnings more than doubled from the year 1999 (Bufkins & Dharan, 2004). Analysts did not question the profitability of Enron as long as net profits continued to grow at 15% plus per year, despite the fact that these profits were actually small as a percentage of revenues. For comparison (Bufkins & Dharan, 2004) shows data on the profitability of major global energy companies and in terms of return on assets, net profit margin and return on equity, Enron's financial performance was one of the lowest for this group. The rapid decline of gross profit margin in Enron's income statement revealed a major red flag that investors and most of the analysts oversaw due to a behavioral bias to overlook negative information.

Other cognitive biases we can notice in both cases are a bandwagon effect, which is explained as individual's opinion being shifted by the idea of what a majority of people chooses or expects to choose (Schmitt-Beck, 2015). Also, selective perception bias - where people perceive what they want to in messages or announcements, while ignoring opposing viewpoints (Walsh, 1988), and anchoring bias - where public rely too much on pre-existing information to make a decision (Furnham & Boo, 2011). Enron had an extra behavioral bias known as overconfidence. Executives were overconfident about the valuation of the company because the difference by their value and what others valued the company was 1,5 billion U.S. dollars also because of their promises of constant innovation and high returns (Malmendier & Tate, 2008).

Using these cognitive biases/behavioral heuristics the author displayed how investigators could have noticed some red flags of the fraud and learned from the mistakes of these two cases that were discussed before. It is hard to notice fraud if you are not a professional investigator or not a professional auditor, but it is important to do your own research before investing rather than trusting a broker's word. Auditors and Analysts are capable to see irregularities in financial statements (Ramzan *et al.,* 2020), but they are people, which means some irrationalities may occur and their perception can influence their decisions. The ideas mentioned in this chapter are arguments on why regulations and laws should be strict for big corporations and that specialists/investigators have a responsibility of noticing irregularities before a potential fraud.

6. DISCUSSION AND FINDINGS

Financial fraud, as mentioned before, can be worse than theft, murder, or corruption, it is an immoral transaction that destroys relationships of trust between groups or organizations and has an impact on individuals' future decisions. A simple explanation of why frauds happen can be excessive greed and a need to control a situation, has been touched previously, the idea still holds that financial misconduct can have different opportunities of emerging. Also, it was explained how deeply victims (by victims I mean customers and family members that were unaware) can be affected by the fraud.

Using the case study of Bernard Madoff, this paper described the immeasurably pain and void it left to victims that trusted their life savings, pension funds, and college savings to the most trusted advisor on Wall Street. For the victims of this crime, the impact extends beyond the financial loss and includes undesired media coverage and perhaps public humiliation. On top of that, this crime could have shaped the lives of individuals for example if middle-aged family lost their children's college savings, which could result in their child not going to college and shaping his future. Also, an elderly family that saved money for a rainy day in Madoff's fund and now cannot pay for surgery, resulting in death or continuing work after retirement. These are just a couple of examples of how such financial misconduct resulted in thousands of other little aftermaths.

When in Enron's case, they manipulated their company's stock, using fraudulent accounting techniques. Using such a practice, they tricked analysts and investors. The collapse of Enron took down one of the biggest accounting firms in the world, due to it being involved with a scam. Around 30,000 people lost their jobs and retirement funds, concluding that people could not find a job in the finance sector, due to their reputation being associated with Enron.

Ex-employee of Enron also published a book about the company and the crime from his perspective called Anatomy of Greed: The Unshredded Truth from an Enron Insider. The movie adaptations and books are a great effort to raise awareness about the problems of financial misconduct and will be available for future generations to learn from fraudsters' mistakes. It is important to talk about this problem when fraud costs 3.89 trillion pounds across the world for businesses, people and organizations, also reducing such losses by 40% would free up more than 76 billion pounds each year (Gee & Button, 2019).

The study found that cognitive biases that influenced chosen case studies were the Halo effect, Ostrich effect, inattentional blindness, bandwagon effect and selective perception bias. (Kleinman & Anandarajan, 2011) Suggests that inattentional blindness should be taught in forensic accounting and auditing classes to broaden student awareness of how "blind spots" could negatively affect the investigation process. Also, the paper showed that it is possible to use behavioral heuristics and cognitive biases to find warning signals and red flags. It is important because potential fraud could be found early and authorities or regulators notified, so that potentially fraudulent companies could be further investigated using technical detection systems or by using professional auditors.

If it is possible to find any benefits from both case studies, then it would be that both cases will be a catalyst for stimulating innovative solutions to address these wide-ranging business challenges. Investigators learned that it is possible to overlook the crime, so new practices will be adopted. Also, SEC made changes to their system after the Madoff scandal, which includes Revitalizing the enforcement division, encouraging greater cooperation by 'insiders', enhancing safeguards for investors' assets, improving risk assessment capabilities, improving internal controls, advocating for whistleblower program, improving fraud detection procedures for examiners and many more (SEC, 2008). Lastly, customers will be wiser to do their own research rather than blindly trusting their broker.

7. RECOMMENDATIONS

- Customers of investment funds should thoroughly read prospectuses, follow up with investment vehicles that hedge fund manager's use and avoid trusting your money to organizations that promise guaranteed, unrealistic, or quick returns.
- If a customer notices any red flags, they should immediately notify regulators or officials for investigation.
- Investigators should thoroughly investigate all red flags that had been noticed.
- Auditors, examiners, or investigators should be professionally trained and have senior-level oversight.
- Investigators should use different detection systems and strategies while conducting examinations.
- A third-party verification team should be used to cross-check SEC investigations.

8. CONCLUSION

In the conclusion the author can say that objectives 1 (To review case studies and describe how chosen financial frauds were formed) and objective 2 (To show the impact of the frauds and psychological side that victims faced due to the financial scams) were reached, using two different examples of financial frauds. Objective 1 was more focused on Enron's case when particular circumstances were subject to fuel the fraud. Bernard Madoff's case was also significant for objective 1, but the researcher used this example to focus more on objective 2, because the fraud was focused more on people and the impact for them was enormous. Objective 3 (To analyze how cognitive psychology is a big part of financial misconduct formation and how can it be helpful in detecting signals and red flags of fraud) was answered using other researchers' works and insights. The chapter investigated them in literature review and using their work, the understanding can be made that cognitive biases and behavioral heuristics can help to detect and prevent financial scams. On top of that, the researcher of this chapter described how these biases and irrationality incite financial misconduct, looking from customers'/investors' perspective and from business owners' perspective. Financial frauds are a broad subject, these anomalies appear very often, because of the nature of greed. As it was discussed in this chapter, financial misconduct can be more harmful to society than regular crimes. They are damaging families, the public, other businesses, and the overall market. It is possible that we are being scammed right now by some company that we trust, but we will not be sure until it is revealed by investigators and other legal bodies. That is why it is important to educate yourselves about financial misconduct and be able to identify signals, that could lead to uncovering fraud in its early stage. Academics have the access to frauds that had already been caught, they have the ability to analyze them and develop new systems so that it would be possible to prevent future misconducts. So, to sum up, companies, if not regulated, can have too much power and influence, which can be manipulated and misused. Such misconducts harm the government and distort the social wellbeing of the community, impacting mental health and removing trust between customers and financial institutions.

DECLARATION

The author declares that the manuscript follows ethical standards and there are no potential conflicts of interest with respect to the research, authorship and/or publication of this chapter.

DISCLAIMER

The contents and views of this chapter are expressed by the author in personal capacity. It is not necessary for the Editor and the Publisher to agree with these viewpoints, and they are not responsible for any duty of care in this regard.

AUTHOR'S NOTE

This chapter is extracted from the unpublished undergraduate project of the principal author. The project was submitted to Coventry University, UK to award the degree.

ACKNOWLEDGMENT

The author extends sincere gratitude to

- The Editor and the International Editorial Advisory Board (IEAB) of this book who initially desk reviewed, arranged a rigorous double/triple blind review process, and conducted a thorough, minute, and critical final review before accepting the chapter for publication.
- All anonymous reviewers who provided very constructive feedbacks for thorough revision, improvement, extension, and fine tuning of the chapter.
- All colleagues, assistants and well-wishers who assisted to complete this task.

REFERENCES

Abatecola, G. (2019). Prioritizing short-termism in behavioural strategy: Lessons from Enron–20 years on. *International Journal of Business and Management*, *14*(4), 60–71. doi:10.5539/ijbm.v14n4p60

Anandarajan, A., & Kleinman, G. (2011). The impact of cognitive biases on fraudulent behaviour: The Leeson case. *International Journal of Behavioural Accounting and Finance*, *2*(1), 40–55. doi:10.1504/IJBAF.2011.038756

Armstrong, M. (2021. August 6). How many websites are there? *Statista Infographics*. https://www.statista.com/chart/19058/how-many-websites-are-there/

Asadov, A. (2021). Financial scams through Ponzi schemes: The case of CIS countries. In A. Rafay (Ed.), *Handbook of Research on Theory and Practice of Financial Crimes* (pp. 271–292). IGI Global. doi:10.4018/978-1-7998-5567-5.ch015

Baxter, T. C. Jr, & Ramasastry, A. (1996). The importance of being honest-lessons from an era of large-scale financial fraud. *Saint Louis University Law Journal*, *41*, 93.

Beneventano, P., Berger, P. D., & Weinberg, B. D. (2012). Predicting run production and run prevention in baseball: The impact of Sabermetrics. *International Journal of Business. Human Technology*, *2*(4), 67–75.

Benston, G. J. (2006). Fair-value accounting: A cautionary tale from Enron. *Journal of Accounting and Public Policy*, *25*(4), 465–484. doi:10.1016/j.jaccpubpol.2006.05.003

Bolton, R. J., & Hand, D. J. (2002). Statistical fraud detection: A review. *Statistical Science*, *17*(3), 235–255. doi:10.1214s/1042727940

Bratton, W. W. (2001). Enron and the dark side of shareholder value. *Tulane Law Review*, *76*, 1275.

Brody, R. G., & Perri, F. S. (2016). Fraud detection suicide: The dark side of white-collar crime. *Journal of Financial Crime*, *23*(4), 786–797. doi:10.1108/JFC-09-2015-0043

Bufkins, W. R., & Dharan, B. G. (2004). Red Flags in Enron's Reporting of Revenues and Key Financial Measures. *Enron: Corporate Fiascos and Their Implications,* 97–110. https://papers.ssrn.com/sol3/papers.cfm?abstract_id=1172222

Columbus, L. (2019). AI is predicting the future of online fraud detection. *Forbes*. https://www.forbes.com/sites/louiscolumbus/2019/08/01/ai-is-predicting-the-future-of-online-fraud-detection/

Davies, D. (2018, June 28). How to get away with financial fraud. *The Guardian*. https://www.theguardian.com/news/2018/jun/28/how-to-get-away-with-financial-fraud

Deakin, S., & Konzelmann, S. J. (2004). Learning from Enron. *Corporate Governance*, *12*(2), 134–142. doi:10.1111/j.1467-8683.2004.00352.x

Edelman, D., & Nicholson, A. (2011). Arthur Anderson auditors and Enron: What happened to their Texas CPA licenses? *Journal of Finance and Accountancy*, *8*, 1–9.

Ekbia, H. R. (2004). How IT mediates organizations: Enron and the California energy crisis. *Journal of Digital Information*, *5*(4).

Ekins, E. (2017, September 19). Poll: Public distrusts wall street regulators as much as wall street, say gov't regulators are ineffective, biased, and selfish. *Cato Institute*. https://www.cato.org/blog/poll-public-distrusts-wall-street-regulators-much-wall-street-say-govt-regulators-are

Frankel, T. (2012). *The Ponzi scheme puzzle: A history and analysis of con artists and victims*. Oxford University Press. doi:10.1093/acprof:osobl/9780199926619.001.0001

Furnham, A., & Boo, H. C. (2011). A literature review of the anchoring effect. *Journal of Socio-Economics*, *40*(1), 35–42. doi:10.1016/j.socec.2010.10.008

Gee, J., & Button, M. (2019). *The financial cost of fraud 2019: The latest data from around the world*. University of Portsmouth.

Ginzl, D. J. (2004). Dumb, dumber, and dumbest: What went wrong at Enron. *Commercial Lending Review*, *19*, 42.

Glodstein, D., Glodstein, S. L., & Fornaro, J. (2010). Fraud trauma syndrome: The victims of the Bernard Madoff scandal. *Journal of Forensic Studies in Accounting and Business*, *2*(1), 1–9.

Gunestas, M., Mehmet, M., & Wijesekera, D. (2010). *Detecting Ponzi and pyramid business schemes in choreographed web services*. In *IFIP International Conference on Digital Forensics* (pp. 133–150). IEEE. 10.1007/978-3-642-15506-2_10

Healy, P. M., & Palepu, K. G. (2003). The fall of Enron. *The Journal of Economic Perspectives*, *17*(2), 3–26. doi:10.1257/089533003765888403

Henriques, D. B. (2018). A case study of a con man: Bernie Madoff and the timeless lessons of history's biggest Ponzi scheme. *Social Research*, *85*(4), 745–766. doi:10.1353or.2018.0048

Heydenburg, M. R. (2015). The Ponzi scheme as a deception operation: The Bernie Madoff case study. *American Intelligence Journal*, *32*(2), 27–34.

Hong, H., & Liskovich, I. (2015). Crime, punishment and the halo effect of corporate social responsibility (No. w21215). Washington: National Bureau of Economic Research.

Hurt, C. (2009). Evil has a new name (and a new narrative): Bernard Madoff. *Detroit College of Law at Michigan State University Law Review*, 947.

Jacobs, P., & Schain, L. (2011). The never-ending attraction of the Ponzi scheme. *Journal of Comprehensive Research*, *9*, 40–46.

Jebb, A., Parrigon, S., & Woo, S. (2017). Exploratory data analysis as a foundation of inductive research. *Human Resource Management Review*, *27*(2), 265–276. doi:10.1016/j.hrmr.2016.08.003

Johnsen, C. G. (2018). Authenticating the leader: Why Bill George believes that a moral compass would have kept Jeffrey Skilling out of jail. *Journal of Business Ethics*, *147*(1), 53–63. doi:10.100710551-015-2968-7

Karlsson, N., Loewenstein, G., & Seppi, D. (2009). The ostrich effect: Selective attention to information. *Journal of Risk and Uncertainty*, *38*(2), 95–115. doi:10.100711166-009-9060-6

Keynes, J. M., Moggridge, D. E., & Johnson, E. S. (1971). The Collected Writings of John Maynard Keynes (Vol. 30, pp. 1971–89). London: Macmillan.

Kleinman, G., & Anandarajan, A. (2011). Inattentional blindness and its relevance to teaching forensic accounting and auditing. *Journal of Accounting Education*, *29*(1), 37–49. doi:10.1016/j.jaccedu.2011.08.002

Koehler, S. A. (2007). The role of suicide notes in death investigation. *Journal of Forensic Nursing*, *3*(2), 87–89. doi:10.1097/01263942-200706000-00007 PMID:17679273

Lewis, L. S. (2010). Madoff's victims and their day in court. *Society*, *47*(5), 439–450. doi:10.100712115-010-9345-z

Malkiel, B. G. (1999). *A Random Walk Down Wall Street: including a life-cycle guide to personal investing*. W.W. Norton & Company.

Malmendier, U., & Tate, G. (2008). Who makes acquisitions? CEO overconfidence and the market's reaction. *Journal of Financial Economics*, *89*(1), 20–43. doi:10.1016/j.jfineco.2007.07.002

Mandell, H. (2015). Imagine what the gentiles must think: Editors of the US Jewish press reflect on covering the Bernard Madoff Scandal. In Journalism, Audiences and Diaspora (pp. 17–33). London: Palgrave Macmillan.

Mandell, H. (2015). The Nazi treatment: Press coverage of Barack Obama and Bernard Madoff from 2008 to 2009. *International Journal of Media and Cultural Politics*, *11*(1), 87–103. doi:10.1386/macp.11.1.87_1

Markopolos, H. (2011). *No one would listen: A true financial thriller*. John Wiley & Sons.

Merle, R. (2018, September 10). A guide to the financial crisis—10 years later. *The Washington Post*. https://www.washingtonpost.com/business/economy/a-guide-to-the-financial-crisis--10-years-later/2018/09/10/114b76ba-af10-11e8-a20b-5f4f84429666_story.html

Michaels, A. C. (2003). Fastow and Arthur Andersen: Some reflections on corporate criminality, victim status, and retribution. *Ohio State Journal of Criminal Law*, *1*, 551.

Mostyn, G. R. (2012). Cognitive load theory: What it is, why it's important for accounting instruction and research. *Issues in Accounting Education*, *27*(1), 227–245. doi:10.2308/iace-50099

Nakitende, M. G., Rafay, A., & Waseem, M. (2021). Frauds in Business Organizations: A Comprehensive Overview. In A. Rafay (Ed.), *Handbook of Research on Theory and Practice of Financial Crimes* (pp. 21–38). IGI Global. doi:10.4018/978-1-7998-5567-5.ch002

Nisbett, R., & Wilson, T. (1977). The halo effect: Evidence for unconscious alteration of judgments. *Journal of Personality and Social Psychology*, *35*(4), 250–256. doi:10.1037/0022-3514.35.4.250

Ofori, E. (2016). Detecting corporate financial fraud using Modified Altman Z-score and Beneish M-score. The case of Enron Corp. *Research Journal of Finance and Accounting*, *7*(4), 59–65.

Pavlo, W. (2018, January 18). White collar crime: Suicide, murder and revenge. *Forbes*. Retrieved from https://www.forbes.com/sites/walterpavlo/2018/01/18/white-collar-crime-suicide-murder-and-revenge/?sh=4b54ea3d74d8

Prabakaran, M. (2010). Business ethics: Should it remain an oxymoron? *MES Journal of Technology and Management*, *1*(1), 83–98.

Pressman, S. (1998). On financial frauds and their causes: Investor overconfidence. *American Journal of Economics and Sociology*, *57*(4), 405–421. doi:10.1111/j.1536-7150.1998.tb03373.x

Quigley, B., & Williams, J. (2013). Madoff: From man to monster. *The Academic Forum*. 28–37. https://www.proquest.com/docview/1639614541?pq-origsite=gscholar&fromopenview=true

Quisenberry, W. L. (2017). Ponzi of all Ponzis: Critical analysis of the Bernie Madoff scheme. *International Journal of Econometrics and Financial Management*, *5*(1), 1–6.

Rafay, A. (Ed.). (2021a). *Money Laundering and Terrorism Financing in Global Financial Systems*. IGI Global. doi:10.4018/978-1-7998-8758-4

Rafay, A. (Ed.). (2021b). *HandBook of Research on Theory and Practice of Financial Crimes*. IGI Global. doi:10.4018/978-1-7998-5567-5

Rafay, A. (Ed.). (2023a). *Concepts, Cases, and Regulations in Financial Fraud and Corruption*. IGI Global. doi:10.4018/978-1-6684-5007-9

Rafay, A. (Ed.). (2023b). *Concepts and Cases of Illicit Finance*. IGI Global. doi:10.4018/978-1-6684-8587-3

Ramzan, M., Ahmad, I., & Rafay, A. (2020). Is auditor independence influenced by non-audit services? A stakeholder's viewpoint. *Pakistan Journal of Commerce and Social Sciences*, *14*(1), 388–408.

Reinstein, A., & McMillan, J. J. (2004). The Enron debacle: More than a perfect storm. *Critical Perspectives on Accounting*, *15*(6-7), 955–970. doi:10.1016/j.cpa.2003.08.006

Reurink, A. (2018). Financial fraud: AQ literature review. *Journal of Economic Surveys*, *32*(5), 1292–1325. doi:10.1111/joes.12294

Robb, G. (2012). Depicting a Female Fraud: Sarah Howe and the Boston Women's Bank. *Nineteenth-Century Contexts*, *34*(5), 445–459. doi:10.1080/08905495.2012.738086

Rosoff, S., Pontell, H., & Tillman, R. (2002). *Profit Without Honor: White-Collar Crime and the Looting of America*. Prentice Hall.

Rosoff, S. M., Pontell, H. N., & Tillman, R. (2002). *Profit without honor: White-collar crime and the looting of America*. Prentice Hall Publishing.

Schmitt-Beck, R. (2015). Bandwagon effect. The International Encyclopedia of Political Communication, 1–5.

Schuchter, A., & Levi, M. (2016). The fraud triangle revisited. *Security Journal*, *29*(2), 107–121. doi:10.1057j.2013.1

SEC. (2008, March). *The Securities and Exchange Commission Post-Madoff Reforms*. Securities and exchange Commission. https://www.sec.gov/spotlight/secpostmadoffreforms.htm

Sims, R. R., & Brinkmann, J. (2003). Enron ethics (or: Culture matters more than codes). *Journal of Business Ethics*, *45*(3), 243–256. doi:10.1023/A:1024194519384

Singh, P. (2013). An exploratory study on internet banking usage in Semi-Urban areas in India. *International Journal of Scientific and Research Publications*, *3*(8), 1–5.

Smith, F. (2010). Madoff ponzi scheme exposes the myth of the sophisticated investor. *University of Baltimore Law Review*, *40*, 215.

Sood, P., & Bhushan, P. (2020). A structured review and theme analysis of financial frauds in the banking industry. *Asian Journal of Business Ethics*, *9*(2), 305–321. doi:10.100713520-020-00111-w

Stolowy, H., Messner, M., Jeanjean, T., & Richard Baker, C. (2014). The construction of a trustworthy investment opportunity: Insights from the Madoff fraud. *Contemporary Accounting Research*, *31*(2), 354–397. doi:10.1111/1911-3846.12039

Thoma, M. (2010, September 2). Too Much "Too Big to Fail"? *Economist's View*. https://economistsview.typepad.com/economistsview/2010/09/too-much-too-big-to-fail.html

Thomas, C. W. (2002). The rise and fall of Enron. *Journal of Accountancy*, *193*(4), 41–52.

Varcarolis, E. M., Carson, V. B., & Shoemaker, N. C. (2006). *Foundations of Psychiatric Mental Health Nursing: A Clinical Approach*. Saunders.

Walsh, J. P. (1988). Selectivity and selective perception: An investigation of managers' belief structures and information processing. *Academy of Management Journal*, *31*(4), 873–896. doi:10.2307/256343

Chapter 12
Accounting Fraud and Bankruptcy: The Case of Wirecard AG

S. Baranidharan
https://orcid.org/0000-0002-7780-4045
CHRIST University (Deemed), India

Clement Chiahemba M. Ajekwe
https://orcid.org/0000-0001-9617-6438
Benue State University, Nigeria

Marie Goretti Nakitende
Uganda Martyrs University, Uganda

ABSTRACT

This chapter examines the scandal at Wirecard AG, a German payment processing and financial services company, that became one of the most valuable companies on the German stock exchange in the 2010s. From 2010 to 2018, Wirecard reported consistent revenue growth and profitability. In 2019, the company reported revenues of €2.8 billion ($3.2 billion). As of September 2018, its market capitalization was over €24 billion ($27 billion). In late 2019, the Wirecard scandal was discovered through investigative reports by the Financial Times, which raised questions about Wirecard's accounting practices. The company faced a major scandal in 2020 when it was revealed that €1.9 billion ($2.1 billion) was missing from its balance sheet. Subsequent investigations revealed a massive accounting fraud that had been going on for years. Subsequently, the company filed for bankruptcy. Multiple Wirecard executives, including its CEO, were charged with fraud and market manipulation. German regulators and auditors were criticized for failing to detect and prevent the fraud.

DOI: 10.4018/979-8-3693-1190-5.ch012

INTRODUCTION

The collapse of Wirecard AG, a German payment processing company, has been one of the biggest corporate scandals in recent years. The company filed for bankruptcy in June 2020, following the discovery of a massive accounting fraud that had been going on for years.

Wirecard, founded in 1999, was once seen as a promising Fintech company that could disrupt the traditional banking industry. The company offered payment processing, card issuing, and other financial services to businesses and individuals globally. Wirecard's share price surged in the early 2010s, and the company became one of the most valuable companies on the German stock exchange.

However, in late 2019, Wirecard's share price began to plummet after a series of investigative reports by the Financial Times raised questions about the company's accounting practices. The reports alleged that Wirecard had overstated its revenue and profits, and that much of its business in Asia was fraudulent. The reports triggered an investigation by the German financial regulator, BaFin, which initially defended Wirecard and even filed a criminal complaint against the FT journalists. However, in June 2020, Wirecard admitted that €1.9 billion ($2.1 billion) was missing from its balance sheet, and the company filed for bankruptcy shortly after.

Subsequent investigations revealed that Wirecard had been engaging in a massive accounting fraud for years, inflating its revenue and profits through a complex network of shell companies and fake transactions. The fraud involved multiple Wirecard executives, including the CEO Markus Braun, who was arrested and charged with fraud and market manipulation. The collapse of Wirecard has had far-reaching consequences. Thousands of Wirecard employees lost their jobs, and many investors lost their life savings. The scandal has also raised serious questions about the role of auditors and regulators in detecting and preventing corporate fraud. The German government has launched an inquiry into the Wirecard scandal, and BaFin has faced criticism for its handling of the case.

Overall, the Wirecard scandal has highlighted the need for greater transparency and accountability in the financial sector, and the importance of robust corporate governance and regulatory oversight. It serves as a cautionary tale of the risks of unchecked corporate greed and the dangers of failing to uphold ethical and legal standards.

BACKGROUND

Wirecard AG was founded in 1999 by Markus Braun, a former consultant at KPMG, and Arndt Roller, a computer science expert. The company initially focused on providing payment solutions to online merchants, enabling them to accept payments through various payment methods, including credit cards, bank transfers, and e-wallets. This was a time when e-commerce was growing rapidly, and online businesses needed a secure and reliable payment processing service.

In the early 2000s, Wirecard expanded its services to include card issuing and acquiring, which allowed the company to offer end-to-end payment solutions to its clients. This meant that Wirecard could provide businesses with everything they needed to accept and process payments, from payment terminals to payment gateway software. The company also entered the mobile payment market, offering digital wallets and mobile payment solutions to consumers. Wirecard's growth accelerated in the 2010s, with the company becoming one of the most valuable companies on the German stock exchange. The company's revenue and profits increased significantly, driven by strong demand for its payment processing services and its expansion into new markets. Wirecard expanded its operations globally, with offices and subsidiaries in more than 30 countries. Wirecard's success was partly due to its innovative business model, which disrupted the traditional banking industry. By providing payment processing services directly to businesses, Wirecard bypassed the need for traditional banks and payment processors, offering faster and more cost-effective payment solutions. The company also leveraged technology to provide clients with real-time data and analytics (Breuer, Boronczyk & Rumpf, 2021), enabling them to make better business decisions. In 2018, Wirecard's market capitalization reached over €24 billion ($27 billion), making it one of the most valuable companies in Germany. The company's success was also recognized internationally, with Wirecard winning numerous awards for its innovative payment solutions.

However, the discovery of the accounting fraud in 2019 and the subsequent bankruptcy of Wirecard has raised questions about the company's rapid growth and the integrity of its financial reporting. The scandal has also highlighted the need for greater transparency and accountability in the financial sector, and the importance of robust corporate governance and regulatory oversight.

CASE NOVELTY

The Wirecard case 2020 stands out as a unique and significant scandal in the financial industry. While accounting frauds and corporate scandals have occurred in the past, the magnitude and impact of the Wirecard case distinguish it from existing cases. Here are a few key differences:

Scale of Fraud

The Wirecard case involved a staggering amount of missing funds, with €1.9 billion ($2.1 billion) being unaccounted for on the company's balance sheet. This level of financial discrepancy sets it apart from many previous scandals.

Industry Disruption

Wirecard was positioned as a disruptor in the traditional banking industry, offering innovative payment processing solutions. The case highlighted the risks associated with disruptive fintech companies and the potential vulnerabilities in their operations.

Regulatory Oversight Failure

The Wirecard scandal exposed significant shortcomings in regulatory oversight. German regulators and auditors faced criticism for failing to detect and prevent the fraud, raising questions about the effectiveness of regulatory systems and the need for improved monitoring and enforcement.

Global Implications

Wirecard's operations spanned multiple countries, and the scandal had global implications. It impacted not only employees and investors but also raised concerns among financial institutions, regulators, and market participants worldwide.

Investor Confidence Impact

Wirecard's collapse resulted in significant losses for investors, including institutional investors, who had placed their trust in the company's financial performance. The case underscored the importance of conducting thorough due diligence and maintaining skepticism regarding financial reporting.

These differences make the Wirecard case a significant event in the history of corporate scandals, emphasizing the need for enhanced transparency, accountability, and regulatory oversight in the financial industry.

WIRECARD AG: COMPANY PROFILE AND OVERVIEW

Wirecard AG was a German payment processing company that provided payment solutions and financial services to businesses and individuals globally. The company was founded in 1999 and headquartered in Aschheim, near Munich, Germany. Wirecard operated in more than 100 countries and had a workforce of around 5,800 employees. The company was listed on the Frankfurt Stock Exchange and was included in German DAX 30 index.

Overview

History and Growth

- Founding of Wirecard AG in 1999
- Initial focus on providing payment solutions to online merchants.
- Expansion into card issuing, acquiring, and other financial services.
- Rapid growth in the 2010s, with the company becoming one of the most valuable companies on the German stock exchange.

Products and Services

- Payment processing solutions for online and offline merchants
- Card issuing and acquiring services.
- Mobile payment solutions
- Risk management and fraud prevention services
- Digital banking solutions

Market Position

- Global player in the payment processing industry
- Competed with other payment processors such as PayPal, Adyen, and Stripe
- Positioned as a disruptor in the traditional banking industry.

Financial Performance

- Consistent revenue growth and profitability until 2019
- Reported revenues of €2.8 billion ($3.2 billion) in 2019
- Market capitalization of over €24 billion ($27 billion) in September 2018

Corporate Governance

- Executive board led by CEO Markus Braun
- Supervisory board consisting of industry experts and investors
- Compliance department responsible for ensuring ethical and legal business practices.

Scandal and Bankruptcy

Discovery of Accounting Irregularities

- Investigative reports by the Financial Times in late 2019 raised questions about Wirecard's accounting practices.
- Reports alleged that Wirecard had overstated its revenue and profits, and that much of its business in Asia was fraudulent.
- Wirecard initially denied the allegations and accused the journalists of market manipulation.

Collapse and Bankruptcy

- In June 2020, Wirecard admitted that €1.9 billion ($2.1 billion) was missing from its balance sheet.
- The company filed for bankruptcy shortly after this announcement.
- Thousands of employees lost their jobs, and many investors lost their life savings.

Investigation and Legal Proceedings

- Subsequent investigations revealed a massive accounting fraud that had been going on for years.
- Multiple Wirecard executives were charged with fraud and market manipulation, including CEO Markus Braun
- German regulators and auditors faced criticism for failing to detect and prevent the fraud

Products and Services

Wirecard AG was a provider of payment processing and digital banking solutions to businesses and consumers. The company offered a wide range of products and services, including:

Payment Processing Solutions

Wirecard provided payment processing solutions to online and offline merchants, enabling them to accept payments from customers through various payment methods, including credit cards, bank transfers, e-wallets, and mobile payments. The company offered payment gateway software, payment terminals, and point-of-sale (POS) systems to businesses, making it easy for them to process payments and manage their transactions.

Card Issuing and Acquiring Services

Wirecard offered card issuing and acquiring services to businesses, enabling them to issue prepaid cards, credit cards, and debit cards to their customers. The company provided end-to-end solutions, including card design, production, and management. Wirecard also offered acquiring services, enabling businesses to accept card payments and settle transactions with card issuers.

Mobile Payment Solutions

Wirecard provided mobile payment solutions to consumers, allowing them to make payments using their smartphones. The company offered digital wallets, mobile payment apps, and contactless payment solutions, making it easy for consumers to make payments on the go.

Risk Management and Fraud Prevention Services

Wirecard offered risk management and fraud prevention services to businesses, helping them to identify and prevent fraudulent transactions. The company used advanced fraud detection algorithms and machine learning techniques to analyse transaction data and detect anomalies, reducing the risk of fraud and chargebacks.

Digital Banking Solutions

Wirecard provided digital banking solutions to businesses and consumers, enabling them to manage their finances online. The company offered white-label banking solutions, allowing businesses to launch their own digital banking services. Wirecard also offered prepaid debit cards, digital wallets, and other banking services to consumers.

Overall, Wirecard's products and services were designed to help businesses and consumers to manage their finances more efficiently and securely. However, the accounting fraud scandal that engulfed the company has raised questions about the integrity of its financial reporting and the quality of its services. Despite this, the payment processing and digital banking industry remains highly competitive, with many innovative companies offering similar products and services.

Market Positioning

Global Player in the Payment Processing Industry

Wirecard AG was a global player in the payment processing industry, offering a wide range of products and services to businesses and consumers. The company had a strong market position in Europe, Asia, and the Americas, with operations in more than 30 countries. Wirecard's revenue and profits grew rapidly in the 2010s, driven by strong demand for its payment processing solutions and its expansion into new markets.

Competed With Other Payment Processors Such as PayPal, Adyen, and Stripe

Wirecard competed with other payment processors such as PayPal, Adyen, and Stripe, all of which offered similar products and services. However, Wirecard's innovative business model and technology-enabled solutions positioned it as a disruptor in the traditional banking industry. By providing payment processing services directly to businesses, Wirecard bypassed the need for traditional banks and payment processors, offering faster and more cost-effective payment solutions.

Positioned as a Disruptor in the Traditional Banking Industry

Wirecard's disruption of the traditional banking industry was recognized by industry experts, with the company winning numerous awards for its innovative payment solutions. In 2018, Wirecard was ranked as the second most innovative company in Germany by Forbes, behind only the technology giant SAP.

Wirecard's market position was also reflected in its market capitalization, which reached over €24 billion ($27 billion) in 2018, making it one of the most valuable companies in Germany. The company's success was partly due to its ability to attract large clients, including major retailers, airlines, and financial institutions.

However, the discovery of the accounting fraud in 2019 and the subsequent bankruptcy of Wirecard has had a significant impact on the company's market position. The scandal has raised questions about the company's financial reporting and the integrity of its services, leading to a loss of confidence among investors and clients. Wirecard's competitors, including PayPal, Adyen, and Stripe, have also benefited from the scandal, with some clients switching to their services.

Overall, Wirecard's market position was highly competitive, with the company positioned as a disruptor in the traditional banking industry. However, the accounting fraud scandal has had a significant impact on the company's market position, highlighting the importance of transparency and accountability in the financial sector.

Wirecard's market position (based on publicly available sources):

- In 2018, Wirecard was valued at over €24 billion ($27 billion), making it one of the most valuable companies in Germany.
- Wirecard was ranked as the second most innovative company in Germany by Forbes in 2018, behind only SAP.
- As of 2019, Wirecard had operations in more than 30 countries, with a strong presence in Europe, Asia, and the Americas.

- Wirecard competed with other payment processors such as PayPal, Adyen, and Stripe, among others.
- Wirecard was positioned as a disruptor in the traditional banking industry, offering innovative payment solutions and bypassing the need for traditional banks and payment processors.

Table 1. Wirecard's business coverage (2010 – 2018)

Year	Number of countries with operations	Number of customers
2010	15	13,000
2011	25	16,000
2012	33	20,000
2013	44	24,000
2014	45	27,000
2015	51	27,000
2016	71	31,000
2017	76	34,000
2018	118	33,000

The Table 1 shows that Wirecard expanded its operations into an increasing number of countries, from 15 in 2010 to 118 in 2018. The company also increased its customer base, with the number of customers growing from 13,000 in 2010 to 33,000 in 2018.

The expansion into new markets was a key part of Wirecard's growth strategy, allowing the company to tap into new sources of revenue and expand its product offerings. Wirecard's acquisition of other companies also played a role in its business coverage growth, allowing the company to enter new markets and add new capabilities to its portfolio.

However, it was important to note that these business coverage data points have come under scrutiny due to the accounting fraud scandal that has affected the company. It was possible that some of the reported data may have been artificially inflated. The scandal has had a significant impact on the company's business coverage, and it remains to be seen how Wirecard will recover from this crisis.

Financial Performance

Wirecard AG had a consistent track record of revenue growth and profitability until the accounting fraud scandal hit the company in 2019. Here was a detailed look at the company's financial performance:

Consistent revenue growth and profitability until 2019

Wirecard had a strong history of revenue growth and profitability. From 2010 to 2018, the company's revenue grew at a compound annual growth rate (CAGR) of 26.7%, from €347 million to €2.1 billion. During this period, the company's net income grew at a CAGR of 34.7%, from €48 million to €347 million. The company's strong financial performance was driven by its expansion into new markets, partnership with key players, and investment in technology.

Reported revenues of €2.8 billion ($3.2 billion) in 2019

In 2019, Wirecard reported revenues of €2.8 billion ($3.2 billion), an increase of 36% compared to the previous year. The company's growth was driven by increased demand for its payment processing and digital banking solutions. However, it later emerged that some of these reported revenues may have been artificially inflated through accounting irregularities.

Market capitalization of over €24 billion ($27 billion) in September 2018

At its peak, Wirecard had a market capitalization of over €24 billion ($27 billion) in September 2018, making it one of the most valuable companies on the German stock exchange. The company's strong financial performance and growth prospects had attracted significant investor interest.

However, the accounting fraud scandal that hit the company in 2019 severely impacted its financial performance and reputation. The company's market capitalization plummeted, and it was eventually forced to file for insolvency. The true extent of the financial impact of the scandal was still under investigation, and it remains to be seen how Wirecard will recover from this crisis.

Table 2. Wirecard's financial data (2010 - 2018)

Year	Revenue (in € millions)	Net income (in € millions)	Total assets (in € millions)	Market capitalization (in € billions)
2010	273.7	29.6	280.9	1.6
2011	394.2	38.3	402.3	3.4
2012	601.0	70.2	741.4	4.7
2013	641.6	82.4	970.8	9.3
2014	892.5	124.4	1,360.2	14.1
2015	1,028.0	156.0	1,779.8	14.9
2016	1,028.0	266.7	2,633.6	16.2
2017	1,488.3	259.3	3,787.8	17.6
2018	2,016.2	347.5	4,144.1	24.6

The financial data table 2 shows that Wirecard experienced rapid growth in the 2010s, with its revenue and net income increasing significantly. The company's market capitalization also grew rapidly, reaching €24.6 billion in 2018. Additionally, Wirecard's total assets grew significantly, reflecting the company's expansion into new markets and the acquisition of new businesses.

However, it was important to note that these financial data points have come under scrutiny due to the accounting fraud scandal that has affected the company. Wirecard's financial reporting has been called into question, and it was possible that some of the reported financial figures may have been artificially inflated. The scandal has had a significant impact on the company's market position, and it remains to be seen how Wirecard will recover from this crisis.

Business Strategies

Wirecard implemented various business strategies throughout its history to drive growth and expand its business. Here were the strategies and their impact on the company:

Expansion Into New Markets

Wirecard entered new markets through organic growth and acquisitions. For example, the company acquired Payment Network AG in 2006 to expand into the Swiss market, and it acquired Citigroup's prepaid card business in 2016 to expand into North America. The company's expansion into new markets helped to increase its customer base and revenue streams.

Partnership With Key Players

Wirecard partnered with key players in the payment industry to increase its reach and offer new services to its customers. For example, the company partnered with Visa to offer mobile payments and with Tencent to offer WeChat Pay to European merchants. These partnerships helped Wirecard to stay competitive and offer innovative services to its customers.

Investment in Technology

Wirecard invested heavily in technology to improve its product offerings and stay ahead of its competitors. The company developed a range of digital banking and payment solutions, such as its mobile payment app boon, which helped to attract new customers and increase revenue.

These business strategies had a positive impact on Wirecard's financial performance. From 2010 to 2018, the company's revenue grew from 347 million euros to 2.1 billion euros, representing a compound annual growth rate (CAGR) of 26.7%. During the same period, the company's net income grew from 48 million euros to 347 million euros, representing a CAGR of 34.7%.

However, it was important to note that the accounting fraud scandal that has affected the company has cast doubt on the accuracy of these financial figures. The true impact of Wirecard's business strategies on its financial performance was currently under investigation.

Corporate Governance

Corporate governance refers to the system of rules, practices, and processes by which a company was directed and controlled. Here was a detailed look at Wirecard's corporate governance structure:

Executive Board

Wirecard was led by a six-member executive board, with Markus Braun serving as CEO and chairman of the board. Braun had been with the company since 2002 and was instrumental in driving its growth and expansion into new markets. However, he resigned from his position in June 2020 following the accounting fraud scandal.

Supervisory Board

Wirecard's supervisory board was responsible for overseeing the company's management and strategic direction. It consisted of nine members, including industry experts and investors, such as former Deutsche

Bank CEO Josef Ackermann and SoftBank executive Pascal Heberling. However, the board has come under scrutiny for failing to detect and prevent the accounting irregularities that led to the scandal.

Compliance Department

Wirecard had a compliance department responsible for ensuring that the company operated ethically and in compliance with all relevant laws and regulations. The department was headed by a chief compliance officer and was responsible for implementing policies and procedures to prevent fraud and other illegal activities. However, it was later revealed that the compliance department had failed to detect and report the accounting irregularities that led to the scandal.

Overall, Wirecard's corporate governance structure was supposed to provide oversight and ensure that the company operated in an ethical and legal manner. However, the accounting fraud scandal highlighted serious deficiencies in the company's governance and raised questions about the effectiveness of its internal controls.

Scandal and Bankruptcy

Escalation of Scandal

- The allegations led to an investigation by the German financial regulator, BaFin, which initially dismissed the accusations as baseless.
- However, further investigations by other media outlets, including the Wall Street Journal, and independent auditors revealed evidence of accounting irregularities and fraud.
- Wirecard eventually admitted that €1.9 billion was missing from its accounts, leading to a sharp decline in its stock price and widespread criticism of the company's management and governance.

Bankruptcy Filing

- Wirecard filed for insolvency in June 2020, following the revelation of the accounting irregularities.
- The company's shares were delisted from the Frankfurt Stock Exchange, and its creditors began the process of recovering their investments.
- Wirecard's collapse was one of the largest corporate bankruptcies in German history and had far-reaching implications for the financial industry and the reputation of the country's regulatory system.

Impact on Stakeholders

- The Wirecard scandal had a significant impact on the company's shareholders, who lost billions of dollars in value because of the fraud.
- The scandal also led to the resignation of CEO Markus Braun, as well as several other executives, and raised questions about the effectiveness of the company's governance structure and internal controls.
- The German government faced criticism for its handling of the scandal and for failing to prevent the collapse of one of the country's largest companies.

In summary, the Wirecard scandal was a major blow to the company's reputation and had far-reaching implications for the financial industry in Germany and beyond. The discovery of accounting irregularities and subsequent bankruptcy filing highlighted serious deficiencies in the company's governance and internal controls and raised questions about the effectiveness of regulatory oversight in the country. The impact on stakeholders, including shareholders, employees, and creditors, was significant and underscored the need for greater transparency and accountability in corporate governance.

Collapse and Bankruptcy

Causes of Collapse

- The collapse of Wirecard was caused by a massive accounting scandal, where the company falsified its accounts to inflate its revenue and profits.
- The company's auditors, EY, failed to uncover the accounting fraud, and the German financial regulator, BaFin, was criticized for its lax oversight of the company.
- The scandal was exacerbated by Wirecard's complex corporate structure, which made it difficult to unravel the extent of the fraud.

Impact on Employees

a. The bankruptcy of Wirecard had a significant impact on its employees, with thousands losing their jobs because of the company's collapse.
b. Many of the affected employees were based in Germany, where Wirecard was one of the country's largest employers in the financial sector.
- c. The collapse of Wirecard also had a ripple effect on the broader economy, with suppliers and other businesses linked to the company also facing financial difficulties.

Impact on Investors

a. The collapse of Wirecard had a devastating impact on investors, with many losing their life savings because of the fraud.
b. The scandal also had a wider impact on the financial industry, with other companies in the sector facing increased scrutiny from investors and regulators.
- c. The reputation of the German financial system was also damaged, with critics arguing that the country's regulatory system had failed to prevent the fraud and protect investors.

Legal Proceedings

a. Following the collapse of Wirecard, several legal proceedings were initiated against the company and its former executives.
b. Markus Braun, the former CEO of Wirecard, was arrested and charged with fraud, market manipulation, and other offenses.
c. Other executives, including the former CFO and COO, were also arrested, and charged with various offenses related to the accounting fraud.

The collapse of Wirecard was a significant event in the financial industry, with the company's bankruptcy highlighting serious deficiencies in corporate governance and regulatory oversight. The impact of the scandal was felt by employees, investors, and the wider economy, and the fallout from the collapse was likely to continue for some time. The legal proceedings against the company and its former executives underscore the need for greater accountability and transparency in corporate governance and for regulators to take a more proactive role in preventing fraud and misconduct in the financial sector.

Parties Involved in the Wirecard Case

Wirecard AG

The German fintech company that was at the centre of the scandal. Wirecard's top executives were accused of perpetrating a massive accounting fraud, which ultimately led to the company's collapse.

Markus Braun

The former CEO of Wirecard, who was arrested and charged with fraud and market manipulation in connection with the scandal. Braun had been the face of Wirecard and was responsible for much of the company's growth and success.

Financial Times

The British newspaper that first raised questions about Wirecard's accounting practices in late 2019. The Financial Times published a series of investigative reports that alleged Wirecard had overstated its revenue and profits, and that much of its business in Asia was fraudulent.

BaFin

The German financial regulator, which has faced criticism for failing to detect and prevent the fraud at Wirecard. BaFin was accused of being too cozy with Wirecard and not doing enough to investigate the company's accounting practices.

Ernst & Young (EY)

The auditing firm responsible for auditing Wirecard's financial statements. EY has also faced criticism for failing to detect the accounting irregularities at Wirecard, despite auditing the company's books for years.

In both negative and positive ways, the parties involved in the Wirecard case were connected by their roles in the company's rise and fall. Wirecard and Markus Braun were instrumental in building the company into a global player in the payment processing industry. However, their alleged fraudulent activities led to the company's downfall and had far-reaching consequences for employees and investors. The Financial Times played a key role in exposing the fraud and raising awareness about the issues at Wirecard, but also faced criticism for potentially benefiting from market manipulation. BaFin and EY were responsible for ensuring compliance and detecting fraud but have faced criticism for failing to fulfil their responsibilities and allowing the fraud to go on for so long. Overall, the case underscores the importance of transparency, ethical business practices, and effective regulatory oversight in the financial industry.

Investigation and Legal Proceedings

Investigation by Authorities and Regulatory Bodies

- Following the discovery of accounting irregularities, German authorities and regulatory bodies launched investigations into Wirecard's practices.
- The German Federal Financial Supervisory Authority (BaFin) and the Financial Reporting Enforcement Panel (FREP) launched investigations into Wirecard's accounting practices and possible market manipulation.
- The investigations revealed that Wirecard had been inflating its revenue and profits for years through fraudulent accounting practices.

Charges Against Executives

- Markus Braun, the former CEO of Wirecard, was arrested and charged with market manipulation, fraud, and other offenses related to the accounting scandal.
- Other senior executives, including the former CFO and COO, were also arrested, and charged with similar offenses.
- The charges against the executives highlight the extent of the fraud at Wirecard and the role of senior management in perpetuating the fraud.

Impact on Auditors and Regulators

- The Wirecard scandal also had a significant impact on the reputation of the auditors and regulators involved in the case.
- EY, Wirecard's auditor, faced criticism for failing to detect the accounting fraud, and the firm's reputation was damaged as a result.
- BaFin, the German financial regulator, was also criticized for its lax oversight of Wirecard and its failure to take action to prevent the fraud.

Ongoing Legal Proceedings

- The legal proceedings against Wirecard and its executives were ongoing, and it was likely to be some time before the full extent of the fraud was uncovered.
- The bankruptcy of Wirecard has complicated the legal proceedings, with creditors and investors seeking to recover their losses from the company's assets.
- The fallout from the scandal was likely to continue for years, as the various legal and regulatory proceedings play out.

The investigation and legal proceedings surrounding the Wirecard scandal have revealed a significant failure in corporate governance and regulatory oversight. The charges against senior executives and the criticism of auditors and regulators highlight the need for greater accountability and transparency in the financial industry. The fallout from the scandal was likely to continue for some time, with investors and other stakeholders seeking to recover their losses and hold those responsible for the fraud accountable.

DEVELOPMENT CHALLENGES

The Wirecard scandal highlights several development challenges that need to be addressed, including:

Weak Corporate Governance

The Wirecard scandal highlights the importance of strong corporate governance in preventing fraud and ensuring ethical business practices. Companies need to have effective board oversight, independent auditors, and robust internal controls to prevent fraud and ensure transparency.

Regulatory Oversight

The scandal also highlights the need for stronger regulatory oversight to prevent fraud and protect investors. Regulators need to have the resources, expertise, and authority to detect and prevent fraud, and to hold companies and executives accountable for illegal activities.

Transparency

The lack of transparency around Wirecard's business practices and financial reporting contributed to the scandal. Companies need to be more transparent about their operations, financial performance, and risk management practices to ensure that investors and other stakeholders have accurate information to make informed decisions.

Ethical Business Practices

The Wirecard scandal also highlights the importance of ethical business practices. Companies need to prioritize ethical conduct and avoid cutting corners or engaging in fraudulent activities to achieve short-term gains. Strong ethical values and practices were essential for building trust with investors, customers, and other stakeholders.

International Business Practices

The scandal also highlights the challenges of doing business in foreign countries, where regulatory oversight may be weaker, and the risk of fraud may be higher. Companies need to have robust risk management practices in place to identify and manage risks associated with international operations, and to ensure compliance with local laws and regulations.

The Wirecard scandal highlights several development challenges that need to be addressed, including the need for stronger corporate governance, regulatory oversight, transparency, ethical business practices, and risk management. Addressing these challenges will help to prevent future scandals and ensure that companies operate ethically and responsibly, benefiting both investors and society.

DELIVERY CHALLENGES

The Wirecard scandal also highlights several delivery challenges that need to be addressed, including:

Digital Payment Processing

Wirecard was a digital payment processing company that offered various payment solutions to online and offline merchants. The scandal shows the challenges of delivering digital payment processing solutions in a fast-paced, constantly evolving industry. Companies need to keep up with technological advancements, regulatory changes, and changing consumer preferences to stay competitive and deliver high-quality services.

Fraud Prevention and Risk Management

Wirecard's fraud and accounting irregularities show the challenges of delivering effective fraud prevention and risk management solutions. Companies need to have robust fraud prevention and risk management systems in place to prevent fraudulent activities, detect potential risks, and mitigate risks that arise. Companies need to continuously monitor and improve their systems to keep up with changing risks and threats.

Compliance and Ethics

Wirecard's scandal highlights the importance of delivering compliance and ethics programs to ensure that companies adhere to legal and ethical standards. Companies need to have strong compliance and ethics programs in place to prevent illegal activities and unethical behaviour. Companies need to prioritize ethical conduct and ensure that their employees, contractors, and partners follow ethical standards.

Auditing and Financial Reporting

The scandal also highlights the challenges of delivering effective auditing and financial reporting. Auditors need to have the expertise, resources, and independence to conduct thorough audits and identify potential fraud and irregularities. Companies need to provide accurate financial reporting and transparent disclosure of their financial performance.

Stakeholder Management

Wirecard's collapse also highlights the challenges of delivering effective stakeholder management. Companies need to communicate effectively with their stakeholders, including employees, investors, customers, and regulators, to build trust and maintain good relationships. Companies need to manage stakeholders' expectations and respond promptly to their concerns and inquiries.

The Wirecard scandal highlights several delivery challenges that need to be addressed, including digital payment processing, fraud prevention and risk management, compliance and ethics, auditing and financial reporting, and stakeholder management. Addressing these challenges will help companies to deliver high-quality services, build trust with their stakeholders, and prevent future scandals.

PRE AND POST FINANCIAL ACCOUNTING FRAUD

Pre-Fraud

- In 2017, Wirecard reported revenues of €1.5 billion and a net income of €267.2 million.
- In 2018, the company reported revenues of €2.1 billion and a net income of €347.5 million.
- In September 2018, the company's market capitalization was over €24 billion.

Post-Fraud

- In June 2020, Wirecard admitted that €1.9 billion ($2.1 billion) was missing from its balance sheet.
- The company filed for bankruptcy in June 2020.
- The company's shares lost over 90% of their value following the revelations of fraud.
- Thousands of employees lost their jobs, and many investors lost their life savings.

CONCLUSION

The case of Wirecard AG was a high-profile example of accounting fraud and corporate malpractice in the financial industry. The company, once regarded as a disruptor in the traditional banking industry, grew rapidly in the 2010s to become one of the most valuable companies on the German stock exchange. However, in 2020, Wirecard faced a major scandal when it was revealed that €1.9 billion ($2.1 billion) was missing from its balance sheet, and the company subsequently filed for bankruptcy. The scandal had far-reaching consequences, with thousands of employees losing their jobs and many investors losing their life savings. The case highlights the importance of corporate governance, regulatory oversight, and ethical business practices, and raises questions about the effectiveness of auditing and accounting standards in detecting and preventing fraud.

The Wirecard case highlights the importance of corporate governance, financial transparency, and accountability in the global financial system. The case also underscores the risks associated with rapid growth and expansion in the fintech industry, where innovation and disruption can sometimes lead to unethical or illegal practices.

The Wirecard scandal has had far-reaching implications for the financial industry, with regulators, investors, and consumers questioning the effectiveness of existing oversight and risk management practices. The case has also led to increased scrutiny of auditors, who were responsible for verifying the accuracy of financial statements and ensuring compliance with accounting standards.

Furthermore, the case raises questions about the role of technology in the financial industry, and the potential for new technologies to be abused or misused for fraudulent purposes. As fintech companies continue to innovate and disrupt traditional financial services, it was critical for regulators and industry leaders to ensure that proper safeguards were in place to prevent financial fraud and misconduct.

Development Outcomes

The Wirecard case has resulted in several development outcomes, including:

- Increased awareness of the risks associated with rapid growth and expansion in the fintech industry, and the need for proper risk management and oversight to prevent financial fraud and misconduct.
- Greater scrutiny of auditors and accounting firms and calls for improved auditing standards and practices to ensure the accuracy and transparency of financial statements.
- The need for stronger corporate governance and ethical business practices, including greater accountability and transparency at all levels of the organization.
- A renewed focus on the importance of financial transparency and reporting, and the need for accurate and reliable financial data to inform investment decisions and protect investors.
- Calls for greater regulatory oversight of the fintech industry, including more rigorous requirements for licensing and compliance with anti-money laundering (AML) and counter-terrorism financing (CTF) regulations.

Overall, the Wirecard case has highlighted the need for stronger regulatory oversight, improved corporate governance, and greater transparency and accountability in the global financial system. It serves as a cautionary tale for the fintech industry and underscores the importance of ethical and responsible business practices in building and maintaining public trust.

Lessons Learned

The Wirecard scandal serves as a cautionary tale of the risks of unchecked corporate greed and the dangers of failing to uphold ethical and legal standards. The case highlights the importance of transparency and accountability in the financial sector, and the need for robust corporate governance and regulatory oversight. The scandal has led to calls for reforms in the auditing and regulatory industry and has raised awareness about the risks of investing in companies with questionable business practices.

The Wirecard case provides several lessons, including:

- Importance of transparency and accountability: Wirecard's downfall highlights the importance of transparency and accountability in business practices. The company's lack of transparency and manipulation of financial statements ultimately led to its collapse.
- Need for effective regulatory oversight: The case also highlights the need for effective regulatory oversight to prevent corporate fraud and malfeasance. The failure of regulators to detect and prevent the accounting fraud at Wirecard was a clear indication of the shortcomings in the regulatory environment.

- The risks of rapid growth: Wirecard's rapid growth was fuelled by aggressive expansion strategies and acquisitions. However, the company's inability to effectively manage this growth, coupled with its fraudulent practices, ultimately led to its collapse.
- Importance of ethical leadership: The role of leadership in setting the tone for ethical behaviour cannot be overstated. Wirecard's CEO Markus Braun was charged with fraud and market manipulation, highlighting the critical role that leadership plays in setting ethical standards and promoting a culture of compliance.
- The impact of corporate scandals: Corporate scandals can have far-reaching consequences, including job losses, financial losses for investors, and damage to a company's reputation. The Wirecard scandal serves as a stark reminder of the need for companies to prioritize ethical behaviour and maintain the trust of their stakeholders.

The Wirecard case study highlights several important lessons for the science of delivery:

- Importance of effective regulation: The case illustrates how ineffective regulation and oversight can allow fraudulent activities to go undetected for years. Effective regulation was crucial for maintaining the integrity of financial markets and protecting investors.
- Need for transparency and accountability: The case highlights the importance of transparency and accountability in business operations. Companies must be transparent about their financial reporting and operations to maintain the trust of investors and stakeholders.
- Importance of ethical leadership: The Wirecard scandal highlights the impact that unethical leadership can have on a company and its stakeholders. It was important for leaders to prioritize ethical behaviour and hold themselves and their employees accountable for ethical conduct.
- Need for effective risk management: The case illustrates the importance of effective risk management to prevent and mitigate the impact of potential risks. Companies must identify and address potential risks in their operations to ensure long-term sustainability.

Overall, the Wirecard case emphasizes the need for effective governance, risk management, transparency, and accountability in business operations to ensure sustainable and ethical delivery of services.

Relentless Focus on Citizen, Shareholder, Investors, Government, Employees: Outcomes

The Wirecard case highlights the importance of a relentless focus on various stakeholders, including citizens, shareholders, investors, government, and employees. Failing to deliver on commitments to these stakeholders can lead to severe consequences, as seen in the case of Wirecard.

Citizens, for instance, rely on financial institutions to provide them with reliable and trustworthy services. Wirecard's accounting fraud led to a loss of trust in the company, leaving citizens vulnerable to financial risks. Similarly, shareholders and investors trusted the company to provide them with accurate financial information, which would inform their investment decisions. The company's failure to deliver on this commitment led to significant financial losses for these stakeholders.

The government also has an interest in ensuring that financial institutions operate in a transparent and accountable manner, to protect citizens and maintain the integrity of the financial system. Wirecard's fraudulent activities raised serious questions about the effectiveness of regulatory oversight in preventing such incidents.

Finally, employees of the company were also impacted by the scandal, losing their jobs, and potentially facing legal consequences for their involvement in the fraud. A relentless focus on ethical and legal business practices, as well as transparency and accountability, can help prevent such outcomes and protect all stakeholders.

In summary, the Wirecard case highlights the need for organizations to prioritize the interests of all stakeholders and ensure that they deliver on their commitments in a transparent and accountable manner. A relentless focus on these principles can help prevent fraudulent activities and protect citizens, shareholders, investors, government, and employees alike.

Multidimensional Response

The response to the Wirecard case involves multiple dimensions, including financial, legal, ethical, and reputational considerations.

From a financial perspective, the case highlights the importance of accurate financial reporting and transparency in business operations. The discovery of accounting irregularities and subsequent collapse of the company resulted in significant financial losses for investors and employees, demonstrating the need for effective financial oversight and risk management.

From a legal perspective, the case illustrates the consequences of fraudulent behaviour, including criminal charges and penalties for executives and regulatory authorities who failed to detect and prevent the fraud. It also highlights the importance of legal and regulatory frameworks that support ethical business practices and hold individuals and organizations accountable for wrongdoing.

From an ethical perspective, the case raises questions about the responsibility of businesses to act in the best interests of their stakeholders, including customers, shareholders, and employees. The alleged fraudulent behaviour and subsequent collapse of the company had devastating consequences for thousands of individuals, underscoring the importance of ethical decision-making and values-based leadership.

From a reputational perspective, the case highlights the importance of maintaining a strong reputation and brand image through effective communication, risk management, and crisis response. The negative publicity and loss of trust resulting from the scandal and bankruptcy have had long-lasting consequences for Wirecard and its stakeholders, demonstrating the need for proactive reputation management and crisis planning.

Overall, the Wirecard case serves as a cautionary tale for businesses and underscores the importance of effective governance, risk management, and ethical decision-making in achieving sustainable success and stakeholder value.

Evidence to Achieve Results

To achieve results, evidence-based decision-making was crucial. In the case of Wirecard, evidence was initially ignored, leading to the massive accounting fraud that eventually led to the company's collapse. It was essential to prioritize evidence-based decision-making at all levels of an organization and establish a culture of transparency and accountability.

Leaders must ensure that there were systems in place to detect and address any irregularities or inconsistencies. In Wirecard's case, there was a failure in the company's auditing and regulatory systems, which allowed the fraud to go undetected for years. It was essential to have robust auditing and regulatory mechanisms in place to detect any issues and address them promptly.

Additionally, there must be a willingness to act on the evidence presented. Wirecard's management initially denied the allegations and accused the journalists of market manipulation, despite the evidence presented. It was crucial to have leaders who were willing to take action based on evidence, even if it means acknowledging mistakes or wrongdoing and taking responsibility.

Overall, evidence-based decision-making, robust auditing and regulatory mechanisms, and a culture of transparency and accountability were critical to achieving results in any organization.

Leadership to Change

The Wirecard case highlights the critical role of leadership in ensuring ethical and legal business practices. Here were some leadership lessons that can be learned from the case:

Prioritize Transparency

Leaders should prioritize transparency in their communication with stakeholders, including employees, investors, and regulators. Wirecard's lack of transparency regarding its accounting practices contributed to the scandal.

Encourage Accountability

Leaders should encourage a culture of accountability within their organizations. This includes holding executives and employees accountable for their actions and implementing processes and systems to detect and prevent fraud.

Foster a Culture of Ethical Behaviour

Leaders should prioritize a culture of ethical behaviour within their organizations. This includes promoting values such as honesty, integrity, and accountability and creating an environment where employees feel comfortable reporting ethical concerns.

Build Trust

Leaders must build trust with stakeholders by consistently demonstrating ethical behaviour and following through on their commitments.

Encourage Collaboration

Leaders should encourage collaboration across different departments and stakeholders to ensure that everyone was working towards the same goals and objectives.

By prioritizing transparency, accountability, ethical behaviour, trust-building, and collaboration, leaders can help prevent similar scandals and ensure the long-term success of their organizations.

Adaptive Implementation

The Wirecard case highlights the importance of adaptive implementation, which was the ability to adjust strategies and approaches in response to changing circumstances. Adaptive implementation requires a flexible mindset and a willingness to learn and improve.

In the case of Wirecard, the company's leadership failed to adapt to the changing circumstances and continued to deny allegations of accounting irregularities even as evidence mounted against them. This lack of adaptability ultimately led to the company's downfall.

On the other hand, adaptive implementation can be seen in the response of regulators and auditors who took action once the fraud was uncovered. They adapted their approaches and implemented new regulations and oversight to prevent similar cases from happening in the future.

The Wirecard case underscores the importance of adaptive implementation in achieving sustainable outcomes, particularly in complex and rapidly changing environments. It requires leaders to be open to feedback, willing to experiment, and able to pivot when necessary.

DECLARATION

The authors declare that the manuscript follows ethical standards and there are no potential conflicts of interest with respect to the research, authorship and/or publication of this chapter.

DISCLAIMER

The contents and views of this chapter are expressed by the authors in personal capacities. It is not necessary for the Editor and the Publisher to agree with these viewpoints, and they are not responsible for any duty of care in this regard.

ACKNOWLEDGMENT

The authors extend sincere gratitude to

- The Editor and the International Editorial Advisory Board (IEAB) of this book who initially desk reviewed, arranged a rigorous double/triple blind review process, and conducted a thorough, minute, and critical final review before accepting the chapter for publication.
- All anonymous reviewers who provided very constructive feedbacks for thorough revision, improvement, extension, and fine tuning of the chapter.
- All colleagues, assistants and well-wishers who assisted to complete this task.

REFERENCES

Breuer, C., Boronczyk, F., & Rumpf, C. (2021). Message personalization and real-time adaptation as next innovations in sport sponsorship management? How run-of-play and team affiliation affect viewer response. *Journal of Business Research, 133*, 309–316. doi:10.1016/j.jbusres.2021.05.003

ADDITIONAL READING

Browne, R. (2020, June 29). The Enron of Germany: Wirecard scandal casts a shadow on corporate governance. *CNBC*. https://www.cnbc.com/2020/06/29/enron-of-germany-wirecard-scandal-casts-a-shadow-on-governance.html

Dorris, B. (2021, April 02). Exposing Fraud at "Germany's Enron". *ACFE Insights*. https://www.acfeinsights.com/acfe-insights/from-president-exposing-fraud-germanys-enron

Investors' Chronicle. (2022, September 21). *Dan McCrum: Lessons from the Wirecard scandal*. ACAST. https://shows.acast.com/investorschronicle/episodes/dan-mccrum-lessons-from-the-wirecard-scandal

McCrum, D. (2020, October 25). Wirecard: the timeline. *Financial Times*. https://www.ft.com/content/284fb1ad-ddc0-45df-a075-0709b36868db

Reuters. (2022, December 06). *The rise and fall of Wirecard*. Reuters. https://www.reuters.com/business/finance/rise-fall-wirecard-2022-12-06/

Section 4
Corruption in Public Finance

Chapter 13
Corruption and the Resource Curse:
The Case of Timor-Leste

Michael King
https://orcid.org/0000-0003-0446-7698
Griffith University, Australia

Abdul Rafay
https://orcid.org/0000-0002-0285-5980
University of Management and Technology, Lahore, Pakistan

ABSTRACT

In Timor-Leste, one of the newest nations in the world, a case of corruption is explored in this chapter, which is associated with the resource curse of official corruption. The case involves an expatriate tax lawyer who worked for the Ministry of Finance and orchestrated a 'taxation miracle' for 'his' adopted country. He was charged for a $3.51 million wire-fraud by the United States Department of Justice and subsequently sentenced to six years of imprisonment. However, the case was found to be more complex than simple fraud and official corruption. The findings indicate that the key elements that led to the fraud were a series of misadventures arising from issues of hiring, management, cybercrime, and weak internal controls. It has also been suggested that the fraud was allowed to perpetuate due to the collusion of several multinational resource companies, costing the Timor-Leste taxpayers as much as $176 million.

INTRODUCTION

The United States (US) Attorney General's wire fraud related charges against Bobby Boye read like to plot of a fantastic international crime thriller:

DOI: 10.4018/979-8-3693-1190-5.ch013

Per the wiring instructions of Opus & Best, Country A wired a total of approximately $3,510,000[1] on Contract payments from a Country A account at the Federal Reserve ... to the Opus & Best 0399 Account secretly controlled by the defendant BOYE ... [who] did knowingly and intentionally conspire and agree with others, known and unknown, to devise a scheme and artifice to defraud Country A, and to obtain money and property from Country A. (United States, June 2014, p.2)

The funds were utilized to acquire four properties in New Jersey, totalling over $1.5 million in cash. Additionally, luxury items like a Bentley, a Range Rover, a Rolls Royce, and designer watches were purchased (US, 2014). The country referred to as "Country A" by US prosecutors in the aforementioned quotation is Timor-Leste, formerly known as East Timor. Timor-Leste has gained notoriety for endemic corruption in its political structures and society at large, as evidenced by various studies (Doig & Tisne, 2009; Drysdale, 2008; Lundahl & Sjöholm, 2008; White, 2017). This reputation is supported by reputable indicators, such as Transparency International's Corruption Perceptions Index, where it has consistently ranked as highly prone to corruption.

However, it is worth noting that there has been some improvement in the corruption ranking of Timor-Leste, which ranked 82 out of 180 countries in 2021, compared to its lowest ranking of 143 in 2011 (TI, 2021). Despite these improvements, Timor-Leste continues to be one of the poorest nations globally, as reported by the World Bank. Although poverty has declined significantly from 2007 to 2014, there is a lack of more recent statistical data due to the government's failure to collect information since 2014 (World Bank, 2022).

The legacy of the 25-year Indonesian occupation and the influences of Portuguese and Indonesian rule have deeply impacted Timor-Leste's bureaucratic practices and societal customs, contributing to the prevalence of corruption (Blunt, 2009). The country's natural resource exploration and exploitation, as well as contract negotiations, present ample opportunities for corruption. Apart from its oil and gas resources, Timor-Leste possesses substantial and relatively untapped marine and land resources suitable for various development purposes (Blunt, 2009).

Regrettably, the study of corruption in Timor-Leste has been neglected by criminologists, and research on this topic is limited, not only in criminology but also in other disciplines such as commerce and accounting.

Corruption cases prevalent in resource-dependent countries like Timor-Leste are not uncommon. In fact, the term 'Dutch disease' is associated, in part, with corruption and lax governmental practices in tax revenues that emerge in resource-rich developing economies. These cases often make headlines when politicians or public officials engage in corrupt activities, such as accepting facilitation payments for services within the scope of their employment.

The criminological and financial crime literature contains well-documented evidence highlighting the vulnerabilities of developing nations to internal fraud and corruption (Doig & Riley, 1998; Kenny, 2007; Otusanya, 2011; Wraith & Simpkins, 2010). Indonesia, for instance, is a country significantly impacted by corruption among government officials, which has permeated all aspects of official life (Nurhidayat & Kusumasari, 2018). Given that Indonesia occupied Timor-Leste for twenty-five years, with Indonesian officials holding all key positions in government and the public sector during that period, the endemic official corruption in Indonesia has had lasting effects on Timor-Leste as well.

One case of corruption in Timor-Leste is examined in this chapter. This case is remarkable because it is one of the few instances of successfully prosecuted expatriate corruption cases in the world. The focus of this article is on this case because it bears a resemblance to other cases and elements of corrupt behaviour and economic crime that are known from the public and private sectors. Valuable insight is aimed to be offered to professionals who wish to research, investigate, and prosecute white-collar, transglobal, financial, and economic crimes through this research.

In this case, a person with a dominant personality finds themselves surrounded by individuals with weaker personalities, creating an environment ripe for personal enrichment, which is often conducive to corruption. However, what sets this case apart from typical instances of corruption is that the perpetrator doesn't merely exploit existing opportunities for corrupt practices but actively engineers' events to expand the reach of corruption.

This case study stands out as one of the few examples of a successful US prosecution involving an expatriate official working for a foreign government agency, namely, the Ministry of Finance in Timor-Leste. Referred to as Timor-Leste's worst fraud in history, it made headlines like "Timor-Leste has been robbed!" (La'o Hamutuk, 2014) and garnered international attention with titles such as '3.5M international con game nets N.J. man 6 years in prison' (Sherman, 2015).

The Timor-Leste fraud presents a complex case study that vividly illustrates how developing countries are susceptible to fraud perpetrated by trusted advisors. The dynamics and outcomes of this case offer valuable insights into the vulnerabilities faced by such countries in dealing with fraudulent activities conducted by individuals in positions of trust.

LITERATURE REVIEW

Corruption and Fraud in Developing Nations

Transparency International defines corruption as the 'abuse of entrusted power for private gain' and describes corruption as follows:

"Corruption can take many forms and can include behaviours like public servants demanding or taking money or favours in exchange for services, politicians misusing public money or granting public jobs or contracts to their sponsors, friends and families, corporations bribing officials to get lucrative deals". (TI, 2023)

Corruption, a widespread issue, is seen as a symptom of poor governance and institutional weaknesses present in almost every country worldwide. No nation is entirely immune to corruption, as it has become a global problem. In the realm of criminology research, the understanding of corruption has evolved from being perceived solely as criminal behavior characteristic of developing economies to encompassing governance methods that support formal practices. Corruption, which manifests through various forms such as bribes, embezzlement, clientelism, patronage, or patrimonialism, is deeply rooted in social relationships (Granovetter, 2007; Rothstein & Varraich, 2017).

Preventing corruption has emerged as a major concern for many developing countries and multilateral institutions, with the World Bank aiming to reduce corruption in these regions (World Bank, 2022). As pointed out by Sullivan (2009), corruption corrodes public trust and undermines the legitimacy of both public and private sector institutions. The adverse effects of corruption can be devastating for a national economy (Doig, 1999; Fantaye, 2004).

Recent research has raised concerns about foreign direct investment potentially fuelling opportunities for corruption in developing countries (Canare, 2017; Gottschalk, 2019; Habib & Zurawicki, 2002). Companies seeking market access or government contracts may resort to bribing officials to achieve their objectives. Underpaid officials in developing countries might be enticed by the significant sums offered by multinational firms. The presence of natural resources and the associated resource rents can further exacerbate this issue (Davis & Tilton, 2005).

The behaviour of foreign firms operating in developing countries, particularly resource-rich ones, is a primary focus of the Organisation for Economic Co-operation and Development (OECD, 2019). The hope of multinational aid institutions and host governments is that foreign direct investment will positively impact the country by fostering openness to the global economic and financial system, rather than fuelling more corruption (Davis & Tilton, 2005). Therefore, increased engagement with foreign firms is considered to potentially elevate standards of transparency and good governance in developing countries.

The possession of natural resources introduces complexities to the relationship between investment and corruption. Typically, the concern is that corruption will negatively affect foreign investment. This concern arises from the belief that firms may be deterred from investing due to the additional costs of dealing with corrupt officials or the risks associated with engaging in contracts under corrupt institutional conditions. However, especially when natural resources are involved, resulting in significant profit motives, firms may be more willing to deal with a corrupt regime or even gain advantages from corruption. The necessity of accessing natural resources narrows firms' locational decisions as they seek profits from a limited and essential natural commodity (David & Tilton, 2005). Consequently, multinational resource extraction firms could benefit from corrupt officials by gaining increased access to resources at lower royalty costs and/or with less regulation. As a result, countries rich in oil and other minerals are particularly susceptible to such corruption (Corden, 1984; Doig & Riley, 1998; Fantaye, 2004).

The term 'Dutch disease' refers to the adverse effects on Dutch manufacturing caused by the discovery of natural gas in the North Sea during the 1960s, which subsequently led to the appreciation of the Dutch real exchange rate (Corden, 1984). The profound impact of this term is more notable in countries with fragile economies, weak institutional structures, corruption, underdeveloped financial systems, and institutional deficiencies concerning the rule of law. Davis (1995) noted that countries relying heavily on rich natural resources may not always be in a sound economic situation, as the exploitation of mineral wealth does not necessarily lead to sustained economic development. Countries with abundant natural resources but lacking strong institutional structures often exhibit weak economic performance. Paradoxically, the revenue derived from oil and other minerals can have harmful effects, particularly on institutions. Corruption, despite an increase in economic wealth, can lead to reduced production levels in the long term due to the weakening of institutions (Boyce & Emery, 2011; Gylfason, 2001).

The OECD (2019) acknowledges that infrastructure development is particularly vulnerable to corruption and fraud due to its size, complexity, investment value, and involvement of numerous stakeholders. The risks related to the integrity of the country and its developing institutions are substantial and should be rigorously assessed at each stage of an infrastructure project cycle.

Background: Timor-Leste

East Timor, originally colonized by the Portuguese in the sixteenth century, was known as Portuguese Timor until 1975 when it faced invasion and occupation by the Indonesian military. In August 1999, after a United Nations–sponsored act of self-determination, Indonesia relinquished control of the territory. Subsequently, in October 1999, the United Nations Transitional Administration in East Timor was established, with an Australia-led peacekeeping force arriving to restore order and provide stability and security for the Timorese people.

Since 1999, Timor-Leste has been the focus of United Nations peacebuilding and international stabilisation missions. The international recognition of Timor-Leste's sovereignty marked the culmination of the most extensive period of state building ever conducted by the United Nations. The most significant of these missions was under the direction of the United Nations Transitional Administration in East Timor, which operated in the country from 1999 until 2002. This mission was entrusted with administering the territory and held exclusive legislative and executive authority. It was also mandated to provide immediate humanitarian and security assistance, build state institutions and public administration, restore the judicial system, and promote 'capacity building' in the local society.

Following a political crisis in 2006, an International Stabilisation Force and the United Nations Integration Mission were introduced to establish internal security and order. From 2006 until 2012, Timor-Leste once again relied on foreign intervention. Even after the violent protests surrounding the 2012 political elections, the country's public sector continued to depend on expatriates to provide various specialized services.

On May 20, 2002, the República Democrática de Timor-Leste (Democratic Republic of Timor-Leste) became the first sovereign state established in the twenty-first century. Its sovereignty was internationally recognized when it became the one-hundred and ninety-first member of the United Nations in September 2002.

Oil Resources

Timor-Leste's economy relies heavily on its extractive industries, particularly the substantial oil reserves in Timor Gap, located in the Timor Sea between Timor-Leste and Australia. All the country's oil is extracted from the Bayu-Undan oil and gas field within the Joint Petroleum Development Area, operated by the United States-based natural resource company, ConocoPhillips. In 2012, Timor-Leste's petroleum revenues peaked at $3.8 billion but experienced a downward trend, thereafter, reaching a record low of $243 million in 2016, primarily due to reduced production and falling global oil prices.

In July 2001, Timor-Leste and Australia signed a memorandum of understanding concerning future revenues from the oil and gas fields in the Timor Sea. The Timor-Leste government heavily relies on revenue from the resources sector, which contributes 80% of the country's total revenue (World Bank, 2022). Production at the Bayu-Undan field commenced in February 2004, producing natural gas located 500 kilometres from Australia and 250 kilometres south of Timor-Leste. ConocoPhillips, a multinational oil and gas company based in Houston, Texas, operates the facility, holding a 57.2% stake in the Bayu-Undan oil and gas field. The company operates in 15 countries and is listed on the Fortune 500.

Woodside Energy Group Ltd (formerly Woodside Petroleum Ltd), an Australian petroleum exploration and production company, is another significant player in the region. Woodside operates oil and gas production in Australia and stands as Australia's largest independent dedicated oil and gas company. Several other joint venture partners, including international multinational resource firms with majority state ownership, work alongside ConocoPhillips in the Bayu-Undan oil and gas field.

The Norway Oil for Development Programme

In 2005, the government of Norway initiated the Oil for Development program in Timor-Leste, aiming to share its extensive experience in managing oil and gas resources gathered over more than five decades. As part of this project, the Norwegian Ministry of Finance financed ten international advisors starting in 2008 to support the Timor-Leste government in various international finance matters related to the natural resources sector.

In 2009, Bobby Boye (also known as Bobby Ajiboye and Bobby Aji-Boye), a US resident, applied to the Norwegian Ministry of Finance for the position of tax advisor in Timor-Leste. Boye was selected among six applicants and stood out as the most qualified candidate. He asserted having significant experience working with 'high-level tax' and the international oil industry. Consequently, the Norwegian authorities offered him employment on December 1, 2009, with a salary of S$340,000 for a one-year contract.

As a Petroleum Tax Advisor (International), Boye's role involved working with Timor-Leste's National Directorate of Petroleum Revenue under the Ministry of Finance. His assignment aimed to develop the National Directorate of Petroleum Revenue as a professional petroleum tax authority capable of auditing and collecting petroleum tax revenue for Timor-Leste. This work encompassed administering Timor-Leste's revenue laws pertaining to the petroleum industry, analysing tax returns and information related to petroleum tax to identify potential tax issues, and conducting necessary tax inquiries and audits.

The position required a master's degree or higher in business administration, chartered accountancy, or taxation, detailed knowledge of international tax issues (including transfer pricing), familiarity with the industrial activities of the petroleum sector, and expertise in petroleum industry accounting information systems. Boye's resume mentioned his membership in the Lincoln's Inn Lawyers' Society in London and his bachelor's degree in law from St John's College, University of Cambridge.

THE SCANDAL

The scandal came to light in June 2014 when Bobby Boye was apprehended by the US Federal Bureau of Investigation (FBI) upon his arrival at Newark International Airport, New Jersey. This arrest was part of the FBI's operation, in collaboration with the Financial Fraud Enforcement Task Force, dedicated to investigating and prosecuting financial crimes. The FBI had been discreetly monitoring Boye's financial activities for several months.

American authorities arrested Boye on charges related to wire fraud, amounting to over $3.51 million. Allegedly, he deceived Timor-Leste representatives into awarding a lucrative legal and tax accounting contract to Opus & Best Services LLC, a sham New York law and accounting firm secretly controlled by Boye, unbeknownst to Timor-Leste (Sherman, 2015). The funds from this deceitful contract were used by Boye to acquire four properties in New Jersey, totalling over $1.5 million in cash, along with three luxury vehicles (a 2012 Bentley for $172,000, a 2012 Range Rover for $100,983, and a 2011 Rolls Royce for $215,000), and two designer watches valued at $20,000 each (US, 2014).

Boye pleaded guilty to one count of conspiracy to commit wire fraud and, in October 2015, received a six-year prison sentence for his actions. In 2019, his attempt to have the sentence commuted proved unsuccessful. He served his full sentence and was released on January 7, 2021. As the prosecution of Boye unfolded, the full extent of the fraud and corruption scandal became apparent to the governments of Norway and Timor-Leste.

METHODOLOGY

This study on 'fraud and corruption' utilized qualitative content analysis as the chosen research approach. Given the specific time frame and focus on a particular case, data collection was conducted through a case-study methodology. Case-study research proves highly relevant for exploratory work that tests a well-developed conceptual framework (Doolin, 1996). By employing a single case study, researchers gain valuable opportunities to delve deep into the phenomenon, enabling a rich description and revealing its underlying structure (Cavaye, 1996).

Moreover, as stated by Yin (2013), a case-study design is particularly suitable when exploring a phenomenon that has not been previously investigated. A key advantage of case studies lies in their ability to generate context-dependent knowledge, aiming to offer authentic and transferable insights (Granovetter, 2007). Therefore, case-study research proves invaluable for exploring underexamined research areas, especially when the objective is to gain a comprehensive understanding of the phenomenon.

Data Collection and Sample

The study employed content analysis to examine the types of documents and information being disclosed. A triangulation approach was adopted to select relevant documents for analysis. Firstly, access to an extensive collection of documents related to the case was granted by the Timor-Leste Institute for Development Monitoring and Analysis (La'o Hamutuk). This organization also provided references to other knowledgeable agencies in the US and Australasia to advise on documents suitable for the sample. Secondly, a search was conducted for documents cited in academic literature, policy papers, newspapers, and industry publications. Inclusion criteria required the documents to be published by governments, their ministries, government-related authorities, or the news media, without any specific exclusion criteria related to geographic area, date, or accessibility.

The final sample comprised 63 documents containing terms such as 'Bobby Boye,' 'Bobby Ajiboye,' 'Bobby Aji-Boye,' and 'Timor Fraud.' These documents were categorized as follows: (a) reports on prior work history (n = 21 documents); (b) documents outlining the tendering contracts of the Ministry of Finance (Norway and Timor-Leste) (n = 17); (c) documents related to the activities or descriptions of the investigative process (n = 9 documents); (d) documents outlining possible future activities (n = 6 documents); (e) documents related to the charges and prosecution (n = 10 documents).

Qualitative Content Analysis

The research conducted an in-depth analysis of case-related documents using a qualitative approach. The analysis combined deductive and inductive methods to effectively structure the content. To facilitate this process, a comprehensive category system was devised, drawing from the theoretical framework. As there were no existing research papers on qualitative content analysis within the realm of criminology and financial crime, additional categories were formulated based on emerging patterns found in the reviewed documents. The coding process was facilitated using NVivo software (version 10).

FINDINGS

The section presents the findings of the case study, commencing with an exploration of Bobby Boye's background and delving into the extent of corruption investigated. The techniques employed by Boye to perpetrate corruption are also discussed. In the analyzed documents, various terms such as 'Bobby Boye,' 'Bobby Ajiboye,' 'Bobby Aji-Boye,' and 'Timor Fraud' appeared between one and 156 times per document. The fraud was either mentioned in conjunction with other topics or served as the primary focus throughout significant portions or the entirety of the documents. As a result, the scope of the examined documents spans a wide range of subjects. While many documents shed light on the conceptualization of wire fraud and the investigation process, only a few addressed the challenges posed by the case.

Boye's Corruption in Timor

According to court records (Doc Id 14), it was observed that Bobby Boye executed the criminal conspiracy in a remarkably composed and premeditated manner. The Court acknowledged Boye's impressive educational and professional background, emphasizing his proficiency in performing the tasks for which he was hired, stating, "*You have great talents because you were able to do the work*" (Doc Id 23). The case study's scrutiny into the fraud and Boye's history uncovered a series of workplace and employment frauds he had perpetrated over the decade leading up to his employment in Timor-Leste, as detailed below.

Boye's Employment History

The Norwegian Ministry of Finance conducted thorough pre-employment screening, including interviews with four references, before offering Bobby Boye a contract. The screening did not reveal any discrepancies in his resume or references (Doc Id 4).

Bobby Abiola Olawale Ajiboye was born in Nigeria on 30 July 1963. Later, he became a US citizen on 23 September 2005, opting to change his name to Bobby Wale Boye (Doc Id 12). He obtained a law degree in Nigeria and pursued higher education at the University of California, Los Angeles (UCLA), earning a Master of Law. Subsequently, he attended the University of Southern California, graduating with a Master of Business Tax (Doc Id 23).

One of Boye's resumes indicated that he received his law training and practicing certificate from Nigeria in 1987. The resume also mentioned his membership in the Lincoln's Inn Lawyers' Society in London and claimed a bachelor's degree in law from St John's College, University of Cambridge.

The first reported instance of Boye's employment fraud occurred when he secured a job with the stock brokerage and securities firm Dean Witter, Discover & Co., a subsidiary of Morgan Stanley in California. On 24 April 2000, without proper authorization from the client, Boye withdrew \$6,500.00 from a client's account (Doc Id 19).

To conceal the fraud, Boye fabricated a life-threatening illness, prompting his employer to place him on paid medical leave and halt any internal investigation. During this time, he began working at KPMG's San Francisco office in the taxation innovation team (Doc Id 24). However, when Dean Witter, Discover & Co. discovered the unauthorized employment in January 2001, they promptly terminated Boye.

Following his departure from KPMG in 2002, Boye assumed the position of Manager of Taxation at the Californian technology firm 3D Systems Corporation, with a yearly salary of \$100,000 (Doc Id 25). Exploiting the company's complex tax structure, Boye orchestrated a scheme that involved overpaying taxes to the Canadian Revenue Authority (CRA) and redirecting the refunds to his personal account. Forensic accountants determined that he received $250,000.00 from this fraudulent activity (Doc Id 26).

In January 2004, Boye faced disciplinary action from the New York Stock Exchange for engaging in trading improprieties in client accounts, and he was subsequently censured by the New York Stock Exchange and the US Securities and Exchange Commission (Doc Id 31).

3D Systems appeared unaware of the disciplinary findings and Boye's bankruptcy filing in September 2004, listing debts of $163,000 primarily from loans and credit cards (Doc Id 34). To rectify the tax payment discrepancies with the Internal Revenue Service and the CRA, the company hired forensic accountants and investigators. Boye left 3D Systems in June 2005, before the forensic accountant's report was presented to management.

In 2006, Boye was arrested for his fraudulent actions at 3D Systems and brought to trial the following year. He pleaded guilty to theft, money laundering, and forgery, with the police presenting evidence linking Bobby Boye and Bobby Ajiboye as the same person. Boye received a three-year prison sentence and was ordered to repay $262,128 to 3D Systems, along with $125,252 for the investigative costs of the forensic accountant (Doc Id 42).

After his release from custody in early 2009, Boye relocated to New Jersey, where he managed to become a lawyer and was admitted to the New York Bar, despite his previous criminal and securities misconduct history. He then applied for and secured a role as a Petroleum Tax Advisor (International) with the Norwegian Ministry of Finance in Timor-Leste, working with the National Directorate of Petroleum Revenue (Doc Id 42).

Techniques of Corruption: The Tendering Panel

Based on the documents analyzed in this research, this section explores the primary methods employed by Boye to facilitate corrupt activities in Timor-Leste. Soon after assuming the role of Petroleum Tax Advisor (International), Boye identified substantial revenue gaps faced by the Timor-Leste government concerning income from oil companies. He contended that these companies were manipulating revenues and royalties from oil and resource production, depriving Timor-Leste of its rightful share. Multinational resource companies used well-known techniques like asset depreciation, transfer pricing, and profit shifting to evade or minimize tax payments, as commonly observed in international corporate practices (Sikka & Willmott, 2010; Taylor & Richardson, 2012; Waris & Seabrooke, 2017).

Before 2010, the Timor-Leste government lacked the resources and expertise to conduct compliance checks on multinational tax returns. When they finally initiated their compliance program, they encountered the typical challenges faced by regulators when auditing multinational companies, including navigating complex jurisdictional issues, international financing, tax havens, and managing relations with other tax regulatory agencies. The absence of adequate government compliance and regulatory functions to enforce tax regulations was further compounded by limited access to records. However, this situation changed in July 2010 when the government modified the law, mandating multinational companies to maintain business records in Timor-Leste and provide access to government agencies for regulatory reviews. This critical development allowed Timor-Leste regulators to carry out investigations, audits, and tax collection, leading to a significant increase in the number of audits conducted from 2008 and 2009 to 2010.

Upon commencing his contract in Timor-Leste, Boye took charge of a special tax task force that initiated a forensic investigation into the tax records of multinational companies operating in the Bayu-Undan oil and gas field. He proposed that the amount owed to the Timor-Leste government could be as high as $3 billion, considering interest and penalties on unpaid taxes (Cronau & Fowler, 2012). In response, ConocoPhillips and other companies strongly protested but ultimately paid over US$362 million in back taxes levied in 2011 and 2012 to avoid further penalties and interest charges. However, they also contested the assessments.

Boye advised the National Directorate of Petroleum Revenue of the Ministry of Finance, Timor-Leste, that they lacked the technical capacity to effectively challenge the taxation teams of large international petroleum companies, which employed intricate international financial structures and tax havens to obscure their proper tax obligations.

Boye suggested that the Ministry of Finance, Timor-Leste seek suitable external legal support. In March 2012, the Ministry of Finance, Timor-Leste requested bids from the following:

"Suitably qualified and experienced international engineering audit firms and or accounting firms with demonstrable experience in petroleum taxation and related engineering issues to assist NDPR [National Directorate of Petroleum Revenue] on technical/engineering and petroleum tax accounting issues that are implicated in the tax audit of oil and gas companies." (Doc Id 37)

Timor-Leste's oil and gas industry (Doc Id. 33). The chosen firm/s were also expected to develop new regulations for computing income tax and allowable deductions within the sector. Boye was the designated point of contact for both tender processes. Notably, Boye served on a seven-member committee responsible for evaluating the tenders, with the committee members relying on his expertise in tax matters to identify the most effective law firm for the project. Among the applicants vying for consideration in the legal tender panel were ten international firms, including renowned companies such as Deloitte and Baker McKenzie. This panel would play a crucial role in shaping the tax laws related to the oil and gas industry in Timor-Leste (Doc Id. 39).

The successful firm was Opus & Best Law Services LLC, a multinational law and accounting firm that was experienced in the mining, oil and gas industries and had offices in New York; it was founded in 1985. Its website stated the following:

We have over 40 top tax professions (sic.), each with decades of high-level oil and gas tax/accounting experience spread across the Americas, Middle East, Europe, Africa and South-East Asia … We provide tax advisory services on all aspects of oil and gas taxation and taxation department operations to corporations. We also assist sovereign government revenue agencies to write tax laws, regulations, tax manuals and rulings (Doc Id 45).

In June 2012, Opus & Best was awarded the exclusive contract after Boye's advice was relied upon by the Ministry to determine the most qualified applicant for the tender. The Ministry further entrusted Boye with the authority to approve reports, invoices, and payments made by the successful law firm. Timor-Leste made payments to Opus & Best in instalments, acknowledging their excellent work that aligned with the contract's benchmarks. The quality of their work was so remarkable that Timor-Leste engaged Opus & Best twice more in subsequent contracts, awarded directly without any competitive bidding (Doc Id 46 and Doc Id 47), based on the outstanding performance under the first contract (Doc Id 47).

In April 2013, Opus & Best Hong Kong attempted to secure a 'Tax Consulting and Advisory Services' contract in Timor-Leste, requesting an advance payment of $250,000.00. However, the Timor-Leste authorities declined the proposal (Doc Id 52). In May 2013, an email from Opus & Best sent an invoice of $630,000 for unspecified services to Timor-Leste, but this payment was not made (Doc Id 51).

A total sum of $3,510,000 (Doc Id 41) was paid to Opus & Best's US-based account in New York. Surprisingly, according to Timor-Leste's Procurement Transparency Portal, the Ministry of Finance awarded contracts worth $7.8 million to Opus & Best in 2012 (Doc Id 60). The whereabouts of the remaining funds remain undetermined.

The Investigation

In June 2014, Boye was apprehended by the FBI in New Jersey as part of an investigation conducted by the Financial Fraud Enforcement Task Force. The FBI had been secretly monitoring Boye's financial activities for several months.

The fraudulent scheme heavily relied on the internet, as Boye and his spouse registered a website and produced content, including detailed biographies of prominent lawyers, accountants, and economists. This was done to create a facade of legitimacy for their fictitious multinational tax and law firm. They aimed to portray it as an established and reputable entity with extensive international expertise in natural resources and boasting prestigious clients across various continents.

Boye's main motive behind establishing this elaborate charade was to secure consulting contracts from the Timor-Leste government. The FBI's criminal complaint revealed that Opus & Best had only Boye as its sole member, and the registered business address was associated with him. Furthermore, he opened a bank account in New York for Opus & Best, being the sole authorized signatory.

Throughout the process, Boye deliberately concealed his true connection with Opus & Best from the Timor-Leste government and failed to disclose any conflicts of interest in pursuing the contracts.

Justice Wolfson, made several observations in her sentencing remarks in October 2015, noting the following:

"Mr. Boye was given a wonderful opportunity. He was going to be on the ground floor of assisting them in moving forward in an economic way ... to do what I would call 'do good' to assist this country in moving forward in a very important way'. [However, the fraud was] 'quite sophisticated and involved' [and Boye knew he was seeking] 'a multi-million-dollar contract of work ... which is why when you created this company you didn't just make it a two or three-person company. You presented it as a dozen people, 20 people who could perform all these different services." (Doc Id 55)

Boye faced serious consequences for his actions. He was charged with five counts of wire fraud, indicating the gravity of his fraudulent activities. Recognizing the weight of the evidence against him, Boye chose to plead guilty to the charges brought against him.

Upon conviction, he was sentenced to six years of imprisonment, signifying the severity of his offense. In addition to the prison sentence, the court also ordered him to repay the ill-gotten gains, amounting to $3.51 million. This restitution was aimed at compensating the victims for the financial losses incurred due to Boye's fraudulent schemes.

The sentence and restitution highlight the commitment of the legal system to hold individuals accountable for their actions and deter others from engaging in similar criminal activities.

Ongoing Consequences

The tax assessment carried out by Boye on behalf of the Timor-Leste government for the multinational companies operating in the Bayu-Undan oil and gas field had significant and enduring implications. In February 2016, ConocoPhillips settled most of its tax disputes with the government for an undisclosed sum. However, it came to light that many of Boye's assessments lacked substantiation, leading to refunds being issued to the involved multinational companies, likely accompanied by interest payments.

Remarkably, evidence indicated that the multinational resource companies were aware of Boye's fraudulent activities two years prior to his FBI arrest. As part of their disputes over taxation assessments, these companies engaged investigators to delve into Boye's background, uncovering falsehoods in his resume and his history of defrauding clients, which led to his banishment from the New York Stock Exchange.

Interestingly, it appeared that the multinationals kept this information hidden, possibly intending to leverage it as part of their litigation strategy to discredit the Timor-Leste government during the taxation disputes.

According to the Timor-Leste Institute for Development Monitoring and Analysis, the actual cost of Boye's fraud extended far beyond the funds received by Opus & Best, estimated at a staggering $176,080,000 (Doc Id 61). This calculation factored in various elements, such as the $10 million cost of forensic reviews of the assessments conducted by legitimate law firms, which the Ministry engaged to unravel Boye's calculations. Additionally, the total amount of interest and penalties incurred in the tax liability, amounting to $17.2 million, was considered. It was customary for multinationals to initially pay or partially pay the tax liability and then challenge the assessment in court. In the case mentioned, the multinationals made an initial payment under protest in 2012 as part of the initial assessments. Upon successful challenge, this amount was refunded, along with the interest awarded during the litigation settlement process.

DISCUSSION

The examination of the 63 documents provided valuable insights into the unfolding of the fraud and the events leading up to it. Throughout its history, Timor-Leste has unfortunately grappled with persistent and systemic corruption, allowing embezzlement, bribery, and fraud to become deeply ingrained within the societal framework.

In many aspects, Boye perfectly exemplified what Sutherland (1949, p. 2) coined as the archetypical White-collar criminal—a person of elevated social standing and respectability. Allard (2014) portrayed him as someone who often signed his emails as 'Bobby W. Boye esq.' and was noted for wearing suits with waistcoats even in the sweltering tropical weather. Boye amassed his wealth within Timor-Leste and was celebrated as a hero by local authorities (Allard, 2014).

Embezzlement, Theft, and Fraud

Corruption manifests in various forms, including embezzlement, theft, and fraud, where individuals exploit their positions of employment to unlawfully acquire money, property, or valuable items. Embezzlement, specifically, involves the misappropriation of public funds or property by those in positions of trust or authority, such as senior officials. Fraud, on the other hand, encompasses the use of deceit or concealment to carry out illicit acts.

These acts of wrongdoing not only erode public trust but also have detrimental effects on governments' ability to provide essential services to their communities (De Vaal & Ebben, 2011; Mo, 2001). Regrettably, Timor-Leste is not immune to such challenges, despite witnessing significant revenues from its natural resources in recent years. The equitable and effective distribution of these resources to benefit the broader community has remained elusive (Berlie, 2012; White, 2017).

Addressing this issue necessitates a concerted effort to foster transparency, accountability, and robust anti-corruption measures. Only through responsible governance and a steadfast commitment to combat corruption can Timor-Leste hope to unlock its full potential and uplift the well-being of its citizens.

Procurement Fraud

In developing economies, procurement fraud emerges as one of the most prevalent fraudulent techniques. Research indicates that substantial revenue losses occur due to inflated contracts or non-delivery of paid products or services (Matthew *et al.*, 2013; Gottschalk & Stanislas, 2017).

In the specific case of Timor-Leste, the fraud was intricately linked to the use of the Internet. The fraudulent Opus & Best website featured falsified employment credentials of accountants and lawyers, along with details of past client engagements. To unsuspecting observers, including members of the tendering panel, the website appeared genuine. This type of fraud is categorized as 'cyber-enabled,' as it leverages technology like the internet to facilitate its execution, though it is not solely reliant on it. In this instance, while the creation of Opus & Best by Boye was essential for the fraud, he also employed non-cyber deception in his communications with the tender committee and the Ministry during the procurement process, as well as in the subsequent supply of legal and accounting services.

A robust public procurement system serves as a cornerstone of good governance, ensuring the accountable use of public funds for the greater benefit of the public. Procurement fraud can take various forms, ranging from providing privileged information to companies for a fee to manipulating the bidding process to favour a particular bidder. To enhance transparency, the Timor-Leste Ministry of Finance established an online Procurement Portal in 2011 to disclose information about government tenders and contracts. However, the portal's effectiveness has been hindered by inconsistent updates, and not all tenders seem to be adequately included on the site.

Employment Screening Failure

Engleman and Kleiner (1998) conducted research revealing that conventional employment screening methods like interviews, references, and resumes are insufficient in safeguarding employers from fraudulent practices or potential legal issues arising from employees' misconduct. Despite being the most common form of employment screening, personal interviews often prove weak in assessing a candidate's integrity, as they mainly focus on social skills without effectively gauging honesty and ethical behavior (Bonanni *et al.*, 2006; Brody, 2010; Engleman & Kleiner, 1998).

Similarly, contacting references and checking resumes also suffer from deficiencies, as applicants tend to provide selective references, and resumes can omit critical details (Brody, 2010; Engleman & Kleiner, 1998). Even background checks, which are commonly conducted, were found to have limited effectiveness in preventing fraud in a study of 1,142 occupational fraud cases by Holtfreter (2005).

Corporate corruption can take various forms, and when perpetrated by upper management, it can prove devastating to an entire organization (Murphy, 1993, as cited in Brody, 2010). While the extent of Boye's potential impact on the Ministry of Finance in Timor-Leste remains debatable, his corrupt activities have undoubtedly had significant and enduring consequences for the country.

The Norwegian Ministry of Finance's vetting process for Boye was inadequate, relying solely on two interviews and two personal references. To exercise proper due diligence in hiring a senior executive, the Ministry should have conducted integrity screenings, verified resumes, and performed checks on media, credit, and criminal history. These searches, especially for a US citizen like Boye, could have been conveniently conducted online at a minimal cost. Moreover, to ensure a more comprehensive background screening of employees, the engagement of private investigators and forensic accountants could have been considered (Brody, 2010; King, 2020). Such measures might have uncovered Boye's prior fraud conviction and Securities and Exchange Commission violation before he was employed, potentially preventing the situation from unfolding as it did.

Organizational Controls

The second tender for accounting and law in Timor-Leste, awarded to Opus & Best, encountered significant challenges that fostered an environment conducive to corruption. Firstly, the tender organization lacked safeguards against misuse and seemed to incentivize improper spending. Secondly, the initial planning for the tender was insufficient, compounded by a lackadaisical approach to administration during implementation. Notably, the Ministry heavily relied on Boye for technical advice, giving him an unprecedented level of involvement compared to other panel members. While not all projects characterized by poor planning and organization lead to fraud, in this case, Boye capitalized on these weaknesses and exploited his familiarity with the process to create a fictitious cyber international law firm that secured the project tender successfully.

As with many developing economies, Timor-Leste heavily depended on international expatriate consultants to provide technical services for government agencies. Ideally, these consultants should have established a system that ensured money expenditure was distributed among various individuals or departments within the organization. Unfortunately, an impartial party to review the tender/bid process and verify the consistency of records with invoices and cash balances was absent. This lack of oversight and shared responsibility, coupled with Boye's influential position, enabled him to execute and conceal the fraudulent activities.

Internal Audit Function

Upon Boye's entry into the Ministry of Finance, the International Monetary Fund (IMF) conducted a review of Timor-Leste's public financial management system, revealing critical shortcomings. These included the absence of an independent external auditor, a nearly non-existent internal auditing system, incomplete budget coverage, and weak budget planning and implementation capacities within ministries. The heavy reliance on foreign international experts also raised concerns about the integrity of procurement and tax administration, impacting the overall effectiveness of public administration (Van Eden *et al.*, 2010).

Within the Ministry, the absence of a robust internal auditor hindered the reconciliation of records with assets, jeopardizing the accuracy of financial records and the protection of assets. Best practice suggests that internal audit committees should operate independently and free from interference by top management (Brennan & McGrath, 2007). Objectivity is enhanced when the internal audit function reports to a high level within the organization, such as an audit committee advising the department head or minister. To combat corruption and facilitation payments, it is crucial for ministers to periodically assign internal auditors to evaluate potential risks. Implementing a public sector code of conduct and identifying conflicts of interest can also serve as effective controls.

Prior to the Boye corruption scandal, Timor-Leste experienced extensive media coverage of allegations of corruption involving government ministers and leaders in 2009. This led to the establishment of the Anti-Corruption Commission (Komisaun Anti Korupsaun) in June 2009, which subsequently referred several cases to the Office of the Prosecutor General for ongoing investigations.

Starting in November 2018, the United Nations Office on Drugs and Crime provided training to investigators and prosecutors within Timor-Leste's Anti-Corruption Commission, aiming to equip them with specialized skills and tools for handling complex corruption cases involving financial transactions. However, according to Berlie's research study on anti-corruption activities in Timor-Leste (2012), a major cause of corruption was the government's lack of follow-up capacity regarding significant projects (p. 260). This lack of follow-up capacity was evident in the events outlined in the case study, despite the IMF's warning to the Ministry of Finance about its deficient internal controls (see Van Eden *et al.*, 2010). Although the Ministry later developed a Procurement Portal, it seems that its intended use has not been effectively implemented.

CONTRIBUTION TO RESEARCH AND LIMITS

The findings of this case study indicate that developing economies, abundant with natural resources, can be susceptible to exploitation by expatriate international advisors who provide much-needed technical support. This research sheds light on how a highly educated expatriate capitalized on weaknesses in the international recruitment process to establish a fabricated international tax and accounting corporate entity, solely existing online, and ultimately securing a multimillion-dollar tender. These findings underscore the significance of understanding corruption and fraud's impact on developing economies, emphasizing the need for robust investigative processes that encompass recruitment, internal audit, and other controls to prevent such crimes.

While this paper's insights contribute significantly to an often-neglected topic, it is noteworthy that the volume of research on corruption, fraud, and fraud prevention by esteemed researchers has grown considerably. Despite this, there remains a glaring lack of research on expatriate corruption by trusted advisors within developing countries. Consequently, further research must address this gap to gain a comprehensive understanding of this evolving facet of corruption and fraud.

It is important to acknowledge that this study focused on a specific case in one developing economy, and the circumstances that allowed Boye to exploit the system might not be widespread. However, the case discussions adequately served the inquiry's objectives and should serve as a cautionary tale for those engaged in investigating and researching corruption and fraud. By learning from these insights, future efforts can be better directed toward preventing and combatting similar incidents in the future.

CONCLUSION

The findings of this research uncover a significant corruption case in Timor-Leste, arguably one of the most profound instances observed within any developing economy. This study highlights that individuals in higher positions of government or society often possess increased opportunities for corruption, especially when they serve as trusted international advisors.

Using content analysis, this study delved into a corruption case within Timor-Leste's Ministry of Finance. It explored the specific corruption technique employed and investigated potential measures to prevent such occurrences. Contrary to the conventional focus on identifying "bad apples" in corruption research, the situation in Timor-Leste reveals a unique scenario where a "bad apple" was imported into an environment that allowed them to fully exploit the lack of controls typically implemented by organizations to prevent and mitigate such events.

DECLARATION

The authors declare that the manuscript follows ethical standards and there are no potential conflicts of interest with respect to the research, authorship and/or publication of this chapter.

DISCLAIMER

The contents and views of this chapter are expressed by the authors in personal capacities. It is not necessary for the Editor and the Publisher to agree with these viewpoints, and they are not responsible for any duty of care in this regard.

ACKNOWLEDGMENT

The authors extend sincere gratitude to

- The Editor and the International Editorial Advisory Board (IEAB) of this book who initially desk reviewed, arranged a rigorous double/triple blind review process, and conducted a thorough, minute, and critical final review before accepting the chapter for publication.
- All anonymous reviewers who provided very constructive feedbacks for thorough revision, improvement, extension, and fine tuning of the chapter.
- All colleagues, assistants and well-wishers who assisted to complete this task.

REFERENCES

Allard, T. (2014, September 10). Big Oil stands by as con man swindles East Timor. *The Sydney Morning Herald*. https://www.smh.com.au/national/big-oil-stands-by-as-con-man-swindles-east-timor-20140909-10eb13.html

Berlie, J. (2012). Anticorruption in East Timor: Implications for development and education. *Asian Education and Development Studies, 1*(3), 251–261. doi:10.1108/20463161211270473

Blunt, P. (2009). The political economy of accountability in Timor-Leste: Implications for public policy. *Public Administration and Development, 29*(2), 89–100. doi:10.1002/pad.522

Bonanni, C., Drysdale, D., Hughes, A., & Doyle, P. (2006). Employee background verification: The cross-referencing effect. *The International Business & Economics Research Journal, 5*(11). doi:10.19030/iber.v5i11.3519

Boyce, J. R., & Emery, J. H. (2011). Is a negative correlation between resource abundance and growth sufficient evidence that there is a 'resource curse'? *Resources Policy, 36*(1), 1–13. doi:10.1016/j.resourpol.2010.08.004

Brennan, N. M., & McGrath, M. (2007). Financial statement fraud: Some lessons from US and European case studies. *Australian Accounting Review, 17*(42), 49–61. doi:10.1111/j.1835-2561.2007.tb00443.x

Brody, R. G. (2010). Beyond the basic background check: Hiring the 'right' employees. *Management Research Review, 33*(3), 210–223. doi:10.1108/01409171011030372

Canare, T. (2017). The effect of corruption on foreign direct investment inflows: Evidence from a panel of Asia-Pacific countries. In M. dela Rama & C. Rowley (Eds.), *The Changing Face of Corruption in the Asia Pacific* (pp. 35–55). Elsevier. doi:10.1016/B978-0-08-101109-6.00003-4

Cavaye, A. L. (1996). Case study research: A multi-faceted research approach for IS. *Information Systems Journal, 6*(3), 227–242. doi:10.1111/j.1365-2575.1996.tb00015.x

Corden, W. M. (1984). Booming sector and Dutch disease economics: Survey and consolidation. *Oxford Economic Papers, 36*(3), 359–380. doi:10.1093/oxfordjournals.oep.a041643

Cronau, P., & Fowler, A. (2012). Miners owe East Timor millions in unpaid taxes [Episode]. Four Corners. Australia: ABC.

Davis, G. (1995). Learning to love the Dutch disease: Evidence from the mineral economies. *World Development, 23*(10), 1765–1779. doi:10.1016/0305-750X(95)00071-J

Davis, G. A., & Tilton, J. E. (2005). The resource curses. *Natural Resources Forum, 29*(3), 233–242). doi:10.1111/j.1477-8947.2005.00133.x

De Vaal, A., & Ebben, W. (2011). Institutions and the relation between corruption and economic growth. *Review of Development Economics, 15*(1), 108–123. doi:10.1111/j.1467-9361.2010.00596.x

Doig, A. (1999). Dealing with corruption: The next steps. *Crime, Law, and Social Change, 29*(2/3), 99–112. doi:10.1023/A:1008390808395

Doig, A., & Riley, S. (1998). Corruption and anti-corruption strategies: Issues and case studies from developing countries. In G. S. Cheema & J. Bonvin (Eds.), *Corruption And Integrity Improvement Initiatives in Developing Economies*. OECD.

Doig, A., & Tisne, M. (2009). A candidate for relegation? Corruption, governance approaches and the (re) construction of post-war states. *Public Administration and Development*, *29*(5), 374–386. doi:10.1002/pad.543

Doolin, B. (1996). Alternative views of case research in information systems. *AJIS. Australasian Journal of Information Systems*, *3*(2). Advance online publication. doi:10.3127/ajis.v3i2.383

Drysdale, J. (2008). Five principles for the management of natural resource revenue: The case of Timor-Leste's petroleum revenue. *Journal of Energy & Natural Resources Law*, *26*(1), 151–174. doi:10.1080/02646811.2008.11435181

Engleman, D., & Kleiner, B. H. (1998). Effective employment screening practices. *Career Development International*, *3*(4), 164–168. doi:10.1108/13620439810214420

Fantaye, D. K. (2004). Fighting corruption and embezzlement in third world countries. *Journal of Criminal Law*, *68*(2), 170–176. doi:10.1350/jcla.68.2.170.29126

Gottschalk, P. (2019). *Fraud and corruption: A convenience perspective*. Universal-Publishers.

Gottschalk, P., & Stanislas, P. (2017). *Public corruption: Regional and national perspectives on procurement fraud*. Routledge. doi:10.1201/9781315277301

Granovetter, M. (2007). The social construction of corruption. In M. Granovetter (Ed.), *On capitalism*. Stanford University Press. doi:10.1515/9780804768368-011

Granovetter, N. N. (2007). Identification of ambiguity in the case study research typology: What is a unit of analysis? *Qualitative Market Research*, *10*(1), 78–97. doi:10.1108/13522750710720413

Gylfason, T. (2001). Natural resources, education, and economic development. *European Economic Review*, *45*(4–6), 847–859. doi:10.1016/S0014-2921(01)00127-1

Habib, M., & Zurawicki, L. (2002). Corruption and foreign direct investment. *Journal of International Business Studies*, *33*(2), 291–307. doi:10.1057/palgrave.jibs.8491017

Holtfreter, K. (2005). Is occupational fraud 'typical' White-collar crime? A comparison of individual and organizational characteristics. *Journal of Criminal Justice*, *33*(4), 353–365. doi:10.1016/j.jcrimjus.2005.04.005

Kenny, C. (2007). *Construction, corruption, and developing countries* (World Bank Policy Research Working Paper No. 4271). World Bank. doi:10.1596/1813-9450-4271

King, M. (2020). Out of obscurity: The contemporary private investigator in Australia. *International Journal of Police Science & Management*, *22*(3), 285–296. doi:10.1177/1461355720931887

La'o Hamutuk. (2014). Timor-Leste has been robbed! La'o Hamutuk. http://laohamutuk.blogspot.com/2014/06/timor-leste-has-been-robbed.html

Lundahl, M., & Sjöholm, F. (2008). The oil resources of Timor-Leste: Curse or blessing? *The Pacific Review*, *21*(1), 67–86. doi:10.1080/09512740701868898

Matthew, K., Patrick, K., & Denise, K. (2013). The effects of fraudulent procurement practices on public procurement performance. *International Journal of Business and Behavioral Sciences*, *3*(1), 17–27.

Mo, P. H. (2001). Corruption and economic growth. *Journal of Comparative Economics*, *29*(1), 66–79. doi:10.1006/jcec.2000.1703

Nurhidayat, I., & Kusumasari, B. (2018). Strengthening the effectiveness of whistleblowing system: A study for the implementation of anti-corruption policy in Indonesia. *Journal of Financial Crime*, *25*(1), 140–154. doi:10.1108/JFC-11-2016-0069

OECD. (2019). *Using extractive revenues for sustainable development: Policy guidance for resource-rich countries, OECD development policy tools*. Organisation for Economic Co-operation and Development

Otusanya, O. J. (2011). Corruption as an obstacle to development in developing countries: A review of literature. *Journal of Money Laundering Control*, *14*(4), 387–422. doi:10.1108/13685201111173857

Rothstein, B., & Varraich, A. (2017). *Making sense of corruption*. Cambridge University Press. doi:10.1017/9781316681596

Sherman, T. (2015, October 15). $3.5M international con game nets NJ man 6 years in prison. *NJ.com*. https://www.nj.com/news/2015/10/35m_international_con_game_nets_nj_man_6_years_in.html

Sikka, P., & Willmott, H. (2010). The dark side of transfer pricing: Its role in tax avoidance and wealth retentiveness. *Critical Perspectives on Accounting*, *21*(4), 342–356. doi:10.1016/j.cpa.2010.02.004

Sullivan, J. D. (2009, February). *The moral compass of companies: Business ethics and corporate governance as anti-corruption tools*. Washington: Global Corporate Governance Forum.

Sutherland, E. H. (1949). *White collar crime*. Dryden Press.

Taylor, G., & Richardson, G. (2012). International corporate tax avoidance practices: Evidence from Australian firms. *The International Journal of Accounting*, *47*(4), 469–496. doi:10.1016/j.intacc.2012.10.004

TI. (2021). *Timor Leste*. Transparency International. https://www.transparency.org/en/countries/timor-leste

TI. (2023). *What is corruption*. Transparency International. https://www.transparency.org/en/what-is-corruption

US. (2014, June 18). Criminal Complaint filed by FBI in U.S. District Court New Jersey.

Van Eden, H., Bessette, F., Pedastsaar, E., & Nayer, H. (2010). *Democratic Republic of Timor-Leste: Public financial management–performance report*. International Monetary Fund Country Report. doi:10.5089/9781455212613.002

Waris, A., & Seabrooke, L. (2017). Arrested development in Africa's global wealth chains: Accountability and hierarchy among 'tax havens. In *The Routledge Companion to Tax Avoidance Research* (pp. 267–286). Routledge. doi:10.4324/9781315673745-18

White, R. (2017). Corruption and the securitisation of nature. *International Journal for Crime. Justice and Social Democracy*, *6*(4), 55–70. doi:10.5204/ijcjsd.v6i4.449

World Bank. (2022). Timor-Leste economic report: Investing in the next generation. https://openknowledge.worldbank.org/bitstream/handle/10986/37604/ P1773510568a060db09183035b08e384fec.pdf?sequence=1&isAllowed=y doi:10.4324/9780203835722

Wraith, R., & Simpkins, E. (2010). *Corruption in developing countries.* Routledge. doi:10.4324/9780203835722

Yin, R. K. (2013). Validity and generalization in future case study evaluations. *Evaluation, 19*(3), 321–332. doi:10.1177/1356389013497081

ENDNOTE

1 All $ are US unless stated otherwise.

Chapter 14
Public Sector Fraud Control in the Caliphate of Umar ibn Abdul-Aziz:
Lessons for Contemporary Nigeria

Adebayo Rafiu Ibrahim
University of Ilorin, Nigeria

Muftau Abdulrauph
Federal College of Education, Iwo, Nigeria

ABSTRACT

The achievements of Islamic caliph Umar bn Abdul-Aziz's in reducing fraud are widely recognized and unparalleled in history after Prophet Muhammad (may peace be upon him). This chapter reviews Umar's strategies to curb fraud in the public sector and extracts insights relevant to contemporary Nigeria. Political officeholders in Nigeria can learn valuable lessons from his wisdom and measures to combat fraud. The study employs a phenomenological methodology, analyzing fraudulent activities in Nigeria through Islamic ethical values. It concludes that public sector fraud is a global phenomenon, but highlights hope based on the Umayyad period, which produced a leader who effectively eliminated corruption. Nigeria can follow a similar path by demonstrating a genuine commitment to fighting fraud among public figures, inspired by Umar bn Abdul-Aziz's remarkable efforts during his caliphate.

INTRODUCTION

Illegal acquisition of wealth which comes under different names and nomenclatures has become a serious and most viable threat to the global economy. Corruption, as it is generally called, is, therefore, a serious pandemic that has ravaged and eaten deep into every fabric of human endeavors leaving no country untouched and no sector unaffected. It is clearly defined by Transparency International (T.I.) as the practice of officials in the public sector, politicians, or civil servants improperly and unlawfully

DOI: 10.4018/979-8-3693-1190-5.ch014

enriching themselves, or those close to them by abuse of public power entrusted to them. This includes embezzlement of funds, election rigging, theft of corporate or public property as well as corrupt practices such as bribery, extortion, or influence peddling[1]. Unfortunately, it has become a disease that proved all medicine applied to it ineffective. In other words, despite the unstopped efforts to eradicate fraudulent activities, it continues to grow in frequency and severity. This global phenomenon has universally penetrated both the private and public sectors to the extent that no country is protected from its taint although developing countries suffer most (Onuora, Akpoveta & Agbomah, 2018). According to the 2022 Corruption Perceptions Index (CPI) of Transparency International, Denmark scored 90 percent in the ranking making it the first country with the least corrupt practices. This is followed by Finland and New Zealand which scored 87% and so ranked second. Norway was ranked fourth scoring 84%, while Singapore and Sweden scored 83% and were ranked 5th respectively. According to the ranking, Afghanistan, Cambodia, Central African Republic, Guatemala, Lebanon, Nigeria and Tajikistan were on the same level scoring 24% thereby ranking them in 150th position, while Somalia scored the least mark at 12% ranking it the most corrupt nation[2]. It is on record that between January and April 2023, a total number of 107,983 reported cases of scams were made and almost $194,133,494 had been lost into all types of scams[3].

Figure 1. January to April 2023 reported cases of scams and amounts lost
Source: www.scamwatch.gov.au

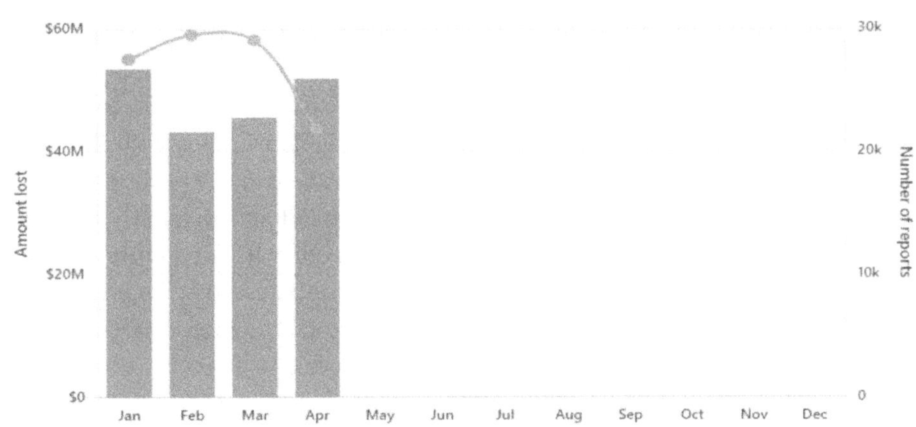

The 2021 report of the KPMG Fraud Barometer revealed how worse this phenomenon is in the UK thus:

From a sector perspective, the UK healthcare sector has continued to be affected by fraud not only from external criminals but from individuals working within the sector. The NHS Counter Fraud Authority estimates that the NHS is vulnerable to 1.14 billion pounds worth of fraud each year. A bill is inevitably picked up by the taxpayers....The trend of cases relating to insider threats may continue to become more prevalent. This year's data found a substantial rise in fraud committed by employees (66 cases in 2021 compared with 44 in 2020) and management (66 cases in 2021 compared with 21 in 2020).

In Cameroon, research showed that virtually all the segments of the public sector are highly corrupt. It was alleged that the police, custom, and tax administration are the most corrupt public institutions in the country (Kingsley, 2015). In Nigeria, the case is not different, it rather goes far beyond control. Cases of fraud and other fraudulent activities have become daily news, especially in the public sector where it begins to become a normal way of life in the midst of civil servants. Fraud scams can be found in many ministries where government officials use the power of their offices to defraud their organizations. The case is not different in the political sphere where vote buying has become the order of the day, and electoral officials are bribed to manipulate or falsify election figures.

The colossal effects of fraud in the public sector in Nigeria have made the country which is once upon a time a major export of agricultural products like groundnuts, palm oil, cocoa, cotton, timber, and hides and skins, becomes an importer of what it produces locally. Virtually all major industries have become ghosts of themselves courtesy of high-rate corruption among those who managed them. It is unbelievable to say that a country that is a strong member of OPEC has no functional oil refinery and so has to export crude oil and import back the refined one at an unaffordable high price subsidized by the Federal Government. In the education sector, Nigeria's higher education system which was regarded as the best in sub-Saharan Africa is deeply in a serious setback, as the nation could hardly meet the demands of staff managing the institutions. There is also little to write home in the health sector of the country because this sector has also been corruptly eaten to the marrow. It is therefore not surprising that Nigeria is conspicuous on the global map of corrupt nations and so, insecurity, criminality and poverty become the order of the day.

It will be a disservice to the country if one fails to mention that successive governments in the country have taken serious steps to check the menace of fraud and corruption in the country. The spread of fraud and its immeasurable effects on socio-economic and political spheres has compelled successive Nigerian governments to establish agencies, commissions, and other bodies with the responsibility of minimizing it to the barest minimum. Other efforts include a probe panel, a commission of inquiry and tribunal, the Money Laundering Act 2003, the Advance Fee Fraud and Related Offence Act of 1995, the Foreign Exchange Act 1995, and the Corrupt Practices and other Related Offence Act 2000 among others (Mathew *et al.*, 2013). Through the various initiatives, some percentages of positive changes could be said to have been recorded particularly in the banking sector. Research carried out on frauds and forgeries in the Nigerian banking sector in 2022, shows that there was a drastic drop in the volume and value of fraud cases in the sector. As against 40, 522 reported cases of incidents of frauds and forgeries in the first quarter (Q1) and second quarter (Q2) of the year 2022, Q2 recorded 27,356 cases representing a 32.49 percent decrease between the periods. In the same vein, the total sum involved in fraud cases which was put at N14.65 billion in Q1 2022 reduced to N8.78 billion in Q2, 2022, a decrease of 40.05 percent. The table below illustrates this further.

The above table shows the fluctuation in reported fraudulent activities in the first and second quarters of 2022. In spite of the reduction in cases reported, the amount involved and amount lost in the first and second quarters respectively, involvement of staff in the fraudulent activities increased by 21.67 percent in the period under review. This possibly, was responsible for the increase in the number of staff whose appointments were terminated from ten to nineteen in the first and second quarters respectively.

Despite all these measures, fraudulent activities continue to be popular in Nigeria. Lack of sincerity and direct and indirect involvement of Nigerian policy-makers, law-enforcement agents, and other stakeholders at all levels are among what renders all attempts against the crime futile. A survey carried out on the prevalence of bribery in relation to several types of public officials in 2016 and 2019 ranked police officers high among others. The figure below shows the percentage of involvement of numerous public officials in Nigeria in bribery in 2016 and 2019.

Table 1. A comparison of fraud activities in the banking sector between Q1 and Q2, 2022

S/N	Variable	Q1	Q2	Percentage (%) change
1.	Total Cases Reported	40,522	27,356	(32.49)
2.	Total Amount Involved	N14,653,505,790.67	N8,784,587,569.59	(40.05)
3.	Total Amount Lost	N1,540,684,616.97	N1,176,131,800.42	(23.66)
4.	Outsider Involvement	34,677	23,440	(32.40)
5.	Insider (Staff) Involvement	60	73	21.67
6.	Appointment Terminated	10	19	90

Source: FITC report on frauds and forgeries in Nigerian banks Quarter 2, 2022

Figure 2. Prevalence of bribery by type of public officials in Nigeria, 2016 and 2019
Source: UNODC: (2019) Corruption in Nigeria: Patterns and Trends

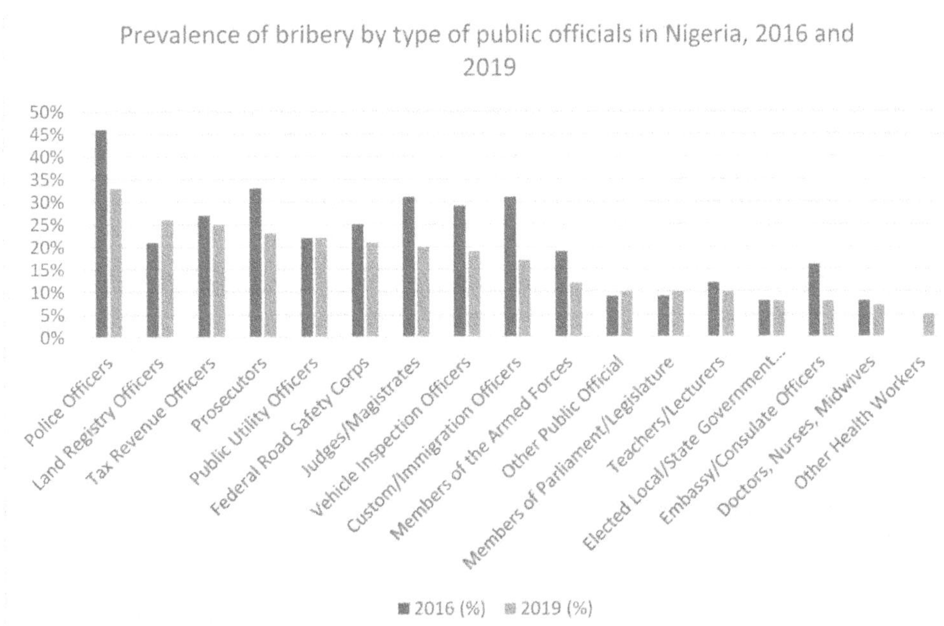

Furthermore, the privatization of government industries and manufacturing companies was a measure put in place for the purpose of reducing state monopolies, government bureaucracy, bad management, and corruption. Such companies so privatized according to Abdulkadir (2008) included the Nigerian Machine Tools, Nigerian Paper Manufacturing Company Limited, Nigerian Sugar Company, Bachita, Ashaka Cement, Benue Cement Company, Calabar Cement, Leyland, Peugeot, etc]; power and steel group [Oshogbo Steel Rolling Mill, Jos Steel Rolling Mill, Ajaokuta Steel Rolling Mill, Aluminum

Smelter Company Limited, National Iron Mining Company Limited, etc]; solid minerals [Nigerian Mining Corporation, Nigerian Uranium Company Limited, etc]. Privatization and government divestiture in the face of fraudulent practices eventually led to job losses, as many companies had to lay off their workers. Three years after its privatization in 2004, Delta Steel, Aladjia stopped production and laid off 2,878 workers; while the Ajaokuta Steel Complex reduced its workforce by 400 percent from 5,000 to 1,000 due to cannibalization of spare parts after its privatization. Other companies which had to fold up were the Aluminum Smelter Company of Nigeria, Osogbo Rolling Mill and Osogbo Machine Tools. The hope that privatization would create employment opportunities by expanding local businesses and increasing the quality of goods and services amongst others was therefore dashed, as it failed to yield the expected results. Privatization is therefore conceived as a means through which political leadership fraudulently acquires themselves or their companies, projects, and enterprises on which huge sums of public money had been sunk.

The unsatisfactory performance of the numerous agencies put in place to curb fraud in Nigeria calls for alternative solutions. Many suggestions have been made by economists and more are still expected. Addressing this situation from an Islamic perspective would therefore not be a wasted effort toward developing the Nigerian economy. Religious values are expected to check fraudulent practices in any society. This is because most religious traditions advocate imbibing virtuous deeds and avoiding the illegal acquisition of wealth at the expense of the community. A highly religious community is therefore expected to have a cream of its public officers with high levels of religiosity who will be less likely to engage in corrupt practices. This view is shared by Treisman (2000) who submits that religion reduces corruption, as it assists in organizing a civil society where citizens are more likely to monitor elites.

CONCEPT AND MEANING OF FRAUD

The word fraud has been defined in different forms by writers based on their specialization and discipline. Onuorah *et al.* (2018) have chronicled various definitions by different authors for the word 'fraud'. According to them, fraud was described by the American Institute of Certified Public Accounts to mean a broad legal concept that is distinguished from error depending on whether the action is intentional or unintentional. Fraud as a concept is a generic term, and it embraces all the multifarious means that human ingenuity can devise which are resorted to by one individual to get an advantage over another by false representation. They equally captured the definition of the FBI which defined fraud as fraudulent conversation and acquisition of money or property by force pretense. Adebisi and Gbegi (2015) described the fraud as an intentional misrepresentation of financial information by one or more individuals among the management, employees, or third parties. It involves the use of criminal deception to obtain unjust or illegal advantages.

From the definitions above, fraud involves dishonesty and abuse of public office for private gain. Fraud is perpetrated in both the public and private sectors of the economy. While describing fraud in the public sector, a number of fraudulent activities involved include bribery, corruption, misuse of authority during public procurement, cash given under the table without records, and gifts to the management.

Public sector fraud originates from both internal and external sources. Internal frauds are the fraud committed by any of the employees within the organization. Examples of internal fraud include but are not limited to procurement fraud such as false invoicing, manipulations in the procurement process, receiving bribes or kickbacks before performing official duties, theft, and skimming, such as removing and selling inventory, cash and consumables, fraudulent expenditures, payroll fraud, such as adding a fake employee to the payroll, manipulation of vouchers, poor Book Keeping, falsification of status report, money laundering and impersonation.

WHY ARE CASES OF FRAUD RAMPANT IN THE PUBLIC SECTOR?

Many factors contributed to the high rate of fraudulent activities in any organization. One of the major factors is weakness in internal control and administrative bureaucracy. Admittedly, the essence of bureaucracy is to ensure that due process is followed in the operations of public service in order to prevent abuse of public funds. However, bureaucracy has conversely become one of the major causes of fraud in the public sector. The stress that people go through to accomplish a task that would have been accomplished in one day in the private sector, could take more than a month to get just a signature from the superior officers. Some employees especially those in the junior cadre exploit the teeming populace in the guise of offering a way of assistance in order to get the job done as soon as possible.

Tribal and ethnic consideration is another critical factor that is responsible for the increase in the number of fraudulent activities in Nigeria. Many people in the public sector are tribally and ethnically inclined. They preferred to favor their kinsmen than to follow the laid down procedures.

Lapses in the operation of anti-graft agencies contributed significantly to the increase in cases of fraudulent activities in the country. There are cases where those that were employed with the aim of reducing fraud in the public sector became the real perpetrators of the fraud. For example, about two or more former chairmen of the Economic and Financial Crimes Commission (EFCC) were dismissed on account of corruption. Also, the Federal government introduced the Treasury Single Account (TSA) and Integrated Payroll and Personnel Information System (IPPIS) with a view to ensuring that the leakages in the government income and expenditures are blocked. The Accountant General of the Federation, the chief accounting officer of the country was recently accused of diverting about 109 billion naira into his personal account. A former Chairman of the defunct Pension Reform Task Team was accused of laundering the pension fund and was jailed for seven years[4]. The Judiciary which is expected to be the hope for the masses is not spared from the plunge of fraud. A former Chief Justice of the Federation was forced to retire on the allegation of receiving bribes and failing to declare his assets as enshrined in the constitution[5]. Of recent, is the case of a Deputy Commissioner of Police, who was charged to court on the allegation of money laundering and drug trafficking[6]. The list is inexhaustible.

The legal system of the country is also not assisting the matter. The procedures through which criminal procedures are being handled called of great concern. A chairman of the defunct Pension Reform Task Team who was accused of mismanaging billions of naira, for instance, on his first appearance in court, was fined a meager and had the gut to dip his hand inside his pocket and handed the fine to the Judge. He was eventually sent to seven years in prison instead of the maximum 14 years prescribed by law on the account that he pleaded for mercy, a sanction that could not serve as a deterrent to potential criminals[7].

As religious as Nigerians claim to be, their religiosity starts and ends within the corners of their churches, mosques or their temples because the application of various religious teaching is not reflected in their day-to-day activities. Many religious leaders are only concerned with the commission that will go to their pocket or religious organization. They are not concerned with the source of funds of their members. In fact, there are cases of some religious leaders involved in money laundry and money rituals.

The societal system also played a major role in the increased number of public sector frauds in Nigeria. Our societies have become so porous to the extent that the source of individual wealth is not questioned again. Unlike the traditional society that served as a check on itself, a young graduate of less than one hundred thousand nairas without any other lawful means of getting additional income could be riding a luxurious car of ten million to the same office where he is being paid without anybody questioning him. This accounted for the prevalence of the Yahoo boys' syndrome in Nigerian society.

UMAR BN ABDUL-AZIZ AT A GLANCE

His full name was Umar bn Abdul-Aziz bn Marwan bn Al-Hakm bn Abi al-As bn Ummayah bn Abdus Shams bn Abdul Manaf. He was born into the family of Abdul-Aziz bn Marwan and Umm Asim bint Asim bn Umar bn Al- Khattab in the year 61H/683AD in the city of Madinah. At a very young age, Umar bn Abdul-Aziz devoted his time to studying under great scholars of Madinah. He studied Literature and Science and was able to collect the entire manuscript of the glorious Qur'an which he memorized and indeed applied its teachings in his day-to-day activities for self-purification. It was reported that Umar bn Abdul-Aziz was educated and mentored by the great scholars and *fuqaha'* of Madinah of that time numbering at least thirty-three, eight of whom were the companions of the Prophet *(May peace be upon him)*, including the famous Abdullah bn Umar. Umar bn Abdul-Aziz became famous with knowledge and piety that he was referred to as the *Imam* of his era by great scholars like Imam Malik, Imam Sufyan bn Uyaynah and Imam Adh-Dhahabi.

Upon the demise of his father, his paternal uncle, Khalifah Abdul-Malik bn Marwan became his guardian. He was beloved to the Khalifah to the extent that he married him to his biological daughter, Fatimah. Umar bn Abdul-Aziz later married additional three wives namely Lamas bint Ail bn al-Hadith, Umm Othman bint Shuayb bn Mayan and Umm Waleed.

Khalifah Umar bn Abdul-Aziz enjoyed special status from the Umayyad royal family. It was observed as stated earlier that Khalifah Abdul-Malik bn Marwan favored him more than some of his children to the extent that he married him to his daughter. Although he could not make significant contributions to the administration of his guardian due to his age, records showed that he performed some advisory role through his frequent reminder notice to Abdul-Malik bn Marwan. He however came to the limelight with his appointment as the governor of Madinah Province by Khalifah Walid bn Abdul-Malik in 87H at the age of 26 years and later extended his office to include Taif in 91H, thereby making him the governor of the entire Hijaz region. His acceptance to become a governor was premised upon three conditions which were approved by Caliph Walid, namely, to deal with people with truth and justice and not to oppress or deprive anyone of his right to the *Baytul Māl*; that he would be allowed to perform hajj at the beginning of the year; and that he would be permitted to make donations to the people of Madinah (As-Sallabi, 2011).

After the demise of Walid bn Abdul-Malik, his brother, Sulyman succeeded him on the throne of Khalifah. Khalifah Sulyman was very close to Umar bn Abdul-Aziz for many reasons. Obviously, due to his personal nature as a lover of truth and justice, Khalifah Sulyman gave him the opportunity to contribute freely to his administration. While Khalifah Sulyman was dying, he consulted the righteous people for advice on who to succeed him and they advised him to nominate Umar bn Adbul-Aziz as his successor which he did. Khalifah Sulyman bn Abdul-Malik died in 99H and was succeeded by Umar bn Abdul-Aziz at the age of thirty-eight years and was popularly referred to as Umar II. He died on Friday

20th Rajab in the year 101H in Hims, Syria, at the age of forty years, while other historical accounts maintained that he died at the age of thirty-nine years and five months after reigning for just two years, five months and four days (As-Sallabi, 2011).

PUBLIC SECTOR FRAUD CONTROL USING UMAR BN ABDUL-AZIZ MODEL

Public sector fraud has been a major problem to the public from time immemorial. The successive dynasties and kingdoms have taken one step or the other toward its control. Public sector fraud took new dimensions during the Umayyad dynasty. Unlike what was obtainable during the reign of the four rightly guided *khalifas* who considered *baytul mal* as sacred and would not allow anyone to spend a penny from the public fund unjustifiably, many of the Umayyad rulers took *baytul mal* as personal belongings of the *khalifahs* and expended lavishly on worthless ceremonies that had no relevance to the public (Rahim, 1983). Public sector fraud became the norm in the administration of the Umayyads from the time of its first ruler Muawiyyah bn Abi Sufyan to the era of Sulyman bn Abdul-Malik. The fraud was not limited to the activities of the *khalifahs* alone but also extended to some of the Umayyad provincial governors who engaged in the illegal acquisition of wealth through the confiscation of private properties in the public name and illegal diversion of public funds into the private property of the Umayyad officials.

On the assumption of Umar bn Abdul-Aziz as the *Khalifah* of the Muslim *Ummah*, he set the agenda of righting the wrongs of the previous *khalifahs* with passion. The approaches adopted by *Khalifah* Umar bn Abdul-Aziz in fighting public sector fraud which was hitherto the order of the day are highly commendable. It will go a long way in addressing the current problems facing the public sector in Nigeria. These are discussed as follows:

Appointment of God-Fearing and Knowledgeable People Into Offices

In fighting public sector fraud, Umar bn Abdul-Aziz being a God-fearing person himself, appointed people of like minds. He maintained that appointing a God-fearing person into the position of authority required little or no supervision, as he already realized that he is holding such a position in trust and would be held accountable for every aspect of his stewardship to Allah (*Subhanahu wa Taala*). While describing the political appointees of Umar bn Abdul-Aziz, many scholars like the famous Imam Ibn Kathir attested to the fact that they were all God fearing and people of proven integrity, when he said: "Many of the Imams declare everyone employed by Umar bn Abdul-Aziz as trustworthy." While corroborating this assertion, Nor (2019) posited thus:

Umar bn Abdulaziz made his line of officers from knowledgeable ulamas and they can be trusted externally and internally. They were highly intelligent and capable of analyzing and practicing the truth well (p. 42).

Provision of Social Amenities

Umar bn Abdul-Aziz adopted positive approaches in fighting against public sector fraud during his reign as the Commander of the Faithfuls. By positive approach, we mean all approaches that ensured easy compliance with the laid principles and practices of the government without necessarily applying force on anyone. This approach equally made people contented and reduced the covetous nature of man in the people. For instance, Umar bn Abdul-Aziz made the provision of social amenities his priority. He accorded priority to the provision of social amenities such as roads, schools, bridges, construction of wells for both human and animals, and housing facilities for the people. Indeed, there were attestations that Umar II attended to every bit of his subjects' needs concentrating fully on their welfare. Through this, he was able to take a larger percentage of the people out of extreme poverty. Once the poverty level is reduced in any society, there is a higher probability of reduced fraud and crime rates in such a society. After all, the major reason why many people engaged in fraudulent practices is their fear of poverty. For an average Nigerian to live a meaningful life, he has to provide basically all the social amenities for himself and his family, whereas, his income cannot cater for such, hence, the reason why many of them engage in fraudulent activities at any slightest opportunity.

It needs to be mentioned that Nigeria is seriously lagging behind in terms of the provision of social infrastructure for its citizens. This is why the World Bank (2022) posited that the country needed about $3 trillion by 2050 for it to cover its infrastructural deficit. A comparative analysis of the infrastructural development index for Egypt, Nigeria and South Africa, the three Africa's biggest economies in all infrastructural groups, namely Information and Communication Technology (ICT), Water and Sanitation, Transport, Electricity and aggregate infrastructure, elucidates this further as indicated in Table 2 below.

Table 2. Infrastructural development index for the top three economies in Africa (2022)

No	Type of Infrastructure	Egypt	Nigeria	South Africa
1.	ICT Composite	33.80	18.76	35.32
2.	Water and Sanitation	99.31	69.22	93.98
3.	Transport	54.54	5.60	22.30
4.	Electricity	33.40	2.42	76.73
5.	aggregate infrastructure	89.91	24.53	81.67

Source: Yusuf, S.A. (2023)

Just and Fair Distribution of Wealth

Umar bn Abdul-Aziz equally ensured that there was a fair distribution of wealth and income among the people. He embarked on a rigorous campaign for truth and justice. He ensured that fair distribution of wealth was the only mean through which the disparities between the rich and the poor could be bridged. To achieve this, he prohibited his governors and powerful figures from having exclusive power over the wealth of the Muslim *Ummah.* Not only did he forbid illegal confiscation of people's property, he made a special public announcement to the people whose properties had been confiscated illegally by his predecessors to come back and take possession of such, and only the unclaimed confiscated properties were returned to *Baitul-mal* for public use (Nor, 2019). This move encouraged the people to increase their economic activities because some people whose properties were confiscated had become impoverished, while those whose properties were not yet confiscated continued to live in fear of having their own properties too confiscated. The overall effect of an increase in commercial activities by the people led to an increase in employment generation for the people and an increase in the revenue generation to the *Baitul-mal* through payment of zakat, *sadaqah, jizyah, kharaj,* and other means through which revenue was being accrued to the public treasury (Tahir, 2020).

Poverty Reduction Policy

Umar II equally ensured that special attention was given to places that were suffering from abject poverty by devoting special spending on them. This he aimed would assist in bringing down the poverty level among the people and improve their productivity. This approach eventually worked out, because a countless number of people were moved out of poverty within the two years and seven months of his administration. It needed to be mentioned here that despite the short reign of his administration, it was difficult to identify the true poor or needy that were supposed to be recipients of zakat. Almost all the people during his reign were rich on average. To buttress this, Yahya bn Said, who happened to be his governor posited thus:

I was sent by Umar bn Abdulaziz to collect zakat from Africa. After collecting it, I intended to give it to poor people. However, I did not find one. Umar bn abdul-Aziz made people rich during his time. I decided to use the Zakat fund to buy and emancipate slaves (Nor, 2015).

Similarly, to confirm the abundance of funds in the *Baitul-mal*, the governor of Kufah wrote a letter to the *Khalifah* informing him of the surplus funds in the public treasury and the absence of the poor and needy to receive them as stipulated by the shariah. Umar bn Abdul-Aziz replied to him thus:

You have told me about abundant funds in Baitul-mal. You can use the funds to pay off the debt of your war team which was not used for vices purposes or even for those who wanted to get married but did not have anything as dowry for the brides. Wassalam (Nor, 2015).

Umar bn Abdul-Aziz was of the view that many people who engaged in fraud were doing so purposely because of fear of poverty. Of course, many people would desist from fraudulent activities once basic amenities such as good roads, basic health care facilities, and standard education were provided for them. Critical insight into the lives of the majority of people engaging in fraudulent practices these days and then was basically their fear of how they would be able to cater to their responsibilities with their limited resources. The *Khalifah* was able to increase revenue generation to the *Baitul-mal* through his numerous public-oriented policies, hence it was easy for him to embark on all his plans for the people.

Self-Sacrifice Policy and Economic Prudency

To guide against public sector fraud, Umar II first identified the purpose of his appointment as the leader of the Muslim community. He realized that the essence of his appointment was to hold his position as a trust for the betterment of the people. Hence, he set up the goal of increasing his spending on the poor and needy and ensured that their means of livelihood were improved. He then considered funds in *Baitul-mal* as a trust which must only be used for the public and not for the personal benefit of the *Khalifah* or his officials. To achieve this, Umar bn Abdul-Aziz started with himself and his family. He did not take a dime from *Baitul-mal* for his personal use. People realized this and advised him to take what Umar bn al-Khattab used to take from *Baitul-mal* during his reign. However, he answered them by saying "Umar had no money whereas my money makes me rich." From this, one could infer that Umar bn Abdul-Aziz followed the footstep of the four rightly-guided *Khalifah* by creating a line of demarcation between his personal property and the public property. It could be likened to the contemporary single treasury account system currently in operation in Nigeria. He was able to monitor all the funds going to the state purse and directed its expenditure accordingly. It was on the basis of this that *Khalifah* Umar bn Abdul-Aziz instructed his governors and all other officials to be prudent in handling the public fund. To know the extent to which Umar bn Abdul-Aziz was economically prudent when it comes to spending public funds, it was reported that his governor in Madinah requested writing materials, and he replied thus:

Once you have read my letter, use less ink, shorten the gaps between your lines and make your words more concise so that they fit on one page, for I certainly hate to exhaust the Muslims' funds on what is of no direct benefit to them (As-Sallabi, 2011).

From the above, it could be derived that one of the means through which Umar bn Abdul-Aziz guarded against public sector fraud is through his economic prudence. He ensured that the recurrent expenditure was reduced to the barest minimum even to the issue of writing materials. He also withdrew many of the personal benefits attached to the office of *khalifah* to ensure more funds were available to cater for the basic need of the government. Once his officials have known the nature of the lifestyle of the *Khalifah*, they also adjusted their own to suit his.

Improving the Living Standard of Public Officials

In a bid to combat public sector fraud and ensure efficiency in the public service, *khalifah* Umar bn Abdul-Aziz made a move towards improving the living standard of the public officials in his domains. He did this by increasing their wages despite reducing his own and depriving himself of some basic royalty treatment. This, according to him, would prevent his officials from being easily tempted to engage in fraudulent acts. He also introduced performance allowance for his officials. It was said that he used to give every official a hundred *Dinar* and two hundred *Dinar* to those who made themselves available to attend to the affairs of the Muslims at all times. Through this, he was able to get his officials motivated.

Blocking Leakages

Khalifah Umar bn Abdul-Aziz equally guided against public sector fraud by blocking every act that could aid or albeit it. The first thing he did in this regard was he prohibited taking gifts for himself when he assumed the leadership position of the Muslim *Ummah*. Likewise, he forbade all his governors and other officials from taking gifts. It was reported that *Khalifah* desired an apple one day, and one of his family members gave him one. When he saw the apple, he was impressed by its color and odor. After looking at it, he asked the boy that brought him the apple to return it to his giver with the message that his message was appreciated and that it had a high place with him but he could not take it. The boy then reminded him that the apple was from the son of his uncle. He also reminded him that the Prophet *(May peace be upon him)* used to take gifts. Umar replied by saying "What is wrong with you? For *Rasullullah (May peace be upon him)*, it was a gift, but for us, in this day, it is a bribe" (Tahir, 2020). This act of *Khalifah* Umar bn Abdul-Aziz is in line with what the Prophet *(May peace be upon him)* ordered to be the code of conduct of every public servant. It could be deduced that taking gifts of any kind by the public official is illegal which has been discouraged by the Prophet *(May peace be upon him)* himself. It was narrated in a hadith reported by Bukhari in his collection when Prophet *(May peace be upon him)* appointed ibn Al-Lutbiyyah as a zakat collector. The hadith read thus:

Abu Humaid al- Sa'idiy RA narrated "The Prophet SAW employed a man from the Al Azdiy tribe as a zakat collector. When the man came back from his assignment, he said, "This is for you as zakat and this is given to me". The Prophet (May peace be upon him) was spontaneously angered and responded by saying; "Let him dwell in his father's or mother's house and see whether it is true that it was given for him or not! And for the sake of the essence of my soul in His hand, no one will take anything from zakat unless he will come on the Day of Judgment the top of his neck is a screaming camel, or a softening cow or a bleating goat". Then he raised his hand so that it was seen us in his white armpit and said: "O Allah surely, I have conveyed, surely, I have conveyed"...(Sahih Bukhari, 2407).

From this hadith, it could be deduced that the Prophet *(May peace be upon him)* was angry at the zakat collector because giving him a gift while discharging his official duty as a zakat collector was likely going to lead to bribery in as much as such a gift will not be given to him had it been that he has not been appointed by the Prophet *(May peace be upon him)* as a zakat collector. The majority of the public officials receiving bribes these days are hiding under the pretense of receiving gifts. Had the society asked them what the Prophet *(May peace be upon him)* asked al-Lutbiyyah, the menace of public sector fraud in this direction would have been reduced.

Removal of Unnecessary Administrative Bureaucracies

Umar bn Abdul-Aziz equally controlled public sector fraud through his removal of many administrative bureaucracies. This he was able to achieve by adopting the system of his grandfather and the second *Khalifah* of the *Ummah.* It was his practice to move around the city to confirm the feelings of the people in his administration and to confirm their immediate needs. Through this, he was able to ascertain the level of compliance of his officials to his directives and to check that the approved projects were executed as budgeted. This made his officials be on their toes because they were aware that *Khalifah* could visit their domain anytime unannounced. He was equally known for his promptness and punctuality. He was noted for completing all the daily work without procrastination. Since he was known for this attitude, it was easier for the people to contact him for any delay from his officials. In addition to this, Umar bn Abdul-Aziz opened up channels of communication between his governors and the citizens in such a way that citizens had free access to the governors and the *khalifah* himself. Through these channels, he ordered his governors to be vigilant and listen to what the citizens were saying. Allowing this accessibility and openness was aimed at stopping oppression and afforded them the opportunity to demand their need.

Punishment of Fraudulent Officials

As human and kind as *Khalifah* Umar bn Abdul-Aziz were to his subjects, he was tough on any case that involved the misappropriation of public funds. It was on record that Umar bn Abdul-Aziz upon his enthronement as the *Khalifah* of the Muslim *Ummah*, released all the political prisoners except those involved in financial misappropriation. He implemented measures to prevent the circulation of counterfeit money because of its adverse effects on the economy. It was reported that a person was brought to his court on the allegation of the production of counterfeit money. He flogged the man and ordered him to be imprisoned. Similarly, it was said that he issued a warrant of arrest for the governor of Khorasan, Yazid bn Abdul-Malik over the public fund bequeathed to him by his brother Sulyman bn Abdul-Malik. Despite the fact that Yazid was a close associate of the *Khalifah*, he ordered his imprisonment saying to him that he could not overlook the rights of the Muslims. This is to show that Umar bn Abdul-Aziz was not discriminatory in his fight against public sector fraud. It could be likened to the way the Prophet *(May peace be upon him)* approached the issue of applying capital punishment in the case of theft that involved a notable figure in Al-Madinah and the people sent Zaid to the Prophet *(May peace be upon him)* to intercede on his behalf. The Prophet *(May peace be upon him)* condemned this act and submitted that such a practice was "what led to the destruction of the generations before them. When the nobles among them committed an offense, they let it go scot-free, but when the ordinary people amongst them committed an offense, they got punished." He then swore that were his daughter, Fatimah guilty of theft, he would have her hand amputated.

From all indications, it can be observed that there are clear differences between the approach adopted by Umar bn Abdul-Aziz and the ones adopted by a majority of the countries these days. For example, in Nigeria, there have been cases of granting a presidential pardon to public officers that engaged in corrupt practices and have been found guilty by the court and imprisoned accordingly. The case of the former governors of Bayelsa and Edo and of recent those of the former governors of Taraba and Plateau states are pointers to this fact. This is definitely setting a bad precedent for the fight against public sector fraud, as the people will assume that no matter the amount they embezzled, a government is coming to grant them a state pardon.

In the same vein, it must be realized that Umar bn Abdul-Aziz took the issue of performance seriously during his tenure. He was not reluctant in appointing any officials that he thought would provide better governance to the people. Likewise, he did not hesitate to terminate the appointment of any officials whose performance was below expectation even if such persons were to be his blood brother. Among the officials dismissed by *Khalifah* Umar bn Abdul-Aziz were Abdullah bn al-Ahtam from Khurasan, Yazid bn al Muhallab and Saleh bn Yazid bn Muslim from Africa, and a host of others. The royal family was not equally exempted from the hiring and firing techniques of the *Khalifah*. Some of the persons from his family that were dismissed on account of wrongdoing included Umar bn al-Walid, who was the son of *Khalifah* Walid bn Abdul Malik. Umar bn Abdul-Aziz accused Umar bn al – Walid of being an unjust leader who lacked all qualities of a good leader and that he was only appointed to the position of authority simply because he was a beloved son of his father. He dismissed Khalid bin ar-Rayyan, the chief security officer of Caliph Sulaiman bin Abdul-Malik and 'Usamah bin Zayd at-Tanukhi who was in charge of the *Kharaj* (Board of Revenue) in Egypt. He was dismissed and imprisoned for being found guilty of brutality and excessive penalization of people.

LESSONS FOR NIGERIA

Leadership by example is seriously lacking in the political and governance sector of most countries. Nigeria's political setup is marred with ethnic and religious sentiments to the extent that those who mismanage the nation's resources are being celebrated and accorded recognition in society. Tukur (1999) identifies some leadership values to have included justice and impartiality, ease and kindness, humility and modesty, moderation and asceticism, integrity, honesty, and service to the community. One doubts if one percent of Nigerian leaders possess these qualities. This, therefore, escalates the high rate of poverty and unemployment in the country despite its abundant human and natural resources. The spirit of materialism in the leadership of the country made them greedily consume the nation's resources and consequently led citizens of the country into the ocean of penury, joblessness, and all sorts of criminal tendencies (Adebayo, 2018). What can one say about a head of state of the country who looted and deposited 90 billion naira in Swiss Banks, while the citizens are languishing in abject poverty? It is amazing when one reads about some governors who are expected to use the resources of their State to better the lot of the people, but such governors ended up siphoning such resources to their foreign personal accounts. About N3.1 billion was said to have been looted by the former Governor of a State to fund two banks in the Gambia and Sierra Leone and purchase some houses in the U.K. and U.S.A.

What is unfortunate there is that the agencies set up to check this inhuman behavior have not performed up to expectation. Mohammed (2013) itemized some fraudulent cases that the instituted EFCC has not been able to bring to the book. Such included the looted N84 billion Naira that was missing at the Nigerian Ports Authority (NPA), N311 billion Naira missing at NNPC, and N400 million alleged to have been mismanaged by one Senator in the failed Hajj Operations in 2005. Nigeria is therefore expected to share the experience of Umar bn Abdul-Aziz who blocked all leakages from the nation's purse through virile, conscious, and determined leadership.

It is true that some governments attempted to retrieve the looted money of the nation from the hands of some unpatriotic leaders. For instance, the Buhari administration claimed to have made cash recoveries from his predecessor to the tune of seventy-eight billion, three hundred and twenty-five million, three hundred and fifty-four thousand, six hundred and thirty-one naira and eighty-two kobo (N78,325,354,631.82); one hundred and eighty-five million, one hundred and nineteen thousand, five hundred and eighty-four dollars, sixty-one cents ($185,119,584.61); three million, five hundred and eight thousand, three hundred and fifty-five pounds and 46 pence (3,508,355.46), and eleven thousand, two hundred and fifty Euros (11,250 Euros) (Adebayo, 2018). While this effort is commendable, the persistence of poverty, unemployment, and untold hardship of the citizens made one doubt the authenticity of the claim. Unlike the administration of Umar bn Abdul-Aziz who was able to retrieve the looted money from the public purse and used it to better the lot of his people, such resources are used on worthless projects that have no direct relevance to the need of the people in Nigeria.

Nigeria also needs to learn lessons from Umar's administration in the aspect of the elimination of sacred cows. The immunity clause in the nation's constitution is being abused by those in power to carry out their fraudulent activities with impunity. They thus use the opportunity to cheat the electorates. According to Adebayo (2018), soon after they are elected to office, they violate even simple traffic rules and shield themselves from those who voted them in. Unlike Umar II who made himself available to his subject to approach him freely, Nigerian leaders become so scarce that one needs to spend months before being opportune to see them.

Another aspect where Nigerians need to borrow a leaf from the administration of Umar II is in the aspect of prompt payment and increment of salary of workers to guard them against fraud. In Nigeria, there are instances where some State governors had to slash the monthly wages of their workers, whereas their monthly own huge emolument and allowances are on the increase. While those in power looted public funds, they resorted to the poor masses for taxes of different magnitudes all in the name of looking inward to internally generated revenues to substitute for shortfalls in oil prices. In addition, the cost of governance is outrageous at the expense of the poor masses. A one-time Governor of the Central Bank of Nigeria, Sanusi Lamido Sanusi raised an alarm on the rate at which the salaries of members of the

National Assemblies namely the Senators and members of the National House of Representatives drain the purse of the nation. According to him, it gulped 25% of the nation's federal budget. Nwabugo (2016) also submitted that the nation is spending more on annual salaries, allowances, and other emoluments of the lawmakers than what lawmakers in the United States of America, and the United Kingdom earn. He concluded that it would take a common Nigerian public worker 1,638 years to collect the annual salary of a Senator. This development perhaps led to the lamentation of Adebayo (2018) thus:

"It is disheartening that most of the states which owe several months' salaries to their workers and several years of pensions to their retired workers could design fantastic salaries for their ex-governors who served for just four or eight years in addition to other take-home gifts. Most of such ex-governors are still serving at the Senate or House of Representative levels and they still enjoy all the benefits of serving officers. In such a case, the wealth of the nation is being unjustly diverted to the purse of the leaders to the detriment of the workers and the provision of essential amenities for the populace."

CONCLUSION

The tenure of Umar bn Abdul-Aziz is a turning point in the history of Muslim leadership and so a model for contemporary leadership especially in the area of checking the menace of public fund fraud. Apart from creating a conducive atmosphere for people to cherish the dignity of labor, Umar II blocked all possible means through which fraudulent activities could thrive. If the Umayyads could produce such an excellent leader during such a period when all hope of practical Islamic leadership seemed to have been lost, then one rests assured that fraud can be a thing of the past courtesy of good leadership as demonstrated by Umar II. As such, governance is expected to be people-oriented rather than leaders' oriented. From all indications, Nigeria has the potential of reducing the high rate of poverty if its resources are guarded against fraudulence, as this is a bane to a prosperous economy and healthy living in the country.

DECLARATION

The authors declare that the manuscript follows ethical standards and there are no potential conflicts of interest with respect to the research, authorship and/or publication of this chapter.

DISCLAIMER

The contents and views of this chapter are expressed by the authors in personal capacities. It is not necessary for the Editor and the Publisher to agree with these viewpoints, and they are not responsible for any duty of care in this regard.

ACKNOWLEDGMENT

The authors extend sincere gratitude to

- The Editor and the International Editorial Advisory Board (IEAB) of this book who initially desk reviewed, arranged a rigorous double/triple blind review process, and conducted a thorough, minute, and critical final review before accepting the chapter for publication.
- All anonymous reviewers who provided very constructive feedbacks for thorough revision, improvement, extension, and fine tuning of the chapter.
- All colleagues, assistants and well-wishers who assisted to complete this task.

REFERENCES

Adebayo, R. I. (2018). The change agenda of *Úmar Bn Ábdul-Áziz* as a model for fighting corruption in Nigeria. *Journal of Islam in Nigeria*, *3*(1), 106–120.

Adebisi, J. F., & Gbegi, D. O. (2015). Fraud and the Nigerian public sector performance: The need for forensic accounting. *International Journal of Business. Human Technology*, *5*(5), 67–78.

As-Sallabi, A. M. (2011). The rightly-guided caliph and great reviver, 'Umar bin 'Abd al-'Aziz: Indicators of renewal and guided reformation on the prophetic path. Riyadh: Darussalam.

Kingsley, K. M. (2015). Fraud and corruption practices in public sector: The Cameroon experience. *Research Journal of Finance and Accounting*, *6*(4), 203–209.

KPMG. (2022). *Fraud Barometer 2021: A snapshot of Fraud in UK*. KPMG. https://kpmg.com/dp/en/home/insights/2022/03/fraud-barometer-annual-report-2021.html

Matthew, R. E., Barnabas, O., Isola, L. A., & Joseph, I. O. (2013). Analysis of corruption and economic growth in Nigeria. *Afro Asian Journal of Social Sciences*, *4*(4.2), 1–19.

Mohammed, U. (2013). Corruption in Nigeria: A Challenge to Sustainable Development in the Fourth Republic. *European Scientific Journal*, *9*(4), 118–137.

Nor, R. M. (2015). Success factors for *Baitulmal* management during the reign of *Khalifah* Umar bn Abdulaziz. *Open Journal of Social Sciences*, *3*(5), 90–94. doi:10.4236/jss.2015.35013

Nor, R. M. (2019). The era of Umar bn AbdulAziz's reign: The hiring and dismissal complex system in government officials. *Malaysian Journal of Social Sciences and Humanities*, *4*(3), 140–146.

Nwabugo, O. (2016). Latest outrageous salaries of top Nigerian politicians revealed. *Buzz Nigeria*. http://buzznigeria.com

Onuora, J. K. J., Akpoveta, E. B., & Agbomah, D. J. (2018). Public sector fraud in Nigeria. *Accounting and Taxation Review*, *2*(4), 125–135.

Rahim, A. (1983). *Islamic History*. Islamic Publications Bureau.

Tahir, I. N. (2020). Poverty alleviation strategies implemented by Umar bn Abd Al Aziz: Lessons for Muslim economists on achieving SDG of poverty alleviation. *International Journal of Economics Management and Accounting*, *28*(2), 483–515.

Treisman, D. (2000). The causes of corruption: A cross-national study. *Journal of Public Economics, 76*(3), 399–457. doi:10.1016/S0047-2727(99)00092-4

Tukur, M. (1999). *Leadership and governance in Nigeria: The Relevance of values*. HudaHuda/Hodder and Stoughton.

UNODC. (2019). *Corruption in Nigeria: Patterns and Trends (Second survey on corruption as experienced by the population.* www.unodc.org

World Bank. (2022). *Nigeria Public Finance Review: Fiscal Adjustment for Better Sustainable Results* (Report No. AUS0002571). Washington, D.C.: World Bank Group. https://documents.worldbank.org/curated/en/099615211172222358/P1750950fbd29d02008429007d1ed499d61

Yusuf, S. A. (2023). *Living in the eye of the storm: What options for Nigeria.* An Inaugural Lecture delivered at the University of Ibadan.

ENDNOTES

1 www.transparency.org
2 www.transparency.org
3 www.scamwatch.gov.au
4 www.vanguardngr.com
5 www.premiumtimesng.com).
6 www.punchng.com
7 www.vanguardngr.com

Chapter 15
The Impact of Corruption on Tax Revenue:
The Case of Türkiye

Nagihan Özkanca Andıç
https://orcid.org/0000-0003-4028-264X
Pamukkale University, Turkey

ABSTRACT

In today's interconnected world, corruption is on the rise, bringing about harmful consequences such as the widespread evasion of taxes, irregular exemptions, and a weakened tax administration. These issues collectively contribute to a decline in tax revenues, affecting both developed and underdeveloped nations. Corruption takes various forms, but corruption involving public employees is particularly destructive, as it not only results in a loss of tax revenue but also gives rise to other social problems. This research aims to investigate the relationship between different types of taxes and corruption, aiming to determine which taxes are more vulnerable to corrupt practices. To achieve this, the study presents a conceptual framework and explores the causes and effects of corruption before conducting a regression analysis to assess its impact on tax revenues in Türkiye.

INTRODUCTION

Since corruption is a social phenomenon, many disciplines in history have addressed and evaluated its causes and consequences and given it importance. In this context, corruption has been studied by many disciplines, from politics to public administration, sociology to anthropology, and economics to law. Each branch of science has defined corruption within its scope. The common aspect of these definitions can be stated as the existence of interest and the fact that people use the power of their position to gain that advantage. In economics, many definitions of corruption can be found in the literature, with the World Bank definition accepted. Corruption is "*the malicious use of public power and resources for personal gain and purposes.*" The reason for the sensitivity to corruption in public finance lies in the enormous

DOI: 10.4018/979-8-3693-1190-5.ch015

advantages that corrupt individuals or institutions can gain. Both direct and indirect financial benefits can be obtained in this area. Individuals can earn directly by paying less taxes or avoiding taxes and indirectly by gaining competitive advantages over foreign investors in the country. On the other hand, widespread corruption among officials can lead to the deterioration and complexity of tax systems and the introduction of special practices that create more opportunities for corruption. Studies on corruption show that corruption has significant economic and social costs. The most cited harm of corruption is that it discourages investors, thus negatively affecting the country's investment, growth, and development (Rafay, 2021). Corruption also negatively affects allocative efficiency and the use of resources. Corrupt government officials prefer to channel investment into large projects where corruption is more difficult to detect. As corruption increases, the waste of resources in the public sector increases budget deficits, which are the source of many economic problems, from inflation to high-interest rates. In the presence of corruption, both the composition of public spending changes and public revenues, especially tax revenues, decrease. This situation significantly impacts the level and composition of public spending, especially on the public financial balance, and reduces the tax system's efficiency. This is because corruption manifests itself in tax avoidance, tax evasion, and illegal tax exemption, resulting in a tax loss for the state. This disrupts the supply of goods and services in the public sector, makes public services incomplete and inefficient, triggers excessive consumption of resources, and results in lower-than-expected realization rates of estimated public revenues. Studies conducted to examine the relationship between public finance and corruption emphasize that the ability of the state to implement effective public financial management is extremely low in countries where corruption is widespread (Nikolov, 2021). Corruption, a covert act by nature, negatively affects macroeconomic factors such as investment, growth, and income distribution in economies. Therefore, the state, whose main purpose is to serve society, has important responsibilities in fighting corruption. The state should perform these tasks at the national and international levels in cooperation with institutions. At the same time, trust in the state should be strengthened by involving the public. With the disappearance of borders between countries due to globalization, corruption is now becoming an international problem. The effects of corruption at the local level are spreading to other countries with the increasing mobility of capital and labour, and the fight against corruption is being taken to an international platform. At this point, supranational associations such as the OECD, the United Nations, and the European Union are trying to fight corruption with projects and studies (Rafay, 2023a). However, since measuring the extent of corruption is impossible, reports and surveys are prepared to fully determine this perception. As a result of these reports and surveys, it becomes possible to perceive the extent of corruption. At this point, the "Corruption Perceptions Index" developed by Transparency International is of interest. According to this index, countries are assigned a value between 0 and 1, and it can be said that in countries with a value of 0, there is no corruption, and in countries with a value of 1, there is corruption. In this study, the concept of corruption is defined, and the causes and effects of corruption are shown. Then, the effect of corruption on tax revenues in Türkiye is evaluated with regression analysis, and the results are evaluated.

THE CONCEPT OF CORRUPTION

Corruption comes from the Latin word "corrumpere," meaning "to destroy, break, hurt"; it corresponds to "corruption" in English and "korroptus" in German. While poverty in the narrow sense is defined as immoral, illegal, and unlawful, the definition of poverty in the broader sense can vary depending on the structure, culture, and socioeconomic dynamics of the place where the definition is made (Gedikli, 2011).

The first definitions of the concept of corruption associated with the history of states can be found in the work of Kau-tiliya called Arthashastra in India in the fourth century BC. Kautiliya stated that it could not be determined whether officials used part of the king's income for themselves and that there were forty diverse types of embezzlement (Bardhan, 1997). According to McMullan (1961), a corrupt official abuse the public power gained in performing his duty or demands gifts of material value without good reason to fulfil his neglected duty. According to Nye (1967), it is defined as a behaviour in which the public sector moves away from its main duty because of private interests such as wealth and the desire for office. According to Huntington (1968), corruption is the abuse or non-exercise of power by public officials to obtain personal benefits. According to Bayley (1989), some outcomes, such as seeking personal benefits and especially bribery, are directly related. On the other hand, Shleifer and Vishny (1993) define corruption as the sale of government property or the abuse of power by public officials for personal gain (McMullan, 1961, Nye 1967, Huntington, 1968, Bailey, 1966, Shleifer & Vishny, 1993).

A clear definition of corruption could not be found in the literature. However, in its broadest sense, corruption is described as "*the abuse of public power for private ends*" (Gray & Kaufman, 1998, Tanzi, 1998). The concept of corruption, in its simplest form, is the poor and unlawful use of the functions entrusted to them by public officials to make a profit. Although this definition explains the concept of corruption in general, it does not contain value judgments accepted by all. Accepting the concept of corruption by all is possible when the value judgments of all societies are brought to a common denominator (Tosun, 2001).

Since countries have different social and cultural structures, the concept of corruption has a different meaning for each country. Corruption arises from the use of the results of production-related activities conducted by public and private sector institutions for the benefit of society as a whole and in the interests of individuals. Corruption is higher in closed economies than in open countries (Olken & Pande 2012).

The Transparency International Organization, on the other hand, considers corruption to be one of the biggest problems facing the modern world and defines it as a structure that deforms the functioning of societies and destroys the cultural and economic structures of societies. The Transparency International Organization states that corruption erodes public policy, causes the inefficient distribution of resources, further impoverishes people experiencing poverty, and, as a result, has repercussions that can topple the government (Amundsen, 1999).

Corruption was not taken seriously by international organizations such as the World Bank, etc., and they considered corruption as their own internal and political problem (Rafay, 2023b). However, due to increasing criticism, the problem of corruption has become a phenomenon that cannot be ignored. The World Bank has developed detailed and broad-based policies to curb corruption. These policies have four dimensions:

- Preventing fraud and corruption in World Bank projects,
- Clarifying a problem related to corruption in the organization,
- Making international efforts to reduce corruption,
- Assisting applicant countries in fighting corruption (Special Report on Corruption and Development Assistance).

Corruption was first discussed when the IMF and the World Bank met in 1996. Solving a political disease like corruption moved to the forefront of national and international development, and the anti-corruption agenda took shape. Since then, it has been known that the World Bank has conducted investigations in many countries and allocated an annual budget for these investigations. In addition, the World Bank stated that it has hundreds of programs created specifically to fight corruption and that an investigation department with more than fifty staff members was created to fight corruption (Wanless, 2013).

The elements that reveal corruption, defined as the abuse of a public office, involve the private and public sectors. However, the widespread opinion in society is that corruption affects the public sector. Since problems related to corruption are more frequent in the public sector, the problem of the cost of corruption to the public economy arises in this case. According to the public economy, restricted economic activities due to state intervention are the main cause of corruption. The causes of corruption are illustrated by Klitgaard (1998) using a simple model.

CORRUPTION (C) = MONOPOLITARY STRUCTURES (M) + DECISION-MAKING (D) -ACCOUNTABILITY (A)

According to Klitgaard (1998), the fact that officials who have the freedom to make decisions on their own do not face the risk of accountability and have monopoly power in the use of resources leads them to try to maximize their interests after a certain period, in other words, corruption. The extent of corruption is determined by accountability, decision-making power, and monopoly power. Although corruption occurs to a greater or lesser extent in all countries, it can be said that it is more evident in societies with a paternalistic structure, where monopoly and decision-making power in the public sector are concentrated on one hand. It can also be said that corruption decreases as the level of accountability and control increases.

Corruption can be divided into political corruption and bureaucratic corruption. Political corruption can be defined as bribes paid for policymaking or contracts involving policymakers to protect their interests. On the other hand, bureaucratic and judicial corruption results from the day-to-day interactions of bureaucrats or judicial officials responsible for implementing existing policies with citizens. The most common forms of corruption include bribery, fraud, embezzlement, and nepotism (Nakitende *et al.*, 2021). Considering that the corrupt behaviour of officials affects the cost structure of businesses and households, economists have long analyzed how corruption affects economic performance, arguing that corruption affects the growth rate (Swaleheen, 2011).

The phenomenon of corruption can occur in all economic systems and directly affects all layers of society, all living beings, and every situation experienced (Balachandrudu, 2006). If there is corruption in a country, it has no transformative effect because the system chosen is capitalism or communism. However, this problem should be studied and addressed, considering the historical and cultural structures of the countries because each country has different structural characteristics.

CAUSES OF CORRUPTION

Since the main basis of corruption is the availability of rents, researchers agree that corruption is likely to occur where restrictions exist. It turns out that government intervention is among the important reasons for the emergence of excessive profits from pensions. If we look at examples in this area, we can see that they include trade restrictions (such as tariffs and import quotas), preferential industrial policies (such as government allocations and tax cuts), price controls, floating exchange rates and foreign exchange allocation programs, and government-controlled credit facilities. (Mauro, 1998).

One of the internal and most important causes of corruption is the bribes paid by foreign companies and their consequences. It can be seen that OECD member countries, with external support, are trying to implement anti-bribery laws intensively. This is because international organizations prefer not to assist until they see that corruption has been contained (World Bank, 1997).

Corruption is an overly broad issue that affects its interlocutors on a global scale. Various international organizations have conducted numerous studies showing the effects and dimensions of corruption. These studies have identified three main causes of corruption: administrative, economic, and social.

Administrative Reasons

Administrative reasons are the problems that occur in public administration and the negative effects caused by them. We can list these reasons as problems arising from bureaucratic processes, problems arising from legal regulations and permits, employment and wage problems in the public sector, problems with the transparency of laws, a lack of accountability mechanisms, problems related to taxation, and a low probability of being audited and punished.

Corruption is more prevalent in developing countries. The reason why there is more corruption in these countries is not that people are more susceptible to corruption but that there is a structure that lends itself to corruption. It is also known that social security options are limited in these countries, which do not have a developed labour market. People suffer from poverty, and laws and resources are inadequate. In addition, public employees receive low wages, and political freedoms are limited. In a system where all these factors are present, the legal institutions and the administration undoubtedly fail to realize this complex relationship (Gray & Kaufman, 1998). As the presence of the state in economic life increases, the bureaucracy will inevitably grow. It is believed that the growing bureaucracy and public administrations that have not completed their institutional structures, especially in underdeveloped and developing countries, are prone to corruption. It is believed that the quality of bureaucracy should be increased by legal sanctions against corruption to prevent corruption from increasing and becoming commonplace after some time.

Economic Reasons

In developing countries, many tasks fall to the state to meet the demands of the growing service network with the increased expectations of the public. However, the inadequacy of scarce resources prevents the fulfilment of these requirements, and the state cannot meet all expectations. Therefore, the division of public services enables corruption. The economic determinants of corruption consist of many different economic variables (Iliman & Tekeli, 2016). As economic factors that cause corruption, we can list the rate of increase of inflation, the share of the state in the economy, the existence of the shadow economy, and the inequitable distribution of income. For example, the decrease in the purchasing power of individuals due to high inflation increases the tendency to corruption, or it is believed that officials who are employed with low wages prefer corruption because they are less likely to be caught when confronted with a bribe that they cannot refuse.

Social Reasons

It can be concluded that the most important reason for corruption is social. The lack of awareness in society and education simultaneously creates the basis for corruption. In this sense, problems such as unplanned urbanization, a high population growth rate, and the inadequacy of non-governmental organizations can be mentioned as social reasons.

From the social point of view, the individual is the basis for the emergence of corruption. Characteristics such as dissatisfaction arising from the nature of the individual are crucial factors in the emergence of corruption. In particular, the individuals' efforts to eliminate their material dissatisfaction and the behaviors they adopt to get increasingly may lead them to perform actions that are outside the bounds of moral values, such as corruption (Sayan & Kışlalı, 2004). At the same time, cultural level and educational level are other factors that draw attention to the increase of individuals' tendency to corruption. From the social point of view, other crucial factors that increase corruption are increasing urbanization due to population growth and migration. Especially due to the increasing urbanization due to migration and the inadequacy of the services provided by the public administration, individuals who benefit from these limited services will become rich in the future and will become prominent in political processes. Politicians try to give these individuals more benefits to win votes (Kongar, 2005).

TYPES OF CORRUPTION

Corruption can occur in many different forms and types. While the types of corruption in the narrow sense can be listed as bribery, embezzlement, and nepotism, we can refer to corruption in the broader sense as extortion, favouritism, patronage, vote trading, lobbying, rent-seeking, profiteering, and manipulation (Aktan, 2001).

Corruption activities can be divided into various categories and can take different forms. These are.

- Bureaucratic corruption by the bureaucracy and political corruption by the political leadership,
- Reducing costs (for the briber) or increasing benefits,
- Inducing or accepting bribes,
- Enforced bribery or collaborative bribery,
- Central or local corruption,
- Foreseeable or arbitrary corruption,
- Corruption with or without money (Tanzi, 1998:9).

From a general theoretical point of view, corruption can be defined in three basic ways. The first is corruption used by natural and legal persons to obtain special financial opportunities and expedite transactions. For example, a person with the right to obtain a passport may obtain it by bribing an official to conduct his business more quickly. The second type of corruption is administrative corruption, in which legal regulations are violated, and the regulations are applied unilaterally. Most of the corruption in the theoretical field falls within the scope of administrative corruption. This type of corruption corresponds to the principal-agent model of corruption. The third type of corruption is corruption which takes over the state and aims to change the rules and regulations in Favor of the corrupt individuals. In this type of corruption, described by the World Bank, it is found that legislation and public policies are shaped not for the people but for the benefit of a few oligarchs, especially immensely powerful businesspeople (Boris, 2005).

EFFECTS OF CORRUPTION

If one examines the literature, one finds that there are two views on the effects of corruption. The group of those who believe that corruption has a positive impact on the economy defines it as "oil the gears," while the group that argues that it is negative calls it "sand in the gears" (Wei, 2000). Within these discussions, it is assumed that corruption is due to the inefficiency of public administration and that the bureaucracy has a cumbersome structure (Méon & Sekkat, 2005; Ünlü & Ulusoy, 2021)). This positive perception of corruption, which lasted until the 1900s, claims that the bureaucracy pursues policies that discourage investment, that corruption provides flexibility in the economic sphere, and that it positively affects growth.

According to the oil-the-wheels view, bribery is expressed as speeding up transactions in public services; "it is assumed that the person who gives the highest amount of bribe is the one who values the good or service in question and the time the most, and that person's work will be solved faster. It is also claimed that, with corruption, the process of supply and demand is effective and fast, and it helps to allocate resources effectively. In addition, there are opinions that officials who receive bribes work harder and remove bureaucratic obstacles, which increases investment. Shleifer and Vishny, looking at this issue from different angles, stated that "*the structures of public institutions and political processes effectively determine the extent of corruption; weak governments that cannot control public institutions will cause high levels of corruption; the more bribes collected, the greater the need for concealment, which is detrimental to economic growth; but coordinated bribes would be less harmful*" (Shleifer & Vishny, 1993).

Another viewpoint on the positive impact of corruption on the economy is that bribe payers are more efficient and effective, thereby increasing the economy's productivity since bribes paid to obtain a public contract represent additional costs for bribe payers. It has been argued that although the marginal propensity to consume of the bribe recipient is low compared to the bribe giver, corruption can increase investment due to the high propensity to invest (Bailey, 1966).

Corruption is an act against the law. When the degeneration caused by corruption leads to corruption in public administration, the legitimacy of administration disappears and governance, the common denominator of administration and communication, suffers. In this way, the legitimacy problem in public administration arises due to corruption. Moreover, it is believed that civil servants who are not involved in corruption, adopt ethical behaviour as a principle, and are among the authorized persons in public administration are lost in this vortex as part of this corruption spiral.

However, in recent studies, opinions have emerged about the negative impact of corruption on economic development and growth, and it has been described as negative by all researchers. Today, the impact of corruption is addressed under four main headings: political, economic, social, and environmental. Regarding political impact, corruption is a major obstacle to democracy and the rule of law. When institutions and organizations in democratic systems abuse their special advantages, they lose their legitimacy. From an economic perspective, corruption causes the erosion of national prosperity. Environmental degradation is another major impact that corruption has just revealed. From a social perspective, reliance on the rules of the law has a shocking effect and makes it difficult to maintain social equilibrium.

Corruption reduces economic growth by reducing foreign direct investment, causing inequality and poverty in the distribution of income, distorting the distribution of labour, causing negative value-added, and distorting the distribution of resources and income. Corruption causes budget deficits, reduces the efficiency of public spending, reduces investment, and negatively affects growth. Corruption reduces investment and tax revenues, limits economic growth, and lowers the quality of public services. Corruption also leads to a decline in tax and non-tax revenues and an increase in borrowing. In countries with high levels of corruption, the share of taxes collected in GDP is lower (Beşel, 2013; Beebejaun *et al.*, 2023).

With corruption, countries' economic growth decreases, public sector efficiency decreases, income inequality increases, and the composition of government spending deteriorates. With many similar effects, public trust in the state is diminished. Moreover, corruption harms countries in many ways—financially, economically, and socially. Countries fighting corruption should primarily try to find solutions that correspond to their structural situation. In this context, it is necessary to make the fight against corruption more effective by taking measures such as ensuring good interaction of citizens with their governments, reducing excessive bureaucratic procedures, ensuring proper distribution of public incentives, introducing legal regulations with high enforcement powers, best protecting people/organizations fighting corruption, and improving salaries and the working environment of public employees. In addition to these internal solutions, countries fighting corruption should try to find external solutions by cooperating with international organizations.

THE RELATIONSHIP BETWEEN CORRUPTION AND TAX REVENUE

One of the most important costs of corruption to economic life is decreased tax revenues. The fact that these revenues, which are the main source of public spending, are decreasing due to corruption also changes the course of expenditures made by the public sector. The lack of sufficient financial resources for spending hinders the public investments that need to be made. As a result of the deterioration of the public expenditure regime, the decline in social welfare comes to the fore. As a result of these negative effects of corruption, the efficiency and diversity of goods and services provided by the public sector also decline. This decline also negatively pressures individuals (Bağdigen & Tuncer, 2004).

The impact of corruption on taxes can be addressed from two points of view: The first is the reduction in the elasticity of public revenues. Since taxes are the main source of income, the decrease in tax revenues because of corruption will increase the other source of income, borrowing, and thus decrease the income elasticity. Second, it leads to inequality in taxes. Taxes are increased to compensate for the decrease in tax revenues due to corruption, in which case taxpayers must pay more taxes. For this reason, imposing, accruing, and collecting taxes is one of the areas most affected by corruption in the public sector. This situation increases tax leakage and tax evasion due to corruption in tax administration and affects the state's tax revenue. In addition to tax revenues, a decrease in fees, goodwill, fiscal revenues, real estate, and corporate revenues occurs, while an increase in borrowing in the case of corruption in non-tax revenues occurs.

Corruption circumvents fiscal (revenue generation) and non-fiscal (income redistribution, environmental protection, etc.) taxation purposes and reduces tax revenues. Reductions in infrastructure services, transfer payments, higher borrowing, or taxation can offset revenue losses from corruption-related tax shortfalls. These options lead to growing budget deficits, significant resource shifts, and negative effects on employment and economic growth (Edling, 2007).

Corruption reduces tax revenues and limits the government's other financing options, including borrowing. This is because spending on debt service alters the priority of another spending, reducing future fiscal flexibility. This creates a vicious cycle and jeopardizes fiscal sustainability. Corruption paves the way for more corruption. Honest taxpayers face lower profit margins if they do not evade taxes. The impact of corruption on tax officials is also significant. Weakening the will of honest tax officials increases the number of corrupt officials and reduces the sense of guilt. Corruption also affects the quality of administration. This is because the authorities act for their interests, not the public. The efficiency of the administration is low because it can occur in the untalented, in tax evasion, and in the informal economy with clientelism and nepotism. At the same time, the tax structure can also promote corruption.

The negative impact of corruption on taxation can be evaluated from two perspectives. Taxes are the main source of revenue for public finances. Corruption and declining tax revenues force the public sector to borrow. As a result, income elasticity will decrease. Another effect of corruption is that it negatively impacts the tax structure. Lower tax revenues due to corruption lead to additional taxes or an increase in tax rates and create additional pressure on taxpayers who pay their taxes regularly (Asher, 2001). Many studies in the literature have found that corruption caused by the tax structure both reduces tax revenues and creates inequity in the distribution of the tax burden. The general result of these studies is that corruption erodes the tax base and reduces the efficiency of public spending by causing budget deficits (Giray, 2005).

Corruption has negative effects, such as a decrease in tax revenues, the inability to achieve a balanced budget, and changes in public spending, as well as negative effects on inefficient economic decisions and misallocating existing resources (Shimpalee & Breuer, 2006). This situation significantly impacts the level and composition of public spending, especially the public fiscal balance. It reduces the tax system's efficiency by causing tax losses to the state through tax avoidance, tax evasion, and illegal tax exemption. This situation disrupts the public sector's supply of goods and services, makes public services incomplete and inefficient, triggers excessive resource consumption, and results in lower-than-expected realization rates of estimated public revenues.

Corruption is more prevalent where there are institutional inefficiencies such as political instability, bureaucratic difficulties, and weak legislative and judicial systems. Indeed, this raises the question of whether the judgment that other factors, rather than corruption, cause low economic growth will prevail. Regression analyses provide some insights in this regard. However, even if political instability and other factors caused by similar institutional inefficiencies can be controlled, corruption is still shown to impact growth (Mauro, 1998).

Corruption has the effect of reducing public revenues and increasing expenditures. Governments are believed to face large budget deficits due to corruption and cannot use fiscal instruments effectively. According to the Asian Development Bank, corruption increases the cost of public goods and services produced by the state by 20-100%, burdens the state with up to 50% of tax revenues, and further increases the country's external debt (Giray, 2005). Therefore, the measures taken to reduce corruption, widely believed to increase tax evasion, were expected to increase tax revenues significantly.

When the dimensions of corruption in Türkiye are examined, it is stated that the cost to the country's economy is approximately four billion dollars. In addition, the fact that Türkiye ranks 101st in the 2022 corruption perception index makes us think that it has failed in the fight against corruption (Euronews, 2023). When we look at corruption from a tax perspective, it is determined that 53.9% of taxpayers try to evade taxes. In this case, governments prefer to collect taxes not on income but on expenditures, and the share of indirect taxes in GDP increases. The fact that the share of indirect taxes in tax revenues is quite high is a situation that increases income inequality. For this reason, it is thought that preventing tax evasion (Rashid & Morshed, 2021) will reduce corruption and reduce income inequality significantly.

ANALYSIS OF THE EFFECT OF CORRUPTION ON TAX REVENUES

Literature Review

Some basic studies in the literature show and measure the impact of corruption on tax revenues, and the results of these studies are as follows:

Ghura (1998) analyzed 39 African countries between 1985 and 1996 to determine how economic policies and levels of corruption affect tax revenues and GDP rates. According to the analysis, the increase in corruption rates reduces the ratio of tax revenues to GDP in the African countries studied.

In a study by Tanzi (1998), it was found that corruption affects tax revenues and has a negative impact on investment. At the same time, it has been shown that GDP, wage variables, and rising public costs lead to budget deficits and reduce the welfare level of individuals. It was found that transparent taxation and structural reforms in taxation can reduce the destructive effects of corruption.

Tanzi and Davoodi (2000) showed the impact of corruption levels on tax and non-tax revenues by analysing about ninety-seven countries between 1980 and 1997. It was concluded that corruption affects total government tax revenues, with a more negative impact on direct taxes than indirect taxes, which are included in total tax revenues.

Rivera-Batiz (2001) concluded in their study that the increase in corruption negatively affected the countries' return on investment and technological progress and decreased the inflow of capital.

Gupta, Davoodi, and Alonso-Terme (2002) examined the impact of corruption on income distribution and poverty and found that corruption negatively affects human capital by disrupting income and wealth distribution and equal opportunity in education.

Fisman and Svensson (2002) sought to analyze the relationship between bribes, taxation, and the growth rate of firms in various sectors in Uganda between 1995-1997. The results of the analysis show that both taxation and corruption rates have a negative impact on the growth rate of the firm. Moreover, it was also found that the negative impact of corruption on the business growth rate will lead to an erosion of the government's total tax revenue in the coming years.

Acconcia, D'Amato & Martina (2003) examined the behaviour of those responsible for overseeing corruption in a simple economic model in which self-interested taxpayers may have incentives to evade taxes and avoid sanctions by bribing officials. It was concluded that tax avoidance and evasion increase in countries where corruption is accepted.

Bağdigen and Beşkaya (2005), in their regression analysis examining the impact of corruption on public revenues for the period 1980–2001 in Türkiye, concluded that high levels of corruption would reduce tax revenues, especially direct tax revenues.

Imam and Jacobs (2007) analyzed twelve countries in the Middle East and explained the relationship between tax revenues and corruption between 1990-2003. The analysis showed that corruption affects commercial and individual taxes more than others. Tax revenues increase if corruption can be reduced, especially in commercial and special excise taxes. Another conclusion was that governments that need to increase tax revenues can do so by minimizing corruption and maximizing social welfare.

Braşoveanu and Obreja Brasoveanu (2009) analyzed the relationship between corruption and the general tax burden in 27 European countries between 1995 and 2008 using the correlation method.

Oral and Sayın (2009) conducted a model test and analysis of the relationship between corruption and the tax system in Türkiye. Using the data from 1985-2007 in Türkiye, they found a short-run and long-run relationship between corruption variables, tax burden, tax revenue from the general budget, the share of direct and indirect taxes in GDP, and the audit rate.

Cerqueti and Coppier (2011) developed a Ramsey economic growth model with a competing but not excluded public good financed by taxes that corrupt tax auditors can avoid. They argued that the relationship between tax rate and tax collection is not unique in a dynamic framework but that the "shame effect" varies depending on the degree of relevance. They concluded that countries with high corruption rates have low growth rates and lower tax revenues.

Bakırtaş (2012) analyzed the relationship between tax revenues and corruption using the method of regression analysis based on the data of the Corruption Perception Index (CPI) published annually by Transparency International for the period 1996–2010 in Türkiye and the realized tax revenues from CBRT funds during this period and significantly concluded that corruption reduces tax revenues. Furthermore, they came to the significant conclusion that corruption reduces tax revenues.

Aghion *et al.* (2016) built an endogenous growth model to analyze the relationships between taxation, corruption, and economic growth, and the model found an inverted U relationship between taxation and growth. It was concluded that corruption reduces optimal taxation.

Jahnke and Weisser (2019) claimed in their study in sub-Saharan countries that corruption affects tax morale and reduces trust in tax authorities, thus indirectly affecting tax morale.

These studies have shown that corruption has an impact on tax revenues. It has been shown to have a negative impact on investment. At the same time, GDP, wage variables, and rising public costs cause budget deficits and reduce the welfare level of citizens. It was found that transparent taxation and structural reforms in taxation can reduce the destructive effects of corruption. Tax revenues as a percentage of GDP tend to decrease in countries with high corruption. This finding suggests that some of the taxes paid by taxpayers do not flow into the government's coffers or that taxes are not paid or are paid incompletely. In either case, the efficiency of tax administration decreases, the degree of proportionality in the tax system declines, and tax fairness is compromised. When governments need to increase tax revenues, minimizing corruption and maximizing social welfare is the right way. Since corruption prevents tax distribution to the base and leads to high tax revenues from a small number of taxpayers, it has been widely believed that it harms society's sense of fairness.

RESEARCH METHODOLOGY AND DATA SET

In this analysis, the data of the Corruption Perception Index (CPI) announced annually by Transparency International for the period 2012-2022 for Türkiye and the realized tax revenues from CBRT funds in this period were taken as the basis. The data obtained for the specified period were analyzed using the SPSS 22.0 (Statistical Program for Social Science) package program.

The first data set used for the analysis is the Corruption Perception Index. This index is announced annually by Transparency International on a country-by-country basis. According to this index, countries are assigned a value between 0 and 10, and it is found that corruption is higher in countries close to 0 and lower in countries close to 10. The study was based on Türkiye's corruption perceptions index data for 2012-2022.

The other dataset used in the analysis is limited to tax revenues realized in Türkiye's budget between 2012-2022. Non-tax revenues included in budget revenues are not included in this dataset.

Table 1. Corruption perceptions index data for Türkiye (2012-2022)

Years	Corruption Perceptions Index
2012	49
2013	50
2014	45
2015	42
2016	41
2017	40
2018	41
2019	39
2020	40
2021	38
2022	36

Source: Transparency International, 2023

Table 2. Central government tax revenues (2012-2022)

Years	Central Government Tax Revenues
2012	277,676,933
2013	317,948,666
2014	348,352,781
2015	407,818,455
2016	459,001,741
2017	536,617,206
2018	621,536,356
2019	673,859,718
2020	833,250,502
2021	1,164, 988,000
2022	2,185,950,000

Source: Transparency International, https://www.transparency.org/ (2023)

ANALYSIS AND FINDINGS

The data set created to measure the relationship between corruption and tax revenues was explained with a simple linear regression analysis. In the analysis, the "corruption perception index" represents the independent variable and "tax revenues" represents the dependent variable. Before starting the regression analysis in the study, a correlation analysis was conducted to check whether there was a relationship between the variables. The results of the correlation analysis in Table 3 show a statistically significant high correlation between the corruption perception index and tax revenues. In other words, corruption strongly influences the change of tax revenues in Türkiye.

Table 3. Correlation analysis

		CPI	Tax Revenues
CPI	Pearson Correlation Sig. (2-tailed) N		.714 .014 11
Tax Revenues	Pearson Correlation Sig. (2-tailed) N	714 .014 11	

The regression analysis results in Table 4 show that a 1-unit improvement in the corruption perception index corresponds to a 0.714 unit increase in tax revenues. This result can be interpreted to mean that the corruption perception index strongly impacts tax revenues. Considering the corruption variable used, this situation can be explained by the fact that the reduction of corruption in Türkiye leads to increased tax revenues.

Table 4. Regression analysis

Model	*B*	T	*p*
Constant		-2.640	0.27
CPI	.714	3.063	0.14

CONCLUSION

Corruption is one of the most important problems in both developed and developing countries. The corruption problem primarily has a staggering impact on the public financial balance of countries. It negatively affects public spending, income distribution, economic stability, and total tax revenues eventually (Güzel, 2021). Corruption manifests itself in several ways, such as bribery of public officials, misappropriation of funds entrusted to the public administration by public officials, and fraud. Corruption varies widely from country to country and even from one region to another and may be observed in various areas, including health, transportation, and education. Although corruption is a measurable concept, it is challenging to measure it because there is no single definition. It varies from culture to culture and is inherently clandestine. In general, it is noticeable that corruption is higher in developed countries than in underdeveloped countries. When Türkiye is evaluated according to Transparency International's Corruption Perception Index, the country's index scores and rankings have decreased in recent years. This indicates that the structural measures Türkiye has taken or will take in the fight against corruption should be strengthened.

Corruption is an important phenomenon affecting the economic conditions of individuals and society in both micro and macroeconomic terms. Corruption arises from the ineffective use of factors of production in the economy or the use of existing factors by authorized economic entities to further their interests. Therefore, corruption in an economy sets in motion a process that leads to a decline in growth and a worsening of income distribution. This situation, which leads to a deterioration of justice, especially in income distribution, disturbs the integrity of society and leads to the separation of social classes. Corruption affects inequality in income distribution through factors such as economic growth, a lopsided tax system, weak social programs, the negative accumulation of human capital, and inequality in education. It leads to a deterioration in the equal and equitable distribution of resources, increases public spending and reduces its efficiency, reduces human capital spending, affects taxes, increases production and transaction costs, reduces the efficiency of public institutions, lowers people's living standards, increases the shadow economy, and causes inflation (Walker-Munro, 2021). As a result, privatization activities have a negative impact on economic growth by reducing productivity. An unfair tax system negatively affects tax revenues, and because of decreasing tax revenues, it decreases public revenues by causing taxpayers to pay more taxes and borrow more.

Governments today rely on tax revenues to provide public services, and damage to this resource through corruption leads to a negative perception of society and a decline in public revenues. Failure to pay or avoid paying the amount of tax due to the use of various instruments of corruption creates discomfort in the eyes of taxpayers. Citizens who pay their taxes on time and regularly will react against the government and avoid paying their taxes on time. In addition, citizens who do not pay their taxes due to corruption will cause an increase in the government deficit. In response to corruption, non-payment of taxes, tax avoidance, or tax evasion may, at a certain point, turn into active and passive tax resistance, even a form of tax revolt.

As can be seen from the data of the Corruption Perception Index, the existence of corruption in Türkiye is an undeniable reality. The damage this situation has caused to the country's internal dynamics is obvious. From this point of view, the regression analysis method was used to investigate the impact of corruption in Türkiye on tax revenues. The results of the simple linear regression analysis show that there is a positive and strong relationship between corruption and tax revenues, and this relationship shows that corruption causes a significant decrease in total tax revenues. The results obtained in the study show parallelism with other studies in the literature. In a general assessment, the analysis confirms that corruption causes a decrease in total tax revenues and that it is possible to increase total tax revenues by reducing corruption. From this point of view, it can be concluded that measures to eliminate corruption contribute to the achievement and protection of tax discipline by increasing tax revenues.

Any corruption or irregularity is a problem, not only for Türkiye but also for the entire world. This problem must be addressed regardless of individuals, and corruption should be prevented appropriately and with absolute determination. Türkiye's growth and development are directly related to preventing corruption. A Türkiye in which corruption and irregularities approach zero can complete its growth and development in a very short time.

DECLARATION

The author declares that the manuscript follows ethical standards and there are no potential conflicts of interest with respect to the research, authorship and/or publication of this chapter.

DISCLAIMER

The contents and views of this chapter are expressed by the author in personal capacity. It is not necessary for the Editor and the Publisher to agree with these viewpoints, and they are not responsible for any duty of care in this regard.

ACKNOWLEDGMENT

The author extends sincere gratitude to

- The Editor and the International Editorial Advisory Board (IEAB) of this book, who initially desk reviewed, arranged a rigorous double/triple-blind review process, and conducted a thorough, minute, and critical final review before accepting the chapter for publication.

- All anonymous reviewers who provided very constructive feedback for thorough revision, improvement, extension, and fine-tuning of the chapter.
- All colleagues, assistants and well-wishers who assisted to complete this task.

REFERENCES

Acconcia, A., D'Amato, M., & Martina, R. (2003). *Corruption and tax evasion with competitive bribes* (Working Paper No. 112). Centre for Studies in Economics and Finance, Università degli studi di salerno.

Aghion, P., Akcigit, U., Cagé, J., & Kerr, W. R. (2016). Taxation, corruption and growth. *European Economic Review*, *86*, 24–51. doi:10.1016/j.euroecorev.2016.01.012

Aktan, C. (2001). *Siyasal Ahlak ve Siyasal Yozlaşma*, Yolsuzlukla Mücadele Stratejileri, içinde Ankara: Hak-İş Yayınları.

Amundsen, I. (1999). Political Corruption: An Introduction to the Issues. Chr. Michelsen Institute.

Asher, M. G. (2001). Design of tax systems and corruption. In *Conference on "Fighting Corruption: Common Challenges and Shared Experiences," Singapore* (pp. 10–11). Cite Seer. https://citeseerx.ist.psu.edu/document?repid=rep1&type=pdf&doi=e7b2483b1fbb522 ef88146a5fdddaf99ce702d6a .

Bagdigen, M., & Beskaya, A. (2005). The impact of corruption on government revenues: The Turkish case. *Yapi Kredi Economic Review, 16*(2), 31–54

Bagdigen, M., & Tunçer, M. (2004). Yolsuzluğun kamu gelirleri üzerine etkisi: Belediye gelirleri üzerine ampirik bir çalışma. *Vergi Dünyası*, *272*, 168–174.

Bakirtaş, D. (2012). The effect of corruption on tax revenues: The case of Türkiye. *Journal of Management and Economics*, *19*(2), 87–98.

Balachandrudu, K. (2006). Understanding political corruption. *Indian Journal of Poultry Science*, *67*(4), 809–816.

Bardhan, P. (1997). Corruption and development: A review of issues. *Journal of Economic Literature*, *35*(3), 1320–1346.

Bayley, C. (1989). *Imperial Meridian: The British Empire and the World 1780-1830*. Pearson.

Bayley, D. H. (1966). The effects of corruption in a developing nation. *The Western Political Quarterly*, *19*(4), 719–732. doi:10.1177/106591296601900410

Beebeejaun, A., Gunputh, R., & Rafay, A. (2023). Base Erosion and Profit Shifting (BEPS) in International Taxation System: The Case of Mauritius in the light of OECD/G20 initiatives. In A. Rafay (Ed.), *Concepts, Cases, and Regulations in Financial Fraud and Corruption* (pp. 259–277). IGI Global. doi:10.4018/978-1-6684-5007-9.ch011

Beşel, F. (2013). *Corruption-economic growth relationship: The case of Türkiye* [Doctoral dissertation), Sakarya University Türkiye].

Boris, B. (2005). Corruption: Concepts, types, causes, and consequences. Washington, DC: Center for International Private Enterprise (CIPE), US Chamber of Commerce.

Braşoveanu, I. V., & Obreja Brasoveanu, L. (2009). Correlation between corruption and tax revenues in EU 27. *Economic Computation and Economic Cybernetics Studies and Research*, *43*(4), 133–142.

Cerqueti, R., & Coppier, R. (2011). Economic growth, corruption and tax evasion. *Economic Modelling*, *28*(1-2), 489–500. doi:10.1016/j.econmod.2010.07.006

Edling, H. (2007). *Preventing corruption in public finance management: A practical guide*. World Bank Group.

EuroNews. (2023, January 31). *Report: The world fails to fight corruption; Türkiye, in which rank?* Euronews. (https://tr.euronews.com/2023/01/31/rapor-dunya-yolsuzlukla-mucadelede-basarisiz-turkiye-kacinci-sirada

Fisman, R., & Svensson, J. (2007). Are corruption and taxation really harmful to growth? Firm level evidence. *Journal of Development Economics*, *83*(1), 63–75. doi:10.1016/j.jdeveco.2005.09.009

Gedikli, A. (2011). Kamu hizmetlerinin yönetimi sürecinde yolsuzluğun derinleştirdiği ekonomik büyüme ve yoksulluk sorunu üzerine bir değerlendirme. *Öneri Dergisi, 9*(36), 169–188.

Ghura, M. D. (1998). *Tax revenue in Sub-Saharan Africa: Effects of economic policies and corruption* (IMF Working Paper No. WP/98/135). International Monetary Fund.

Giray, F. (2011). Yolsuzluk ve yolsuzluğun vergi yapisi üzerine etkileri. *İstanbul Üniversitesi Siyasal Bilgiler Fakültesi Dergisi, 32*, 111–137.

Gray, C. W., & Kaufmann, D. (1998). Corruption and Development. *Maliye Dergisi*, *35*(1), 128.

Gupta, S., Davoodi, H., & Alonso-Terme, R. (2002). Does corruption affect income inequality and poverty? *Economics of Governance*, *3*(1), 23–45. doi:10.1007101010100039

Güzel, S. (2021). The Role of Tax Systems in Preventing Corruption. In A. Rafay (Ed.), *Handbook of Research on Theory and Practice of Financial Crimes* (pp. 397–427). IGI Global. doi:10.4018/978-1-7998-5567-5.ch020

Huntington, S. P. (1968). *Political order in changing societies*. Yale university press.

Iliman, T., & Tekeli, R. (2016). Dünya'da ve Türkiye'de yolsuzluk algısı. *Adnan Menderes Üniversitesi Sosyal Bilimler Enstitüsü Dergisi*, *3*(2), 62–84. doi:10.30803/adusobed.287988

Imam, P. A., & Jacobs, D. (2014). Effect of corruption on tax revenues in the Middle East. *Review of Middle East Economics and Finance*, *10*(1), 1–24. doi:10.1515/rmeef-2014-0001

Jahnke, B., & Weisser, R. A. (2019). How does petty corruption affect tax morale in Sub-Saharan Africa? *European Journal of Political Economy*, *60*, 101751. doi:10.1016/j.ejpoleco.2018.09.003

Klitgaard, R. (1988). *Controlling Corruption*. University of California Press. doi:10.1525/9780520911185

Kongar, E. (2005). Kamuda Rüşvetin Toplumsal Nedenleri. *Yolsuzluk ile Savaşım Stratejileri Uluslararası Sempozyumu, 29*.

Mauro, P. (1998). Corruption: Causes, consequences, and agenda for further research. *Finance & Development*, 11–14. http://syahia.atreides.online.fr/iae/ethics/corruption.pdf

McMullan, M. (1961). A theory of corruption. *The Sociological Review*, *9*(2), 181–201. doi:10.1111/j.1467-954X.1961.tb01093.x

Méon, P. G., & Sekkat, K. (2005). Does corruption grease or sand the wheels of growth? *Public Choice*, *122*(1-2), 69–97. doi:10.100711127-005-3988-0

Nakitende, M. G., Rafay, A., & Waseem, M. (2021). Frauds in Business Organizations: A Comprehensive Overview. In A. Rafay (Ed.), *Handbook of Research on Theory and Practice of Financial Crimes* (pp. 21–38). IGI Global. doi:10.4018/978-1-7998-5567-5.ch002

Nikolov, N. (2021). Conflict of Interest for Corruption and Abuse of Public Power: The Case of European Legislation. In A. Rafay (Ed.), *Handbook of Research on Theory and Practice of Financial Crimes* (pp. 105–131). IGI Global. doi:10.4018/978-1-7998-5567-5.ch007

Nye, J. S. (1967). Corruption and political development: A cost-benefit analysis. *The American Political Science Review*, *61*(2), 417–427. doi:10.2307/1953254

Olken, B. A., & Pande, R. (2012). Corruption in developing countries. *Annual Review of Economics*, *4*(1), 479–509. doi:10.1146/annurev-economics-080511-110917

Oral, B. G., & Sayın, F. (2009). Mali yolsuzluğun yansımaları: Türkiye için eşbütünleşme analizi. *İstanbul Üniversitesi İktisat Fakültesi Maliye Araştırma Merkezi Konferansları, Prof. Dr. Şerafettin Aksoy'a Armağan, 141*, 176.

Rafay, A. (Ed.). (2021). *HandBook of Research on Theory and Practice of Financial Crimes*. IGI Global. doi:10.4018/978-1-7998-5567-5

Rafay, A. (Ed.). (2023a). *Concepts, Cases, and Regulations in Financial Fraud and Corruption*. IGI Global. doi:10.4018/978-1-6684-5007-9

Rafay, A. (Ed.). (2023b). *Concepts and Cases of Illicit Finance*. IGI Global. doi:10.4018/978-1-6684-8587-3

Rashid, M. H., & Morshed, A. (2021). Firms' Characteristics and Tax Evasion. In A. Rafay (Ed.), *Handbook of Research on Theory and Practice of Financial Crimes* (pp. 428–451). IGI Global., doi:10.4018/978-1-7998-5567-5.ch022

Rivera-Batiz, F. L. (2001). International financial liberalization, corruption, and economic growth. *Review of International Economics*, *9*(4), 727–737. doi:10.1111/1467-9396.00309

Sayan, İ. Ö., & Kışlalı, M. (2004). Yolsuzluk Üzerine Ekonometrik Bir Çalışma. *Amme Idaresi Dergisi*, *37*(2), 31–50.

Shimpalee, P. L., & Breuer, J. B. (2006). Currency crises and institutions. *Journal of International Money and Finance*, *25*(1), 125–145. doi:10.1016/j.jimonfin.2005.10.008

Shleifer, A., & Vishny, R. W. (1993). Corruption. *The Quarterly Journal of Economics*, *108*(3), 599–617. doi:10.2307/2118402

Swaleheen, M. (2011). Economic growth with endogenous corruption: An empirical study. *Public Choice*, *146*(1-2), 23–41. doi:10.100711127-009-9581-1

Tanzi, V. (1998). Corruption around the world: Causes, consequences, scope, and cures. *Staff Papers - International Monetary Fund. International Monetary Fund*, *45*(4), 559–594. doi:10.2307/3867585

Tanzi, V., & Davoodi, H. (1997). *Corruption, public investment, and growth* (IMF Working Paper, WP/97/139). International Monetary Fund.

Tanzi, V., & Davoodi, H. R. (2000). *Corruption, growth and public Finances* (IMF Working Paper, WP/00/182). International Monetary Fund.

Tosun, U. (2001). Yolsuzluğun ekonomik etkileri: Yolsuzluk ve büyüme arasındaki ilişki. *Kamu Tercihi ve Anayasal İktisat Dergisi*, *4*, 3–8.

Ünlü, H., & Ulusoy, M. K. (2021). Innovation and Corruption in Türkiye: "Grease the Wheels" or "Sand the Wheels". In A. Rafay (Ed.), *Handbook of Research on Theory and Practice of Financial Crimes* (pp. 80–103). IGI Global. doi:10.4018/978-1-7998-5567-5.ch006

Walker-Munro, B. (2021). Tax Enforcement in the Black Economy: Tackling Disruptive Challenge. In A. Rafay (Ed.), *Handbook of Research on Theory and Practice of Financial Crimes* (pp. 356–380). IGI Global. doi:10.4018/978-1-7998-5567-5.ch019

Wanless, M. (2013). The World's Bank fight against corruption: 'See nothing, hear nothing, say nothing,'. *Hydra*, *1*(2), 38–48.

Wei, S. J. (2000). *Bribery in the economies: Grease or sand?*. The Brookings Institution, Harvard University, NBER.

World Bank. (1997). *Helping countries combat corruption: The role of the World Bank* (Working Paper No. 24687). Washington, D.C.: World Bank Group. https://documents.worldbank.org/curated/en/799831538245192753/Helping-countries-combat-corruption-the-role-of-the-World-Bank

Chapter 16

Difference Between the Real and Estimated Size of a Company: A Potential Cause of Tax Evasion

Gerardo Reyes Ruiz
https://orcid.org/0000-0003-0212-2952
Centro de Estudios Superiores Navales (CESNAV), Mexico

ABSTRACT

Small and medium-sized enterprises (SMEs) hold a crucial role in modern economies, contributing significantly to wealth generation and job creation. This study aims to explore the correlation between specific financial ratios and construct a synthetic measure to understand the business size of selected Catalan SMEs. Using discriminant analysis, the methodology calculates and explains company size, considering synthetic dimensions generated through principal components analysis with a set of financial ratios as input variables. By utilizing this information, the study precisely explains the "size" classification variable, detecting discrepancies between reported and actual company sizes to address potential tax evasion. The valuation of the classification process determines the necessary adjustments between real and estimated sizes, providing valuable insights into the business sizes of analyzed Catalan SMEs.

INTRODUCTION

The significance of studying small and medium-sized enterprises (SMEs) lies in their transcendence and relevance for a country's economic development. Despite facing challenges in economic and political contexts, it has become increasingly crucial to implement models that foster the sector's pertinent growth, aligning with the demands of global competition.

SMEs play a vital role in generating employment and supporting both national and international economies. Notably, between 2011 and 2020, European SMEs created a staggering 85% of new jobs, contributing to the generation of 1.1 million new jobs annually. Comparatively, the annual job creation

DOI: 10.4018/979-8-3693-1190-5.ch016

rate of SMEs at the community level during this period was twice that of large European companies, with an average annual increase of 1% compared to 0.5%, respectively (Government of Spain, 2019).

These SMEs can be categorized into two forms of emergence and classification. The first category comprises proper companies with a well-defined organization and structure, guided by business management (owner of the firm) and the presence of paid work within the formal sector of the economy. On the other hand, the second category consists of SMEs that originated from family backgrounds and were primarily focused on survival, neglecting the opportunity cost of capital or investment required for their growth (Rao *et al.*, 2021).

Considering these facts, it is imperative to acknowledge the importance of SMEs and create an enabling environment that empowers their sustainable development, ensuring they continue to be crucial drivers of economic growth and job creation.

SMEs offer numerous advantages, making them a significant engine of a country's development. Their inherent flexibility enables them to adjust their plant size and technical processes as needed, fostering adaptability. With their dynamic nature, SMEs have the potential for substantial growth, possibly evolving into large companies and providing employment opportunities for a considerable portion of the population.

However, SMEs also face certain disadvantages. They often struggle to reinvest their profits to improve equipment and production techniques. Additionally, a lack of specialized and trained personnel results in non-competitive salaries and deficiencies in production quality due to minimal or absent quality controls. Organizational shortcomings lead to issues like insufficient sales, weak competitiveness, subpar customer service, high prices, poor location, inadequate inventory control, tax problems, and challenges in accessing technology, supplies, market information, credit, and support services (Gherghina *et al.*, 2020).

Research indicates that small firms located in business concentrations can overcome some of these obstacles, and using financial information, some can even be classified as medium-sized firms using a Probit model (Vier Machado, 2016; Greene, 2017).

Thus, the current study aims to classify Catalan companies based on size through the analysis of financial ratios. The objective is to provide a criterion for measuring business size, eschewing the classic approach based mainly on employee count (Curado *et al.*, 2021). Instead, multivariate techniques will be employed to generate synthetic variables, which will then be used in a subsequent analysis to develop a more nuanced measure of business size. This approach recognizes that setting quantitative limits for variables to determine small, medium, or large companies does not generally account for the diverse factors affecting business classification.

BACKGROUND

Since 2004, SMEs have been responsible for over 65.4% of employment in EU member countries, 69% in non-EU member countries, 61.9% in Asia, 55.43% in North America, and 66.9% in Latin America (Castelleti, 2005). These percentages have been on the rise, underscoring the undeniable importance of these companies in supporting more than half of the economically active population worldwide. Understanding and striving for excellence in SMEs is crucial not only for their own success but also for the prosperity of the countries they operate in (OECD, 2018).

In Europe, SMEs exhibit distinct characteristics. Approximately 93% of all companies have less than 10 employees, 6% fall within the range of 10 to 249 employees, and only 0.2% have 250 or more employees (Zevallos, 2007). Meanwhile, in Latin America, SMEs constitute a significant proportion of the business landscape, representing an average of 90% to 98.5% of all companies in countries like Uruguay, Guatemala, Argentina, Brazil, Chile, and Mexico (OECD/CAF, 2019). Despite facing chronic challenges in their establishment and sustenance, such as excessive bureaucracy and lack of supportive government programs, Latin American entrepreneurs show remarkable tenacity and confidence in venturing into business (OECD, 2017).

The analysis of financial statements has proven crucial in predicting the bankruptcy of companies (Chen *et al.*, 2021). The groundbreaking work by Altman (1968), using Linear Discriminant Analysis on financial ratios, enabled the probability of insolvency prediction for selected companies (Kliestik *et al.*, 2020). This financial statement analysis has also been instrumental in studying business size, as it provides insights into a company's operations.

Knowing a company's accurate size through its financial information holds significant importance, especially concerning tax evasion. Companies that misrepresent their size are breaching their tax responsibilities. Inaccurate reporting of business size can lead to undeserved tax benefits or evasion, impacting both the company's rights and obligations (OECD, 2022). This empirical study reveals that many companies tend to report a smaller size than reality to reduce their financial contribution to the State, leading to implications such as inadequate support for workers or lower contributions and royalties paid to employees.

In conclusion, understanding the dynamics and accurate financial reporting of SMEs is essential for fostering their growth and ensuring fair and responsible contributions to the economy and society at large.

MAIN FOCUS OF THE CHAPTER

Issues, Controversies, Problems

Since the early 1990s Urías, (1992) has aimed to investigate and analyze the impact of a company's[1] management on its current position and predict its future development, facilitating consequential decision-making based on accounting information. Over the years, a three-stage approach to AFS has been proposed: 1) Examination, 2) Analysis and interpretation, and 3) Prescription (Urías, 1992; Rivero, 1991; Ittelson, 2020).

During the first stage, a thorough examination of accounting documents, including the balance sheet, profit and loss account, and statement of origin, is emphasized. Specific procedures such as mass comparisons of assets, percentages, index numbers, ratios, trends, etc., are employed to ensure accuracy and reliability. In the second stage, the information gathered in the initial phase is meticulously analyzed, leading to comprehensive conclusions about the company's present state and the efficacy of its management.

In the final stage, predictions are made, and viable solutions are proposed to enhance the company's situation in the short and medium term. This forward-looking approach seeks to improve the company's performance, positioning it for success in the future. The AFS plays a vital role in providing valuable insights for decision-makers, enabling them to steer the company towards growth and prosperity.

Objectives and Precautions in the Use of Financial Ratios

Ratios are fundamental arithmetic expressions derived from economic or financial figures extracted from accounting information. These expressions can be categorized as simple (between figures of the same type within the balance sheet or income statement) or compound (between figures or aggregates from various sources). The primary purpose of utilizing financial ratios is to facilitate the interpretation of financial statements, presenting the information in the form of indexes or percentages. This, in turn, aids in developing a comprehensive financial diagnosis of the company's standing (Tran, Nguyen & To, 2020; Laitinen, 2018).

In essence, a ratio represents a relationship between two numbers, often encompassing key accounts from the Balance Sheet or the Profit and Loss Statement (Hilkevics & Semakina, 2019). The derived ratios offer vital information to assist interested parties in making informed decisions about the company (Ozyesil, 2020). Though the calculation of ratios is relatively straightforward, their interpretation can be overlooked, leading to a mere technical application without fully understanding their significance (Myšková & Hájek, 2017).

One significant issue worth emphasizing is the proliferation of ratios due to their ease of construction, creating a new challenge in selecting the most relevant ones for specific analyses. There is no one-size-fits-all answer to the question of which ratios to use, as it depends on numerous factors, including the analysis's objective, the perspective of the analyst, and the prevailing economic reality. Experience plays a crucial role in defining a relevant set of ratios that align with the unique context of the analysis (Faello, 2015).

The selection of appropriate ratios[2] is a complex task that requires careful consideration and expertise to ensure their meaningful application in providing valuable insights into a company's financial health and performance.

Logical Relations in the Formation of Ratios

As previously mentioned, ratios are arithmetic expressions. When constructing ratios, the specialized literature outlines specific logical relationships that should be considered among their elements. Therefore, three types of logical relationships have been proposed for the construction of ratios (Davidson, 2020):

An economic relationship between the components of the ratio must exist, meaning that the elements being compared should have a meaningful connection or relevance to each other in the context of the analysis.

The components of the ratio must be expressed in common values, ensuring that the units or measurements of the elements are compatible and can be meaningfully compared.

A functional relationship between the components is required, implying that the elements should interact in a way that provides valuable insights or meaningful information about the aspect of the business being examined.

Adhering to these logical relationships ensures that ratios are constructed thoughtfully and systematically, enhancing their usefulness in financial analysis and decision-making processes.

The Definition of SME

One of the primary challenges in studying the differences in economic and financial structures among businesses of different sizes is the classification criteria used for categorizing companies as large, medium, or small (Ježovita, 2015). The problem lies not only in selecting the appropriate variable but also in determining the cutoff points for each considered variable. The review of criteria used in this context leads to the following observations:

- The criteria used are generally one-dimensional, with two classic approaches being the number of employees or sales figures. However, the first approach underestimates the size of companies based on capital, as it focuses solely on labor without considering technological differences among sectors or the inclusion of temporary and unpaid work like that of corporate partners. The second approach presents a dilemma as it combines size with varying degrees of efficiency, leading to different groups even with the same number of workers and volume of assets but different sales volumes.
- There is no consensus on the limits to be established for each criterion. Some authors define SMEs as companies with fewer than 100 workers, while others set the limit at up to 500 workers.
- The lack of uniform criteria and cutoff points across studies complicates comparisons of results, hindering the implementation of consistent financing criteria based on company size.

This lack of agreement also extends to various definitions of SMEs by institutions and public administrations, especially concerning eligibility for specific subsidies. To unify criteria, the EU recommends that an SME should employ less than 250 people, have a billing volume not exceeding 40 million euros or an annual balance not exceeding 27 million euros, and meet the criterion of independence. Additionally, small companies are defined as those with no more than 50 workers, a turnover not exceeding 7 million euros, a balance sheet not exceeding 5 million euros, and also meeting the independence criterion (Boedo & Calvo, 2001).

The importance of accounting-financial information for understanding the real situation of any company cannot be overstated. From Financial Statements to financial ratios derived from them, knowing both the present and future of a company is of utmost significance. The future of a company determines the achievements of all its stakeholders, making the use of financial ratios crucial in establishing a more representative and reliable business size.

Though there is no universally accepted methodology for determining company size, multiple research studies propose innovative methodologies, particularly utilizing accounting-financial information (Thanh Binh *et al.*, 2020; Karlsson, 2021; Brijlal, Enow & Isaacs, 2014). The business size likely depends on factors such as the economic sector, region, territory, and autonomy of the company. Nevertheless, studies that provide information and statistical evidence for estimating business size based on accounting-financial information are invaluable.

In the following section, solutions and recommendations will be presented to support the selection of correct financial variables that aid in estimating the business size of a group of Catalan companies. This statistical evidence will shed light on scenarios where there is a higher probability of tax evasion among these Catalan companies.

Solutions and Recommendations

Undoubtedly, data quality is a highly desirable characteristic in any analytical process. However, it is crucial to acknowledge the presence of imperfections such as missing values, outliers, inconsistencies, and duplicate data, which can distort the dataset. Anomalies within data groups are often overlooked during most data grouping processes (Foorthuis, 2021). To manage these anomalies effectively, it is recommended to partition the dataset and treat the subset of anomalies separately, ensuring they do not interfere with the primary clustering process. Several methods can be employed to manage anomalies, but it is essential to address them during the pre-processing stage.

Certain algorithms, like CURE (Cai & Liang, 2018) and DBSCAN (Deng, 2020; Behara, Bhaskar, & Chung, 2021), have been developed to work with outliers. In this context, relevant ratios serve as explanatory variables, allowing companies to be classified based on their size through a specific procedure. However, in most cases, the selection of these explanatory variables has been empirical in nature, lacking theoretical support. This means that no theoretical model guides the choice of independent variables in previous studies.

Multicollinearity is an important consideration in the selection of ratios, as it pertains to the correlation between chosen variables. Eliminating certain ratios, unless they are exact linear combinations of others, may lead to information loss and a reduction in the model's predictive power (Robinson, 2020). Additionally, the assumption of normality in statistical techniques does not hold for ratios, as many studies have found that they follow a non-normal distribution (Agwor, 2014). Furthermore, the instability of ratios over time poses another challenge for models, given that they rely on a specific time horizon for estimation. Ratios can undergo changes over time due to economic cycles, market fluctuations, technological advancements, and other factors (Boedo & Calvo, 2001).

Hence, it is important to acknowledge that achieving normality for baseline variables in this analysis has not been fully realized, and partial asymmetry was assumed for some of them (Mahmoudabadi & Barzegar, 2009).

DATA

The definition of business size commonly relies on quantitative criteria, such as the number of employees, total assets, and sales figures (Curado *et al.*, 2021). However, the establishment of specific quantitative thresholds for these variables lacks a discriminative method to categorize companies into small, medium, or micro-enterprises. To address this, our study utilized a comprehensive database comprising 12,658 SMEs in Catalonia, along with 22 financial ratios, resulting in the integration of 278,476 records for analysis. All records are exclusively from the year 2020, as presented in Table 1.

METHODOLOGY

In the initial phase of this study, we applied Principal Component Analysis (PCA) to the selected financial ratios from Table 1. PCA is a powerful multivariate method aimed at transforming complex statistical information involving multiple quantitative variables calibrated in different units of measurement into a more manageable form with fewer new variables. This transformation minimizes information loss while optimally representing observations from a higher-dimensional space into a lower-dimensional space (Nobi, Tuhin & Lee, 2021; Jolliffe & Cadima, 2016; Hahs-Vaughn, 2017). By doing so, PCA helps identify possible latent variables that underlie the data and also converts the original correlated variables into new, uncorrelated ones, facilitating data interpretation (Shinmura, 2016; Tsoulfidis & Athanasiadis, 2022).

Table 1. Initial financial ratios and those considered for analysis

No.	Concept	Label	Ratio
1	Current assets	act_circ	Act circ explot / Actiu net
2	Net asset	act_net_	Act net explot / Actiu net
3	Profitability of sales	altres_d	Altres desp explot / Ing explot
4	Liquidity	cash_flo	Cash Flow/creditors a c/t
5	Operation	consums_	Consumerexploitot / Ing explot
6	Credits	creditor	Creditors c/t / Passiu remunerat
7	Personnel expenses per employee	desp_per	Desp personal / n treballadors
8	Own funds	fons_pro	Fons propis / passiu remunerat
9	External financing of fixed assets	immob_ne	Immob net explot / Actiu net
10	Margin	marge	Marge
11	Indebtedness	rec_alie	Rec aliens ll/t / passiu remunerat
12	General resources	recursos	Recursos Generats
13	Economic profitability	rendib1	Rendibilitat econòmica
14	Financial profit	rendibil	Rendibilitat financera
15	Financial Expense Coverage	rene_d	Rene / Desp financeres
16	Cash Coverage	rene_i	Rene / Ing explot
17	Rotation	rotació	Rotació
18	Solvency	tresorer	Tresoreria/Ingressos explot
19	Asset Productivity	vab_ac	VAB / Act net explot
20	Productivity of fixed assets	vab_im	VAB / Immob net explot
21	Income Productivity	vab_in	VAB / Ing explot
22	VAB (gross value added) per occupant	vab_nom	VAB/ Nombre treb

Source: Author's Calculation

The PCA process involves obtaining linear combinations of the original variables that are orthogonal to each other, yielding a subset of new variables known as principal components (Omprakash & Gokila, 2018. These principal components are ordered based on their variance in decreasing order, explaining the percentage of variability of the data for each component (Härdle & Simar, 2016; Hahs-Vaughn, 2017). Thus, each observation in the sample has scores in each of the selected principal components, enabling the ordering of observations based on multivariate information. For this study, the principal components were obtained by diagonalizing the correlation matrix since the ratios have different units of measurement, and each variable contributes equally to the analysis.

Next, the obtained latent variables were fed into a Discriminant Analysis (DA) to elucidate a synthetic measure (Boedeker & Kearns, 2019) of the business size of Catalan SMEs. DA is a multivariate statistical technique used for classifying objects into different groups based on observed characteristics. It seeks to find a linear combination of several independent variables (as ensured by the earlier PCA) that maximizes the differences between classification groups while minimizing the differences within each group. The resulting linear discriminant function is a weighted linear combination of the observed characteristics, with the weights representing the relative importance and impact of the features in the discriminant function. Consequently, objects are classified into specific groups based on the scores obtained through the discriminant function (Dias, Brito & Amaral, 2021).

It is essential to acknowledge that DA relies on several assumptions, including the assumption that each group follows a multivariate normal distribution, that the covariance matrices of each group are identical, and that the covariance matrices, prior probabilities, and classification errors are known. Deviations from these assumptions may lead to erroneous results.

In conclusion, we employed DA in this study because it allowed us to select the variables with the greatest discriminant power, which were previously generated using PCA. This two-step approach aids in understanding the patterns that distinguish distinct groups of companies based on their business size.

RESULTS AND DISCUSSIONS

In this section, we will first conduct a Principal Component Analysis (PCA) to present the primary findings. Subsequently, we will delve into the key results of the Data Analysis (DA). However, before delving into these analyses, we will begin by showing an examination of the financial ratios. This preliminary step will aid in the selection of the most significant contributors to our study.

Analysis of Financial Ratios

Working with financial ratios can be inherently complex, primarily due to their construction, often leading to issues of linear dependency between several of them. In the case of the ratios presented in Table 1, a meticulous analysis was conducted, revealing four initial groups (see Table 2). However, a crucial challenge emerged as these ratios did not exhibit a behavior consistent with a univariate normal distribution (see Table 3). Consequently, any parametric statistical inference, such as Analysis of Variance (ANOVA) or Pearson's correlation coefficient, both of which rely on normality assumptions, had to be ruled out at this stage. Employing such techniques would have yielded fragile results and erroneous conclusions.

Alternatively, assuming normality in the ratios would allow for ANOVA (Ardelean, 2017) to be applied, revealing two significant findings. First, it would indicate a lack of equality of variances among the groups of the tamany ratio. Second, it would identify three ratios likely to be excluded from the study: 1) rotation, rec_alie; 2) immob_ne, and 3) act_circ. These three ratios exhibited significant differences among the subgroups in which the tamany factor was divided.

Given these challenges and insights, it becomes imperative to explore alternative non-parametric approaches to ensure the robustness of our analysis and draw meaningful conclusions from the financial ratio data.

Table 2. Grouping of the initially selected ratios

Group	No.	Concept	Label	Ratio
A	1	Own funds	fons_pro	Fons propis / passiu remunerat
	2	Indebtedness	rec_alie	Rec aliens ll/t / passiu remunerat
	3	Credits	creditor	Creditors c/t / Passiu remunerat
B	4	Net asset	act_net_	Act net explot / Actiu net
	5	External financing of fixed assets	immob_ne	Immob net explot / Actiu net
	6	Current assets	act_circ	Act circ explot / Actiu net
C	7	Operation	consums_	Consums explot / Ing explot
	8	Profitability of sales	altres_d	Altres desp explot / Ing explot
	9	Income Productivity	vab_in	VAB / Ing explot
	10	Cash Coverage	rene_i	Rene / Ing explot
	11	Solvency	tresorer	Tresoreria/Ingressos explot
D	12	Financial profit	rendibil	Rendibilitat financera
	13	Economic profitability	rendib1	Rendibilitat econòmica
	14	Margin	marge	Marge
	15	Rotation	rotació	Rotació
	16	Productivity of fixed assets	vab_im	VAB / Immob net explot
	17	General resources	recursos	Recursos Generats
	18	Liquidity	cash_flo	Cash Flow / creditors a c/t
	19	Financial Expense Coverage	rene_d	Rene / Desp financeres
	20	Asset Productivity	vab_ac	VAB / Act net explot
	21	VAB (gross value added) per occupant	vab_nom	VAB/ Nombre treb
	22	Personnel expenses per employee	desp_per	Desp personal / n treballadors

Source: Author's Calculation

Another significant challenge arose from the high degree of multicollinearity observed among certain ratios. This became evident during the implementation of a PCA, where all ratios were considered, resulting in a synthetic correlation matrix that was not positively defined. Consequently, the presence of multicollinearity necessitates the careful selection and discrimination of certain ratios to ensure the attainment of more robust and reliable results.

Graphically, drawing value judgments becomes intricate due to the absence of direct discernible relationships a priori, as depicted in Figure 1. The complexities introduced by multicollinearity make it challenging to establish clear and straightforward connections between the ratios under consideration.

To verify the issue of linear dependence, a multiple linear regression was conducted, excluding the constant term, with each of the 22 ratios taken as endogenous variables and the remaining ratios as exogenous variables. Regardless of the chosen endogenous variable, the result consistently yielded a "Near Singular Matrix" message, rendering the regression infeasible. This outcome confirms that some of the ratios are exact linear combinations of other financial ratios, which is logically expected.

Table 3. Descriptive statistics for each ratio and its normality test

Concept	ACT_CIRC	ACT_NET_	ALTRES_D	CASH_FLO	CONSUMS_	CREDITOR
Mean	0.708276	0.979248	0.143915	0.142742	0.549918	0.598940
Median	0.747253	0.989576	0.127434	0.106417	0.569334	0.602096
Maximum	0.994574	1.050.000	0.502165	0.864286	0.976852	1.221.790
Minimum	0.082866	0.831131	0.000000	-0.227273	-0.161458	0.054054
Std. Dev.	0.186787	0.027223	0.080202	0.128084	0.199817	0.194523
Skewness	-0.758372	-1.998.640	1.105.267	1.570.903	-0.500683	-0.060804
Kurtosis	2.847.768	7.434.143	4.192.336	6.078.085	2.779.711	2.470.745
Jarque-Bera	1.225.552	18797.06	3.327.011	10203.16	5.544.519	1.555.346
Probability	0.000000	0.000000	0.000000	0.000000	0.000000	0.000000
Concept	**DESP_PER**	**FONS_PRO**	**IMMOB_NE**	**MARGE**	**REC_ALIE**	**RECURSOS**
Mean	2.171.083	0.279642	0.270971	0.029426	0.121417	3.660.175
Median	2.081.818	0.254209	0.231102	0.028080	0.086957	2.600.000
Maximum	4.700.000	0.870130	0.831897	0.132184	0.561001	2.250.000
Minimum	0.575758	-0.354978	0.002580	-0.066886	0.000000	-7.200.000
Std. Dev.	7.380.503	0.183599	0.183363	0.021574	0.118713	3.516.287
Skewness	0.466162	0.479587	0.800863	0.314733	0.882035	1.678.234
Kurtosis	3.064.230	3.046.158	2.902.975	4.973.456	2.830.043	6.896.744
Jarque-Bera	4.606.211	4.863.549	1.358.067	2.263.016	1.656.524	13950.43
Probability	0.000000	0.000000	0.000000	0.000000	0.000000	0.000000
Concept	**RENDIB1**	**RENDIBIL**	**RENE_D**	**RENE_I**	**ROTACI**	**TRESORER**
Mean	0.053635	0.128085	2.670.975	0.028405	1.924.304	0.052789
Median	0.049180	0.102899	2.000.000	0.027061	1.843.534	0.039216
Maximum	0.201117	0.706667	1.750.000	0.129555	4.461.124	0.351351
Minimum	-0.096014	-0.424419	-5.350.000	-0.068182	0.129730	0.000000
Std. Dev.	0.039118	0.156985	2.510.854	0.021725	0.733695	0.052236
Skewness	0.416861	0.429416	1.302.754	0.293810	0.517476	1.393.762
Kurtosis	3.955.600	4.022.874	6.786.215	4.975.837	2.960.674	5.228.141
Jarque-Bera	8.482.255	9.408.393	11141.20	2.241.113	5.657.449	6.716.602
Probability	0.000000	0.000000	0.000000	0.000000	0.000000	0.000000
Concept	**VAB_AC**	**VAB_IM**	**VAB_IN**	**VAB_NOM**		
Mean	0.569462	3.118.930	0.306168	2.798.534		
Median	0.508027	2.282.263	0.283876	2.657.738		
Maximum	1.754.190	1.685.714	0.824490	7.700.000		
Minimum	0.009174	0.029024	0.005711	0.848485		
Std. Dev.	0.322062	2.549.153	0.158381	1.012.659		
Skewness	0.807116	1.692.892	0.583454	0.712943		
Kurtosis	3.174.538	6.685.061	2.737.325	3.602.812		
Jarque-Bera	1.390.381	13208.20	7.545.597	1.263.970		
Probability	0.000000	0.000000	0.000000	0.000000		

Source: Author's Calculation

Figure 1. Multiple representations of the 22 financial ratios
Source: Authors elaboration based on the Eviews program.

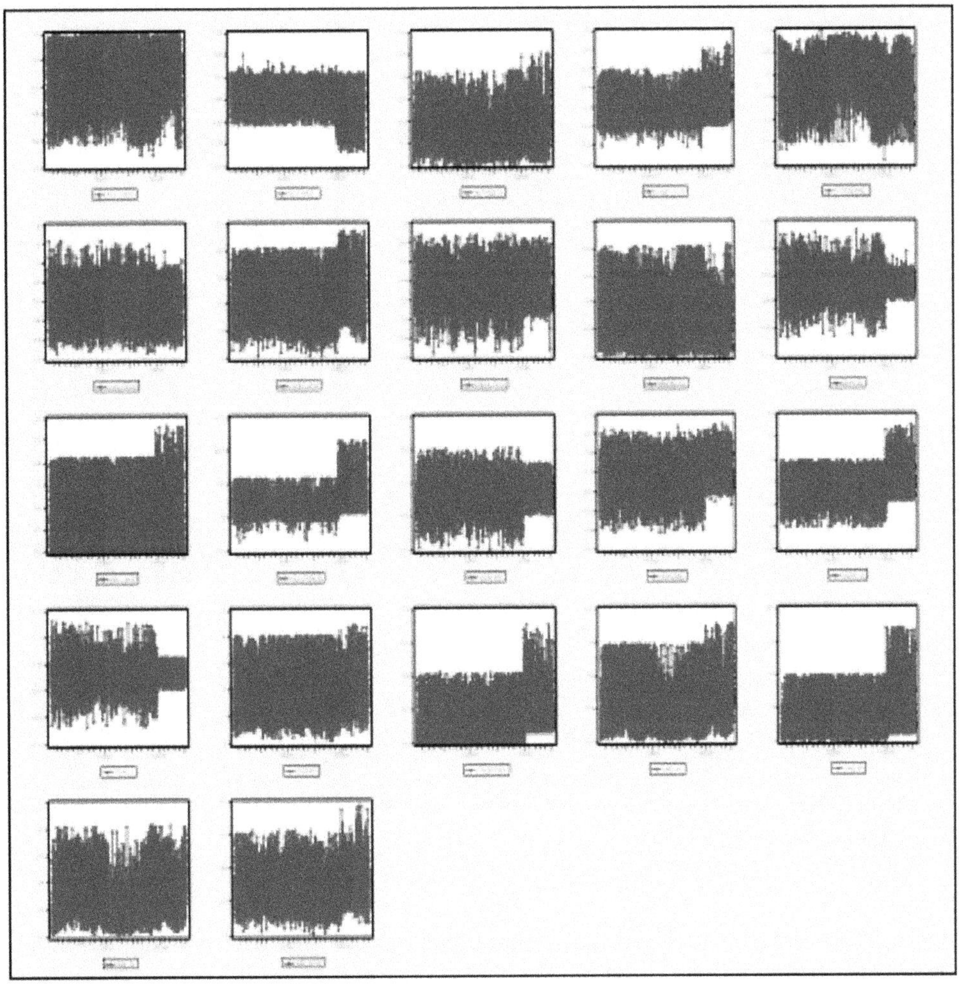

The presence of such linear relationships can also be observed when omitting a specific variable, like act_circ, for instance. Upon attempting to explain the ratio altres_d using the remaining ratios, the results presented in Table 4 were obtained. These findings further emphasize the extent of linear dependence among the financial ratios and underscore the necessity of addressing this challenge for a more accurate and meaningful analysis.

Based on the analysis, a strong linear relationship was observed between nearly all the ratios included in the study. This was evident from the coefficient of determination (r2) being equal to one and the majority of t-statistics exceeding two, indicating statistical significance. However, due to the regression model lacking a constant term, judgments about first-order correlation were not feasible, and the Durbin-Watson (d) test could not be employed.

Table 4. Linear dependence between the ratios

Variable	Coefficient	Std. Error	t-Statistic	Prob.
CASH_FLO	-9.63E-14	1.10E-14	-8.744889	0.0000
CONSUMS_	-1.000000	1.14E-14	-8.75E+13	0.0000
CREDITOR	1.000000	3.26E-14	3.07E+13	0.0000
DESP_PER	-5.32E-15	3.21E-16	-16.58892	0.0000
FONS_PRO	1.000000	3.29E-14	3.04E+13	0.0000
IMMOB_NE	4.27E-15	7.61E-15	0.561940	0.5742
MARGE	-1.52E-11	2.35E-13	-64.64628	0.0000
REC_ALIE	1.000000	3.28E-14	3.05E+13	0.0000
RECURSOS	-2.97E-16	2.77E-17	-10.69459	0.0000
RENDIB1	1.61E-12	6.23E-14	25.88477	0.0000
RENDIBIL	-8.71E-14	8.24E-15	-10.57439	0.0000
RENE_D	6.05E-15	4.43E-16	13.64236	0.0000
RENE_I	1.21E-11	2.17E-13	55.69137	0.0000
ROTACI	4.21E-14	2.53E-15	16.61078	0.0000
TRESORER	4.56E-14	1.72E-14	2.650537	0.0080
VAB_AC	-2.53E-13	7.97E-15	-31.74186	0.0000
VAB_IM	-9.69E-16	5.08E-16	-1.904872	0.0568
VAB_IN	-1.000000	1.98E-14	-5.06E+13	0.0000
VAB_NOM	3.46E-15	2.43E-16	14.25310	0.0000
ACT_NET_	-2.78E-12	3.21E-14	-86.60744	0.0000

R-squared	1.000000	Mean dependent var	0.143915
Adjusted R-squared	1.000000	S.D. dependent var	0.080202
S.E. of regression	9.40E-14	Akaike info criterion	-57.15134
Sum squared resid	1.12E-22	Schwarz criterion	-57.13958
Log likelihood	361730.9	F-statistic	4.85E+26
Durbin-Watson stat	1.963626	Prob(F-statistic)	0.000000

Source: Author's Calculation based on Eviews.

To address the assumption of normality, non-parametric tests were utilized, despite their lower power, to avoid making assumptions about the data distribution. Nonetheless, the runs test revealed that none of the ratios exhibited randomness or independence, implying that the sampling of companies was not random. Consequently, the use of non-parametric tests like Siegel and Castellan (2009) may lead to erroneous conclusions.

For instance, applying the Kruskal-Walli's test assuming independence indicated significant differences in the arithmetic mean for certain ratio groups like rotació, rec_alie, immob_ne, act_circ, and tresorer, possibly suggesting their exclusion from the study. On the other hand, the median test identified additional ratios, such as altres_d, treasure, r, and rene_d, showing significant differences between the tamany ratio groups. This emphasized the risk of making poor ratio selections.

To overcome these challenges and facilitate ratio discrimination, an analysis of distances between each identified group's ratios concerning the tamany ratio was performed. The Chebychev distance (Haryati, Surono & Suparman, 2021) standardized by the absolute value of the standard deviation for each ratio was used for a better understanding of these distances. The results for the ratios in Table 1 were as follows:

Block A: The ratio exhibiting the greatest distance concerning the tamany ratio was rec_alie, making it suitable for omission in the corresponding PCA.

Block B: The ratio act_net_ showed the highest distance concerning the tamany ratio, making it appropriate for exclusion from the PCA.

Block C: Unexpectedly, the ratio rene_i displayed the greatest distance concerning the tamany ratio. However, including this ratio in the PCA yielded a correlation matrix that was not positively defined. Conversely, altres_d showed the smallest distance with the tamany ratio. By omitting altres_d, more robust PCA results were obtained. Consequently, altres_d was excluded from further consideration.

Taking these analyses into account, Table 5 presents the selected financial ratios, which will serve as input for the subsequent PCA.

Table 5. Grouping of the selected financial ratios

Group	No.	Concept	Label	Ratio
A	1	Fondos propios	fons_pro	Fons propis/passiu remunerat
	2	Créditos	creditor	Creditors c/t/Passiu remunerat
B	3	Financiación ajena del inmovilizado	immob_ne	Immob net explot/Actiu net
	4	act_circ	act_circ	Act circ explot/Actiu net
C	5	Operación	consums_	Consums explot/Ing explot
	6	Productividad del ingreso	vab_in	VAB/Ing explot
	7	Coberetura de efectivo	rene_i	Rene/Ing explot
	8	Solvencia	tresorer	Tresoreria/Ingressos explot
D	9	Rentabilidad financiera	rendibil	Rendibilitat financera
	10	Rentabilidad económica	rendib1	Rendibilitat econòmica
	11	Margen	marge	Marge
	12	Rotación	rotació	Rotació
	13	Productividad del inmovilizado	vab_im	VAB/Immob net explot
	14	Recursos generales	recursos	Recursos Generats
	15	Liquidez	cash_flo	Cash Flow/creditors a c/t
	16	Cobertura de Gastod financieros	rene_d	Rene/Desp financeres
	17	Productividad del activo	vab_ac	VAB/Act net explot
	18	VAB (valor añadido bruto) por ocupante	vab_nom	VAB/Nombre treb
	19	Gastos de personal por empleado	desp_per	Desp personal/n treballadors

Source: Author's Calculation

Principal Component Analysis (PCA)

PCA (Principal Component Analysis) is a widely employed factor extraction technique utilized to create uncorrelated linear combinations of observed variables (Tsoulfidis & Athanasiadis, 2022). The primary component captures the maximum variance present in the data, while successive components explain progressively smaller proportions of the variance and remain uncorrelated with one another. Another valuable aspect of PCA is its applicability in obtaining the initial factorial solution, even when dealing with a singular correlation matrix.

In the context of our study, PCA was performed on the selected ratios from Table 5, and through the sedimentation line, we identified 6 components or latent variables (Figure 2).

The KMO and Bartlett test results for the six components were obtained from Table 6. Additionally, Table 7 displays the matrix of commonalities for these six components or latent variables, while Table 8 presents the total variance matrix explained by these six latent variables.

Figure 2. Sedimentation line
Source: Author's elaboration with SPSS results.

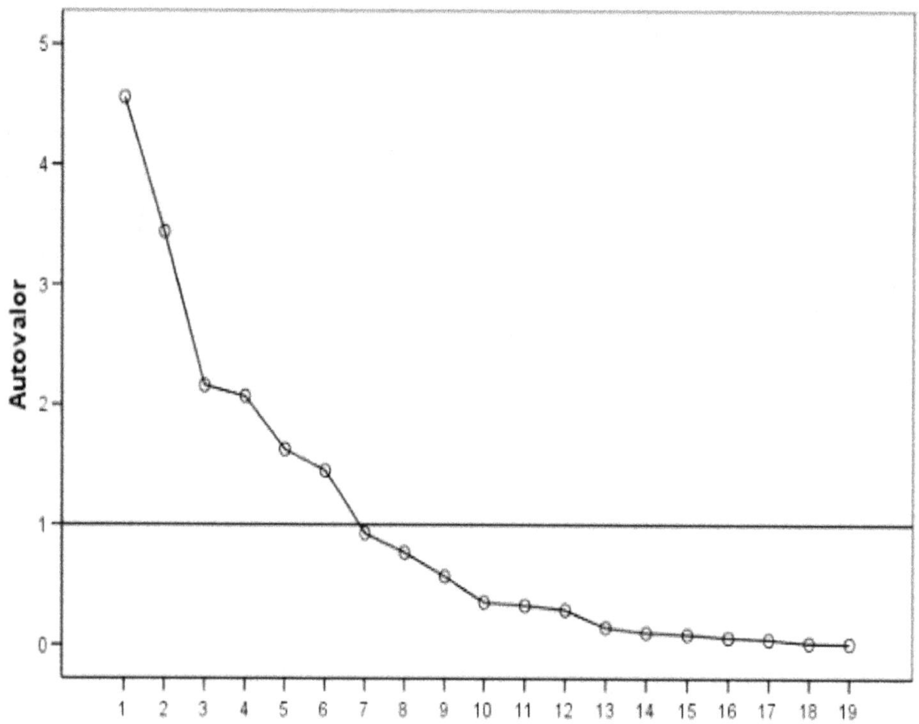

Table 6. KMO and Bartlett's test using a PCA

Sample adequacy measure of Kaiser-Meyer-Olkin.		,698
Sphericity test of Bartlett	Chi squared approximate	260998,4
	degrees of freedom	171
	Sig.	,000

Source: Author's Calculation

Table 7. Matrix of commonalities obtained through a PCA

	Initial	Extraction
Rendibilitat financera	1,000	,722
Rendibilitat econòmica	1,000	,878
Marge	1,000	,919
Rotació	1,000	,934
Fons propis / passiu remunerat	1,000	,844
Creditors c/t / Passiu remunerat	1,000	,840
Immob net explot / Actiu net	1,000	,934
Act circ explot / Actiu net	1,000	,933
Consums explot / Ing explot	1,000	,922
VAB / Ing explot	1,000	,956
VAB / Immob net explot	1,000	,799
VAB / Act net explot	1,000	,943
Desp personal / n treballadors	1,000	,923
VAB/ Nombre treb	1,000	,937
Tresoreria/Ingressos explot	1,000	,269
Recursos Generats	1,000	,382
Cash Flow / creditors a c/t	1,000	,735
Rene / Ing explot	1,000	,911
Rene / Desp financeres	1,000	,523

Extraction Method: Principal Component Analysis.

Source: Author's Calculation

The Kaiser-Meyer-Olkin (KMO) measure of sample adequacy was used to test the strength of association between the selected ratios, yielding a coefficient very close to 70%, indicating a good level of association. Concurrently, Bartlett's sphericity test was employed to assess the adequacy of the correlation matrix. The hypothesis that the determinant of the correlation matrix is equal to one was rejected, given a significance of less than 5%, implying that the model is not inadequate.

Together, these results indicate that PCA analysis is both feasible and appropriate for this study. The six components account for 80.536% of the total variance of the selected ratios (refer to Table 8). Although the synthetic variables are not labeled, a PCA was performed using Varimax normalization rotation with Kaiser, as shown in Table 9

Table 8. Explained total variance matrix obtained by PCA

Total explained variance.

Component	Initial eigenvalues			Sums of squared saturations of extraction			Sum of squared loadings of rotation		
	Total	% of the variance	% accumulated	Total	% of the variance	% accumulated	Total	% of the variance	% accumulated
1	4,559	23,996	23,996	4,559	23,996	23,996	3,695	19,449	19,449
2	3,439	18,098	42,094	3,439	18,098	42,094	2,837	14,933	34,382
3	2,159	11,362	53,456	2,159	11,362	53,456	2,684	14,125	48,507
4	2,070	10,894	64,350	2,070	10,894	64,350	2,445	12,867	61,374
5	1,626	8,556	72,906	1,626	8,556	72,906	2,048	10,781	72,155
6	1,450	7,630	80,536	1,450	7,630	80,536	1,592	8,381	80,536
7	,929	4,891	85,427						
8	,769	4,047	89,474						
9	,569	2,995	92,469						
10	,354	1,862	94,330						
11	,327	1,721	96,052						
12	,290	1,529	97,580						
13	,145	,766	98,346						
14	,101	,530	98,876						
15	,085	,448	99,324						
16	,059	,311	99,635						
17	,044	,234	99,869						
18	,015	,080	99,949						
19	,010	,051	100,000						

Extraction Method: Principal Component Analysis.

Source: Author's Calculations

Similarly, Table 9 presents the comparison between the matrix of components and the matrix of rotating components. The latter is utilized to maximize the total variance explained by each component estimated using PCA.

Table 9. Matrix of components vs. the array of rotating components using a PCA

	Component					
	1	2	3	4	5	6
Rendibilitat financera						
Rendibilitat econòmica						
Marge						
Rotació						
Fons propis / passiu remunerat						
Creditors c/t / Passiu remunerat						
Immob net explot / Actiu net						
Act circ explot / Actiu net						
Consums explot / Ing explot						
VAB / Ing explot						
VAB / Immob net explot						
VAB / Act net explot						
Desp personal / n treballadors						
VAB/ Nombre treb						
Tresoreria/Ingressos explot						
Recursos Generats						
Cash Flow / creditors a c/t						
Rene / Ing explot	,7					
Rene / Desp financeres						

Extraction Method: Principal Component Analysis.
a 6 extracted components

	Component					
		2	3	4	5	6
Rendibilitat financera						
Rendibilitat econòmica						
Marge						
Rotació						
Fons propis / passiu remunerat						
Creditors c/t / Passiu remunerat						
Immob net explot / Actiu net						
Act circ explot / Actiu net						
Consums explot / Ing explot						
VAB / Ing explot						
VAB / Immob net explot						
VAB / Act net explot						
Desp personal / n treballadors						
VAB/ Nombre treb						
Tresoreria/Ingressos explot						
Recursos Generats						
Cash Flow / creditors a c/t				,622		
Rene / Ing explot	,9					
Rene / Desp financeres	,6					

Extraction Method: Principal Component Analysis.
Rotation method: Varimax normalization with Kaiser.
a.The rotation has converged in 6 iterations.

Note: Correlations less than 0.6 in absolute value have been suppressed.
Source: Author's Calculations

It is important to highlight that Principal Component Analysis (PCA) yielded more insightful results compared to Factor Analysis (FA) (Chen & Zhou, 2018) in terms of the number of latent variables. The FA generated only four latent factors (refer to Table 10), which accounted for 57.525% of the total variance of the selected ratios. Conversely, PCA achieved a higher percentage of total explained variance, reaching 80.536%. While the four factors in FA led to the same results as PCA, especially in the context of reducing variable dimensions, FA would have been more favorable. In this scenario, using four latent factors in FA produced similar test statistics as PCA (see Table 11).

Table 10. Total explained variance of the factors extracted through an AF

Factor	Initial eigenvalues			Sums of the squared loadings of the extraction			Sums of the squared saturations of the rotation		
	Total	% variance	% accumulated	Total	% variance	% accumulated	Total	% variance	% accumulated
1	4.559	23.996	23.996	4.277	22.512	22.512	3.409	17.940	17.940
2	3.439	18.098	42.094	3.162	16.643	39.155	2.742	14.430	32.370
3	2.159	11.362	53.456	1.840	9.585	48.840	2.543	13.909	46.279
4	2.070	10.894	64.350	1,65	8.584	57.525	2.137	11.245	57.525
5	1.626	8.556	72.906						
6	1.450	7.630	80.536						
7	.929	4.891	85.427						
8	.769	4.047	89.474						
9	.569	2.995	92.469						
10	.354	1.862	94.330						
11	.327	1.721	96.052						
12	.290	1.529	97.580						
13	.145	.766	98.346						
14	.101	.530	98.876						
15	.085	.448	99.324						
16	.069	.311	99.535						
17	.044	.234	99.869						
18	.015	.080	99.949						
19	.010	.051	100.000						

Source: Author's calculations.

Table 11. Total explained variance of the factors extracted using an AF

Sample adequacy measure of Kaiser-Meyer-Olkin.		,698
Sphericity test of Bartlett	Chi squared approximate	260998,4
	degrees of freedom	171
	Sig.	,000

Source: Author's calculations.

It is essential to discuss the Principal Axes Factorization, commonly known as Factor Analysis, as it is a method employed to extract factors from the original correlation matrix. The process starts with initial estimates of commonalities by inserting the squares of the multiple correlation coefficients on the main diagonal of the matrix. The resulting factor loadings are then used to re-estimate the commonalities and replace the previous estimates. This iteration continues until convergence is achieved based on the extraction criterion.

However, the goal of this study is to explore a greater number of synthetic variables and examine their association with the size of companies. Consequently, Principal Component Analysis (PCA) was chosen for this purpose. The scores obtained through PCA have a mean of 0 and variance equal to the square of the multiple correlations between the estimated factorial scores and the true factorial values. It is worth noting that these scores can still be correlated even when the factors are orthogonal.

One important consideration is that the correlation matrix is calculated using Pearson's correlation coefficient, which measures linear association. Thus, while two variables may be perfectly related, a non-linear relationship would not be adequately captured by the Pearson correlation test. Furthermore, normality in the ratios is assumed for the calculation of this coefficient. To address this, the level of concordance with the Spearman correlation coefficient (Frey, 2018) was assessed, as it does not rely on the assumption of normality. By comparing the Pearson correlation matrix with the Spearman correlation matrix, the difference between them was calculated, and the determinant of this difference matrix was used to quantify the level of error in the measurements. The calculated determinant was found to be very close to zero (1.02763 x 10 -30), indicating that using Pearson's correlation coefficient in PCA is valid and does not significantly affect the results. Although Pearson's coefficient allows for cause-effect analysis, it is important to note that using the Spearman correlation coefficient would prevent making

Table 12. Synthetic variables to be analyzed using an AD

No.	Label	Variable
1	F01	Factor01
2	F02	Factor02
3	F03	Factor03
4	F04	Factor04
5	F05	Factor05
6	F06	Factor06
7	número_e	Number of employees
8	Tamany	Business size

Source: Author's calculations.

value judgments about potential cause-effect relationships between the ratios since it is non-parametric.

With the latest results, the dimension of the problem was successfully reduced, and instead of using 19 selected ratios, 6 independent and uncorrelated variables (latent variables) were utilized. Typified factorial scores were calculated for these six components, and they were standardized to ensure homogeneity in the subsequent Discriminant Analysis (DA). The variables used as input for the DA are presented in Table 12.

Discriminant Analysis (DA)

The six synthetic variables obtained through PCA, along with the variable representing the number of employees in 2020, exhibited univariate normality issues when subjected to the Jarque-Bera test (Aslam, Sherwani & Saleem, 2021) (refer to Table 13).

Table 13. Results of the Jarque-Bera test

	FACTOR1	FACTOR02	FACTOR03	FACTOR04	FACTOR05	FACTOR06	EMP_2002
Mean	-2.31E-12	-1.81E-12	9.08E-13	1.03E-12	-4.74E-13	8.53E-13	10.70398
Median	-0.031284	-0.104791	0.056657	-0.120248	-0.113794	-0.050867	8.000000
Maximum	4.022478	3.421737	3.510298	4.032051	3.996283	4.347965	245.0000
Minimum	-4.535290	-2.336568	-2.917688	-3.200732	-2.946192	-4.499070	1.000000
Std. Dev.	1.000000	1.000000	1.000000	1.000000	1.000000	1.000000	10.67817
Skewness	-0.142793	0.416481	-0.117654	0.484072	0.485847	0.213561	4.709507
Kurtosis	4.260840	2.562898	2.690508	3.084496	3.070916	2.981031	57.15522
Jarque-Bera	881.4587	466.7019	79.72179	498.1149	500.6331	96.40785	1593593.
Probability	0.000000	0.000000	0.000000	0.000000	0.000000	0.000000	0.000000
Observations	12658	12658	12658	12658	12658	12658	12658

Source: Author's calculations based on Eviews.

On the other hand, among the variables examined, the one that showed the strongest linear relationship (71.3159%) with the tamany variable was the variable representing the number of employees in 2020. This notable result can be attributed to its linear correlation coefficient, which surpassed 70% (refer to Table 14).

The validity of this finding is further supported by the structure matrix (see Table 15), which clearly demonstrates that the variable representing the number of employees in 2020 contributed the most information to discriminant function 1. Impressively, this variable retained 99.8% of the total explained variance, solidifying its significance in the analysis.

Table 14. Correlation matrix

	FACTOR1	FACTOR02	FACTOR03	FACTOR04	FACTOR05	FACTOR06	EMP_2002	TAMANY
FACTOR1	1.000000	-6.27E-12	-2.14E-12	1.87E-12	-2.44E-12	2.19E-12	-0.038403	-0.024366
FACTOR02	-6.27E-12	1.000000	2.98E-12	-5.31E-12	1.88E-12	8.07E-13	0.146135	0.116763
FACTOR03	-2.14E-12	2.98E-12	1.000000	4.56E-13	3.87E-12	-3.52E-12	0.028377	0.019847
FACTOR04	1.87E-12	-5.31E-12	4.56E-13	1.000000	-3.22E-12	-2.28E-12	0.058828	0.070179
FACTOR05	-2.44E-12	1.88E-12	3.87E-12	-3.22E-12	1.000000	-6.08E-12	0.045620	0.085520
FACTOR06	2.19E-12	8.07E-13	-3.52E-12	-2.28E-12	-6.08E-12	1.000000	0.049876	0.049326
EMP_2002	-0.038403	0.146135	0.028377	0.058828	0.045620	0.049876	1.000000	0.713159
TAMANY	-0.024366	0.116763	0.019847	0.070179	0.085520	0.049326	0.713159	1.000000

Source: Own elaboration based on Eviews.

Table 15. Structure matrix

	Function	
	1	2
Number of employees	,998*	-,049
REGR factor score 5 for analysis 1	,051	,687*
REGR factor score 4 for analysis 1	,040	,626*
REGR factor score 6 for analysis 1	,034	,272*
REGR factor score 2 for analysis 1	,097	,154*
REGR factor score 1 for analysis 1	-,026	,136*
REGR factor score 3 for analysis 1	,018	-,021*

Pooled intra-group correlations between the discriminant variables and the standardized canonical discriminant functions.
Variables ordered by the size of the correlation with the function.

*. Highest absolute correlation between each variable and any discriminant function.

Source: Author's calculations based on SPSS.

Table 16. Variable Tammany (frequencies)

		Frequency	%	% valid	% accumulated
Valid	1	7642	60,4	60,4	60,4
	2	4901	38,7	38,7	99,1
	3	115	,9	,9	100,0
	Total	12658	100,0	100,0	

Source: Author's calculations.

During the Discriminant Analysis (DA), the grouping variable was labeled as "Tammany," and it involved defining three distinct subgroups of companies: 1 (Micro), 2 (Small), and 3 (Medium). The integration of the grouping variable is displayed in Table 16.

Upon applying the multivariate technique of Discriminant Analysis (DA) to the variables listed in Table 12, it was observed that all the variables exhibited statistical significance in the test of equality of means. However, the Box's M test (see Table 17), which examines the equality of covariance matrices, revealed distinct heterogeneity among the variances of these variables.

Table 17. Results for Box's M test

M of Box		12025,123
F	Aprox.	212,305
	'reedom 1	56
	'reedom 2	259671,731
	Sig.	,000

It tests the null hypothesis that the population covariance matrices are equal.

Source: Author's calculations.

The latest finding suggests substantial distinctions among the analyzed subgroups of companies regarding their ability to explain company size variance. This disparity is logical, given that the data dispersion within the micro-companies' subgroup does not necessarily exhibit homogeneity with the medium-sized companies subgroup. The analysis also yielded an important outcome concerning the Wilks Lambda for the discriminant canonical functions. Significantly, each of the functions achieved a level of significance below 5%. This statistical significance (as indicated in Table 20) implies that discrimination is not only possible but also meaningful. From Table 18, it is evident that discriminant function 1 accounts for the highest percentage of variability (99.4%), while discriminant function 2 shows limited association between the discriminant scores and the involved groups (6%). In other words, distinguishing a company from subgroup 2 (Small) from subgroup 3 (Medium) is not as straightforward.

The validation of this final result is presented in Table 19, where the discriminant scores for the centroids of the subgroups are displayed.

The analysis reveals a distinct pattern: discriminant function 1 exhibits stronger discrimination, whereas discriminant function 2's discrimination is not entirely confirmed. Nonetheless, both discriminant functions are statistically significant, as confirmed by the Wilks lambda test (refer to Table 20). When each discriminant function achieves a statistical significance level (p-value) of less than 5%, it indicates their individual importance and contribution to the analysis.

Figure 3 displays the scores calculated through a Discriminant Analysis (DA) for the two discriminant functions.

Table 18. Results for the eigenvalues

Function	Self value	variance %	% accumulated	Canonical correlation
1	1,596 [a]	99,4	99,4	,784
2	,009 [a]	,6	100,0	,095

a. The first 2 canonical discriminant functions have been used in the analysis.

Source: Author's calculations.

Table 19. Functions for the centroids

Tamany	Function	
	1	2
1	-,839	-,044
2	1,103	,087
3	8,775	-,747

Unstandardized canonical discriminant functions evaluated at group means.

Source: Author's calculations.

Table 20. Results for the Wilks Lambda

Contrast of functions	Wilks' Lambda	Chi squared	df	Sig.
1 a la 2	,382	12183,980	14	,000
2	,991	115,488	6	,000

Source: Author's calculations.

Similarly, Figure 4 illustrates the dispersion (scatter) of the scores calculated using a Discriminant Analysis (DA) for the two discriminant functions.

It is worth noting that the implementation of DA multivariate analysis and cross-variation resulted in an impressive 89.9% accuracy in classification. Additionally, Table 21 presents the frequency statistics for the variable "Tammany" alongside its respective predicted group.

Lastly, Figure 5 displays the distribution of both the estimated business size and the actual business size, providing a visual representation of the classification assessment.

Figure 3. Scores using a DA for discriminant functions
Source: Author's calculations based on Eviews.

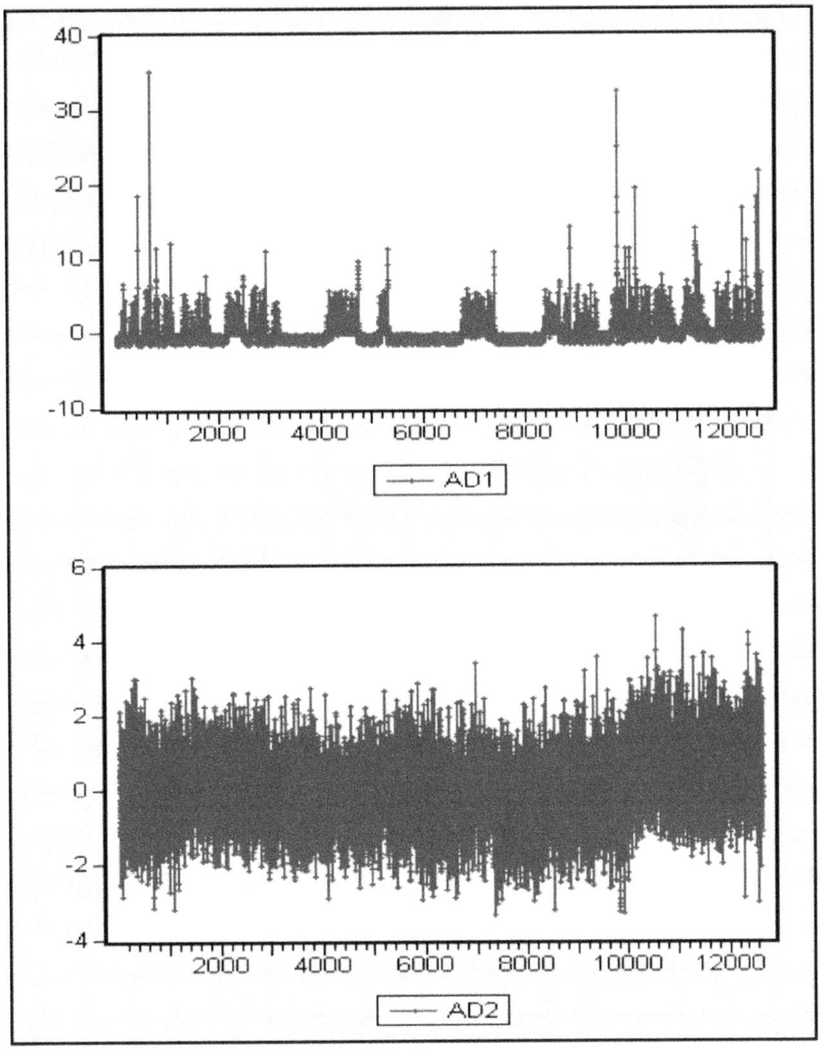

As depicted in Graph 5, a noteworthy observation arises when analyzing the reported business sizes of companies compared to their classifications based on accounting-financial data. It is evident that a considerable proportion of companies indicating a business size of 1 (Micro) can be accurately classified as size 2 (Small) companies. Conversely, among the companies reporting a business size of 2 (Small), slightly less than half can be categorized as size 1 (Micro), making this classification particularly noteworthy in our analysis.

The most intriguing aspect emerges when considering companies that reported a business size of 3 (Medium). Surprisingly, none of these companies were classified in the same category. Instead, most of them could be accurately classified as size 1 (Micro), with a smaller portion falling into size 2 (Small). These stark differences between the reported size and the estimated size based on accounting information call for a thorough review of the companies' rights and obligations to prevent potential tax evasion.

Figure 4. Scores were calculated for the two discriminant functions
Source: Own elaboration based on Eviews.

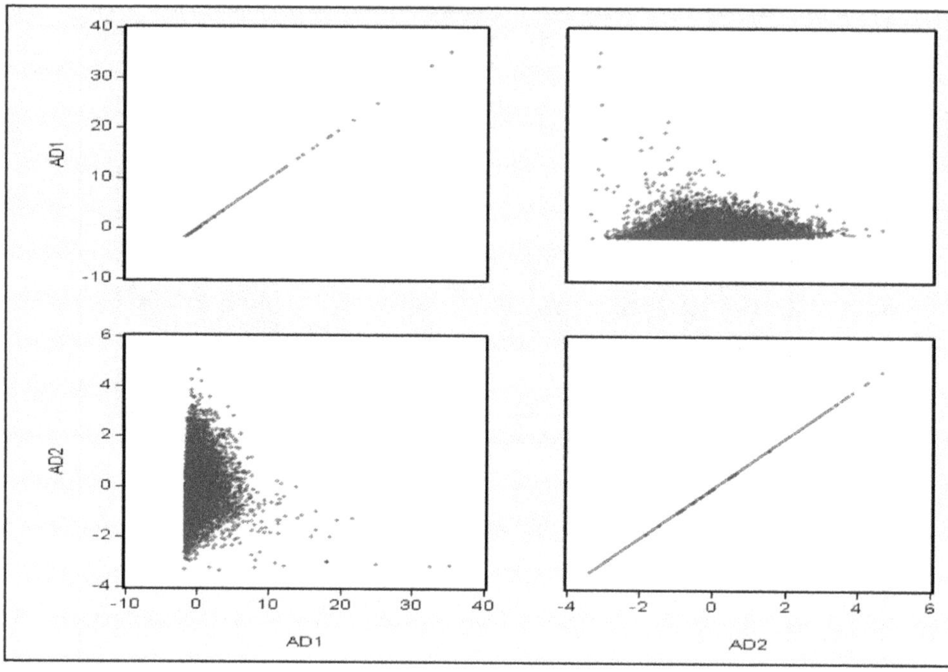

Table 21. Actual and forecast business size

Real size		Frequency	Percentage	Percentage valid	Percentage accumulated
Valid	1	7642	60.4	60.4	60.4
	2	4901	38.7	38.7	99.1
	3	115	.9	.9	100.0
	Total	12658	100.0	100.0	

Forecast size		Frequency	Percentage	Percentage valid	Percentage accumulated
Valid	1	8680	68.6	68.6	68.6
	2	3774	29.8	29.8	98.4
	3	204	1.6	1.6	100.0
	Total	12658	100.0	100.0	

Source: Author's calculations.

In conclusion, the findings highlight a clear disparity between the reported business size and the size determined through accounting-financial information. This divergence underscores the importance of addressing discrepancies and emphasizes the need for accurate reporting to ensure compliance with tax regulations.

Figure 5. Classification through a DA
Source: Author's calculations.

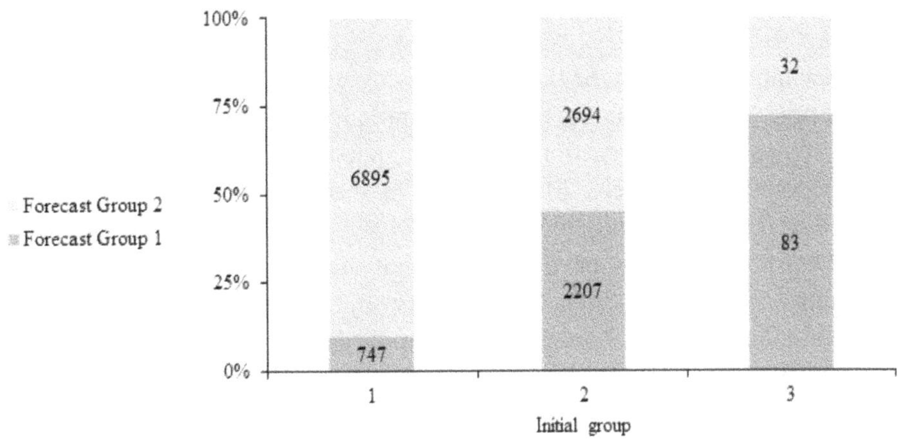

FUTURE RESEARCH DIRECTIONS

In today's globalized world, the significance of human capital, training, and technology transfer as pivotal elements for organizational success is widely acknowledged. Small and Medium Enterprises (SMEs) play a crucial role in any country or region, not only contributing to wealth generation but also job creation (Healy, O'Dwyer & Ledwith, 2017). These enterprises employ more than half of the world's economically active population, underscoring the need to understand their dynamics and how they bolster their workforce (Zevallos, 2007).

Within the Latin American context, SMEs have constituted nearly 90% (in the case of Uruguay) and 98.5% of all companies in countries such as Argentina, Brazil, Chile, Guatemala, and Mexico (Zevallos, 2003). However, the existence of these companies is fraught with challenges, including excessive bureaucracy, slow procedures, lack of confidence in regulations, and insufficient support from federal governments regarding programs exclusively tailored for SMEs (Guaipatín, 2003). Despite such obstacles, the determination and conviction of some entrepreneurs to establish and operate these businesses amid adversity are noteworthy.

SMEs play a pivotal role in the economic development of a country or region, owing to their dynamism and high growth potential, which could eventually lead them to become large companies and significantly impact the population (Azari, Madsen & Moen, 2017). They possess great flexibility in personnel management, enabling adjustments in workforce size and technical processes (Bani-Hani & AL-Hawary, 2009). However, these enterprises also face challenges such as reinvesting profits, upgrading equipment, and adopting advanced production techniques. Often, they struggle to attract specialized and trained personnel, resulting in non-competitive wages (Engidaw, 2022). The absence of skilled employees can lead to deficient production quality due to minimal or absent quality controls in various processes (Knezović, Bušatlić, and Riđić, 2020).

Furthermore, the presence of qualified personnel in SMEs brings about additional issues, including organizational challenges, competitive weaknesses, inventory control problems, tax issues, limited access to financing, difficulties in adopting cutting-edge technology, challenges with suppliers, entry into competitive markets, and obtaining relevant information, credits, and support services tailored to SMEs (Camisón & Villar-López, 2010). These factors may lead to subpar customer service, soaring prices, poor product quality, excessive fixed assets, and limited local impact, among other repercussions (Hayes, Chawla & Kathawala, 2016).

In the context of technology transfer, SMEs are increasingly recognizing their relevance. Such transfer occurs through various means, including targeted training for technology management, consultancy services, training of students with international exposure, personnel exchange, and informal scientific collaborations (De Moortel & Crispeels, 2018; Shmeleva *et al.*, 2021; Giones, Kleine & Tegtmeier, 2021; Budiman, 2018; Sezal & Giumelli, 2022).

Studies from the early 21st century have indicated that the competitive success factors for SMEs may vary across countries (Rubio & Aragón, 2002). However, two recurring elements are the quality of human resources within the company and the level of knowledge, skills, and behavior exhibited by the workforce, which significantly impact the SME's success (Clarke, Seng & Whiting, 2011; Hutchinson & Quintas, 2008).

Research examining the influence of science and engineering-trained human resources on economic growth and well-being worldwide further reinforces the importance of skilled labor across companies of varied sizes, including SMEs (Torre, 2014; Maitra, 2018). For instance, studies have highlighted the critical role of innovation in the economic development of countries and have explored the underutilization of science and technology graduates in the SME sector in the UK, with a focus on their potential contribution to these enterprises (Castelblanco & Robledo, 2014; Febriani & Dewobroto, 2018).

In conclusion, skilled labor at all levels constitutes a determining factor for the success of organizations, particularly for SMEs. Their ability to adapt, innovate, and attract qualified personnel significantly impacts their growth, productivity, and overall contribution to economic development.

CONCLUSION

The empirical findings of this study demonstrate the feasibility of classifying companies based on their accounting-financial information. These results have important implications, potentially leading to more accurate tax capture, as certain companies previously considered micro-sized could be appropriately classified as small ones. Moreover, this methodology could identify companies that may have a significant potential for employment generation if they are found to be larger in size. While the results obtained in this research contribute to the understanding of SMEs' economic growth and innovative potential in a given country or region, further investigation is warranted.

Despite the statistical challenges in constructing the selected financial ratios for PCA, the ratios still enabled considerable Discriminant Analysis (DA) results. However, to ensure the consistency of these findings, independent sampling, like systematic random sampling, should be employed to verify the results' robustness. Through DA, it was evident that two linear functions can effectively discriminate among the three groups of companies. The cross-validation technique yielded a reliability level of 89.9% in predicting company size for 2020 based on the synthetic variables generated by PCA and the variable representing the number of employees in 2020. Notably, this approach facilitated distinguishing micro and small companies quite well. Nevertheless, discriminating between small and medium-sized companies proved less clear-cut.

The variable related to the number of employees in 2020 contributed significantly to the discrimination process, underscoring the importance of reinforcing the results with an accounting analysis. However, the synthetic measure obtained for explaining company size through the selected ratios might be biased due to data nature. To address this, it is recommended to transform the data or enhance the database with more relevant financial ratios for the sector, thus validating the results.

While the study pursued its purpose effectively through traditional statistical procedures, the data's nature calls for the consideration of alternative techniques in the analysis, such as Probit (Logit) models with three categorizations or neural network analysis. Employing these methods could strengthen the relationship between the ratios or aid in constructing additional synthetic financial ratios that offer more comprehensive insights into business size.

In conclusion, the study's outcomes provide valuable insights into classifying companies based on accounting-financial information. These findings have potential implications for tax assessment and identifying employment-generating companies. Nevertheless, further analysis and refinement of methodologies may be needed to ensure accuracy and enhance the understanding of SMEs' impact on economic growth and innovation.

DECLARATION

The author declares that the manuscript follows ethical standards and there are no potential conflicts of interest with respect to the research, authorship and/or publication of this chapter.

DISCLAIMER

The contents and views of this chapter are expressed by the author in personal capacity. It is not necessary for the Editor and the Publisher to agree with these viewpoints, and they are not responsible for any duty of care in this regard.

REFERENCES

Agwor, T. C. (2014). The normal distribution of financial accounting ratios as indicators of business status. *European Journal of Business and Management*, *6*(35), 215–222.

Altman, E. I. (1968). Financial ratios, discriminant analysis and the prediction of corporate bankruptcy. *The Journal of Finance*, *23*(4), 589–609. doi:10.1111/j.1540-6261.1968.tb00843.x

Ardelean, F. A. (2017). Case study using analysis of variance to determine groups' variations. *MATEC Web of Conferences, vol. 126. Annual Session of Scientific Papers IMT ORADEA 2017*. Baile Felix SPA, Romania. 10.1051/matecconf/201712604008

Aslam, M., Sherwani, R. A. K., & Saleem, M. (2021). Vague data analysis using neutrosophic Jarque-Bera test. *PLoS One*, *16*(12), e0260689. doi:10.1371/journal.pone.0260689 PMID:34855840

Azari, M. J., Madsen, T. K., & Moen, O. (2017). Antecedent and outcomes of innovation-based growth strategies for exporting SMEs. *Journal of Small Business and Enterprise Development*, *24*(4), 733–752. doi:10.1108/JSBED-08-2016-0125

Bani-Hani, J. S., & AL-Hawary, F. (2009). The impact of core competencies on competitive advantage: Strategic challenge. *International Bulletin of Business Administration*, *6*(6), 93–104.

Behara, K. N. S., Bhaskar, A., & Chung, E. (2021). A DBSCAN-based framework to mine travel patterns from origin-destination matrices: Proof-of-concept on proxy static OD from Brisbane. *Transportation Research Part C, Emerging Technologies*, *131*, 103370. doi:10.1016/j.trc.2021.103370

Boedeker, P., & Kearns, N. T. (2019). Linear discriminant analysis for prediction of group membership: A user-friendly primer. *Advances in Methods and Practices in Psychological Science*, *2*(3), 250–263. doi:10.1177/2515245919849378

Boedo, L., & Calvo, A. R. (2001). Incidencia del tamaño sobre el comportamiento financiero de la empresa. Un análisis empírico con PYMES Gallegas. *Revista Galega de Economía*, *10*(2), 1–23.

Brijlal, P., Enow, S., & Isaacs, E. B. H. (2014). The use of financial management practices by small, medium and micro enterprises: A perspective from South Africa. *Industry and Higher Education*, *28*(5), 341–350. doi:10.5367/ihe.2014.0223

Budiman, A. (2018). Employee transfer: A review of recent literature. *Journal of Public Administration Studies*, *3*(1), 33–36. doi:10.21776/ub.jpas.2018.003.01.5

Cai, M., & Liang, Y. (2018). An Improved CURE Algorithm. In Z. Shi, C. Pennartz, & T. Huang (Eds.), *Intelligence Science II. ICIS 2018. IFIP Advances in Information and Communication Technology* (Vol. 539). Springer. doi:10.1007/978-3-030-01313-4_11

Camisón, C., & Villar-López, A. (2010). Effect of SMEs' international experience on foreign intensity and economic performance: The mediating role of internationally exploitable assets and competitive strategy. *Journal of Small Business Management*, *48*(2), 116–151. doi:10.1111/j.1540-627X.2010.00289.x

Castelblanco, J., & Robledo, J. (2014). Relación entre el PIB y algunos indicadores de Ciencia y Tecnología: Colombia vs. Corea del Sur. *Escenarios: Empresa y territorio, 3*(3). https://esumer.edu.co/revistas/index.php/escenarios/article/view/88

Castelleti, O. (2005). Experiencia Italiana: Los Distritos Industriales. *Ibero-American Seminar on Business Cooperation*. Santiago de Chile, Chile. http://iberpyme.sela.org/Chile0505/ProgramaTrabajoChile.htm

Chen, Y., & Zhou, Y. (2018). Robust principal component analysis with matrix factorization. *IEEE International Conference on Acoustics, Speech and Signal Processing (ICASSP)*, (pp. 2411–2415). IEEE. 10.1109/ICASSP.2018.8462041

Chen, Y. S., Lin, C. K., Lo, C. M., Chen, S. F., & Liao, Q. J. (2021). Comparable studies of financial bankruptcy prediction using advanced hybrid intelligent classification models to provide early warning in the electronics industry. *Mathematics*, *9*(20), 2622. doi:10.3390/math9202622

Clarke, M., Seng, D., & Whiting, R. H. (2011). Intellectual capital and firm performance in Australia. *Journal of Intellectual Capital*, *12*(4), 505–530. doi:10.1108/14691931111181706

Curado, C., Tai, S. H. T., Oliveira, M., & Sarmento, J. M. (2021). Levels and dimensions of diversity in small businesses: Contributions for performance. *International Journal of Productivity and Performance Management, 71*(8), 3138–3159. doi:10.1108/IJPPM-12-2020-0628

Davidson, W. III. (2020). *Financial Statement Analysis: Basis for Management Advice (AICPA Book 18)* (1st ed.). John Wiley & Sons. doi:10.1002/9781119743217

De Moortel, K., & Crispeels, T. (2018). International university-university technology transfer: Strategic management framework. *Technological Forecasting and Social Change, 135*, 145–155. doi:10.1016/j.techfore.2018.05.002

Deng, D. (2020). *DBSCAN Clustering Algorithm Based on Density*. 2020 7th International Forum on Electrical Engineering and Automation (IFEEA), Hefei, China. 10.1109/IFEEA51475.2020.00199

Dias, S., Brito, P., & Amaral, P. (2021). Discriminant analysis of distributional data via fractional programming. *European Journal of Operational Research, 294*(1), 206–218. doi:10.1016/j.ejor.2021.01.025

Engidaw, A. E. (2022). Small businesses and their challenges during COVID-19 pandemic in developing countries: In the case of Ethiopia. *Journal of Innovation and Entrepreneurship, 11*(1), 1. doi:10.118613731-021-00191-3 PMID:35036286

Faello, J. (2015). Understanding the Limitations of Financial Ratios. *Academy of Accounting and Financial Studies Journal, 19*(3), 75–86.

Febriani, E., & Dewobroto, W. S. (2018). Problems and requirement analysis as a first step to connect researchers and small and medium enterprises (SMEs). *Cogent Business & Management, 5*(1), 1513774. doi:10.1080/23311975.2018.1513774

Foorthuis, R. (2021). On the nature and types of anomalies: A review of deviations in data. *International Journal of Data Science and Analytics, 12*(4), 297–331. doi:10.100741060-021-00265-1 PMID:34368422

Frey, B. (2018). Spearman correlation coefficient. In *The SAGE encyclopedia of educational research, measurement, and evaluation* (Vol. 1–4). SAGE Publications, Inc., doi:10.4135/9781506326139

Gherghina, S. C., Botezatu, M. A., Hosszu, A., & Simionescu, L. N. (2020). Small and Medium-Sized Enterprises (SMEs): The engine of economic growth through investments and innovation. *Sustainability (Basel), 12*(1), 347. doi:10.3390u12010347

Giones, F., Kleine, K., & Tegtmeier, S. (2021). Students as scientists' co-pilots at the onset of technology transfer: A two-way learning process. *The Journal of Technology Transfer, 47*(5), 1373–1394. doi:10.100710961-021-09880-3

Government of Spain. (2019). *Marco estratégico en política de PYME 2030*. Government of Spain. https://industria.gob.es/es-es/Servicios/MarcoEstrategicoPYME/Marco%20Estratégico%20PYME.pdf

Greene, H. W. (2017). *Econometric analysis*. Pearson.

Guaipatín, A. (2003). *Observatorio MIPYME: Compilación estadística para 12 países de la Región*. New York: Banco Interamericano de Desarrollo. https://www.iadb.org/es

Hahs-Vaughn, D. L. (2017). *Applied multivariate statistical concepts*. Routledge.

Härdle, W. K., & Simar, L. (2016). *Applied multivariate statistical analysis* (4th ed.). Springer.

Haryati, A. E., Surono, S., & Suparman, S. (2021). Implementation of Minkowski-Chebyshev distance in fuzzy subtractive clustering. *EKSAKTA: Journal of Sciences and Data Analysis*, *2*(2), 82–87. doi:10.20885/EKSAKTA.vol2.iss2.art1

Hayes, J. P., Chawla, S. K., & Kathawala, Y. (2016). A comparative study of problems encountered in the development of small businesses in the U.S. and Mexico. *Journal of Developing Areas*, *49*(3), 395–406. doi:10.1353/jda.2015.0175

Healy, B., O'Dwyer, M., & Ledwith, A. (2017). An exploration of product advantage and its antecedents in SMEs. *Journal of Small Business and Enterprise Development*, *25*(1), 129–146. doi:10.1108/JSBED-06-2017-0206

Hilkevics, S., & Semakina, V. (2019). The classification and comparison of business ratios analysis methods. *Insights into Regional Development*, *1*(1), 48–57. doi:10.9770/ird.2019.1.1(4)

Hutchinson, V., & Quintas, P. (2008). Do SMEs do knowledge management?: Or simply manage what they know? *International Small Business Journal*, *26*(2), 131–154. doi:10.1177/0266242607086571

Ittelson, T. (2020). *Financial statements: A step-by-step guide to understanding and creating financial reports* (3rd ed.). Career Press.

Ježovita, A. (2015). Variations between financial ratios for evaluating financial position related to the size of a company. *Review of Innovation and Competitiveness: A Journal of Economic and Social Research*, *1*(1), 115–136. https://hrcak.srce.hr/155600

Jolliffe, I., & Cadima, J. (2016). Principal component analysis: A review and recent developments. *Philosophical Transactions - Royal Society. Mathematical, Physical, and Engineering Sciences*, *374*(2065), 20150202. doi:10.1098/rsta.2015.0202 PMID:26953178

Karlsson, J. (2021). Firm size and growth barriers: A data-driven approach. *Small Business Economics*, *57*(3), 1319–1338. doi:10.100711187-020-00350-y

Kliestik, T., Valaskova, K., Lazaroiu, G., Kovacova, M., & Vrbka, J. (2020). Remaining financially healthy and competitive: The role of financial predictors. *Journal of Competitiveness*, *12*(1), 74–92. doi:10.7441/joc.2020.01.05

Knezović, E., Bušatlić, S., & Riđić, O. (2020). Strategic human resource management in small and medium enterprises. *International Journal of Human Resources Development and Management*, *20*(2), 114–139. doi:10.1504/IJHRDM.2020.106255

Laitinen, E. (2018). Financial reporting: Long-term change of financial ratios. *American Journal of Industrial and Business Management*, *8*(9), 1893–1927. doi:10.4236/ajibm.2018.89128

Lin, S.-W., & Chen, S.-C. (2009). PSOLDA: A particle swarm optimization approach for enhancing the classification accuracy rate of linear discriminant analysis. *Applied Soft Computing*, *9*(3), 1008–1015. doi:10.1016/j.asoc.2009.01.001

Mahmoudabadi, H., & Barzegar, E. (2009). Investigating statistical distribution of financial ratios of accepted companies in Tehran's stock exchange. *Journal of Accounting Advances*, *1*(1(57/3)), 171–189.

Maitra, B. (2018). Investment in physical, human capital, economic growth and life expectancy in Bangladesh: An empirical investigation. *South Asia Economic Journal*, *19*(2), 251–269. doi:10.1177/1391561418799110

Myšková, R., & Hájek, P. (2017). Comprehensive assessment of firm financial performance using financial ratios and linguistic analysis of annual reports. *Journal of International Students*, *10*(4), 96–108. doi:10.14254/2071-8330.2017/10-4/7

Nobi, A., Tuhin, K. H., & Lee, J. W. (2021). Application of principal component analysis on temporal evolution of COVID-19. *PLoS One*, *16*(12), e0260899. doi:10.1371/journal.pone.0260899 PMID:34855909

OECD. (2017). *Enhancing the contributions of SMEs in a global and digitalised economy*. Meeting of the OECD Council at Ministerial Level, Paris, France. https://www.oecd.org/industry/C-MIN-2017-8-EN.pdf

OECD. (2018). *Fostering greater SME participation in a globally integrated economy*. SME Ministerial Conference (Plenary session 3), Mexico City, Mexico. https://www.oecd.org/cfe/smes/ministerial/documents/2018-SME-Ministerial-Conference-Plenary-Session-3.pdf

OECD. (2022). *Glossary of tax terms*. OECD. https://www.oecd.org/ctp/glossaryoftaxterms.htm

OECD/CAF. (2019). *Latin America and the Caribbean 2019: Policies for competitive SMEs in the Pacific Alliance and participating South American countries, SME Policy Index*. OECD Publishing. doi:10.1787/d9e1e5f0-

Omprakash, S., & Gokila, S. (2018). Principal component analysis-A survey. *International Journal of Advanced Research in Computer and Communication Engineering*, *7*(8), 63–66. doi:10.17148/IJARCCE.2018.7814

Ozyesil, M. (2020). An application of financial ratio analysis on concordat firms: A model suggestion on construction firms listed in Borsa Istanbul. *Journal of Economics and Behavioral Studies*, *11*(6J), 10–22. doi:10.22610/jebs.v11i6(J).3001

PIMEC. (2022). *Web site Servicio de Estudios de Pimec (Micro, petita i mitjana empresa de Catalunya)*. PIMEC. https://www.pimec.org/es/pimec-comerc/observatorio/estudios

Rao, P., Kumar, S., Chavan, M., & Lim, W. M. (2021). A systematic literature review on SME financing: Trends and future directions. *Journal of Small Business Management*, *61*(3), 1247–1277. doi:10.1080/00472778.2021.1955123

Rivero, P. (1991). *Análisis de Balances y Estados Complementarios*. Ediciones Pirámide.

Robinson, T. R. (2020). *International Financial Statement Analysis (CFA Institute Investment Series)*. Wiley.

Rubio, A., & Aragón, A. (2002). Factores explicativos del éxito competitivo. Un estudio empírico en la PYME. *Cuadernos de Gestión*, *2*(1), 49–63.

Sezal, M. A., & Giumelli, F. (2022). Technology transfer and defence sector dynamics: The case of the Netherlands. *European Security*, *31*(4), 558–575. doi:10.1080/09662839.2022.2028277

Shinmura, S. (2016). *New theory for discriminant analysis after R. Fisher*. Springer. doi:10.1007/978-981-10-2164-0

Shmeleva, N., Gamidullaeva, L., Tolstykh, T., & Lazarenko, D. (2021). Challenges and opportunities for technology transfer networks in the context of open innovation: Russian experience. *Journal of Open Innovation*, *7*(3), 197. doi:10.3390/joitmc7030197

Siegel, S., & Castellan, N. J. (2009). *Estadística no paramétrica. Aplicada a las ciencias de la conducta*. Editorial Trillas.

Sosa, M. C. (2011). Breve inventario de los principales ratios financieros utilizados en el análisis financiero empresarial. *Observatorio de la Economía Latinoamericana*, *152*, 1–23.

Thanh Binh, V. T., Tran, N. M., Thanh, D. M., & Phamd, H. H. (2020). Firm size, business sector and quality of accounting information systems: Evidence from Vietnam. *Accounting*, *6*(3), 327–334. doi:10.5267/j.ac.2020.2.002

Torre, F. (2014). Contribución de la Ciencia e Ingeniería en el desarrollo económico. *The Twelfth Latin American and Caribbean Conference for Engineering and Technology*. Guayaquil, Ecuador. Retrieved from https://www.laccei.org/LACCEI2014-Guayaquil/RefereedPapers/RP080.pdf

Tran, Q. T., Nguyen, N. K. D., & To, P. Q. A. (2020). Financial ratios affecting disclosure level in interim report of Vietnamese listed enterprises. *The Journal of Asian Finance. Economics and Business*, *7*(10), 43–50. doi:10.13106/jafeb.2020.vol7.no10.043

Tsoulfidis, L., & Athanasiadis, I. (2022). A new method of identifying key industries: A principal component analysis. *Journal of Economic Structures*, *11*(1), 1–23. doi:10.118640008-022-00261-z

Urías, J. (1992). *Análisis de Estados Financieros*. McGraw-Hill.

Vier Machado, H. P. (2016). Growth of small businesses: A literature review and perspectives of studies. Gest. Prod., São Carlos, 23(2), 419–432. https://doi.org/ doi:10.1590/0104-530X1759-14

Zevallos, E. (2003). Micro, pequeñas y medianas empresas en América Latina. *Revista de la CEPAL*, *79*(79), 53–70. doi:10.18356/da461f83-es

Zevallos, E. (2007). *Restricciones del entorno a la competitividad empresarial en América Latina*. Bolivia: Fundación para el Desarrollo Sostenible (FUNDES). http://www.sela.org/es/centro-de-documentacion/base-de-datos-documental/bdd/28689/ restricciones-del-entorno-a-la-competitividad-empresarial-en-america-latina

ENDNOTES

1 Thanks to the Pimec Studies Service (Micro, medium and small company of Catalonia) for the transfer of the database to carry out this work (PIMEC, 2022).

2 In the work of Sosa (2011) a series of ratios are proposed to be used in a business financial analysis that intends to answer this question.

Compilation of References

Abatecola, G. (2019). Prioritizing short-termism in behavioural strategy: Lessons from Enron–20 years on. *International Journal of Business and Management*, *14*(4), 60–71. doi:10.5539/ijbm.v14n4p60

Abdullah, F., Mohamad, N. S., & Yunos, Z. (2018). Safeguarding Malaysia's cyberspace against cyber threats: Contributions by cyber security Malaysia. *OIC-Cert Journal of Cyber Security*, *1*(1), 22–31.

Abou-El-Sood, H., & El-Sayed, D. (2022). Abnormal disclosure tone, earnings management and earnings quality. *Journal of Applied Accounting Research*, *23*(2), 402–433. doi:10.1108/JAAR-07-2020-0139

Abu-Shanab, E., & Matalqa, S. (2015). Security and fraud issues of E-Banking. *International Journal of Computer Networks and Applications*, *2*(4), 179–188.

Acconcia, A., D'Amato, M., & Martina, R. (2003). *Corruption and tax evasion with competitive bribes* (Working Paper No. 112). Centre for Studies in Economics and Finance, Università degli studi di salerno.

Acemoglu, D., & Johnson, S. (2005). Unbundling institutions. *Journal of Political Economy*, *113*(5), 949–995. doi:10.1086/432166

Adebayo, R. I. (2018). The change agenda of *Úmar Bn Ábdul-Á*ziz as a model for fighting corruption in Nigeria. *Journal of Islam in Nigeria*, *3*(1), 106–120.

Adebisi, J. F., & Gbegi, D. O. (2015). Fraud and the Nigerian public sector performance: The need for forensic accounting. *International Journal of Business. Human Technology*, *5*(5), 67–78.

Aghion, P., Akcigit, U., Cagé, J., & Kerr, W. R. (2016). Taxation, corruption and growth. *European Economic Review*, *86*, 24–51. doi:10.1016/j.euroecorev.2016.01.012

Agwor, T. C. (2014). The normal distribution of financial accounting ratios as indicators of business status. *European Journal of Business and Management*, *6*(35), 215–222.

Ahmad, I., Iqbal, S., Jamil, S., & Kamran, M. (2021). A Systematic literature review of E-Banking frauds: Current scenario and security techniques. *Linguistica Antverpiensia*, *2*(2), 3509–3517.

Ahmadpour, A., & Shahsavari, M. (2016). Earnings management and the effect of earnings quality in relation to bankruptcy level. *Iranian Journal of Management Studies*, *9*(1), 77–99.

Aidt, T. (2003). Economic analysis of corruption: A survey. *Economic Journal (London)*, *113*(491), 632–652. doi:10.1046/j.0013-0133.2003.00171.x

Aixalá, J., & Fabro, G. (2008). Does the impact of institutional quality on economic growth depend on initial income level? *Economic Affairs*, *28*(3), 45–49. doi:10.1111/j.1468-0270.2008.00844.x

Akdemir, N., & Lawless, C. J. (2020). Exploring the human factor in cyber-enabled and cyber dependent crime victimization: A lifestyle routine activities approach. *Internet Research*, *30*(6), 1665–1687. doi:10.1108/INTR-10-2019-0400

Akdemir, N., & Yenal, S. (2020). Card-Not-Present fraud victimization: A routine activities approach to understand the risk factors. *Güvenlik Bilimleri Dergisi*, *9*(1), 243–268. doi:10.28956/gbd.736179

Akram, T., Ramakrishnan, S. A. I., & Naveed, M. (2022). (Forthcoming). Prevalence of money laundering and terrorism financing through stock market: A comprehensive conceptual review paper. *Journal of Money Laundering Control*. doi:10.1108/JMLC-06-2022-0094

Aktan, C. (2001). *Siyasal Ahlak ve Siyasal Yozlaşma*, Yolsuzlukla Mücadele Stratejileri, içinde Ankara: Hak-İş Yayınları.

Alam, M. K. (2018). *Situational Victimization Among Adolescents Exploring the Role of Morality, Self-control and Lifestyle Risk*. Degree Project in Criminology master's Program, Criminology. Malmo Universitet.

Albrecht, C., Duffin, K. M., Hawkins, S., & Morales Rocha, V. M. (2019). The use of cryptocurrencies in the money laundering process. *Journal of Money Laundering Control*, *22*(2), 210–216. doi:10.1108/JMLC-12-2017-0074

AlDaajeh, S., Saleous, H., Alrabaee, S., Barka, E., Breitinger, F., & Choo, K. K. R. (2022). The role of national cybersecurity strategies on the improvement of cybersecurity education. *Computers & Security*, *119*, 102754. doi:10.1016/j.cose.2022.102754

Ali, M. J., Razzaque, R. M., & Ahmed, K. (2018). Real earnings management and financial statement fraud: Evidence from Malaysia. *International Journal of Accounting & Information Management*, *26*(4), 508–526. doi:10.1108/IJAIM-03-2017-0039

Ali, M., Lei, S., & Wei, X. Y. (2018). The mediating role of the employee relations climate in the relationship between strategic HRM and organizational performance in Chinese banks. *Journal of Innovation & Knowledge*, *3*(3), 115–122. doi:10.1016/j.jik.2016.12.003

Allard, T. (2014, September 10). Big Oil stands by as con man swindles East Timor. *The Sydney Morning Herald*. https://www.smh.com.au/national/big-oil-stands-by-as-con-man-swindles-east-timor-20140909-10eb13.html

Alsayed, A., & Bilgrami, A. (2017). E-Banking security: Internet hacking, phishing attacks, analysis, and prevention of fraudulent activities. *International Journal of Emerging Technology and Advanced Engineering*, *7*(1), 109–115.

Al-Shattarat, B., Hussainey, K., & Al-Shattarat, W. (2022). The impact of abnormal real earnings management to meet earnings benchmarks on future operating performance. *International Review of Financial Analysis*, *81*, 101264. doi:10.1016/j.irfa.2018.10.001

Altman, E. I. (1968). Financial ratios, discriminant analysis and the prediction of corporate bankruptcy. *The Journal of Finance*, *23*(4), 589–609. doi:10.1111/j.1540-6261.1968.tb00843.x

Amjad, R., Rafay, A., Arshed, N., Munir, M., & Amjad, M. (2021). Non-Linear impact of globalization on financial crimes: A case of developing economies. *Journal of Money Laundering Control*, *25*(2), 358–375. doi:10.1108/JMLC-03-2021-0023

Amundsen, I. (1999). Political Corruption: An Introduction to the Issues. Chr. Michelsen Institute.

Anandarajan, A., & Kleinman, G. (2011). The impact of cognitive biases on fraudulent behaviour: The Leeson case. *International Journal of Behavioural Accounting and Finance*, *2*(1), 40–55. doi:10.1504/IJBAF.2011.038756

Anand, V., Ashforth, B. E., & Joshi, M. (2004). Business as usual: The acceptance and perpetuation of corruption in organizations. *The Academy of Management Perspectives*, *18*(2), 39–53. doi:10.5465/ame.2004.13837437

Anastasiadou, E., & Chrissos Anestics, M. (2020). The coronavirus' effects on consumer behavior and supermarket activities: Insights from Greece and Sweden. *The International Journal of Sociology and Social Policy*, *40*(9/10), 893–907. doi:10.1108/IJSSP-07-2020-0275

Anderson, J. H., & Gray, C. W. (2007). Transforming judicial systems in Europe and Central Asia. In F. Bourguignon & B. Pleskovic (Eds.) *Annual World Bank Conference on Development Economics – Regional: Beyond Transition*, (pp. 329–356). World Bank.

Andoh-Baidoo, F. K., & Osatuyi, B. (2009). Examining online banking initiatives in Nigeria: A value network approach. *The Electronic Journal on Information Systems in Developing Countries*, *38*(1), 1–14. doi:10.1002/j.1681-4835.2009.tb00264.x

Andreas, P., & Nadelmann, E. (2008). *Policing the globe: Criminalization and crime control in international relations*. Oxford University Press.

Andreas, P., & Wallman, J. (2009). Illicit markets and violence: What is the relationship? *Crime, Law, and Social Change*, *52*(3), 225–229. doi:10.100710611-009-9200-6

Andrews, C. J. (2008). Greenhouse gas emissions along the rural-urban gradient. *Journal of Environmental Planning and Management*, *51*(6), 847–870. doi:10.1080/09640560802423780

An, H., Lee, Y. W., & Zhang, T. (2014). Do corporations manage earnings to meet/exceed analyst forecasts? Evidence from pension plan assumption changes. *Review of Accounting Studies*, *19*(2), 698–735. doi:10.100711142-013-9261-8

Antonescu, M., & Birăub, R. (2015). Financial and non-financial implications of cybercrime in emerging countries. *Procedia Economics and Finance*, *32*, 618–621. doi:10.1016/S2212-5671(15)01440-9

Apau, R., Koranteng, F. N., & Gyamfi, S. A. (2019). Cyber-crime and its effects on E-commerce technologies. *Journal of Information*, *5*(1), 39–59. doi:10.18488/journal.104.2019.51.39.59

APG. (1997). *Members & Observers - Sri Lanka*. Asia Pacific Group. http://www.apgml.org/members-and-observers/members/details.aspx ?m=ff29a4ed-30d0-416b-a234-39aa780a2c9f

APG. (2022). *What is mone laudering*. Asia Pacific Group. http://www.apgml.org/about-us/page.aspx?p=5620f71b-1858-4ca1-85d7-f9eae97210a7

Arango, L. G., Deccache, E., Bonatto, B. D., Arango, H., & Pamplona, E. O. (2017). Study of electricity theft impact on the economy of a regulated electricity company. *Journal of Control. Automation and Electrical Systems*, *28*(4), 567–575.

Ardelean, F. A. (2017). Case study using analysis of variance to determine groups' variations. *MATEC Web of Conferences, vol. 126. Annual Session of Scientific Papers IMT ORADEA 2017*. Baile Felix SPA, Romania. 10.1051/matecconf/201712604008

Ariza, L. R., Ferrero, J. M., & Sànchez, M. B. (2015). Consequences of earnings management for corporate reputation. Evidence from family firms. *Accounting Research Journal*, *29*(4), 457–474. doi:10.1108/ARJ-02-2015-0017

Armstrong, M. (2021. August 6). How many websites are there? *Statista Infographics*. https://www.statista.com/chart/19058/how-many-websites-are-there/

Armstrong, C. S., Blouin, J. L., & Larcker, D. F. (2012). The incentives for tax planning. *Journal of Accounting and Economics*, *5*(1), 391–411. doi:10.1016/j.jacceco.2011.04.001

Arnaud, B. P. (2016, January 31). La Grande Peste de Marseille de 1720 n'est pas venue d'Asie. Le bacile tueur était sur place. *Science & Avenir*. https://www.sciencesetavenir.fr/archeo-paleo/archeologie/la-grande-peste-de-marseille-de-1720-n-est-pas-venue-d-asie-le-bacille-tueur-etait-sur-place_104165

Asadov, A. (2021). Financial scams through Ponzi schemes: The case of CIS countries. In A. Rafay (Ed.), *Handbook of Research on Theory and Practice of Financial Crimes* (pp. 271–292). IGI Global. doi:10.4018/978-1-7998-5567-5.ch015

Asher, M. G. (2001). Design of tax systems and corruption. In *Conference on "Fighting Corruption: Common Challenges and Shared Experiences," Singapore* (pp. 10–11). Cite Seer. https://citeseerx.ist.psu.edu/document?repid=rep1&type=pdf&doi=e7b2483b1fbb522 ef88146a5fdddaf99ce702d6a .

Aslam, M., Sherwani, R. A. K., & Saleem, M. (2021). Vague data analysis using neutrosophic Jarque-Bera test. *PLoS One*, *16*(12), e0260689. doi:10.1371/journal.pone.0260689 PMID:34855840

As-Sallabi, A. M. (2011). The rightly-guided caliph and great reviver, 'Umar bin 'Abd al-'Aziz: Indicators of renewal and guided reformation on the prophetic path. Riyadh: Darussalam.

Associated Press. (2016, December 16). Genovese family mobsters busted for offshore gambling ring. *Fox News*. https://www.foxnews.com/us/genovese-family-mobsters-busted-for-offshore-gambling-ring

ATF. (2015, February). Fact sheet - Explosives Enforcement Officer (EEO). *Bureau of Alcohol, Tobacco, Firearms, and Explosives, United States Department of Justice*. https://www.atf.gov/file/10976/download

ATF. (2018, May). Fact sheet - tobacco enforcement. *Bureau of Alcohol, Tobacco, Firearms, and Explosives, United States Department of Justice*. https://www.atf.gov/resource-center/fact-sheet/fact-sheet-tobacco-enforcement

Athanasakou, V., Strong, N. C., & Walker, M. (2011). The market reward for achieving analyst earnings expectations: Does managing expectations or earnings matter? *Journal of Business Finance & Accounting*, *38*(2), 58–94. doi:10.1111/j.1468-5957.2010.02219.x

Audoin-Rouzeau, F. (2003). *Les chemin de la peste. Le rat, la puce et l'homme*. Presses Universitaires de Rennes. doi:10.4000/books.pur.8382

Azari, M. J., Madsen, T. K., & Moen, O. (2017). Antecedent and outcomes of innovation-based growth strategies for exporting SMEs. *Journal of Small Business and Enterprise Development*, *24*(4), 733–752. doi:10.1108/JSBED-08-2016-0125

Aziani, A., Kulick, J., Norman, N., & Prieger, J. E. (2017). Empty discarded pack data and the prevalence of illicit trade in cigarettes. SSRN *Electronic Journal*. https://ssrn.com/abstract=2906015 doi:10.2139/ssrn.2906015

Aziani, A., Dugato, M., & Meneghini, C. (2020). A methodology for estimating the illicit consumption of cigarettes at the country level. *Global Crime*, *21*(2), 154–184. doi:10.1080/17440572.2020.1724786

Azizi, F. (2018). Effect of information asymmetry and mutual funds ownership on earnings management in companies listed in Tehran Stock Exchange. *International Journal of Management. Accounting and Economics*, *5*(7), 516–534.

Back, S., & Guerette, R. T. (2021). Cyber place management and crime prevention: The effectiveness of cybersecurity awareness training against phishing attacks. *Journal of Contemporary Criminal Justice*, *37*(3), 427–451. doi:10.1177/10439862211001628

Badiora, A. I. (2022). Predictors of future travel intentions to Lagos Megacity: Exploring the crime-risk perceptions. [AJHTM]. *African Journal of Hospitality and Tourism Management*, *3*(2), 1–22. doi:10.47963/ajhtm.v3i2.831

Bagdigen, M., & Beskaya, A. (2005). The impact of corruption on government revenues: The Turkish case. *Yapi Kredi Economic Review*, *16*(2), 31–54

Bagdigen, M., & Tunçer, M. (2004). Yolsuzluğun kamu gelirleri üzerine etkisi: Belediye gelirleri üzerine ampirik bir çalışma. *Vergi Dünyası, 272*, 168–174.

Baker, A., Goodman, J. D., & Mueller, B. (2015, June 14). Beyond the chokehold: The path to Eric Garner's death. *New York Times*. https://www.nytimes.com

Baker, W. E., & Faulkner, R. R. (1993). The social organization of conspiracy: Illegal networks in the heavy electrical equipment industry. *American Sociological Review, 58*(6), 837–860. doi:10.2307/2095954

Bakirtaş, D. (2012). The effect of corruption on tax revenues: The case of Türkiye. *Journal of Management and Economics, 19*(2), 87–98.

Balachandrudu, K. (2006). Understanding political corruption. *Indian Journal of Poultry Science, 67*(4), 809–816.

Balachndran, B., Hanno, D., & Hanghang, T. (2013). Tax-induced earnings management within a dividend imputation system. *Australian Tax Forum, 28*(3), 555–582.

Baltagi, B. H., & Levin, D. (1986). Estimating dynamic demand for cigarettes using panel data: The effects of bootlegging, taxation and advertising reconsidered. *The Review of Economics and Statistics, 68*(1), 148–155. doi:10.2307/1924938

Banerjee, A. V. (1997). A theory of misgovernance. *The Quarterly Journal of Economics, 112*(4), 1289–1332. doi:10.1162/003355300555484

Banerjee, A. V., & Duflo, E. (2019). *Good economics for hard times*. PublicAffairs.

Bani-Hani, J. S., & AL-Hawary, F. (2009). The impact of core competencies on competitive advantage: Strategic challenge. *International Bulletin of Business Administration, 6*(6), 93–104.

Bansal, M., Kumar, A., Bhattacharyya, A., & Bashir, H. A. (2022). Predictors of revenue shifting and expense shifting: Evidence from an emerging economy. *Journal of Contemporary Accounting & Economics, 19*(1), 100339. doi:10.1016/j.jcae.2022.100339

Barak, G. (Ed.). (2015). *The Routledge international handbook of the crimes of the powerful*. Routledge. doi:10.4324/9781315815350

Bardhan, P. (1997). Corruption and development: A review of issues. *Journal of Economic Literature, 35*(3), 1320–1346.

Bardhan, P. (2021). *Indian Polity and economy: A mirror to difficult times*. Frontpage.

Barnes, P. (2010). Stock market efficiency, insider dealing and market abuse: The UK experience. *International Journal of Business Governance and Ethics, 5*(1-2), 38–50. doi:10.1504/IJBGE.2010.029554

Bartov, E., Givoly, D., & Hayn, C. (2002). The rewards to meeting or beating earnings expectations. *Journal of Accounting and Economics, 33*(2), 173–204. doi:10.1016/S0165-4101(02)00045-9

Basel Committee Report on Banking Supervision. (1998). *Risk Management for Electronic Banking and Electronic Money Activities*. Basel: Bank of International Settlements.

Bashir, M. A., Ali, M. H., Wai, L. M., Hossain, M. I., & Rahaman, M. S. (2020). Mediating effect of customer perceived value on the relationship between service quality and customer satisfaction of E-Banking in Bangladesh. *International Journal of Advanced Science and Technology, 29*(2), 3590–3606.

Baskaran, T., Min, B., & Uppal, Y. (2015). Election cycles and electricity provision: Evidence from a quasi-experiment with Indian special elections. *Journal of Public Economics, 126*, 64–73. doi:10.1016/j.jpubeco.2015.03.011

Basyir, M. (2021). Malaysians suffered RM2.23 billion losses from cyber-crime frauds. *New Straits Times*. https://www.nst.com.my/news/crime-courts/2021/07/708911/malaysians-suffered-rm223-billion-losses-cyber-crime-frauds

Baucus, M. S., & Baucus, D. A. (1997). Paying the piper: An empirical examination of longer-term financial consequences of illegal corporate behavior. *Academy of Management Journal*, *40*(1), 129–151. doi:10.2307/257023

Baxter, T. C. Jr, & Ramasastry, A. (1996). The importance of being honest-lessons from an era of large-scale financial fraud. *Saint Louis University Law Journal*, *41*, 93.

Bayley, C. (1989). *Imperial Meridian: The British Empire and the World 1780-1830*. Pearson.

Bayley, D. H. (1966). The effects of corruption in a developing nation. *The Western Political Quarterly*, *19*(4), 719–732. doi:10.1177/106591296601900410

Bazilian, M., Nakhooda, S., & Van de Graaf, T. (2014). Energy governance and poverty. *Energy Research & Social Science*, *1*, 217–225. doi:10.1016/j.erss.2014.03.006

BBC. (2009, February 26). US raids target Mexican drug gang. *BBC News*. http://news.bbc.co.uk

Becker, C. L., Defond, M. L., Jiambalvo, J., & Subramanyam, K. R. (1998). The effect of audit on earnings management. *Contemporary Accounting Research*, *15*(1), 1–25. doi:10.1111/j.1911-3846.1998.tb00547.x

Becker, G. S. (1968). Crime and punishment: An economic approach. *Journal of Political Economy*, *76*(2), 169–217. doi:10.1086/259394

Becker, G. S. (1968a). *The Economic approach to human behavior*. University of Chicago Press.

Beebeejaun, A., Gunputh, R., & Rafay, A. (2023). Base Erosion and Profit Shifting (BEPS) in International Taxation System: The Case of Mauritius in the light of OECD/G20 initiatives. In A. Rafay (Ed.), *Concepts, Cases, and Regulations in Financial Fraud and Corruption* (pp. 259–277). IGI Global. doi:10.4018/978-1-6684-5007-9.ch011

Behara, K. N. S., Bhaskar, A., & Chung, E. (2021). A DBSCAN-based framework to mine travel patterns from origin-destination matrices: Proof-of-concept on proxy static OD from Brisbane. *Transportation Research Part C, Emerging Technologies*, *131*, 103370. doi:10.1016/j.trc.2021.103370

Bellanova, R., & Glouftsios, G. (2022). Controlling the Schengen Information System (SIS II): The infrastructural politics of fragility and maintenance. *Geopolitics*, *27*(1), 160–184. doi:10.1080/14650045.2020.1830765

Belverd, E., Powers, M., & Şenyiğit, Y. B. (2018). Earnings management: A review of selected cases. *Muhasebe Enstitüsü Dergisi*, *16*(59), 23–36.

Bénassy-Quéré, A., Coupet, M., & Mayer, T. (2007). Institutional determinants of foreign direct investment. *World Economy*, *30*(5), 764–782. doi:10.1111/j.1467-9701.2007.01022.x

Bender, W., & Palmer, C. (2016, August 4). Joey Merlino arrested in federal mob crackdown. *The Philadelphia Inquirer*. https://www.inquirer.com

Beneish, M. D. (1997). Detecting GAAP violation: Implications for assessing earnings management among firms with extreme financial performance. *Journal of Accounting and Public Policy*, *16*(3), 271–309. doi:10.1016/S0278-4254(97)00023-9

Beneish, M. D. (1999). Incentives and penalties related to earnings overstatements that violate GAAP. *The Accounting Review*, *74*(4), 425–457. doi:10.2308/accr.1999.74.4.425

Beneventano, P., Berger, P. D., & Weinberg, B. D. (2012). Predicting run production and run prevention in baseball: The impact of Sabermetrics. *International Journal of Business. Human Technology*, *2*(4), 67–75.

Benson, M. L., & Simpson, S. S. (2014). *Understanding White-Collar crime. An opportunity perspective*. Routledge. doi:10.4324/9780203762363

Benston, G. J. (2006). Fair-value accounting: A cautionary tale from Enron. *Journal of Accounting and Public Policy*, *25*(4), 465–484. doi:10.1016/j.jaccpubpol.2006.05.003

Bereskin, F. L., Hsu, P., & Rotenberg, W. (2018). The real effects of real earnings management: Evidence from innovation. *Contemporary Accounting Research*, *35*(1), 525–557. doi:10.1111/1911-3846.12376

Berg, L. A., & Desai, D. (2013). *Background paper: overview on the rule of law and sustainable development for the global dialogue on rule of law and the post-2015 development agenda*. UNDP.

Bergstresser, D., Desai, M., & Rauh, J. (2006). Earnings manipulation, pension assumptions, and managerial investment decisions. *The Quarterly Journal of Economics*, *121*(1), 157–195.

Berlie, J. (2012). Anticorruption in East Timor: Implications for development and education. *Asian Education and Development Studies*, *1*(3), 251–261. doi:10.1108/20463161211270473

Beşel, F. (2013). *Corruption-economic growth relationship: The case of Türkiye* [Doctoral dissertation), Sakarya University Türkiye].

Beyer, B. D., Nabar, S. M., & Rapley, E. T. (2018). Real earnings management by benchmark-beating firms: Implications for future profitability. *Accounting Horizons*, *32*(4), 59–84. doi:10.2308/acch-52167

Bhagwati, J., & Panagariya, A. (2012). *India's tryst with destiny: Debunking myths that undermine progress and addressing new challenges*. HarperCollins Publishers.

Bhojraj, S., Hribar, P., Picconi, M., & McInnis, J. (2009). Making sense of cents: An examination of firms that marginally miss or beat analyst forecasts. *The Journal of Finance*, *64*(5), 2361–2388. doi:10.1111/j.1540-6261.2009.01503.x

BIG. (2021). *Basel AML Index 2021*. Basel Institute of Governance. https://baselgovernance.org/publications/basel-aml-index-2021

BIG. (2022). *About us*. Basel Institute of Governance. https://baselgovernance.org/about-us

Bingham, T. (2011). *The rule of law*. Penguin.

Biraben, J. N. (1968). Certain demographic characteristics of the plague epidemic in France, 1720-1722. *Daedalus*, *97*(2), 536–545. PMID:11609518

Biraben, J. N. (1975). Les hommes et la peste en France et dans les pays européens et méditerranéens des origines à 1850. *Population*, *30*(6), 1143–1144. doi:10.2307/1531209

Bishop, J. M. (2018). Does cigarette smuggling prop up smoking rates? *American Journal of Health Economics*, *4*(1), 80–104. doi:10.1162/ajhe_a_00094

Blunt, P. (2009). The political economy of accountability in Timor-Leste: Implications for public policy. *Public Administration and Development*, *29*(2), 89–100. doi:10.1002/pad.522

Boedeker, P., & Kearns, N. T. (2019). Linear discriminant analysis for prediction of group membership: A user-friendly primer. *Advances in Methods and Practices in Psychological Science*, *2*(3), 250–263. doi:10.1177/2515245919849378

Boedo, L., & Calvo, A. R. (2001). Incidencia del tamaño sobre el comportamiento financiero de la empresa. Un análisis empírico con PYMES Gallegas. *Revista Galega de Economía*, *10*(2), 1–23.

Bolton, R. J., & Hand, D. J. (2002). Statistical fraud detection: A review. *Statistical Science*, *17*(3), 235–255. doi:10.1214s/1042727940

Bonanni, C., Drysdale, D., Hughes, A., & Doyle, P. (2006). Employee background verification: The cross-referencing effect. *The International Business & Economics Research Journal*, *5*(11). doi:10.19030/iber.v5i11.3519

Boris, B. (2005). Corruption: Concepts, types, causes, and consequences. Washington, DC: Center for International Private Enterprise (CIPE), US Chamber of Commerce.

Boros, C., & Cusick, J. (2017, November 22). Bought and paid for – how Romania's media is pressured by corporate and political masters. *Open Democracy*. https://www.opendemocracy.net/en/bought-and-paid-for-how-romania-s-media-is-pressured-by-corporate-and-polit/

Bos, K. I., Herbig, A., Sahl, J., Waglechner, N., Fourment, M., Forrest, S. A., Klunk, J., Schuenemann, V. J., Poinar, D., Kuch, M., Golding, G. B., Dutour, O., Keim, P., Wagner, D. M., Holmes, E. C., Krause, J., & Poinar, H. N. (2016). Eighteenth century Yersinia pestis genomes reveal the long-term persistence of an historical plague focus. *eLife*, *5*, e12994. doi:10.7554/eLife.12994 PMID:26795402

Box, S. (1983). *Crime, power and ideological mystification*. Tavistock.

Boyce, J. R., & Emery, J. H. (2011). Is a negative correlation between resource abundance and growth sufficient evidence that there is a 'resource curse'? *Resources Policy*, *36*(1), 1–13. doi:10.1016/j.resourpol.2010.08.004

Boyum, D., & Kleiman, M. A. (2003). Breaking the drug-crime link. *The Public Interest*, *152*, 19–38.

Braga, A. A., Kennedy, D. M., & Tita, G. E. (2002). New approaches to the strategic prevention of gang and group-involved violence. *Gangs in America*, *3*, 271–286. doi:10.4135/9781452232201.n17

Braga, A. A., Kennedy, D. M., Waring, E. J., & Piehl, A. M. (2001). Problem-oriented policing, deterrence, and youth violence: An evaluation of Boston's operation ceasefire. *Journal of Research in Crime and Delinquency*, *38*(3), 195–226. doi:10.1177/0022427801038003001

Braga, A. A., Turchan, B., Papachristos, A. V., & Hureau, D. M. (2019). Hot spots policing of small geographic areas effects on crime. *Campbell Systematic Reviews*, *15*(3), e1046. doi:10.1002/cl2.1046 PMID:37133274

Braga, A. A., & Weisburd, D. L. (2012). The effects of focused deterrence strategies on crime: A systematic review and meta-analysis of the empirical evidence. *Journal of Research in Crime and Delinquency*, *49*(3), 323–358. doi:10.1177/0022427811419368

Braga, A. A., & Weisburd, D. L. (2015). Focused deterrence and the prevention of violent gun injuries: Practice, theoretical principles, and scientific evidence. *Annual Review of Public Health*, *36*(1), 55–68. doi:10.1146/annurev-publhealth-031914-122444 PMID:25494051

Braga, A. A., Weisburd, D. L., Waring, E. J., Mazerolle, L. G., Spelman, W., & Gajewski, F. (1999). Problem-oriented policing in violent crime places: A randomized controlled experiment. *Criminology*, *37*(3), 541–580. doi:10.1111/j.1745-9125.1999.tb00496.x

Braga, A. A., Weisburd, D., & Turchan, B. (2018). Focused deterrence strategies and crime control: An updated systematic review and meta-analysis of the empirical evidence. *Criminology & Public Policy*, *17*(1), 205–250. doi:10.1111/1745-9133.12353

Braga, A. A., Weisburd, D., & Turchan, B. (2019). Focused deterrence strategies effects on crime: A systematic review. *Campbell Systematic Reviews*, *15*(3), e1051. doi:10.1002/cl2.1051 PMID:37133287

Braşoveanu, I. V., & Obreja Brasoveanu, L. (2009). Correlation between corruption and tax revenues in EU 27. *Economic Computation and Economic Cybernetics Studies and Research*, *43*(4), 133–142.

Bratton, W. W. (2001). Enron and the dark side of shareholder value. *Tulane Law Review*, *76*, 1275.

Brennan, N. M., & McGrath, M. (2007). Financial statement fraud: Some lessons from US and European case studies. *Australian Accounting Review*, *17*(42), 49–61. doi:10.1111/j.1835-2561.2007.tb00443.x

Breuer, C., Boronczyk, F., & Rumpf, C. (2021). Message personalization and real-time adaptation as next innovations in sport sponsorship management? How run-of-play and team affiliation affect viewer response. *Journal of Business Research*, *133*, 309–316. doi:10.1016/j.jbusres.2021.05.003

Brijlal, P., Enow, S., & Isaacs, E. B. H. (2014). The use of financial management practices by small, medium and micro enterprises: A perspective from South Africa. *Industry and Higher Education*, *28*(5), 341–350. doi:10.5367/ihe.2014.0223

Brody, R. G. (2010). Beyond the basic background check: Hiring the 'right' employees. *Management Research Review*, *33*(3), 210–223. doi:10.1108/01409171011030372

Brody, R. G., & Perri, F. S. (2016). Fraud detection suicide: The dark side of white-collar crime. *Journal of Financial Crime*, *23*(4), 786–797. doi:10.1108/JFC-09-2015-0043

Brooks, C. (2019). Federal Law Enforcement Officers, 2016 – Statistical Tables. *US Department of Justice, Office of Justice Programs, Bureau of Justice Statistics* (NCJ 251922). https://tinyurl.com/2wr6zkhy

Brouwer, E. (2018, August 2018). Schengen entry bans for political reasons? The Case of Lyudmyla Kozlovska. *Verfassungsblog: On Matters Constitutional*. https://verfassungsblog.de/schengen-entry-bans-for-political-reasons-the-case-of-lyudmyla-kozlovska/

Brouwer, E. (2021). Schengen and the administration of exclusion: Legal remedies caught in between entry bans, risk assessment and artificial intelligence. *European Journal of Migration and Law*, *23*(4), 485–507. doi:10.1163/15718166-12340115

Brown, R., & Gillespie, S. (2015). Overseas financial investigation of organised crime. *Journal of Money Laundering Control*, *18*(3), 371–381. doi:10.1108/JMLC-03-2014-0010

Budiman, A. (2018). Employee transfer: A review of recent literature. *Journal of Public Administration Studies*, *3*(1), 33–36. doi:10.21776/ub.jpas.2018.003.01.5

Bufkins, W. R., & Dharan, B. G. (2004). Red Flags in Enron's Reporting of Revenues and Key Financial Measures. *Enron: Corporate Fiascos and Their Implications*, 97–110. https://papers.ssrn.com/sol3/papers.cfm?abstract_id=1172222

Buil-Gil, D., Lord, N., & Barrett, E. (2021). The dynamics of business, cybersecurity and cyber-victimization: Foregrounding the internal guardian in prevention. *Victims & Offenders*, *16*(3), 286–315. doi:10.1080/15564886.2020.1814468

Buti, G. (2020). *Colère de dieu, mémoire des hommes. La peste en Provence 1720-2020*. Les éditions du Cerf.

Butkiewicz, J. L., & Yanikkaya, H. (2006). Institutional quality and economic growth: Maintenance of the rule of law or democratic institutions, or both? *Economic Modelling*, *23*(4), 648–661. doi:10.1016/j.econmod.2006.03.004

Byard, D., Hossain, M., & Mitra, S. (2007). US oil companies' earnings management in response to hurricanes Katrina and Rita. *Journal of Accounting and Public Policy*, *26*(6), 733–748. doi:10.1016/j.jaccpubpol.2007.10.006

CA LAO. (2022, January). How much does it cost to incarcerate an inmate? *California Legislative Analyst's Office*. https://lao.ca.gov/policyareas/cj/6_cj_inmatecost

Caiden, G. E., Dwivedi, O. P., & Jabbra, J. (2001). Where Corruption Lives. Bloomfield: Kumarian Press.

Cai, M., & Liang, Y. (2018). An Improved CURE Algorithm. In Z. Shi, C. Pennartz, & T. Huang (Eds.), *Intelligence Science II. ICIS 2018. IFIP Advances in Information and Communication Technology* (Vol. 539). Springer. doi:10.1007/978-3-030-01313-4_11

Cameron, I. (2003). UN targeted sanctions, legal safeguards and the European Convention on Human Rights. *Nordic Journal of International Law*, *72*(2), 159–214. doi:10.1163/157181003322560556

Camisón, C., & Villar-López, A. (2010). Effect of SMEs' international experience on foreign intensity and economic performance: The mediating role of internationally exploitable assets and competitive strategy. *Journal of Small Business Management*, *48*(2), 116–151. doi:10.1111/j.1540-627X.2010.00289.x

Campa, D., & Cmacho-Miñan, M. D. M. (2014). Earnings management among bankrupt non-listed firms: Evidence from Spain. *Revista Española de Financiación y Contabilidad*, *43*(1), 3–21. doi:10.1080/02102412.2014.890820

Campaign for Tobacco-Free Kids. (2021). *Cigarette tax increases by state per year 2000-2021*. Tobacco Free Kids. https://www.tobaccofreekids.org/assets/factsheets/0275.pdf

Canare, T. (2017). The effect of corruption on foreign direct investment inflows: Evidence from a panel of Asia-Pacific countries. In M. dela Rama & C. Rowley (Eds.), *The Changing Face of Corruption in the Asia Pacific* (pp. 35–55). Elsevier. doi:10.1016/B978-0-08-101109-6.00003-4

Carpenter, C. S., & Nguyen, H. V. (2021). Intended and unintended effects of banning menthol cigarettes. *The Journal of Law & Economics*, *64*(3), 629–650. doi:10.1086/713978

Carrière, C., Courdurié, M., & Rebuffat, F. (1968). *Marseille ville morte: la peste de 1720*. Jeanne Laffite.

Castelblanco, J., & Robledo, J. (2014). Relación entre el PIB y algunos indicadores de Ciencia y Tecnología: Colombia vs. Corea del Sur. *Escenarios: Empresa y territorio, 3*(3). https://esumer.edu.co/revistas/index.php/escenarios/article/view/88

Castelleti, O. (2005). Experiencia Italiana: Los Distritos Industriales. *Ibero-American Seminar on Business Cooperation*. Santiago de Chile, Chile. http://iberpyme.sela.org/Chile0505/ProgramaTrabajoChile.htm

Caulkins, J. P., Kleiman, M. A. R., & Kulick, J. D. (2010). *Drug production and trafficking, counterdrug policies, and security and governance in Afghanistan*. New York University Center on International Cooperation.

Caulkins, J. P., Larson, R. C., & Rich, T. F. (1993). Geography's impact on the success of focused local drug enforcement operations. *Socio-Economic Planning Sciences*, *27*(2), 119–130. doi:10.1016/0038-0121(93)90012-8

Cavaye, A. L. (1996). Case study research: A multi-faceted research approach for IS. *Information Systems Journal*, *6*(3), 227–242. doi:10.1111/j.1365-2575.1996.tb00015.x

Caylor, M. L., & Chambers, D. J. (2015). Reaching into the cookie jar? Why conservative accounting is sometimes a problem. *Journal of Corporate Accounting & Finance*, *26*(5), 73–77. doi:10.1002/jcaf.22066

CBSL. (2019, October 21). *The Financial Action Task Force delisted Sri Lanka from the grey list*. Central Bank of Sri Lanka. https://www.cbsl.gov.lk/en/node/6701#:~:text=The%20Financial%20Action%20Task%20Force%20(FATF)%2C%20the%20global%20policy,as%20%E2%80%9Cthe%20Grey%20List%E2%80%9D

CBSL. (2020, May 12). *Delisting of Sri Lanka by the Eropean Commission from its list of high risk 3rd countries.* Central Bank of Sri Lanka. https://www.cbsl.gov.lk/en/news/delisting-of-sri-lanka-by-european-commission-from-its-list-of-high-risk-3rd-countries

CDC. (2021). *The Tax Burden on Tobacco, 1970-2019.* Centers for Disease Control and Prevention, United States Department of Health and Human Services. https://chronicdata.cdc.gov/Policy/The-Tax-Burden-on-Tobacco-1970-2019/7nwe-3aj9

Ceccato, V. (2019). Crime and control in the digital era. *Criminal Justice Review, 44*(1), 5–10. doi:10.1177/0734016818818688

Cerqueti, R., & Coppier, R. (2011). Economic growth, corruption and tax evasion. *Economic Modelling, 28*(1-2), 489–500. doi:10.1016/j.econmod.2010.07.006

Chaimaa, B., Najib, E., & Rachid, H. (2021). E-banking overview: Concepts, challenges and solutions. *Wireless Personal Communications, 117*(2), 1059–1078. doi:10.100711277-020-07911-0

Chaturvedi, A., & Meena, A. (2016). Analyzing the impacts of phishing and vishing attacks in internet banking. *International Journal of Advanced Research in Computer Science and Software Engineering, 6*(3), 16–21.

Chemali, H. H. (2020, December 10). The European Magnitsky Law—A milestone with a lot of potential. *Atlantic Council.* https://www.atlanticcouncil.org/blogs/new-atlanticist/the-european-magnitsky-law-a-milestone-with-a-lot-of-potential/#:~:text=The%20European%20Magnitsky%20Act%20has%20some%20limitations%2C%20but,States%20and%20Europe%20to%20coordinate%20their%20efforts%20together

Chen, J. Z. (2009). *The choice between real and accounting earnings management* [Doctoral Dissertation). University of Houston]. https://pdfs.semanticscholar.org/491e/97e6eaca3e6d2cf8986cb8e03b5a5568cf2f.pdf

Chen, Y. S., Lin, C. K., Lo, C. M., Chen, S. F., & Liao, Q. J. (2021). Comparable studies of financial bankruptcy prediction using advanced hybrid intelligent classification models to provide early warning in the electronics industry. *Mathematics, 9*(20), 2622. doi:10.3390/math9202622

Chen, Y., & Zhou, Y. (2018). Robust principal component analysis with matrix factorization. *IEEE International Conference on Acoustics, Speech and Signal Processing (ICASSP)*, (pp. 2411–2415). IEEE. 10.1109/ICASSP.2018.8462041

Chhabra, S. (2016). Earning management: A study. *Splint International Journal of Professionals, 3*(11), 40–44.

Chi, J., Hayatdavoudi, L., Kruszona, S., Rowe, B., & Kleiman, M. A. R. (2014, April). *Reducing drug violence in Mexico: Options for implementing targeted enforcement.* UCLA Luskin School of Public Affairs. https://www.ojp.gov/pdffiles1/nij/grants/246358.pdf

Chiemeke, S. C., Evwiekpaefe, A. E., & Chete, F. O. (2006). The adoption of Internet banking in Nigeria: An empirical investigation. *Journal of Internet Banking and Commerce, 11*(3), 1–10.

Chin, A. J., Wafa, S. A. W. S. K., & Ooi, A. Y. (2009). The effect of internet trust and social influence towards willingness to purchase online in Labuan, Malaysia. *International Business Research, 2*(2), 72–81. doi:10.5539/ibr.v2n2p72

Chionis, D., & Chalkia, A. (2016). Illicit tobacco trade in Greece: The rising share of illicit consumption during crisis. *Trends in Organized Crime, 19*(3), 236–253. doi:10.100712117-016-9273-4

Chiou, L., & Muehlegger, E. (2008). Crossing the line: Direct estimation of cross-border cigarette sales and the effect on tax revenue. *The B.E. Journal of Economic Analysis & Policy, 8*(1), 48. doi:10.2202/1935-1682.2027

Choi, K. S., Cho, S., & Lee, J. R. (2019). Cyberbullying and traditional bullying victimization among Korean youth: Application of cyber-routine activities theory with latent class analysis. *Computers in Human Behavior, 100*, 1–10. doi:10.1016/j.chb.2019.06.007

Christensen, T. E., Huffman, A., Lewis-Western, M. F., & Scott, R. (2022). Accruals earnings management proxies: Prudent business decisions or earnings manipulation? *Journal of Business Finance & Accounting, 49*(3-4), 536–587. doi:10.1111/jbfa.12585

Cizmaziova, L. (2021). *Sanctions as a tool for asset recovery: A global perspective (CIFAR Research Paper).* CIFAR. https://cifar.eu/wp-content/uploads/2021/05/CiFAR_Sanctions-as-a-Tool-for-Asset-Recovery_Global-Perspective.pdf

Clarke, M., Seng, D., & Whiting, R. H. (2011). Intellectual capital and firm performance in Australia. *Journal of Intellectual Capital, 12*(4), 505–530. doi:10.1108/14691931111181706

Clow, K. E., Baack, D., & Fogliasso, C. (1998). Reducing perceived risk through advertising service quality cues. *Journal of Professional Services Marketing, 16*(2), 151–162. doi:10.1300/J090v16n02_08

Cohen, L. E., & Felson, M. (1979). Social change and crime rate trends: A routine activity approach. *American Sociological Review, 44*(4), 588–608. doi:10.2307/2094589

Cohen, L. E., Kluegel, J. R., & Land, K. C. (1981). Social inequality and predatory criminal victimization: An exposition and test of a formal theory. *American Sociological Review, 46*(5), 505–524. doi:10.2307/2094935

Columbus, L. (2019). AI is predicting the future of online fraud detection. *Forbes.* https://www.forbes.com/sites/louiscolumbus/2019/08/01/ai-is-predicting-the-future-of-online-fraud-detection/

Cook, S., Giommoni, L., Trajtenberg Pareja, N., Levi, M., & Williams, M. L. (2023). Fear of economic cybercrime across Europe: A multilevel application of Routine Activity Theory. *British Journal of Criminology, 63*(2), 384–406. doi:10.1093/bjc/azac021

Cooter, R., & Ulen, T. (2016). *Law and economics.* Addison-Wesley.

Corden, W. M. (1984). Booming sector and Dutch disease economics: Survey and consolidation. *Oxford Economic Papers, 36*(3), 359–380. doi:10.1093/oxfordjournals.oep.a041643

Corsaro, N., & Engel, R. S. (2015). Most challenging of contexts. *Criminology & Public Policy, 14*(3), 471–505. doi:10.1111/1745-9133.12142

Cosgrove, E. (2005). Examining targeted sanctions: Are travel bans effective? In C. Staibano & P. Wallensteen (Eds.), *International Sanctions: Between Wars and Words* (pp. 225–246). Routledge.

Cronau, P., & Fowler, A. (2012). Miners owe East Timor millions in unpaid taxes [Episode]. Four Corners. Australia: ABC.

Crudele, J. (2015, November 5). This teacher-turned-arms dealer is lucky he only got 15 years. *New York Post.* https://nypost.com/

Cubbin, J., & Stern, J. (2006). The impact of regulatory governance and privatization on electricity industry generation capacity in developing economies. *The World Bank Economic Review, 20*(1), 115–141. doi:10.1093/wber/lhj004

Curado, C., Tai, S. H. T., Oliveira, M., & Sarmento, J. M. (2021). Levels and dimensions of diversity in small businesses: Contributions for performance. *International Journal of Productivity and Performance Management, 71*(8), 3138–3159. doi:10.1108/IJPPM-12-2020-0628

Cussatt, M., Huang, L., & Pollard, T. J. (2018). Accounting quality under U.S. GAAP versus IFRS: The case of Germany. *Journal of International Accounting Research, 17*(3), 21–41. doi:10.2308/jiar-51997

Dam, K. W. (2007). *The law-growth nexus: The rule of law and economic development.* Brookings Institution Press.

Das, G. (2013). *India grows at night.* Penguin.

Das-Gupta, A. (2015). Corruption. In K. Basu & A. Maertens (Eds.), *The New Oxford Companion to Economics in India* (Vol. I). Oxford University Press.

Dashora, K. (2011). Cybercrime in the society: Problems and preventions. *Journal of Alternative Perspectives in the Social Sciences*, *3*(1), 240–259.

Davidson, W. III. (2020). *Financial Statement Analysis: Basis for Management Advice (AICPA Book 18)* (1st ed.). John Wiley & Sons. doi:10.1002/9781119743217

Davies, D. (2018, June 28). How to get away with financial fraud. *The Guardian*. https://www.theguardian.com/news/2018/jun/28/how-to-get-away-with-financial-fraud

Davis, G. A., & Tilton, J. E. (2005). The resource curses. *Natural Resources Forum*, *29*(3), 233–242). doi:10.1111/j.1477-8947.2005.00133.x

Davis, G. (1995). Learning to love the Dutch disease: Evidence from the mineral economies. *World Development*, *23*(10), 1765–1779. doi:10.1016/0305-750X(95)00071-J

De Kimpe, L., Walrave, M., Verdegem, P., & Ponnet, K. (2022). What we think we know about cybersecurity: An investigation of the relationship between perceived knowledge, internet trust, and protection motivation in a cybercrime context. *Behaviour & Information Technology*, *41*(8), 1796–1808. doi:10.1080/0144929X.2021.1905066

De Moortel, K., & Crispeels, T. (2018). International university-university technology transfer: Strategic management framework. *Technological Forecasting and Social Change*, *135*, 145–155. doi:10.1016/j.techfore.2018.05.002

De Vaal, A., & Ebben, W. (2011). Institutions and the relation between corruption and economic growth. *Review of Development Economics*, *15*(1), 108–123. doi:10.1111/j.1467-9361.2010.00596.x

Deakin, S., & Konzelmann, S. J. (2004). Learning from Enron. *Corporate Governance*, *12*(2), 134–142. doi:10.1111/j.1467-8683.2004.00352.x

Dechow, P. M., Ge, W., Larson, C. R., & Sloan, R. G. (2011). Predicting material accounting misstatements. *Contemporary Accounting Research*, *28*(1), 17–82. doi:10.1111/j.1911-3846.2010.01041.x

Dechow, P. M., & Skinner, D. J. (2000). Earnings management: Reconciling the views of accounting academics, practitioners, and regulators. *Accounting Horizons*, *14*(2), 235–250. doi:10.2308/acch.2000.14.2.235

Dechow, P. M., Sloan, R. G., & Sweeney, A. P. (1995). Detecting earnings management. *The Accounting Review*, 193–225.

Dechow, P. M., Sloan, R. G., & Sweeney, A. P. (1996). Causes and consequences of earnings manipulation: An analysis of firms subject to enforcement actions by the SEC. *Contemporary Accounting Research*, *13*(1), 1–36. doi:10.1111/j.1911-3846.1996.tb00489.x

DeCicca, P., Kenkel, D., & Liu, F. (2013). Excise tax avoidance: The case of state cigarette taxes. *Journal of Health Economics*, *32*(6), 1130–1141. doi:10.1016/j.jhealeco.2013.08.005 PMID:24140760

Degeorge, F., Patel, J., & Zeckhauser, R. (1999). Earnings management to exceed thresholds. *The Journal of Business*, *72*(1), 1–33. doi:10.1086/209601

Deng, D. (2020). *DBSCAN Clustering Algorithm Based on Density*. 2020 7th International Forum on Electrical Engineering and Automation (IFEEA), Hefei, China. 10.1109/IFEEA51475.2020.00199

Department of State. (2015). *The global illicit trade in tobacco: A threat to national security*. DoS. https://2009-2017.state.gov/documents/organization/250513.pdf

Depuru, S. S. S. R., Wang, L., & Devabhaktuni, V. (2011). Electricity theft: Overview, issues, prevention and a smart meter-based approach to control theft. *Energy Policy*, *39*(2), 1007–1015. doi:10.1016/j.enpol.2010.11.037

Devaux, C. A. (2013). Small oversights that led of the Great Plague of Marseille (1720-1723): Lessons from the past. *Infection, Genetics and Evolution*, *14*, 169–185. doi:10.1016/j.meegid.2012.11.016 PMID:23246639

DHS. (2014). Intellectual property rights seizures statistics: Fiscal year 2013. *Department of Homeland Security*. https://tinyurl.com/3vtrpp43

DHS. (2020). Intellectual property rights seizures statistics: Fiscal year 2019. *Department of Homeland Security*. https://tinyurl.com/2p8ktjrt

Dias, S., Brito, P., & Amaral, P. (2021). Discriminant analysis of distributional data via fractional programming. *European Journal of Operational Research*, *294*(1), 206–218. doi:10.1016/j.ejor.2021.01.025

Dichev, I. D., Graham, J. R., Harvey, C. R., & Rajgopal, S. (2013). Earnings quality: Evidence from the field. *Journal of Accounting and Economics*, *56*(3), 1–33. doi:10.1016/j.jacceco.2013.05.004

Dickenson, M. (2014). The impact of leadership removal on Mexican drug trafficking organizations. *Journal of Quantitative Criminology*, *30*(4), 651–676. doi:10.100710940-014-9218-5

Dionisie, D., & Checchi, F. (2008). *Corruption and anti-corruption agencies in Eastern Europe and the CIS: A practitioners' experience*. United Nations Development Programme.

Doig, A. (1999). Dealing with corruption: The next steps. *Crime, Law, and Social Change*, *29*(2/3), 99–112. doi:10.1023/A:1008390808395

Doig, A., & Riley, S. (1998). Corruption and anti-corruption strategies: Issues and case studies from developing countries. In G. S. Cheema & J. Bonvin (Eds.), *Corruption And Integrity Improvement Initiatives in Developing Economies*. OECD.

Doig, A., & Tisne, M. (2009). A candidate for relegation? Corruption, governance approaches and the (re)construction of post-war states. *Public Administration and Development*, *29*(5), 374–386. doi:10.1002/pad.543

Dollar, D., & Kraay, A. (2003). Institutions, trade, and growth. *Journal of Monetary Economics*, *50*(1), 133–162. doi:10.1016/S0304-3932(02)00206-4

Doolin, B. (1996). Alternative views of case research in information systems. *AJIS. Australasian Journal of Information Systems*, *3*(2). Advance online publication. doi:10.3127/ajis.v3i2.383

Drakopoulou, A., Konstantinou, A., & Koros, D. (2020). Border management at the external Schengen borders: border controls, return operations, and obstacles to effective remedies in Greece. In S. Carrera & M. Stefan (Eds.), *Fundamental Rights Challenges in Border Controls and Expulsion of Irregular Immigrants in the European Union: Complaint Mechanisms and Access to Justice* (pp. 175–196). Routledge. doi:10.4324/9780429203275-11

Drèze, J. (2018). On corruption. In B. C. Nirmal, B.C& Bandyopadyay, S. (Eds.) Combating Corruption, Black Money and Money Laundering: Issues and Challenges Ahead. New Delhi: Satyam Law International.

Drysdale, J. (2008). Five principles for the management of natural resource revenue: The case of Timor-Leste's petroleum revenue. *Journal of Energy & Natural Resources Law*, *26*(1), 151–174. doi:10.1080/02646811.2008.11435181

Dumitrescu, E. I., & Hurlin, C. (2012). Testing for Granger non-causality in heterogeneous panels. *Economic Modelling*, *29*(4), 1450–1460. doi:10.1016/j.econmod.2012.02.014

Duo, Y., Hope, O., Thomas, W. B., & Zou, Y. (2016). Individual large shareholders, earnings management and capital market consequences. *Journal of Business Finance & Accounting*, *43*(7), 872–902.

Dyntu, V., & Dykyi, O. (2018). Cryptocurrency in the system of money laundering. *Baltic Journal of Economic Studies, 4*(5), 75–81. doi:10.30525/2256-0742/2018-4-5-75-81

Dyreng, S. D., Hillegeist, S. A., & Penalva, F. (2022). Earnings management to avoid debt covenant violations and future performance. *European Accounting Review, 31*(2), 311–343. doi:10.1080/09638180.2020.1826337

Dyson, C. (2015, April 12). King George County has earned a dubious distinction for the role it plays in the highly profitable world of cigarette smuggling. *The Free Lance-Star*. https://fredericksburg.com

EC. (2022). *Money Laundering*. European Commission. European Commiccion. https://ec.europa.eu/home-affairs/policies/internal-security/organised-crime-and-human-trafficking/money-laundering_en#:~:text=EU%20legal%20measures%20against%20money,it%20through%20law%20enforcement%20response

Eck, J. E., & Clarke, R. V. (2003). Classifying common police problems: A routine activity approach. *Crime Prevention Studies, 16*, 7–39.

Edelman, D., & Nicholson, A. (2011). Arthur Anderson auditors and Enron: What happened to their Texas CPA licenses? *Journal of Finance and Accountancy, 8*, 1–9.

Edling, H. (2007). *Preventing corruption in public finance management: A practical guide*. World Bank Group.

Ehsan, S., Tariq, A., Nazir, M. S., Shabbir, M. S., Shabbir, R., Lopez, L. B., & Ullah, W. (2022). Nexus between corporate social responsibility and earnings management: Sustainable or opportunistic. *MDE. Managerial and Decision Economics, 43*(2), 478–495. doi:10.1002/mde.3396

Eigen, P. (2005). *Corruption Perception Index*. Transparency International.

Ekbia, H. R. (2004). How IT mediates organizations: Enron and the California energy crisis. *Journal of Digital Information, 5*(4).

Ekins, E. (2017, September 19). Poll: Public distrusts wall street regulators as much as wall street, say gov't regulators are ineffective, biased, and selfish. *Cato Institute*. https://www.cato.org/blog/poll-public-distrusts-wall-street-regulators-much-wall-street-say-govt-regulators-are

El Diri, M. (2017). *Introduction to Earnings Management*. Springer.

Elbasani, A. (2018). International promotion of rule of law: Facing connections between patronage, crime and judiciary corruption. In *Rule of law in the Eestern Balkans: Exploring the new EU enlargement strategy and necessary steps ahead.* Aspen Institute. https://www.aspeninstitute.de/wp-content/uploads/Reader-Rule-of-Law.pdf#page=28

Elstein, A. (Nov. 13, 2016). High taxes and limited enforcement have New York City awash in illegal booze and cigarettes. *Crain's New York Business*. https://www.crainsnewyork.com/

Eneji, S. E., Angib, M. U., Ibe, W. E., & Ekwegh, K. C. (2019). A study of electronic banking fraud, fraud detection and control. *International Journal of Innovative Science and Research Technology, 4*(3), 708–711.

Engidaw, A. E. (2022). Small businesses and their challenges during COVID-19 pandemic in developing countries: In the case of Ethiopia. *Journal of Innovation and Entrepreneurship, 11*(1), 1. doi:10.118613731-021-00191-3 PMID:35036286

Engleman, D., & Kleiner, B. H. (1998). Effective employment screening practices. *Career Development International, 3*(4), 164–168. doi:10.1108/13620439810214420

Enomoto, M., Kimura, F., & Yamaguchi, T. (2015). Accrual-based and real earnings management: An international comparison for investor protection. *Journal of Contemporary Accounting & Economics, 11*(3), 183–198. doi:10.1016/j.jcae.2015.07.001

Erdogdu, E. (2014). The political economy of electricity market liberalization: A cross-country approach. *The Energy Journal (Cambridge, Mass.)*, *35*(3), 91–128. doi:10.5547/01956574.35.3.5

Euractiv. (2010, January 29). *EU investigates possible insider trading by terrorists.* Euractiv.com. https://www.euractiv.com/section/financial-regulation/news/eu-investigates-possible-insider-trading-by-terrorists/

EUR-Lex. (2019). *Second generation Schengen Information System (SIS II).* EUR-Lex. https://eur-lex.europa.eu/legal-content/RO/TXT/?uri=LEGISSUM%3Al14544

EuroNews. (2023, January 31). *Report: The world fails to fight corruption; Türkiye, in which rank?* Euronews. (https://tr.euronews.com/2023/01/31/rapor-dunya-yolsuzlukla-mucadelede-basarisiz-turkiye-kacinci-sirada

European Commission. (2021). *Restrictive measures (sanctions).* EC. https://ec.europa.eu/info/business-economy-euro/banking-and-finance/international-relations/restrictive-measures-sanctions_en

European Commission. (n.d.). *Migration and Home Affairs.* EC. https://ec.europa.eu/home-affairs/policies/schengen-borders-and-visa/schengen-information-system/alerts-and-data-sis_en

European Council. (2022). *EU sanctions against Russia explained.* EC. https://www.consilium.europa.eu/en/policies/sanctions/restrictive-measures-against-russia-over-ukraine/sanctions-against-russia-explained/

Everett, J., Neu, D., & Rahaman, A. S. (2006). The global fight against corruption: A Foucaultian, virtues-ethics framing. *Journal of Business Ethics*, *65*(1), 1–12. doi:10.100710551-005-8715-8

Fadare, O. A. (2015). A survey on perceived risk and intention of adopting internet banking. *Journal of Internet Banking and Commerce*, *21*(1), 144.

Faello, J. (2015). Understanding the Limitations of Financial Ratios. *Academy of Accounting and Financial Studies Journal*, *19*(3), 75–86.

Faisal, S. H. S., & Ismail, F. (2022). Cybersecurity threats and best practices of working from home. *Journal of Techno-Social*, *13*(2), 1–5.

Fantaye, D. K. (2004). Fighting corruption and embezzlement in third world countries. *Journal of Criminal Law*, *68*(2), 170–176. doi:10.1350/jcla.68.2.170.29126

FATF. (2012). FATF report: Illicit tobacco trade. *Financial Action Task Force.* https://tinyurl.com/2uytf5ay

FATF. (2012, July 17). *Revisions to the Financial Action Task Force (FATF) Standard - Information note to the executive board* (IMF Policy Papers). International Monetary Fund. https://www.imf.org/en/Publications/Policy-Papers/Issues/2016/12/31/Revisions-to-the-Financial-Action-Task-Force-FATF-Standard-Information-Note-to-the-PP4683

FATF. (2016, February 19). Consolidated FATF strategy on combatting terrorist financing. *Financial Action Task Force.* https://tinyurl.com/y9fuwt8t

FATF. (2020, December). Trade-based money laundering: Trends and developments. *Financial Action Task Force.* https://www.fatf-gafi.org/media/fatf/content/Trade-Based-Money-Laundering-Trends-and-Developments.pdf

FATF. (2021, October). *FATF Methodology for assessing compliance with the FATF Recommendations and the effectiveness of AML/CFT systems.* Financial Action Task Force. https://www.fatf-gafi.org/publications/mutualevaluations/documents/fatf-methodology.html

FATF. (2022). International standards on combating money laundering and the financing of terrorism & proliferation: The FATF recommendations: Updated March 2022. *Financial Action Task Force.* https://tinyurl.com/3fbncvur https://tinyurl.com/yptjyvca

FATF. (2022a). *Frequently asked questions.* Financial Action Task Force. https://www.fatf-gafi.org/en/pages/frequently-asked-questions.html

FATF. (2022b). *About.* Financial Action Task Force. Retrieved fom https://www.fatf-gafi.org/about/

FDA. (2018). Illicit trade in tobacco products after implementation of an FDA product standard. *United States Department of Health and Human Services.* https://tinyurl.com/3crar53d

FDA. (2020). Justification of estimates for appropriations committees: Fiscal year 2021. *Food and Drug Administration, United States Department of Health and Human Services.* https://www.fda.gov/media/135078/download

Febriani, E., & Dewobroto, W. S. (2018). Problems and requirement analysis as a first step to connect researchers and small and medium enterprises (SMEs). *Cogent Business & Management, 5*(1), 1513774. doi:10.1080/23311975.2018.1513774

Fedpol. (2020a). *Money Laundering Reporting Office Switzerland MROS.* Fedpol. https://www.fedpol.admin.ch/fedpol/en/home/kriminalitaet/geldwaescherei.html

Fedpol. (2020b). *The Schengen Information System SIS.* FedPol. https://www. fedpol.admin.ch/fedpol/en/home/polizei-zusammenarbeit/international/schengen /sis.html

Fedpol. (2020c). *At the centre of policing in Switzerland – fedpol in focus.* Fedpol. https://www.fedpol.admin.ch/fedpol/en/home/fedpol/fedpol.html

Finckenauer, J. O. (2005). Problems of definition: What is organized crime? *Trends in Organized Crime, 8*(3), 63–83. doi:10.100712117-005-1038-4

Fisher, R. J. (1993). Social desirability bias and the validity of indirect questioning. *The Journal of Consumer Research, 20*(2), 303–315. doi:10.1086/209351

Fisman, R., & Svensson, J. (2007). Are corruption and taxation really harmful to growth? Firm level evidence. *Journal of Development Economics, 83*(1), 63–75. doi:10.1016/j.jdeveco.2005.09.009

FIU-SL. (2014). *National Risk Assessment Report.* Financial Intelligence Unit of Sri Lanka Central Bank of Sri Lanka. https://fiu.gov.sl/reports/national-risk-assessment-report-nra-report/

FIU-SL. (2016). *APG Co-Chair (for 2016-2018) acceptance speech by Director of the Financial Intelligence Unit of Sri Lanka.* Financial Intelligence Unit of Sri Lanka Central Bank of Sri Lanka. FIU-SL: http://www.fiusrilanka.gov.lk/docs/Other/APG_Co-Chair_Acceptance_Speech.pdf

FIU-SL. (2020). *FIU-SL Annual Report.* Financial Intelligence Unit of Sri Lanka Central Bank of Sri Lanka. https://fiu.gov.sl/reports/annual-reports/

Fjeldstad, O. H., & Tungodden, B. (2003). Fiscal corruption: A vice or a virtue? *World Development, 31*(8), 1459–1467. doi:10.1016/S0305-750X(03)00089-5

Flitter, E., Dawson, S., & Hosenball, M. (2013, March 13). Exclusive: U.S. plans to let spy agencies scour Americans' finances. *Reuters.* https://www.reuters.com/article/usa-banks-spying-idINDEE92C0EH20130313

Foorthuis, R. (2021). On the nature and types of anomalies: A review of deviations in data. *International Journal of Data Science and Analytics, 12*(4), 297–331. doi:10.100741060-021-00265-1 PMID:34368422

Franceschetti, B. M. (2018). *Financial Crises and Earnings Management Behavior.* Springer International Publishing. doi:10.1007/978-3-319-54121-1

Francis, J. R., Maydew, E. L., & Sparks, H. C. (1999). The role of big 6 auditors in the credible reporting of accruals. *Auditing*, *18*(2), 17–35. doi:10.2308/aud.1999.18.2.17

Frankel, T. (2012). *The Ponzi scheme puzzle: A history and analysis of con artists and victims*. Oxford University Press. doi:10.1093/acprof:osobl/9780199926619.001.0001

Freitas-Lemos, R., Stein, J. S., Tegge, A. N., Kaplan, B. A., Heckman, B. W., Cummings, K. M., & Bickel, W. K. (2021). The illegal experimental tobacco marketplace I: Effects of vaping product bans. *Nicotine & Tobacco Research: Official Journal of the Society for Research on Nicotine and Tobacco*, *23*(10), 1744–1753. doi:10.1093/ntr/ntab088 PMID:33955478

Frey, B. (2018). Spearman correlation coefficient. In *The SAGE encyclopedia of educational research, measurement, and evaluation* (Vol. 1–4). SAGE Publications, Inc., doi:10.4135/9781506326139

Friedrichs, D. (2009). *Trusted Criminals: White Collar Crime in Contemporary Society*. Wadsworth.

Furnham, A., & Boo, H. C. (2011). A literature review of the anchoring effect. *Journal of Socio-Economics*, *40*(1), 35–42. doi:10.1016/j.socec.2010.10.008

Gainsborough, M. (2006). *Country study report: Vietnam 2006*. Transparency International.

Galbraith, J. W., & Kaiserman, M. (1997). Taxation, smuggling and demand for cigarettes in Canada: Evidence from time-series data. *Journal of Health Economics*, *16*(3), 287–301. doi:10.1016/S0167-6296(96)00525-5 PMID:10169302

Garba, A. A., Siraj, M. M., & Othman, S. H. (2022). An assessment of cybersecurity awareness level among Northeastern University students in Nigeria. *Iranian Journal of Electrical and Computer Engineering*, *12*(1), 572–584. doi:10.11591/ijece.v12i1.pp572-584

Gaur, V., & Gupta, E. (2016). The determinants of electricity theft: An empirical analysis of Indian states. *Energy Policy*, *93*, 127–136. doi:10.1016/j.enpol.2016.02.048

Gedikli, A. (2011). Kamu hizmetlerinin yönetimi sürecinde yolsuzluğun derinleştirdiği ekonomik büyüme ve yoksulluk sorunu üzerine bir değerlendirme. *Öneri Dergisi, 9*(36), 169–188.

Gee, J., & Button, M. (2019). *The financial cost of fraud 2019: The latest data from around the world*. University of Portsmouth.

General Accounting Office. (2004, May). *Cigarette smuggling: Federal law enforcement efforts and seizures increasing*. GAO-04-641. https://www.gao.gov/new.items/d04641.pdf

Gertler, M., & Kiyotaki, N. (2010). Financial intermediation and credit policy in business cycle analysis. In *Handbook of Monetary Economics* (Vol. 3, pp. 547–599). Elsevier.

Gherghina, S. C., Botezatu, M. A., Hosszu, A., & Simionescu, L. N. (2020). Small and Medium-Sized Enterprises (SMEs): The engine of economic growth through investments and innovation. *Sustainability (Basel)*, *12*(1), 347. doi:10.3390u12010347

Ghura, M. D. (1998). *Tax revenue in Sub-Saharan Africa: Effects of economic policies and corruption* (IMF Working Paper No. WP/98/135). International Monetary Fund.

Gill, A., Biger, N., Mand, H. S., & Mathur, N. (2013). Earnings management, firm performance, and the value of Indian manufacturing firms. *International Research Journal of Finance and Economics*, *116*(1), 120–132.

Ginzl, D. J. (2004). Dumb, dumber, and dumbest: What went wrong at Enron. *Commercial Lending Review*, *19*, 42.

Giones, F., Kleine, K., & Tegtmeier, S. (2021). Students as scientists' co-pilots at the onset of technology transfer: A two-way learning process. *The Journal of Technology Transfer*, *47*(5), 1373–1394. doi:10.100710961-021-09880-3

Giray, F. (2011). Yolsuzluk ve yolsuzluğun vergi yapisi üzerine etkileri. *İstanbul Üniversitesi Siyasal Bilgiler Fakültesi Dergisi, 32*, 111–137.

Glaeser, E. L., La Porta, R., Lopez-de-Silanes, F., & Shleifer, A. (2004). Do institutions cause growth? *Journal of Economic Growth*, *9*(3), 271–303. doi:10.1023/B:JOEG.0000038933.16398.ed

Glauner, P., Valtchev, P., State, R., & Duarte, D. (2018). *Non-technical losses in the 21st century: Causes, economic effects, detection and perspectives*. Research Gate. https://www.researchgate.net/publication/325297875_Non-Technical_Losses_in_the_21st_Century_Causes_Economic_Effects_Detection_and_Perspectives

Glodstein, D., Glodstein, S. L., & Fornaro, J. (2010). Fraud trauma syndrome: The victims of the Bernard Madoff scandal. *Journal of Forensic Studies in Accounting and Business*, *2*(1), 1–9.

Goel, R. K. (2008). Cigarette smuggling: Price vs. nonprice incentives. *Applied Economics Letters*, *15*(8), 587–592. doi:10.1080/13504850600721981

Goldkamp, J. S., & Vîlcică, E. (2008). Targeted enforcement and adverse system side effects: The generation of fugitives in Philadelphia. *Criminology*, *46*(2), 371–409. doi:10.1111/j.1745-9125.2008.00113.x

Goldstein, P. J. (1985). The drugs/violence nexus: A tripartite conceptual framework. *Journal of Drug Issues*, *15*(4), 493–506. doi:10.1177/002204268501500406

Goldstein, P. J. (1989). Drugs and violent crime. In N. A. Weiner & M. E. Wolfgang (Eds.), *Pathways to Criminal Violence* (pp. 16–48). Sage Publications.

Gottschalk, P. (2019). *Fraud and corruption: A convenience perspective*. Universal-Publishers.

Gottschalk, P., & Stanislas, P. (2017). *Public corruption: Regional and national perspectives on procurement fraud*. Routledge. doi:10.1201/9781315277301

Goudie, A., & Stasavage, D. (1997). *Corruption: The Issues* (OECD Development Centre Working Paper No. 122). Paris: OECD Publishing.

Government of Spain. (2019). *Marco estratégico en política de PYME 2030*. Government of Spain. https://industria.gob.es/es-es/Servicios/MarcoEstrategicoPYME/Marco%20Estratégico%20 PYME.pdf

Graham, J. R., Harvey, C. R., & Rajgopal, S. (2005). The economic implications of corporate financial reporting. *Journal of Accounting and Economics*, *40*(1), 3–73. doi:10.1016/j.jacceco.2005.01.002

Granger, C. W. (1969). Investigating causal relations by econometric models and cross-spectral methods. *Econometrica*, *37*(3), 424–438. doi:10.2307/1912791

Granovetter, M. (2007). The social construction of corruption. In M. Granovetter (Ed.), *On capitalism*. Stanford University Press. doi:10.1515/9780804768368-011

Granovetter, N. N. (2007). Identification of ambiguity in the case study research typology: What is a unit of analysis? *Qualitative Market Research*, *10*(1), 78–97. doi:10.1108/13522750710720413

Gray, C. W., & Kaufmann, D. (1998). Corruption and Development. *Maliye Dergisi*, *35*(1), 128.

Green, F. (2012, September 5). Va., US aim to crack down on cigarette smuggling. *Richmond Times-Dispatch*. http://www.richmond.com

Green, F. (2015a, March 14). Garner case brings cigarette trafficking to light. *Richmond Times-Dispatch.* http://www.richmond.com

Green, F. (2015b, March 28). Cigarette trafficking spawning other crimes and possibly violence. *Richmond Times-Dispatch.* http://www.richmond.com

Green, F. (2015c, December 20). Major player in cigarette trafficking to be sentenced Tuesday. *Richmond Times-Dispatch*, 1A.

Green, F. (2016, July 25). 2 plead not guilty in cigarette case. *Richmond Times-Dispatch*, 6B.

Greene, H. W. (2017). *Econometric analysis.* Pearson.

Guaipatín, A. (2003). *Observatorio MIPYME: Compilación estadística para 12 países de la Región.* New York: Banco Interamericano de Desarrollo. https://www.iadb.org/es

Gual, J., & Trillas, F. (2006). Telecommunications policies: Measurement and determinants. *Review of Network Economics*, *5*(2), 249–272. doi:10.2202/1446-9022.1097

Guedes, I., Martins, M., & Cardoso, C. S. (2022). Exploring the determinants of victimization and fear of online identity theft: An empirical study. *Security Journal*, 1–26. doi:10.105741284-022-00350-5

Gunestas, M., Mehmet, M., & Wijesekera, D. (2010). *Detecting Ponzi and pyramid business schemes in choreographed web services.* In *IFIP International Conference on Digital Forensics* (pp. 133–150). IEEE. 10.1007/978-3-642-15506-2_10

Gunny, K., & Zhang, T. C. (2014). Do managers use meeting analyst forecasts to signal private information? Evidence from patent citations. *Journal of Business Finance & Accounting*, *41*(8), 950–973. doi:10.1111/jbfa.12082

Gupta, S., Davoodi, H., & Alonso-Terme, R. (2002). Does corruption affect income inequality and poverty? *Economics of Governance*, *3*(1), 23–45. doi:10.1007101010100039

Güzel, S. (2021). The Role of Tax Systems in Preventing Corruption. In A. Rafay (Ed.), *Handbook of Research on Theory and Practice of Financial Crimes* (pp. 397–427). IGI Global. doi:10.4018/978-1-7998-5567-5.ch020

Gylfason, T. (2001). Natural resources, education, and economic development. *European Economic Review*, *45*(4–6), 847–859. doi:10.1016/S0014-2921(01)00127-1

Habib, M., & Zurawicki, L. (2002). Corruption and foreign direct investment. *Journal of International Business Studies*, *33*(2), 291–307. doi:10.1057/palgrave.jibs.8491017

Hadfield, G. K., & Weingast, B. R. (2014). Microfoundations of the rule of law. *Annual Review of Political Science*, *17*(1), 21–42. doi:10.1146/annurev-polisci-100711-135226

Hahs-Vaughn, D. L. (2017). *Applied multivariate statistical concepts.* Routledge.

Hakim, M. P., Zanetta, D., & da Cunha, D. T. (2021). Should I stay, or should I go? Consumers' perceived risk and visit to restaurants during the COVID-19 pandemic in Brazil. *Food Research International*, *141*, 110152. [REMOVED HYPERLINK FIELD] doi:10.1016/j.foodres.2021.110152 PMID:33642018

Hamir, M. A. (1999). Keynote Address. In K. Frimpong & G. Jacques (Eds.), *Corruption, democracy and good governance in Africa: Essays on accountability and ethical behavior.* Lightbooks.

Hani, P. (2020). Impact of frauds on the Indian Banking sector. *International Journal of Creative research Thoughts*, *8*(4), 1602–1607.

Hanif, N., Javaid, A., Arshed, N., & Rafay, A. (2023). (Forthcoming). Foreign exploration of immature markets and incidence of money laundering. *Journal of Money Laundering Control*. doi:10.1108/JMLC-10-2022-0153

Hanretty, C., & Koop, C. (2013). Shall the law set them free? The formal and actual independence of regulatory agencies. *Regulation & Governance*, *7*(2), 195–214. doi:10.1111/j.1748-5991.2012.01156.x

Hansen, L. (2021). Regulatory ambiguity: The underbelly of insider trading. In A. Rafay (Ed.), *Handbook of Research on Theory and Practice of Financial Crimes* (pp. 132–148). IGI Global., doi:10.4018/978-1-7998-5567-5.ch008

Härdle, W. K., & Simar, L. (2016). *Applied multivariate statistical analysis* (4th ed.). Springer.

Harrington, W. (1988). Enforcement leverage when penalties are restricted. *Journal of Public Economics*, *37*(1), 29–53. doi:10.1016/0047-2727(88)90003-5

Haryati, A. E., Surono, S., & Suparman, S. (2021). Implementation of Minkowski-Chebyshev distance in fuzzy subtractive clustering. *EKSAKTA: Journal of Sciences and Data Analysis*, *2*(2), 82–87. doi:10.20885/EKSAKTA.vol2.iss2.art1

Hasan, M. S., Rahman, R. A., Abdillah, S. F. H. B. T., & Omar, N. (2015). Perception and awareness of young internet users towards cybercrime: Evidence from Malaysia. *Journal of Social Sciences*, *11*(4), 395–404. doi:10.3844/jssp.2015.395.404

Hashemi, S. A., & Rabiee, H. (2011). The relation between real earnings management and accounting earnings management: Evidence from Iran. *Business and Management Review*, *1*(8), 25–33.

Hashim, J., Haniff, M. N., & Rahman, I. K. A. (2012). Tax waiver year effect on earnings management practices in Malaysia. *Journal of Financial Reporting and Accounting*, *10*(2), 171–189. doi:10.1108/19852511211273714

Hayes, J. P., Chawla, S. K., & Kathawala, Y. (2016). A comparative study of problems encountered in the development of small businesses in the U.S. and Mexico. *Journal of Developing Areas*, *49*(3), 395–406. doi:10.1353/jda.2015.0175

Healy, B., O'Dwyer, M., & Ledwith, A. (2017). An exploration of product advantage and its antecedents in SMEs. *Journal of Small Business and Enterprise Development*, *25*(1), 129–146. doi:10.1108/JSBED-06-2017-0206

Healy, P. M. (1985). The effect of bonus schemes on accounting decisions. *Journal of Accounting and Economics*, *7*(1-3), 85–107. doi:10.1016/0165-4101(85)90029-1

Healy, P. M., & Palepu, K. G. (2003). The fall of Enron. *The Journal of Economic Perspectives*, *17*(2), 3–26. doi:10.1257/089533003765888403

Healy, P. M., & Wahlen, J. M. (1999). A review of the earnings management literature and its implications for standard setting. *Accounting Horizons*, *13*(4), 365–383. doi:10.2308/acch.1999.13.4.365

Heinrich, P. A. (2015). *Generation iStalk: An examination of the prior relationship between victims of stalking and offenders* [Master's Thesis Marshall Digital Scholar]. Marshall University.

Henriques, D. B. (2018). A case study of a con man: Bernie Madoff and the timeless lessons of history's biggest Ponzi scheme. *Social Research*, *85*(4), 745–766. doi:10.1353or.2018.0048

Herawaty, T., & Tresna, P. W. (2019). The influence of lifestyle on the process of purchase decision (A study on android users community). *Review of Integrative Business and Economics Research*, *8*(S I2), 344–351.

Heydenburg, M. R. (2015). The Ponzi scheme as a deception operation: The Bernie Madoff case study. *American Intelligence Journal*, *32*(2), 27–34.

Hilkevics, S., & Semakina, V. (2019). The classification and comparison of business ratios analysis methods. *Insights into Regional Development*, *1*(1), 48–57. doi:10.9770/ird.2019.1.1(4)

Hobbs, D. (2003). Organized Crime and Violence. In W. Heitmeyer & J. Hagan (Eds.), *International Handbook of Violence Research* (pp. 679–699). Springer. doi:10.1007/978-0-306-48039-3_33

Holtfreter, K. (2005). Is occupational fraud 'typical' White-collar crime? A comparison of individual and organizational characteristics. *Journal of Criminal Justice*, *33*(4), 353–365. doi:10.1016/j.jcrimjus.2005.04.005

Hong, H., & Liskovich, I. (2015). Crime, punishment and the halo effect of corporate social responsibility (No. w21215). Washington: National Bureau of Economic Research.

Hou, Q., Jin, Q., Yang, R., Yuan, H., & Zhang, G. (2015). Performance commitments of controlling shareholders and earnings management. *Contemporary Accounting Research*, *32*(3), 1099–1127. doi:10.1111/1911-3846.12111

Hsieh, M.-L., & Wang, S. Y. K. (2018). Routine activities in a virtual space: A Taiwanese case of an ATM hacking spree. *International Journal of Cyber Criminology*, *12*(1), 333–352.

Hsieh, S. J., Su, Y., & Chang, C. C. A. (2020). The role of discretionary pension accruals in earnings management. *Journal of Applied Accounting Research*, *22*(1), 1–21. doi:10.1108/JAAR-06-2019-0095

Huda, M. S., & McDonald, M. (2016). Regional cooperation on energy in South Asia: Unraveling the political challenges in implementing transnational pipelines and electricity grids. *Energy Policy*, *98*, 73–83. doi:10.1016/j.enpol.2016.07.046

Huntington, S. P. (1968). *Political order in changing societies.* Yale university press.

Hurt, C. (2009). Evil has a new name (and a new narrative): Bernard Madoff. *Detroit College of Law at Michigan State University Law Review*, 947.

Hurtt, D. N., Kreuze, J. G., & Langsam, S. A. (2000). Auditing to combat revenue recognition fraud. *Journal of Corporate Accounting & Finance*, *11*(4), 51–59. doi:10.1002/1097-0053(200005/06)11:4<51::AID-JCAF8>3.0.CO;2-V

Hutchinson, V., & Quintas, P. (2008). Do SMEs do knowledge management?: Or simply manage what they know? *International Small Business Journal*, *26*(2), 131–154. doi:10.1177/0266242607086571

Ibrahim, S., Xu, L., & Rogers, G. (2011). Real and accrual-based earnings management and its legal consequences: Evidence from seasoned equity offerings. *Accounting Research Journal*, *24*(1), 50–78. doi:10.1108/10309611111148779

Iliman, T., & Tekeli, R. (2016). Dünya'da ve Türkiye'de yolsuzluk algısı. *Adnan Menderes Üniversitesi Sosyal Bilimler Enstitüsü Dergisi*, *3*(2), 62–84. doi:10.30803/adusobed.287988

Imam, P. A., & Jacobs, D. (2014). Effect of corruption on tax revenues in the Middle East. *Review of Middle East Economics and Finance*, *10*(1), 1–24. doi:10.1515/rmeef-2014-0001

IMF. (2000). *Anti-money laundering/combating the financing of terrorism (AML/CFT).* International Monetary Fund. https://www.imf.org/external/np/leg/amlcft/eng/aml1.htm#:~:text=Terrorist% 20financing%20involves%20the%20 solicitation,both%20legal%20and%20illicit%20sources.

Immigration and Customs Enforcement. (2013, January 27). Mohamad Youssef Hammoud sentenced to 30 years in terrorism financing case. *United States Department of Homeland Security.* https://tinyurl.com/9x9sk552

Ingle, A., & Pardeshi, R. (2012). Internet banking in India: Challenges and opportunities. *IBMRD's. Journal of Management Research*, *1*(1), 13–18.

IntelBrief. (2021, March 12). *Emerging terrorist financing threats and trends.* The Sofan Center. IntelBrief: https://thesoufancenter.org/intelbrief-2021-march-12/

Interpol. (2022). *Fighting money laundering goes hand in hand with investigating the crimes it is linked to.* Interpol. https://www.interpol.int/en/Crimes/Financial-crime/Money-laundering#:~:text=Money%20laundering%20is%20concealing%20or, drug%20trafficking%2C%20robbery%20or%20extortion.

Iqbal, N. (2017, October 19). Tareen's employees involved in insider trading, counsel tells SC. *Dawn.* https://www.dawn.com/news/1364754

Iqbal, W. (2019). Impact of perceived risk on customer's online purchase intention towards branded apparels. *Journal of Marketing Strategies, 1*(1), 38–62. doi:10.52633/jms.v1i1.3

Isa, M. Y. M., Ibrahim, W. N. W., & Mohamed, Z. (2021). The relationship between financial literacy and public awareness on combating the threat of cybercrime in Malaysia. *The Journal of Industrial Distribution and Business, 12*(12), 1–10.

Ittelson, T. (2020). *Financial statements: A step-by-step guide to understanding and creating financial reports* (3rd ed.). Career Press.

Jackall, R. (1997). *Wild cowboys: Urban marauders and the forces of order.* Harvard University Press.

Jacobs, B. A., Topalli, V., & Wright, R. (2000). Managing retaliation: Drug robbery and informal sanction threats. *Criminology, 38*(1), 171–198. doi:10.1111/j.1745-9125.2000.tb00887.x

Jacobs, P., & Schain, L. (2011). The never-ending attraction of the Ponzi scheme. *Journal of Comprehensive Research, 9*, 40–46.

Jahnke, B., & Weisser, R. A. (2019). How does petty corruption affect tax morale in Sub-Saharan Africa? *European Journal of Political Economy, 60*, 101751. doi:10.1016/j.ejpoleco.2018.09.003

Jain, A. K. (2001). Corruption: A review. *Journal of Economic Surveys, 15*(1), 71–121. doi:10.1111/1467-6419.00133

Jalan, B. (2019). *Resurgent India: Politics, economics and governance.* HarperCollins Publishers India.

Jamil, F. (2013). On the electricity shortage, price and electricity theft nexus. *Energy Policy, 54*, 267–272. doi:10.1016/j.enpol.2012.11.034

Jamil, F., & Ahmad, E. (2010). The relationship between electricity consumption, electricity prices and GDP in Pakistan. *Energy Policy, 38*(10), 6016–6025. doi:10.1016/j.enpol.2010.05.057

Janazzo, D. (2021, January 28). EU menthol cigarette ban survey. *Foundation for a Smoke Free World.* https://www.smokefreeworld.org/eu-menthol-cigarette-ban-survey-2

Jarvenpaa, S. L., Tractinsky, N., & Vitale, M. (2000). Consumer trust in an internet store. *Information Technology and Management, 1*(1/2), 45–71. doi:10.1023/A:1019104520776

Javaid, A., & Arshed, N. (2022). Demand for money laundering in developing countries and its deterrence: A quantitative analysis. *Journal of Money Laundering Control, 25*(3), 625–636. doi:10.1108/JMLC-06-2021-0063

Jayasekara, S. D. (2021). How effective are the current global standards in combating money laundering and terrorist financing? *Journal of Money Laundering Control, 24*(2), 257–267. doi:10.1108/JMLC-05-2020-0047

Jebb, A., Parrigon, S., & Woo, S. (2017). Exploratory data analysis as a foundation of inductive research. *Human Resource Management Review, 27*(2), 265–276. doi:10.1016/j.hrmr.2016.08.003

Jeffrey, C., & Harriss, J. (2014). Corruption. In *Keywords for modern India.* Oxford University Press.

Jeyanthi, P. M., Mansurali, A., Harish, V., & Krishnaveni, V. D. (2019). Significance of fraud analytics in Indian banking sectors. *Journal of Critical Reviews, 7*(4), 209–213.

Ježovita, A. (2015). Variations between financial ratios for evaluating financial position related to the size of a company. *Review of Innovation and Competitiveness: A Journal of Economic and Social Research, 1*(1), 115–136. https://hrcak.srce.hr/155600

Jimenez, R., Serebrisky, T., & Mercado, J. (2014). *Power lost: sizing electricity losses in transmission and distribution systems in Latin America and the Caribbean.* IADB. https://publications.iadb.org/en/publication/16883/power-lost-sizing-electricity-losses-transmission-and-distribution-systems-latin

Johan, M. R. M., Syed, M. A. M., & Adnan, H. M. (2022). Digital media and online buying considerations among generation Z in Malaysia. *Jurnal Intelek, 17*(1), 164–180. doi:10.24191/ji.v17i1.15920

John, S. N., Anele, C., Kennedy, O. O., Olajide, F., & Kennedy, C. G. (2016, December). Realtime fraud detection in the banking sector using data mining techniques/algorithm. In 2016 international conference on computational science and computational intelligence (CSCI) (pp. 1186–1191). IEEE.

Johnsen, C. G. (2018). Authenticating the leader: Why Bill George believes that a moral compass would have kept Jeffrey Skilling out of jail. *Journal of Business Ethics, 147*(1), 53–63. doi:10.100710551-015-2968-7

Johnson, S. D., & Nikolovska, M. (2022). The effect of COVID-19 restrictions on routine activities and online crime. *Journal of Quantitative Criminology*, 1–20. [REMOVED HYPERLINK FIELD] doi:10.100710940-022-09564-7 PMID:36532607

Jolliffe, I., & Cadima, J. (2016). Principal component analysis: A review and recent developments. *Philosophical Transactions - Royal Society. Mathematical, Physical, and Engineering Sciences, 374*(2065), 20150202. doi:10.1098/rsta.2015.0202 PMID:26953178

Jones, N. (2021, May 14). The shape of fraud and cybercrime: 10 things we learned from 2020. *Computerweekly.com.* Retrieved from https://www.computerweekly.com/opinion/The-shape-of-fraud-and-cyber-crime-10-things-we-learned-from-2020

Jones, K. L., Krishnan, G. V., & Melendrez, K. (2010). Do models of discretionary accruals detect actual cases of fraudulent and restated earnings? An empirical evaluation. *Contemporary Accounting Research, 25*(2), 499–531. doi:10.1506/car.25.2.8

Joossens, L., & Raw, M. (2012). From cigarette smuggling to illicit tobacco trade. *Tobacco Control, 21*(2), 230–234. doi:10.1136/tobaccocontrol-2011-050205 PMID:22345257

Jordan, G., Leskovar, R., & Marič, M. (2018). Impact of fear of identity theft and perceived risk on online purchase intention. *Organizacija, 51*(2), 146–155. doi:10.2478/orga-2018-0007

Joseph, K. L. (2010). The politics of power: Electricity reform in India. *Energy Policy, 38*(1), 503–511. doi:10.1016/j.enpol.2009.09.041

Joskow, P. L., & Rose, N. L. (1989). The effects of economic regulation. Handbook of Industrial Organization, 2, 1449-1506.

Junger, M., Montoya, L., Hartel, P., & Heydari, M. (2017). Towards the normalization of cybercrime victimization: A routine activities analysis of cybercrime in Europe. *2017 International Conference on Cyber Situational Awareness, Data Analytics and Assessment.* IEEE. 10.1109/CyberSA.2017.8073391

Kagan, J. (2021, July 25). *Combating the Financing of Terrorism (CFT) Definition* Investopedia. *Investiopedia.* https://www.investopedia.com/terms/c/combating-financing-terrorism-cft.asp

Kaleniuk, D. (2021). *The EU must stop serving as a playground for corrupt Ukrainian oligarchs and officials.* Atlantic Council. https://www.atlanticcouncil.org/blogs /ukrainealert/the-eu-must-stop-serving-as-a-playground-for-corrupt-ukrainian-oligarchs-and-officials/

Kallunki, J. P., & Martikainen, M. (2003). Earnings management as a predictor of future profitability of Finnish firms. *European Accounting Review*, *12*(2), 311–325. doi:10.1080/0963818032000089409

Karklins, R. (2002). Typology of post-communist corruption. *Problems of Post-Communism*, *49*(4), 22–32. doi:10.1080/10758216.2002.11655993

Karlsson, J. (2021). Firm size and growth barriers: A data-driven approach. *Small Business Economics*, *57*(3), 1319–1338. doi:10.100711187-020-00350-y

Karlsson, N., Loewenstein, G., & Seppi, D. (2009). The ostrich effect: Selective attention to information. *Journal of Risk and Uncertainty*, *38*(2), 95–115. doi:10.100711166-009-9060-6

Karmakar, A. K., & Jana, S. K. (2018). Corruption in India - An introspective view. In S. Bandyopadyay & B. C. Nirmal (Eds.), *Combating Corruption, Black Money and Money Laundering: Issues and Challenges.* Satyam Law International.

Karmakar, A. K., & Jana, S. K. (2022). Governance reform from global perspectives: Some dimensions. In R. C. Das (Ed.), *Social Sector Spending, Governance and Economic Development - Theoretical and Empirical Perspectives from Across the World* (Vol. I). Routledge.

Kaufmann, D., Kraay, A., & Mastruzzi, M. (2011). The worldwide governance indicators: Methodology and analytical issues. *Hague Journal on the Rule of Law*, *3*(2), 220–246. doi:10.1017/S1876404511200046

Kennedy, D. M. (1997). Pulling levers: Chronic offenders, high-crime settings, and a theory of prevention. *Valparaiso University Law Review. Valparaiso University. School of Law*, *31*(2), 449–484.

Kennedy, D. M., & Braga, A. (2006). Advocate: Old wine in new bottles: Policing and the lessons of pulling levers. In D. Weisburd (Ed.), *Police Innovation* (1st ed., pp. 155–170). Cambridge University Press. doi:10.1017/CBO9780511489334.008

Kenny, C. (2007). *Construction, corruption, and developing countries* (World Bank Policy Research Working Paper No. 4271). World Bank. doi:10.1596/1813-9450-4271

Kessides, I. N. (2012). The impacts of electricity sector reforms in developing countries. *The Electricity Journal*, *25*(6), 79–88. doi:10.1016/j.tej.2012.07.002

Keynes, J. M., Moggridge, D. E., & Johnson, E. S. (1971). The Collected Writings of John Maynard Keynes (Vol. 30, pp. 1971–89). London: Macmillan.

Kibets, D., Lepei, O., Prokopenko, O., Chorna, A., & Shelukhin, M. (2019). Anti-Fraud technologies in E-Banking. *Journal of Legal, Ethical and Regulatory Issues*, *22*(SI2), 1–6.

Kiener, R. (2018). Art. 55. In C. Auer, M. Müller, & B. Schindler (Eds.), *VwVG Kommentar.* Dike.

Kigerl, A. (2012). Routine activity theory and the determinants of high cybercrime countries. *Social Science Computer Review*, *30*(4), 470–486. doi:10.1177/0894439311422689

Kigerl, A. (2021). Routine activity theory and malware, fraud, and spam at the national level. *Crime, Law, and Social Change*, *76*(2), 109–130. doi:10.100710611-021-09957-y

Kighir, A., Omar, N., & Mohamed, N. (2013). Opportunities, motivations and approaches of earnings management: A structured theoretical review of the corporate virus. *International Journal of Auditing Technology*, *1*(3-4), 312–329. doi:10.1504/IJAUDIT.2013.057730

Kim, D. J., Ferrin, D. L., & Rao, H. R. (2008). A trust-based consumer decision-making model in electronic commerce: The role of trust, perceived risk, and their antecedents. *Decision Support Systems*, *44*(2), 544–564. doi:10.1016/j.dss.2007.07.001

Kim, J. B., Song, B. Y., & Wang, Z. (2017). Special purpose entities and bank loan contracting. *Journal of Banking & Finance*, *74*, 133–152. doi:10.1016/j.jbankfin.2016.10.006

Kindhäuser, U. (2015). Strafprozessrecht, 4th ed. Baden-Baden, 219, Nomos.

King, M. (2020). Out of obscurity: The contemporary private investigator in Australia. *International Journal of Police Science & Management*, *22*(3), 285–296. doi:10.1177/1461355720931887

Kingsley, K. M. (2015). Fraud and corruption practices in public sector: The Cameroon experience. *Research Journal of Finance and Accounting*, *6*(4), 203–209.

Kinnvall, C., & Lindén, J. (2010). Dialogical selves between security and insecurity: Migration, multiculturalism, and the challenge of the global. *Theory & Psychology*, *20*(5), 595–619. doi:10.1177/0959354309360077

Kirwan, G. H., Fullwood, C., & Rooney, B. (2018). Risk factors for social networking site scam victimization among Malaysian students. *Cyberpsychology, Behavior, and Social Networking*, *21*(2), 123–128. [REMOVED HYPERLINK FIELD] doi:10.1089/cyber.2016.0714 PMID:29048944

Kleiman, M. A. R. (1993). Enforcement swamping: A positive-feedback mechanism in rates of illicit activity. *Mathematical and Computer Modelling*, *17*(2), 65–75. doi:10.1016/0895-7177(93)90240-Y

Kleiman, M. A. R. (2009). *When brute force fails: How to have less crime and less punishment*. Princeton University Press. doi:10.1515/9781400831265

Kleiman, M. A. R. (2011). Surgical strikes in the drug wars: Smarter policies for both sides of the border. *Foreign Affairs*, *90*(5), 89–101.

Kleiman, M. A. R., & Kilmer, B. (2009). The dynamics of deterrence. *Proceedings of the National Academy of Sciences of the United States of America*, *106*(34), 14230–14235. doi:10.1073/pnas.0905513106 PMID:19706505

Kleinman, G., & Anandarajan, A. (2011). Inattentional blindness and its relevance to teaching forensic accounting and auditing. *Journal of Accounting Education*, *29*(1), 37–49. doi:10.1016/j.jaccedu.2011.08.002

Kliestik, T., Valaskova, K., Lazaroiu, G., Kovacova, M., & Vrbka, J. (2020). Remaining financially healthy and competitive: The role of financial predictors. *Journal of Competitiveness*, *12*(1), 74–92. doi:10.7441/joc.2020.01.05

Klitgaard, R. (1988). *Controlling Corruption*. University of California Press. doi:10.1525/9780520911185

Klitgaard, R. (1991). *Controlling corruption*. University of California Press.

Knack, S., & Keefer, P. (1995). Institutions and economic performance: Cross-country tests using alternative institutional measures. *Economics and Politics*, *7*(3), 207–227. doi:10.1111/j.1468-0343.1995.tb00111.x

Knezović, E., Bušatlić, S., & Riđić, O. (2020). Strategic human resource management in small and medium enterprises. *International Journal of Human Resources Development and Management*, *20*(2), 114–139. doi:10.1504/IJHRDM.2020.106255

Knight, B., Chigudu, H., & Tandon, R. (2006). *Reviving democracy: Citizens at the heart of Governance*. Earthscan Publications.

Kochan, N., & Goodyear, R. (2011). *Corruption: The new corporate challenge*. Palgrave Macmillan. doi:10.1057/9780230343344

Koehler, S. A. (2007). The role of suicide notes in death investigation. *Journal of Forensic Nursing*, *3*(2), 87–89. [REMOVED HYPERLINK FIELD] doi:10.1097/01263942-200706000-00007 PMID:17679273

Kongar, E. (2005). Kamuda Rüşvetin Toplumsal Nedenleri. *Yolsuzluk ile Savaşım Stratejileri Uluslararası Sempozyumu, 29.*

KPMG. (2022). *Fraud Barometer 2021: A snapshot of Fraud in UK*. KPMG. https://kpmg.com/dp/en/home/insights/2022/03/fraud-barometer-annual-report-2021.html

Kühne, H. H. (2020). Die internationale Bekämpfung von Wirtschaftskriminalität und die Konstitution des Verdachts. *Goltdammer's Archiv für Strafrecht*, 356–363.

Kühne, H. H. (2010). *Strafprozessrecht: eine systematische Darstellung des deutschen und europäischen Strafverfahrensrechts*. CF Müller GmbH.

Kulick, J., & Prieger, J. E. (2019). Empty discarded pack data and the prevalence of illicit trade in cigarettes in California. SSRN *Electronic Journal*. https://ssrn.com/ abstract=3320922. doi:10.2139/ssrn.3320922

Kulick, J., Prieger, J., & Kleiman, M. A. R. (2016). Unintended consequences of cigarette prohibition, regulation, and taxation. *International Journal of Law, Crime and Justice*, *46*, 69–85. doi:10.1016/j.ijlcj.2016.03.002

Kuo, T.-L. (2021). *Criminal Victimization in Taiwan: An Opportunity Perspective*. [Doctor of Philosophy Thesis, University College London].

Kupatadze, A. (2021). Corruption and illicit tobacco trade. *Journal of Illicit Economies and Development*, *3*(2), 217–223. doi:10.31389/jied.94

Kurti, M. K., Schroth, K. R., Ackerman, C., Kennedy, M., Jeong, M., & Delnevo, C. D. (2020). Availability of menthol cigarettes in Oakland, California after a partial flavor ban. *Preventive Medicine Reports*, *20*, 101200. doi:10.1016/j.pmedr.2020.101200 PMID:32995144

Kuzic, J., Fisher, J., & Scollary, A. (2002). Electronic commerce benefits, challenges and success factors in the Australian banking and finance industry. *ECIS 2002 Proceedings*, *60*, 1607–1616.

Kyckr. (2022, February 3). *AML Fines 2021*. Kyckr. https://www.kyckr.com/aml-fines-2021/

La'o Hamutuk. (2014). Timor-Leste has been robbed! La'o Hamutuk. http://laohamutuk.blogspot.com/2014/06/timor-leste-has-been-robbed.html

Labelle, H. (2010, October 26). Response to global crises must prioritize zero tolerance for corruption. *Transparency International*. https://www.transparency.org/en/press/20101026-global-crisis-zero-tolerance-for-corruption

LaFaive, M., Nesbit, T., & Drenkard, S. (2016). Cigarette taxes and smuggling: A 2016 update. *Mackinac Center for Public Policy*. https://www.mackinac.org/S2016-09

Laitinen, E. (2018). Financial reporting: Long-term change of financial ratios. *American Journal of Industrial and Business Management*, *8*(9), 1893–1927. doi:10.4236/ajibm.2018.89128

Lallie, H. S., Shepherd, L. A., Nurse, J. R. C., Erola, A., Epiphaniou, G., Maple, C., & Bellekens, X. (2021). Cyber security in the age of COVID-19: A timeline and analysis of cyber-crime and cyber-attacks during the pandemic. *Computers & Security*, *105*, 102248. [REMOVED HYPERLINK FIELD] doi:10.1016/j.cose.2021.102248 PMID:36540648

Lando, H., & Shavell, S. (2004). The advantage of focusing law enforcement effort. *International Review of Law and Economics*, *24*(2), 209–218. doi:10.1016/j.irle.2004.08.005

Lane, D. (2002). *Russian Banking: Evolution, problems, and prospects*. Edward Elgar. doi:10.4337/9781781950586

Lange, D. (2008). A multidimensional conceptualization of organizational corruption control. *Academy of Management Review*, *33*(3), 685–709. doi:10.5465/amr.2008.32465742

Lanier, D. Jr, Wempe, W. F., & Swink, M. (2019). Supply chain power and real earnings management: Stock market perceptions, financial performances effects, and implications for suppliers. *The Journal of Supply Chain Management*, *55*(1), 48–70. doi:10.1111/jscm.12186

Lascoumes, P., & Nagels, C. (2014). *Sociologie des élites délinquantes; De la criminalité en col blanc à la corruption politique*. Armand Colin.

Lavallée, E., Razafindrakoto, M., & Roubaud, F. (2008). *Les mécanismes à l'origine de la corruption: une analyse sur micro-données africaines* (Working Paper No. DT/2008-08). Paris: DIAL.

Law, S. H., & Bany-Ariffin, A. N. (2008). Institutional infrastructure and economic performance: Dynamic panel data evidence. *Transition Studies Review*, *15*(3), 542–557. doi:10.100711300-008-0026-1

Law, S. H., Lim, T. C., & Ismail, N. W. (2013). Institutions and economic development: A Granger causality analysis of panel data evidence. *Economic Systems*, *37*(4), 610–624. doi:10.1016/j.ecosys.2013.05.005

Lee, C. S. (2021). Online fraud victimization in China: A case study of Baidu Tieba. *Victims & Offenders*, *16*(3), 343–362. doi:10.1080/15564886.2020.1838372

Leskiewicz, J., & Mourre, C. (1964). La peste de 1720 à Marseille et les Intendents du Bureau de Santé", Ch. Mourre," Provence Historique, t. XIV, fasc. 52, 1963: [recenzja]/JL. Kwartalnik Historii Kultury Materialnej, 12(4)

Leukfeldt, E. R. (2014). Phishing for suitable targets in The Netherlands: Routine activity theory and phishing victimization. *Cyberpsychology, Behavior, and Social Networking*, *17*(8), 551–555. [REMOVED HYPERLINK FIELD] doi:10.1089/cyber.2014.0008 PMID:25080013

Levy, B., & Spiller, P. T. (1994). The institutional foundations of regulatory commitment: A comparative analysis of telecommunications regulation. *Journal of Law Economics and Organization*, *10*(2), 201–246.

Lewis, F. B. (2015). Costly 'Throw-Ups': Electricity theft and power disruptions. *The Electricity Journal*, *28*(7), 118–135. doi:10.1016/j.tej.2015.07.009

Lewis, L. S. (2010). Madoff's victims and their day in court. *Society*, *47*(5), 439–450. doi:10.100712115-010-9345-z

Lew, J. F. (2009). Pension actuarial incentive for earnings management. *Asia Pacific Management Review*, *14*(3), 313–334.

Li, L., Sommarribas, A., & Baltes-Löhr, C. (2014). Good practices in the return and reintegration of irregular migrants: Member states' entry bans policy & use of readmission agreements between member states and third countries - Luxembourg. Walferdange: University of Luxembourg.

Li, M., Huang, L., Tan, C. H., & Wei, K. K. (2013). Helpfulness of online product reviews as seen by consumers: Source and content features. *International Journal of Electronic Commerce*, *17*(4), 101–136. doi:10.2753/JEC1086-4415170404

Lin, S.-W., & Chen, S.-C. (2009). PSOLDA: A particle swarm optimization approach for enhancing the classification accuracy rate of linear discriminant analysis. *Applied Soft Computing*, *9*(3), 1008–1015. doi:10.1016/j.asoc.2009.01.001

Li, Y., Li, X., Xiang, E., & Djajadikerta, H. G. (2020). Financial distress, internal control, and earnings management: Evidence from China. *Journal of Contemporary Accounting & Economics*, *16*(3), 100210. doi:10.1016/j.jcae.2020.100210

Li, Z., Sha, Y., Song, X., Yang, K., Zhao, K., Jiang, Z., & Zhang, Q. (2019). Impact of risk perception on customer purchase behavior: A meta-analysis. *Journal of Business and Industrial Marketing*, *35*(1), 76–96. doi:10.1108/JBIM-12-2018-0381

Logan, T. K., & Walker, R. (2021). The gender safety gap: Examining the impact of victimization history, perceived risk, and personal control. *Journal of Interpersonal Violence*, *36*(1-2), 603–631. [REMOVED HYPERLINK FIELD] doi:10.1177/0886260517729405 PMID:29294904

Loonam, M., & O'Loughlin, D. (2008). An observation analysis of e-service quality in online banking. *Journal of Financial Services Marketing*, *13*(2), 164–178. doi:10.1057/fsm.2008.13

Lovenheim, M. F. (2008). How far to the border? The extent and impact of cross-border casual cigarette smuggling. *National Tax Journal*, *61*(1), 7–33. doi:10.17310/ntj.2008.1.01

Lundahl, M., & Sjöholm, F. (2008). The oil resources of Timor-Leste: Curse or blessing? *The Pacific Review*, *21*(1), 67–86. doi:10.1080/09512740701868898

Luong, L. (2015). *Earnings management through accrual-based analysis: Case study: Stockmann Oy Abp 2005-2014* [Doctoral Dissertation, Nyland's Swedish University of Applied Sciences].

Lynch, J. P., & Sabol, W. J. (2004). Assessing the effects of mass incarceration on informal social control in communities. *Criminology & Public Policy*, *3*(2), 267–294. doi:10.1111/j.1745-9133.2004.tb00042.x

Mahdi, M. D. H., Rezaul, K. M., & Rahman, M. A. (2010, February). Credit fraud detection in the banking sector in UK: a focus on e-business. In *2010 Fourth International Conference on Digital Society* (pp. 232–237). IEEE. 10.1109/ICDS.2010.45

Mahmoudabadi, H., & Barzegar, E. (2009). Investigating statistical distribution of financial ratios of accepted companies in Tehran's stock exchange. *Journal of Accounting Advances*, *1*(1(57/3)), 171–189.

Maiorano, F., & Stern, J. (2007). Institutions and telecommunications infrastructure in low and middle-income countries: The case of mobile telephony. *Utilities Policy*, *15*(3), 165–181. doi:10.1016/j.jup.2007.04.001

Maitra, B. (2018). Investment in physical, human capital, economic growth and life expectancy in Bangladesh: An empirical investigation. *South Asia Economic Journal*, *19*(2), 251–269. doi:10.1177/1391561418799110

Majcher, I. (2019a). Conclusion: Schengen-Wide Entry Ban: A Triple Peine? In The European Union Returns Directive and its Compatibility with International Human Rights Law (pp. 333–342). Brill Nijhoff.

Majcher, I. (2019b). The European Union returns directive and its compatibility with international human rights law: Analysis of return decision, entry ban, detention, and removal. In *The European Union Returns Directive and its Compatibility with International Human Rights Law*. Brill Nijhoff.

Majcher, I. (2020). The Schengen-wide entry ban: How are non-citizens' personal data protected? *Journal of Ethnic and Migration Studies*, *48*(8), 1944–1960. doi:10.1080/1369183X.2020.1796279

Malkiel, B. G. (1999). *A Random Walk Down Wall Street: including a life-cycle guide to personal investing*. W.W. Norton & Company.

Malmendier, U., & Tate, G. (2008). Who makes acquisitions? CEO overconfidence and the market's reaction. *Journal of Financial Economics*, *89*(1), 20–43. doi:10.1016/j.jfineco.2007.07.002

Mandell, H. (2015). Imagine what the gentiles must think: Editors of the US Jewish press reflect on covering the Bernard Madoff Scandal. In Journalism, Audiences and Diaspora (pp. 17–33). London: Palgrave Macmillan.

Mandell, H. (2015). The Nazi treatment: Press coverage of Barack Obama and Bernard Madoff from 2008 to 2009. *International Journal of Media and Cultural Politics*, *11*(1), 87–103. doi:10.1386/macp.11.1.87_1

Mangala, D., & Soni, L. (2023). A systematic literature review on frauds in banking sector. *Journal of Financial Crime*, *30*(1), 285–301. doi:10.1108/JFC-12-2021-0263

Mannan, M., & Van Oorschot, P. C. (2008, July). Security and usability: the gap in real-world online banking. In *Proceedings of the 2007 Workshop on New Security Paradigms* (pp. 1–14). ACM. 10.1145/1600176.1600178

Marafon, D. L., Basso, K., Espartel, L. B., de Barcellos, M. D., & Rech, E. (2018). Perceived risk and intention to use internet banking: The effects of self-confidence and risk acceptance. *International Journal of Bank Marketing*, *36*(2), 277–289. doi:10.1108/IJBM-11-2016-0166

Marangoz, C. (2013). *Illegal electricity use in Türkiye: Causes and policy implications* [Doctoral dissertation, Vanderbilt University].

Markopolos, H. (2011). *No one would listen: A true financial thriller*. John Wiley & Sons.

Matthew, R. E., Barnabas, O., Isola, L. A., & Joseph, I. O. (2013). Analysis of corruption and economic growth in Nigeria. *Afro Asian Journal of Social Sciences, 4*(4.2), 1–19.

Matthew, K., Patrick, K., & Denise, K. (2013). The effects of fraudulent procurement practices on public procurement performance. *International Journal of Business and Behavioral Sciences*, *3*(1), 17–27.

Mauro, P. (1998). Corruption: Causes, consequences, and agenda for further research. *Finance & Development*, 11–14. http://syahia.atreides.online.fr/iae/ethics/corruption.pdf

Mavragani, A., Nikolaou, I., & Tsagarakis, K. (2016). Open economy, institutional quality, and environmental performance: A macroeconomic approach. *Sustainability (Basel)*, *8*(7), 601. doi:10.3390u8070601

Mazerolle, L., Soole, D. W., & Rombouts, S. (2006). Street-level drug law enforcement: A meta-analytical review. *Journal of Experimental Criminology*, *2*(4), 409–435. doi:10.100711292-006-9017-6

Mc Gonigle, B. N. (2011). *Procedural justice? Victim participation in international criminal proceedings* [Doctoral Dissertation, The Netherlands Institute of Human Rights, Utrecht University].

McDermott, R. (2010). *UK Bribery Act 2010—a blessing in disguise? Construction industry briefing*. KPMG.

McEwen, A., & Straus, L. (2009). Counterfeit tobacco in London: Local crime requires an international solution. *Trends in Organized Crime*, *12*(3-4), 251–259. doi:10.100712117-009-9068-y

McMullan, M. (1961). A theory of corruption. *The Sociological Review*, *9*(2), 181–201. doi:10.1111/j.1467-954X.1961.tb01093.x

Mears, D. P., Reisig, M. D., Scaggs, S., & Holtfreter, K. (2016). Efforts to reduce consumer fraud victimization among the elderly. *Crime and Delinquency*, *62*(9), 1235–1259. doi:10.1177/0011128714555759

Mendelski, M. (2010). Where does the European Union make a difference? *Rule of law development in South-Eastern Europe (APSA 2010 Annual Meeting Paper.* SSRN. https://papers.ssrn.com/sol3/papers.cfm?abstract_id=1644729

Mendelski, M. (2015). The EU's pathological power: The failure of external rule of law promotion in South Eastern Europe. *Southeastern Europe. L'Europe du Sud-Est*, *39*(3), 318–346. doi:10.1163/18763332-03903003

Méon, P. G., & Sekkat, K. (2005). Does corruption grease or sand the wheels of growth? *Public Choice*, *122*(1-2), 69–97. doi:10.100711127-005-3988-0

Merle, R. (2018, September 10). A guide to the financial crisis—10 years later. *The Washington Post*. https://www.washingtonpost.com/business/economy/a-guide-to-the-financial-crisis--10-years-later/2018/09/10/114b76ba-af10-11e8-a20b-5f4f84429666_story.html

Merton, R. K. (1938). Social structure and anomie. *American Sociological Review*, *3*(5), 319–328. doi:10.2307/2084686

Meskaran, F., Ismail, Z., & Shanmugam, B. (2013). Online purchase intention: Effects of trust and security perception. *Australian Journal of Basic and Applied Sciences*, *7*(6), 307–315.

Michaels, A. C. (2003). Fastow and Arthur Andersen: Some reflections on corporate criminality, victim status, and retribution. *Ohio State Journal of Criminal Law*, *1*, 551.

Michalowski, R. (2013). What is crime? Why is criminology? Presented at the *annual meeting of the* American Society of Criminology.

Michelet, J. (2016). *Histoire de France* (Vol. XVII). Lacroix et Cie. (Original work published 1877)

Min, B., & Golden, M. (2014). Electoral cycles in electricity losses in India. *Energy Policy*, *65*, 619–625. doi:10.1016/j.enpol.2013.09.060

Ministry of Justice and Security. (2021). *Entry ban*. IND. https://ind.nl/en/Pages/Entry-ban.aspx

Miranda, K. F., Machado, M. A. V., & Machedo, L. A. F. (2018). Investor sentiment and earnings management: Does analysts monitoring matter? *Revista de administração Mackenzie*, *19*(4), 1–29.

Misangyi, V. F., Weaver, G. R., & Elms, H. (2008). Ending corruption: The interplay among institutional logics, resources, and institutional entrepreneurs. *Academy of Management Review*, *33*(3), 750–770. doi:10.5465/amr.2008.32465769

Mississippi Office of the State Auditor. (2009, April 15). *State Auditor and Tax Commissioner Uncover Warehouse Containing Estimated $20 Million Of Contraband Tobacco* [Press release]. MS OSA. https://tinyurl.com/sz4cyvuv

Moeller, K., & Hesse, M. (2013). Drug market disruption and systemic violence: Cannabis markets in Copenhagen. *European Journal of Criminology*, *10*(2), 206–221. doi:10.1177/1477370812467568

Mohammed, U. (2013). Corruption in Nigeria: A Challenge to Sustainable Development in the Fourth Republic. *European Scientific Journal*, *9*(4), 118–137.

Mohanram, P. S. (2003). How to manage earnings management. *Accounting World*, *10*(1), 1–12.

Moiseienko, A. (2018). Legal Protections from the accusations of corruption. In Corruption and Targeted Sanctions: Law and Policy of Anti-Corruption Entry Bans (pp. 177–211). Brill Nijhoff. doi:10.1163/9789004390478_006

Moiseienko, A. (2019). *Corruption and targeted sanctions: Law and policy of anti-corruption entry bans*. BRILL. doi:10.1163/9789004390478

Moiseienko, A. (2021). Due process and unilateral targeted sanctions. In C. Beaucillon (Ed.), *Research Handbook on Unilateral and Extraterritorial Sanctions*. Edward Elgar Publishing. doi:10.4337/9781839107856.00033

Mo, P. H. (2001). Corruption and economic growth. *Journal of Comparative Economics*, *29*(1), 66–79. doi:10.1006/jcec.2000.1703

Morais, A. I., & Pinto, I. (2019). Pension plans assumptions: The case of discount rate. *Accounting Research Journal*, *32*(1), 36–49. doi:10.1108/ARJ-02-2018-0041

Mosebach, M., & Simko, P. (2010). Discretionary accruals and the emergence of profitability. *Journal of Accounting, Auditing & Finance, 25*(3), 351–374. doi:10.1177/0148558X1002500304

Mostafa, R. B. (2020). Mobile banking service quality: A new avenue for customer value co-creation. *International Journal of Bank Marketing, 38*(5), 1107–1132. doi:10.1108/IJBM-11-2019-0421

Mostyn, G. R. (2012). Cognitive load theory: What it is, why it's important for accounting instruction and research. *Issues in Accounting Education, 27*(1), 227–245. doi:10.2308/iace-50099

Mouton, P. (2001). *La malédiction du Grand-Saint-Antoine: 25 mai 1720: la peste entre à Marseille*. Autres Temps.

Muhamad, F. H., Muhammad, M. Z., Muhamad, S. F., & Samad, N. S. A. (2021). Awareness on Financial Cybercrimes among youth: Experience, exposure and effect. *Proceedings of the First International Conference on Society 5*.0. IEEE.

Muhtasim, D. A., Tan, S. Y., Hassan, M. A., Pavel, M. I., & Susmit, S. (2022). Customer Satisfaction with digital wallet services: An analysis of security factors. *International Journal of Advanced Computer Science and Applications, 13*(1), 195–206. doi:10.14569/IJACSA.2022.0130124

Mukherjee, K., & Tripathy, D. (2010, November 26). India probes 21 companies in bribes-for-loans scandal. *Reuters*. https://www.reuters.com/article/us-india-corruption-idUSTRE6AO19P20101126

Mulford, C. W., & Comiskey, E. (2002). *The Financial Numbers Game: Detecting Creative Accounting Practices*. John Wiley & Sons.

Muniandy, L., Muniandy, B., & Samsudin, Z. (2017). CyberSecurity behavior among higher education students in Malaysia. *Journal of Information Assurance and Cybersecurity, 800299*, 1–13. doi:10.5171/2017.800299

Munksgaard, R., Décary-Hétu, D., Malm, A., & Nouvian, A. (2021). Distributing tobacco in the dark: Assessing the regional structure and shipping patterns of illicit tobacco in crypto markets. *Global Crime, 22*(1), 1–21. doi:10.1080/17440572.2020.1799787

Myšková, R., & Hájek, P. (2017). Comprehensive assessment of firm financial performance using financial ratios and linguistic analysis of annual reports. *Journal of International Students, 10*(4), 96–108. doi:10.14254/2071-8330.2017/10-4/7

Nakitende, M. G., Rafay, A., & Waseem, M. (2021). Frauds in Business Organizations: A Comprehensive Overview. In A. Rafay (Ed.), *Handbook of Research on Theory and Practice of Financial Crimes* (pp. 21–38). IGI Global. doi:10.4018/978-1-7998-5567-5.ch002

National Network for Safe Communities. (n.d.). *Group violence intervention*. MSC. https://nnscommunities.org/strategies/group-violence-intervention

Nepal, R., & Jamasb, T. (2015). Caught between theory and practice: Government, market, and regulatory failure in electricity sector reforms. *Economic Analysis and Policy, 46*, 16–24. doi:10.1016/j.eap.2015.03.001

Never, B. (2015). Social norms, trust and control of power theft in Uganda: Does bulk metering work for MSEs? *Energy Policy, 82*, 197–206. doi:10.1016/j.enpol.2015.03.020

New York State Office of the Attorney General. (2013, May 16). *A.G. Schneiderman & NYPD Commissioner Kelly Announce Take Down of Massive Eastern Seaboard Unstamped Cigarette Trafficking Enterprise*. NY SoAG. https://tinyurl.com/u8j2cbhs

New York State Office of the Governor. (2014, July 14). *Governor Cuomo Announces New Cigarette Strike Force Seizes Nearly $1.7 Million in Contraband and Cash Within First 6 Months*. NY SoAG. https://tinyurl.com/mkzeynjn

New York State Office of the Governor. (2017, August 3). *Governor Cuomo Announces $6.6 Million in Illegal Tobacco Removed from New York State Streets in 2017.* NY SoAG. https://tinyurl.com/3mke4cbp

Ngcamu, B. S., & Mantzaris, E. (2021). Biased and falsified reporting: The Government's perspectives. In *Addressing Xenophobia in South Africa: Drivers, Responses and Lessons from the Durban Untold Stories.* Emerald Publishing Limited. doi:10.1108/978-1-80262-479-320211006

Nguyen, C. M., Barrash, J., Koenigs, A. L., Bechara, A., Tranel, D., & Denburg, N. L. (2013). Decision-making deficits in normal elderly persons associated with executive personality disturbances. *International Psychogeriatrics, 25*(11), 1811–1819. [REMOVED HYPERLINK FIELD] doi:10.1017/S1041610213001270 PMID:23906413

Nickerson, C. (2022). Routine activities theory. *Simply Psychology.* https://www.simplypsychology.org/routine-activities-theory.html

Nikolov, N. (2021). Conflict of Interest for Corruption and Abuse of Public Power: The Case of European Legislation. In A. Rafay (Ed.), *Handbook of Research on Theory and Practice of Financial Crimes* (pp. 105–131). IGI Global. doi:10.4018/978-1-7998-5567-5.ch007

Nisbett, R., & Wilson, T. (1977). The halo effect: Evidence for unconscious alteration of judgments. *Journal of Personality and Social Psychology, 35*(4), 250–256. doi:10.1037/0022-3514.35.4.250

Nobi, A., Tuhin, K. H., & Lee, J. W. (2021). Application of principal component analysis on temporal evolution of COVID-19. *PLoS One, 16*(12), e0260899. doi:10.1371/journal.pone.0260899 PMID:34855909

Nor, R. M. (2015). Success factors for *Baitulmal* management during the reign of *Khalifah* Umar bn Abdulaziz. *Open Journal of Social Sciences, 3*(5), 90–94. doi:10.4236/jss.2015.35013

Nor, R. M. (2019). The era of Umar bn AbdulAziz's reign: The hiring and dismissal complex system in government officials. *Malaysian Journal of Social Sciences and Humanities, 4*(3), 140–146.

North, D. C. (1991). Institutions. *The Journal of Economic Perspectives, 5*(1), 97–112. doi:10.1257/jep.5.1.97

Northeast-Group. (2021). *Electricity theft and non-technical losses.* Northeast Group. https://Northeast-Group.com/2021/10/20/electricity-theft-non-technical-losses/

Nuradzimmah, D. (2022, March 14). Online scammers rake in RM1.6 billion, over 51,000 reports lodged in 2 years. *New Straits Times.* https://www.nst.com.my/news/nation/2022/03/779915/online-scammers-rake-rm16-billion-over-51000-reports-lodged-2-years

Nurhidayat, I., & Kusumasari, B. (2018). Strengthening the effectiveness of whistleblowing system: A study for the implementation of anti-corruption policy in Indonesia. *Journal of Financial Crime, 25*(1), 140–154. doi:10.1108/JFC-11-2016-0069

Nwabugo, O. (2016). Latest outrageous salaries of top Nigerian politicians revealed. *Buzz Nigeria.* http://buzznigeria.com

Nye, J. S. (1967). Corruption and political development: A cost-benefit analysis. *The American Political Science Review, 61*(2), 417–427. doi:10.2307/1953254

O'Connor, R. J., Bansal-Travers, M., Carter, L. P., & Cummings, K. M. (2012). What would menthol smokers do if menthol in cigarettes were banned? Behavioral intentions and simulated demand. *Addiction (Abingdon, England), 107*(7), 1330–1338. doi:10.1111/j.1360-0443.2012.03822.x PMID:22471735

Oberlechner, T., & Hocking, S. (2004). Information sources, news, and rumors in financial markets: Insights into the foreign exchange market. *Journal of Economic Psychology, 25*(3), 407–424. doi:10.1016/S0167-4870(02)00189-7

OECD. (2016, April 18). Illicit trade: Converging criminal networks. *Organisation for Economic Co-operation and Development*. https://www.oecd.org/corruption-integrity/reports/charting-illicit-trade-9789264251847-en.html

OECD. (2017). *Enhancing the contributions of SMEs in a global and digitalised economy*. Meeting of the OECD Council at Ministerial Level, Paris, France. https://www.oecd.org/industry/C-MIN-2017-8-EN.pdf

OECD. (2018). *Fostering greater SME participation in a globally integrated economy*. SME Ministerial Conference (Plenary session 3), Mexico City, Mexico. https://www.oecd.org/cfe/smes/ministerial/documents/2018-SME-Ministerial-Conference-Plenary-Session-3.pdf

OECD. (2019). *Using extractive revenues for sustainable development: Policy guidance for resource-rich countries, OECD development policy tools*. Organisation for Economic Co-operation and Development

OECD. (2022). *Glossary of tax terms*. OECD. https://www.oecd.org/ctp/glossaryoftaxterms.htm

OECD/CAF. (2019). *Latin America and the Caribbean 2019: Policies for competitive SMEs in the Pacific Alliance and participating South American countries, SME Policy Index*. OECD Publishing. doi:10.1787/d9e1e5f0-

Office of the Inspector General. (2009, September). The Bureau of Alcohol, Tobacco, Firearms and Explosives' efforts to prevent the diversion of tobacco. *United States Department of Justice, Office of the Inspector General, Evaluation and Inspections Division*. OIG. http://oig.justice.gov/reports/ATF/e0905.pdf

Ofgem. (2014). *Tackling Electricity Theft - The way forward*. Ofgem. https://www.Ofgem.gov.uk/sites/default/files/docs/2014/03/electricitytheft-iafinal_0.pdf

Ofori, E. (2016). Detecting corporate financial fraud using Modified Altman Z-score and Beneish M-score. The case of Enron Corp. *Research Journal of Finance and Accounting*, *7*(4), 59–65.

Oğuz, F., Akkemik, K. A., & Göksal, K. (2014). Can law impose competition? A critical discussion and evidence from the Turkish electricity generation market. *Renewable & Sustainable Energy Reviews*, *30*, 381–387. doi:10.1016/j.rser.2013.10.024

Oki, O. & in Buffalo City. *International Conference on Electrical, Computer, Communications and Mechatronics Engineering (ICECCME)*. (pp. 1–6). doi:10.1109/ICECCME52200.2021.9590998

Olken, B. A., & Pande, R. (2012). Corruption in developing countries. *Annual Review of Economics*, *4*(1), 479–509. doi:10.1146/annurev-economics-080511-110917

Omar, N., Rahman, R. A., Danbatta, B. L., & Sulaiman, S. (2014). Management disclosure and earnings management practices in reducing the implication risk. *Procedia: Social and Behavioral Sciences*, *145*, 88–96. doi:10.1016/j.sbspro.2014.06.014

Omprakash, S., & Gokila, S. (2018). Principal component analysis-A survey. *International Journal of Advanced Research in Computer and Communication Engineering*, *7*(8), 63–66. doi:10.17148/IJARCCE.2018.7814

Omri, A. (2014). An international literature survey on energy-economic growth nexus: Evidence from country-specific studies. *Renewable & Sustainable Energy Reviews*, *38*, 951–959. doi:10.1016/j.rser.2014.07.084

Onuora, J. K. J., Akpoveta, E. B., & Agbomah, D. J. (2018). Public sector fraud in Nigeria. *Accounting and Taxation Review*, *2*(4), 125–135.

Oral, B. G., & Sayın, F. (2009). Mali yolsuzluğun yansımaları: Türkiye için eşbütünleşme analizi. *İstanbul Üniversitesi İktisat Fakültesi Maliye Araştırma Merkezi Konferansları, Prof. Dr. Şerafettin Aksoy'a Armağan*, *141*, 176.

Örnebring, H. (2012). Clientelism, elites, and the media in Central and Eastern Europe. *The International Journal of Press/Politics*, *17*(4), 497–515. doi:10.1177/1940161212454329

Osma, B. G., Gomez-Conde, J., & Lopez-Valeiras, E. (2022). Management control systems and real earnings management: Effects on firm performance. *Management Accounting Research*, *55*, 100781. doi:10.1016/j.mar.2021.100781

Otusanya, O. J. (2011). Corruption as an obstacle to development in developing countries: A review of literature. *Journal of Money Laundering Control*, *14*(4), 387–422. doi:10.1108/13685201111173857

Oxford Analytica. (2021). Russia's EU entry bans may close these sanctions round. *Emerald Expert Briefings*, (oxan-es).

Ozturk, I. (2010). A literature survey on energy–growth nexus. *Energy Policy*, *38*(1), 340–349. doi:10.1016/j.enpol.2009.09.024

Ozyesil, M. (2020). An application of financial ratio analysis on concordat firms: A model suggestion on construction firms listed in Borsa Istanbul. *Journal of Economics and Behavioral Studies*, *11*(6J), 10–22. doi:10.22610/jebs.v11i6(J).3001

Papazoglou, M. P. (2003, December). Service-oriented computing: Concepts, characteristics and directions. In *Proceedings of the Fourth International Conference on Web Information Systems Engineering, 2003. WISE 2003.* (pp. 3–12). IEEE. 10.1109/WISE.2003.1254461

Papon, P. (1760). Stories of the great day of history. Plague of Marseille in 1720. In H. Gautier (Ed.), *Vaugirard Press.*

Park, H. (2003). Determinants of corruption: À cross-national Aanalysis. *Multinational Business Review*, *11*(2), 29–48. doi:10.1108/1525383X200300010

Paul, C., Schaefer, A. G., & Clarke, C. P. (2011). *The challenge of violent drug-trafficking organizations: An assessment of Mexican security based on existing RAND research on urban unrest, insurgency, and defense-sector reform.* RAND National Defense Research Institute.

Pavlo, W. (2018, January 18). White collar crime: Suicide, murder and revenge. *Forbes.* Retrieved from https://www.forbes.com/sites/walterpavlo/2018/01/18/white-collar-crime-suicide-murder-and-revenge/?sh=4b54ea3d74d8

Payne, J. E. (2010). A survey of the electricity consumption-growth literature. *Applied Energy*, *87*(3), 723–731. doi:10.1016/j.apenergy.2009.06.034

Payton, M. E., Young, L. J., & Young, J. H. (1989). Bounds for the difference between median and mean of beta and negative binomial distributions. *Metrika*, *36*(1), 347–354. doi:10.1007/BF02614111

Pelfrey, W. V. Jr. (2015). Cigarette trafficking, smurfing, and volume buying policy, investigation, and methodology recommendations from a case study. *Criminal Justice Policy Review*, *26*(7), 713–726. doi:10.1177/0887403414540518

Penman, S. H. (2009). Accounting for intangible assets: There is also an income statement. *Abacus*, *45*(3), 358–371. doi:10.1111/j.1467-6281.2009.00293.x

Perols, J. L., & Lougee, B. A. (2011). The relation between earnings management and financial statement fraud. *Advances in Accounting*, *27*(1), 39–53. doi:10.1016/j.adiac.2010.10.004

Perrin, B., Rémy, M., & Roubaty, R. (2011). Electronic evidence in Swiss criminal procedure. *Digital Evidence & Electronic Signature Law Review*, *8*, 70.

Pierini, J. P. (2014). Violation of ECHR procedural guarantees and redress using the example of the Italian trial in absentia. *Zeitschrift für die gesamte Strafrechtswissenschaft,* 951.

Pieth, M. (2016). *Schweizerisches Strafprozessrecht* (3rd Revised Ed.). Helbing Lichtenhahn.

PIMEC. (2022). *Web site Servicio de Estudios de Pimec (Micro, petita i mitjana empresa de Catalunya)*. PIMEC. https://www.pimec.org/es/pimec-comerc/observatorio/estudios

Pinto, J., Leana, C. R., & Pil, F. K. (2008). Corrupt organizations or organzations of corrupt individuals? Two types of organization-level corruption. *Academy of Management Review*, *33*(3), 685–709. doi:10.5465/amr.2008.32465726

Polinsky, M. A., & Shavell, S. (2007). The theory of public enforcement of law. In M. A. Polinksy & S. Shavell (Eds.), *Handbook of Law and Economics* (Vol. 1, pp. 403–454). Elsevier.

Popova, M., & Post, V. (2018). Prosecuting high-level corruption in Eastern Europe. *Communist and Post-Communist Studies*, *51*(3), 231–244. doi:10.1016/j.postcomstud.2018.06.004

Prabakaran, M. (2010). Business ethics: Should it remain an oxymoron? *MES Journal of Technology and Management*, *1*(1), 83–98.

Pressman, S. (1998). On financial frauds and their causes: Investor overconfidence. *American Journal of Economics and Sociology*, *57*(4), 405–421. doi:10.1111/j.1536-7150.1998.tb03373.x

Prieger, J. E., & Kulick, J. (2014). Unintended consequences of enforcement in illicit markets. *Economics Letters*, *125*(2), 295–297. doi:10.1016/j.econlet.2014.09.025

Prieger, J. E., & Kulick, J. (2015). Violence in illicit markets: Unintended consequences and the search for paradoxical effects of enforcement. *The B.E. Journal of Economic Analysis & Policy*, *15*(3), 1263–1295. doi:10.1515/bejeap-2014-0184

Prieger, J. E., & Kulick, J. (2018). Cigarette taxes and illicit trade in Europe. *Economic Inquiry*, *56*(3), 1706–1723. doi:10.1111/ecin.12564

Putra, A. M., Pagalung, G., & Habbe, A. H. (2018). Culture and corruption-driven agency costs and earnings management. Evidence from southeast Asian countries. *Intangible Capital*, *14*(4), 499–517. doi:10.3926/ic.1289

Quigley, B., & Williams, J. (2013). Madoff: From man to monster. *The Academic Forum*. 28–37. https://www.proquest.com/docview/1639614541?pq-origsite=gscholar&fromopenview=true

Quisenberry, W. L. (2017). Ponzi of all Ponzis: Critical analysis of the Bernie Madoff scheme. *International Journal of Econometrics and Financial Management*, *5*(1), 1–6.

Rafay, A. (Ed.). (2019). *FinTech as Disruptive Technology for Financial Institutions*. IGI Global. doi:10.4018/978-1-5225-7805-5

Rafay, A. (Ed.). (2021a). *HandBook of Research on Theory and Practice of Financial Crimes*. IGI Global. doi:10.4018/978-1-7998-5567-5

Rafay, A. (Ed.). (2021b). *Money Laundering and Terrorism Financing in Global Financial Systems*. IGI Global. doi:10.4018/978-1-7998-8758-4

Rafay, A. (Ed.). (2023a). *Concepts, Cases, and Regulations in Financial Fraud and Corruption*. IGI Global. doi:10.4018/978-1-6684-507-9

Rafay, A. (Ed.). (2023b). *Concepts and Cases of Illicit Finance*. IGI Global. doi:10.4018/978-1-6684-8587-3

Rafay, A., & Ajmal, M. M. (2014). Earnings management through deferred taxes recognized under IAS 12: Evidence from Pakistan. *Lahore Journal of Business*, *3*(1), 1–19. doi:10.35536/ljb.2014.v3.i1.a1

Rafay, A., Chen, Y., Naeem, M. A. B., & Ijaz, M. (2018). Analyzing the impact of credit ratings on firm performance and stock returns: An Evidence from Taiwan. *Indian Economic Review*, *22*(3), 767–786.

Rafay, A., & Gilani, U. J. (2016). Banking Competition and Stability: Evidence from Inter-continental Markets. *DLSU Business and Economics Review*, *25*(2), 24–40.

Rahim, A. (1983). *Islamic History*. Islamic Publications Bureau.

Rahman, R. A., & Anwar, I. S. K. (2014). Effectiveness of fraud prevention and detection techniques in Malaysian Islamic banks. *Procedia: Social and Behavioral Sciences*, *145*, 97–102. doi:10.1016/j.sbspro.2014.06.015

Rajan, R. (2019). *The third pillar: How markets and the state leave the community*. HarperCollins Publishers India.

Ramamoorti, S., Morrison, D., & Koletar, J. W. (2009). *Bringing Freud to Fraud: Understanding the state-of-mind of the C-level suite/white collar offender through "ABC" analysis*. Institute for Fraud Prevention (IFP) at West Virginia University. https://ecommons.udayton.edu/acc_fac_pub/71/

Ramana, S. V., & Krishna, S. G. (2017). A study on impact of fraud in Indian banking sector (With special reference on retail banking products). *International Journal of Academic Research and Development*, *2*(6), 544–547.

Ramírez-Orellana, A., Martínez-Romero, M. J., & Mariño-Garrido, T. (2017). Measuring fraud and earnings management by a case of study: Evidence from an international family business. *European Journal of Family Business*, *7*(1-2), 41–53. doi:10.1016/j.ejfb.2017.10.001

Rampini, A. A., & Viswanathan, S. (2010). Collateral, risk management, and the distribution of debt capacity. *The Journal of Finance*, *65*(6), 2293–2322. doi:10.1111/j.1540-6261.2010.01616.x

Rampini, A. A., & Viswanathan, S. (2019). Financial intermediary capital. *The Review of Economic Studies*, *86*(1), 413–455. doi:10.1093/restud/rdy020

Ramzan, M., Ahmad, I., & Rafay, A. (2020). Is auditor independence influenced by non-audit services? A stakeholder's viewpoint. *Pakistan Journal of Commerce and Social Sciences*, *14*(1), 388–408.

Ramzan, M., Ahmad, I., & Rafay, A. (2020). Is auditor independence influenced by Non-audit services? A stakeholder's viewpoint. *Pakistan Journal of Commerce and Social Sciences*, *14*(1), 388–408.

Rao, P., Kumar, S., Chavan, M., & Lim, W. M. (2021). A systematic literature review on SME financing: Trends and future directions. *Journal of Small Business Management*, *61*(3), 1247–1277. doi:10.1080/00472778.2021.1955123

Raphael, S. (2014). The effects of conviction and incarceration on future employment outcomes. In D. P. Farrington & J. Murray (Eds.), Advances in Criminological Theory: Vol. 18. *Labeling Theory: Empirical Tests* (pp. 237–262). Transaction Publishers.

Rapoport, M. (2011, March 9). Rewriting pension history. *Wall Street Journal*.

Rashid, M. H., & Morshed, A. (2021). Firms' Characteristics and Tax Evasion. In A. Rafay (Ed.), *Handbook of Research on Theory and Practice of Financial Crimes* (pp. 428–451). IGI Global., doi:10.4018/978-1-7998-5567-5.ch022

Reinstein, A., & McMillan, J. J. (2004). The Enron debacle: More than a perfect storm. *Critical Perspectives on Accounting*, *15*(6-7), 955–970. doi:10.1016/j.cpa.2003.08.006

Reurink, A. (2018). Financial fraud: AQ literature review. *Journal of Economic Surveys*, *32*(5), 1292–1325. doi:10.1111/joes.12294

Reuter, P. (2012). *Draining development?: Controlling flows of illicit funds from developing countries* (Report 66815). The World Bank. https://documents1.worldbank.org/curated/en/305601468178737192/text/668150PUB0EPI0067848B09780821388693.txt

Reuter, P., & Majmundar, M. (Eds.). (2015). Understanding the US illicit tobacco market: Characteristics, policy context, and lessons from international experiences. National Academies of Science and Engineering, National Research Council, Committee on the Illicit Tobacco Market: Collection and Analysis of the International Experience and Division of Behavioral and Social Sciences and Education, Committee on Law and Justice; Institute of Medicine, Board on Population Health and Public Health Practice. National Academies Press.

Reuter, P. (2009). Systemic violence in drug markets. *Crime, Law, and Social Change*, *52*(3), 275–284. doi:10.100710611-009-9197-x

Reyns, B. W., Henson, B., & Fisher, B. S. (2016). Guardians of the cyber galaxy: An empirical and theoretical analysis of the guardianship concept from routine activity theory as it applies to online forms of victimization. *Journal of Contemporary Criminal Justice*, *32*(2), 148–168. doi:10.1177/1043986215621378

Riedo, C., Fiolka, G., & Niggli, M. A. (2011). Strafprozessrecht sowie Rechtshilfe in Strafsachen. 1st ed. Basel, 425. Retrieved from Helbing Lichtenhahn Verlag.

Rigobon, R., & Rodrik, D. (2005). Rule of law, democracy, openness, and income: Estimating the interrelationships. *Economics of Transition*, *13*(3), 533–564. doi:10.1111/j.1468-0351.2005.00226.x

Rivera-Batiz, F. L. (2001). International financial liberalization, corruption, and economic growth. *Review of International Economics*, *9*(4), 727–737. doi:10.1111/1467-9396.00309

Rivero, P. (1991). *Análisis de Balances y Estados Complementarios*. Ediciones Pirámide.

Robb, G. (2012). Depicting a Female Fraud: Sarah Howe and the Boston Women's Bank. *Nineteenth-Century Contexts*, *34*(5), 445–459. doi:10.1080/08905495.2012.738086

Robinson, T. R. (2020). *International Financial Statement Analysis (CFA Institute Investment Series)*. Wiley.

Rodrik, D. (2000). Institutions for high-quality growth: What they are and how to acquire them. *Studies in Comparative International Development*, *35*(3), 3–31. doi:10.1007/BF02699764

Rodrik, D., Subramanian, A., & Trebbi, F. (2004). Institutions rule: The primacy of institutions over geography and integration in economic development. *Journal of Economic Growth*, *9*(2), 131–165. doi:10.1023/B:JOEG.0000031425.72248.85

Rose, D. R., & Clear, T. R. (1998). Incarceration, social capital, and crime: Implications for social disorganization theory. *Criminology*, *36*(3), 441–480. doi:10.1111/j.1745-9125.1998.tb01255.x

Rosenfeld, R. (2016). *Documenting and explaining the 2015 homicide rise: Research directions*. National Institute of Justice, Office of Justice Programs, US Department of Justice.

Rosner, R. L. (2003). Earnings manipulation in failing firms. *Contemporary Accounting Research*, *20*(2), 361–408. doi:10.1506/8EVN-9KRB-3AE4-EE81

Rosoff, S. M., Pontell, H. N., & Tillman, R. (2002). *Profit without honor: White-collar crime and the looting of America*. Prentice Hall Publishing.

Rosoff, S., Pontell, H., & Tillman, R. (2002). *Profit Without Honor: White-Collar Crime and the Looting of America*. Prentice Hall.

Ross, H. (2015). Measures to control illicit tobacco trade. *University of Illinois at Chicago, Institute for Health Research and Policy, Tobacconomics*. UIC. https://tinyurl.com/nm3n6hu4

Rothe, D., & Kauzlarich, D. (2022). *Crimes of the powerful: White-collar crime and beyond*. Routledge. doi:10.4324/9781003124603

Rothstein, B., & Varraich, A. (2017). *Making sense of corruption*. Cambridge University Press. doi:10.1017/9781316681596

Roychowdhury, S. (2006). Earnings management through real activities manipulation. *Journal of Accounting and Economics*, *42*(3), 335–370. doi:10.1016/j.jacceco.2006.01.002

Rubio, A., & Aragón, A. (2002). Factores explicativos del éxito competitivo. Un estudio empírico en la PYME. *Cuadernos de Gestión*, *2*(1), 49–63.

Ruggiero, V. (2021). The Crimes of the powerful: Between force and consensus. *Social Sciences (Basel, Switzerland)*, *10*(2), 51. doi:10.3390ocsci10020051

Rutz, J. (2014, November). Austria's Return Policy: Application of entry bans policy and use of readmission agreements. *European Migration Network (EMN)*. https://www.emn.at/wp-content/uploads/2017/01/EMNReturnStudy2014_AT-NCP_eng.pdf

Saad, M. E., Abdullah, S. N. H. S., & Murah, M. Z. (2018). Cyber romance scam victimization analysis using routine activity theory versus apriori algorithm. *International Journal of Advanced Computer Science and Applications*, *9*(12), 479–485. doi:10.14569/IJACSA.2018.091267

Saba, R. R., Beard, T. R., Ekelund, R. B. Jr, & Ressler, R. W. (1995). The demand for cigarette smuggling. *Economic Inquiry*, *33*(2), 189–202. doi:10.1111/j.1465-7295.1995.tb01856.x

Sadiq, M., & Shafie, R. B. (2017). The quality of financial reporting and its measurements. *International Journal of Economic Perspectives*, *11*(1), 392–401.

Safdar, R., & Yan, C. (2016). Managing accruals for income smoothing: Empirical evidence from Pakistan. *Journal of Accounting in Emerging Economies*, *6*(4), 372–387. doi:10.1108/JAEE-07-2014-0038

Salehi, M., & Alipour, M. (2010). E-banking in emerging economy: Empirical evidence of Iran. *International Journal of Economics and Finance*, *2*(1), 201–209. doi:10.5539/ijef.v2n1p201

Sanction Scanner. (2020). *Effects of money laundering on development*. Sanction Scanner. https://sanctionscanner.com/blog/effects-of-money-laundering-on-development-291

Sanderson, T. M. (2004). Transnational terror and organized crime: Blurring the lines. *SAIS Review (Paul H. Nitze School of Advanced International Studies)*, *24*(1), 49–61. doi:10.1353ais.2004.0020

Saranya, K., & Gunasri, K. S. (2013). Challenges in E-banking. *International Journal of Scientific Research and Management (IJSRM)*, *22*, 27.

Saridakis, G., Benson, V., Ezingeard, J. N., & Tennakoon, H. (2016). Individual information security, user behavior and cybervictimization: An empirical study of social networking users. *Technological Forecasting and Social Change*, *102*, 320–330. doi:10.1016/j.techfore.2015.08.012

Sayan, İ. Ö., & Kışlalı, M. (2004). Yolsuzluk Üzerine Ekonometrik Bir Çalışma. *Amme Idaresi Dergisi*, *37*(2), 31–50.

Schilit, H. M., & Perler, J. (2010). *Financial Shenanigans* (3rd ed.). McGraw-Hill.

Schmitt-Beck, R. (2015). Bandwagon effect. The International Encyclopedia of Political Communication, 1–5.

Schneider, S., & Hurst, C. (2008). Obstacles to an integrated, joint forces approach to organized crime enforcement: A Canadian case study. *Policing*, *31*(3), 359–379. doi:10.1108/13639510810895759

Schrand, C., & Wong, M. H. F. (2003). Earnings management using the valuation allowance for deferred tax assets under SFAS No. 109. *Contemporary Accounting Research*, *20*(3), 579–611. doi:10.1506/480D-098U-607R-5D9W

Schuchter, A., & Levi, M. (2016). The fraud triangle revisited. *Security Journal, 29*(2), 107–121. doi:10.1057j.2013.1

SEC. (2008, March). *The Securities and Exchange Commission Post-Madoff Reforms.* Securities and exchange Commission. https://www.sec.gov/spotlight/secpostmadoffreforms.htm

SECP. (2017, April 27). *SECP files criminal case of insider trading against a bank employee.* Retrieved from https://www.secp.gov.pk/media-center/press-releases/secp-files-criminal-case-of-insider-trading-against-a-bank-employee/

Sen, S., & Sen, A. (2019). *India Emerging: From Policy Paralysis to Hyper Economics.* Bloomsbury Publishing.

Sezal, M. A., & Giumelli, F. (2022). Technology transfer and defence sector dynamics: The case of the Netherlands. *European Security, 31*(4), 558–575. doi:10.1080/09662839.2022.2028277

Shah, M. (2019). A Case study on increasing of banking fraud in India. *Parichay: Maharaja Surajmal Institute Journal of Applied Research, 2*(1), 20–23.

Shams, R., Sobhan, A., Vrontis, D., Belyaeva, Z., & Vukovic, D. (2021). Detection of financial fraud risk: Implications for financial stability. *Journal of Operational Risk, 15*(4), 1–13.

Sharma, R. (2022). *Grey List.* EDUCBA. https://www.educba.com/grey-list/

Sharma, N., & Sharma, D. (2017). An empirical study on banking frauds in India-with a special reference to role of employee awareness in banking frauds. *International Journal of Business and Management, 3*(1), 2055–2066.

Shelley, L. (2015, November 28). How to beat Islamic State? Crack down on cigarette smuggling. *The Guardian.* https://www.theguardian.com/commentisfree/2015/nov/27/isis-cigarette-smuggling-isis-middle-east

Shelley, L. I. (2018). *Dark commerce: How a new illicit economy is threatening our future.* Princeton University Press. doi:10.2307/j.ctv346n56

Shelley, L. I. (2020). Illicit trade and terrorism. *Perspectives on Terrorism, 14*(4), 7–20.

Shelley, L. I., & Melzer, S. A. (2008). The nexus of organized crime and terrorism: Two case studies in cigarette smuggling. *International Journal of Comparative and Applied Criminal Justice, 32*(1), 43–63. doi:10.1080/01924036.2008.9678777

Sherman, T. (2015, October 15). $3.5M international con game nets NJ man 6 years in prison. *NJ.com.* https://www.nj.com/news/2015/10/35m_international_con_game_nets_nj_man_6_years_in.html

Shimpalee, P. L., & Breuer, J. B. (2006). Currency crises and institutions. *Journal of International Money and Finance, 25*(1), 125–145. doi:10.1016/j.jimonfin.2005.10.008

Shinmura, S. (2016). *New theory for discriminant analysis after R. Fisher.* Springer. doi:10.1007/978-981-10-2164-0

Shleifer, A., & Vishny, R. W. (1993). Corruption. *The Quarterly Journal of Economics, 108*(3), 599–617. doi:10.2307/2118402

Shmeleva, N., Gamidullaeva, L., Tolstykh, T., & Lazarenko, D. (2021). Challenges and opportunities for technology transfer networks in the context of open innovation: Russian experience. *Journal of Open Innovation, 7*(3), 197. doi:10.3390/joitmc7030197

Shover, N. (2007). Generative worlds of white-collar crime. In H. Pontell & G. Geis (Eds.), *International Handbook of White-Collar and Corporate Crime.* Springer. doi:10.1007/978-0-387-34111-8_4

Siegel, S., & Castellan, N. J. (2009). *Estadística no paramétrica. Aplicada a las ciencias de la conducta.* Editorial Trillas.

Sikka, P., & Willmott, H. (2010). The dark side of transfer pricing: Its role in tax avoidance and wealth retentiveness. *Critical Perspectives on Accounting, 21*(4), 342–356. doi:10.1016/j.cpa.2010.02.004

Simmons, D., & Quinton, M. (2021, March 24). Covid fraud: £34.5m stolen in pandemic scams. *BBC*. https://www.bbc.co.uk/news/technology-56499886

Sims, R. R., & Brinkmann, J. (2003). Enron ethics (or: Culture matters more than codes). *Journal of Business Ethics*, *45*(3), 243–256. doi:10.1023/A:1024194519384

Singh, R. (2010, December 27). RBI joins bribes-for-loans scam probe. *Economic Times*. https://economictimes.indiatimes.com/news/politics-and-nation/rbi-joins-bribes-for-loans-scam-probe/articleshow/7169716.cms?from=mdr

Singh, M. M., Frank, R., & Zainon, W. M. N. W. (2021). Cyber-criminology defense in pervasive environment: A study of cybercrimes in Malaysia. *Bulletin of Electrical Engineering and Informatics*, *10*(3), 1658–1668. doi:10.11591/eei.v10i3.3028

Singh, P. (2013). An exploratory study on internet banking usage in Semi-Urban areas in India. *International Journal of Scientific and Research Publications*, *3*(8), 1–5.

Skoryk, M. (2019). Theoretical aspects of the transformation of the institute of corruption in Eastern Europe. *Baltic Journal of Economic Studies*, *5*(1), 201–206. doi:10.30525/2256-0742/2019-5-1-201-206

Small, K., & Taylor, B. (2006). State and local law enforcement response to transnational crime. *Trends in Organized Crime*, *10*(2), 5–17. doi:10.100712117-006-1033-4

Smith, F. (2010). Madoff ponzi scheme exposes the myth of the sophisticated investor. *University of Baltimore Law Review*, *40*, 215.

Smith, K. C., Stillman, F., Bone, L., Yancey, N., Price, E., Belin, P., & Kromm, E. E. (2007). Buying and selling "loosies" in Baltimore: The informal exchange of cigarettes in the community context. *Journal of Urban Health*, *84*(4), 494–507. doi:10.100711524-007-9189-z PMID:17431795

Smith, T. B. (2004). Electricity theft: A comparative analysis. *Energy Policy*, *32*(18), 2067–2076. doi:10.1016/S0301-4215(03)00182-4

Sofian, F. N. R. M., Mohd-Sabrun, I., & Muhamad, R. (2022). Past, present, and future of corporate social responsibility and earnings management research. *Australasian Accounting. Business and Finance Journal*, *16*(2), 116–144.

Song, H. J., Lynch, M. J., & Cochran, J. K. (2016). A Macro-Social exploratory analysis of the rate of interstate cyber-victimization. *American Journal of Criminal Justice*, *41*(3), 583–601. doi:10.100712103-015-9308-4

Sood, P., & Bhushan, P. (2020). A structured review and theme analysis of financial frauds in the banking industry. *Asian Journal of Business Ethics*, *9*(2), 305–321. doi:10.100713520-020-00111-w

Sosa, M. C. (2011). Breve inventario de los principales ratios financieros utilizados en el análisis financiero empresarial. *Observatorio de la Economía Latinoamericana*, *152*, 1–23.

Spyrou, M. A., Tukhbatova, R. I., Feldman, M., Drath, J., Kacki, S., Beltran de Heredia, J., Arnold, S., Sitdikov, A. G., Castex, D., Wahl, J., Gazimzyanov, I. R., Nurgaliev, D. K., Herbig, A., Bos, K. I., & Krause, J. (2016). Historical Y. pestis Genomes Reveal the European Black Death as the Source of Ancient and Modern Plague Pandemics. *Cell Host & Microbe*, *19*(6), 874–881. doi:10.1016/j.chom.2016.05.012 PMID:27281573

Staff, R. (2008). *Tobacco and terror: How cigarette smuggling is funding our enemies abroad.* United States House of Representatives, Committee on Homeland Security. https://tinyurl.com/2p8d9pfz

Stallworth, H. L., & Digregorio, D. (2004). Improper revenue recognition: To help clients avoid SEC violations, internal auditors need to understand the revenue management practices that can lead to material misstatements. *Internal Auditor*, *61*(3), 53–57.

Stancu, I., & Rece, D. (2009). The Relationship between economic growth and money laundering—a Linear Regression Model. *Theoretical & Applied Economics*, *16*(9), 1–8.

Steadman, K. U. (2011). *Essays on electricity theft*. State University of New York at Binghamton.

Stehr, M. (2005). Cigarette tax avoidance and evasion. *Journal of Health Economics*, *24*(2), 277–297. doi:10.1016/j.jhealeco.2004.08.005 PMID:15721046

Stein, L. C. D., & Wang, C. C. Y. (2015). *Economic uncertainty and earnings management* (Working Paper 16-103). Harvard Business School Accounting & Management Unit.

Stern, J., & Holder, S. (1999). Regulatory governance: criteria for assessing the performance of regulatory systems: an application to infrastructure industries in the developing countries of Asia. *Utilities Policy*, *8*(1), 33–50. doi:10.1016/S0957-1787(99)00008-9

Stofkova, K. R., Laitkep, D., & Stofkova, Z. (2022). Shopping behavior in the context of the digital economy. *Journal of Risk and Financial Management*, *15*(2), 39. doi:10.3390/jrfm15020039

Stoklosa, M. (2019). No surge in illicit cigarettes after implementation of menthol ban in Nova Scotia. *Tobacco Control*, *28*(6), 702–704. doi:10.1136/tobaccocontrol-2018-054552 PMID:30309981

Stolowy, H., Messner, M., Jeanjean, T., & Richard Baker, C. (2014). The construction of a trustworthy investment opportunity: Insights from the Madoff fraud. *Contemporary Accounting Research*, *31*(2), 354–397. doi:10.1111/1911-3846.12039

Stuckenberg, C. F. (1998). Untersuchungen zur Unschuldsvermutung, 1st ed. Berlin: de Gruyter. DEG. doi:10.1515/9783110906349

Sullivan, J. D. (2009, February). *The moral compass of companies: Business ethics and corporate governance as anti-corruption tools*. Washington: Global Corporate Governance Forum.

Sumartono, S., Urumsah, D., & Hamdani, R. (2020). Skills of the forensic accountants in revealing fraud in public sector: The Case of Indonesia. *Journal of Accounting and Investment*, *21*(1), 180–194.

Sutherland, E. H. (1940). White-collar criminality. *American Sociological Review*, *5*(1), 1–12. doi:10.2307/2083937

Sutherland, E. H. (1945). Is "white collar crime" crime? *American Sociological Review*, *10*(2), 132–139. doi:10.2307/2085628

Sutherland, E. H. (1949). *White collar crime*. Dryden.

Sutherland, E. H. (1973). Development of the theory. In K. Schuessler (Ed.), *Edwin H. Sutherland on analyzing crime Chicago*. University of Chicago Press.

Sviatun, O., Goncharuk, O., Roman, C., Kuzmenko, O., & Kozych, I. V. (2021). Combating cybercrime: Economic and legal aspects. *WSEAS Transactions on Business and Economics*, *18*, 751–762. doi:10.37394/23207.2021.18.72

Swaleheen, M. (2011). Economic growth with endogenous corruption: An empirical study. *Public Choice*, *146*(1-2), 23–41. doi:10.100711127-009-9581-1

Swissinfo. (2022, April 13). *Swiss tighten Russia sanctions and increase support for refugee*. Swiss Info. https://www.swissinfo.ch/eng/swiss-tighten-russia-sanctions-and-increase-support-for-refugees/47515750

Tahir, I. N. (2020). Poverty alleviation strategies implemented by Umar bn Abd Al Aziz: Lessons for Muslim economists on achieving SDG of poverty alleviation. *International Journal of Economics Management and Accounting*, *28*(2), 483–515.

Tamekamta, A. (2021). Terrorism and privatization of state spaces in the Sahel: Case of the Polisario Front. *Revista Universitară de Sociologie*, *17*(1), 186–196.

Tamyez, P. F. (2022). The challenges and solutions of cybersecurity among Malaysian companies. In *Research Anthology on Business Aspects of Cybersecurity* (pp. 676–693). IGI Global. doi:10.4018/978-1-6684-3698-1.ch031

Tanzi, V., & Davoodi, H. (1997). *Corruption, public investment, and growth* (IMF Working Paper, WP/97/139). International Monetary Fund.

Tanzi, V., & Davoodi, H. R. (2000). *Corruption, growth and public Finances* (IMF Working Paper, WP/00/182). International Monetary Fund.

Tanzi, V. (1998). Corruption around the world: Causes, consequences, scope, and cures. *Staff Papers - International Monetary Fund. International Monetary Fund*, *45*(4), 559–594. doi:10.2307/3867585

Taşdöven, H., Emhan, A., & Dönmez, M. (2012). Liderlik tarzı ve mizaç-karakter ilişkisi: Polis teşkilatında bir uygulama. *Yönetim ve Ekonomi Dergisi*, *19*(2), 165–177.

Taylor, G., & Richardson, G. (2012). International corporate tax avoidance practices: Evidence from Australian firms. *The International Journal of Accounting*, *47*(4), 469–496. doi:10.1016/j.intacc.2012.10.004

Taylor, R. W., Caeti, T. J., Loper, D. K., Fritsch, E. J., & Liederbach, J. (2006). *Digital crime and digital terrorism*. Pearson Prentice Hall.

Teichmann, F. (2017). Bribery and corruption–Challenges and potential solutions in multinational corporations. *SEER: Journal for Labour and Social Affairs in Eastern Europe*, *20*(2), 247–268. doi:10.5771/1435-2869-2017-2-247

Teichmann, F. (2021). Einreiseverbote aufgrund ausländischer Strafverfahren – Straf- und verwaltungsverfahrensrechtliche Herausforderungen für das schweizerische Bundesamt für Polizei (Fedpol). *Kriminalistik*, *1*, 48–53.

Teichmann, F. (2021). Korruption in osteuropäischen Staatsanwaltschaften und ihre Implikationen für Rechtshilfe - und Wirtschaftsstrafverfahren. *Kriminalistik*.

Teichmann, F. M., & Sergi, B. S. (2018). *Compliance in Multinational Corporations: Business Risks in Bribery, Money Laundering, Terrorism Financing and Sanctions*. Emerald Group Publishing. doi:10.1108/9781787568679

Teixeira, J. F., & Rodrigues, L. L. (2022). Earnings management: A bibliometric analysis. *International Journal of Accounting & Information Management*, *30*(5), 664–683. doi:10.1108/IJAIM-12-2021-0259

Thanh Binh, V. T., Tran, N. M., Thanh, D. M., & Phamd, H. H. (2020). Firm size, business sector and quality of accounting information systems: Evidence from Vietnam. *Accounting*, *6*(3), 327–334. doi:10.5267/j.ac.2020.2.002

Tharshini, N. K., Hassan, Z., & Mas'ud, F. (2021). Cybercrime threat landscape amid the movement control order in Malaysia. *International Journal of Business and Society*, *22*(3), 1589–1601. doi:10.33736/ijbs.4323.2021

Tharshini, N. K., Mas'ud, F., & Hassan, Z. (2022). Level of cybercrime threat during the outbreak of COVID-19 pandemic: A study in Malaysia. *International Journal of Academic Research in Business & Social Sciences*, *12*(5), 40–51.

The Express Tribune. (2016, November 23). PTI leader had returned Rs73.1 million: SECP. *The Eastern Tribune*. https://tribune.com.pk/story/1240182/pti-leader-returned-rs73-1-million-secp

The Federal Council. (2022, February 28). *Switzerland adopts EU sanctions against Russia.* The Federal Council. https://www.admin.ch/gov/en/start/documentation/media-releases.msg-id-87386.html

The White House. (2022, July 13). *The White House Announces Newly Designated High Intensity Drug Trafficking Areas* [Press release]. The White House. https://tinyurl.com/y74yzhbe

Thoma, M. (2010, September 2). Too Much "Too Big to Fail"? *Economist's View.* https://economistsview.typepad.com/economistsview/2010/09/too-much-too-big-to-fail.html

Thomas, B., Clergue, J., Schaad, A., & Dacier, M. (2004). A comparison of conventional and online fraud. *Conference on Securing Critical Infrastructures* (pp. 25–27). IEEE.

Thomas, C. W. (2002). The rise and fall of Enron. *Journal of Accountancy, 193*(4), 41–52.

Thursby, J. G., & Thursby, M. C. (2000). Interstate cigarette bootlegging: Extent, revenue losses, and effects of federal intervention. *National Tax Journal, 53*(1), 59–77. doi:10.17310/ntj.2000.1.04

TI. (2006). *Global Corruption Report 2006: Corruption and Health.* Transparency International.

TI. (2021). *Corruption perceptions index.* Transparency International: https://www.transparency.org/en/cpi/2021

TI. (2021). *Timor Leste.* Transparency International. https://www.transparency.org/en/countries/timor-leste

TI. (2023). *What is corruption.* Transparency International. https://www.transparency.org/en/what-is-corruption

Tiba, S., & Omri, A. (2017). Literature survey on the relationships between energy, environment and economic growth. *Renewable & Sustainable Energy Reviews, 69*, 1129–1146. doi:10.1016/j.rser.2016.09.113

Tientcheu, P. P. (2021). *Security Awareness Strategies Used in the Prevention of Cybercrime by Cybercriminals.* [MS Thesis. Walden University].

Time Warner Inc. (2010). *Time Warner Annual Report, 2009.* Annual Report Owl. https://www.annualreportowl.com/Time%20Warner%20Cable/2009/Annual%20Report

Topalli, V., Wright, R., & Fornango, R. (2002). Drug dealers, robbery and retaliation: Vulnerability, deterrence and the contagion of violence. *British Journal of Criminology, 42*(2), 337–351. doi:10.1093/bjc/42.2.337

Torre, F. (2014). Contribución de la Ciencia e Ingeniería en el desarrollo económico. *The Twelfth Latin American and Caribbean Conference for Engineering and Technology.* Guayaquil, Ecuador. Retrieved from https://www.laccei.org/LACCEI2014-Guayaquil/RefereedPapers/RP080.pdf

Torsello, D., & Venard, B. (2016). The anthropology of corruption. *Journal of Management Inquiry, 25*(1), 34–54. doi:10.1177/1056492615579081

Tosun, U. (2001). Yolsuzluğun ekonomik etkileri: Yolsuzluk ve büyüme arasındaki ilişki. *Kamu Tercihi ve Anayasal İktisat Dergisi, 4*, 3–8.

Toumeh, A. A., & Yahya, S. (2019). A review of earnings management techniques: An IFRS perspective. *Global Business and Management Research, 11*(3), 1–13.

Tran, Q. T., Nguyen, N. K. D., & To, P. Q. A. (2020). Financial ratios affecting disclosure level in interim report of Vietnamese listed enterprises. *The Journal of Asian Finance. Economics and Business, 7*(10), 43–50. doi:10.13106/jafeb.2020.vol7.no10.043

Transparency International. (2014). *Leaving the corrupt at the door: From denial of entry to passport sales.* Federal Council. https://transparency.eu/wp-content/uploads/2018/02/Golden-Visas-TI-S-Leaving-the-Corrupt-at-the-Door.pdf

Transparency International. (2020). *World Map*. Transparency International. https://www.transparency.org/en/cpi/2019/results.

Travis, J., & Waul, M. (2003). Prisoners once removed: The impact of incarceration and reentry on children, families, and communities. *The Urban Institute*. https://webarchive.urban.org/publications/210900.html

Treisman, D. (2000). The causes of corruption: A cross-national study. *Journal of Public Economics*, *76*(3), 399–457. doi:10.1016/S0047-2727(99)00092-4

Tsoulfidis, L., & Athanasiadis, I. (2022). A new method of identifying key industries: A principal component analysis. *Journal of Economic Structures*, *11*(1), 1–23. doi:10.118640008-022-00261-z

TTB. (2016). FY 2017 president's budget. *Alcohol and Tobacco Tax and Trade Bureau, United States Department of the Treasury*. https://www.ttb.gov/images/pdfs/fy2017-enacted.pdf

TTB. (2021). Congressional Budget Justification and Annual Performance Plan and Report. *Alcohol and Tobacco Tax and Trade Bureau, United States Department of the Treasury*. TTB. https://www.ttb.gov/images/pdfs/fy2022-cj.pdf

Tukur, M. (1999). *Leadership and governance in Nigeria: The Relevance of values*. HudaHuda/Hodder and Stoughton.

Ulep, V. G., Lavares, M. P., & Francisco, A. (2021). Measuring the capacity to combat illicit tobacco trade in 160 countries. *Globalization and Health*, *17*(1), 1–8. doi:10.118612992-021-00783-4 PMID:34789289

Ullah, K., Arentsen, M. J., & Lovett, J. C. (2017). Institutional determinants of power sector reform in Pakistan. *Energy Policy*, *102*, 332–339. doi:10.1016/j.enpol.2016.12.019

United States Attorney's Office. (2015, March 12). *Ten members and associates of decavalcante organized crime family arrested* [press release]. USAO. https://tinyurl.com/mkars347

Ünlü, H., & Ulusoy, M. K. (2021). Innovation and Corruption in Türkiye: "Grease the Wheels" or "Sand the Wheels". In A. Rafay (Ed.), *Handbook of Research on Theory and Practice of Financial Crimes* (pp. 80–103). IGI Global. doi:10.4018/978-1-7998-5567-5.ch006

UNODC. (1988). *United Nations Convention against Illicit Traffic in Narcotics Drugs and Psychotropic Substances*. United Nations Office on Drugs and Crimes. https://www.unodc.org/unodc/en/treaties/illicit-trafficking.html

UNODC. (2011). *Money Laudering*. United Nations Office on Drugs and Crimes. https://www.unodc.org/unodc/en/money-laundering/overview.html

UNODC. (2019). *Corruption in Nigeria: Patterns and Trends (Second survey on corruption as experienced by the population.* www.unodc.org

UNODC. (2022). *Combatting Terrorist Financing*. United Nations Office on Drugs and Crimes. https://www.unodc.org/unodc/en/terrorism/expertise /combating-terrorist-financing.html

Urías, J. (1992). *Análisis de Estados Financieros*. McGraw-Hill.

US. (2014, June 18). Criminal Complaint filed by FBI in U.S. District Court New Jersey.

Usman, A. K., & Shah, M. H. (1970). Critical success factors for preventing e-banking fraud. *Journal of Internet Banking and Commerce*, *18*(2), 1–14.

Vagner, L., Valaskova, K., Durana, P., & Lazaroiu, G. (2021). Earnings management: A bibliometric analysis. *Economia e Sociologia*, *14*(1), 249–262.

Vaithilingam, S., & Nair, M. (2007). Factors affecting money laundering: Lesson for developing countries. *Journal of Money Laundering Control, 10*(3), 352–366. doi:10.1108/13685200710763506

Van Eden, H., Bessette, F., Pedastsaar, E., & Nayer, H. (2010). *Democratic Republic of Timor-Leste: Public financial management–performance report.* International Monetary Fund Country Report. doi:10.5089/9781455212613.002

Varcarolis, E. M., Carson, V. B., & Shoemaker, N. C. (2006). *Foundations of Psychiatric Mental Health Nursing: A Clinical Approach.* Saunders.

Varma, P. K. (2019). *Chanakya's View: Understanding India in Transition.* Tranquebar Press.

Vaughan, D. (2007). Beyond macro- and micro-levels of analysis, organizations, and the cultural fix. In H. Pontell & G. Geis (Eds.), *International Handbook of White-Collar and Corporate Crime.* Springer. doi:10.1007/978-0-387-34111-8_1

Vier Machado, H. P. (2016). Growth of small businesses: A literature review and perspectives of studies. Gest. Prod., São Carlos, 23(2), 419–432. https://doi.org/ doi:10.1590/0104-530X1759-14

Villarreal, A., & Silva, B. F. A. (2006). Social cohesion, criminal victimization and perceived risk of crime in Brazilian neighborhoods. *Social Forces, 84*(3), 1725–1753. doi:10.1353of.2006.0073

Viswanathan, V. N. (2008). *Corruption and Human Rights.* Allied Publishers.

Vitaux, J. (2021). *Les grandes pandémies de l'histoire: De la peste au Covid.* Archipoche.

Von Arnim, H. H. (2003). Korruption in politik und verwaltung. In H. H. Von Arnim (Ed.), *Korruption. Netzwerke in Politik, Ämtern und Wirtschaft.* Knaur.

von Lampe, K., Kurti, M., Johnson, J., & Rengifo, A. F. (2016). "I wouldn't take my chances on the street": Navigating illegal cigarette purchases in the South Bronx. *Journal of Research in Crime and Delinquency, 53*(5), 654–680. doi:10.1177/0022427816637888

Wade, R. (1985). The market for public office: Why the Indian state is not better at development. *World Development, 13*(4), 467–497. doi:10.1016/0305-750X(85)90052-X

Walker-Munro, B. (2021). Tax Enforcement in the Black Economy: Tackling Disruptive Challenge. In A. Rafay (Ed.), *Handbook of Research on Theory and Practice of Financial Crimes* (pp. 356–380). IGI Global. doi:10.4018/978-1-7998-5567-5.ch019

Walsh, J. P. (1988). Selectivity and selective perception: An investigation of managers' belief structures and information processing. *Academy of Management Journal, 31*(4), 873–896. doi:10.2307/256343

Wang, Y., Butterfield, S., & Campbell, M. (2017). Effects of earnings management, compensation, insider equity holding on tax structure. *International Management Review, 13*(2), 5–15.

Wanless, M. (2013). The World's Bank fight against corruption: 'See nothing, hear nothing, say nothing,'. *Hydra, 1*(2), 38–48.

Waris, A., & Seabrooke, L. (2017). Arrested development in Africa's global wealth chains: Accountability and hierarchy among 'tax havens. In *The Routledge Companion to Tax Avoidance Research* (pp. 267–286). Routledge. doi:10.4324/9781315673745-18

Wasiuzzaman, S., Sahafzadeh, I., & Nejad, N. R. (2015). Prospect theory, industry characteristics and earnings management: A study of Malaysian industries. *Review of Accounting and Finance, 14*(3), 324–347. doi:10.1108/RAF-07-2014-0075

Watkins, A., & Apuzzo, M. (2018, January 19). Trump envisions an A.T.F. without the A or T. *New York Times*. http://www.nytimes.com

WDI. (2022). *Data Bank: World Development Indicators*. The World Bank. https://databank.worldbank.org/source/world-development-indicators

Wei, S. J. (1999). *Corruption in economic development: Beneficial grease, minor annoyance, or major obstacle?* (World Bank Policy Research Working Paper). National Bureau of Economic Research.

Wei, S. J. (2000). *Bribery in the economies: Grease or sand?*. The Brookings Institution, Harvard University, NBER.

Wei, L., Peng, M., & Wu, W. X. (2021). Financial literacy and fraud detection - Evidence from China. *International Review of Economics & Finance*, *76*(C), 478–494. doi:10.1016/j.iref.2021.06.017

Weisburd, D., Wyckoff, L. A., Ready, J., Eck, J. E., Hinkle, J. C., & Gajewski, F. (2006). Does crime just move around the corner? A controlled study of spatial displacement and diffusion of crime control benefits. *Criminology*, *44*(3), 549–592. doi:10.1111/j.1745-9125.2006.00057.x

Wen, T. S., Satar, N. M., Ishak, N. A., & Ating, R. (2020). Consumer intention towards online shopping in Malaysia. *The International Journal of Accounting*, *5*(27), 93–117.

White, R. (2017). Corruption and the securitisation of nature. *International Journal for Crime. Justice and Social Democracy*, *6*(4), 55–70. doi:10.5204/ijcjsd.v6i4.449

Whitty, M. T. (2020). Is there a scam for everyone? Psychologically profiling cyber scam victims. *European Journal on Criminal Policy and Research*, *26*(3), 399–409. doi:10.100710610-020-09458-z

Wijayatunga, P. D., Fernando, W. J. L. S., & Shrestha, R. M. (2004). Impact of distributed and independent power generation on greenhouse gas emissions: Sri Lanka. *Energy Conversion and Management*, *45*(20), 3193–3206. doi:10.1016/j.enconman.2004.01.009

Wikipedia. (2023). *Cyberterrorism*. https://en.wikipedia.org/wiki/Cyberterrorism

Wilkitzki, P. (1995). On judicial mutual assistance in criminal matters between the states of Western and Eastern Europe. *European Journal on Criminal Policy and Research*, *3*(4), 91–98. doi:10.1007/BF02243036

Wilson, C., Sheridan, L., & Garratt-Reed, D. (2022). Examining cyberstalking perpetration and victimization: A scoping review. *Trauma, Violence & Abuse*, *15248380221082937*. Advance online publication. doi:10.1177/15248380221082937 PMID:35387506

Winarso, W. (2020). The impact of perceived of cyber fraud, ease of use and risk perception on the behavior of using e-commerce systems in Indonesia. *Journal of Critical Reviews*, *7*(4), 2394–5125.

Winther, T. (2012). Electricity theft as a relational issue: A comparative look at Zanzibar, Tanzania, and the Sunderban Islands, India. *Energy for Sustainable Development*, *16*(1), 111–119. doi:10.1016/j.esd.2011.11.002

World Bank. (1997). *Helping countries combat corruption: The role of the World Bank* (Working Paper No. 24687). Washington, D.C.: World Bank Group. https://documents.worldbank.org/curated/en/799831538245192753/Helping-countries-combat-corruption-the-role-of-the-World-Bank

World Bank. (2001). *Governance and Corruption*. World Bank Group.

World Bank. (2022). *Nigeria Public Finance Review: Fiscal Adjustment for Better Sustainable Results* (Report No. AUS0002571). Washington, D.C.: World Bank Group. https://documents.worldbank.org/curated/en/099615211172222358/P1750950fbd29d02008429007d1ed499d61

World Bank. (2022). Timor-Leste economic report: Investing in the next generation. https://openknowledge.worldbank.org/bitstream/handle/10986/37604/ P1773510568a060db09183035b08e384fec.pdf?sequence=1&isAllowed=y doi:10.4324/9780203835722

World Justice Project. (2020). *Rule of Law Index.* World Justice Project. https://worldjusticeproject.org/sites/default/files/documents/WJP-ROLI-2020-Online_0.pdf. (Accessed 09.05.2020).

Wu, K., Noorian, Z., Vassileva, J., & Adaji, I. (2015). How buyers perceive the credibility of advisors in online marketplace: Review balance, review count and misattribution. *Journal of Trust Management*, *2*(1), 1–18. doi:10.118640493-015-0013-5

Wyatt, E. (2010, July 22). Dell to pay $100 million settlement. *The New York Times*. https://www.nytimes.com/2010/07/23/business/23dell.html#:~:text=Dell%2C%20agreed%20Thursday%20to%20pay,pad%20its%20quarterly%20earnings%20statements.

Xian, C., Sun, F., & Zhang, Y. (2015). Book-tax differences: Are they affected by equity-based compensation? *Accounting Research Journal*, *28*(3), 300–318. doi:10.1108/ARJ-12-2013-0088

Xu, R. Z., Taylor, G. K., & Dugan, M. T. (2007). Review of real earnings management literature. *Journal of Accounting Literature*, *26*, 195–228.

Xu, W. (2016). Accruals Management to avoid losses. *Journal of Business Finance & Accounting*, *43*(9), 1095–1120. doi:10.1111/jbfa.12215

Yin, R. K. (2013). Validity and generalization in future case study evaluations. *Evaluation*, *19*(3), 321–332. doi:10.1177/1356389013497081

Yogesh, A., & Choudhary, S. K. (2014). *Combating corruption: The Indian case.* Orient BlackSwan.

Yoon, S. J. (2002). The antecedents and consequences of trust in online-purchase decisions. *Journal of Interactive Marketing*, *16*(2), 47–63. doi:10.1002/dir.10008

Yurtseven, Ç. (2015). The causes of electricity theft: An econometric analysis of the case of Türkiye. *Utilities Policy*, *37*, 70–78. doi:10.1016/j.jup.2015.06.008

Yusof, S. A. (2015). Household bargaining, financial decision-making and risk tolerance. *International Journal of Business and Society*, *16*(2), 221–236.

Yusuf, S. A. (2023). *Living in the eye of the storm: What options for Nigeria.* An Inaugural Lecture delivered at the University of Ibadan.

Zabyelina, Y. (2020). The Long arm of anti-corruption: Extraterritoriality and anti-corruption targeted sanctions. *Global Policy*, *11*(4), 535–540. doi:10.1111/1758-5899.12850

Zahari, A. I., Bilu, R., & Said, J. (2019). The role of familiarity, trust and awareness towards online fraud. *Journal of Research and Opinion*, *6*(9), 2470–2480.

Zatoński, M., Herbeć, A., Zatoński, W., Przewoźniak, K., Janik-Koncewicz, K., Mons, U., Fong, G. T., Demjén, T., Tountas, Y., Trofor, A. C., Fernández, E., McNeil, A., Willemsen, M., Hummel, K., Quah, A. C. K., & Kyriakos, C. N. (2018). Characterising smokers of menthol and flavoured cigarettes, their attitudes towards tobacco regulation, and the anticipated impact of the Tobacco Products Directive on their smoking and quitting behaviours: The EUREST-PLUS ITC Europe Surveys. *Tobacco Induced Diseases*, *16*(Suppl. 2), A4. doi:10.18332/tid/96294 PMID:31516460

Zeng, T. (2014). Earnings management around tax rate reduction: Evidence from China's 2007 corporate tax reform. *Asian Review of Accounting*, *22*(3), 304–317. doi:10.1108/ARA-01-2014-0012

Zevallos, E. (2007). *Restricciones del entorno a la competitividad empresarial en América Latina*. Bolivia: Fundación para el Desarrollo Sostenible (FUNDES). http://www.sela.org/es/centro-de-documentacion/base-de-datos-documental/bdd/28689/ restricciones-del-entorno-a-la-competitividad-empresarial-en-america-latina

Zevallos, E. (2003). Micro, pequeñas y medianas empresas en América Latina. *Revista de la CEPAL*, *79*(79), 53–70. doi:10.18356/da461f83-es

Zgaga, B. (2018). Slovene media owned by oligarchs, corrupt politicians. *Reporters without borders*. https://rsf.org/en/slovene-media-owned-oligarchs-corrupt-politicians

Zhang, Y., Bian, J., & Zhu, W. (2013). Trust fraud: A crucial challenge for China's e-commerce market. *Electronic Commerce Research and Applications*, *12*(5), 299–308. doi:10.1016/j.elerap.2012.11.005

Zhao, Y., Chen, K. H., Zhang, Y., & Davis, M. (2012). Takeover protection and managerial myopia: Evidence from real earnings management. *Journal of Accounting and Public Policy*, *31*(1), 109–135. doi:10.1016/j.jaccpubpol.2011.08.004

Zhou, D., & Habib, A. (2013). Accounting standards and earnings management: Evidence from China'. *Accounting Perspectives*, *12*(3), 213–236. doi:10.1111/1911-3838.12016

Zimmer, L. (1990). Proactive policing against street-level drug trafficking. *American Journal of Police*, *9*(1), 43–74.

Zimring, F. E. (2011). *The city that became safe: New York's lessons for urban crime and its control*. Oxford University Press. doi:10.1093/acprof:oso/9780199844425.001.0001

Zulkipli, N. H. N., Rashid, N. A. M., Zolkeplay, A. F., & Buja, A. G. (2021). Synthesizing cybersecurity issues and challenges for the elderly. *Turkish Journal of Computer and Mathematics Education*, *12*(5), 1775–1781.

About the Contributors

Abdul Rafay is a practitioner cum academician. For more than 25 years, Mr. Rafay has been working as a freelance advisor, consultant & trainer to a wide variety of public & private sector national and multinational companies in the areas of Corporate Finance, Financial Policy & Implementation, Auditing & Assurance, Accountancy, Corporate Tax Management, Financial Technology, and System Consultancy. He has been providing consultancy to various industries including Textile, Auto Assembling, Footwear, Industrial/Agro Chemicals, Ice Cream/Dairies, Glass/Ceramics, Healthcare, Mining/Natural Resources, Packaging/Paper Sacking, Steel/Pipe Casting, Rice Processing, Brokerage/Co-operative Financing, Software Development, Real Estate, Printing/Publishing, and Construction/Civil Engineering, etc. Mr. Rafay is a Fellow member of the Institute of Chartered Accountants of Pakistan. He is also a member of various national and international professional bodies including the Institute of Internal Auditors (IIA), USA; Association of Certified Fraud Examiners (ACFE), USA. Since 2001, he has been a lifetime member of the Lahore Tax Bar Association. He has served as Co-regional Director (Founding) of Lahore-Islamabad Chapter of Professional Risk Managers International Association (PRMIA), Washington, USA (2011-2013). In 2012, he was nominated as Member: Education & Training Committee (ETCOM) of The Institute of Chartered Accountants of Pakistan (ICAP). He is also a member of ICAP's "Islamic Finance working group" which is closely in liaison with the State Bank of Pakistan and other stakeholders for Islamic Finance Accounting and Auditing Standards. He is an Alumnus of Rausing Executive Development Center (REDC), Lahore University of Management Sciences (LUMS), Pakistan. In 2014, International Finance Corporation (World Bank Group) selected him for Training of Trainers (ToT) for Corporate Governance Action Planning for SMEs. He is also an approved trainer for the Institute of Financial Markets of Pakistan (IFMP) established by the Securities and Exchange Commission of Pakistan (SECP), the corporate regulator. In 2013, his name got included in the list of "Certified Directors" as per Clause (xi) of The Code of Corporate Governance 2012 issued by SECP. Currently, he is on the board of a Listed Company as an Independent Director. For the last 27 years, Mr. Rafay has also been associated with teaching in some of the top business schools of Pakistan. His specialized subjects of interest include Strategic Corporate Finance, Financial Crimes, Financial Derivatives, Investments/Portfolio Analysis, International Financial Reporting Standards, Corporate Restructuring (Mergers & Acquisitions), Financial Statement Analysis & Corporate Taxation. He also served as an instructor in Civil Services Academy, Pakistan to train the CSS Officers selected by the Federal Public Service Commission of Pakistan (FPSC). Currently, he is a Professor of Finance & Accounting at the University of Management & Technology, Pakistan. He has published more than two dozen research papers in SSCI, ESCI and Scopus indexed journals published by reputed global publishers including Emerald, Sage, Taylor & Francis, Routledge and IGI Global. He contributed multiple chapters in Books edited by International Editors. He also edited international books on FinTech, Islamic Finance, Financial Crimes, Money Laundering, Terrorism Financing, Energy Finance, Environmental Finance and Technological/Financial Frauds published by IGI Global, USA.

***

Abdulrauph Muftau is a lecturer in the Department of Islamic Studies, Federal College of Education, Iwo, Osun State. He had his early education in Ilorin, Kwara State. He had his first and Master's degrees in Islamic Studies from the University of Ilorin. He is currently pursuing his doctoral degree from the same University. He specializes in Islamic economic system with particular interest in Islamic insurance.

Clement Chiahemba M. Ajekwe holds a PhD in Accounting from Benue State University, Nigeria, and an MSc from the London School of Economics, UK. Currently, he is an Associate Professor of Accounting at Benue State University, Nigeria. He is a member of the Chartered Institute of Management Accountants of the United Kingdom and the Institute of Chartered Accountants of Nigeria. Dr. Ajekwe has more than thirty years of academic experience. He has taught undergraduate and graduate students and supervised undergraduate projects, Master's degree dissertations and PhD theses. Dr. Ajekwe is an accomplished researcher; he has several publications in peer-reviewed Journals and Chapters in Edited Books. In addition, he has had twelve years of professional management experience in corporate Nigeria.

Tooba Akram holds a PhD in Management Sciences in area of Forensic Finance from University of Technology Malaysia, Johor. Her research interests mainly includes financial markets, and financial crimes. She is a young dynamic researcher and a refined professional with 11 years of diversified post-qualification experience in management and financial sector embraces Project Management, Operations Management, Administration, Financial Modeling & Business Analysis, Financial Administration, followed by Financial Markets, Investigations, Financial fraud examination, Compliance AML/CFT, FinCrime Research, and Academic Finance. She published more than 5 publications during last 2 years.

Adnan Ali holds a PhD from the Faculty of Management, Universiti Teknologi Malaysia (UTM), Malaysia. Currently, he is Assistant Professor at Shaheed Benazir Bhutto University (SBBU), Sheringal Dir (U) Pakistan. His research interest revolves around Management, focusing on Sustainable Development, Economics, Natural Resources, Financial Economics, Corporate Social Responsibility, Finance, Shadow Economy, International Business and Trade, Institutional Quality, and Microfinance Institutions. Further, Dr. Ali has great expertise in multidisciplinary areas considering Bibliometric Analysis. He possesses more than 13 years of Teaching and Research experience at various Public sector Universities in Pakistan.Dr. Ali previously served as Management Associate at the Small and Medium Enterprises Development Authority (SMEDA), Pakistan, and has first-hand experience with Industry and Entrepreneurship Development. Besides, Dr. Ali publishes more than 17 articles in SSCI, ESCI, Web of Science, and Scopus Indexed journals. He also presented at several national and international conferences and won first prize. He publishes in The Quarterly Review of Economics and Finance, Resources Policy, International Journal of Finance & Economics, Environment, Development and Sustainability, Journal of the Knowledge Economy, and Heliyon to mention a few. He delivered several sessions on how to publish in high-impact journals and bibliometrics analysis at UTM, Malaysian, and Sohar University, Oman. He also served on a board of reviewers for many impact full journals. Moreover, Dr. Ali has served as Research Leader and Research Member in various projects and received grants to support the research, which speaks to his ability to conduct rigorous and impactful research. Dr. Ali also served as an organizer for conducting International conferences at Kuala Lumpur and National an International conferences at SBBU, Sheringal Dir Upper.

Au Yong Hui Nee holds a PhD in Technology Management from Universiti Sains Malaysia and Master in Economics from the University of Tsukuba, Japan. She was also trained by the World Bank. Currently, she is an Associate Professor of Economics at Universiti Tunku Abdul Rahman. She is the Dean of the Faculty of Business and Finance. Her research interests include Behavioural Economics, Digital Economy, Environment, Social & Governance (ESG), International Economics, Real Estate Economics. She possesses almost two decades of experience as a manager at government agency and Fortune 500 multinational companies. She is involved in international research grants and consultation projects in China, Indonesia, Japan, Pakistan, Taiwan and the United Kingdom. She published more than 30 indexed papers/book chapters. She serves as the chief editor of a book published by Singapore-based World Scientific Publishing, reviewer editor of Switzerland-based Frontiers Media journal and editor of five peer-reviewed international journals. She was a Monbukagakusho Scholar and awarded the Tun Razak Youth Leadership Award, best oral presentation award and best paper awards.

Priyanthi Bagchi holds M.A. and M.Phil. from the University of Calcutta, India. Currently, she is an assistant professor in the Department of Economics, School of Professional Studies at Netaji Subhas Open University, West Bengal, India. She is the recipient of many awards and prizes. She has published papers in reputed journals and edited books.

Sonia Ruxandra Boticiu is a research associate at Teichmann International (Schweiz) AG, Switzerland. She holds an undergraduate and a graduate degree in law from the University of Craiova, Romania. Her research focuses on Eastern Europe.

Kuah Yoke Chin holds a PhD in Finance from Universiti Tunku Abdul Rahman University, Malaysia. Currently, she is an Assistant Professor and Head of Department for the Faculty of Business & Finance at the same university. Her research interest fields are stock market and foreign exchange exposure.

Martynas Damulis holds a master's degree in International Financial Analysis from Jönköping University, Sweden. Currently, he is working as an International Custody Settlement Associate at Danske Bank, Lithuania.

Daniel Giordino is a PhD candidate at the University of Turin, Italy. His research interests include Circular Economy, Sustainability, and Digital Innovation.

Ruchi Gupta holds a PhD in Commerce from Kalinga University Naya Raipur, India. Currently, she is an Assistant Professor of Accounting at The ICFAI University, Raipur, India. Dr. Ruchi has more than twelve years of academic experience. She is an accomplished researcher; she has several publications in peer-reviewed Journals and Chapters in Edited Books.

Shilpi Gupta is an ICWA and MBA (Finance). She has research interests in the area of behavioral finance, Banking, digitalization and stock market.

Rafiu Ibrahim Adebayo is a Professor of Islamic Studies in the Department of Religions, University of Ilorin. He specializes in Islamic Thought with emphasis on Islamization of Knowledge and Contemporary issues. He obtained all his higher academic qualifications of Bachelor of Arts in Education, Master of Arts and PhD, all in Islamic Studies from the University of Ilorin in 1990, 1995 and 2003 respectively. He has offered his services to the University of Ilorin in several capacities. He served as a Member of the University E-Learning Committee and as the Director of the Centre for Affiliated Institutions between August 2018 and April 2021. Professor Adebayo is highly prolific and has published extensively in local, national and international reputable journals. Currently, he is the pioneer Provost of the Federal College of Education, Iwo, Osun State.

Gamze Kargın Akkoç holds a PhD in Economics from Ankara Yıldırım Beyazıt University, Turkey specializing in Regulated Industries and Institutional Economics. Earlier she received her Master of Arts (MA) degree in Economics from Ankara Yıldırım Beyazıt University. Currently, Gamze Kargın Akkoç is a Research Assistant and Instructor in the Department of Economics in the Faculty of Political Sciences at Ankara Yıldırım Beyazıt University (AYBU), Turkey.

Asim K. Karmakar is an Assistant Professor in Economics, School of Professional Studies, Netaji Subhas Open University, West Bengal, India. He has written several texts, edited and co edited books published by Springer, IGI Global, Emerald UK and others as well as research articles in national and international journals of repute. He has received two national and four International awards.

Somnath Karmakar is currently a research scholar, at University of Gour Banga, Malda West Bengal, India. He has published many researches in home and abroad in peered reviewed journals and edited books including Emerald publishing, United Kingdom.

Michael King holds a PhD from Queensland University of Technology, Australia. Currently, he is a faculty member at Griffith University Australia. Michael is a Financial Crime, Money Laundering, and Criminology specialist who researches illicit financial flows, white-collar and financial crime, policing, corruption and regulatory offenses. Prior to accepting a role at Griffith University Michael taught at the esteemed Australian Graduate School of Policing and Security, Charles Sturt University, where he was the Convenor for a number of financial crime subjects including: Criminology of Financial Crime, Forensic Accounting and Corporate Governance. Michael was a sessional lecturer within the Bachelor of Justice program in the Faculty of Law, School of Justice Queensland University of Technology. Michael was awarded the QUT Outstanding Doctoral Thesis Award for this research on the policing of economic crime by Australian corporate investigators.

Marie G Nakitende holds a PhD in Management from Cardinal Stritch University, USA. Faculty Dean, Senior Lecturer, in the Faculty of Business Administration and Management at Uganda Martyrs University, Uganda. She published many research papers in international journals.

Muhammad Naveed holds a PhD in Finance from University of Technology Malaysia. Currently he is working as a Dean/Principle of Bahria Business School at Bahria University, Islamabad, Pakistan. Dr. Naveed is recognized as an expert on Dynamic Financial Modelling, Business Schools Accreditation, Corporate Governance and Sustainability, Financial Democracy, Knowledge Economy, Economic Sensitivity and Customized Modelling, Silicon Valley Research Framework, Business Incubation, Research Innovation & Commercialization. Dr. Naveed been honored invited as Guest Speaker and Chair in more than 50 Global Forums including Oxford University, LSE, Cambridge University, Silicon Valley, Melbourne University, Stanford University and many other world renowned knowledge partners and R&D Institutions.

Fuat Oğuz holds a PhD from George Mason University, USA. Earlier he earned his master's degree in Applied Economics from the American University. Currently, he is a professor of Economics at Yildirim Beyazit University, Ankara. His main research areas are law and economics, regulatory economics, infrastructure industries, and Austrian economics. In the economics of regulation, he worked mainly on electricity and telecommunications regulations and legal issues surrounding the regulatory policy. His work on Austrian economics focuses on the theory of knowledge and the role of tacit knowledge in economic processes.

Nagihan Özkanca Andıç holds a PhD in Public Finance from the University of Pamukkale, Turkey. Currently, she is an Assistant Professor at the same university. Her research interests include public economics, welfare economics, taxation, and regulations. She possesses 12 years of experience as a consultant to multinational companies. She published more than 20 papers and book chapters.

James E. Prieger holds a PhD in Economics from the University of California, Berkeley, USA. Previously he did his BA at Yale University, USA. Currently, he is a professor at the School of Public Policy at Pepperdine University, USA. He specializes in regulatory economics, public policy concerning health and the internet, industrial organization, and applied econometrics. Previously, he was an assistant professor in the Department of Economics at the University of California, Davis. Dr. Prieger is a Senior Economist at BOTEC Analysis, where he has led research teams on illicit tobacco markets and other tobacco-related policy issues. He is a senior fellow at the Reason Foundation, where he has studied the regulation of alternative tobacco products. He has published about four dozen articles in refereed academic journals and chapters in books.

Suresh Ramakrishnan holds a PhD in Finance. Currently, he is an associate professor of accounting & finance at University of Technology Malaysia. His research interests include Capital Structure, IPOs and CSR. He published a large number of research papers in journals of repute.

Gerardo Reyes Ruiz holds a Ph.D. in Business Studies from the University of Barcelona, Spain. Currently, he is a research professor at the Center for Higher Naval Studies (CESNAV) in Mexico. His research interests include Academic Evaluation, the generation of Human Resources, the National System of Science and Technology, New Technologies, Marketing, and the Maritime and Port environment. All of them with an econometric, statistical, and mathematical approach (qualitative and quantitative). He has more than 10 years of experience as an advisor/consultant to government, and multinational companies, and a researcher in various public institutions. He published more than 50 papers/book chapters/books.

Baranidharan S. holds a PhD in Finance from Christ University, India. Currently, he holds 5 years of research experience, 2 years of Industrial experience, and 6 years of teaching experience. He has published 4 patents, and 37 research articles in international and national journals indexed in Scopus, WoS, Proquest, ABDC, etc.,

Fabian Teichmann studied economic science and finance at Bocconi University in Italy, management at Harvard, and accounting, finance and law at the University of St. Gallen in Switzerland. At the head of Teichmann International (Schweiz) AG, Law Firm and Notary Office in St. Gallen, is attorney-at-law Dr. iur. Dr. rer. pol. He graduated as a doctor of law from the University of Zurich, and acquired a doctorate in economic sciences at the University of Kassel in Germany. Dr. Teichmann also holds an LL.M. in International Financial and Commercial Law as well as a M.Sc. in Psychology and Neuroscience of Mental Health from King's College London. Dr. Teichmann has published both books and articles in well-known professional journals on various topics relating to law and economic science. He has a particular interest in criminal law and criminology. Dr. Teichmann lectures on these topics at several universities.

Janitha Thilakaratne holds a BSc. Accounting Special Degree (First Class Honors) from the University of Sri Jayewardenepura, Sri Lanka and was awarded the Chartered Institute of Management Accountants (CIMA) Gold Medal (awarded to the student who had obtained the highest overall Grade Point Average (GPA) in the final year and the best student in the field of Management Accounting of the B.Sc. Accounting Special Degree) in 2016. She is also an Associate Chartered Accountant of the Institute of Chartered Accountants of Sri Lanka (ICASL) and was the winner of the Second in Order of Merit prizes at both Certificate in Accounting and Business I and II examinations conducted by the ICASL in 2012 and 2013 respectively. She is also a member of the ICASL Toastmasters Club since 2019. She worked as an Audit Associate at the PricewaterhouseCoopers, Sri Lanka from 2014 – 2018. Further, she was appointed as a Sworn Translator (Sinhala-English) in 2020. She has published newspaper articles concerning her area of expertise and currently she serves as an Assistant Director at the Financial Intelligence Unit of the Central Bank of Sri Lanka.

Ivan Topalovic located in Monaco is a specialist in corruption. He defended his thesis on corruption at the University Paris Dauphine - PSL in Paris (France).

Wei Chooi Yi holds a PhD in Economic Education from Sultan Idris Education University, Malaysia. Currently, she is an Assistant Professor at the University Tunku Abdul Rahman (UTAR), Malaysia. Her research interest fields are Banking products and Facilities, Behavioral Finance, Social Development, Educational Economics and Finance.

Index

L

M

O

P

R

S

T

U

V

W

www.ingramcontent.com/pod-product-compliance
Lightning Source LLC
LaVergne TN
LVHW062116300926
849161LV00010B/2472